'A roundho[illegible]
Sunday Tim[illegible]

[illegible] a [illegible] p off

[illegible]ly's new biography is long overdue but does Hong Kong's most [illegible]son proud . . . engaging, enthusiastic and empathetic.'
[illegible]outh China Morning Post Magazine

'The first noteworthy treatment of its subject – and a definitive one at that . . . Fascinating.'
New York Times Book Review

'Proof that dogged research and sharp insight lie at the foundation of any successful biography . . . a definitive work to satisfy Lee's fans and spark curiosity in a new generation.'
Associated Press

'At last, Bruce Lee has the powerful biography he deserves. Matthew Polly's book is packed with new information and sharp insights. It will thrill Lee's fans and fascinate the unfamiliar. Bravo!'
Jonathan Eig, author of *Ali: A Life* and *Luckiest Man: The Life and Death of Lou Gehrig*

'You won't find a better match of biographer and subject than Matthew Polly and Bruce Lee . . . Polly tells Bruce Lee's story with clarity and empathy, tearing away the myths to reveal Lee's most interesting persona yet: the man himself. A definitive biography, told with passion and punch.'
Brian Jay Jones, author of *George Lucas: A Life* and *Jim Henson: The Biography*

'With this meticulously researched, beautifully realised work, Matthew Polly has written the definitive account. It moves with the authority, grace and economy of Lee himself.'
Jimmy McDonough, author of *Shakey: Neil Young's Biography* and *Soul Survivor: A Biography of Al Green*

'This thorough, well-sourced biography from Polly is an engrossing examination of the life of a martial arts movie star and his shocking, early death . . . Polly wonderfully profiles the man who constructed a new, masculine Asian archetype and ushered kung fu into pop culture.'
Publisher's Weekly

also by matthew polly

tapped out

american shaolin

bruce lee

a life

matthew polly

SIMON &
SCHUSTER

London · New York · Sydney · Toronto · New Delhi

First published in the United States by Simon & Schuster, Inc., 2018
First published in Great Britain by Simon & Schuster UK Ltd, 2018
This paperback edition published by Simon & Schuster UK Ltd, 2019

3 5 7 9 10 8 6 4

Simon & Schuster UK Ltd
1st Floor
222 Gray's Inn Road
London WC1X 8HB

www.simonandschuster.co.uk
www.simonandschuster.com.au
www.simonandschuster.co.in

Simon & Schuster Australia, Sydney
Simon & Schuster India, New Delhi

A CIP catalogue record for this book is available from the British Library.

Paperback ISBN: 978-1-4711-7572-5
eBook ISBN: 978-1-4711-7571-8

Interior design by Ruth Lee-Mui
Printed and bound by CPI Group (UK) Ltd, Croydon, CR0 4YY

For M.C.

May you dream big.

And in memory of my father,

Dr. Richard Polly,

1942–2017

"Knowing others is Wisdom,
Knowing yourself is Enlightenment."

—Lao-tzu

contents

bruce lee

Crowds outside Kowloon Funeral Parlour for Bruce Lee's Hong Kong funeral, July 25, 1973. *(David Tadman)*

Steve McQueen places his gloves on Bruce's casket. James Coburn on the left; Linda, Shannon, and Brandon Lee sitting on the right. Seattle funeral, July 30, 1973. *(Bettmann/Getty Images)*

prologue

tale of two funerals

The crowd of mourners began gathering on the evening of July 24, 1973, outside the Kowloon Funeral Parlour in anticipation of the ceremony the next morning. As the appointed hour of 10 a.m. drew closer, their numbers swelled and multiplied until over fifteen thousand Hong Kong residents stood behind police barricades, looked down from balconies, or perched precariously on the city's famous neon signs to catch a final glimpse of their idol's coffin. Five days earlier Bruce Lee had died at the age of thirty-two. Several hundred extra police officers were detailed to control the crowd. Wearing lime green shorts and short-sleeved shirts, black shoes, knee socks, and billed caps, the cops looked like overgrown Boy Scouts on a summer trip.

The *South China Morning Post* described the scene as "a carnival." When the crowd spotted one of Bruce's celebrity friends entering the funeral home, they clapped and cheered. Wearing sunglasses to hide tears, the famous arrived one after another to pay their respects to the man who had put Hong Kong cinema on the world map: Shih Kien, the villain in *Enter the Dragon*; Nancy Kwan, the star of *The World of Suzie Wong*; Nora Miao,

Lee's longtime costar; pop singer Samuel Hui, a childhood friend; even Lo Wei, who directed two of Bruce's films. One of the few famous faces to skip the event was Betty Ting Pei in whose apartment Lee had died. Much to the disappointment of the throng, Betty chose to stay home where she was reported to be under heavy sedation. She sent a wreath instead with a note, "To Bruce from Ting Pei." Next to it a tearful six-year-old boy dropped a spray of flowers with a simple message, "From a little fan."

"For the scores of fans who had stayed the night, the saddest moment was the arrival of Lee's wife Linda," reported *The China Mail.* A black Mercedes pulled to the curb, and Raymond Chow, Bruce's business partner and the head of Golden Harvest studios, opened Linda's door and gave her a hand. Linda was dressed in all white—the Chinese color for mourning—a white double-breasted long coat down to her knees, white slacks, and a white turtleneck. Her light brown hair was cut short. Big round sunglasses covered her red eyes. She appeared dangerously thin as if she hadn't eaten for days. Leaning on Raymond's arm, Linda was surrounded by a group of Golden Harvest employees who helped push her through the crowd surrounding the front door. "Outside the crush was tremendous," Linda later said. "I recalled the old newsreel shots of the funeral of Rudolph Valentino."

The five hundred VIP mourners inside the cramped funeral home fell silent as the twenty-eight-year-old widow entered. At the front of the parlor was an altar with a movie-poster-sized photo of Bruce wearing sunglasses surrounded by a display of ribbons, flowers, and a Chinese banner saying, "A Star Sinks in the Sea of Art." Three joss sticks and two candles burned in front of his picture. The walls were covered with thousands of tributes—Chinese calligraphy on strips of white silk.

Raymond and Linda bowed before the altar three times before Chow escorted her over to the section reserved for family. Bruce's older brother, Peter, and his wife, Eunice Lam, stood solemnly. Linda was helped out of her fashionable long coat and into a white, hooded, burlap mourning gown per Chinese custom. Her two children, eight-year-old Brandon and four-year-old Shannon, were brought in from a side entrance and dressed in white burlap as well. A white bandanna was tied around Brandon's head. Shannon, too young to understand what was happening, played happily while Brandon glared angrily.

A Chinese band struck up a traditional funeral song, which sounded like "Auld Lang Syne." Bruce's HK$40,000 bronze casket was brought into the room. The top half of the coffin was opened. Inside was a protective enclosure of glass covering Bruce's body to prevent anyone from touching him. Linda had dressed her husband in the blue Chinese outfit he had worn in *Enter the Dragon* and liked to wear around the house because it was comfortable. Beneath the glass, Bruce's face looked gray and distorted despite heavy makeup. Friends filed past the open casket to see him one last time. Press photographers jostled with the invited guests to get a better angle; many simply raised their cameras above their heads and snapped away furiously. As Linda made her way to her husband's side, she looked heartbreakingly close to collapse. Covering her face with a trembling hand, Linda burst into tears. "It was a frightful time," she later confessed to friends.

Seeing his hearse begin to depart, Bruce's fans went wild with grief. Three hundred policemen surrounding the funeral parlor were forced to link arms and form a human chain to hold back the surging crowds. Eventually, reinforcements were called as women and children were repeatedly plucked clear of the barrier to prevent them from being crushed. Old men wept, young girls fainted, and many people were hospitalized for shock and minor injuries. "It was terrible alright," remembers Peter Lee. For hours afterward, police with loudspeakers were still patrolling the streets urging people to return to their homes.

Many mourners refused to leave because they knew this was the last time they would be near their hero. The Hong Kong tabloids had angrily reported that Linda planned to bury her husband in America, making it nearly impossible for the average Chinese fan to visit his grave. Under the headline, "Lee's Body Flies to America Tomorrow," the *Oriental Daily* wrote, "Linda has stuck to her guns regarding several things about Lee's death. She is obviously holding some kind of grudge. From the start, Linda wanted to ship Lee's body back to America for autopsy, but due to legal restrictions, she relented. However, the body will be sent to America for burial."

In life, Bruce Lee sought to straddle East and West. In death, he only had one body, and his Western widow had to pick a side. She chose her hometown. "I decided to bury Bruce in the peace and calm of Seattle," Linda explained. "I think his happiest times were spent in Seattle, and I intended to return there with my children to live." Seattle was where Linda had grown up, gone to college, and fallen in love with Bruce Lee.

Her hometown had the added benefit of being a tranquil place for a funeral, unlike the mass mania of Hong Kong. In Asia, Bruce was bigger than the Beatles, but in America, *Enter the Dragon* had yet to be released. He was an obscure TV actor whose death garnered only a handful of short obituaries, several of which contained glaring errors. The *Los Angeles Times* wrote that Linda was his "Swedish-born" wife and in a shameful they-all-look-alike mistake added that Bruce was "the hero of such films as *Five Fingers of Death*." (The popular Shaw Bros. kung fu movie actually starred Lieh Lo.) To ensure a serene Seattle funeral, Linda sent a telegram to Warner Brothers executives, insisting on "a quiet and private service with no publicity."

Plane tickets that had been purchased by Warner Bros. to take Bruce and Linda to New York for his guest appearance on *The Tonight Show Starring Johnny Carson* were exchanged for the passage of Bruce's body and the family to Seattle. On Thursday, July 26, Linda and the children went to Hong Kong's Kai Tak Airport and boarded Northwest Orient Airlines Flight #4. Joining them were Andre Morgan, who, as the representative from Golden Harvest, was tasked with organizing and paying for the funeral; Charles Loke, a Chinese cameraman, who was recording the event for a documentary; and Rebu Hui, Linda's best friend. "She kept me sane and I don't know what I would have done without her," says Linda. "I fell asleep immediately on the plane and slept like an unconscious person—my brain had finally shut down."

While Bruce's older brother, Peter, lived in Hong Kong, the rest of

Bruce's immediate family had followed him to America—his younger brother, Robert, his older sisters, Agnes and Phoebe, and his mother, Grace Ho. They were waiting in the Seattle airport when Linda and the children arrived. Weeping, Grace grabbed Linda and refused to let go.

Andre Morgan met with the funeral director of the Butterworth Mortuary on 300 East Pine Street. They discussed which plot to buy at the Lake View Cemetery.

"Do you want him buried with his kind?" the funeral director asked.

"What does that mean?"

The funeral director took a deep breath and looked left to right, right to left before whispering, "We have a Chinese section."

"Oh really? Show me."

The Chinese cemetery was a small isolated area next to the equipment shed. The Caucasian cemetery was, Morgan says, "as big as Arlington." Andre opted for the latter, picking out a location under big trees with a nice view of the mountain. "I bought two plots, side by side. One for Bruce, one for Linda," Morgan recalls. "That afternoon I went and saw Linda at her mother's home and said, 'I hope you don't mind that I bought two plots.' "

The funeral in Seattle was held on Monday, July 30, 1973. Unlike in Hong Kong, fewer than two dozen fans and only a couple of reporters were camped outside. Gathered inside were a hundred or so relatives, friends, and former students, including Jesse Glover. As an African American growing up in 1950s Seattle, Glover became obsessed with the martial arts but had difficulty finding anyone willing to teach a black student. Bruce was the first kung fu teacher in America to accept students regardless of race or ethnicity. For years, Jesse and Bruce had been as close as brothers. "I was unable to conceal the emotions that surged to the surface," Jesse says, "and I broke down and cried like a baby."

A contingent of Bruce's Hollywood pals had flown up from Los Angeles—Ted Ashley, the chairman of Warner Bros., James Coburn, and Steve McQueen. Everyone was surprised to see McQueen, who generally shunned funerals. "I cared about Bruce," McQueen explained. "I felt like saying good-bye to a friend."

During the eulogies, Ted Ashley opined, "In 35 years in the moviemaking business, I have never known anyone who wanted more and tried harder for perfection than Bruce. It could be viewed as a pity that Bruce passed on right at the beginning of his realization that he would 'make it big.' I have a sense of sadness mingling with the realization that, while he may not have gotten up that ladder, he at least got his foot on it."

Instead of traditional funeral music, Linda chose to play recordings of Bruce's favorite songs: Frank Sinatra's "My Way," Tom Jones's "The Impossible Dream," and the Blood, Sweat, & Tears version of "And When I Die." In her eulogy, Linda said that the lyrics of the last song spoke to Bruce's philosophy: "When I die and when I'm gone, there will be one child born in this world to carry on."

Looking considerably less shaken on her home territory, Linda went on to say, "Bruce believed the individual represents the whole of mankind whether he lives in the Orient or elsewhere. He believed man struggles to find the life outside himself, not realizing that the life he seeks is within him. The soul is an embryo of the body of man. The day of death is a day of awakening. The spirit lives on." Adding her own view, she concluded, "When our day of awakening comes, we will meet him again."

After the service, the mourners made their way to Bruce's open casket, covered with white, yellow, and red flowers making up the Taoist yin and yang symbol. "When I looked into the coffin and saw the pale imitation of what used to be Bruce I felt a wild anger and the need to strike out at something," Jesse Glover recalls.

Bruce's gravestone was hand-carved in Hong Kong and shipped over. Per Linda's instructions, the stonemason placed a photo of Bruce at the top and etched beneath it his name in English and Chinese characters and his birth and death dates—Nov. 27, 1940–July 20, 1973. Linda also chose to have carved into the stone, "FOUNDER OF JEET KUNE DO." At the base, the stonemason attached a marble carving of an open book. On the left page was the Taoist yin and yang symbol; on the right page were the words, "Your Inspiration Continues to Guide Us Towards Our Personal Liberation."

The pallbearers were Steve McQueen, James Coburn, Bruce's assistant

Jeet Kune Do instructors, Taky Kimura and Dan Inosanto, his younger brother, Robert Lee, and Peter Chin, a family friend from Los Angeles. At the gravesite, James Coburn stepped forward and spoke the last words: "Farewell, brother. It has been an honor to share this space in time with you. As a friend and as a teacher, you have brought my physical, spiritual, and psychological selves together. Thank you. May peace be with you." Then he dropped the white gloves he had worn as a pallbearer into the open grave and the others followed suit.

Linda stood up and quickly thanked everyone for coming. Bruce's mother, Grace Ho, wearing a blue button coat and dark sunglasses, was so distraught with grief two relatives had to help her walk away. As the crowd thinned and the mourners returned to their cars, the last person to remain was Jesse Glover. When the workmen came to fill the grave, Jesse took one of their shovels and shooed them away. It was a uniquely American moment—a black man in a suit with tears running down his face filling a Chinese grave in a white cemetery. Jesse says, "It didn't seem right that Bruce should be covered by strange hands."

act i

little dragon

"Every talent must unfold itself in fighting."

—Friedrich Nietzsche

Bruce Lee's parents, Grace Ho and Li Hoi Chuen, circa 1950s. *(David Tadman)*

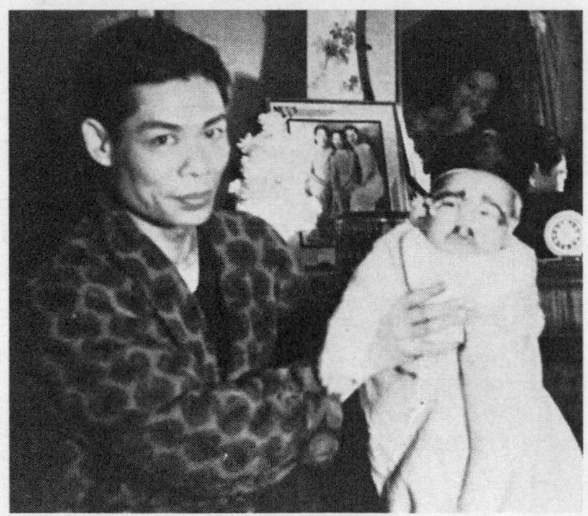

Backstage: Li Hoi Chuen holding his infant son, Bruce, with his face painted in Cantonese Opera makeup, circa December 1940. *(David Tadman)*

one

sick man of asia

Ten-year-old Li Hoi Chuen stood barefoot on the dirt road outside a corrugated tin roof restaurant on the outskirts of Foshan City in southern China. He wore threadbare clothes passed down to him from his three older brothers. As urban pedestrians wandered down the street, Hoi Chuen sang out in Cantonese the restaurant's specials of the day: "Friends, countrymen, come, come, come and try our fresh stewed beef brisket, water spinach with fermented tofu, frog legs on lotus leaf, congee with century egg, and sweet and sour pork." His tender voice rose up and down with each menu item, a dancing falsetto. Among the hundreds of peasant boys employed by restaurants across the city to hawk their menus, there was something special about the way Hoi Chuen sang—a wry, ironic undercurrent. On this particular day a famous Cantonese Opera singer passed by the restaurant, heard the humor in the young boy's voice, and invited him to become his apprentice. Bruce Lee's father ran all the way back to his small village to tell his parents the good news.

The year was 1914. Revolutionary forces had recently overthrown the

Qing Dynasty and established a constitutional republic, putting an end to four thousand years of imperial rule. The new government had a weak grip on power, various factions vied for control, popular revolts had erupted in major cities, bandits roamed the land, and the peasantry struggled to survive.

The suffering was particularly intense in the Li household. Hoi Chuen was the fourth of six siblings. His father, Li Jun Biao, suffered so many ill turns of fortune neighbors believed he was cursed. A severe fever in childhood damaged Jun Biao's throat to the point where he could barely speak, causing many to assume he was a deaf-mute. He struggled to find enough work to feed his family. Along with a part-time job as a security guard, he was also a fisherman. He often took his boys with him to catch supper.

Hoi Chuen's parents were overjoyed that their son would be apprenticed to an opera singer. It meant one less mouth to feed and a potential career for one of their children. On the appointed day, Hoi Chuen left his home to begin his training—an incredibly brutal dawn-to-dusk regimen of acting, singing, acrobatics, and kung fu (also spelled "gung fu") training. Unlike its more staid European counterpart, Chinese Opera featured extravagant costumes, bright full-face makeup, falsetto singing, Olympic-class gymnastics, and both weapon and empty-handed stage combat.

After years of schooling, Li Hoi Chuen joined the senior actors on the stages of Foshan. His specialty was comedic roles. In 1928, his opera troupe decided to move sixty miles south to Hong Kong in search of larger and wealthier audiences. Ever loyal to his family, Hoi Chuen invited several of his brothers to join him in the British colony and helped them find jobs as waiters and busboys. Hoi Chuen was still supporting his acting career with part-time work in a restaurant.

As Hoi Chuen and his opera troupe performed across the colony, their fame grew to the point where they were invited to give a private performance at the palatial home called Idlewild, of Sir Robert Hotung Bosman, the richest man in Hong Kong. It was here that Bruce's father and mother, Li Hoi Chuen and Grace Ho, first laid eyes on each other from across China's economic, cultural, and racial divide. The maternal side of Bruce's family was as wealthy and influential as his father's was poor and powerless.

Grace Ho was a member of the Eurasian Bosman-Hotung clan—Hong Kong's equivalent of the Rockefellers or the Kennedys. Her grandfather was Charles Henri Maurice Bosman. Although many have thought Bosman was German Catholic, Bruce Lee's great-grandfather was actually Dutch-Jewish. He was born Mozes Hartog Bosman in Rotterdam on August 29, 1839.

Mozes joined the Dutch East Asia Company as a teenager and arrived in Hong Kong in 1859. His fortune was made in the coolie trade. He shipped Chinese peasant laborers to Dutch Guiana to work the sugar plantations after African slavery was abolished and to California to build the Central Pacific Railroad. His business success led him to be appointed the Dutch consul to Hong Kong in 1866. Given the anti-Semitism of the time, all of his letters to the Netherlands minister of foreign affairs were signed "M Bosman."

Soon after his arrival in Hong Kong, Bosman purchased a Chinese concubine named Sze Tai. The teenage girl had grown up on Chongming Island, Shanghai, in a good family, as evidenced by her bound feet. (Girls from wealthy families, who did not need their feet to work, could afford to have them bound.) But when her father died, her family fell on hard times, and the girl was literally "sold down the river" to settle debts. Sze Tai produced six children. Since the father was from Holland, they were given the Chinese surname "Ho."

Mozes Hartog Bosman fell into serious financial difficulty and went bankrupt in 1869. He abandoned his Chinese family, moved to California, and changed his name to Charles Henri Maurice Bosman. To protect her children, Sze Tai became the fourth concubine to a Chinese cattle merchant, Kwok Chung. He had little interest in providing for her Eurasian children and barely gave them enough money to eat, but Sze Tai convinced him to pay for the children's tuition to the prestigious Central School (now Queen's College), where they learned English.

Robert Hotung was the eldest son of Sze Tai's six children with Bosman. He grew up to become the comprador (foreign agent) for Jardine Matheson, the largest trading conglomerate in East Asia. He made his fortune in shipping, insurance, real estate, and opium. By the age of thirty-five, Bruce Lee's great-uncle was the wealthiest man in Hong Kong.

To help him with his varied business interests, Robert Hotung hired his younger brother, Ho Kom Tong, who quickly became the second-richest man in Hong Kong. Bruce Lee's grandfather's two great passions were Cantonese Opera acting (he performed onstage in support of fund-raising events for charity) and women. Ho Kom Tong married at the age of nineteen and soon after began taking concubines until he reached twelve in total in Hong Kong. In the household he maintained in Shanghai for business, Ho Kom Tong kept his thirteenth concubine, a Eurasian lady named Ms. Cheung. In Shanghai, he also had a secret British mistress, who provided him with another daughter, his thirtieth child, in 1911. Her name was Grace Ho, or Ho Oi Yee in Chinese. Nothing is known about Grace Ho's English mother or why she gave up her little girl, but Grace was raised by Ms. Cheung as her daughter.

As the one half English, one quarter Dutch-Jewish, and one quarter Han Chinese child of an elite Eurasian family in colonial Shanghai, Grace Ho's upbringing was very European. Instead of learning to read Chinese characters, she was taught English and French. As a teenager, she studied Western medicine in hopes of becoming a nurse. She also converted to Catholicism, no doubt attracted to its absolute insistence on monogamy and condemnation of polygamy.

Grace saw firsthand how miserable it made her adoptive mother to compete with a dozen other concubines for the attention of one man. Grace was determined to live a very different life. "She wasn't happy with her father's traditional, sinful ways," says Phoebe Lee, Bruce's older sister. Instead of accepting an arranged marriage as was common for Chinese and Eurasians of her class, Grace ran off to Hong Kong when she was eighteen and moved in with her Uncle Robert. Grace became a socialite in Hong Kong, filling her days with fashionable social gatherings. She was wealthy, independent, and single throughout her early twenties—a rarity for a Chinese woman in that era—until the day Li Hoi Chuen's opera troupe came to Sir Robert Hotung's Idlewild mansion.

Sir Robert intended the event for his friends, but his niece, Grace Ho, asked her uncle to allow her to attend. She had little experience with traditional Chinese art forms and wanted to see her first Cantonese Opera, which was considered a lowbrow, vaudevillian entertainment for the Chinese masses.

Li Hoi Chuen and his troupe rode the Star Ferry from Kowloon to Hong Kong Island and trekked up to Idlewild at 8 Seymour Road, Mid-Levels. The actors painted their faces with thick makeup, donned their ornate costumes, and tested their kung fu weapons before marching into the courtyard to entertain this private audience of Eurasian elites.

Grace was intrigued and delighted by the performances, but the longer she watched the more her attention was drawn to a handsome young actor with excellent comedic timing. "Just in those ten minutes or so when Dad was on stage," says Robert Lee, Bruce's younger brother, "Mom was deeply moved by his performance technique and developed feelings for him." She fell in love because he made her laugh.

In 1930s China it was unheard of for a woman to pursue a man, but Grace sought out Li Hoi Chuen and charmed him. It was doubly scandalous for the daughter of a wealthy family to become enamored with a struggling actor. Marriage was a financial institution with little room for romance. Grace was supposed to wed a wealthy Eurasian scion, not the son of illiterate Chinese peasants.

Her entire clan was against the relationship. Threats were made. Pressure was applied. "But Mom was very independent, strong-willed, and adaptable," says Robert, "and she finally made up her mind she wanted to be with Dad." As the child of two cultures, Grace's choice was a microcosm of the conflict between Western individualism and Chinese tradition, romanticism versus family obligation. In traditional China's patriarchal, polygamous culture, Grace Ho wed for love. She wasn't formally disowned, but her decision to elope caused a rupture and she was financially cut off. Grace went from being a wealthy socialite to the wife of a Chinese actor.

If Grace had any regrets, she never spoke of them. After her romantic rebellion against her family, she settled comfortably into the life of a simple Chinese wife. She dressed plainly, only wearing a cheongsam on special occasions. She loved to knit and play mahjong with her friends. Her personality embodied the Chinese ideal for a woman—*wenrou* (温柔)—quiet, gentle, and tender. "My mother was very patient, very kind, capable of controlling her emotions," says Phoebe. "She was very refined, didn't talk much, smiling all day, a traditional kind of woman."

Confucius modeled Chinese society on the patriarchal family—the emperor as the stern but benevolent father and the people as his obedient children. As the most successful member of his family, it was Li Hoi Chuen's duty to support his entire clan—to serve as its emperor. When Li Hoi Chuen's father died, he supported his mother as was expected of a filial son. "My father gave all his salary to his mother, and my mother did the same," Phoebe says. "My grandmother would only take a little and give it all back to my father. When he tried to refuse, she would tell him to take the money as if it were from her." When one of Hoi Chuen's older brothers also passed away unexpectedly, he moved his brother's widow and her five children into his and Grace's tiny apartment.

As his wife, it was Grace's duty to support her husband and to produce offspring, especially male heirs. (A popular Chinese saying—*duo zi duo fu* (多子多福)—"the more sons, the more happiness.") To the utter delight of her husband, Grace's first child was a boy. Tragically, he died when he was three months old. Even though infant mortality rates were much higher than now, the loss of a boy was still considered an evil portent, maybe even a sign of a curse.

When Grace was eight months pregnant with their second child, the family adopted an infant girl and named her Phoebe. It was odd timing—Hoi Chuen was struggling to support his mother and his dead brother's family; he didn't need any more mouths to feed. One explanation is Phoebe was a bad omen insurance policy. Superstition dictated the second child must be a girl; if Grace was pregnant with a boy, he was in danger unless he had an older sister. The more likely scenario is Phoebe wasn't a random orphan girl. Hoi Chuen fathered her with another woman, who, after she gave birth to a daughter instead of a highly valued son, gave the girl to Hoi Chuen to raise. For her part, Phoebe, who is sensitive about the topic, claims to be a blood relative to her siblings: "Even though we had different personalities, we were close. Blood is thicker than water, our genes are the same!"

A month after Phoebe's adoption, Grace gave birth to another daughter, not a son. She was named Agnes. "Phoebe is my adopted daughter," Li Hoi Chuen told U.S. Immigration officials in 1941. "She is about 40 days older than my own daughter, Agnes."

After Agnes, Grace was soon pregnant again and gave birth to a son, Peter, on October 23, 1939. His ear was immediately pierced. Even though he had two older sisters, Peter was still considered to be in danger from the mythical ghouls who steal little boys. Because their first son had died in infancy, any boy born afterward had to be given girl's clothing, a girl's nickname, and a pierced ear to trick the boy-hunting devil. It was an ancient custom and in this case it worked. Peter would live a long life, despite another demon roaming the land, killing children and adults in massive numbers—the Empire of Japan.

For two thousand years, China viewed itself as the most advanced civilization on earth—the country's name *Jong Guo* (中國) literally means "Center Country." The arrival of European colonialists with their superior military technology shook Chinese chauvinism to its core. When the Qing government tried to stop British traders from importing opium, which was causing an epidemic of addiction, the United Kingdom launched the First Opium War (1839–42) and crushed Chinese opposition. Suing for peace, the Qing emperor gave away Hong Kong—a rocky island with a population of only seven thousand fishermen—and opened a few treaty ports. Instead of appeasing the big-nosed barbarians, the concessions displayed a weakness that whetted the appetites of Western imperialists. Britain, France, and America seized more territory, including sections of Shanghai, the country's most important commercial city.

The Chinese people viewed the loss of Shanghai to Westerners as a grievous insult. It marked the beginning of what Chinese patriots called the "Century of Humiliation." In 1899, an uprising of Chinese martial artists (called Boxers), convinced that the mystical powers of kung fu could stop foreign bullets, converged on Beijing with the slogan "Support the Qing government and exterminate the foreigners." It turned out their kung fu could not stop high-speed metal projectiles and the Boxers along with the Chinese army backing them were slaughtered by a seven-nation alliance of Britain, France, America, Germany, Italy, Austria-Hungary, and Japan. The failure of their government and kung fu to protect the Chinese people shattered their self-confidence and brought down the Qing Dynasty in 1912, resulting in decades of chaos, warlordism, and civil war. China became known as the "Sick Man of Asia."

Unlike China, which was unable to adapt quickly enough, Japan rapidly adopted Western military technology and imperial policies. Imitating what the Europeans had done in the Americas, Africa, and Asia, the Japanese sought to kick all the Westerners out of East Asia and colonize it for themselves. They set their sights on the Sick Man. After grabbing territory along China's periphery (the Senkaku Islands, Taiwan, Korea, Manchuria), the Japanese launched a full-scale invasion of the mainland on July 7, 1937, advancing rapidly and killing millions.

The British colony of Hong Kong served as a critical supply line in support of Chinese resistance and as a refugee camp—the population of the island increased by 63 percent (over 600,000). After the outbreak of war between England and Germany in 1939, the British publicly kept up their trademark stiff upper lip, convincing their Chinese subjects they were safely protected by the invincible British navy and the superiority of the white race. But in private, the British government realized that "Hong Kong could not be expected to hold out for long" against a Japanese invasion and that "delaying action was the best to be hoped for."

In this time of war and under the false sense of Pax Britannica security, Li Hoi Chuen and Grace Ho made a fateful decision. In the fall of 1939, Hoi Chuen's opera troupe was invited for a year-long tour of America. The objective was to raise funds from the overseas Chinese community to support the war effort. The catch was he couldn't bring along his entire family, just one person. As Japanese forces were pushing ever closer to Hong Kong, Grace had to decide if she would join him and leave her three infant children (Peter was less than two months old) under the care of her mother-in-law or let her husband travel halfway around the world for a year all by himself. It was Grace's mother-in-law who convinced Grace to accompany her son. "My paternal grandmother said she should go with him or he might be tempted by someone else," Phoebe says with a chuckle. "She told my mother not to worry, so long as Grandma is here, no one is going to mistreat these three kids. So my mom went with him. Agnes, Peter, and I stayed in Hong Kong."

Hoi Chuen applied for a twelve-month nonimmigrant visa to the United States on November 15, 1939. His stated reason for coming to America was "theatrical work only," and he listed his occupation as "actor." On Grace's application, she wrote her purpose was "accompanying my husband." She fudged her occupation as "actress, wardrobe woman." In fact, she was a housewife and mother.

The entire extended family went to the Hong Kong Harbor docks. Through their tears, Hoi Chuen and Grace kissed their infant children goodbye and walked up the ramp to their steamer ship, SS *President Coolidge*, for their long voyage to America. It was the first time either of them had left Asia.

After a three-week journey with a stop in Honolulu, the *President Coolidge* finally sailed into San Francisco Bay on December 8, 1939. Hoi Chuen and Grace gazed up in wonder at the recently built, two-year-old Golden Gate Bridge—the tallest and longest suspension bridge in the world. As the steamer slowly made its way through the bay, the couple could see the federal prison on Alcatraz Island and the 1939 World's Fair being hosted on Treasure Island, featuring an eighty-foot statue of Pacifica, goddess of the Pacific Ocean. The *Coolidge* docked at Angel Island, called "The Ellis Island of the West." Chinese immigrants seeking permanent residence were often detained for months. The 1882 Chinese Exclusion Act, which was not repealed until 1943, prohibited all immigration of low-skilled Chinese laborers. Since Hoi Chuen and Grace arrived on a one-year cultural worker visa, they were processed relatively quickly.

Greeted by a representative from the Mandarin Theatre, who had sponsored their visas, Hoi Chuen and Grace were guided through the streets of Chinatown. It was the largest enclave of Chinese outside Asia and the only neighborhood in San Francisco where Chinese could own property. Rebuilt after the 1906 earthquake, this warren of three- and four-story brick buildings over a twenty-four-block area had long been a major tourist attraction with its numerous restaurants, gambling dens, and brothels. The nightclub Forbidden City was famed for its exotic Oriental performances. Li Po, which catered to a gay clientele, advertised itself as a "jovial and informal Chinatown cocktail lounge" where one could find "love, passion, and nighttime." At every intersection, Chinese boys hawked Chinese- and English-language newspapers. The headline story in the *San Francisco Chronicle* was the trial of a local labor leader as a Communist.

Hoi Chuen and Grace walked down the busiest section of Grant Street in the heart of Chinatown to visit his place of work for the next year, the Mandarin Theatre. Built in 1924 with a distinctive green, red, and gold arched awning, the Mandarin Theatre was a key player in Chinatown's live opera (and later cinema) culture for decades. Its main competition was the Great China Theatre just one block east on Jackson Street. The two venues were constantly trying to out-bill each other by importing superior opera talent from China. It was as part of this rivalry that the Mandarin had booked Hoi Chuen's troupe, posting bonds with the Immigration Department for each actor and paying the talent far more than they could have earned in Hong Kong.

Hoi Chuen and Grace lived at the Mandarin Theatre's boardinghouse on 18 Trenton Street, a block away from the Chinese Hospital, the cornerstone of the neighborhood. It turned out to be a fortunate location. The Chinese Hospital was the only medical facility at the time that would treat Chinese patients. Grace discovered she was pregnant again in April.

As her due date approached, Hoi Chuen's troupe was scheduled to perform in New York City. With great reluctance, he left his very pregnant wife alone in a foreign city and traveled by train across the country. Grace hid her anxiety behind a fixed smile. When she went into labor a few weeks later, neighbors helped her walk down the street to the hospital.

A healthy baby boy—five eighths Han Chinese, one quarter English, and one eighth Dutch-Jewish—was born at 7:12 a.m. on November 27, 1940.

The neighbors called the Le Qian Qiu Theatre in New York's Chinatown to leave a message for Hoi Chuen: It's a boy! When he heard the good news that night, Hoi Chuen celebrated with the entire cast by passing out cigarettes—the Chinese equivalent of passing out cigars.

The first question all his fellow actors asked was: "What are his astrological signs?" The Chinese zodiac not only assigns one of twelve animals—rat, ox, tiger, rabbit, dragon, snake, horse, goat, monkey, rooster, dog, and pig—to the year of a person's birth (called the outer animal), but also the month (inner animal), the day (true animal), and the hour (secret animal). Of the twelve birth signs, the dragon is considered the most powerful and propitious. Chinese emperors took the dragon as their symbol, causing it to be associated with leadership and authority. Many Chinese parents tried to time a pregnancy in the hopes that their child would be born in the year, month, day, or hour of the dragon.

Hoi Chuen proudly told everyone that his boy was born in the year of the dragon, the month of the pig, the day of the dog, and the hour of the dragon. Two dragon signs, especially if one was the year, were considered exceptionally auspicious. The troupe all congratulated him: "Your son is destined for greatness."

Back in San Francisco, Grace needed to pick out an American name for her son, a natural-born citizen of the United States. When Li Hoi Chuen applied for his nonimmigrant visa, his surname was changed from "Li" to the Anglicized version "Lee"—Lee Hoi Chuen. And so on the boy's birth certificate his last name was also written down as "Lee," a subtle shift in spelling demarking a break with the past and a new beginning. For the first name, Grace, who spoke little English, turned to a Chinese American friend for help. He consulted with the midwife, Mary E. Glover, who delivered the baby and signed the birth certificate. She suggested Bruce.

Alone with her son, Grace selected his Chinese name: Li Jun Fan

(李震藩). “Li” was the family surname. “Jun” was part of Hoi Chuen’s father’s name (Li Jun Biao) and meant “shake up, rouse, or excite.” And “Fan” is the Chinese character for San Francisco. So Bruce Lee’s Chinese name meant “Shake Up and Excite San Francisco.”

Hoi Chuen returned to his wife and newborn son as fast as he could. Grace would later joke with friends that he arrived with his face still covered in bright Cantonese Opera paint. Hoi Chuen decided his father’s life had been so cursed by misfortune that it would be unlucky to use the same “Jun” character (震) in his son’s name. He changed it to a slightly different “Jun” character (振), meaning “echo, reverberate, or resound.” Hoi Chuen didn’t like “Bruce” either, but since it was already recorded on the birth certificate, it was too late. He complained, “I can’t pronounce it.”

Li Hoi Chuen came to America to raise funds from the overseas Chinese community to support the war effort back home. As part of that process, he made a number of close friends. One of them was Esther Eng, a pioneering female film director who specialized in patriotic war movies. While filming *Golden Gate Girl*, she needed a newborn girl for several scenes and asked Hoi Chuen if she could borrow Bruce. He hesitated. Knowing intimately the vagaries of the artistic life, he didn’t want his children to follow in his footsteps, but as a traditional Chinese man he deeply believed in *guanxi* (關係), the system of relationships, connections, personal favors, and reciprocity that undergirds and binds Chinese society together. When he later explained why he decided to “lend out” his son, Hoi Chuen said that Chinese people have to help each other out, especially abroad. “Dad was very concerned about reciprocity among friends,” says Robert Lee.

Born on the road between curtain calls, Bruce Lee faced his first movie camera before he was old enough to crawl. It was his first and last cross-dressing performance. In one brief scene, two-month-old Bruce is rocked to sleep in a wicker bassinet, wearing a lacy bonnet and girl’s blouse. His mother, Grace, was flustered to see her delicate child so transfigured for the camera. In another close-up, a warmly wrapped baby Bruce cries inconsolably, eyes squeezed shut, mouth agape, arms flapping, chubby cheeks and double chin reverberating as the sound echoes through San Francisco.

Because Bruce was too young to travel, the Li family overstayed their visa by five months. It had been nearly a year and a half since Hoi Chuen and Grace had seen their other young children. They were anxious to go home.

But they worried Bruce might not be allowed to return to the United States. Discriminatory anti-Chinese immigration officials frequently denied American-born Chinese children reentry into the country by claiming they had "repatriated" (i.e., given up their U.S. citizenship) or questioning the validity of their paperwork. To ensure this didn't happen to their son, Hoi Chuen and Grace hired the appropriately named law firm of White & White, submitted documentary evidence of Bruce's birth in San Francisco, applied for a Citizen's Return Form for their son, and submitted to questioning under oath by the U.S. Immigration and Naturalization Services. Attached to Bruce's application for return was a photo of the chubby, healthy, three-month-old boy with a smattering of hair and pierced left ear. The stated reason for leaving the United States was "a temporary visit abroad." The visit would last eighteen years.

Departing from the port of San Francisco, they stepped onto the deck of the SS *President Pierce* on April 6, 1941, for the eighteen-day journey back to Hong Kong. Hoi Chuen must have considered his time away a rousing success. His wife had given birth to a second son—an heir and a spare. As one of the most famous actors on the tour, Hoi Chuen had helped stir the patriotic hearts of many Chinese Americans. "Upon hearing my father sing such pieces as 'Prime Minister Uniting the Six Kingdoms,' 'Martyrs for the Ming Royal Family,' and 'The Crimson Knights,' many overseas Chinese were moved to volunteer and donate," says Robert Lee.

Every little bit of reciprocity was necessary and needed, because Bruce and his parents were returning home to a situation that was turning from bad to worse.

No one was happier to see her son and daughter-in-law return safely to their old apartment on Mau Lam Street than Grandma Li, who was already seventy years old. She had carefully watched over Phoebe, Agnes, and Peter for eighteen months, as well as her widowed daughter-in-law and five children in a tiny two-bedroom, one-bathroom flat. Everyone was overjoyed to meet the newest member of the family, Bruce Jun Fan. Grandma Li nicknamed him Tiny Phoenix—the female counterpart to the dragon in Chinese mythology—in order to keep him safe from the ox ghosts and snake spirits, who liked to hurt little boys. "Though Dad didn't much like this girl's name, he was always very respectful of his mother's wishes," says Robert Lee, "and so went along with it." The excitement and delight of the reunion was soon dampened by terrible news abroad and at home.

World War II was engulfing the planet in fire and blood. Japanese forces were driving deep into China's heartland. In Europe, the German Luftwaffe was bombing British cities and German U-boats were sinking supply ships from America. Hong Kong was cut off from both China and Britain, helpless and alone.

As the Chinese and the British fought for their very survival, so did young Bruce Jun Fan Lee. Born in San Francisco's peaceful chill air, the chubby infant boy fell dangerously ill in Hong Kong's humid, cockroach-infested, wartime environment. A cholera outbreak was ravaging the colony. Bruce Jun Fan became so weak and thin his parents feared he might die. Having already lost one boy, Grace constantly hovered over her ailing son. "I think I spoiled him because he was so sick," Grace later said. Because of his near-fatal illness, Bruce Lee grew up frailer than the other children. He could not walk without stumbling until he was four years old.

On December 8, 1941, the day everyone had feared for years finally arrived in the British colony. Eight hours after their sneak attack on Pearl Harbor, Japan invaded Hong Kong, declaring war on America and Britain at the same time. The Allied garrison of British, Canadian, Indian, and a small group of Chinese volunteers was outnumbered four to one (Japanese 52,000; Allied 14,000).

Thousands of civilians were killed as the battle raged through Kowloon on the southern tip of mainland China and across the harbor into Hong

Kong Island. One of those who nearly died was Bruce's father, Hoi Chuen. Like many Cantonese Opera singers, he was an opium smoker. When Hoi Chuen was sharing a pipe with a fellow actor at a neighborhood opium den, a bomb from a Japanese plane crashed through the roof, smashed his friend in the bed next to his, and plunged down into the basement, carrying his friend's body with it. The bomb failed to explode—the only reason Hoi Chuen survived.

It took less than three weeks for the Japanese to conquer the exposed imperial outpost on December 25, 1941—known forever after in Hong Kong as "Black Christmas." It was the first time a British colony had ever surrendered to an invading force. Whatever resentment the Chinese felt about the British and their laissez-faire colonial rule was nothing compared to their horror at the totalitarian brutality of their new Japanese masters, who decided the best way to control the colony was to depopulate it. Anyone who did not have residence or employment was forced to leave. Those who remained suffered under a reign of terror. Ten thousand women were gang-raped. In the three years and eight months of Japanese occupation, the population dropped from 1.5 million to 600,000. One third escaped, mostly to the nearby Portuguese colony of Macau, one third survived by whatever means necessary, and the rest were starved or killed. Japanese sentries regularly shot or beheaded passing Chinese who failed to bow. Random civilians were killed for jujitsu practice, being thrown roughly to the ground repeatedly until unable to move and then bayoneted. An average of three hundred corpses were collected from the streets every day for the duration of the occupation—those who weren't murdered died from disease or malnourishment.

Li Hoi Chuen was the only breadwinner for a household of thirteen people. If forced to flee to Macau, it was unlikely all family members would survive, especially his infant son, Bruce, who had barely recovered from his near-fatal illness. Fortunately for Hoi Chuen and his dependents, the Japanese had a fondness for Chinese Opera. The head of the Japanese Ministry of Media, Wakuda Kosuke, made an offer to all the famous opera performers—including Hoi Chuen, who was one of the four great comedic "clown" actors—that they couldn't refuse. What exactly was said is unknown. "Dad never talked to anyone about it," says Robert Lee. "But considering the Japanese tactic of using food rationing to threaten people, we can only imagine he had no other choice." Phoebe says, "The Japanese forced my father to perform, but they didn't pay him with money. They paid him with rice instead, so we had rice for one meal once a week. The rest of the time we ground up tapioca to make *bok-chan* (Cantonese pancakes)."

The Japanese believed the continuation of opera performances created an impression of peace throughout their so-called Greater East Asia Co-Prosperity Sphere, so Hoi Chuen's job as an opera actor gave his family a slightly elevated status. Grace would later tell her children that when the Japanese soldiers came around, she only had to claim her husband was a Chinese Opera actor and they wouldn't give her any trouble.

In densely populated prewar Hong Kong, the most valuable asset was real estate. By removing two thirds of its people, the Japanese inadvertently flooded the housing market with available properties. Suddenly, the few like Hoi Chuen who had decent jobs and food rations could dramatically improve their lot. About a year into the occupation, he moved his thirteen-member family into a four-thousand-square-foot apartment—extremely spacious by Hong Kong standards. The flat's biggest selling point was its location at 218 Nathan Road, Kowloon. It was directly across a small park from the Japanese occupation headquarters, making the neighborhood safe from the desperate criminality of starving locals trying to survive. Over the next two years, Hoi Chuen cleverly purchased at depressed prices four more apartments as rental properties.

Even for lucky families like the Lis, life was a daily fight for survival, filled with deprivation, misery, and humiliation. A strict nighttime curfew was enforced along with a requirement of absolute silence. One night during the occupation, one of Bruce's aunts was loudly playing mahjong at a friend's apartment, causing Japanese soldiers to kick in the door and order them to stop. When Auntie objected in an even louder voice, a Japanese soldier slapped her across the face, forced her to bow, and made her apologize one hundred times.

The collective shame and loss of face suffered during the occupation led many to overstate their resistance after it was over. In one of the earliest tales the family liked to tell about Bruce Jun Fan, the patriotic toddler reportedly would stand on the apartment's balcony and "shake his fist defiantly at Japanese planes flying overhead." It's a prideful image with one small problem. By the time young Bruce, born November 27, 1940, was old enough to stand and raise a clenched hand, the Japanese had already lost air superiority over the colony to the Allies. If Bruce ever shook his fist at a foreign plane, it was an American one. "I was in Macau for the war," Marciano Baptista, a classmate of Bruce's older brother, Peter, says. "American planes attacked the power and oil stations in '43, '44. We still shook our fists at them, because they were causing chaos."

While the Allies controlled the air for several years, the liberation of Hong Kong had to wait until after Hiroshima, Nagasaki, and the surrender of Japan on August 15, 1945. Both Chinese and American officials expected control of Hong Kong to be returned to China, but the British, who considered restoration of colonial rule a matter of honor and a necessity for their Asian commercial interests, raced a Royal Navy task force to Hong Kong to accept the Japanese surrender and reclaim Hong Kong for themselves on August 30.

In retrospect, it was the best possible outcome for the people of Hong Kong. China was about to be consumed by a civil war between the Nationalists and the Communists, led by Mao Zedong, that would further tear the country apart and then sink it into decades of isolation and turmoil. In contrast, Hong Kongers would flourish, especially families like the Lis, who enjoyed their most prosperous period following the bitterness of the Three Year Eight Month Occupation.

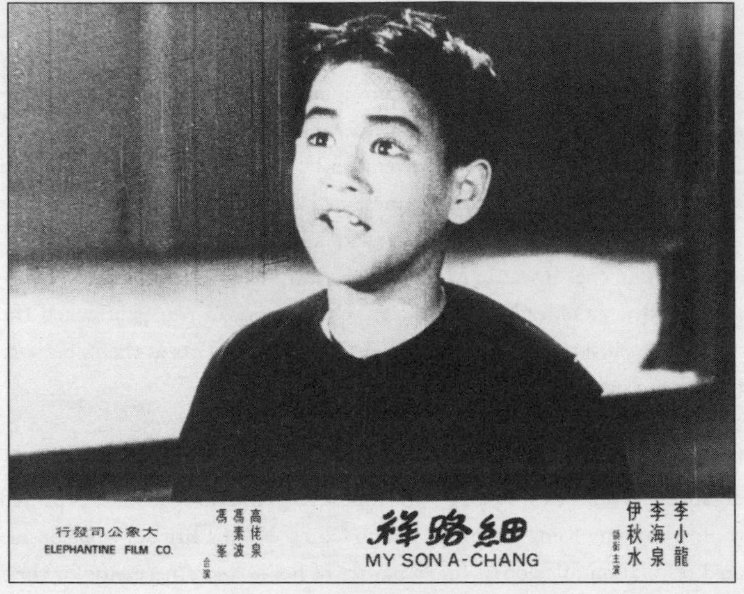

大象公司發行
ELEPHANTINE FILM CO.
高佬泉
馮素波
馮峯
合演
細路祥
MY SON A-CHANG
李小龍
李海泉
伊秋水
藝術主演

Ten-year-old Bruce Lee's first starring role as an orphan in *My Son A-Chang* (1950)—also called *The Kid*. *(Courtesy of Hong Kong Heritage Museum)*

In the movie *The Orphan* (1960), Bruce's troubled teenage character pulls a knife on his teacher. *(Courtesy of Hong Kong Heritage Museum)*

two

boomtown

After Hong Kong was liberated, everyone who had been banished came flooding back, along with hundreds of thousands of refugees from China's civil war. The first to arrive packed themselves into every available room—each divided into ten or more "bed spaces"—until there was nothing left for the remainders but the hillside shantytowns. In five years, the population jumped from 600,000 to three million, and rental prices went through the roof. Suddenly, Li Hoi Chuen was not only an actor but also a successful landlord.

Owning four apartments did not make him a tycoon—he was not in the top one percent like Bruce's great-uncle Robert Hotung—but it did secure his large family's financial future. "My parents were not real rich, but we never had to worry about food or clothing," Bruce told friends later in life. In fact, the family was more than comfortable. By the Third World standards of postwar Hong Kong, they were affluent and could afford the latest luxuries. "By 1950, we had a TV, a fridge, a car, and a driver," Phoebe recalls. "We didn't have a sense of social classes, but if you had a TV, you must be in the upper class." Along with a driver, they also had two live-in servants, plus a cat, a tankful of goldfish, and five wolfhounds. Through a combination of talent, shrewdness, and luck, Hoi Chuen had climbed a long way from his impoverished childhood.

After the deprivations of the occupation, the children flourished in their newfound prosperity. Phoebe and Bruce were the extroverted, fun-loving siblings, while Peter and Agnes were the introverted, studious ones. "They didn't talk much and were serious about everything they did," says Phoebe. "Bruce and I were different. We would fight one minute and then be fine the next. We were lazy, but I wasn't as lazy as him. If we were too lazy, our father would scold and not feed us."

The illness and frailty that haunted Bruce during the occupation lost its grip after the liberation. He became so hyperactive his family nicknamed him "Never Sits Still." He was forever jumping, talking, playing, or moving. Peter remembers that if Bruce was ever quiet for a long period his mother thought he must be sick. "He almost had a disorder which filled him with too much extra energy like a wild horse that had been tied up," says Robert. When he wasn't knocking over furniture in a whirlwind of chaos, Bruce was questioning everything his parents told him to do, earning him yet another nickname, "Why Baby." (His skeptical attitude toward authority lasted his entire life. The director of *The Big Boss* (1971) called Bruce in exasperation, "The Why Dragon.")

His parents discovered the only way to calm Bruce down—his "off-switch"—was to hand him a comic book. He would read quietly for hours. Prior to the advent of television in Hong Kong in 1957, comic books and magazines, like *The Children's Paradise*, were a major form of entertainment. Bruce started with kung fu comic books and graduated to sword-and-sorcery martial arts (in Chinese, *wuxia*) novels—devoting much of his spare time to bookstores. Bruce read so much his mother believed it caused him to be nearsighted. "He used to spend hours in bed reading comic books with small type without my permission," recalls Grace. "I think that is what contributed to his poor eyesight." Bruce began wearing corrective glasses at the age of six.

All of those comic books and fantasy novels created a rich inner life. As he read, Bruce imagined himself as the story's hero. Once Grace rebuked her son for acting selfishly, "You are really no use, child. You seem to hardly have any soft spot for your own family." To defend himself, Bruce told a story, "If we were ever walking in the forest and came across a tiger, I'd stay and fight the tiger and let the rest of you escape."

Along with the rental properties and his salary as a stage actor, Hoi Chuen developed a new source of income: the movies. Before the war, the managing director of China's biggest studio, Lianhua, was Bruce's great-uncle Robert Hotung. Its head office was initially in Hong Kong until it became clear that Shanghai was the Mecca of Chinese filmmaking. As Shanghai's influence grew, initiating the first golden age of Chinese cinema in the 1930s, Hong Kong turned into a regional branch office, making cheap flicks in the local dialect, Cantonese. The Japanese invasion effectively halted all movie production until 1945. The only Hong Kong film made during the three years and eight months of subjugation was the Japanese propaganda film *The Battle for Hong Kong* (1942). The cast was mostly Japanese, but many Hong Kong film personalities were forcefully asked to participate, including Bruce's father. He courageously refused. This wise decision saved his career—those who appeared in the movie were blacklisted after the war as collaborators.

After liberation, the continuing civil war in mainland China caused many Shanghai artists to relocate to Hong Kong. The initial trickle of migrating talent transformed into a flood after Mao Zedong's victory in 1949 and the Communist Party's decision to close their market, ban all foreign films, and only allow the production of government-censored propaganda movies. By 1950, Hong Kong was the Hollywood of the East, the center of the Chinese filmmaking world.

As a famous stage actor and one of the few to survive the occupation with his reputation intact, Hoi Chuen was well positioned to take advantage of the boom in movie productions. He became a character actor in dozens of films, often playing for laughs a comic archetype—the miserly rich guy who gets his comeuppance—a Chinese Scrooge. While movie actors weren't paid well by modern standards, it was far more lucrative than stage work. "The money he made for shooting a movie was about half the price of an apartment back then," says Takkie Yeung, the Hong Kong director of *The Brilliant Life of Bruce Lee.*

As part of the nascent movie industry, Hoi Chuen was friendly with all the major players, often inviting them over to his home. He also brought his children on-set with him. None of them took to the jungle-gym-like backlots with as much excitement as "Never Sits Still." "Bruce climbed the wooden ladders to reach the suspended studio lights. We were afraid he would lose his grip. He wanted to touch everything from the cameras to the sound equipment," remembers one of the actresses, Feng So Po. "He was so naughty they taught him hand games to distract him."

When Bruce was six years old, the director of his father's latest film saw him on-set and was so impressed that he offered him a part. At first, both Bruce and his father thought he was joking. "Bruce was wide eyed, open mouthed, and deliriously happy," says his mother, Grace. It was his first part—playing a runaway boy who becomes a pickpocket and is run over by a truck—in the Cantonese tearjerker *The Birth of Mankind* (1946). A forgettable flick that flopped at the box office, it is only notable for typecasting young Bruce as a tough, wily street urchin with a heart of gold, a kind of Artful Dodger. It was a character he would play repeatedly for the rest of his childhood acting career.

In his next film, *Wealth Is like a Dream* (1948), he once again was cast as a lost boy on his own after the war. His father, Hoi Chuen, was a costar in the film and the movie promoters, seeking to play off the family connection and his father's fame, gave Bruce a new stage name, Little Hoi Chuen. The newspapers even advertised "Cameo by Wonder Kid Little Li Hoi Chuen." Bruce's career, down to his diminutive screen name, began in the shadow of Hoi Chuen's star. The son would spend the rest of his life determined to outshine his father.

Bruce's first chance to win a victory in this Oedipal battle came with his fifth film, *My Son A-Chang* (also titled *The Kid*) in 1950. Based on a popular comic book by Po-Wan Yuen, it was by the standards of the time a serious, big-budget film. The director, Feng Feng, interviewed a number of child actors but none of them was right for the title role of A-Chang—a tough, wily street urchin with a heart of gold—until he saw the fiendish energy of Bruce's previous screen work. Director Feng personally visited 218 Nathan

Road to ask for the father's blessing but was, to his surprise, rebuffed. A leading role in a major movie threatened to turn what was an extracurricular activity into a full-time career, and Hoi Chuen, to his credit, was not at all certain he wanted his son to follow in his theatrical footsteps. He hoped his children would become well-educated middle-class professionals—doctors, lawyers, bankers. Director Feng praised his son's talent, spoke of his destiny as an entertainer, and, when all this failed, offered Hoi Chuen a major role in the film—as the miserly, rich boss who is secretly a soft touch—so he could keep an eye on his boy during filming. "Finally, Dad agreed," says Robert, "and this decision would change Bruce's life."

Following the civil war in China, the early 1950s Hong Kong film community was politically charged and ideologically divided between left-wing Communist sympathizers and right-wing Nationalists. *My Son A-Chang* is a solid example of socialist agitprop. Bruce, as A-Chang, is an orphan boy living with his uncle, a teacher who is paid so poorly he can't afford to send his nephew to school. Hoi Chuen, playing Boss Hong, the owner of a sweatshop, hires A-Chang's uncle as his private secretary and arranges for A-Chang to attend a private school, where he is bullied as the new kid, gets into a fight, and is promptly expelled. A-Chang then falls in with a gang of former war veterans who have been forced by the cruel capitalist system into a life of crime. "We have to steal to survive," says the leader, Flying Blade Lee.

After a bungled attempt to rob Boss Hong's factory ends in murder, Flying Blade nobly agrees to take all the blame, instructing his fellow hoodlums to flee and reform their ways: "No more crime. Find a proper job. You just have to work hard. Give A-Chang my share of the money, so he and his uncle can farm in villages." The movie ends with A-Chang and his uncle, the former teacher, happily heading to the countryside to restart their lives as peasants. The movie predates the Cultural Revolution by twenty-five years, where teachers and intellectuals were forcibly relocated to the countryside to be reeducated as peasants.

Politics aside, ten-year-old Bruce's performance displays a range of emotions and raw talent. In one scene he is humorously imitating his teacher; in another, he puffs himself up with cocky bravado by throwing his shoulders back and thumbing his nose at an opponent—one of his signature moves as an adult actor. In an elaborately choreographed fight, he fearlessly jumps onto the back of the evil factory foreman, who shakes him off and takes a wild swing. Bruce ducks it and head-butts his adult enemy in the stomach like a charging ram. When one of the foreman's punches finally lands, young Bruce rips open his shirt, pulls out a knife tucked inside his pants, and charges at the foreman, who runs away in terror. Bruce would later re-create this scene in real life, getting himself into serious trouble.

For Bruce Lee fans, the movie is most notable for the new screen name given to the lead actor. Previously known as Little Hoi Chuen, the film's opening credits list him as Li Long (李龍) or "Dragon Li." Given his pint-sized stature, this was quickly converted to Li Xiao Long (李小龍) or "Little Dragon Li." Bruce loved his new screen name so much he insisted on using it in his private life. From then on, all of his friends called him Little Dragon Li, many of them having no idea that his birth name was Li Jun Fan. If names have a magical power, this film marked the moment when Bruce Jun Fan Little Dragon Li Lee's personal life and movie persona began to merge, overlap, and bleed into each other.

My Son A-Chang opened in late May of 1950. It was a box office and critical success. Plans were immediately made for a sequel, but the project was soon scuttled by Bruce's father, who refused to allow his son to appear in it. His general concerns about his children following in his footsteps into the topsy-turvy entertainment industry had become very specific in regards to Bruce, who was becoming as rebellious and difficult to handle as the characters he played in his films.

Hoi Chuen had always kept a close eye on his baby boy. He frequently took Bruce on special fishing trips and backstage during stage performances. To strengthen his body, Hoi Chuen would often bring Bruce, starting at the age of seven, along with him to King's Park in the morning to practice Tai Chi together. The slow meditative art form, which uses soft to conquer hard and stillness to conquer speed, was Bruce Lee's first style of martial arts and a test of his patience. "Dad also wanted to use Tai Chi as a way to help with Bruce's hyperactive tendencies," says Robert. Bruce enjoyed the special father-son time, but not Tai Chi. "I got tired of it quickly," he later explained. "It was no fun for a kid. Just a bunch of old men." In addition, he found its techniques useless for what was quickly becoming his favorite extracurricular activity—fighting.

Bruce's mother, Grace, was a devout Catholic and personal friends with many European and American nuns and priests. Wanting her children to have the best possible education, she enrolled them in the finest Catholic schools in the British colony. "To send her children to whichever parochial school was as easy as placing a phone call for her," says Robert. For their elementary school education, Grace sent her daughters to St. Mary's School run by European nuns and her sons to Tak Sun, an all-boys parochial school.

When Bruce entered Tak Sun at the age of six, he was at a distinct disadvantage. Physically weaker and smaller than the other boys with perhaps lingering balance issues from his childhood illness, he was never able to learn how to ride a bike. He was also terrified of the water. "Bruce was already quite mischievous. Our sisters thought they'd 'teach him a lesson' by holding him underwater at the Lai Chi Kok Amusement Park swimming pavilion and not letting him come back up," says Robert. "It scared him so badly he never dared to swim again." Severely nearsighted, Bruce wore thick, horn-rim glasses, and his ear was pierced to protect him from boy-stealing snake demons. "He even wore an earring to school, inviting much teasing from his classmates," says Robert.

Most scrawny, four-eyed boys would have hidden in the corner, downcast, lost in fantasy. But not Bruce. Just like his character in *My Son A-Chang*, he was pugnacious and short-tempered. Anyone who teased him or made him lose face, he fought right then, right there. It didn't matter if they were bigger or smaller, taller or shorter, older or younger, he fought them all, until he developed a reputation and the other boys stopped picking on him.

While Bruce started out defending himself against insults, he quickly acquired a taste for combat and was soon instigating fights himself. His reputation shifted from someone you didn't want to mess with to the boy it was best to avoid. Parents began warning their sons to stay away from him.

"We were playing marbles," Anthony Yuk Cheung, his third-grade classmate, recalls. "He took a shot put and smashed some of our marbles.

We went to another corner of the playground. He followed us and ruined the rest of our marbles. I ran away, but he chased me, so I fought him. That was the first time in my life. There is a Chinese saying, 'Corner a dog in a dead-end street, and it will turn and bite.' "

Bruce's remarkably forgiving Catholic instructors, who had a boys-will-be-boys approach to discipline, plotted ways to keep the Little Dragon contained. "He was a real pain in the neck for any teacher, a proverbial devil in the holy water soup," remembers Brother Henry, one of his teachers. "I waged a battle on his hyperactive problem and won it. The strategy was simple—Bruce was basically a good boy and a maverick if you understood him and handled him right. He was a live wire charged with I do not know how many kilowatts. So each morning my first step was to preempt that energy and tire him out before he caused trouble. I gave him all the odd jobs I could think of: opening all the windows, cleaning blackboards, getting the register from the office, and running errands all over school. When that didn't work I sent him to the headmaster with a note, 'Sending you Bruce to have a few moments of peace.' Looking back on who he became as a man, I'm glad I did not suppress or snuff him out."

Bruce hated school. Sitting still in a classroom was nearly impossible for him. He fidgeted and couldn't focus on the lessons. While he loved reading comic books and martial arts novels, he despised his textbooks, refusing to crack them open. He was a bright child who got terrible grades because he refused to do his homework. What must have made this even worse for Bruce was the fact that his older brother, Peter, was a model student—the scholarly overachiever who aced all his exams. "Dad was very fond of Peter, because he was studious, had a bright future, and, like himself, was very quiet," says Robert.

To help her wayward son, Grace hired a private tutor for Bruce. Acting like an obedient child, he would dutifully leave the house to visit the tutor, carrying an armload of books. An hour or two later the tutor would call Grace, "Where's Bruce?" When Bruce returned home—his clothes ragged and torn, his books unopened—he'd swear he had been with the tutor the entire time. "Bruce was generally off with friends, fighting in the street," recalls Grace. "He didn't know the tutor had just called. I'd ask him where he'd been, and he'd tell me he just finished studying."

Bruce had joined a gang. Or to be more precise he had formed his own gang. The Little Dragon didn't take orders—he gave them. His classmates say he had a half dozen or so "followers," who did his bidding. Two of them would remain loyal to him his entire life. Wu Ngan was the son of the main servant in the Li household. Growing up together, they were like brothers. Wu Ngan would later become Bruce's manservant when they were adults. There was no one Bruce trusted more. The other was Unicorn Chan, a childhood actor Bruce had met on the set of *The Birth of Mankind* (1946). Unicorn would later help Bruce as an adult revive his movie career in Hong Kong.

Unlike in the movie *My Son A-Chang*, these boys were not street urchins. They were mostly middle-class kids attending prestigious parochial schools. They were rabble-rousers, not gangsters, causing minor trouble, not committing serious crimes. Besides getting into fights, their main leisure activity was pranks. "One night, when our maid went out for the evening, Bruce moved all the furniture in her room to different spots," remembers Grace. "The nearest light was in the center of the room, so when she returned she banged and bumped into almost every chair and table until she reached it. Afterward, she was furious and came to me saying she knew it was Bruce. I promised I would talk to him but found it very hard to keep from laughing myself."

As he grew older the pranks became more sophisticated and aggressive, especially if he felt he was avenging his family or his friends. At the age of ten, Bruce and Wu Ngan tried to sneak into the Dongle Theatre at the corner of Nathan and Nullah Roads. Bruce made it inside but Wu Ngan was caught by the South Asian ticket-taker, scolded, and smacked across the head. Filled with rage, Bruce rushed outside and yelled for the man to stop, resulting in both of them being punished. They spent the next two weeks plotting their revenge. They bought piping-hot, fragrant roast squid from a nearby food stall, to which they secretly added a laxative, and then offered it, with profuse apologies, to the ticket-taker. Now most ten-year-old pranksters would have stopped here, but not Bruce. Instead, the boys hid inside one of the bathroom stalls with a carefully prepared bucket full of excrement waiting for the ticket-taker to relieve himself. When the laxative-laced squid forced him to the bathroom, the boys stuck a four-inch firecracker into the crap-filled bucket, lit it, and slid the bucket under the stall door right in front of the ticket-taker. When it blew, it covered the man in feces. Bruce was banned from the theater for six months.

Grace, who later worried she had spoiled Bruce, played the good cop. She scolded, cajoled, and pleaded with him, hiding many of his infractions from his father. When Bruce went too far, like with the movie ticket-taker, Grace called in the enforcer. "Bruce knew how much his father hated violence," says Grace. "I would always threaten to tell on him if he didn't start behaving. He always promised to, but he kept fighting."

While Hoi Chuen played the comic clown onstage and in the movies, his primary role at home was as the stern, emotionally distant disciplinarian—an archetype familiar to most Chinese children. "Each time Bruce did something wrong, my father would punish all of us," Phoebe recalls, chuckling. "It was our responsibility to look after our younger brother. He'd twist our ears, close the door, and make us kneel. He would say, 'Dare to misbehave now?' Then he would hit each of us—boys with a bamboo stick, and girls with a rolled-up newspaper. Bruce would ask why the girls only got hit with a newspaper. Dad would say, 'Because sisters are girls, and newspapers don't hurt so much, but you boys misbehave so much, you won't think it hurts enough.' Often he didn't have to hit Bruce—he could scare Bruce with just one look. Dad had this awe about him."

The bad grades, the constant fighting, the increasingly violent pranks—Little Dragon was bringing disgrace on his family, making his parents lose face. After his stunt with the ticket-taker at the Dongle Theatre, something had to be done. Besides his comic books, the only thing Bruce truly loved was acting. While his mother could barely drag him out of bed in the mornings for school, she had no trouble waking him to go to the film studio in the wee hours. (To avoid the loud city noises of Hong Kong and its nearby airport, studios did most of their filming at night. It wasn't until the 1960s that they began to record the audio separately and dub it in.) "Bruce was a natural," Robert says. "Awakened in the middle of the night, he was on his feet and in character right away."

Since no other type of punishment seemed to work, his father put him in a movie-acting "time out," until he started to behave. He barred the Little Dragon from taking part in the sequel to *My Son A-Chang*. For the rest of 1950, Bruce did not appear in another film. After much begging from Bruce, they allowed him to make one movie in 1951, *The Beginning of Man*, but since his behavior did not improve, they banned him again. The Little Dragon did not appear on-screen again until 1953, a two-year hiatus.

Far from being stage parents, Hoi Chuen and Grace viewed acting as a privilege, not a career, to be taken away if Bruce didn't study hard. Hoi Chuen had grown up so poor he couldn't afford to attend school. He didn't want one of his sons to miss out on a good education—or make the same mistakes he had.

Hong Kong was still awash in opium a century after its conquest. While the colonial government had officially banned the drug in 1908, enforcement was lax. Up until the 1960s, the number of opium addicts, especially in the entertainment industry, continued to grow. One of them was Bruce's father. "It helps my theater voice," Hoi Chuen claimed, "and sweetens my singing." Opium was to Chinese Opera singers what heroin was to American jazz musicians. A Cantonese slang term for smoking opium was "chewing rhyme."

Hoi Chuen's favorite acting role, and his most famous performance, was in the play *Two Opium Addicts Sweep the Dike*. This comedy about two bony, skinny opium fiends sent to do cleanup work in Guangzhou after the government prohibited opium required (allowed) the two lead actors, Li Hoi Chuen and Sun-Ma Sze-Tsang, to smoke opium onstage night after night.

It was perfect casting for Hoi Chuen, who had done plenty of personal research into the subject. In his bedroom at home, he had a king-sized opium bed. Many famous actors and directors visited the apartment to get their fix. "Dad loved to lie on the right side, leaving the left side free for guests," says Phoebe. As a young girl, she curried favor by assisting him and his friends. "Why did I get along best with my father? My father taught me how to light up the pipe and give it to him to smoke."

Sometime in the early 1950s, opium drew Hoi Chuen deeper and deeper into its euphoric, languid, sweet oblivion. He lost interest in anything but sleep and smoking more. According to Grace, he was close to the children when they were younger, but as they got older he changed and had very little to do with his family: "He spent most of his time in his room studying or sleeping and didn't sit with the family except at meals." Bruce later told his wife, Linda, his father was "an absentee parent," who, because of his habit, "was often not mentally there for him."

Besides the emotional costs, there were the financial. "Only rich people could smoke opium at that time," Phoebe says. "You couldn't smoke if you didn't have the money. It was a very fashionable thing!" Hoi Chuen had over a dozen mouths to feed, plus the giant monkey on his back. The cost of supplying his habit and the ravaging effect addiction had on his acting career threatened his family's upper-class status. Bruce frequently complained to his teenage friends about his father's "stinginess" and the lack of spending money. For years Grace pleaded with her husband to quit without success.

The effect of the father's addiction on his children was to exaggerate their natural inclinations. The sensitive, studious Peter buried his head in his homework and focused on individual sports, becoming an elite fencer. He was the son everyone in the family expected to be the first to attend college. In sharp contrast, hyperactive Bruce appeared to be heading to jail. He exhibited many of the classic symptoms of a child of a drug-abusing parent: aggression, distrust of authority figures, and excessive need to be in control.

Following in the footsteps of his older brother, ten-year-old Bruce entered La Salle in September 1951 as a fifth-grader. Run by the Catholic Lasallian Brothers, La Salle, located at the time on Perth Street, was one of the most prestigious secondary schools in Hong Kong. Most of its students were upper- and middle-class Chinese and Eurasians, although there were a number of scholarship students. Its great advantage was the entire curriculum was taught in English, producing bilingual graduates. This guaranteed a decent job in the British colony. "You could join the police, a bank, the civil service," says Marciano Baptista, a classmate of Bruce's older brother, Peter. Without his elite education at La Salle, Bruce Lee would never have made it in Hollywood, where the ability to speak English is a prerequisite, especially for Asian actors.

English was one of the few subjects in which Bruce excelled. Overall, he was a terrible student, especially in math. "He never got beyond the stage of simple addition and subtractions—and he managed to stay in school at all only because he bullied other youngsters into doing his homework for him," says Linda Lee. His mother joked, "By the time he was ten, that was as far as he could count." One of his classmates says that he let Bruce peep at his test paper during exams for 50 cents. Despite the bullying and bribery, Bruce was held back twice in the five years he attended La Salle. It was far more common back then than it is now to be asked to repeat a grade, but Bruce was still considered a particularly poor student, one of the worst in his class, while Peter was one of the best.

Like many Hong Kong bad boys (called in Cantonese slang "teddy boys"), Bruce's favorite time was recess. Out from under the thumb of the adult authority figures, he set out to establish control by recruiting his classmates into his crew. He flitted from one boy to another, joking, cajoling, and promising. "He would often put his arm around his schoolmates and just say to them, 'If anyone is causing you trouble, just let me know and I will take up the matter with them,' " recalls classmate Pau Siu Hung. Other boys he tried to win over with his cutup sense of humor. For laughs and attention, he would imitate King Kong, inflating his barrel chest, pounding it with his fists, and shrieking like an ape. He often called himself the Monkey King. "He was always talking and liked to make jokes so he always had lots of friends," recalls the introverted Peter. His contemporaries remember him strutting around the playground with a "bounce," his heels hardly touching the ground. Michael Lai, a childhood friend, describes young Bruce's personality as "teeth brushing," slang for boastful, cocky, a peacock.

Bruce was not, according to his peers, a bully in the classic sense: a sadist who takes pleasure in humiliating weaker boys. Rather he was a gang leader, offering protection to those willing to follow him. Robert Lee, who idolizes his older brother and tends to paint him in the most positive light, says, "Bruce was more often like a hero in a chivalry movie—always trying to defend the weak from the strong, like a knight-errant-type character." This was true for members of his crew, whom he looked after and fiercely protected. In return, they hailed him as "big brother," did his homework, and let him cheat off their tests. "He had a mesmerizing leadership that made people submit," says Michael Lai.

"From boyhood to adolescence, I was a bit of a troublemaker and was greatly disapproved of by my elders," Bruce later told reporters. "I was extremely mischievous and aggressive." He focused his aggression on his rivals, the leaders of other cliques. The Little Dragon believed everyone should follow him—respect his authority. "Bruce picked on the boys who liked to show off and tried to look confident," recalls classmate Dennis Ho. "He would go and put those boys right." To any boy who wouldn't bend to Bruce's will, a challenge was issued. The battles took place behind the hill overlooking La Salle. "You didn't have to ask Bruce twice to fight," says Robert. In fact, you didn't have to ask once. He won more often than he lost, but the hypercompetitive Bruce hated losing so much he refused to admit defeat. "When he lost, we'd ask him how it happened," says Michael Lai, "and he'd always come up with excuses for himself, because he was like the boss of everyone and needed to win."

Bruce's chief rival was David Lee, a tough boy with whom most people didn't mess. They battled several times. In their last contest, it got heated, and both Bruce and David pulled out their switchblades. The fight was stopped after Bruce lightly cut David's arm, drawing first blood. The injury wasn't serious, but neither boy wanted to take their enmity any further. The use of weapons, instead of just fists and feet, shocked the more timid sensibilities of their middle-class La Salle classmates. Only the most rebellious teddy boys, like Bruce and David, carried weapons on their persons to school. Bruce owned a switchblade, brass knuckles, and other improvised devices. "In school, our favorite weapon was bathroom chains used to flush toilets," Bruce explained. "Those days, kids improvised all kinds of weapons—even shoes with razors."

With their gang life obsessions, these La Salle boys were, in their middle-class way, imitating their elders. The Triads (Chinese mafia) had been operating in the colony since the beginning of the opium trade, but their influence didn't take off until after Mao Zedong's victory in 1949. "The communists purged the Triads, so the criminals all came down to Hong Kong," says William Cheung, a friend of Bruce's. "A lot of kids got hooked up with them, some very reluctantly. By 1954, they were quite established." The influx of hundreds of thousands of desperate Chinese refugees, including ex-soldiers and Triad members, proved a volatile mix, spreading corruption and violence across the Kowloon side of the colony.

Another cultural shift affecting Bruce and his crew was growing Chinese nationalism. The failure of the British to defend the colony against the Japanese had shattered the myth of white superiority, and many Chinese resented the reestablishment of British colonial rule after the war. "The British were the ruling class. They were the minority but they ran the city," Bruce later told American friends. "They lived up on the hills with the big cars and beautiful homes, while the rest of the population, who lived below, struggled and sweat their asses off to make a living. You saw so much poverty among the Chinese people that eventually it was natural to hate the filthy-rich British. They made the most money and had the best jobs because the color of their skin was white."

After school was over, the La Salle boys engaged in an extracurricular activity they called "Limey Bashing." "We used to stroll along the street, looking for trouble," says Michael Lai. "We had much ethnic pride. We liked to beat up the British boys." The closest target was King George V (KGV), the nearby private school for English kids and other European expats. Bruce and his marauding band of boys would head up the hill separating La Salle and KGV hoping to encounter a group of British boys. Once contact was made, the taunting, insulting, and pushing would begin until tempers overcame common sense, and the fighting finally got under way. Bruce always took the lead, punching and kicking his way to schoolboy glory. "There were constant fights between the expats and local kids," recalls Steve Garcia, a Eurasian classmate of Bruce's. "They had disdain for us."

As the boys reached puberty, KGV offered another source of attraction and opportunity for conflict: females. "They were after our girls," says Anders Nelsson, a graduate of King George V, who later had a small role in Bruce's movie *Way of the Dragon*. "Of course, we went after theirs too at Maryknoll and the other all-girl Chinese schools. There's a Cantonese expression, 'The local ginger is not hot.' I guess they seemed more exotic to us, being Asian girls." It was Hong Kong's version of *West Side Story* with British Jets and Chinese Sharks.

After a two-year time-out from the movie industry (1951–53), Bruce's parents grudgingly gave in to their son's entreaties to revive his acting career. Hoi Chuen and Grace had hoped the ban would force their son to concentrate on his studies, but it had been in vain—Bruce's grades and behavior only got worse, not better. They agreed to let the Little Dragon return to films but on the strict condition that he behave himself. This decision was made easier by the caliber of the team Bruce was joining.

In 1952, a group of the top Cantonese movie directors, actors, and writers had set up their own production company—Union Film Enterprises, or Chung-luen in Cantonese. The expressed goal of this leftist collective was to produce high-quality, socially conscious films. "Cinema should entertain as well as educate audiences to the ethical, to serve the community, to be patriotic, and to take pride in our cultural heritage," explained one of its founders. The flood of nearly a million refugees from the mainland had created a great deal of stress, division, and hardship in the colony. The didactic message of Chung-luen's films was the need for unity, charity, and sacrifice among the Chinese people and government assistance from above. They were socialists not Communists. "Dad was very supportive of Chung-luen's ideals," says Robert. "He was confident they would have a positive effect on Bruce's development."

Perhaps the effect Bruce's father was most looking to develop in his son was a sense of humility and teamwork. All Chung-luen films used the same troupe of a dozen or so actors, mostly adults with Bruce as the token teenage boy. In the spirit of the organization, most of their films were ensemble pieces rather than star vehicles. Bruce typically played secondary roles, appearing onscreen an average of about twenty minutes with about thirty lines of dialogue.

He had one of his biggest roles in his first Chung-luen film, *The Guiding Light* (1953). The plot of the movie: A foster child, who is bounced from home to home, ends up on the streets until he is rescued by a doctor and his kindhearted wife who runs an orphanage for blind girls. The doctor, whose motto is "Kids can always be taught," adopts the homeless boy (played by Bruce) as his apprentice. When Bruce's character grows up, he discovers the cure for blindness. The movie ends with a direct-to-camera plea: "Every child can be just like him. Poor handicapped children are waiting for your love, for education and nurturing."

Between 1953 and 1955, Bruce appeared in ten of Chung-luen's message-driven melodramas: *The Guiding Light*, *A Mother's Tears*, *Sins of the Father*, *Ten-Million People*, *In the Face of Demolition*, *Love*, *An Orphan's Tragedy*, *The Faithful Wife*, *Orphan's Song*, and *Debt Between Mother and Son*. These three years were the most prolific of Bruce's entire film career, comprising nearly half of his oeuvre. His small roles in these movies established Bruce in the public mind as a character actor, not a star, someone whose face they might recognize but whose name they probably couldn't recall.

Chung-luen provided Bruce with an elite education in how to make quality films about serious subjects at a Hong Kong pace. Most of the film shoots lasted only twelve days. The company's ideals also deeply influenced Bruce as an adult filmmaker. He grew up wanting to make patriotic, educational movies about China's cultural heritage.

The money wasn't half bad either for a teenage boy. He earned the equivalent of US$2,000 per film in 2017 dollars. This started a habit he would continue his entire life of purchasing extravagant items with his movie earnings. "After one film, he bought himself a little monkey. One day the monkey somehow got into the cage of our cousin Frank's pet bird and ripped it to pieces," says Robert. "When our cousin found his bird dead, he literally beat the monkey up, making the monkey so mad it bit me. My mother told Bruce the monkey had to go. Bruce didn't want to give it up at first, but finally agreed to begrudgingly."

The artistic union of Chung-luen didn't last long. After three years, ego and infighting split the principals apart and the most talented dispersed to other production companies. No longer part of a highly creative and prolific team, Bruce found roles more difficult to come by. He only appeared in five films in the next five years. Without this creative outlet and structure, his teenage attention turned back to fighting and troublemaking.

After five years at La Salle, Bruce was expelled in 1956. For a respected middle-class family—his father a famous stage actor, his mother a member of the richest clan in Hong Kong—this was a terrible embarrassment. The level of shame can be measured by the degree to which the family has tried to cover up the reason. Phoebe has claimed it was his grades: "Bruce was very lazy. The school only allowed students to repeat a grade once. After his first repetition, his school didn't give him a second chance." In fact, Bruce was held back twice. According to his classmates repeating a grade was fairly common and certainly not cause for expulsion.

In his biography of his brother, Robert Lee writes, "Because Bruce was simply too mischievous—always getting into fights and playing hooky from the time he started studying Wing Chun at the age of fourteen, and showing up for school in outrageous getups—they finally threw him out." In fact, La Salle's attendance records for Bruce show he rarely if ever missed school. All evidence indicates that Bruce didn't start practicing Wing Chun until after he was kicked out of La Salle. Since the school did not have a strict dress code, outrageous getups could not have been a reason for expulsion. And fighting was extremely common among the boys—Bruce had been getting into scraps with his schoolmates from the moment he entered La Salle.

According to his classmates, there were two incidents in his last year at La Salle that led to Bruce's expulsion. The first involved the PE teacher, who all the boys nicknamed Coolie Lo (Coolie because he had dark skin, like a peasant or unskilled laborer; Lo means "guy" or "man"). To warm up at the beginning of class, he made the boys run around the soccer field three times. To motivate the slackers and stragglers, Coolie Lo would hit the back of their legs. "He would run with the class, staying at the end and encouraging the boys along, chanting, 'You're too slow. Need to catch up,' " says classmate Pau Siu Hung.

One day, Bruce, who got paddled plenty by his father at home, decided he was tired of being switched by Coolie Lo. According to Robert's version of the event, "There was a P.E. teacher who liked to hit the students with a ruler, an injustice to which Bruce was not keen to submit. He gave the teacher a fearsome glare and blocked the incoming ruler with his arm. And just like that, he was no longer allowed to go to P.E., but had to stay in the classroom and review his lessons."

Dennis Ho, a classmate of Bruce's, differs with Robert's account. "He is trying to soften the situation," Dennis says. "To my recollection (the scene sinks into my mind deeply), it was a long reed of grass not a ruler. I was running beside Bruce or slightly behind him when it happened." Coolie Lo whipped Bruce's legs with the reed, and it really hurt. Bruce stopped dead in his tracks. "He put his hand in a pocket, took out his switchblade, and pointed it at Coolie Lo," says Dennis. The Little Dragon was re-creating the scene from *My Son A-Chang* where his character pulled a knife on an adult who had hit him. "Coolie Lo turned and ran away. Bruce chased after him with his knife. They ran around and around until Coolie Lo fled to the principal's office. After that, Bruce got kicked out of class."

Remarkably, pulling a knife on his teacher only got Bruce suspended from PE class, not expelled, in part out of deference to his powerful parents. If Bruce was remorseful, he didn't show it. While he was in suspension, he would stand by the window and make ape movements and faces to distract the students on the field.

His schoolmates say it was another incident that finally caused him to be expelled. "It is something we still talk about whenever we touch on the subject of Bruce," says Dennis Ho. According to Dennis and another classmate who wishes to remain anonymous, all the boys spent their lunchtimes messing around on the hill behind La Salle. On one particular lunch break in 1956, Bruce forced one of the boys to drop his pants. No one is exactly sure why Bruce focused on this particular boy. "Maybe Bruce wanted to show off or he was bored," says Dennis. "He was in a mood." After pantsing the boy, Bruce dragged out a can of red paint he had lifted from a construction site and painted the boy's private parts red.

When the boy's parents found out what had happened, the father went to the school's principal and kicked up a fuss, insisting that Bruce be punished. Bruce was a terrible student, who had been held back twice. He was constantly getting into fights and causing trouble. He had pulled a knife on his PE teacher. While he could be charming and the Catholic Brothers saw goodness in him, this bullying prank was the final straw. Bruce was unceremoniously booted from La Salle.

It was a tremendous loss of face for his proud family. As his mother searched for a new school for Bruce, his frustrated father grounded him for a year—no movie work, no nights out with friends, only school and home.

Ip Man and Bruce Lee practicing *chi sao* (sticky hands), summer 1963. *(David Tadman)*

three

ip man

Kung fu was not a popular hobby in Hong Kong when Bruce Lee was growing up. In the cosmopolitan colony, good society shunned the martial arts. Sophisticates associated it with the rural countryside, China's feudal past, and Triad criminality. The event that reignited interest in kung fu and made it trendy was a challenge match in 1954 between two rivals who represented the conflict between tradition and Westernization, tearing at the heart of Chinese society.

Wu Gongyi was the traditionalist, the fifty-three-year-old head of the Hong Kong Tai Chi association. Chen Kefu was the thirty-four-year-old modernizer who had studied White Crane kung fu, Japanese judo, and Western boxing. In a bold move for a man of his age, it was the Tai Chi master who set the chain of events into motion by publishing an open letter declaring his willingness to meet practitioners of any other school "at any time and any place" for "mutual study" of the martial arts. The open challenge drew a published response from Chen Kefu, which developed into a war of words that the Hong Kong tabloids eagerly hyped. It was old versus young, past versus future, purity versus fusion, closed versus open, nationalism versus globalism.

As their conflict simmered in the newspapers, a disaster rocked the colony on Christmas night of 1953. A raging fire destroyed a squatter shantytown in the Shek Kip Mei area of New Kowloon, leaving 53,000 homeless. The government called it "unquestionably the worst catastrophe the Colony has ever suffered." In response, the two combatants agreed to turn their duel into the centerpiece of a charitable relief event—"a joint exhibition of martial arts" complete with an entire evening of kung fu exhibitions and opera singing. It was scheduled to be held in Macau, because Hong Kong colonial officials, who had fresh historical memories of the Boxer Rebellion, refused to sanction a martial arts duel in their territory.

A parade of celebrities, journalists, and gamblers took the ferry from Hong Kong to Macau to attend what was being hyped as the Fight of the Century. The start of the contest between the old master, Gongyi, and the younger fighter, Kefu, had all the hallmarks of an amateur match between two inexperienced contestants—lots of tense flailing and missing. Finally, in the middle of the first round, the younger fighter clocked the old master in the jaw, knocking him into the ropes, but the older man counterpunched the young fighter hard enough in the nose to draw a gush of blood. The judges, who were even less qualified than the fighters, rang the bell early to end the round. After some cautious sparring to start the second, the younger fighter bloodied the old master's mouth, only to receive another blow to his already broken nose in response. The sight of more gore caused the skittish judges to ring the bell early again and stop the contest. After a hurried consultation, they declared the contest at an end with no winner announced. This nondecision infuriated the audience, especially the legion of gamblers who were unable to settle their massive wagers.

The silver lining of the messy, inconclusive ending was it kept the contest a central topic of conversation for weeks. Everyone had an opinion and the debate raged. One Chinese newspaper reported, "Since the bout, everyone in Hong Kong and Macau has been discussing it with great enthusiasm, and the streets and alleys are filled with talk of the martial arts."

Almost overnight, kung fu became fashionable in the colony. Inspired by the contest between the old Tai Chi master and the young mixed martial arts fighter, new students flooded tiny martial arts studios and took to building rooftops to participate in their own semiorganized bare-knuckle challenge matches—called in Cantonese *beimo* (比武). Young Bruce Lee, already a veteran street fighter, was drawn to the competition of these illicit rooftop contests. This led him to a decision that would change his life. He began the formal study of kung fu.

After calling in some favors, Bruce's mother enrolled her difficult fifteen-year-old son at St. Francis Xavier (SFX) on September 10, 1956. Compared to La Salle, SFX was more like a reform school—its discipline stricter, the school style more Spartan and humble. SFX's Catholic Brothers never gave up on a troubled child and were skilled at turning them around. "Many of those boys would have ended up on the street if not for the Brothers," says Johnny Hung, St. Francis Xavier's alumni chairman.

The Brothers had a challenge in Bruce, because, despite promises to his parents to amend his ways, he and his crew were still roaming the back alleys of Kowloon looking for brawls. He won more often than he lost, but he hated losing so much he decided to upgrade his skills. "As a kid in Hong Kong," Bruce recalled for *Black Belt* magazine in October 1967, "I was a punk and went looking for fights. We used chains and pens with knives hidden inside. Then, one day, I wondered what would happen if I didn't have my gang behind me if I got into a fight." Like many young toughs, the Little Dragon didn't study the martial arts to become a better person but a better street fighter—not for self-defense but self-offense. "I only took up kung fu," Bruce confided, "when I began to feel insecure."

The first friend he made at SFX was Hawkins Cheung, who, like Bruce, was a short scrappy kid from an upper-class home. "Being from well-to-do families, we would sometimes have our drivers pick up one another if we wanted to hang out for the weekend," says Hawkins. Their friendship developed quickly and they became close. "Bruce's nickname at school was 'Gorilla,' because he was muscular and walked around with his arms at his sides. Everyone feared him, but I was the only one who called him 'Chicken Legs.' He'd get really mad and chase me all over the schoolyard with his big upper body and chicken legs underneath."

In their after-school adventures, Hawkins and Bruce fell in with another neighborhood tough, William Cheung (no relation to Hawkins). The son of a police officer, William was older, bigger, and a much better fighter than Bruce. Their growing friendship forced the Little Dragon to make a difficult decision: he could either avoid William and maintain his status as the leader of his little pack of SFX teddy boys or swallow his pride, hail William as "Big Brother," and become one of his followers. Most alpha males are unable to subsume their egos and as a consequence never improve or grow. In contrast, Bruce cleverly chose to *temporarily* follow William until he had enough time to study William's techniques and become the better fighter. In the short term, he had to be submissive; in the long run he planned to reverse the power dynamic. This strategy, which Bruce employed throughout his life, was the key to his success. He later repeated this technique with Steve McQueen in Hollywood in order to learn how to become a movie star.

Bruce discovered that William's street talent was the result of his study of an obscure style of kung fu called Wing Chun. In China, there are hundreds of martial arts styles. You can walk from one village to the next and encounter a half dozen different masters teaching radically different systems, each with its own mythical origin story. Wing Chun's legend is unique because it is one of the very few styles whose founder is a woman.

When the Manchus began conquering China in the seventeenth century, the Shaolin Temple was a rebel base for the Han Chinese. It was eventually destroyed and the martial monks and nuns forced to flee. One refugee was a nun named Ng Mui, who had developed a simplified system more suitable to the height, weight, and strength of women. Her first student was a beautiful young girl named Yim Wing Chun who was being pressured by a bandit warlord into marriage. She told the warlord she would only wed a man who could defeat her in unarmed combat. Employing the efficient techniques taught to her by the Shaolin nun, Yim Wing Chun dispatched the bandit with ease and the new style was named after her.

Wing Chun's growing popularity in Hong Kong was largely due to one man, Ip Man. Born in 1893 to a wealthy merchant family in Foshan, the same city where Bruce's father was discovered, Ip Man fled with only the clothes on his back to Hong Kong after the Communist takeover of China in 1949.

Destitute and rumored to have an opium habit, Ip Man began teaching Wing Chun as a way out of poverty. He quickly acquired a coterie of angry young men, who were attracted by his talent, even temper, and quick wit.

To help his students become better fighters, he taught them the basics of Wing Chun, which emphasizes close quarters combat—low kicks, lightning-quick short punches, blocks, and traps—the ideal style for fighting inside narrow alleyways. The main training technique was called *chi sao* (sticky hands). A form of sensitivity training, like Tai Chi's pushing hands, two partners touch their forearms together and then try to block, trap, and hit their opponent while maintaining constant contact.

To help his disciples control their rage and improve as human beings, Ip Man also taught Taoist philosophy—"be calm like water"—and employed his sense of humor. "He always told me, 'Relax! Relax! Don't get excited!' " says Hawkins Cheung. "But whenever I practiced *chi sao* with someone, I became angry when struck. I wanted to kill my opponent. When I saw Ip Man stick hands with others, he was very relaxed and talked to his partner. He never landed a blow on his students, but he would put a student in an awkward position and make the fellow students laugh at the sight. He was the funniest old man. Ip Man never exhibited a killing attitude. The students would swing their hands, and Ip Man would smile and merely control the movements."

Without telling his parents, Bruce asked William Cheung to introduce him to Ip Man, who accepted the fifteen-year-old movie actor as his disciple and then sent him to learn the basics from Wong Shun Leung. (In most kung fu schools, the master only teaches the senior students, who in turn instruct the beginners.) Twenty-one years old and a veteran of dozens of bare-knuckle *beimo* challenge matches, Wong Shun Leung was considered the best fighter in the school and one of the toughest in Hong Kong. His admirers called him *Gong Sau Wong* (講手王), "King of the Talking Hands."

The King's first impression of the Little Dragon, who showed up sporting sunglasses and carefully coiffed hair, was not positive. "William brought in an Elvis-like youngster," says Wong Shun Leung. "His manner was very frivolous as though he thought he was smart. After he went away, I told William that I did not welcome this young man." William must have given Bruce an earful, because the second time they met, Bruce was on his best behavior. "He dressed properly and was more polite," says Wong. The Little Dragon, who rebelled against most authority figures, had decided to once again *temporarily* kowtow until he could become a better fighter than not only William but also Wong Shun Leung. In his typical brash and straightforward manner, Bruce did not hide his intentions. "He asked me when he would be able to win over William and me," recalls Wong, still stunned by the memory. "He asked too much."

So singular was his determination to best his superiors that Bruce would play a trick on his fellow students to secure private lessons. He would make sure he was the first to arrive at Wong Shun Leung's apartment studio and then claim he had something to do immediately but would return shortly. "Please wait for me! Don't go out! I beg you, please don't! Thank you very much!" he'd shout at Wong, before running down the stairs to wait for his classmates. When they showed up at the apartment building, he said to them, "The master has just gone out. His family said he had something important to do and will not be free. So I think we have to see him on another day." After that, he pushed them down the road and onto a bus, before coming back to Wong Shun Leung for his individual lesson. When Wong learned of the ruse, he couldn't help but laugh at its cleverness. "I did not try to persecute him," says Wong. "That was Bruce Lee, competitive and aggressive. If he wanted anything, he would try to have it at any price."

His fellow Wing Chun brothers were not as amused. Most of them were from working-class backgrounds and already resented the good-looking, privileged movie actor. His brashness and entitled attitude only made them angrier. Some of them apparently went to Ip Man and called on him to expel Bruce from the school. According to William Cheung, one of the arguments they made was kung fu should only be taught to Chinese, and because Bruce was Eurasian, or "mixed blood" in Cantonese slang, he had to go. "They said, 'We can't teach Chinese kung fu to an impure Chinese,' " claims William. "Bruce didn't belong to Caucasians or Chinese. He was in between as he was mixed blood. At that time many Chinese people didn't accept someone like that." Ip Man refused to expel Bruce, but the Little Dragon was encouraged to study exclusively with Wong Shun Leung and avoid the main class until things settled down.

Unable to expel him, his Wing Chun seniors knocked Bruce around during class. "These guys, some of them assistant instructors, gave me a hard time when I first studied Wing Chun," Bruce later recalled. "I was just a skinny kid of fifteen." The hazing Bruce endured only steeled his resolve and made him more determined than ever to prove he was better than them. "He became fanatical," says older brother Peter. "He practiced diligently day and night." If Bruce was passionate about a subject, he was an extraordinarily fast learner. He took to Wing Chun like he had been born with a clenched fist. "Less than a year after Bruce had been training at the school, he had progressed so far that a lot of the seniors had trouble sparring or doing *chi sao* with him," says William.

While Bruce's competitive spirit was extreme, it was not unique. Ip Man pitted his students against each other. "Everyone wanted to be top dog," says Hawkins. "We would purposely hold back information that we gathered, and not let others know what we learned." Ip Man also encouraged his students to continue their "research" on the streets. "Ip Man said, 'Don't believe me, as I may be tricking you. Go out and have a fight. Test it out,' " remembers Hawkins.

After class the boys would head to the Shek Kip Mei area looking for easy marks. "We were real bad guys," says Hawkins. "We would go up and touch or pull the target. If the guy was hot-tempered, he would try to push or hit us and we would initiate our timing from his move. If the guy got hurt, we would say, 'What's the matter with you? I was just talking to you, and you tried to hit me first, Mr. Chan.' The target would say, 'I'm not Mr. Chan!' To which we would reply, 'We thought you were Mr. Chan and are very sorry we made a mistake!' "

For Ip Man's school it was a form of fist-to-mouth marketing. His students were developing a reputation for being the baddest boys on the street. Unfortunately, it also drew the attention of the police. Bruce and Hawkins were put down on a police list of juvenile delinquents. "Mom and Dad only realized Bruce had been studying Wing Chun about a year later, when they heard about him getting into even more trouble than before," says Robert.

To avoid police scrutiny, the boys took to the rooftops for secret "crossing hands" matches against other rival kung fu schools. These events typically involved more bluster than brutality—serious injuries were exceedingly rare because the participants' skill level was low and matches were usually stopped as soon as anyone drew blood. They were about bragging rights and resulted in long-standing feuds. Practitioners of Hung Gar, Choy Lay Fat, White Crane, Praying Mantis, and other popular styles gradually grew more and more resentful of the success of upstart Wing Chun fighters.

As Bruce advanced quickly in the style, it soon came his turn to take up Wing Chun's mantle in a *beimo* challenge match. Egged on by his classmates, Bruce challenged the assistant instructor from a rival Choy Lay Fat school named Chung. He asked Wong Shun Leung to be his cornerman. On May 2, 1958, Bruce and Wong Shun Leung made their way through the streets of Kowloon City to the apartment building on Union Road whose rooftop would serve as the challenge site. Wong was surprised to discover the area near the building filled with riffraff buzzing about the upcoming match. "The atmosphere was very tense and heavy as if a great thunderstorm was going to break out," says Wong. "On our way, many meddling youngsters pointed their fingers at us. Bruce was very delighted. I sensed that he was very proud of himself."

As the crowd grew larger, Wong asked Bruce, "How come there are so many people? Did you tell them to come here?"

Bruce denied it. "Maybe they learnt the news from the other side."

When they reached their destination, Bruce wanted to go straight up, but Wong pulled him back and said, "Walk on." They ducked into an alleyway and used a back entrance to fake out the crowd. Despite their precautions, twenty or thirty meddlers were already seated on the parapet of the roof by the time Bruce and Wong arrived.

When Bruce's opponent, Chung, and his crew showed up, everyone greeted each other. Chung's side asked Wong Shun Leung to act as the referee. He tried to rebuff them—"I represent the Wing Chun school"—but they insisted, praising his reputation for fairness. "They were so sincere that I could hardly refuse them," remembers Wong.

He called Chung and Bruce to the center of the eighteen-by-eighteen-foot rooftop for instructions. "A match must follow rules, even if it is a friendly match. You all are young people; you are not qualified to represent your clans. More importantly, this is not a duel. We have two rounds. One round will last two minutes. No matter whose side wins, the comparison will end after two rounds. This is a friendly match—you all should aim at promoting friendship. Do you both understand what I mean?" Bruce and Chung nodded.

Bruce stood in the center in a Wing Chun stance, left hand forward, right hand slightly back. Chung circled Bruce until he saw an opening. He lunged forward with a roar and punched Bruce in the jaw, causing him to retreat in pain. Bruce's mouth was covered in blood. After circling some more, Chung lunged out again, striking Bruce in the left eye. Angry, Bruce slid forward with an aggressive series of Wing Chun chain punches, but because he was not calm his blows did not land decisively and he left himself open to counterpunches to his nose and cheek. As they exchanged wild swings, the timekeeper ended the round. From the damage to Bruce's face, it was clear to everyone he had lost the first round.

"Leung!" Bruce shouted at his cornerman. "Is my eye swollen?"

"Yes," said Wong Shun Leung. "It's bruised. Your nose is bleeding also, but it's O.K."

"My performance today is bad," Bruce said, shaking his head in frustration. "If I am hurt too badly, my father will notice it. I think we better take it as a draw and end the match now."

"Bruce, if you do not continue in the second round, it means that you surrender. How can it be regarded as a draw?" Wong Shun Leung cajoled his reluctant fighter. "You are capable to fight on. Your opponent is wheezing now. If you withdraw, you will regret it. Whether you win or not is not important, but you must try your best. If you fight on, you will win."

"I will win?" Bruce asked, his competitive nature battling against his fear of humiliation. "Leung, are you sure?"

"Yes," Wong Shun Leung replied. "Why should I deceive you? Don't worry about your technique. This is a fight, not a performance. When you are close to him, step up and punch only his face. Do not worry whether you have been hit. Try to get close and attack. And be calm."

Encouraged, Bruce nodded his head to show he understood as the timekeeper signaled the beginning of the second and final round.

Bruce stood in the center of the rooftop with an air of composure he lacked in the first round. He feinted at Chung, causing him to jump back. Bruce smirked. He feinted again, making Chung jump again. Bruce grinned. The third time Bruce faked an attack, Chung stepped back only a half step while throwing a right punch. Seeing his opponent off balance, Bruce made use of the opening and swiftly charged forward. His left punch slammed into Chung's face. Bruce took another step forward and smacked Chung with a right to the jaw so hard several of Chung's false teeth were knocked across the roof. Blood gushed from Chung's mouth, and his legs were wobbly as he stumbled backward. With a yell, Bruce continued to rain heavy punches on Chung's face. Finally, Chung fell beside the water tank on the roof. Chung's friends ran forward to stop the match. Several of them criticized Wong Shun Leung for not stopping it earlier. Bruce was overjoyed. He raised his hands in the air in victory.

As soon as he arrived home with his black eye and busted lip, Bruce went into hiding for fear his father would find out. One of the servants gave him a hardboiled egg to put on his eye to help reduce the swelling. When his little brother, Robert, asked if he was hurt, Bruce bragged, "These are just surface-level wounds on me! You should have seen the other guy—I sent a few of his teeth flying!" In his diary, Bruce wrote, "Against Chinese boxer student of Lung Chi Chuen (4 years training). Results: Won (that guy got fainted [*sic*], one tooth got out, but I got a black eye)."

Unable to conceal his injury from his parents for long, his father blew up. He cursed his son for embarrassing the family and wasting his life with fighting. Phoebe recalls, "What I remember most clearly is that Bruce said to Dad: 'I'm not good at studying. But I'm good at fighting. I will fight to make a name.' "

Details of the match quickly made their way back to Ip Man, whose reaction was very different from Bruce's father. He pulled Wong Shun Leung aside to praise him: "If some day Bruce achieves something in the martial arts, it is because you didn't let him quit after the first round."

Buoyed by his triumph, Bruce's confidence and fighting spirit increased. He became even more obsessed with Wing Chun. "The contest taught him that success does not come naturally, one had to train and fight," says Wong Shun Leung. "Every day he practiced boxing, side kicks, wooden dummy and so on. When he had finished with all this, he would sit down and meditate on what he had done. He trained himself in this way for a long time."

As Bruce's skill in Wing Chun increased, he assumed the role of teacher to his clique of followers at St. Francis Xavier. He was always practicing his moves on the playground and instructing eager classmates during recess. Because Bruce had been held back twice at La Salle, he was two years older than most of his classmates and they looked up to him as a "big brother." Rolf Clausnitzer, whose younger brother was a schoolmate of Bruce's, says, "One of Bruce's favorite stunts was to stand on one leg and with the other fend off a number of 'attackers,' pivoting as required. His speed, maneuverability, and control were such that it was almost impossible to close in on him without getting kicked."

Bruce's recess lessons were noticed by the school's sports master, Brother Edward, a German missionary and former prizefighter. "When he came to our school, I knew at once he was a boxer," says Brother Edward. "His mother came here quite often. She wanted us to look after the boy." Brother Edward took Bruce under his wing and encouraged him to join SFX's newly formed Western boxing team. He invited Bruce to put on the boxing gloves for a friendly sparring match. Using Wing Chun techniques, Bruce was able to hold his own. "One day there was an announcement of an inter-school boxing championship," says Hawkins. "Bruce and I had a reputation in the school for being the naughtiest, so Brother Edward suggested that we get involved."

Every year, the two all-British private schools—King George V, which catered to the children of British businessmen, and St. George's, filled with the kids of British military officers—held an interschool Western boxing tournament. This event represented a chance for the mostly Chinese and Eurasian students of St. Francis Xavier to take their "Limey Bashing" off the streets and into the boxing ring. The previous year, in 1957, only one St. Francis Xavier student had competed, Steve Garcia, who won his weight class. Brother Edward convinced Bruce and another student, Ronnie, to join Steve Garcia in the 1958 tournament to be held at St. George's.

Bruce only had a couple of months to prepare for the boxing championship. Brother Edward gave him a crash course in the basics of Western pugilism. Bruce also turned to Wong Shun Leung for instruction in how to modify his Wing Chun for a contest that included boxing gloves and outlawed kicks. "I attacked his weak points and guided him to make full use of his strong points," says Wong.

On March 29, 1958, about thirty teenage participants gathered in St. George's gymnasium along with family, friends, and classmates. Except for St. Francis Xavier's three fighters—Steve Garcia, Bruce, and Ronnie—the rest were British boys from King George V and St. George's. The thirty boys were spread unevenly in a half dozen or so weight classes. In Bruce's group, he faced only two opponents—a boy from St. George's and KGV's returning champion, Gary Elms, who had won in his weight class the previous three years in a row. The tournament brackets were set by the sports masters from St. George's and KGV. In the first round, they matched Gary Elms against the boy from St. George's—Bruce was given a bye to fight the winner in the finals. "Bruce was unknown and the sports masters thought he would be a walkover, because Gary Elms was considered the best in that weight class," Steve Garcia says.

Rolf Clausnitzer, who attended KGV, remembers Gary not as a particularly skilled fighter but rather as a scrappy little guy, who bragged to everyone that his uncle was a professional boxer. "Although he was considerably lighter and smaller, that didn't stop him from pestering me and others," says Rolf. "I'd wrestle him to the ground, pinch his nostrils and force grass into his mouth to make him say 'Uncle,' but he would never submit. As soon as I got up in frustration, he'd jump me again. He was one tough nut."

Gary easily won his first-round match in the afternoon. He and Bruce tried to keep busy and stay focused for the next several hours until the finals in the evening. Like war, boxing tournaments consist of long periods of boredom punctuated by moments of sheer terror. During this down period, Bruce's friend, Hawkins Cheung, engaged in a little psychological warfare: "I spoke to the champ and warned him that he was facing the Gorilla now, who was an expert in kung fu, so he'd better watch out!"

After all the waiting, the referee called Bruce and Gary to the center of the ring and gave his instructions. The bell rang for the round to begin. Gary bounced on his toes in a classic Western boxing stance. Bruce shifted to a Wing Chun stance. Visually it was a clash of civilizations: boxing versus kung fu. "Many foreign [British] students, male and female, jeered at Bruce," says Wong

Shun Leung. With his lightning speed, Bruce immediately attacked Gary's centerline with a series of short straight Wing Chun punches to Gary's face, bulldozing him back and dropping him to the canvas. But Gary immediately jumped back up. Their first exchange set the tone for the next three 3-minute rounds. Bruce attacked with a series of quick but weak straight punches. Gary countered with a jab or two. As their bodies clashed into each other, Gary went down and then popped back up for more. "When Bruce gradually took control of the situation, the attitude of the spectators changed," says Wong.

Styles make fights, but rules make styles. Although Bruce was dominating the contest, he was pushing against the limits of using Wing Chun in a Western boxing match. Wing Chun's short, quick, rapid straight punches were designed for bare-knuckle alley brawls. The thick padding on boxing gloves made them mostly harmless in the ring. "There were a few knockdowns, but, because of the eight oz. gloves used, they were not that effective," Steve Garcia says. "And some of the knockdowns were ruled as pushes and throws, because of the Wing Chun moves. Bruce was warned a couple of times." While the Little Dragon could knock down his scrappy, tough opponent, he couldn't knock him out. "Gary was completely baffled by Bruce's speed and skill and had no answer for them, as he did not land one power punch on Bruce," Rolf Clausnitzer says. "But Gary was amazingly resilient. He was knocked down several times, but rebounded each time and did not seem to be any worse for wear."

Friends who went to congratulate Bruce after his unanimous decision victory expected to find him elated. Instead, the young perfectionist was shaking his head and looking far from pleased with himself. "Damn it, I couldn't knock the guy out," Bruce complained. "He kept backing away, and my punches weren't penetrating because of the gloves." Bruce swore that he would redouble his training until he could achieve the power he wanted.

While Bruce would continue to fight in the streets and rooftops of Hong Kong, this was the first and last officially organized sports combat tournament he would ever participate in. He didn't like the way the rules constrained the effectiveness of his techniques. As he grew older and better as a martial artist, he studiously avoided boxing and point karate tournaments. He would only agree, when challenged, to bare-knuckle "crossing hands" contests.

Margaret Leung and Bruce Lee practicing the cha-cha, circa 1957. *(David Tadman)*

Bruce Lee's only time playing a "refined gentleman," in *Thunderstorm* (1957). *(Courtesy of the Hong Kong Heritage Museum)*

four

banished

Around the time Bruce took up Wing Chun, he also began to take an interest in girls. Peter noticed the hormonal shift by measuring the amount of time Bruce spent grooming in front of the mirror: "He would spend up to 15 minutes getting his hair just right, making sure his tie was properly adjusted."

As Bruce turned his attention to the young ladies around him, many of them returned the favor. He was a good-looking movie actor from a well-off family with a reputation for being a troublemaker. That frisson of danger wrapped in a respectable upper-class package was a heady mix for the straitlaced Chinese schoolgirls of 1950s Hong Kong. It was a conservative, old-fashioned era. "No one had sex or anything," says Nancy Kwan, the star of *The World of Suzie Wong*. "It was kissing and dating and sending love notes." Bruce's sister Phoebe says, "Nowadays, people are not that restrained. Back then, if you held a boy's hand you would have to bring him to your father, because when we started to hold hands, we were not that far from marriage."

The first girl in Bruce's life was Margaret Leung. She was also a child actor (screen name: Man Lan) from a prominent film family. Her mother was a producer and her father an actor-director. Their mothers introduced the two of them when she was eleven and Bruce was thirteen. By all accounts, their relationship was purely platonic: she was more of a gal-pal than a girlfriend. "Adolescent Bruce was actually very prone to feel shy in front of young women," says Robert. "Bruce's favorite thing to do in front of the ladies was show off his muscles. He liked to ask them to try to use their finger nails to try to pinch up a bit of fat, and when they couldn't he'd laugh proudly." Margaret, like Bruce, had a rebellious streak and she was also a bit of a tomboy. Bruce would often tease her by saying, "If she didn't wear a skirt and have a figure, I'd surely treat her as my sworn brother."

As they got older, they would go out to the nightclubs for dinner and dancing. "We used to go dancing at Hotel Carlton, the Shatin Inn, and the Champagne Night Club, just opposite the Miramar Hotel," Margaret says. "The one with more money would pay more, but we always shared the bill." In the mid-1950s, Hong Kong kids were jitterbugging to clean-cut American pop like Bill Haley's "Rock Around the Clock." Anders Nelsson, a musician who had a part in *Way of the Dragon*, says, "The scene was more Pat Boone than Little Richard." It wasn't until 1957 that Elvis Presley rolled up on Hong Kong's shores and teens like Bruce began greasing back their hair and gyrating in their blue suede shoes.

Nights out with Bruce were fun for Margaret because he was an excellent dancer and charming company. They were also a little bit scary, because the evenings often ended in a brawl. When asked if she felt safe going out with a tough guy like Bruce, Margaret shrugged and smiled, "Fifty/fifty. Half because he was a good fighter. The other half because he always got into fights." On fight nights, Margaret was not only his dance partner but also his getaway driver. "I was his savior," she says. "Every time he engaged in a fight, I was always somewhere nearby, waiting in my car with the engine running. He would jump in, and I'd floor it."

While Bruce and Margaret were palling around like buddies, Bruce took a romantic interest in another young woman, Amy Chan, who would later become famous in Asia by her film name, Pak Yan (白茵). "Neither of us had much money to spend, so we went to Kowloon Tong, near where the MTR station is today," Amy says. "The gardens over there had trees. We would shake the trees to make the flowers fall, yellow and white, like sandalwood flowers." On the weekends, they often joined a larger group of friends for a "tea dance" at Chungking Mansions from 4 to 6 p.m. Tea dances were the cheaper "happy hour" version of a nightclub with a less well-known singer and band.

Amy remembers that Bruce was different depending on how big the group was. "If there were a lot of people having a good time, then he would have an insanely good time," she says. "But when there were only a few people around, he was very quiet. He would rationally analyze things and teach you things you didn't know, like how to be a good person. But he was very masculine, extremely manly. No matter what he said, he was very definitive about it."

While there was a real attraction between Bruce and Amy, their relationship didn't become too serious. As a teenager, Bruce seemed to have an ironic wariness of romantic attachments. When he was fifteen he wrote this playful poem about love and relationships.

Follow her she fly; fly from
her she follows.
. . .
Fall from a tree, fall from
above, for heaven's sake, don't
fall in love.
If you want to know the
value of money, try and
go to borrow some.
. . .
It's better to have loved and
lost, than wed and be forever bitter.
The bigger they are, the harder they fall.

If any one of the young women in his life could be considered Bruce's high school sweetheart, it was Pearl Tso. "She was the one real romance of his youth," says Robert Lee. Pearl's family and Bruce's were extremely close. "Her dad was a friend of my father from the stage," Phoebe says. "Pearl's mum, Eva Tso, was really close with my mum, just like sisters. She came over to our house every day, just to hang out." Bruce called Eva "Auntie Tso," and treated her like a second mother, often confiding in her secrets he didn't want to share with his parents. The two moms looked on their children's budding romance merrily, imagining them joining the families together in marriage. Pearl, who was also a child movie actor, studied ballet. In part to impress her, Bruce took up dancing. He frequently visited her home after school to "practice."

As a teenager, Bruce's obsession with kung fu was rivaled only by his love of dancing. He spent many afternoons at the neighborhood "cold tea house" on Jordan Road, where customers came to drink herbal teas, listen to the jukebox, and, if they were young and energetic, dance. These tea shops were a place where teenage boys and girls could mingle and flirt freely. Bruce thought of dancing as a good way to train himself not to be so shy around women.

From the Lindy Hop to the boogie-woogie, from jitterbug to jive, he followed all the latest fads, seeking to master every move. "He was good at jive," says Dennis Ho, his classmate. "Boy was he good." Most of these styles arrived in Hong Kong from U.S. and British servicemen stationed in the colony and the Hollywood movies and radio stations that catered to them. (Hong Kong was a port of call during the Korean War from 1950 to 1953.) But in 1957 a dance fad originating in Cuba swept its way through Latin America and then to the Philippines before hopping over to Hong Kong. It was called cha-cha. This swivel-hipped, triple-stepped style—one, two, cha-cha-cha—took the colony by storm.

No one was more passionate or serious about cha-cha than Bruce Lee.

"He didn't pick it up by idly watching people at the tea house," says Robert, "but rather found a Philippine woman who owned a dance studio in Tsim Sha Tsui, where she taught wealthy women to dance cha-cha." As part of his homework, he kept a personal notebook of "Cha Cha Fancy Steps" that numbered over a hundred, including moves like "Banana Boat" and "Rubbing & Double." He even invented a few of his own steps by mixing kung fu with cha-cha, creating his own crisp, fresh, and unique style.

Typical of his competitive character, Bruce turned his obsession into a contest with his friends to see who knew the most moves. "At school, I knew some Filipino friends who were pretty good, so I would pick up steps to show up Bruce," says Hawkins. "The next time I saw Bruce, he had a bunch of new steps! I later found out he went to my Filipino friend's dance instructor to learn more steps. I went to the same dance instructor and tried to persuade him not to teach Bruce."

Having bested all his friends, Bruce set his sights on a wider competition. An ambitious nightclub was sponsoring an "All-Hong Kong Cha-Cha Dance Championship." "He could barely wait to enter the contest," says Robert. "The matter he gave most thought to at the time was who should be his dance partner." Bruce's problem was he had too many girlfriends, so he ended up selecting as his dance partner ten-year-old brother Robert. "By picking me, he avoided stirring up any jealousy among his female admirers."

As clever and competitive as Bruce was, he probably also had another motivation for his choice. The Chinese are obsessed with family and worship children, especially sons. Picking his lovable little brother would appeal to the judges' sentimental hearts, giving the partners a cuteness edge in the contest. The two siblings practiced every day for two months. "Bruce was a really great teacher," says Robert. "Every day he'd repeat the three-minute dance for me so that I very quickly learned it. I wasn't nervous at all when it came time for the contest."

Robert was right not to be nervous. The adorable brothers were a lock even before they stepped onto the dance floor and did their charming cha-cha routine. "Bruce was very happy," says Robert. "He carried around the championship flag like a photo to show all his friends everywhere he went." Of all his youthful accomplishments—the boxing match, the challenge fights, the starring movie roles—he was most proud of being, as he bragged to all his friends for the rest of his life, "The Cha-Cha Champion of Hong Kong."

For Bruce's future as a martial arts movie actor, his background as a dancer was crucial to his success. "Since they both involve physical movement and because you must maintain a flow either in dancing or fighting there was, to him, a relationship," says Linda Lee. Many great martial arts fighters have tried their hand (and feet) at movies only to fail miserably because what works on the street often looks stiff and awkward on-screen. "There was a sort of innate balance and rhythm within all his [movie] fights," says Hong Kong film director Michael Kaye, "and he was constantly looking for ever more complicated rhythms."

After Chung-luen Studios disbanded in 1955, Bruce found acting work hard to come by. As with many child actors, his teenage years were a tough transition. Too old for scrappy, lovable orphan roles, he attempted to play against type and broaden his range with mixed results.

A cutup in class, it was natural for Bruce to try his hand at a comedy. His first and only was *Sweet Time Together* (1956). The film starred Sun-Ma Sze-Tsang, the same actor who played Li Hoi Chuen's drug buddy in the play *Two Opium Addicts Sweep the Dike*. By costarring in a comedy with Sun-Ma, Bruce was once again walking in his father's shadow.

In this age-reversal slapstick farce, deluded ladies' man Sun-Ma Sze-Tsang escapes from a jealous husband by exchanging clothing with a doltish teenager played by sixteen-year-old Bruce Lee. With Sun-Ma pretending to be a child and Bruce an adult, they find themselves caught in increasingly absurd romantic situations. By the closing credits, neither lover ends up with the girl of their desires.

The only thing funny about the movie is watching the King of Kung Fu as a teenager, stammering and twitching like a fool. One of Bruce's childhood idols was Jerry Lewis, and Bruce does a credible imitation of the master down to the buckteeth, white sailor boy outfit, and black horn-rim glasses.

For his next big movie, *Thunderstorm* (1957), Bruce moved in the opposite direction, playing a "refined gentleman" in a tragedy. His character, Chow Chung, is in every way the opposite of his previous scrappy orphan roles: proper, sincere, naive, dutiful, and rich. In love with the housemaid of his wealthy family, both he and she die when he makes a final attempt to save her from imminent danger.

The cognitive dissonance between the refined gentleman role and his own temperament must have affected his performance, because it is as stiff as the mandarin collar he wears throughout the film. Critics panned the movie, singling out the Little Dragon's performance as "rigid," "artificial," and "over-eager." It was a tremendous disappointment for Bruce, who had high hopes for the film. But it proved a valuable lesson: he was a much better actor when he could invest his own personality into a role.

The Little Dragon had the chance in his next film, *Darling Girl* (1957). It starred his gal-pal and dance partner, Margaret Leung, and was directed by her father in an effort to make his daughter a star. In this light romantic comedy, Margaret plays a spoiled rich girl—not a stretch for her—competing with a rival over a guy. During a nightclub scene, Bruce has a walk-on role as a fashionable toff, wearing a dress shirt, tie, and sweater vest. Margaret asks Bruce's character to dance the cha-cha with her to make her love interest jealous. Their dance routine has the ease and comfort of two people who have practiced together for a long time. The only bit of acting required on Bruce's part is when Margaret's love interest angrily confronts Bruce's character and instead of attacking back he flees in terror. It is the only time in life or on film that the Little Dragon ever ran away from a fight.

Bruce didn't appear in another film for the next three years. It was the longest break of his acting career since it had begun in earnest as a six-year-old. It is not clear if the roles simply dried up after his less than stellar attempts at playing against type or if his father banned him from making more films after he was expelled from La Salle and continued to get into trouble at St. Francis Xavier. What is obvious is that Bruce, like many teenage boys, was feeling increasingly resentful of his father's authority, especially as he watched his old man descend deeper into opium addiction.

One particularly vivid anecdote from his teenage years captures his state of mind. "I was getting disgusted seeing old Tai Chi men putting on demonstrations—having guys come up from the audience to punch their stomachs," Bruce later told friends. "One day while I was watching this demonstration, I didn't like the way this old man smiled when the young volunteer couldn't hurt him. When the old man asked for another volunteer, I went up. The old man, smiling, exposed his stomach as the target. But instead, I deliberately let go my right as hard as I could towards his ribs. I heard a crack as the old man crumbled to the floor moaning. You know I was such a smart-assed punk, I just looked down at the old man and laughed, 'Sorry, I missed. Next time don't show off.' "

It is hard not to see this old Tai Chi street performer as a stand-in for Bruce's father.

The British colonized Hong Kong for the express purpose of selling opium to the Chinese. In one of the great historical ironies, a century later colonial officials reversed this position. Concerned with the growing number of addicts, the government established the Advisory Committee for the Prohibition of Drugs in 1959 to eradicate the damaging effects of opium on its subjects.

By all accounts, the Hong Kong police force—from the Chinese beat cops at the bottom of the ladder all the way to the British officers at the top—was deeply corrupt. The new government mandate to disrupt the opium trade was taken as an opportunity to shake down opium den owners and wealthy opium smokers, like Bruce's father, Hoi Chuen.

"A British bigwig officer showed up at our house with a bunch of underlings, pulled out all of Dad's opium pipes and paraphernalia, spread it out on the table, and eloquently held forth about how British law did not permit the smoking of opium, and so on," remembers Robert. "Actually, he had only one goal, which was money, but he couldn't come right out and say that, so he would just put you in an awkward position until you coughed up enough to satisfy him. Mom finally gave him five-hundred dollars, which, at the time, was enough to feed the ten of us for several months."

The humiliation, the embarrassment, the loss of face was too much for a proud man like Hoi Chuen to take. It was his rock bottom. "After that, Dad made the decision to quit smoking," says Robert, "after years of persistent urging from my mother."

Few classes of drugs are more addictive or have more painful withdrawal symptoms than opioids. In the first day, the addict suffers muscle aches, runny nose, sweats, fever, racing heart, anxiety, and insomnia. By the third day, it turns into stomach cramps, diarrhea, vomiting, depression, and terrible drug cravings. Hoi Chuen detoxed at home using the time-honored Chinese method—tapering off his drug consumption by drinking rice wine spiked with small pieces of cooked opium for a week before finally quitting cold turkey. "It was very difficult for him to stop," Phoebe recalls. "He had diarrhea often." After this brutal ordeal, Hoi Chuen never touched opium again.

Having dealt with the father's drug addiction, the family turned to confront Bruce's problem with violence. He had come up with a new way to start fights and test out his Wing Chun. Ever the actor, he would dress up in a traditional Chinese costume—mandarin collar, flowing robe—and wander around the streets with everyone else in Western-style clothing. Standing out like a sore thumb, he waited for someone to make a joke or stare at him for too long. "What are you looking at? Do I look weird or something?" Most would shy away and apologize. Bruce used those who didn't as punching dummies.

In corrupt, Triad-infested Hong Kong, the police had higher priorities than a rambunctious teen picking fights. But in 1959, the inevitable happened. He roughed up a teenager with powerful parents. They demanded action from the police. The police went to Bruce's school and confronted St. Francis Xavier's headmaster, who called in his mother. The cops said,

"Hey, either your son stops what he is doing or we will have to arrest him, because we just can't let him go out there and pick fights all day long."

When his terrified mother arrived home, she explained the situation to her husband. "No good! He can't go on like this!" his father shouted. Grace pulled her eighteen-year-old son aside for a serious talk about his future. Nothing his parents had tried could convince Bruce to stop fighting. If he stayed in Hong Kong, he would likely end up in jail. The movie roles had dried up. He could not make a living with one or two small parts a year in low-budget flicks. He also had no chance of attending one of Hong Kong's highly selective universities. It was unlikely he would even graduate from high school. His report card from St. Francis Xavier ranked him forty-one out of forty-two students, and noted his conduct was "very poor."

But Bruce Jun Fan Lee had the unique advantage of being an American citizen. If he returned to the land of his birth, he could attend a remedial high school and get his diploma. He might even get into a local college and only have to pay in-state tuition. As with millions of immigrants before him, America represented a fresh start, a chance for a new beginning. He was heading down a dark road in Hong Kong. The change in environment might do him good.

There was one final reason the move made sense. At the time, every American male was required by law to register for the military draft when he turned eighteen. Bruce either had to sign up or give up his U.S. citizenship.

Despite the clear logic, Bruce understandably didn't want to leave his friends and family. It felt like punishment, like he was being sent away, cast off, banished. "Bruce didn't want to go, but his father forced him," says Hawkins. "Bruce feared his father and had to comply." Phoebe says, "Dad's intuition was to let him 'eat bitter' [suffer] in the U.S."

After the initial indignation and resentment began to recede, Bruce started to see his situation from his parents' perspective. He realized he needed a dramatic change of setting. "He told me once that if he had stayed in Hong Kong, he probably would have joined a gang and been knifed to death," says Nancy Kwan.

By nature, Bruce was optimistic and independent. The trip to America was beginning to feel like an adventure. He started planning in detail for his future life. First, he needed to clear his name. "Prior to any Hong Kong resident leaving for a new country, you had to check with the police station to make sure your record was clean," says Hawkins. "Bruce applied for this certificate, and found that our names were on a blacklist of known juvenile delinquents. He called me at home. 'Hawkins, big trouble,' Bruce exclaimed. 'Our names are on a known gangster list. I'm going down to the police station to clear my name, and while I'm there, I'll clear yours, too.' I thanked him. A few days later, a police investigator came to my house and questioned me about gang relations. Bruce's efforts to clear me actually got me more in trouble. My father had to pay off this investigator to have my name wiped from the record, or else I wouldn't have been able to attend college in Australia. I hated Bruce for that!"

Next Bruce turned his mind to his future profession. In a journal entry from November 30, 1958, he wrote, "Now I try to find out my career—whether as a doctor or another? If as a doctor, I must study hard." His heart was set on a job in the medical field. Besides doctor, he also considered becoming a pharmacist. In one of his earliest English-language letters, also dated November 1958, he reached out to a family friend attending medical school to ask for his advice: "I intend to study medicine or pharmacy in the future. As I am ignorant on that subject, can you please explain to me the qualification of being a doctor or pharmacist step-by-step? Do you think I can succeed when, at present, I don't know anything about it?"

Since the reply letter is lost, it is unknown what advice Bruce received. Whatever it was, it seemed to change his mind. He began toying with the idea of dental school. His friends found it hilarious that the same boy who was an expert in knocking out teeth wanted to fix them. "I cracked up and laughed in his face!" says Hawkins. " 'You, a dentist?' I said. 'Your patients would lose all their teeth.' "

While he was studying medicine or pharmacy or dentistry in America, Bruce knew he would need a way to support himself. His father had promised to pay for his expenses in the U.S., but Bruce, whose pride was still wounded by his banishment, didn't want his father's help. He wanted to be independent. To make money on the side, he planned to teach Wing Chun. "I replied that he didn't have much to teach at the time," says Hawkins. "We had both only learned up to the second Wing Chun form."

Bruce decided it would be useful to pick up a flashy kung fu style to impress potential American students. One of his father's close friends, Master Shiu Hon Sang, was an expert in northern kung fu, known for its acrobatic leaps and high kicks. "Bruce learned northern style for showmanship," says Hawkins. The deal was Master Sang would teach Bruce his fancy forms in return for Bruce instructing him in cha-cha. Bruce went to Master Sang's kung fu club every morning at 7 a.m. for two months to exchange lessons. Master Sang later jokingly complained it turned out to be a bad deal for him: Bruce was such a fast learner he mastered the movements of several complex forms, while Master Sang never quite got the hang of the basic cha-cha steps.

His parents had hoped that America would change Bruce, but it was the verdict to send him away that transformed him from a teenage punk into a more mature and sober young man. "After this decision was made, Bruce suddenly changed," says Robert. "Mr. 'Never Sits Still' suddenly decided to calm down and even to take his studies seriously. He would often stay home for long hours doing homework and reviewing his courses of his own accord." In his diary entry for December 1, 1958, Bruce wrote, "Spent more time on Math and English (especially conversation)." The change in Bruce's behavior was so dramatic his parents at first believed he must have gotten into some serious mess again. Seeing her son at home studying made his mother so uneasy she called his school to see if he was in trouble. Only after his father took the time to have a long conversation with Bruce did his parents finally realize their wayward son was becoming more mature.

Across cultures, the martial arts have served three basic purposes: warfare (combat, street fighting), sports (boxing, MMA), and entertainment (stage combat, pro wrestling, kung fu movies). Eastern martial arts added a fourth category: spiritual practice. Kung fu was understood to be a method of moving meditation. Its deepest goal was to lead its adherents toward enlightenment.

As Bruce was rounding out his martial arts skills with flashy northern kung fu in the mornings, he continued his study of the practical Wing Chun in the afternoons. Wong Shun Leung instructed him in the physical aspects, while Ip Man gave guidance on the psychological and philosophical dimensions. It was Ip Man's wise instruction that led to a transformative spiritual epiphany. Two years later in 1961, Bruce recounted the experience in a remarkably insightful college essay.

> About four years of hard training in the art of gung fu, I began to understand and felt the principles of gentleness—the art of neutralizing the effect of the opponent's effort and minimizing expenditure of one's energy. All this must be done in calmness and without striving. It sounded simple, but in actual application it was difficult. The moment I engaged in combat with an opponent, my mind was completely perturbed and unstable. Especially after a series of exchanging blows and kicks, all my theory of gentleness was gone. My only thought left was somehow or another I must beat him and win.
>
> My instructor, Professor Ip Man, would come up to me and say, "Relax and calm your mind. Forget about yourself and follow the opponent's movement. Let your mind do the counter-movement without any interfering deliberation. Above all, learn the art of detachment."
>
> That was it! I must relax. However, right there I had already done something contradictory, against my will. That was when I said I must relax, the demand for effort in "must" was already inconsistent with the effortlessness in "relax." When my acute self-consciousness grew to what the psychologists called "double-blind" type, my instructor would again approach me and say, "Preserve yourself by following the natural bends of things and don't interfere. Remember never be in frontal opposition to any problem, but control it by swinging with it. Don't practice this week. Go home and think about it."

> The following week I stayed home. After spending many hours in meditation and practice, I gave up and went sailing alone in a junk. On the sea, I thought of all my past training and got mad at myself and punched at the water. Right then at that moment, a thought suddenly struck me: Wasn't this water the essence of kung fu? I struck it just now, but it did not suffer hurt. Although it seemed weak, it could penetrate the hardest substance in the world. That was it! I wanted to be like the nature of water.
>
> I lay on the boat and felt that I had united with Tao; I had become one with nature. The whole world to me was unitary.

This mystical moment had a profound effect on the young man. Kung fu became his religion, his path to enlightenment. He became intensely interested in Taoism, the ancient Chinese philosophy that focuses on being one with nature, going with the flow, bending like a reed in the wind—"Be water, my friend," as Bruce would later famously say. He was self-aware enough to realize many of his problems were the result of his need to be in control, to assert his will. He was a dragon, a fire element—his anger burning those around him. Taoism and kung fu served as a psychological self-corrective, water to douse the flames.

The joke in China is kung fu is a way to trick thirteen-year-old boys into meditating. Bruce had started his martial arts path as a punk. From this instant forward, he would speak and think more and more like a Taoist monk. This internal dichotomy and conflict between his punkish personality and monkish insights would define his adult life.

Ironically, just as preparations for him to leave Hong Kong were nearly complete the Little Dragon was offered one of the best movie roles of his life. Ever since he starred in the film *My Son A-Chang* (1950), he had been waiting for another leading role. After nine years of playing secondary parts, he finally had his chance in *The Orphan*. The plot was a familiar one for Bruce: His character, Ah Sum, orphaned during the war, becomes a pickpocket for a street gang. He is caught and given a choice: jail or school. He takes school, and under the guidance of a kindhearted principal slowly reforms himself. When his old gang tries to strong-arm him into one last raid, he refuses and they cut off his ear.

The update to this shopworn story line is Bruce's performance. Too old to play scrappy but lovable street urchins, he instead makes his character, Ah Sum, emotionally unhinged and psychologically wounded. One moment he is snarling, the next laughing manically, and all the while spewing out a fetid stew of Cantonese street slang. While he clearly fashioned the role after another one of his screen idols, James Dean (*The Orphan* is Hong Kong's version of *Rebel Without a Cause*), he brought in elements from his own roguish life. Whenever the schoolmaster tries to reach out to help him, Bruce's character ignores him by breaking into an elaborate cha-cha routine. After a female teacher inadvertently insults him, he pulls a switchblade and threatens her. This confrontation leads to perhaps the most realistic fight scene of his career when several of his classmates awkwardly try to wrestle the knife out of his hand and they all end up falling over each other.

The Orphan was both a critical and commercial success. A leading film critic at the time, Ting Yut, exalted Bruce's performance in bringing the lead character to life. Opening on March 3, 1960, in an unprecedented eleven theaters, the film broke the previous box office record, grossing more than HK$400,000 in its first run. It also became the first Hong Kong movie to break into the international market. It was shown at the Milan Film Festival.

Teenage boys were so taken with Bruce's swaggering portrayal of Ah Sum—the gangster who defied authority, battled against his teacher, and turned his school upside down—that they began to emulate the way he smoked cigarettes and cha-cha danced. One concerned high school principal felt the need to hang a banner across the school's entrance reading: "No one is allowed to imitate Little Dragon Lee's Ah Sum in *The Orphan*!"

In the week before he left, Bruce and his sister Agnes went to an old fortune-teller to find out his fate in America. The crone told him what she undoubtedly repeated to thousands of other anxious clients: someday he would be rich and famous. "We laughed about it," says Agnes, "but I always felt it was going to happen." Despite this auspicious prophecy, Bruce's stomach twisted in knots as the day of departure approached. "The night before he left, when I had almost fallen asleep, he came into my room, sat by my bed, and said, 'I'm going to leave for America to study. I don't know what it's going to be like over there,' " recalls Robert. "I understood his sighs—he was afraid, and didn't know what his future would hold."

On the afternoon of April 29, 1959, Bruce headed to Victoria Harbor. His parents bought him a one-way ticket on the SS *President Wilson*, a high-end ocean liner, for the eighteen-day voyage to San Francisco. He was joined by several of his friends and most of his family. One person missing was his father, Hoi Chuen. "We people of Shunde County have an old custom—a father can't see off his son on a voyage," says Robert. One imagines him pacing at home—a swirling mix of anger, guilt, disappointment, remorse, and hope—wondering if he had made the right decision and if he would ever see his second son again. At the dock, Bruce's mother, Grace, gave him US$100 for expenses and a warning: Unless he made something of himself, he was not to come back. Bruce promised to behave and only return "when I've made some money."

As the boarding horn blew, Bruce hugged his family, friends, and girlfriend, Pearl. "After many years of being as close as twins, we would be apart for the first time," says Hawkins. One dear friend who couldn't make it was his dance partner, Margaret Leung. She was in the hospital for a minor operation. "He asked someone to send me a note. Bruce wrote: 'I hope the doctor cuts you in two,' " Margaret says, laughing at the memory. "What a jerk!" Bruce promised Pearl he would write her frequently. His eleven-year-old brother handed him a card: "To dearest Bruce, Please don't be sad in the ship. From your loving brother, Robert." Bruce kept the note his entire life.

It was customary for passengers leaving on long journeys to buy several rolls of ribbons. Once on deck, they would hold one end and toss the rolls down to their family and friends remaining on the docks. Both sides would hold on to each end of the ribbon until the boat had pulled far enough away to stretch the ribbon to its limits and it broke. "On the ship, he threw five or six ribbons to us," says Robert. "Me and my sisters caught them and saw the ship depart." Watching Bruce wave goodbye, Hawkins says, "I saw him cry." When the ribbons broke, his mother wept uncontrollably. Bruce was out of sight, heading off to an unknown future on the other side of the world.

act ii

gold mountain

Daddy has gone to Gold Mountain
To earn money.
He will earn gold and silver,
Ten thousand taels.
When he returns,
We will build a house and buy farmland.

—Cantonese nursery rhyme, circa 1850

Bruce Lee outside Ruby Chow's restaurant in Seattle, circa 1960. *(David Tadman)*

five

native son

After gold was discovered at Sutter's Mill in California in 1848, mining companies searched the world for a compliant workforce. With the gradual abolition of African slave labor, coolie traders in southern China, like Bruce's great-grandfather, offered an alternative source. Using deceptive promises of quick riches and clever marketing—California became known in Chinese as *Jinshan* (Gold Mountain)—they signed Chinese peasants to coercive contracts and shipped them across the Pacific. From 1850 to 1852, the number of Chinese in California rose from 500 to 25,000.

When the gold ran dry, this cheap labor force was hired to build the Central Pacific Railroad in 1863. The Chinese became to the West what the Negro was to the South and the Celt to the East. From the perspective of California businessmen, the Chinese were ideal employees: as guest workers under exploitative contracts and aliens ineligible for citizenship, they were willing to work harder for less money and less likely to organize or strike than their European immigrant counterparts. "They are quiet, peaceable, tractable, free from drunkenness," wrote Mark Twain. "A disorderly Chinaman is rare, and a lazy one does not exist."

In contrast, white working-class immigrants, especially the Irish, saw the quiet, tractable Chinese as unwanted competition and set about finding ways to eliminate these men, who they called "Nagurs," "Celestials," and "Moon-eyed Lepers." Instead of seeking common ground, the American labor movement rallied European-immigrant workers against the Chinese, declaring in 1870: "We are inflexibly opposed to all attempts on the part of capitalists to cheapen and degrade American labor by the introduction of a servile class of laborers from China."

Whereas Chinese workers were once praised, they were now vilified. The *Daily Alta California* editorialized: "The Chinese are morally a far worse class to have among us than the Negro. They are idolatrous in their religion—in their disposition cunning and deceitful, and in their habits libidinous and offensive. They can never become like us." Chinatowns began to be portrayed as dens of inequity, filled with opium and prostitution. As the American economy descended into the "Long Depression" of the 1870s, the exploding population of Chinese on the West Coast was seen as a threat. By the early 1880s, it had grown to 370,000—representing one quarter of the entire able-bodied labor force. Dark conspiratorial talk arose of the "Yellow Peril"—the fear that an Asiatic horde would descend on the New World and overwhelm the white majority.

In 1881, the anti-Chinese anger of the white working class moved congressional lawmakers to propose the Chinese Exclusion Act. It was the first time the nation had ever seriously considered banning an entire immigrant group based on race, ethnicity, or country of origin. "Why not discriminate?" asked California senator John F. Miller. "America is a land resonant with the sweet voices of flaxen-haired children. We must preserve American Anglo-Saxon civilization without contamination or adulteration from the gangrene of Oriental civilization." President Chester A. Arthur vetoed the bill, fearful of how it might affect trade with China. The public erupted in anger. Across the West the president was hanged in effigy, his image burned by enraged mobs. A compromise bill was introduced the next year barring all Chinese laborers. It passed and was signed by President Arthur.

Instead of dampening passions, the 1882 Chinese Exclusion Act inflamed them. Banning new Chinese was not enough, they all had to go. White vigilantes subjected Chinese communities to a period of genocidal violence and terror known as "the Driving Out." In Seattle in 1885, a mob forced most of the Chinese laborers to leave town. Six hundred Chinese merchants who refused to abandon their goods were rounded up by force and herded to the Northern Pacific Railroad train station, built by Chinese sweat, and shipped to Portland. The secretary of war had to dispatch troops to Seattle to stop more anti-Chinese pogroms.

For the next sixty years, the Chinese in America were marginalized and ghettoized in their Chinatowns—a distrusted, despised, and discriminated against minority. The turning point was Pearl Harbor. Suddenly, 120,000 Japanese Americans were rounded up and sent to internment camps, while the American attitude toward China underwent a dramatic enemy-of-my-enemy change. Almost overnight the backward and semi-colonized country of China became a valuable ally, and its people hailed as heroic freedom fighters. To prevent China from surrendering to the Japanese and keep them fighting on America's side, President Franklin Roosevelt sent a letter on October 11, 1943, urging Congress to "be big enough to correct a historic mistake," and "silence the distorted Japanese propaganda" by repealing the Chinese Exclusion Act.

After the war was over, the need for more scientists, engineers, and doctors led to further liberalizations of immigration law and exceptions for skilled workers. The result was a second great wave of Chinese immigrants—mostly highly educated "Uptown Chinese" from Taiwan and Hong Kong. While the first wave had led to the "Yellow Peril" fear of Chinese immigrants, the second wave caused white America to hold up the Chinese as a "model minority," capable, as *U.S. News & World Report* declared in 1966, of "winning wealth and respect by dint of its own hard work."

On a passenger liner in the middle of the Pacific Ocean in 1959, Bruce Lee was part of this second wave. Educated, well-to-do, and already an

American citizen, his success would fundamentally alter the perception of the Chinese in America.

However disappointed Bruce's parents might have been in their son, they made every effort to ease his journey to a strange land. When Bruce's ship made its first port of call in Osaka, Japan, on May 4, 1959, the first face he saw on the dock belonged to his older brother, Peter, who was studying in Tokyo. "He took me on the train from Osaka directly to Tokyo for sightseeing," Bruce wrote to a friend. He was shocked at how much more advanced Tokyo was than Hong Kong. "It's as pretty as any Western country. I've never seen so much automobile traffic. The city is full of excitement. Hong Kong falls way behind!" His initial impression was the seed for Bruce's lifelong admiration for and envy of the Japanese.

When his ship docked in Honolulu on May 17, Bruce was greeted by two Cantonese Opera actors—friends of his father. They introduced him to a wealthy Chinese benefactor, Mr. Tang. "He and I hit it off right away, like we'd known each other forever," Bruce wrote. "He studies Hung style boxing and loves the National Art. He envies my skill and knowledge of Wing Chun and hopes that I can stay longer in Hawaii to teach him boxing, and to find a school for me to teach at." As a welcoming gesture to the young man, Mr. Tang invited the group to the finest Chinese restaurant in Honolulu. Bruce marveled: "One bowl of shark fin soup is already US$25! I think after eating it for the first time I, myself, will never have any opportunity to eat another US$25 gourmet dish again."

The ever-gregarious Bruce made a number of friends on the ship. "There were two Americans who live in our cabin room. Both are studying law. We chit-chatted," Bruce wrote. "I also met my school friend's older brother, Mr. Chang. We basically did everything together. This person studies Choy Lay Fut boxing and has definite interest and admiration for Wing Chun." He even befriended and impressed the ship's band members, who asked him to teach a cha-cha class to the first-class passengers.

"After I taught for 15 minutes, there came a life saving demonstration. Everybody had to go below deck and put on their life-jackets. This is very bothersome!"

Despite his extroverted personality and his family's best efforts, it was still a lonely journey filled with intense feelings of anxiety and loss. "Dearest Pearl, after our departure I miss you very much," the heartsick young man wrote to his high school sweetheart. "At night I can't sleep and I take out all the photos which you gave me and look at them over and over again. I love you."

On May 17, 1959, eighteen years after departing America, Bruce "Reverberate San Francisco" Lee returned to his birthplace. Dressed in a sharp dark suit, light tie, and sunglasses, Bruce was met at the docks by Quan Ging Ho, a friend of Bruce's father. He had worked at the Mandarin Theatre (since renamed the Sun Sing Theatre) when Hoi Chuen was performing in San Francisco in 1940. The plan was for Bruce to stay with Mr. Quan over the summer until he moved to Seattle in the fall to finish his high school education.

As they walked from the docks, Mr. Quan served as an excited tour guide to San Francisco's Chinatown, the neon-lit, colorfully painted neighborhood hemmed in between the financial district to the south, the dockworkers along the bay to the east, the Italian neighborhood to the north, and the financial elite of Nob Hill to the west. One can only imagine the disorientation Bruce must have felt staring at this miniature simulacrum of Hong Kong with its Chinese grocery stores, chop suey restaurants, gaudy gift shops, and ornate theaters—so much the same and yet everything just a bit off.

Bruce arrived at Mr. Quan's tiny apartment at 654 Jackson Street to discover his accommodation was a single bed squeezed in the corner of the main room between other pieces of furniture. The bathroom and kitchen, located down a narrow hallway, were shared with the residents of the other units. Although his living conditions in Hong Kong with thirteen other family members had been cramped, this space was depressing and claustrophobic. At least at home there were servants. Bruce was experiencing the shock of going from Third World rich to First World poor.

Mr. Quan found work for Bruce as a waiter at the Kum Hom Restaurant just across the street from their apartment. Bruce, who had never previously held a job other than movie actor, quickly proved unsuited for the service industry and lasted barely a week. A better fit for his personality proved to be teaching—it allowed him to display his charm and demonstrate his talent. What the Bay Area Chinese community wanted to learn from a handsome eighteen-year-old fresh off the boat was not the ancient art of kung fu, but the newest steps of the dance craze cha-cha.

His dance classes took place at the KMT Building, the Claremont and Leamington Hotels, and numerous association halls in San Francisco and Oakland. "There were 30 of us and Bruce charged one dollar a person," remembers Harriet Lee, one of his dance students. "He showed us some very different cha-cha moves than we were used to. Everyone liked him. He told very funny jokes. He was a pure entertainer."

During intermission in his cha-cha classes, Bruce would dazzle his students with Wing Chun performances. One of the people stunned by Bruce's talent was George Lee, a forty-year-old machinist from Alameda: "I had never seen anyone as fast as he was. Heck, I never dreamed anyone could be that fast."

George pulled Bruce aside after the class was over and breathlessly asked, "What style was that?"

"Wing Chun," Bruce beamed.

"I have been training in gung fu for the past 15 years and I've never seen anything like what you are doing," George said. "What are your plans?"

"I'm moving to Seattle for school."

"Well, when you are back this way, I would like to get a group and have you for our instructor."

As the fall semester approached, Peter arrived in San Francisco to help Bruce move and make certain, on behalf of the family, that his younger brother was not in any trouble. Afterward Peter planned to travel east to the University of Wisconsin where he had gained admission. It was quite an honor—only the most elite Hong Kong students were accepted to American universities. Peter would go on to earn a PhD in physics and become a respected scientist at Hong Kong's Royal Observatory.

Peter found Bruce to be as outwardly buoyant and confident as before. By all measures, his summer in the Bay Area had been put to good effect. He had reaffirmed his legal identity as an American citizen by acquiring a driver's license and registering for the draft. His cha-cha teaching gig had put some spending money in his pocket and the praise he received for his kung fu skills had given him an inkling of an alternative career path.

But beneath the bravado Bruce's subconscious was unsettled. "We slept together in an old double bed," Peter says. "Every once in a while Bruce would be taken with a dream and start punching and yelling, and once, literally tore his pajamas apart as he punched and kicked out in a violent demonstration. Then he'd start kicking and throwing his covers off us before settling back for the rest of the night. He was tight and tense even in his sleep."

Bruce had reason for concern. In Seattle, he was going to face two things that had tripped him up before: school and a stern authority figure.

When Bruce's father, Li Hoi Chuen, toured America, one of his closest friends in the opera troupe, Ping Chow, became gravely ill in New York City. He was nursed back to health by a young Chinese American woman named Ruby. Born on a Seattle fishing dock, Ruby was the eldest daughter in a family of ten children. Her family was so poor that her brothers would knock on the back doors of Chinatown restaurants and ask for leftover food. Strong-willed and unyielding from an early age, Ruby divorced her first husband and moved to Manhattan where she fell in love with Ping Chow.

They married, returned to Seattle, and opened the first Chinese restaurant outside Chinatown. They chose a large three-story home on the corner of Broadway and Jefferson in the First Hill neighborhood. Many Chinese laughed at Ruby and said she would never make it up there, but her restaurant soon became a hangout for white CEOs, politicians, and journalists. Ping, who spoke little English, was the cook, while the loquacious Ruby transformed her job as hostess into a kind of unofficial spokeswoman for the Chinese community. When the Chinese had a problem with the city, its police, or immigration officials, they went to Ruby. Police would come to her to arbitrate neighborhood conflicts in Chinatown. Over the years, she housed hundreds of Chinese immigrants searching for a new life in the rooms above her restaurant.

As the son of one of Ping Chow's oldest friends, Bruce was under the impression he would be treated like an honored guest with no more serious responsibilities than occasionally babysitting Ruby's youngest son, Mark. Instead Ruby put him in a tiny forty-square-foot bedroom—formerly a walk-in closet under the staircase with one naked bulb, a wooden fruit box for a desk, and peeling plaster for decor—and promptly assigned him the most menial tasks as the restaurant's busboy, dishwasher, janitor, scullion.

It was exactly what Bruce's father wanted. Hoi Chuen had sent his son to America to "eat bitter." Having grown up poor, he believed that suffering built character, and his wife, who was raised in Hong Kong's wealthiest clan, had spoiled the boy. His son needed a wake-up call, a reality check. Bruce wrote Hawkins, "Now I am really on my own. Since the day I stepped into this country, I didn't spend any money from my father. Now I am working as a waiter for a part time job after school. I'm telling you it's tough, boy!"

While his father had cut Bruce off, his mother, Grace, secretly sent money to Ruby to help with his upkeep, pad his paycheck, and prevent Ruby from evicting Bruce. Grace knew her son well. He might be trapped in a walk-in closet and forced to clean dishes, but he didn't have to like it. Bruce made his displeasure known by refusing to give Ruby Chow face. In Chinese culture, younger people are expected to address their elders either formally or with a familial appellation, like "Uncle" or "Auntie." As a form of protest, Bruce simply called her "Ruby," an appalling breach of etiquette.

"You should call me 'Mrs. Chow' or else 'Auntie Chow,' " she reprimanded him.

"You're not my auntie," Bruce shot back, "so why should I call you 'Auntie'?"

His insolent attitude toward his elders—what is called in Cantonese "not thick, nor thin"—provoked one of the cooks into threatening Bruce with a cleaver. "Use it," Bruce yelled at the cook. "Take a swing. I dare you." Other employees intervened, forcing the cook to back down.

Bruce complained to anyone who would listen, including Ruby Chow, that he was a victim of exploitation, an indentured servant. He declared his situation the modern equivalent of the coolie trade. Ruby disliked Bruce and detested his criticism. "He was not the sort of person you want your children to grow up like," she later said. "He was wild and undisciplined. He had no respect."

For the three years that Bruce cleaned dishes and lived above Ruby's restaurant, their relationship was one of open hostility. He called her "the dragon lady." But despite his resistance, Ruby gave structure to Bruce's life. By the time he left her service, he had been transformed from a spoiled street punk into someone intent on making something of himself.

Every morning Bruce walked down Broadway to attend Edison Technical High School on 811 East Olive Street. It offered vocational training and adult education to older students, many former military in their mid-twenties, who wanted to complete their high school education or pick up a trade. With a purpose and drive he lacked in Hong Kong, Bruce forced himself to grind through his math and science courses and found himself actually enjoying history and philosophy. He never became an academic whiz, like his brother, but he maintained a 2.6 grade point average and graduated with a high school diploma in eighteen months, a feat his family would have considered impossible only a few years prior.

During his first few months in Seattle, his main extracurricular activity was the Chinese Youth Club. He joined because the head instructor, Fook Young, was one of his father's friends and Bruce looked on him as an uncle. Uncle Fook was well versed in several styles of kung fu and taught Bruce the basics of Praying Mantis, Eagle Claw, and Tai Chi. When Bruce left Hong Kong, he had only three years of training in Wing Chun and considered himself to be the sixth-best student in Ip Man's school of several dozen disciples. His greatest desire was to improve so much that he would be number one when he returned to Hong Kong. His problem was nobody in America practiced the relatively obscure style of Wing Chun. While he was away, his classmates would be getting better and better. To shortcut their advantage, he decided to search out the secrets of other kung fu styles to combine them into a super-system. He wanted to become the best kung fu artist in the world.

The Chinese Youth Club was where Bruce practiced his other great passion—dancing. He was committed to kung fu, but he often felt that cha-cha was more fun. "I don't do much for my spare time except studying and practicing Wing Chun," he wrote to his friend Hawkins. "Now and then a South American will come and teach me some of his terrific fancy steps and have mine in return. His steps are really wonderful and exotic!" Bruce's dueling obsessions were obvious just from looking at his hands: his right was enlarged and heavily callused from pounding his knuckles against wooden dummies but his left was slender and unmarred. "I'm saving it for dancing," Bruce joked with friends.

Bruce Lee's first public performance in America was at the 1959 Seattle Seafair. Billed as a kung fu exhibition, the announcer informed the crowd that the show would be delayed for a cha-cha demonstration. Onto the stage sashayed Bruce and a young female partner. They gracefully danced through twenty different routines until the crowd grew restless. Next up were the kung fu routines from the Chinese Youth Club. The first to perform was a two-hundred-pounder doing a powerful traditional form as the announcer explained each technique and its purpose. The last person to demonstrate was Bruce Lee, who the announcer introduced as just arriving from California. He did a beautiful Southern Praying Mantis form filled with intricate hand movements, which he emphasized by popping his knuckles.

The most excited and dazzled member of the audience was a young African American named Jesse Glover. As a boy growing up in Seattle, Jesse became obsessed with the martial arts after a drunken, racist cop shattered his jaw with a nightstick. Jesse wanted revenge, but he couldn't find any Asian instructor who would teach a black teenager. It wasn't until he joined the Air Force and was stationed at Ramstein Air Base in Germany that Jesse began to formally study judo. After his enlistment ended in his mid-twenties, he joined the Seattle Judo Club where he became a black belt and an assistant instructor. He had recently become fascinated by kung fu but again couldn't find anyone who would accept him as a student. As fate would have it, Jesse lived only four blocks from Ruby Chow's restaurant and was enrolled in Edison Technical High School.

When Jesse discovered his connection to Bruce, he made sure to walk ahead of him each morning to school. Every time he passed a telephone pole he would punch and kick it, pretending like he didn't notice Bruce behind him. For days Jesse did this without eliciting a reaction. Finally he screwed up his courage and asked, "Is your name Bruce Lee?"

"Bruce Lee is my name. What do you want?"

"Do you practice kung fu?"

"I do."

"Would you teach me?" Jesse asked, his heart in his mouth. When Bruce hesitated, Jesse continued, "I am very anxious to learn. I went to California looking for instruction but I couldn't find anyone who would teach me."

Bruce looked at Jesse for a long time, weighing the request in his mind. These were the words Bruce had dreamed of hearing since his buddy Hawkins had cast doubt on his plans to teach Wing Chun in America. But he couldn't have imagined his first serious entreaty would come from an African American. For centuries there was an unwritten prohibition against teaching outsiders kung fu. Why share your secret weapon with potential enemies? Bruce had nearly been kicked out of Ip Man's school when it was discovered he was not fully Chinese. While attitudes were changing and a handful of San Francisco kung fu studios were beginning to allow a token number of white members, nobody would teach black students. If Bruce accepted Jesse as his first disciple, he knew he would receive criticism from conservative Chinese chauvinists like Ruby Chow. (Sure enough, after she discovered Bruce had an African American student, she rebuked him, "You are teaching black guys this and that. They are going to use it to beat up on the Chinese.")

"It would have to be in a place where we could practice in secret," Bruce finally said.

"We could use my apartment," Jesse suggested.

"Do you live alone?"

"I have two roommates."

"They will have to leave when I teach you."

"I will get rid of them."

After school they walked back to Ruby Chow's restaurant as Bruce gave a short lecture on the history of kung fu. When they arrived, Bruce didn't invite Jesse inside. "Some of them don't like blacks," Bruce explained matter-of-factly. "It would be better for everyone if you remain outside. I have to work. I'll meet you at your apartment at six."

Bruce arrived on time at Jesse's apartment on the southeast corner of Seventh and James. Once he was certain no one else was home he said to Jesse, "Let's get on with it. Do you know any martial arts?"

"I did a little boxing in the Air Force and I'm currently practicing judo."

"I don't know much about boxing or judo," Bruce said. "Will you show me your judo?"

Jesse began with *Osoto Gari* (a hip toss and leg sweep). He was expecting Bruce to give a little resistance. When he didn't, the throw ended up a lot faster and stronger than Jesse anticipated and Bruce's head narrowly missed the sharp metal corner of Jesse's bed. It could have killed or maimed him, but Bruce showed no reaction.

"Not bad," Bruce said, clinically, "but I don't like the way you have to hold on to your opponent to throw. Now I'll show you Wing Chun. I want you to try to hit me any way you can."

Jesse threw jabs, hooks, and haymakers as fast as he could, but none made contact. Bruce blocked each one and countered by sticking his fist right in front of Jesse's face. Once Bruce had demonstrated he could stop all of Jesse's punches from long range, he gave him a lesson in short-range sticky hands (*chi sao*). Every time he touched Jesse's hands Jesse was helpless to do anything. If he tried to push forward, his motion was diverted. When he tried to pull back, Bruce stuck his fist in Jesse's face. "He controlled me at will," Jesse remembers. "He could do things I hadn't even thought possible."

Bruce Lee had converted his first soul to the Church of Kung Fu.

From that night on, Bruce and Jesse were inseparable. They practiced outside every day during lunch period under a metal stairwell and after school in Jesse's apartment. Bruce had found a friend and a training partner; Jesse, a master. After a month, Jesse convinced Bruce to accept his roommate, Ed

Hart, as a student. Ed was a two-hundred-pound former professional boxer and veteran bar brawler who could knock out a man with either hand, but in his first lesson with Bruce he was no more effective than Jesse had been. Bruce easily tied him up like a pretzel.

Jesse became Bruce's best PR agent. He couldn't stop talking about how amazing his new teacher was. Pretty soon several students at the Seattle Judo Club, where Jesse was an assistant instructor, began inquiring if they could learn from Bruce. One of them was Skip Ellsworth, who grew up as the only white kid on an Indian reservation, fighting Native American youths on a daily basis amid dismal poverty. "During Bruce's very brief first demonstration of his kung fu, he hit me in the chest with both palms so hard that my feet left the ground and I flew backwards for what seemed like ten feet before I slammed into a wall," Skip remembers. "Nothing like that had ever happened to me before. It only took Bruce Lee approximately two seconds to make a true believer out of me."

Just as he had at La Salle and St. Francis Xavier, Bruce was building his own gang of friend-followers at Edison Tech. Lee found his recruits among Seattle's now vanished street-fighting scene, which consisted of a couple hundred deprived kids of various ethnicities from areas like Lake City and Renton who fought for turf and status with fists, knives, razors, and an occasional gun. To increase his crew's numbers, Bruce began giving his own one-man shows.

On Asian Cultural Appreciation Day at Edison Tech, Bruce gave a performance of "Kung Fu," which the poster outside the auditorium helpfully explained was a Chinese martial art. About forty students showed up to see Bruce Lee walk onstage wearing glasses, a suit, and tie. He appeared to be the stereotypical studious Chinese teenager. Speaking in a Hong Kong accent that made his *r*'s sound like *w*'s, Bruce launched into a potted folkloric history of kung fu: It had been kept secret from foreigners to keep them from using it against the Chinese as they had gunpowder; Buddhist monks had developed lethal techniques based on the ways animals and insects fought. To demonstrate, Bruce first assumed the Eagle stance with his hand extended in a claw, then transformed into a Praying Mantis with his forearms making piano-hammer strikes, then a White Crane with its wings spread and its legs raised in a defensive position, and finally a Monkey's Stealing a Peach, a euphemism for ripping your opponent's testicles.

"It was a beautiful performance, sort of a cross between ballet and mime," remembers James DeMile. "But it sure as hell didn't look like fighting and Bruce looked about as dangerous as Don Knotts. The audience began to titter."

Bruce went stock still, his visage darkening. The audience fell quiet very quickly. Bruce looked directly at DeMile, who had been smirking, and said, "You look like you can fight. How about coming up here for a minute?"

Like a newcomer to prison, Bruce had picked out the baddest dude on the yard to challenge. DeMile was twenty years old and 220 pounds. He could indeed fight. He was a champion boxer and street brawler, who rarely went anywhere without a gun in his pocket. He was currently on probation.

As DeMile jumped onto the stage, Lee said he would be demonstrating his own style of martial arts called Wing Chun, which was developed by a Buddhist nun over four hundred years ago and emphasized close quarters combat. Bruce turned to DeMile: "Hit me as hard as you can with either hand whenever you are ready."

DeMile was afraid he might kill the little Chinese kid with one punch. He needn't have worried. Bruce proceeded to do to DeMile what he had already done to Jesse Glover and Ed Hart. He brushed away every punch as easily as you would a baby, and countered with punches of his own, which he stopped millimeters from DeMile's nose. For the finale, he tied DeMile's arms into knots with one hand, while, to add insult to injury, knocking on DeMile's forehead with the other. "Is anyone home?" Bruce asked to the laughter of the audience.

"I was as helpless as if I was in some giant roll of flypaper. It was like a slow-motion nightmare," DeMile recalls. "After the demonstration, I swallowed what little was left of my pride and asked him if he'd teach me some of his techniques."

To his crew of Jesse Glover, Ed Hart, and Skip Ellsworth, Bruce added James DeMile and Leroy Garcia, a grizzly bear of a young man who was also in the audience for Bruce's performance and must have been grateful he wasn't the one singled out to volunteer. Over the next few months more blue-collar young men from Edison Tech and the Seattle Judo Club joined: Tak Miyabe, Charlie Woo, Howard Hall, Pat Hooks, and Jesse's younger brother, Mike. It was the most racially diverse group of students—white, black, brown, and yellow—in the history of the Chinese martial arts.

The final addition was Taky Kimura, who was thirty years old and owned an Asian supermarket at Eighth and Madison. Like many in the group, Taky carried deep emotional wounds from childhood. His were a result of his incarceration during World War II in a Japanese internment camp. "I thought I was white, until they sent me to the camps," Taky recalled. "They took away my identity because if I wasn't white and I wasn't free and I wasn't American then who was I? When I got out of the camps I was a derelict, except I don't drink. I was walking around half-ashamed even to be alive. And then I hear about this Chinese kid giving kung fu lessons in a parking lot near my supermarket. And there he is, bubbling with pride, knocking these big white guys all over the place easy as you please. And I got excited about something for the first time in fifteen years. So I started training and bit by bit I began to get back the things I thought I'd lost forever."

The crew practiced wherever they could find an open space—parks, parking lots, and when it rained, underground parking garages. Sometimes they practiced behind Ruby Chow's restaurant where they fastened a wooden dummy to the fire escape. Every time they hit the dummy it shook the ancient wooden columns and made a terrible noise that caused Ruby and the senior cooks to loudly complain—much to Bruce's ornery delight.

Classes were so informal they could barely be considered classes. The crew never called Bruce master or *sifu*, just Bruce. He didn't charge them anything, and he didn't so much teach them as use them to further his own pursuit of kung fu perfection. "We were all dummies for Bruce to train on," Jesse noted. "He was caught up in his own development and had little patience for teaching those who were not quick to learn." Bruce was like a brilliant young professor who refuses to teach introductory freshmen lectures and only keeps a group of graduate students to assist him with his own research and discoveries.

One of these was the now famous one-inch punch. Bruce always wanted to increase the power of his punches from shorter and shorter distances. By working on his coordination and timing Bruce learned how to torque his body to create the maximum amount of acceleration. "His punch got stronger with practice," Jesse says.

One day, a 230-pound man, who had heard rumors of Bruce's one-inch punch, approached him and said, "I don't see how you can get any power from that distance."

"I'll be happy to show you," Bruce smiled.

The next instant the man was flying eight feet through the air with a look of frozen terror on his face. After crashing into a wall and slumping to the floor, the only thing the man could say was, "I see, I see."

Bruce's tough young friends loved him—they were receiving a world-class education from a budding genius for free—and he returned their affection. "I don't think Bruce ever again had friends with whom he was so open," Skip Ellsworth says, "or who cared for him as much." They were a tight crew, hanging out together before and after practices. They constantly went to the movies. Bruce introduced them to Chinese kung fu and Japanese samurai flicks but failed to convince them of the comedic genius of Jerry Lewis. "I hated comedies," Jesse Glover recalls, "and we would end up going to separate shows."

After a workout they would go to the Tai Tung Restaurant on 655 South King Street in Chinatown. "The advantage for us is we could always find something on the menu that we could afford," says Skip. Bruce was a voracious eater—he could consume massive quantities without gaining any weight. He was also a voracious talker. His topics of conversation were kung fu, philosophy, cha-cha, and Hong Kong. He worked though his homesickness by describing the sights of Hong Kong and the places that he was going to show them when they went there together. He also liked to debate life goals with Jesse.

"I want to be rich and famous," Bruce would say, before adding, "and the best kung fu man in the world!"

"I just want to be happy," Jesse would reply. "Money can't buy a good life."

"It can," Bruce insisted.

"Name me one rich person who is happy," Jesse would purposely bait Bruce.

"You're crazy," Bruce would shout angrily. "You're crazy!"

Jesse also liked to tease Bruce about how much gum he chewed, nearly four packs a day.

"I have a cavity in my back tooth," Bruce explained. "The gum eases the pain."

"You're the crazy one," Jesse said. "Gum just makes it worse. You should go to a dentist."

"I hate dentists," said Bruce. It took weeks of cajoling, but Jesse finally convinced Bruce to have his tooth filled.

Bruce liked being fashionable. He wore shoes with Cuban heels because they made him an inch taller. When he first came to America, his prize possession was a raccoon skin coat his father had given him. He wore it everywhere until his friends told him raccoon wasn't in vogue. He immediately put it in mothballs.

As a prank, Bruce would dress up in his snappiest suit, swagger into a downtown restaurant with his students acting as his bodyguards, and pretend to be the son of the Chinese ambassador. "Bruce would act like he couldn't speak English," says Jesse, "and Howard, Ed, and I would pretend to translate his wishes to the waitress."

English was Bruce's biggest initial hurdle in America. He was proficient but not fluent. He constantly had to translate from Cantonese to English in his head. Whenever he got excited, which was often, he tripped over certain words and syllables. "I don't think I ever heard him say my name without stuttering," says Jesse. "He always had to repeat the 'J' several times before he could spit it out." He was extremely sensitive about his stutter—no one dared make fun of him about it. His around-the-clock bull sessions with his boys were a way of attacking the problem through total immersion. His English improved rapidly, although he never completely mastered it.

Bruce's street-tough students introduced him to another crucial aspect of American culture—guns. Leroy Garcia and Skip Ellsworth taught Bruce how to shoot pistols, revolvers, rifles, and shotguns. They gave him his first gun, a Colt .25 caliber semiautomatic pistol with black handle grips. "Bruce totally loved it," says Skip. He enjoyed dressing up like a Western gunslinger with Leroy's nine-inch-barrel .357 strapped to his side, a 30-06 in his hand, and a cowboy hat on his head. His interest was less in hunting than in being a quick-draw artist. He and Leroy would practice using blank cartridges. After a short period of time, Leroy refused to play, since the blank wads hurt like hell and Bruce always won.

His friends had less success teaching him how to drive. Leroy Garcia let Bruce practice with his little Fiat. "Bruce was as poor at driving as he was good at kung fu," says Jesse. "Every time I rode with him I felt like the trip might be my last." Bruce was an aggressive and often distracted driver who zoomed up on cars, tailgated, and passed without leaving enough room to pull back if something went wrong. It was a combination of luck and his incredibly quick reflexes that kept him out of a serious accident. For a couple of years he longed to buy his own sports car to complete his image. "It was always on his mind," says Jesse, "and he mentioned it at least once a day." Finally he was able to scrape together enough money to buy a 1957 Ford. He was so proud of it he almost wore off the paint washing it so often.

But perhaps the greatest gift his students gave to Bruce was forcing him to evolve as a martial artist. When he arrived he was wedded to Chinese kung fu, convinced of its superiority. But the sheer size of Americans made him adapt. Techniques that worked in Ip Man's class were easily thwarted by opponents who were eight inches taller and a hundred pounds heavier. His students, all veteran fighters and martial artists, also introduced him to the American combat scene. From them he began to learn the value of certain judo throws and chokes and appreciate the power of Western boxing's punches and fluidity of its footwork. Bruce became an avid fan of pugilism and began borrowing moves from its champions: Muhammad Ali's footwork and timing, Sugar Ray Robinson's bobs and weaves. At this point Bruce still thought of himself as a Kung Fu Man, but he was beginning to merge the best of East and West. It was an approach that would last the rest of his life, characterize his own art, and eventually lead to a new paradigm in the martial arts.

As Bruce and his merry band of mayhem continued to practice in public parks and parking lots, word began to spread about this little Chinese kid and what he could do. Crowds began to gather when they trained and individuals asked about joining the class. Since his arrival in America, Bruce had been giving dancing lessons for money. Now he realized he might be able to do the same with kung fu. To do so, he would need a permanent location. The crew pooled their money and rented the only place they could afford—a two-story storefront at 651 South Weller in a dilapidated section of Chinatown. Gypsies lived in the storefront across the street, hobos camped out in a nearby vacant lot, and derelicts inhabited an abandoned hotel three doors down, but the gang couldn't have been happier. "We felt like we were on top of the world," says Skip.

Bruce conceived of the space less as a traditional kung fu *kwoon* (school) than as a private clubhouse. The original ten charter members of his crew chipped in $10 a month to cover the $100 rent and in return continued to receive free instruction. Anyone accepted as a student afterward paid tuition directly to Bruce. Training took place on the 120-square-foot first floor where spectators could watch from the sidewalk. The large room on the second floor was reserved as a hangout spot for the charter members. In less than a year, Bruce had opened his own kung fu studio, a remarkable achievement for a fresh-off-the-boat nineteen-year-old.

Anxious to increase enrollment, Bruce took his act on the road, like his father before him, treading the boards in a traveling kung fu show. His troupe performed at the International Trade Fair, Seafair, the World's Fair, the Chinese New Year celebrations in Seattle and Vancouver, the Fremont Street Fair, and the University Street Fair. As part of his showmanship and salesmanship, Bruce asked his friends to wear kung fu uniforms, bow to him on stage, and call him *sifu*. By workshopping his material in front of various live audiences, Bruce slowly created his onstage persona—a funny, philosophical, and fearsome character—which he would play, with slight variations, for the rest of his life.

The crew had a rowdy blast. Their one concern was Bruce's vulnerability to heat. "The only time I started to worry was when the stage lights made him sweat," says Jesse. "Whenever he got overheated his control would fade and I would get the hell knocked out of me." During their demonstration in Vancouver, Bruce accidentally hit Jesse four or five times, leaving him with a sore temple, swollen lip, and a bloody nose.

Bruce didn't go looking for fights in Seattle, but he struggled to control himself when fights came looking for him. And they often did. Bruce had a "cocky" walk that attracted attention and he was fearless about going places where Chinese were not typically welcome. One night four guys approached Bruce and his white date, making racist remarks about the chink and his blond chick. Bruce went ballistic and was going to blast all four of them until his date forced him to walk away. Bruce was less inclined to turn the other cheek when he was with one of his boys. An incident broke out at an "all black" pool hall near 23rd and Madison between Bruce, Skip, and several of the regulars. Skip and Bruce also engaged in a brief skirmish at a cowboy honky-tonk in Montana. "Bruce could end any physical confrontation within three or four seconds," says Skip. "He was one of the best fighters who ever lived."

Bruce's public demonstrations were another source of conflict. He peppered his performances with blunt analysis and dismissive critiques of competing styles of martial arts. For every two people he recruited to his school, he offended at least one. As inspiring and infectious as he was to his followers, he came off as brash and egotistical to his detractors.

One of them was Yoichi Nakachi, a twenty-nine-year-old Japanese classmate at Edison Technical. During Bruce's first demonstration at Edison he had asserted that soft styles like Chinese kung fu were superior to hard styles like Japanese karate. Yoichi, a black belt in karate and veteran street fighter, took offense. He and a buddy showed up at Bruce's next performance at Yesler Terrace. After it was over, Yoichi sent his friend backstage to issue a challenge on his behalf. Uncharacteristically, Bruce hesitated and then checked with his crew to make sure he wouldn't lose face with them if he didn't accept. When they told him he didn't have anything to prove to them, he refused the challenge.

For the next several weeks at school, Yoichi tried to provoke Bruce, sneering at him in the cafeteria, bumping into him in the hallway. Other Chinese guys came up to Bruce and told him if he wasn't willing to fight this Japanese punk, they would. "I'm not going to let anyone prod me into a fight," Bruce told them.

Finally, Yoichi pushed Bruce too far. In the school's basement lounge, Yoichi sent a friend over to Bruce with a note that read: "If Bruce Lee wants to go to the hospital, walk over to me." Bruce left the lounge and waited for Jesse to come out of class. He was so angry he could hardly speak.

"What's wrong?" Jesse asked.

"I'm going to fight that son of a bitch," Bruce sputtered. "Will you be my second?"

"Let's go," Jesse said as they headed for the basement lounge.

"I want to fight him on the third floor."

"I don't know," Jesse hesitated. "We could get expelled."

"I hadn't thought of that," Bruce said, remembering his expulsion from La Salle. "Where do you suggest?"

"The downtown YMCA would be better. If anyone comes in during the fight we can always say it's just friendly sparring."

"Agreed," Bruce said. "Will you arrange it? I'm too angry right now. I don't trust myself near him."

Bruce, Jesse, Ed Hart, and Howard Hall waited at the bus stop in front of the school for Yoichi and two of his Japanese friends.

"You insulted me and my country," Yoichi declared.

Bruce was furious. Jesse was afraid the fight was going to happen right there. Bruce looked away in an effort to control his rage. Yoichi kept moving into Bruce's line of vision in an attempt to break down his confidence. When the bus finally arrived Yoichi sat in front of Bruce and started to discuss the rules in an abrasive manner.

"Forget the rules," Bruce snarled, the veins in his neck bulging. "I'm going all out."

"Why don't you stop talking," Jesse said to Yoichi. "We will move to different seats." Jesse spent the rest of the trip downtown trying to calm Bruce down and get him to agree not to go all out. He was afraid Bruce might kill Yoichi.

When they reached the Y, Bruce, Ed, Howard, and Jesse went directly to the handball court. Yoichi and his two friends went to a bathroom where he changed into a white karate gi. Bruce tested the wood floors with his shoes and decided to go barefoot. He took off his dress shirt and did a couple of deep knee bends in his undershirt.

As the two young men faced off, Bruce wanted to make one thing clear: "You challenged me, right?"

"Ya, ya, ya," Yoichi said.

"You asked for this fight?"

"Ya, ya, ya."

"All right," Bruce said.

Jesse, who was the referee, stepped out to explain the rules: the fight would consist of three two-minute rounds with the winner being the man who won two of the three. Ed Hart, serving as timekeeper, pulled out his stopwatch.

Bruce stood in a relaxed Wing Chun stance: right foot forward, right hand pointing at Yoichi's nose, left palm next to right elbow. Yoichi started in a classic karate stance with one leg extended behind him, one hand facing Bruce with palm out, the other hand in a fist chambered at his waist.

"Ready? Set, go!" Jesse shouted.

Yoichi immediately switched to a cat stance and flicked a quick front snap kick at Bruce's groin. Bruce deflected it with his right forearm, followed with his left fist to Yoichi's face, and then immediately launched a series of rapid Wing Chun chain punches. Each blow rippled Yoichi's face like waves on a lake. Bruce smacked Yoichi across the entire handball court without getting counterpunched once. Yoichi flailed at him but all his blows were blocked by Bruce's forearms. Bruce controlled the centerline and his defenses could not be penetrated. As Yoichi's back slammed into the wall he grabbed Bruce's arms and pulled to the side. Bruce responded by twisting his hips and delivering a double-fist punch—his right connected with

Yoichi's face at the same moment his left blasted Yoichi's chest. The power of the impact lifted Yoichi off his feet and sent him flying back six feet in the air. Bruce ran forward and kicked Yoichi in the face as soon as his knees hit the floor. Blood sprayed from Yoichi's nose. He collapsed in a heap as if he was dead.

"Stop!" Jesse screamed.

Jesse and Ed Hart ran over to Yoichi to check his pulse. After a few moments, he regained consciousness. The first question from Yoichi's lips was: "How long did it take him to defeat me?"

Hart looked at his stopwatch. It read eleven seconds. Feeling sorry for the guy, Ed doubled it: "twenty-two seconds."

As Yoichi pulled himself off the floor, he said, "I want a rematch. I didn't train properly for this fight. I want to do it again."

"I never wanted to fight you in the first place," Bruce replied. "There's no point in fighting again. As far as I'm concerned this is over. I will never talk to anyone else about what happened."

As everyone left, Bruce made his friends promise they wouldn't discuss the fight with outsiders. Yoichi's buddies leaked the details to the rest of the school. To save face, Yoichi asked Bruce if he could become his disciple and take private lessons with him. Bruce told him he would have to join his club's formal class and learn with the rest of the beginners. Yoichi swallowed his pride and attended classes for a month before dropping out.

"A lot of people took exception to the things Bruce said," recalls Taky Kimura, "but when they saw what he could do, they all wanted to join him."

At home in Hong Kong, Grace Ho and her son, proudly wearing his University of Washington Huskies sweatshirt, June 1963. *(David Tadman)*

At Kai Tak Airport, Grace Ho, Li Hoi Chuen, Bruce Lee, actress Mary Wong, cousin-in-law Nguyen Yu Ming with daughter, and Eva Tso, June 1963. *(David Tadman)*

six

husky

Much to the surprise of his friends and family in Hong Kong, Bruce gained admission to the University of Washington on March 27, 1961. For a boy who had been held back, expelled, and regarded as a lost cause, it was a remarkable turn of events. When his father heard the news, he danced around the apartment singing, "We picked the right horse to bet on!" For the first time in a long time, he had given his father face and reason to be proud. Only the very best (or the very richest) Hong Kong students attended a university in Britain or America.

Aside from a few core requirements in math and science, Bruce primarily picked classes that matched his interests. He signed up for courses in gymnastics, dance, judo, drawing, and public speaking. His major was drama. Whenever he had the chance, he explored the spiritual nature of kung fu. For a freshman English essay he wrote, "Gung fu is a special skill, a fine art rather than just a physical exercise. . . . The core principle of Gung fu is *Tao*—the spontaneity of the universe." For a poetry assignment, he described a mystical experience while walking along Lake Washington: "In the moonlight I slowly move to a Gung Fu form; Body and soul are as though fused into one."

It was not until his junior year that Bruce's intellectual curiosity led him to branch out into new areas of inquiry. He took two courses in psychology (General Psychology and Psychology of Adjustment) and two philosophy classes (Intro to Philosophy and Chinese Philosophy). These two subjects became lifelong passions. After college he added hundreds of philosophy and psychology books to his personal library of over 2,500 books, carefully reading and transcribing his favorite passages in his notebooks. His favorite authors included Thomas Aquinas, David Hume, René Descartes, Carl Jung, and Carl Rogers. He would later tell reporters that his major in college was philosophy, even though he never officially switched from drama and only took two classes in the subject.

His interest did not translate into good grades. His GPA after his freshman year was 1.84. Even in gymnastics he only scored a C. (In his later Hong Kong kung fu movies, all of his handsprings and backflips were done by a Cantonese Opera–trained stunt double.) After having achieved the unexpected goal of actually getting into college, he lost focus, slipped back into old habits, and only studied enough to get by. His more studious classmates thought of him as a jock and jokingly nicknamed him Beefcake. "Bruce talked to me about martial arts, philosophy, and girls, but he never mentioned academics," recalls Eunice Lam, who was dating his older brother, Peter. "If you wanted him to shut his mouth, the best way was to ask him about his studies."

Although he never joined a fraternity, he went to a number of frat parties with his classmate and kung fu student Skip Ellsworth, who pledged Delta Kappa Epsilon. It was yet another chance for Bruce to be the life of the party. He would demonstrate his one-inch punch, two-finger pushups, sticky hands, and various kung fu forms, especially Praying Mantis, to the delight and amazement of the frat boys. He taught the sorority girls how to cha-cha. It was Bruce's first introduction to the affluent children of America's elite, and their positive reaction to his talents opened his eyes about how important kung fu could be to him in the States. "How would they treat me if they knew I lived in a closet and worked as dishwasher in a Chinese restaurant?" Bruce would half joke with Skip. Seeing how their comfortable lives compared to his meager circumstances inflamed Lee's ambition to succeed in America.

One area of campus life that held no interest for Bruce was the growing student activism of the early 1960s. Although he was generally aware of the changes sweeping across the country—the civil rights movement and antiwar protests—he did not watch the news on TV or subscribe to a newspaper. His focus was on the personal not the political, self-improvement not social change, making himself better at martial arts not making the world a better place. It was a curious blind spot considering he was nearly drafted to fight in Vietnam.

At the University of Washington, Reserve Officers' Training Corps (ROTC) was mandatory for every male student. Like almost everyone on campus, Bruce resented the required early morning drills. He skipped so many marching exercises that he was finally ordered to get up at 4 a.m. and march for hours to make up the lost time. When the drill sergeant noticed that Bruce was chewing gum, he bellowed, "Swallow that, soldier!" Bruce spit it on the ground instead.

As the sergeant glowered at him, Bruce grinned. "It's bad for my health!"

After the exercises were over, the furious sergeant got in Bruce's face and warned him, "The next time I say, 'Swallow, soldier,' you'd better swallow!"

Bruce erupted, "Son of a bitch, if you ever speak to me like that again, I will knock you on your ass!"

For a moment as they glared at each other, it seemed like violence might ensue, but the sergeant, seeing the fire in Bruce's eyes, wisely decided to back down. He walked away, shaking his head and mumbling, "Poor misguided kid."

Bruce Jun Fan Lee signed up for the draft, as was required of all American men between the ages of eighteen and twenty-five, but was rejected by the draft board. He was categorized as 4-F, medically unfit for service, after the physical examination revealed he had one undescended testicle. Bruce had been born with this defect, called cryptorchidism. The two risks associated with it are infertility and testicular cancer. For years, Bruce was convinced he could never be a father. Seven years later in 1969, he underwent an operation to remove the undescended testicle at St. John's Hospital in Santa Monica.

During his first year in America, Bruce and his high school sweetheart, Pearl, slowly grew apart. Their letters became less and less frequent. Hoping to salvage their long-distance relationship, Pearl flew to Seattle to see Bruce, but he forgot to pick her up from the airport. After waiting for hours, she grew so angry she hopped a flight to San Francisco. When Bruce realized his mistake, he made numerous phone calls to beg her forgiveness, but she refused to accept his apology.

After Pearl, Bruce dated a number of young women, but none for any length of time. He was a charmer and a bit of a player. "If a pretty girl was anywhere near, Bruce would perk up and start a spontaneous kung fu demo," says James DeMile. "He would point to me and explain how fast and tough I was and then promptly knock me over and under." Bruce liked to take his dates to the movies. "R, how could we let the valuable but short autumn days slip away without doing them full justice," he wrote one of his girlfriends. "Write me a letter telling me which movie you haven't seen and I'll invite you to see it this Sunday. That will suit you, won't it, my dear young lady? With my best wishes for all kinds of luck. I am, Bruce."

It wasn't until his first year of college that Bruce fell head over heels in love. He was lounging with friends in the student center, the HUB, when he noticed a stunning Japanese American sophomore named Amy Sanbo sitting in a far corner. Entranced, Bruce left his friends and moved to a nearby table to get a closer look. When she walked past him to go to class, he suddenly said, "Hello," and grabbed her forearm with his index finger and thumb. He squeezed with such power that Amy's knees buckled and she nearly dropped her books on the floor.

"Let go of me before I really get angry!" she exclaimed. When he did, she asked, "Why did you do that?"

"I was just showing my friends how much power can be exerted with only two fingers."

"What a jerk!" she said as she marched away.

While not a particularly suave approach, it left an impression, literally—the black-and-blue bruise on her arm lasted for days. For the next several weeks wherever Amy went Bruce popped up out of nowhere. Trying to make it up to her, Bruce would ask, "How do you feel? Are you okay? My name is Bruce Lee." He would bring up any random topic of conversation just to talk to her.

Bruce pursued Amy with the same single-minded devotion as he did kung fu perfection. In love, as in combat, his strategy was to overwhelm the target. One day she stepped on a nail at ballet practice and needed crutches to get to class. When Bruce saw her struggling up a long flight of concrete stairs north of the football field, he ran to her and offered to help.

"No, I'll do it myself," she said. "Give me my crutches back, and I'll do it myself."

Ignoring her protests, he picked her up and carried her, her textbooks, her crutches, and her heavy coat to the top. He did this every day until her foot healed. And it wasn't just those stairs. After school he carried her to the third floor of her apartment, and anywhere else he thought would be difficult. His chivalry won her over. "Not only was it quite a feat of strength, it was a grand gesture," Amy recalls. "It more than made up for his past indiscretion."

What followed over the next two years was a tempestuous, on-again-off-again relationship. The magnetism was mutual and physical. Both of them were beautiful and both were dancers. "When I perform it's almost orgasmic. It is very sexual, and Bruce was like that, too," Amy says. "I'm horribly attracted to talent, and Bruce was a kinetic genius. He could just look at a movement and assimilate it, absorb it, become that movement. He moved in a way that no other Asians moved."

When she challenged him to do a pirouette, he pulled it off in one try. She also teased him about the stiffness of his cha-cha. "Why don't you put a little funk into it?" After placing some R&B records on the turntable, he was quickly able to feel the music and get down. "It's very hard to teach someone that, but Bruce had it," Amy recalls. "He could get funky."

"More than anything else, what I liked most about Bruce was that he never apologized for being Oriental," Amy says. "In a time when so many

Asians were trying to convince themselves they were white, Bruce was so proud to be Chinese he was busting with it."

One day on campus, Bruce pulled her into an open office in Parrington Hall on the pretext that they could study together there in privacy. It turned out to belong to Theodore Roethke, the university's internationally acclaimed, Pulitzer Prize–winning poet. When Roethke walked in and caught them, he declared, "I'm Roethke, the poet! What are you doing in my room?"

Amy froze, but Bruce stood up, walked right over to him, and stuck out his hand. "I'm Bruce *Sifu* Lee, kung fu master. Good to meet you."

"What is kung fu?" Roethke asked.

Delighted by the question, Bruce went to the chalkboard and launched into a fifteen-minute lecture on kung fu, complete with diagrams and an explanation of the principles of yin and yang. Amy wanted to crawl under the door, but Roethke was mesmerized. When Bruce finished, Roethke said, "I think I understand. Thank you. Please come back anytime you want to talk more about kung fu." The next day, Roethke recounted the story to his class: "I met a young man, and he is supposed to be a master of the martial arts. He seemed pretty lethal."

The difficulty in Bruce and Amy's relationship stemmed from their divergent upbringings. Bruce had a traditional 1950s view of gender roles, whereas Amy was a 1960s proto-feminist. One of her earliest memories was of armed soldiers rummaging through her mother's underwear in the Tule Lake relocation camp where they had been interned with other Japanese Americans during World War II. Amy came out of the experience determined that she would never be caged again. Besides studying ballet, Amy was working her way through college by singing with a jazz band, a risqué activity for the prim Japanese American community. Amy dreamed of an artistic career—singing, dancing, and acting.

Bruce had his own artistic dreams, which were so big and difficult to achieve, he felt she should prioritize his over hers. "Your whole thing is Bruce Lee," Sanbo complained. "All your thoughts, all your goals are Bruce Lee. I haven't heard anything about Amy."

"But my goals are so exciting I want to share them with you," Bruce replied, unable to understand why this made her even angrier.

Amy loved Bruce, but he drove her crazy. She felt he was suffocating her—always wanting to know where she was going and with whom. Whenever she wanted to go to Chinatown without him, Bruce insisted that one of his kung fu students serve as her bodyguard. "Who the hell are your thugs supposed to defend me from?" she shouted at him. "I grew up in Chinatown!"

Bruce repeatedly asked Amy to marry him. He offered her his grandmother's ring—a sapphire on a white cross. Amy was torn. He was so much fun to be around and they had so much in common. She believed they could be together forever, but she was also afraid they might kill each other. She worried he just wanted to lock her down, keep her by his side all the time. She wasn't ready for that kind of commitment and she didn't think deep down he was ready for the responsibility. "I'm taking care of my mother who is ill," Amy said. "Are you capable of supporting us?"

When she finally dumped him for good during the spring semester of 1963, Bruce was devastated. For weeks, he could barely leave his room. "Bruce was heartbroken," Jesse Glover recalls. "He didn't do anything during this period except draw pictures of Amy and talk to his close friends about the emotions that he felt."

Bruce's primary focus in college was his kung fu club. Before he enrolled as a freshman at the University of Washington in 1961, he planned to open his club to the public and turn it into a commercial school, which would allow him to quit his hated job at Ruby Chow's. Instead, his second student, Ed Hart, moved to Brooklyn to find work, and no sooner had he left than other members began to drop out. Within two months the original group dwindled down to such a small number that Bruce was unable to cover the rent. In May 1961, Bruce wrote to Ed Hart, "I don't have a club anymore; in fact, we still owe $80 for it, as everybody is out of a job and couldn't keep it up. Also, I have stopped teaching as I have to have a part time job to tide me over my financial problems. . . . I miss you very much, and I hope that you can come back to Seattle."

With the loss of their clubhouse, Bruce and his crew were back to square one, practicing in parks and students' apartments. On the weekends, Bruce held lessons with the remaining core members—Jesse Glover, Taky Kimura, James DeMile, Howard Hall—at Leroy Garcia's house. During the week, he and Skip Ellsworth instructed a group of University of Washington students on the green used for outdoor concerts. This went on for about a year before Bruce was able to scrape together enough money to rent a basement space on King Street in Seattle's Chinatown and officially open his first public school or *kwoon*.

Bruce Jun Fan Lee named it the Jun Fan Gung Fu Institute after himself—a very American thing to do. It was the first step in his American dream to create a chain of kung fu schools across the country. In September of 1962, he wrote a letter to his former sweetheart, Pearl Tso, laying out the mission statement for his life:

> In every industry, in every profession, ideas are what America is looking for. Ideas have made America what she is, and one good idea will make a man what he wants to be. . . .
>
> Gung fu is the best of all martial arts; yet the Chinese derivatives of judo and karate, which are only basics of gung fu, are flourishing all over the U.S. This so happens because no one has heard of this supreme art; also there are no competent instructors. . . .
>
> I believe my long years of practice back up my title to become the first instructor of this movement. There are yet years ahead of me to polish my technique and character. My aim, therefore, is to establish a first Gung Fu Institute that will spread all over the U.S. (I have set the time limit of 10 to 15 years to complete the whole project.) My reason in doing this is not the sole objective of making money. The motives are many and among them are: I like to let the world know about the greatness of this Chinese art; I enjoy teaching and helping people; I like to have a well-to-do home for my family; I like to originate something; and the last but yet one of the most important is because gung fu is part of myself. . . .
>
> I feel I have this great creative and spiritual force within me that is greater than faith, greater than ambition, greater than confidence, greater than determination, greater than vision. It is all of these combined. . . .

> I may now own nothing but a little place down in a basement, but once my imagination has got up a full head of steam, I can see painted on a canvas of my mind a picture of a fine, big five or six story Gung Fu Institute with branches all over the States.

Twenty-one-year-old Bruce Lee concluded by framing his career goals as part of a spiritual quest. He didn't just want worldly success—he also desired inner peace.

> All in all, the goal of my planning and doing is to find the true meaning of life—peace of mind. I know that the sum of all possessions I mentioned does not necessarily add up to peace of mind; however, it can be if I devote my energy to real accomplishment of self rather than neurotic combat. In order to achieve this peace of mind, the teaching of detachment of Taoism and Zen prove to be valuable.

The first obstacle to Bruce's grand plans came from his senior student, Jesse Glover. He and several other original club members, who were used to training with Bruce for free, were put off by Bruce's efforts to formalize and commercialize his art. At first, Jesse and the others avoided Bruce's new school. "I found it a little difficult to start calling someone who I had been running around with for two years, *Sifu*," Jesse says, using the Chinese word for "Master." Annoyed, Bruce made it clear he wasn't going to share his secrets or reveal his best techniques to anyone who wasn't "strongly in his corner." This provoked Jesse, who was almost as prideful as Bruce, to split away and take Leroy Garcia and James DeMile with him. The breakup was in many ways more painful for Bruce than the one with Amy Sanbo.

The rebel faction opened their own school, not a franchise of the Jun Fan Gung Fu Institute but a competitor, in the basement of the New Richmond Hotel. The market for kung fu in Seattle in 1962 was not big enough to support two *kwoons* and Jesse's school closed in five months. He tried again, opening a second school on Pike Street in 1963. Jesse did the teaching and James DeMile was responsible for recruiting. As the school was struggling to survive with only a handful of students, DeMile made a trip to Bruce's brand-new studio on University Way with its fifty-plus disciples.

After the divorce, the relationship between Jesse, Jim, and Bruce was overtly friendly and polite but carried an undertow of hurt feelings and betrayal. That day a handful of Bruce's students cornered DeMile and asked, "Why did you and Jesse stop training with Bruce?"

"We didn't like some of the changes he was making," DeMile bluntly told them. "We felt like he was holding things back, leaving out important pieces of what make his system work."

When the students later reported back to Bruce what DeMile had said, he erupted. Bruce recognized immediately that the criticism was a crude attempt to steal students away from him, and thus a threat to his livelihood.

The next time DeMile showed up, Lee was in anything but a peaceful frame of mind. He confronted DeMile and asked in a voice pinched with rage: "Why did you say those things?"

"They asked me a question and I told them the truth," DeMile replied defensively.

Bruce pointed his finger into DeMile's chest and declared, "You have no right to make comments to my class."

"You are right," DeMile backed down. "I'm sorry."

Still furious, Bruce slapped a pair of gloves he was holding into his open palm. He seemed ready to attack.

DeMile thought to himself, "To fight Bruce when he is calm is insanity, but to do it when he is mad is to invite certain death." DeMile slipped his hand into his coat pocket and curled his index finger around the trigger of a handgun. If Bruce leapt at him, DeMile planned to blow a hole in him.

"I apologize again. I was wrong. I'm sorry," DeMile said, as he slowly backed away, turned around, and walked out the door. It was the last time the two young men ever spoke.

In the summer of 1963, four years after his banishment, Bruce Lee returned to Hong Kong for a three-month vacation. He had left by boat as an embarrassment and was arriving by airplane as a success. Dressed in his sharpest suit and tie, Bruce was greeted at Kai Tak Airport by his mother, father, younger brother, Robert, auntie Eva Tso, cousin Nguyen Yu Ming, and Mary Wong, his costar from *Thunderstorm* (1957). Robert, who was beginning his career in music, invited a photojournalist from the *Overseas Chinese Daily News* to capture the event.

It was a powerful moment of reconciliation between father and son. As is Chinese custom, Bruce brought back gifts for his family—symbolic proof of his prosperity in a foreign land. He handed to his father a hundred dollar bill, the amount his parents had given him when he left in 1959, and a brand-new overcoat.

"Dad, this is for you," Bruce said. "I bought it myself as a gift for you."

Hoi Chuen grabbed his son, whom he had once called "a useless person," and embraced him. Bruce's eyes grew moist and tears streamed down his face.

"I shouldn't have treated you like this," Hoi Chuen said, his voice choking with emotion.

"No, Dad, you were right," Bruce replied. "I wouldn't have changed my outlook on life otherwise."

In the photos, Hoi Chuen is wearing his new overcoat and beaming from ear to ear, his grin electric. "I had never seen a smile like that on Dad's face," recalls Robert.

His son, who was lost, was now found.

Waiting at the family apartment on Nathan Road were more friends and a multi-course catered banquet, a feast and a celebration for the prodigal son's return. Everyone was amazed at how much Bruce had matured. He was more confident and secure in himself. His sense of humor kept everyone laughing. He was proud of what he had accomplished in America. As the banquet wound down, he switched into a University of Washington sweatshirt. He dazzled his family with a demonstration of his hard-won kung fu skills. "When he left he was an above average student of the martial arts," says Robert, "but when he returned it was obvious he possessed a very special talent." Bruce also surprised them with his philosophical side, which they had never seen in him before. He was less self-centered and self-involved and more in tune with everyone around him. His life seemed to have a purpose.

After four years of training and teaching kung fu in the States, Bruce wanted to test his skill level against the Hong Kong masters. He visited a number of different schools to learn their best techniques. In the process, he often tried to alter and improve them. But instead of praising his innovations, the old masters rebuked him for corrupting tradition. Their negative reaction caused Bruce to become increasingly disillusioned with the conservatism of traditional kung fu.

His most important test came at Ip Man's school where he competed in sticky hands (*chi sao*) with his martial brothers and teachers. When he left in 1959, Bruce considered himself the sixth-best in the school. After four years away, he had only moved up to fourth. He was still unable to best his teacher, Wong Shun Leung, or his master, Ip Man—plus one of Ip Man's assistant instructors. While anyone else would have considered this decent progress—all three were many years his senior—Bruce, ever the perfectionist, was so frustrated he briefly considered quitting the martial arts completely. But after he cooled down, he became even more determined to be better than them. He decided he would have to train fanatically and develop more modifications to circumvent their classical techniques.

During his period of doubt with the martial arts, Bruce flirted with the idea of reviving his acting career. He hoped to act in at least one quickie Hong Kong movie during his summer break. After all, the film he starred in before he left, *The Orphan* (1960), was a critical and box office hit. When it was released, one of Hong Kong's greatest action directors, Chang Cheh (*The One-Armed Swordsman*, *Five Deadly Venoms*), was so impressed by Bruce's performance he went to his new studio, Shaw Brothers, and asked them to sign the Little Dragon, but by this time Bruce had already left for America.

Having heard the positive buzz about his last role, Bruce approached some of his old contacts expecting multiple offers. He soon discovered, however, that four years is forever in the movie business. His father, who had retired, couldn't help and many of his old colleagues had no time for a former actor. One evening as he was strolling along the beach, he saw Christine Pai Lu-Ming, his costar from *Sweet Time Together* (1956), and went over to say, "Hi." Christine walked straight past him without even bothering to glance in his direction. Bruce was crushed. No matter how hard he knocked on the film industry's doors they were all locked and the passwords changed.

Although he couldn't land an acting gig, he did have a delightful chance to serve as an acting coach. While he was away, one of his old flames, Amy Chan (Pak Yan), had begun what would become a long and illustrious film and TV career. When she heard Bruce was back in town, she called him up. "They keep casting me as sly girls," she coyly said. "Can you teach me how to be bad?" After the heartbreaking dissolution of his relationship with Amy Sanbo, it was an offer he couldn't refuse. They spent many nights dining and dancing at the Carlton Hotel in Tai Po.

To make sure he looked his best for all his dates, Bruce had the family's private tailor make him cool custom clothes that he helped design. He was so fussy he ironed them himself, because he was afraid the house servants wouldn't do it right. As Bruce explained to an American friend, "This is Hong Kong—they respect your clothing first before they respect you!"

His taste in fashion occasionally got him into trouble. One evening he went out with a female friend, Eunice Lam, to the Eagle Nest in the Hilton Hotel, the most luxurious club on Hong Kong Island. He wore a new black formal suit with a shimmering purple shirt and became the center of attention on the dance floor with his sensational cha-cha dragon steps. On the ferry back to the Kowloon side, Bruce took off his jacket in the humid Hong Kong evening. His striking purple shirt drew the attention of two hooligans, who began to mock and curse him for looking like a dandy. Bruce smiled at them and said, "You'd better keep your mouths shut or you will be in trouble later."

When they reached the Star Ferry Pier, the ruffians alighted first and waited near the flagpole at the corner of the pier. Bruce guided Eunice past them and toward her home. The thugs followed, taunting Bruce: "Where are you going so fast? Do you have to hurry home to momma?"

Eunice was terrified, but Bruce was calm and composed. When the thugs got too close, Bruce spun to face them. Suddenly Eunice heard screaming and looked back. One of the ruffians was on the ground grabbing his leg in terrible pain; the other was fleeing in terror. Bruce smiled at her and said, "Just treated him to my shin kick!"

When Bruce's cousin Frank, who was a few years older, heard the story he shook his head and made a joke about Bruce's growing maturity. "If that had been a few years ago," Frank said, "Bruce would have beaten them all up as soon as they got off the ferry."

Bruce invited his brightest American student, Doug Palmer, to visit him in Hong Kong. After a year studying with Bruce as a senior in high school, Doug had gone on to Yale University where he was majoring in Mandarin and East Asian Studies. Before Palmer arrived, Bruce wrote him a letter warning him of the heat wave and drought that had plunged the colony into misery: "Man, believe me it's hot. The water supply here is coming to a crisis—it is only on for a few hours every fourth day. The temperature is 95 degrees and it's like living in hell."

As soon as Doug stepped off the plane, it felt like he had entered a sauna. Then he caught a whiff of Hong Kong's distinctive odor: a thick tropical salt air, suffused with a stew of exotic foods, rotting garbage, and human sweat. "The ride from the airport was exhilarating," recalls Doug, "through narrow streets of pushcarts and lorries and weaving taxis, between tall tenement and office buildings with crowded shops at street level, and colorful signs in Chinese characters. Swarms of people filled the sidewalks, sitting in front of shops, standing at food stalls, coolies in undershirts and old ladies in black pajama-like pantsuits rubbing shoulders with businessmen in Western suits. Despite the drought and debilitating heat, the beggars and refugees, the filth, it was everything I had hoped for."

When Doug, who was six-foot-four and 220 pounds, walked into the apartment, Bruce's entire family stood back and gasped. "We had seen tall British guys before," recalls Robert, "but it was like a giant came to visit. We had to let it sink in a bit." At dinner in the main room of the apartment, Bruce began Doug's education in Chinese etiquette. The first course was soup and Doug sat up straight, raised his soup spoon to his mouth, and took care not to slurp. He didn't realize that eating quietly is taken as a sign that you don't like the taste of the food. Bruce leaned over and whispered in his ear, "Make a little noise."

Bruce took Doug to visit Ip Man in his apartment at the top of a high-rise. "He was a smiling man with a twinkle in his eyes, slight and getting on in years but still fit," recalls Doug. Before they arrived, Bruce made Doug promise that he wouldn't do or say anything to reveal he was Bruce's student. Ip Man was old-school and didn't believe kung fu should be taught to foreigners. As Doug sat in the corner pretending to be clueless, he had the opportunity to watch two of the most famous kung fu artists of the twentieth century practice *chi sao* for hours in their undershirts. It was the first time Doug had ever seen Bruce unable to dominate someone.

A week before Doug and Bruce were to leave for the States, Bruce returned to the apartment with a tentative, bow-legged walk and quickly changed his tight pants for loose-fitting black pajama pants he borrowed from his father.

"What's wrong?" Robert asked.

"I've been circumcised," replied Bruce.

"What is circumcision?" Robert asked.

Bruce lowered his pants as all the men in the family gathered around to inspect the surgeon's handiwork. As Bruce described the procedure in gory detail, Robert exclaimed, "Why? Why?"

"It's what they do in America," Bruce said. "I'm American. I want to look the part."

"How bad does it hurt?" Robert asked, pointing at the sutures and bandages. "Are you going to rest for a few days?"

"No, it's really no big deal," Bruce replied with manly assurance. "I'll walk tomorrow to get some exercise."

The next day he left the house only to return fifteen minutes later bleeding and in severe pain. Like it or not, Bruce had to rest up for the next few days until he healed. Every morning his father, brother, and cousin would conduct an inspection to note the progress he was making.

At the end of July as Doug and Bruce packed to leave, Bruce and Hoi Chuen hugged, their reconciliation complete. It was the last time Bruce would see his father alive.

Linda, Bruce, and Brandon Lee, circa 1965. *(Photo 12 / Alamy Stock Photo)*

seven

sunny side of the bay

Linda Emery was born in Everett, Washington, on March 21, 1945, to a Baptist family of Swedish, Irish, and English descent. Her father, Everett, passed away when she was five and her mother, Vivian, struggled to raise Linda and her older sister on her own. Vivian took a job at Sears and later got remarried to a man, who was, in Linda's words, "in no way like a father. He was not a good person." Linda was a quiet but determined child—shy, thoughtful, introverted, humble, prone to self-doubt and yet fiercely loyal, reliable in a crisis, and unbreakable. Brown-haired and blue-eyed, she was pretty in a girl-next-door way, although she never considered herself to be particularly attractive.

Growing up poor in Seattle, Linda attended Garfield High, a tough, inner-city school, which was 40 percent black, 40 percent white, and 20 percent Asian. She was a good student, serious about her academics. She planned to be the first woman in her family to attend college. Seeing how her mother suffered in low-wage jobs, Linda dreamed of becoming a doctor. She was proud to make the cheerleading squad. Her best friend was Sue Ann Kay, an extroverted Chinese American. Linda briefly dated a half-Japanese boy in high school until her mother found out and forbade her. It was okay for Linda to have Asian girlfriends but not boyfriends.

One day during her senior year Linda was hanging by the lockers with Sue Ann and some of her cheerleading friends when a former homecoming queen swept into the school—Amy Sanbo. On her arm was a devilishly handsome young man wearing a custom-tailored black suit, skinny black tie, shimmering purple shirt, a hat with a skinny brim, and a long beige coat. The sight of Amy and her dashing new boyfriend set envious tongues wagging, especially among the clique of cheerleaders at the end of the hallway.

"Who is that?" asked Linda.

"Oh, that's Bruce Lee," answered Sue Ann Kay. "Isn't he beautiful?"

"Um, yeah," the cheerleaders collectively swooned.

"It's like he walked straight out of *West Side Story*," one of them giggled.

"Yes, he looks like George Chakiris," said Linda, "suave, debonair, big city."

"He's here to lecture in Mr. Wilson's class on Chinese philosophy," Sue Ann said.

"How do you know him?" Linda asked.

"I take kung fu lessons from him."

The girls burst out laughing: "I bet." "Is that what you call it?"

Linda's eyes followed Bruce as he walked down the hall, laughing and talking and throwing playful punches with some of the kids. She was more than a little impressed.

That summer Linda took a job with her mom at Sears as she prepared to enter the University of Washington in the fall. Her thoughts often turned to Bruce Lee. She would tease her friend about her dreamy kung fu teacher: "Is he why you are studying all that strange self-defense stuff?"

"Why don't you come to a lesson with me and see what it's like," Sue Ann dared.

One Sunday morning in August 1963, Linda went with Sue Ann to Chinatown. The young women entered a run-down building on King Street through a half door that faced the sidewalk, went down a dingy, dark staircase, and emerged in a basement room with concrete walls, bare light bulbs, and no other decoration. Linda thought to herself, "Oh brother! What did I get myself into now?" It would not be the last time she had such a thought.

Despite the surroundings, the atmosphere in the room was cheerful and welcoming. A dozen students were talking and stretching before class started. Sue Ann saluted Bruce, who had recently returned from Hong Kong, as he came over to greet them. Initially, Linda found him to be a bit cocky, but if anything this made him even more attractive to a young woman who often struggled with self-doubt. She joined the club and became a regular pretty face in Bruce's classes. "I don't know if I was more interested in kung fu or the teacher," she says.

After Sunday morning classes, Bruce would take a group of students out for a long, joyous Chinese lunch. "Bruce used to make me laugh till I hurt," Linda recalls. Food was frequently followed by a film, usually a samurai movie. "All the while Bruce would provide a running commentary about the action," Linda wryly notes. One weekend Bruce thrilled the group by taking them to see his final film, *The Orphan* (1960). None of them knew Bruce had been a child star in Hong Kong. As they entered the theater, Bruce just offhandedly said, "Oh yeah, I'm in the movie." Bruce may have played it off like it was no big deal, but the experience bowled Linda over: "Seeing him on the screen in a theater in Seattle's Chinatown made me realize there was more to this man than I had thought."

When the 1963 fall semester at the University of Washington rolled around, Linda enrolled as a premed student and signed up for some intense science courses. Instead of hitting the books, however, she spent much of her time hanging around Bruce and his followers. Soon Linda was cutting classes and her freshman year nearly turned into a disaster. "Studying, and becoming captivated by Bruce were not compatible," she says. But as gaga as she was for him, she never considered herself glamorous enough for him to return her affection. "He was so dashing and charming, he could have had his choice of dates," she says.

Little did she know that Bruce was rebounding from a broken heart at the hands of a flashy woman who was not that into him. Being worshipped was a nice change of pace for the prideful young man with big plans. Once the fall semester started, Bruce moved his Jun Fan Gung Fu Institute from its dingy basement in Chinatown to 4750 University Way near the campus. It was the largest and most expensive place he had ever rented, nearly three thousand square feet occupying the entire ground floor of an apartment building. In the back was a small bedroom. After three years busing tables, Bruce officially gave Ruby Chow his notice and moved out of her broom closet. He was now all in on his dream to become the Ray Kroc of kung fu. He needed a helpmate. Who better than a besotted disciple?

One afternoon on the University of Washington's outdoor concert green, fenced in by trees and Grecian columns on one end, Bruce and his kung fu students were racing from one end to the other. When Linda lagged behind the rest of the students, Bruce tackled her to the ground. She thought he was going to show her a new kung fu maneuver, but instead he held her down. When she finally stopped laughing, he asked if she wanted to go to dinner at the Space Needle.

She paused, thinking it was an expensive place for the entire class, and asked, "You mean all of us?"

"No, only you and me," he replied.

Stunned, she was only able to nod yes in response.

On the afternoon of October 15, 1963, Linda, who knew her mother wouldn't approve of her dating a Chinese guy, told her she was spending the night at her friend's house. Once Linda arrived she borrowed one of her friend's fashionable dresses and coats, because she didn't own anything appropriate to wear to the hottest restaurant in town. The Space Needle had just been built for the 1962 Seattle World's Fair and its revolving restaurant towered over the city.

Bruce pulled up to her friend's house that evening in his black, souped-up '57 Ford. He was wearing the same outfit he had worn to Garfield High the first time Linda had seen him—the black custom-tailored suit and shimmering purple shirt. He reminded her once again of her screen idol George Chakiris, the leader of the Sharks in *West Side Story*. "I was instantly charmed," she recalls.

Prior to the date, Linda was nervous about how she might keep up a conversation with the object of her desire now that she was going to be alone with him and did not have the security of the group. Bruce solved that concern. "He could always talk enough for the both of us," she recalls. He regaled her with his life story but he was most excited to discuss his future plans for a chain of kung fu schools. Linda wanted to ask him why he had picked her to ask out but was too shy to bring it up. She did not realize at the time that he was selling her on his dreams. "I was totally captivated by his magnetism and the energy which flowed from him," she says.

After dinner, Bruce presented her with a memento, a tiny Scandinavian kewpie doll. Bruce had braided the doll's hair into pigtails, because Linda often walked into the Student Union Building with wet hair in pigtails after her swimming class. As he dropped her off down the block from her home he lightly kissed her on the mouth. "It was the end of the perfect evening," Linda says.

Five days later he wrote her this love note: "To the sweetest girl, from the man who appreciates her: To live content with small means; to seek elegance rather than luxury, and refinement rather than fashion, to be worthy, not respectable, and wealthy, not rich; to study hard, think quietly, talk gently, act frankly; to bear all cheerfully, do all bravely, await occasions, hurry never. In other words, to let the spiritual, unbidden and unconscious grow up through the common. Bruce."

Linda was sold.

In secret from her mother, she was soon splitting her time between Bruce's kung fu classes and his windowless bedroom. "You could sleep forever in the room because the sun never appeared to let you know the time of day," Linda says. She would often pick Bruce up in the morning only to discover he was still asleep with no clue what time it was. The two of them got hooked on soap operas. Every day after classes, they'd run back to his place to watch *General Hospital*. Afterward Bruce would take her to the Chinese restaurant across the street where the cook, Ah Sam, would make Bruce his favorite meal—oyster sauce beef and shrimp with black bean sauce. Then Linda would have to go home and try to eat a full dinner again with her family. "My mother was beginning to think I was anorexic because I ate such small portions," she says.

Her first year of college became a clandestine operation of juggling her hush-hush boyfriend and her suspicious mother. "It took quite a bit of maneuvering and a little help from my friends," Linda recalls. In the process, her schoolwork fell through the cracks. "It's your fault I'm not getting my work done," she complained to him. He would smile and lend a hand on her English papers. He was no help at all in chemistry or calculus, but he was a prolific writer, knocking out essays during the commercials.

Now that Bruce had a serious girlfriend who was invested in his dreams, he turned his attention to professionalizing his operation. He issued a prospectus for his Jun Fan Gung Fu Institute. The regular fee was $22 per month and $17 for juniors. The illustrated prospectus warned that kung fu could *not* be mastered in three easy lessons. Intelligent thinking and hard work were required. Emphasizing the simplicity of his Wing Chun–based style, he promised that "techniques are smooth, short, and extremely fast; they are direct, to the point and are stripped down to their essential purpose without any wasted motions." In a pitch directed at a more upscale, suburban market, he promised that kung fu would develop confidence, humility, coordination, adaptability, and respect for others. He did not mention street fighting.

Bruce Lee was as much a salesman as he was a showman. As a child actor he had learned from an early age how to work the media. When he first came to America one of his odd jobs was as a newspaper "stuffer" (inserting loose advertisements inside the printed pages) for *The Seattle Times*. Within a year he was stuffing quotes inside *Seattle Times* profiles of him—a remarkable achievement given how bigoted the paper was at the time. The jaw-dropping Chinglish headline for his first interview was: "Lee Hopes for Rotsa Ruck." The reporter, Weldon Johnson, opened with this line: "At first Kung Fu sounds like a variety of Chow Mein. And after you think about it, you're pretty sure it is—but it really isn't." In the article, Bruce makes a public case for why the University of Washington should include kung fu as part of its curriculum. Weldon, who apparently found Chinglish hilarious, concluded by noting that if this were to happen it would "make Lee, Kung Fu and Chow Mein manufacturers velly happy."

Bruce quickly realized that the best way to put American reporters at ease was to appropriate hoary Oriental jokes and tell them himself. "I don't drink or smoke, but I do chew gum," he liked to pun with interviewers, "because Fu Man Chu." Another of his favorites: "Seven hundred million Chinese can't be Wong." The strategy worked. He began to receive positive coverage for his TV appearances and public performances. Reporters found him charming, not threatening.

The good publicity and his hard work helped put his Jun Fan Gung

Fu Institute in the black. By the end of his junior year, he had more than fifty students, enough to cover his expenses and place a little extra spending money in his pocket. His girlfriend was enthusiastic about supporting his career. "I was the yin to his yang, generally quieter and calmer," she recalls. "It seemed only natural that I should occasionally run interference for him so that he could devote his time to his work." His assistant instructor, Taky Kimura, was trusted and respected—someone Bruce could put in charge while he was away. It was time to expand his empire. Seattle was too provincial and had too few potential students to support another school. If he wanted to make his mark and make a living teaching martial arts, he would have to open his second branch in the epicenter of kung fu in America—the Bay Area. To do that, Bruce would need a partner.

In his mid-forties and a welder by trade, James Yimm Lee was a hard man—a hard drinker and fighter. As a teenager, he had been a gymnast, weightlifter, and amateur boxer. Throughout his twenties and thirties, he studied jujitsu and Sil Lum kung fu. His specialty was Iron Palm. He could stack up five bricks, ask you which one you wanted him to break, and then shatter your pick while leaving the rest intact. Beneath his tough-as-nails exterior was a gentler, more intellectual side. Seeing there were very few English-language martial arts books available to enthusiasts, he began self-publishing his own titles and selling them through his mail-order business. His first work was *Modern Kung Fu Karate: Iron, Poison Hand Training*, which Bruce Lee bought and read cover-to-cover.

After the modest success of his first title, James agreed to publish a book on Sil Lum kung fu with his teacher, T. Y. Wong, one of San Francisco's most venerated masters. The two men fell out over the proceeds. Master Wong accused James of shorting him $10. Jimmy denied it, became furious, and left Wong's *kwoon* forever. With his business partner, Al Novak, one of the few Caucasians with extensive kung fu training at the time, James decided to set up his own school. The two of them were sick of traditional kung fu's fancy forms, which they believed were impractical in real-life encounters, and decided to offer a more current curriculum by applying a boxing gym setting to kung fu instruction. They opened the East Wing Modern Kung Fu Club in a dilapidated space on Broadway and Garnet Street in Oakland. As with Bruce in Seattle, their first students were mostly non-Chinese looking for more realistic training—cops, bouncers, and street fighters.

When their school failed to attract enough members to cover the rent, they changed the venue to James's two-car garage on 3039 Monticello Avenue. It was a smaller and less convenient space, and James's wife, Katherine, complained about the holes James and his crew were accidentally punching and kicking into the walls while sparring. James needed to find a way to attract more students and move his club out of his home. He considered bringing in a new teacher.

For the last few years, people close to James had been singing the praises of Bruce Lee. His brother-in-law, Robert, and his friend George Lee had both taken cha-cha dance lessons with Bruce when he first came to America in 1959 and been amazed by his Wing Chun demonstrations. In 1962, another friend, Wally Jay, had visited Bruce's school in Seattle while traveling with his judo team and returned deeply impressed by what he had witnessed. Wally's words carried weight with James. Not only was he one of the most respected martial arts instructors in the Bay Area, but Wally also had an eye for talent. His biannual luau served as a showcase for some of the best martial artists in the Bay Area.

James called his old high school buddy Allen Joe. The two of them shared an interest in bodybuilding and martial arts and often trained together. Allen was planning a trip with his family to Seattle for the 1962 World's Fair.

"When you get there, will you look up this Bruce Lee kid for me?" James asked. "Scout him out and see if he's as good as everyone says."

Allen and his family arrived to a city in the thick of World's Fair mania. Seattle was overrun with tourists—traffic was jammed, lines were long, and hotels sold out. Fortuitously, the hotel Allen had booked was only a half block from Ruby Chow's restaurant. After a day maneuvering his children through the colossal crowds at the World of Science and the World of Century 21 exhibits, Allen Joe plopped down at the bar at Ruby Chow's and ordered a single malt Scotch.

"Is Bruce Lee here?" Allen asked the waitress who delivered his drink.

"He is off for the night," she replied, "but will probably be back after 11:00 p.m."

Well into his second drink, Allen looked up and saw the waitress pointing to a dapper, handsome, and bespectacled young man. Sizing up his slight frame and neatly pressed gray flannel suit, Allen Joe was incredulous. "That . . . is Bruce Lee?" he thought to himself. "The kid looks like a fashion model."

"Are you Bruce Lee?" Allen Joe asked as Bruce approached the bar.

"Who wants to know?" he responded suspiciously.

"I was told about you from Robert and Harriet Lee. They took dance lessons from you in Oakland," Allen explained, trying to put Bruce at ease. "They said you are pretty good at Gung Fu."

Those were the magic words. Bruce's face lit up with excitement as he asked, "You practice Gung Fu?"

"Yes, with Robert's brother-in-law, James Lee."

Bruce was all smiles now. "Come on, let's get a bite to eat."

Bruce led Allen out of Ruby Chow's and down the block toward a hamburger joint with Bruce delivering his life story at a fast clip. He explained how he had been teaching kung fu in Seattle for the past three years. He also recounted his meeting with Wally Jay and his admiration for the jujitsu master.

As Bruce paused his narration, Allen Joe jumped in to explain that he was here at the behest of James Lee, a serious practitioner who ran his own school, built his own equipment, and even published his own martial arts books.

"You mean, THE James Lee?" Bruce gushed. "I own all his books!"

"Would you like to meet him?" Allen asked.

"Absolutely," Bruce said.

As they reached the door to the burger joint, Bruce stopped Allen on the sidewalk.

"Before we go in," Bruce told him, "I want you to try to hit me as hard as you can."

The next day, Allen Joe called James Lee to report the encounter. He kept his appraisal short and simple: "James, the kid is amazing."

With this confirmation, James set up a phone call with Bruce and invited him to stay at his house the next time he was down to visit. As soon as

Bruce could rearrange his work and class schedule, he jumped into his black Ford and drove twelve hours south to Oakland.

The two men greeted each other at James's doorstep. It was an unlikely pairing. James was old enough to be Bruce's father. But both of them were former teenage street fighters who were obsessed with the martial arts and contemptuous of the classical approach to teaching it. They wanted to create something new.

James warmly welcomed Bruce and invited him inside to meet his wife and children over tea in the living room. Once the formalities were over, James ushered Bruce into his California garage filled with his inventions—self-made martial arts training equipment. Bruce pointed to a spring-loaded punching board and asked with boyish zeal, "So, how does this thing work?" Soon the entire house was shaking as the two men pounded the various contraptions in the garage.

After working up a sweat, Bruce turned to James and said, "Try to hit me as hard as you can."

Bruce dominated James as easily as he had everyone in Seattle. The next day, James Lee called Allen Joe to report the encounter. He also kept his appraisal short and simple: "Allen, the kid is amazing."

Over the next year, Bruce and James built a strong friendship and slowly recognized the benefits of teaming up. For Bruce, James was an established figure with extensive connections in the Bay Area scene. For James, Bruce was a young genius who was inventing a new style of martial arts that modified tradition for the realities of street combat. He also saw in Bruce someone who might be able to attract enough students to open a proper *kwoon*.

In the spring of 1963, James agreed to turn his tiny two-car-garage school into the second branch of Bruce's Jun Fan Gung Fu Institute. The plan was for Bruce, once he finished his junior year in June 1964, to come down to Oakland for the summer to help James open a new franchise in a new location. Bruce would be the head instructor and James his assistant. The force of Bruce's talent and personality had turned a much older and more established martial artist into one of his students. "The superiority of his gung fu is more refined and effective than that which I have learned in all my years," James proclaimed. "I have changed all my gung fu techniques to his methods."

To cement their relationship, publicize their upcoming venture, and generate some much-needed cash, James and Bruce agreed to publish a book together. It was the first and only one Bruce Lee authored during his lifetime. In 1963, there were only a handful of English-language books about Chinese martial arts. James and Bruce planned for their book, *Chinese Gung Fu: The Philosophical Art of Self-Defense*, to be the first in a series—an introductory primer and training manual for beginners. The book opened with author testimonials from James Lee, Wally Jay, and Ed Parker, one of the most influential martial artists in the country. Bruce emphasized his philosophical perspective on kung fu with a short essay on the Taoist principles of yin and yang. The bulk of the book was a collection of illustrated drawings and photographs of basic kung fu techniques, most of them from styles other than Wing Chun.

For the photo shoot, Bruce invited his original Seattle crew—Jesse Glover, Charlie Wu, and Taky Kimura—to perform in the parking lot next to Ruby Chow's restaurant. Bruce directed all the action, staging each shot for the cameraman. It all went smoothly until the cover photo. As Bruce stood with one leg bent and the other extended straight out into the air, the camera malfunctioned. As the photographer anxiously tried to correct the flaw, Bruce yelled at him, much to the amusement of his crew, "Hurry up and fix the damn thing before my leg falls off!"

It cost $600 to print one thousand copies, which James sold through his mail-order business for $5. Profits from the book helped Bruce pay off various expenses. "His primary reason for doing the book was that he needed the money," Jesse says.

A secondary reason was to declare war on traditional kung fu styles. James was still furious that his old master, T. Y. Wong, had accused James of stiffing him. But he was even angrier that everything he had learned from T. Y. Wong was useless against Bruce's more modern approach. "Jimmy spent years training in classical gung fu," says Gary Cagaanan, a longtime student of James's, "and he felt, after having met and trained with Bruce, that he'd wasted precious years learning sets and forms and not learning how to fight."

In a direct shot at the classical styles taught in San Francisco, Bruce and

James included a section entitled "Difference in Gung Fu Styles," in which Bruce opened by writing, "The technique of a superior system of Gung Fu is based on simplicity. It is only the half-cultivated systems that are full of unnecessary wasted motions." What followed was a photo-by-photo case study of Bruce dismantling the exact same techniques T. Y. Wong had championed in the book he had published with James. The insult was not lost on T. Y. Wong or the San Francisco kung fu community. After the book became available, Master Wong told his students Bruce Lee was "a dissident with bad manners."

Initially Bruce was extremely proud to be a published author. He sent a signed copy to his old Wing Chun friend and mentor, William Cheung, in Hong Kong. William, who remembered Bruce as a punkish teenager, was taken aback that his "little brother" was presenting himself as a master in America. To put him back in his place, William, somewhat enviously, disparaged the quality of the book. "Your letter is kind of stressing doubt on our friendship," Bruce replied, stung by the criticism. "The book you read is a basic book I've written somewhere in 1963 and I'm in the process of completing a much more thorough book on the Tao of Gung Fu."

Bruce never got around to finishing this follow-up volume, although he continued to write extensive notes for it the rest of his life. Some of these notes were published posthumously as *The Tao of Jeet Kune Do*. Over the years Bruce grew embarrassed of his first book, because his unpolished debut gave the impression he was a traditional kung fu practitioner. "So great was his need to liberate himself from classical martial arts in later years," says Linda, "he asked the publishers to cease production of this book."

With all of his trips to Oakland during his junior year, Bruce was increasingly distracted and floundering academically. He was only taking two classes per semester and was not on track to graduate on time, even if he managed to improve his lousy grades. Anxious to launch his kung fu empire, he made the decision to withdraw from the University of Washington after his junior year and move in with James and his family in Oakland. He told friends he intended to complete college in California.

Bruce asked Taky Kimura to run the Seattle branch of the Jun Fan Gung Fu Institute while he established the Oakland franchise. Bruce promised to visit Seattle whenever possible to teach seminars and update Kimura on new techniques, but he planned to base himself in the Bay Area until an opportunity arose to start a new franchise in another city.

Bruce timed his arrival in Oakland for Wally Jay's summer luau. The Hawaiian party, held at Colombo Hall, was expected to draw over a thousand ticket buyers for the food, singing, and martial arts performances. On the bill were "Hawaiian songbird" Lena Machado and a little-known kung fu instructor from Seattle. It was Bruce and James's first opportunity to publicize their partnership.

Weaving his way past platters of roasted pig, huge trays of chicken long-rice, ten-gallon pots of poi, and plates of lomi lomi salmon and sliced pineapples, Bruce made his way to the stage. He ignored the stairs and just leapt onto the raised platform. Without pause he launched into a traditional kung fu form. His movements were fluid and popped with contained power. The crowd watched politely, thinking the young man showed promise but he was nothing special.

As if sensing the mood of the crowd, Bruce stopped in the middle of the form, turned to the audience, and asked in a cocky, condescending voice, "How could you expect to fight like that?" The abrupt change in tone caught everyone off-guard, especially the traditional martial arts people in the crowd. "There is no way a person is going to fight you in the street with a set pattern." Stepping back he launched into a Northern Shaolin form complete with wide crescent kicks over his head. Again, he stopped mid-form to criticize what he'd just expertly performed. "Classical methods like these are a form of paralysis. Too many practitioners are just blindly rehearsing these systematic routines and stunts."

There was red-faced grumbling from the crowd. They had expected a dynamic demonstration, perhaps leavened with some corny jokes, not a lecture full of put-downs. "His demonstration of the ineffectiveness of traditional forms upset and embarrassed the traditionalists in the audience," remembers Leo Fong, a friend and student of James's.

"My approach is scientific street fighting," Bruce declared as he let loose a flurry of Wing Chun punches. "These techniques are smooth, short, and extremely fast—stripped down to their essential purpose without any wasted motions. Does anyone think he can block one of my punches?"

Immediately two volunteers, big football player types, charged up the stairs. Smiling at their size and making a joke about their eagerness, Bruce pulled the first one close to him and explained to him and the crowd, "I'm going to start from seven feet away, close the gap between us, and tap you on the forehead without you blocking my hand. Got it?"

"Got it," the first volunteer replied.

"Are you ready?"

"Yes."

In a blur, Bruce launched himself across the stage and tagged the football player's forehead an instant ahead of his block.

"Next," Bruce said to scattered laughter.

Having seen what happened to his friend, the second volunteer raised his hands in tense anticipation. As soon as Bruce twitched, the guy swept a block across his face. Bruce reassessed in microseconds, waiting for the block to pass, before thumping him on the forehead.

A mixture of applause and hard stares followed Bruce as he left the stage. While his talent was obvious, many felt insulted. Asian martial arts etiquette demanded public courtesy—criticism of other styles was reserved for private conversations. "Bruce had speed and coordination like no one I had ever seen," Leo Fong recalls. "But I worried his attitude was gonna lead to trouble."

James wasn't concerned at all. He loved that his young partner had stuck a thumb in the eye of the classicists. After the performance, James gleefully invited his students and close friends over to his house on Monday for a private meeting with Bruce.

Gathered on that evening were many of James's current students and others who were open to a more modern approach to the martial arts: Al Novak, Leo Fong, George Lee, and a newcomer from Stockton named Bob Baker. James informed the group that he and Bruce were going to start a new school together. James was moving operations from his garage to a new location on Broadway Avenue along Oakland's "Auto Row" and hoped to open in about a month.

To close the sale with the group, Bruce demonstrated a technique none of them had ever seen before—his one-inch punch. He moved the coffee table to the side, grabbed a hefty Oakland phone book, handed it to Bob Baker, the tallest man in the room, and instructed him to hold it tight against his chest. Standing in front of Bob, Bruce extended his right hand until his middle finger touched the phone book, then curled his hand into a fist, an inch or two from the target. In that moment everyone seemed to inhale in unison as Bruce snapped his hips, straightened his back leg, and drove his fist, faster than the eye could see, into the phone book.

The group was stunned. "Bruce knocked him over the couch," recalls Leo Fong, "and Baker's legs went straight up and over. I thought he'd go through the living room window."

Bruce explained that real punching power was generated not from the shoulder and arms but from the entire body working in unison. The more the muscles relaxed, he said, the more power they could generate—softness combining with hardness like yin and yang. "The martial arts should be functional and practical," Bruce said. "The classical mess does not stifle me."

Bruce's performance and modern perspective captivated the room. "This young martial artist was way ahead of his time," Leo Fong says.

Seeing the effect Bruce's talent had on everyone, James smiled and updated the group on the schedule. "Until the new school is ready, we'll continue practicing in the garage," he explained. "Classes resume tomorrow."

On July 24, 1964, James and Bruce filed a simple permit with the city to open the Jun Fan Gung Fu Institute, which they described as a "Chinese Self-Defense School," on 4157 Broadway. Formerly an upholstery store, it was a humble space, located on the first floor of a two-story brick building. Bruce wanted it to be an exclusive club. No signage was put out front. The only way to hear about it was word-of-mouth. Anyone who wanted to join had to apply and be screened by Bruce. He only accepted advanced, dedicated students with high moral character. Anyone who answered the question "Why do you want to learn martial arts?" with a violent answer like "Because I want to beat up my neighbor" was rejected. It was an unusual way to launch a new venture. Because of the strictness of the admission process and Bruce's relative obscurity as an instructor, the school struggled to sign up new members.

As his own skills advanced, Bruce became increasingly convinced that one style does not fit all. For example, taller fighters required different techniques than shorter, faster students than slower, more aggressive personalities than more timid. Bruce tailored his instruction to the specific strengths of each student. "Bruce showed me some moves that were not taught to the majority of the class and he told me to keep them to myself," says George Lee. "He felt that since no one person was the same each individual needed different teaching."

Bruce didn't believe a student should bend to tradition but rather the tradition to the individual. As a result, his classes, although strict, were informal. Sometimes he would work out and other times he would lecture. He didn't line people up to practice set moves in unison like in Japanese karate. He preferred to pair people up to practice techniques and spar. His motto was: "Develop the tools, refine the tools, then dissolve the tools."

While Bruce had set up this second branch to fit his preferences as an instructor, it was not an ideal business model. They were only charging $15 per month for training. Seven or eight students were not enough to cover the rent. To attract more members and survive as a teacher, he was going to have to make a name for himself and do it soon, because his responsibilities were about to get much heavier.

A tried and true way for a young man to knock up his girlfriend is to tell her he's leaving for someplace so dangerous he might never come back. Vietnam, perhaps, or even worse, Oakland. Normal precautions tend to be disregarded. And so it was with Bruce and Linda. They had been dating in secret for eight months. As the date of his departure in July 1964 approached, weeks of tearful goodbye sex led to the discovery that Linda was pregnant.

Linda claims that Bruce "was happy" about the news. While he may have presented a cheery face to her, he was uncertain what to do. Linda was dreadfully in love with him, but his career had barely begun. It was the reverse of his relationship with Amy Sanbo. This time he was the one with doubts. "The idea of commitment scared him to death," Linda recalls. "He wanted to be financially secure before undertaking the responsibilities of a wife and family."

The situation remained unresolved as Taky Kimura chauffeured Bruce and his distraught, pregnant girlfriend to the airport. Standing at the gate for Oakland, Bruce saw the tears in Linda's eyes. He said simply, "I'll be back," and then he was gone.

It felt to Linda like the bottom had dropped out of her life. Her stomach churned. Fears raced through her mind. "What if I never see him again?" she thought. "What if he feels trapped? What if he changes his mind? What if he goes on to bigger and better things and forgets about me?"

Over a series of phone calls, Bruce sought the counsel of Taky Kimura, his most trusted friend and advisor. Taky told Bruce he should marry her—he wouldn't find a better wife. "I respected Linda highly," Taky says. "She was sincere, devoted, and had depth."

After two and half months of agonizing, Bruce finally made a decision. He wrote to Linda and told her he wanted her with him and would return to Seattle to get her. Linda was elated. Bruce slowly warmed to the idea. For years he had worried that his undescended testicle might mean he was infertile. He was delighted he would be a father. "He wanted a child," Linda says. "That was very important to him. This child would be his." He became more excited after convincing himself that the child would be a boy. "In fact, we only chose a boy's name for the unborn baby," Bruce later said. "We didn't even bother thinking of a girl's name." Given how highly prized male heirs were in Chinese society, this was Bruce's chance to make his dad proud. While Peter might have been his father's favorite, Bruce was certain he would be the one to provide Li Hoi Chuen with his first grandson.

The obstacle the young couple faced was Linda's family, especially her mother, who had no idea about the relationship or even Bruce's existence. To keep it clandestine, Linda had gone so far as to set up a private post office box in Seattle, so Bruce could write her in secret. "Bruce and I decided on the coward's way out," Linda says. "We'd get married, run away to Oakland, then call my mom and tell her. A friend of mine had done this a couple of months earlier and after the dust had settled, everyone had survived."

Because he couldn't afford a wedding ring, James Lee's wife, Katherine, loaned Bruce hers for the ceremony. He returned to Seattle on Wednesday, August 12, with the borrowed ring. Bruce and Linda went to the King

County Courthouse to apply for a marriage license. The law required blood tests and a three-day wait before a couple could marry. This turned out to be the undoing of their covert operation. The young couple did not realize that the local newspaper published marriage applicants' names in its Vital Statistics section nor did they know that Linda's maiden aunt Sally was a devoted reader of that section. No sooner had her old eyes lit upon a family scandal than she was dialing Linda's mom to tell her that Linda C. Emery and a Bruce J. F. Lee had declared their intent to marry. Vivian marched into Linda's room, shook the newspaper in her face, and yelled, "What's this! Is this you?"

Her mother called a family powwow to change her daughter's mind. Two aunts, one uncle, a grandmother, and her stepfather showed up for this come-to-Jesus meeting. "They arrived on Saturday and we all sat around the living room as if there had been a death in the family," Linda says. "It was awful."

Bruce had never liked keeping the relationship a secret, only agreeing at Linda's insistence. And he most certainly hated being told what he could and couldn't do.

"I want to marry your daughter. We are leaving on Monday," Bruce declared to her hostile family. "I'm Chinese, by the way."

The joke didn't lighten the mood. Race was the underlying issue for the family and the country. Miscegenation was the gay marriage of that era. While the state of Washington had long allowed interracial marriages, it was still illegal in seventeen other states. It wasn't until 1967 that the Supreme Court outlawed all antimiscegenation laws in the aptly named case, *Loving v. Virginia*.

"If you marry, you will suffer prejudice," one of the aunts argued. "And so will your children."

"Times are changing," Linda argued.

"Not that fast."

"Maybe not, but I don't care."

"How long has this been going on?" Linda's mother demanded.

"A year."

"You've been lying to me for a year?" Mrs. Emery cried out. "After everything I've done for you, how could you do that to me?"

"I'm sorry, I knew you wouldn't understand."

Her uncle turned to Bruce. "How will you support her? What do you do for a living?"

"I teach gung fu," Bruce proudly declared.

"You teach *what*?"

"What about college?" Linda's mother asked her. "You're a good student, premed. What about your dream of becoming a doctor?"

"School can wait," Linda said.

"What's the rush? Why can't this wait?"

Neither Bruce nor Linda would answer.

Sensing a secret, her furious stepfather charged up to her room and ransacked it until he found a shoebox filled with the couple's correspondence. Once he read their letters, he returned downstairs and announced to her mother, "Your precious daughter is pregnant."

Surprisingly, this revelation didn't change the family's mind. "Why don't you put marriage off for a year?" the assemblage argued. "Have your baby and then see how you feel." They would rather Linda be a single mother and raise a bastard child than marry a ne'er-do-well Chinaman.

"I will not wait," Linda declared.

As the hours wore on and the tears and recriminations flowed, her uncle offered to take Linda for a drive to reason with her. Her uncle considered himself a devout Christian. "This is against God's word," he told her in the car. "God doesn't want the races to mix. You are committing a sin."

"God loves all his children," Linda responded.

Her uncle quoted Deuteronomy 7:3–4, "You shall not intermarry with them, giving your daughters to their sons or taking their daughters for your sons, for they would turn away your sons from following me, to serve other gods. Then the anger of the Lord would be kindled against you, and he would destroy you."

"I don't believe that," she quietly replied. "Everyone is equal in the eyes of the Lord, and God commands us to treat everyone equally."

"If you do this," her uncle warned, "you will be kicked out of the family."

If Saturday was bad, the intervention on Sunday was even worse. "A perfectly horrible day," Linda recalls. "This was the day of tears." Any pretense of persuasion was gone. All the arguments had been gone over and over again. It was now a battle of wills. The family threatened her with banishment, and Linda insisted nothing could change her mind. She had fought too hard to win Bruce. She wasn't going to give him up for anyone, even her family. "I had decided I was not going to be talked out of it," she recalls.

Exhausted and frustrated, her mother tried to dissuade Bruce with her strongest put-down: "You don't want to marry Linda. She doesn't know how to cook. She doesn't know how to clean, iron, or sew. She doesn't know how to do anything."

"She'll learn," Bruce said.

And that was that. Realizing she had lost and unwilling to disown her beloved daughter, Vivian tossed in the towel. "If you are going to get married, it has to be in a church."

Vivian had stopped going to church years back, but if her daughter was going to marry, the wedding needed to be sanctified. Vivian considered herself the family historian. She had detailed records of births, marriages, and deaths. Her daughter's wedding had to be properly recorded.

Linda and Bruce agreed to a church wedding. Arrangements were quickly made with the minister of Seattle's Congregational Church. On August 17, 1964, the minister performed the rushed service. There were no flowers. Linda wore a sleeveless, brown, floral dress and Bruce his favorite Hong Kong–tailored suit. Taky Kimura was Bruce's best man. Only Linda's mother and her grandmother showed up from her side. The conservative Christian uncle drove back to Everett and refused to attend, as did the rest of her family. (When Linda saw that uncle again about ten years after Bruce's death, he put his arm around her and said, "Welcome back to the family.") When the service was over, Vivian complained, "Bruce could have brought some flowers, anyway."

As Linda had anticipated, the dust eventually settled and everyone survived. Bruce was able to charm Linda's mother and she grew to love him dearly. He would joke, "You know, Mom, you've got the greatest legs of any woman of your age I've ever seen!" Linda impressed Bruce's siblings and friends with her steadiness and calm strength. "As a bachelor, Bruce liked to have affairs with beautiful, flashy girls, but he married a quiet, sensitive girl who knew how to listen and would let him have his way," Peter said. "He knew what real beauty was, and he knew she would take care of the family. Although Linda is American, she is very, very similar in character to many Chinese girls." Bruce concurred, telling a reporter in 1966, "Linda is more Oriental than some of the Chinese I know. She is quiet, calm, and doesn't yak-yak-yak all the time."

Bruce avoided a conflict with his own parents by not telling them he was marrying a non-Chinese girl until after the wedding. His father and mother were not pleased. He had to spend months convincing them everything was okay before they agreed Linda was welcome in Hong Kong. "If she is your choice," his mother finally conceded, "then she is our choice."

Without perhaps intending it, Bruce had followed in his father's footsteps and married a woman quite similar to his mother. Both Linda Emery and Grace Ho were *wenrou* (温柔)—quiet, gentle, and tender. Both fell in love with actors after watching one of their charismatic performances. Both women vigorously pursued the object of their adoration. And both defied their families to marry broke Chinamen with big dreams.

The main difference was the unexpected pregnancy. That Bruce consented to marry Linda, despite his reservations, made her even more devoted to him. "I was certainly not the type of beauty, which Bruce usually dated before our marriage," she says. "But I could give him repose, tranquility, understanding, and true love." She learned how to be the perfect partner for a brilliant, volatile, and extroverted man, and he came to love her for it. "We are two halves that make a whole," Bruce told friends.

Marrying Linda turned out to be the best decision Bruce made in his life. "Nobody has ever given Linda the credit she deserves. This woman has been one hell of a pillar of strength," says Taky Kimura, expressing a widely held view. "I don't think Bruce would have aspired to the heights that he did without her support."

The heights would come later. At the present moment, the newlyweds were two college dropouts with a baby on the way and barely a dime between them. They moved in with Jimmy's family to save money. In return, Linda served as a nanny to Jimmy's children and nursemaid to his wife, Katherine, who had recently been diagnosed with a terminal case of cancer.

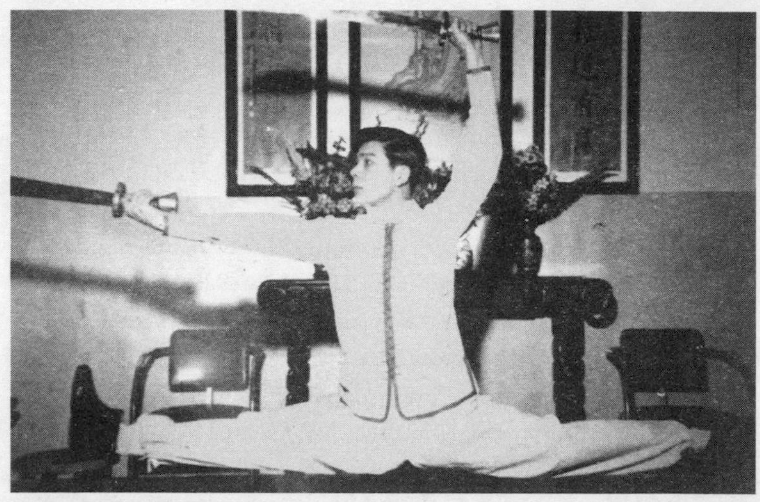

This photo of Wong Jack Man appeared in a front-page story about his challenge fight with Bruce Lee in the *Chinese Pacific Weekly* on January 28, 1965. *(Courtesy of Robert Louie)*

Bruce with James Yimm Lee, who crafted the tombstone and kicking shield, November 1967. *(David Tadman)*

eight

face-off in oakland

1964 was a peak year for Japanese martial arts. Judo was accepted into competition at the Summer Olympics in Tokyo. Karate was one of the hottest fads in America. Elvis Presley and Sean Connery were devoted students. At every West Coast fair there were inevitably demonstrations of Japanese styles alongside square dancers and Miss Teenage contests. Even royalty took up karate. In Europe, the kings of both Spain and Greece boasted of earning black belts.

Riding the wave of karate's popularity was Ed Parker, a thirty-three-year-old Hawaiian-born Mormon and Kenpo karate instructor with several schools in Utah and Southern California. Parker had quickly realized the best way to promote the martial arts, his dojos, and himself was to cater to the movie community. In 1956, Parker opened franchises in Pasadena and Beverly Hills where he eventually taught so many celebrities—including Robert Wagner, Blake Edwards, Robert Conrad, Natalie Wood, George Hamilton, Warren Beatty, and Elvis Presley—that *Time* magazine referred to him as the "High Priest and Prophet of the Hollywood Sect." Parker parlayed his position into a minor career as a stuntman and actor with roles in Lucille Ball's *The Lucy Show* (1963), Blake Edwards's *Revenge of the Pink Panther* (1978), and *Kill the Golden Goose* (1979).

In the summer of 1964, Parker sought to bring his two worlds together with his Long Beach International Karate Championships. The objective was for the country's top martial artists to demonstrate and compete in front of an audience of enthusiasts and Hollywood insiders. Parker spent the months prior to the event sending invitations to established names and searching out new talent. His friend James Lee asked Parker to come up to Oakland to check out Bruce Lee. "Jimmy knew once I observed Bruce's extraordinary talent I would use my influence to help Bruce gain recognition," says Parker. Bruce's skills ("he made the air pop when he hit") and his controversial views earned him a ticket to Long Beach. "Bruce was very anti-classical," says Parker. "So I told him that if he were to come down to the tournament and demonstrate, people would have a better cross section of the martial arts world." After years of regional theater, Bruce finally had his chance to perform on Broadway.

When Bruce landed in Long Beach, Parker assigned Dan Inosanto, his top instructor, to serve as his minder. "Mr. Parker gave me $75 and said, 'Make sure he eats properly, and show him the area,' " recalls Inosanto. Within moments of meeting Inosanto, Bruce made his by now standard request: "Hit me as hard as you can." Dan threw his best punch. "I was completely flabbergasted!" Inosanto says. "He controlled me like a baby. I couldn't sleep that night. It seemed as though everything I'd done in the past was obsolete."

The night before the tournament many of the invited performers and fighters gathered in a vacant ballroom at their hotel for an impromptu exchange of techniques. Bruce strolled in wearing a black leather jacket and jeans. No one there knew who he was, but Tsutomu Ohshima, the first Japanese man to teach karate in America, took one glance at the way Bruce moved when he walked and said to his student, "That one is the only one here who can do anything."

The Long Beach Championships, held at the eight-thousand-seat Municipal Auditorium on August 2, was a great success. Thousands of people showed up to watch masters from all styles and systems demonstrate and compete. Bruce, still relatively unknown, was one of the minor presenters, scheduled during the sluggish part of the afternoon. When he took the floor wearing a black kung fu uniform with white cuffs, the air conditioner was down and the crowd was getting restless in the muggy heat after watching hours of competition.

Parker introduced Bruce as a practitioner of the little-known Chinese art of kung fu. Taky Kimura joined Bruce in the center of the auditorium to serve as his assistant. Bruce's demonstration was a modified version of the one he'd given at Wally Jay's luau. He sent a volunteer flying with his one-inch punch. He performed two-finger push-ups. He demonstrated Wing Chun self-defense techniques and a lightning-quick sticky hands drill with Kimura.

All of these were crowd-pleasers, but the centerpiece of his performance was the lecture he delivered criticizing classical systems and advocating a more modern approach. "He got up there and began to flawlessly imitate all these other styles," remembers Barney Scollan, an eighteen-year-old competitor in the tournament that morning who was disqualified for kicking his opponent in the groin, "and then one-by-one he began to dissect them and explain why they wouldn't work. And the things he was saying made a lot of sense. He even made an absolute mockery of the horse stance."

In front of an audience packed with karate traditionalists, who had spent thousands of hours practicing the horse stance, Bruce fearlessly argued for liberation: "Teachers should never impose their favorite patterns on their students. They should be finding out what works for them, and what does not work for them. The individual is more important than the style."

As he intended, Bruce's provocative performance polarized the audience. "There was a high percentage of people who were in awe of him," recalls Dan Inosanto, "but then there was another group who was really upset."

Clarence Lee, a San Francisco karate instructor, says, "Guys were practically lining up to fight Bruce Lee after his performance in Long Beach."

Just like on the Hong Kong playgrounds of his youth, Bruce's brash manner had divided the world into those who were for and those who were against him. "Bruce made a number of enemies that night," says Scollan, "as well as a number of followers."

Ed Parker, who filmed Bruce's performance on a 16mm camera, was not fussed by the controversy. If anything, it amused him. That night he invited Bruce to join him for a VIP dinner at a Chinese restaurant with Jhoon Rhee, the "Father of American Tae Kwon Do," and Mike Stone, who had defeated Chuck Norris to win the karate tournament. The first thing Bruce did at the restaurant was pull back his sleeves and ask everyone to feel his forearms, which were as hard as iron pipes. "My first impression was, obviously, that he was very arrogant because his talk had put down karate people," Mike Stone remembers, "but I actually ended up liking him very much."

The Long Beach tournament proved to be Bruce's debutante ball, his coming out into society. Mike Stone would become Bruce's first high-profile student, Jhoon Rhee an ally and supporter, and Ed Parker a role model. His performance that afternoon would end up launching his Hollywood career.

When Bruce returned to Hong Kong in the summer of 1963, he failed to secure a movie role for himself, but his efforts did put him back on the industry's radar. Shaw Bros. Studio hired Bruce to accompany Diana Chang Chung-wen, as she promoted her latest movie, *The Amorous Lotus Pan*, in California. Bruce's job was to dance the cha-cha with Diana—whose voluptuous figure and sexy demeanor earned her the nickname "the Mandarin Marilyn Monroe"—onstage each night and to serve as a low-key bodyguard for the duration of her tour. For Bruce the gig was an opportunity to promote his kung fu schools in America. He only accepted the role as Diana's sidekick on the condition he be allowed to give a martial arts demonstration at each stop.

After several performances in Los Angeles, the pair made their way back to San Francisco in late August. Upon his return home, Bruce had a lot on his mind. James Lee was in the hospital with his dying wife, Katherine; Linda, who was pregnant, was tending to James and Katherine's distraught children; and the Oakland branch was struggling. On top of all that, he was scheduled to appear in the Sun Sing Theatre, the same stage where his father had performed two decades earlier. This was his best chance to recruit more students for his new school, but he knew he would be facing a hostile audience. Word of his criticism of classical martial arts at Wally Jay's luau and the Long Beach Karate Championships had spread through San Francisco's Chinatown. A number of traditional kung fu students and old masters bought tickets to see if this arrogant Wing Chun practitioner would dare insult them to their faces.

To lighten the tense atmosphere, Bruce opened with a joke, based on the vertical placement of Chinese text versus English's horizontal sentences. "Honored guests, my new book is on sale in the lobby, which reminds me, I have noticed that unlike the Chinese, Westerners don't appreciate what they read. When people read in the East, you can see they like it," Bruce explained, moving his head up and down as if saying *yes*, "but when a Westerner reads, they go like this," now turning his head side to side as if saying *no*, "because they don't really enjoy it."

The crowd laughed, seemingly put at ease, expecting Bruce would be conciliatory. They were mistaken.

Bruce called up his new stage partner, Dan Inosanto, who had traveled with Bruce from Los Angeles. Using Inosanto as a target, Bruce emphasized the practicality and efficiency of Wing Chun, making the point of how his system was free of so many of the wasted motions found in other traditional kung fu styles. To underline his assertion, he imitated some of Northern Shaolin's wide kicks. "Why would you kick high and leave yourself open," he said, pausing to allow Inosanto to counter. "Instead you can kick low and punch high."

Ignoring the crowd's discomfort, Bruce continued his criticism. "In China, 80 percent of what they teach is nonsense. Here, in America, it is 90 percent." Angry murmurs arose from the audience. "These old tigers," he said, clearly referring to San Francisco's traditional masters, "they have no teeth."

The insult was too much.

A lit cigarette was angrily flicked toward the stage. More followed. It was the Chinese equivalent of throwing rotten fruit.

"Bruce was saying these things that were offensive to the Chinese martial arts," explains Inosanto, "and they didn't like that sort of attitude coming from a young *sifu*."

A man in back stood up and shouted, "That's not kung fu!"

"Sir, would you care to join me on stage so I can demonstrate?" Bruce asked with a smile.

The man waved his hand in dismissal before heading for the exit: "You don't know kung fu!"

"Would anyone else care to volunteer?" Bruce asked, anxious to win back the crowd.

A hand shot up from one of the seats near the stage. It belonged to Kenneth Wong, a teenage kung fu student of one of San Francisco's "old tigers." Bruce quickly motioned Kenneth to join him.

"When Bruce called Kenneth up, we began cheering and hollering and egging him on," recalls Adeline Fong, who attended the demonstration with a big group of Kenneth's kung fu classmates.

Like Bruce, Kenneth was considered a brash prodigy, as cocky as he was talented. Instead of using the stairs, Kenneth just leapt onto center stage, eliciting howls from his friends and laughter from the rest of the audience.

After thanking the teenager for participating, Bruce explained the challenge. "I will stand back seven feet from you, close the gap, and tap your forehead," he said. "You can use either hand or both to try to block me. Do you understand?"

"Yes," Kenneth replied, his smile as wide as Bruce's.

As the two confident young men faced each other, the crowd shouted support for Kenneth. Like a shot, Bruce slipped forward and jabbed his fingers at Kenneth's forehead. Just as fast, Kenneth cleanly blocked Bruce's hand. The audience roared and heckled Bruce, who stepped back and motioned to go again. Annoyed at his surprising failure, Bruce went harder and faster. At the last possible millisecond, Bruce feinted, causing Kenneth to miss, and then cracked Kenneth's forehead forcefully enough to knock him back a step. Kenneth angrily raised his fists in front of him and stepped into an offensive stance. For a moment, it seemed as if a real fight was going to break out.

The crowd erupted. Boos rained down from the balcony. Someone shouted, "That wasn't fair!" Dozens of lit cigarettes were flicked onto the stage. Realizing the crowd was on the verge of a riot, Bruce stepped back from Kenneth, smiled, and said, "Thank you for participating." More cigarette butts skittered across the stage.

His face tight and eyes gleaming, Bruce stepped to the edge of the stage and issued a statement whose exact meaning became a hot topic of debate. "I would like to let everybody know that any time my Chinatown brothers want to *research* my Wing Chun, they are welcome to find me at my school in Oakland."

Almost as soon as the words left his mouth, Bruce exited stage left. The audience turned to each other in surprise: did he really just issue an open challenge to all of Chinatown?

News of Bruce's controversial performance spread quickly and it grew with each retelling. He had insulted all of Chinatown! So disrespectful! We must teach this cha-cha-dancing, pretty-boy actor from Seattle a lesson! Pretty soon the people who hadn't been there were even more outraged than those in the audience that night.

One of those outraged was David Chin. He was twenty-one and a senior kung fu student of one of the venerated San Francisco masters Bruce Lee had insulted. For weeks he urged a response. The challenge could not go unanswered. But the elders advised letting it go. The hot blood of young men led to violence, and violence drew unwanted attention from white authorities. The ancient ones remembered the pogroms against the Chinese. They knew Chinatown's survival depended on appearing unthreatening, by keeping its face inscrutable and neck bent. Some even reasoned that Bruce's final pronouncement wasn't intended as a challenge at all. The young man was simply advertising for his school, inviting prospective students to study under him. Besides, why should anyone in San Francisco care about a two-bit kung fu instructor in Oakland? His school would most likely fail and when it did that would be the last anybody ever heard of him.

David would not be dissuaded. He gathered two of his friends, Bing Chan and Ronald "Ya Ya" Wu, at the popular Jackson Street Café. They chose the location to meet with one of its waiters by the name of Wong Jack Man. Their purpose was to pen a formal letter "accepting" Bruce's perceived open challenge. While the three friends had grown up in Chinatown, the twenty-three-year-old Wong was fresh off the boat from Hong Kong. Clean-cut, tall and thin with a placid mien, Wong looked more like a wispy scholar than a martial artist, but he was a skilled practitioner of Northern Shaolin kung fu. His recent demonstrations of its intricate forms and kicking techniques had impressed the local community. Wong had dreams of quitting his job as a waiter and starting his own kung fu school. Unlike Bruce Lee, he revered traditional kung fu and wanted to transmit to Chinatown students exactly what his masters had taught him.

Once the letter was complete, Wong Jack Man insisted on signing his name at the bottom. David Chin claims he objected: "Wait a minute. I'm supposed to go challenge the guy."

"Well, I'm going to open a *kwoon*," Wong replied. He believed that beating Bruce Lee would give him sufficient prestige to attract enough students to launch his own kung fu school.

If it was an insult that started the ball rolling, it was ambition that moved it down the field. Wong Jack Man and Bruce Lee were two young men, both in their early twenties, who wanted to make a life for themselves as minorities in a hostile land. One was a traditionalist, the other a rebel—for one to succeed the other had to fail.

David Chin drove his beige Pontiac Tempest across the Bay Bridge to Oakland to hand-deliver the challenge letter with Wong Jack Man's name at the bottom. When he entered the studio and asked to speak to Mr. Lee, Bruce responded, "Yeah, you're looking for me?" He put down the Chinese *wuxia* novel he was reading. It was *The Legend of the Condor Heroes*, the tale of two kung fu brothers protecting China from Genghis Khan and the Mongol invaders. The brothers fall out and become rivals.

"He was real cocky," Chin remembers. "He stared at me and then put his feet up on the desk. After I handed him the letter, he looked at it and laughed, and said, 'Okay, that's no problem. Set the date.' "

What David didn't realize was Bruce might have been a brash pretty boy, but he wasn't a pretender. Other than books, fighting was the only thing that seemed to calm Bruce Lee down. In the chaos of what he called "the fresh, alive, and constantly changing nature of combat," he found a sort of peace. The adrenaline rush forced his hyperactive brain to hyperfocus.

No, he wasn't frightened, more like excited. Nor was he surprised. At the Sun Sing Theatre, he had jabbed a thumb in the eye of Chinatown's kung fu community. Bruce Lee was twenty-four years old and he wanted to revolutionize the martial arts.

Although he would later claim that he hadn't intended to issue an open challenge, he was smart enough to know that's how the audience might interpret his words. This wasn't his first challenge match. He knew if you stood on a stage in front of an audience of martial artists and claimed your style was the best someone would volunteer to test the theory.

Over the next several weeks, negotiations ensued between Bruce and David Chin, serving as Wong Jack Man's fight manager, over the time and place. Bruce didn't care when it happened but he was insistent on where. If the Chinatown crowd wanted to test him, they would have to come to Oakland and do it on his turf. "The only condition is you have to fight in my school," Bruce told David. "I won't go out."

As the talks dragged on through September into October, Bruce grew increasingly frustrated and annoyed. It was an anxious time in his life. His new Oakland branch had only attracted a handful of students, maybe a dozen on a good day. His business partner, James Lee, was despondent and drinking heavily after burying Katherine on October 5. Bruce's pregnant wife, Linda, was left to look after James's two grieving children, Greglon and Karena.

The outcome of the fight would determine Bruce's fate. If he lost, his small crop of current students would likely drift away and no new ones would sign up to learn from a young master who had just been humiliated. He would be forced to close his school and go back to his previous job in a Chinese restaurant washing dishes.

To prevent either fighter from backing out, David Chin, as the go-between, kept the hostility level high with provocative taunts. "David was saying one thing to Wong Jack Man and another thing to Bruce, until Bruce was fit to be tied and said bring him on!" recalls Leo Fong, one of Bruce's students.

By the time the appointed date finally arrived, a weekday in early November, Bruce's short fuse was already lit. "Few men had a quicker temper," Linda says.

Around 6 p.m., after twilight, Wong Jack Man, David Chin, and four of David's friends arrived at Bruce's *kwoon*. Inside they found Bruce, Linda, and James. Bruce was pacing in the center of the room.

Seeing the Oakland team was outnumbered and unsure if more people would arrive, James walked to the door and bolted it shut, locking everyone inside. He then crossed to the rear of the studio to stand next to Linda. It was where he kept a concealed handgun in case the situation spun out of hand. "It was not a friendly atmosphere," David remembers. "The challenge was real."

The two combatants had never met before. David Chin stepped up to introduce them, "Bruce Lee, this is—"

Bruce waved David away, directing his question at Wong Jack Man, "Were you at the Sun Sing Theatre?"

"No," Wong Jack Man replied, "but I heard what you said."

David interjected, "This is supposed to be a friendly match, just light sparring to demonstrate who has the superior technique—"

"You shut up," Bruce hissed at David in Cantonese. "You've already gotten your friend killed."

These threatening words knocked the San Francisco crew back on their heels. The level of hostility was more than they had anticipated. They pulled into a huddle to confer. When they broke, David Chin tried to set some basic ground rules, "No hitting on the face. No kicking in the groin—"

"I'm not standing for any of that!" declared Bruce. "You've made the challenge—so I'm making the rules. So far as I'm concerned, there are no rules. It's all out."

Watching from the back, Linda smiled to herself. She didn't speak Cantonese and couldn't follow the back-and-forth, but she had faith in her man. "I suppose I should have been nervous," she later recalled. "Yet the truth is that I could not have been calmer. I was not in the least concerned for Bruce; I was absolutely certain that he could take care of himself."

"Come on," Bruce said impatiently to Wong Jack Man.

As Wong Jack Man stepped forward to face Bruce Lee, the two of them represented the clash between tradition and modernity. What Bruce Lee mocked Wong Jack Man wanted to preserve. Brash and outspoken, Bruce was dressed in a white tank top and jeans. Introverted and thoughtful, Wong Jack Man was wearing a traditional black kung fu uniform with long sleeves and flowing pants. Neither of the two participants, nor the small private audience watching, could have known that what followed would become the most famous challenge match in kung fu history, retold and reinvented countless times in books, plays, and movies.

For a tense moment the two young men just stared at each other. On paper it was a classic Chinese match: Wong Jack Man's northern high-kicking style versus Bruce Lee's southern fists of fury. At five-feet-ten and about the same weight as Bruce, Wong Jack Man was longer and leaner and would be expected to use his reach advantage and superior kicking ability to keep the fight at a distance and pick his opponent apart. Bruce would need to get in close and turn the contest into a brawl to win.

Wong Jack Man bowed his head as Bruce shifted into a Wing Chun stance. Then Wong stepped forward and reached out his right hand. He would later claim he intended to shake hands ("touch gloves") in a sportsmanlike manner before the match began. Whatever his intentions, it was a costly mistake. Amped up and coiled tight, Bruce sprung forward with a low kick to the shins and a four-finger spear straight at Wong Jack Man's eyes. The attack struck the orbital bone, just narrowly missing his eyeball. Wong was temporarily stunned and blinded. Bruce immediately followed with a series of Wing Chun chain punches. His intent was to re-create the eleven-second defeat he had delivered in Seattle to the Japanese karate guy. "If you get in a fight, you've got to take the guy out in the first ten seconds," says James, explaining Bruce's philosophy. "You can't give him a chance. Just destroy him."

"That opening move," recalls Wong, "set the tone for the fight. He really wanted to kill me."

Trying to survive Bruce's initial onslaught, Wong Jack Man backpedaled and swung his arms defensively in wide circles. "Wong Jack Man backed off, and Bruce Lee kept coming in. He kept coming with rotary punches," David Chin recalls. "Wong Jack Man kept backing up and blocking it. The rotary punches coming in, fast." In the middle of his attack, Bruce switched his stance and snapped a kick at Wong's groin. Wong used his knees to block the kick.

It was a chaotic, aggressive, and fast-paced opening frame. Wong Jack Man was extremely evasive, warding off Bruce's strikes with his open-handed windmill defense.

But unable to blunt Bruce's aggression and fearing for his life, Wong Jack Man panicked—his fight-or-flight instinct kicking in. He turned his back and began to run, while still swinging his arms in a wide arc to protect the back of his head from Bruce's incoming punches. "Wong tried to run away," Chin says. "His back was facing Bruce."

Attached to the main room of the school was a storage room. Trying to escape, Wong Jack Man dashed for the door as Bruce chased, aiming punches at the back of Wong's head. The two of them sped through the narrow room and out a second door back into the main room. As Wong came careening out of the storage room with Bruce in hot pursuit, he suddenly stopped, whirled around, and windmilled a karate chop to Bruce's neck. The blow staggered Bruce. It was Wong Jack Man's secret weapon.

Prior to the fight, Wong had strapped on a pair of leather wrist bracelets studded with metal spikes. He then carefully hid them from everyone, including his own supporters, underneath his long sleeves. "I was surprised," Chin says. "I didn't expect it either." Wong kept them a secret for a very good reason. In challenge matches, hidden weapons—razors in shoes, brass knuckles in gloves—are strictly forbidden. If anyone had known beforehand, Wong would have been forced to remove the bracelets.

When Bruce felt the blood on his neck and realized the deception, he went berserk. "Bruce was really upset," Chin recalls. "The pain, I mean from one of those wrist braces. Wong wore long sleeves to cover it." Bruce bellowed and charged. His frenzied punches pushed Wong Jack Man backward toward a dangerous spot in the main hall. Bruce's kung fu studio was previously an upholstery store and there were two showcase windows with raised platforms to display mannequins. On the defensive, Wong Jack Man backpedaled toward the raised platform. Unaware of his surroundings, he tripped on the platform and crashed into the window. Slumped at a 45-degree angle, Wong was trapped, unable to stand up or roll away.

Bruce leapt on top of Wong and rained down punches. "Yield!" Bruce demanded. "Give up!"

David Chin and the others from San Francisco rushed in and separated the two combatants, shouting, "That's enough! That's enough!" Wong Jack Man had prearranged with them to intervene if things went badly for him. "Before there was an understanding we'd break the fight, see," Chin says.

Bruce yelled in Cantonese, "Admit you lost! Say it! Admit you lost!" Wong kept silent as his friends pulled him dazed and confused from the ground.

After Bruce Lee calmed down a bit, he walked over to Wong Jack Man. Just as he had after the challenge match with the Japanese karate guy, Bruce asked Wong not to discuss the fight. He didn't want the story getting out. Wong nodded in agreement.

The entire fight lasted about three minutes.

Chastened, the San Francisco crew shuffled out of the studio with their heads down. The mood on the ride home was somber. "No one said much," David Chin recalls, chuckling.

The next day Ben Der, a friend of Bruce's, went to San Francisco's Chinatown anxious to learn what had happened. "The day before, everybody was talking about it," he remembers, "saying how exciting it was gonna be. So I purposefully went down to Chinatown the next afternoon to see what everyone was saying. And it was dead quiet. Nobody was saying anything. And that's how I knew Bruce Lee won that fight."

Having been banished from Hong Kong for fighting, Bruce was intimately aware of how the aftermath of a fight can cause deeper injuries than the brawl itself. He visited the Jackson Street Café a week after the match to smooth things over with Wong Jack Man. A hostile relationship with all of Chinatown was not in Bruce's best interests.

"Hey man, I was just trying to advertise because I got a new school, man," Bruce said to Wong as a way of explaining his outburst at the Sun Sing Theatre. "I didn't intend to make a public challenge. Look, you and I share a kung fu lineage. We are like martial arts cousins. Besides, we are both Chinamen in a Caucasian country. We should be working together, not against each other. There's no reason for bad feelings. Why are we fighting?"

Wong Jack Man, who was sporting a black eye and still smarting from his defeat, just stared at Bruce and refused to respond. Bruce eventually walked away.

Bruce had wanted to keep the fight secret, but a challenge match associated, however tangentially, with Hong Kong's most alluring actress, Diana Chang, was too juicy to be ignored. In late November, a gossip column in Hong Kong's *Ming Pao Daily* newspaper ran a highly fictionalized version of the event entitled "Diana Chang Attracts Swarm of Butterflies, Bruce Lee Fights and Suffers Light Injury." In this imaginative retelling, Wong Jack Man, referred to as an "overseas brother," was stalking Diana Chang, forcing Bruce Lee to challenge him to defend her honor. In this version, the fight was evenly matched until the final round when Bruce was knocked down and defeated.

> Diana Chang is in San Francisco, and her beauty has charmed and dumbfounded our young overseas brothers. Among them, one has pursued her quite strongly, sticking to her without regard for death, like the shadow follows the form. Diana Chang was pursued by this person until she was at a loss over what to do. . . .
>
> Unexpectedly, Bruce Lee, with a look in his eyes and *qi* in his heart, one night actually invited this overseas young man to fight. The result of the fight was the two were evenly matched, both suffering injury, but Bruce Lee was knocked down in the last encounter. . . .
>
> After this incident the overseas brother realized his victory over Bruce Lee was only due to luck, and he ran off to hide somewhere the next day, not daring to again bother Diana Chang.

Since *Ming Pao Daily* was Hong Kong's equivalent of *The New York Times*, the local San Francisco Chinese-language newspaper, *Chinese Pacific Weekly*, republished the article on November 26, 1964. When Bruce heard about it, he hit the roof. Not only had someone broken their word and spilled the beans about the fight but the local newspaper was claiming he lost! He approached the *Chinese Pacific Weekly* to tell his side of the story. On December 17, 1964, they published his response.

Bruce said the fight had nothing to do with Diana Chang. He blamed David Chin, who had convinced Wong Jack Man that Bruce had issued an open challenge to all of Chinatown when in fact he had only been advertising his new school. Bruce maintained that he won the fight after several punches startled Wong Jack Man and he took off running. Upon wrestling Wong to the ground, Bruce said he raised his fist and asked, "Do you yield?" Wong Jack Man twice exclaimed, "I yield, I yield."

Having been fingered as the instigator, David Chin answered with a letter to the *Chinese Pacific Weekly* on January 7, 1965. He maintained that the cause of the match was Bruce's open challenge at the Sun Sing Theatre. Wong Jack Man had only gone to Oakland for "an exchange of experience" (meaning: light sparring), but Bruce, who was very angry and agitated, had the door locked and insisted on "a contest to decide whose skill was high and whose low" (meaning: no rules, full contact). Chin claimed neither party won or lost—it was a tie. "They were separated by bystanders so as to avoid any injuries or hurt feelings."

Now that this story had blown up into a full-fledged tabloid controversy, it was inevitable that even the introverted Wong Jack Man would feel he had to respond. He agreed to be interviewed for a January 28, 1965, front-page story complete with a photo of him in a kung fu uniform performing the splits with double sabers.

> Wong Jack Man, who lives and works in this city, admitted that he is the "Overseas Chinese Brother" that fought with Bruce Lee at an Oakland martial arts school. . . . Wong Jack Man admits that he was not there when Bruce Lee was on stage "challenging the Overseas Chinese community," but says several of his friends were eyewitnesses, and all say that

> Lee did indeed invite the Chinese community to "come when they will to 'research.' "
>
> . . . Wong Jack Man says that at about 6:05 Lee stood in the middle of the school and asked him to step forward. Wong says that, according to the rules of the martial arts world, he extended a hand of friendship, but Lee started attacking. . . . Wong says that neither man ever fell to the ground, but both participants were swayed and both "grazed" their opponent. . . .
>
> Wong Jack Man denies that Bruce Lee knocked him back until he was against the wall, or that he was taken down to the ground and forced to plead "mercy."
>
> . . . He says that in the future he will not argue his case again in the newspaper, and if he is made to fight again, he will instead hold a public exhibition so that everyone can see with their own eyes.

In Wong Jack Man's mind that last sentence was an open challenge to Bruce: if he disagreed with Wong's version of events they could fight again in public. Bruce ignored the taunt and refused to reply publicly. (In private, he nicknamed Wong Jack Man "The Runner.") He saw little reason for a rematch against a fighter who had cheated and lost.

Immediately after the fight with Wong Jack Man ended and the San Francisco group departed, Linda expected her husband would be elated. Instead she found him sitting in the back of the school with his head in his hands—dejected and physically drained. Ever the perfectionist, Bruce Lee was angry about his performance, exactly as he had been after he won the boxing match in Hong Kong as a teenager. For Bruce an ugly win was almost as bad as a defeat. "His performance had been neither crisp nor efficient," Linda recalls. "The fight, he realized, ought to have ended with a few seconds of him striking the first blows—instead of which, it had dragged on for three minutes. In addition, at the end, Bruce had felt unusually winded which proved to him he was far from perfect condition. So he began to dissect the fight, analyzing where he had gone wrong and seeking to find ways where he could have improved his performance. It did not take him long to realize that the basis of his art, the Wing Chun style, was insufficient."

Bruce later told one of his friends, "It really bugged me after the fight. It was the first time I felt something wrong with the way I was fighting. The fight took too long and I didn't know what to do when he ran. Getting my fists bruised from punching the sonavabitch's head was kinda stupid. I knew right then, I had to do something about my fighting."

For the past few years he had publicly criticized classical martial arts, while, at the same time, holding up traditional Wing Chun as the answer. But his mother style had let him down. Its short, quick techniques were useless against an opponent who stayed out of range and refused to engage. And its training methods—the wooden dummy, sticky hands—were inadequate preparation for a lengthy encounter. Despite a decade of relentless practice, Bruce Lee, whose body was basically one fast twitch muscle, lacked the cardiovascular endurance for more than one three-minute round of combat.

The match with Wong Jack Man proved to be an epiphany for Bruce. It was the turning point that led him to abandon his traditional style of kung fu. For years, he had preached the individual was more important than the style. After his ugly win, he finally accepted this truth for himself. Modifying a few techniques was insufficient. He needed to start from scratch and formulate his own personal brand of martial arts.

Bruce also began to question his career goals. The tabloid controversy and negative press over his match with Wong Jack Man soured him on the Bay Area martial arts scene. He had made a number of powerful enemies. Given that his two schools in Oakland and Seattle were struggling, he wondered if he wanted to spend the rest of his life teaching martial arts.

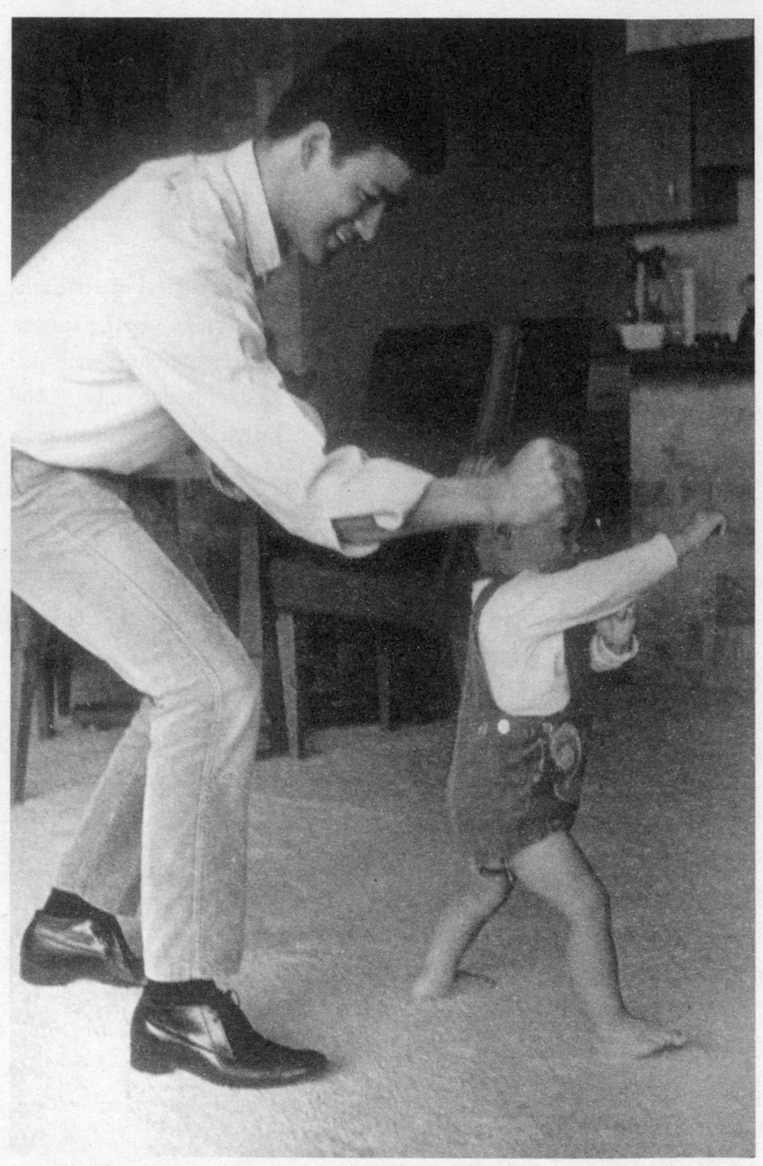

Teaching Brandon kung fu in Barrington Plaza apartment, 1966. *(Moviestore collection Ltd / Alamy Stock Photo)*

nine

hollywood calling

Prior to the Internet, Hollywood hair salons were central information hubs for the movie industry, where well-connected insiders plugged in for updates. Jay Sebring was the first hairstylist to realize that the same service Hollywood's leading ladies had long enjoyed could be offered, at a premium, to its powerful men. At a time when barbers charged men two dollars for a buzz cut and Brylcreem, Sebring could command $50 for styling with scissors, a blow-dry, and hairspray—plus all the latest industry gossip. Very quickly an hour in his barber chair became the most coveted appointment in Hollywood. His celebrity clients included Warren Beatty, Steve McQueen, Paul Newman, Frank Sinatra, and Kirk Douglas. He even designed the Doors' Jim Morrison's free-flowing locks.

One afternoon in early 1965, Sebring was styling the hair of William Dozier, a dapper, Madison Avenue–type TV producer. Dozier was developing a Charlie Chan spinoff series entitled *Charlie Chan's Number One Son*. The pitch: after the murder of Charlie Chan, the fictional Honolulu detective, his eldest son must avenge his death and continue his legacy. Dozier wanted it to be an action thriller—a "Chinese James Bond." His radical idea was to cast an actual Chinese actor for a Chinese role. Back then in the yellow-face era, white actors invariably played Asian parts with taped eyes and painted faces. In sixteen films, Charlie Chan was portrayed by Warner Oland, a Swedish actor. As a result, there was only a tiny pool of Asian actors with any serious experience—mostly they played villains in World War II dramas and pigtailed coolies in Westerns.

"I need to find an Oriental actor who speaks English and can handle action," Dozier complained to Sebring. "Someone with leading man charisma."

Sebring, who was one of Ed Parker's karate students and had attended his 1964 Long Beach International Karate Championships several months earlier, responded immediately, "I have your guy."

"Who is he?"

"Bruce Lee."

"Never heard of him."

"There's film of him at Long Beach," Sebring said. "He will blow you away."

"Can I see it?" Dozier excitedly asked.

On January 21, 1965, Jay Sebring and Ed Parker drove the film over for a screening at Dozier's offices in 20th Century Fox. As soon as he saw it, Dozier knew he'd found his man. He immediately phoned James Lee's home in Oakland.

And just like that Bruce Lee was discovered by Hollywood.

"Bruce was out when the call came through and I spoke to Dozier," Linda recalls. "Although I had never heard of him and he didn't tell me what he wanted, it sounded very hopeful. When Bruce returned his call, Dozier explained that he was interested in him for his new TV series. Understandably, we were both very excited."

It was an extraordinary opportunity. Previously, the only Asian to ever star in an American TV series was the Chinese American actress Anna May Wong, in *The Gallery of Madame Liu-Tsong* (1951). No Asian male actor had ever played the protagonist on a network TV show. There were so few roles for Asians in Hollywood that Bruce Lee, who was a veteran of twenty Hong

Kong movies, never even considered acting in America. "When I went back to the States, I really didn't think, I mean, I said, 'Here I am with a Chinese face.' I mean not prejudice or anything but being realistic thinking, 'How many times in film is a Chinese required?' " Bruce explained in an *Esquire* interview. "And when it is required, it is always branded as the typical, you know, 'Dung ta la la ta dung dung dung,' that type you know what I mean. I said, 'To hell with it.' "

If Bruce landed the part, he would achieve something historic. He would be the Jackie Robinson of Asian actors. He would also, perhaps more importantly to him, finally step out of his father's shadow and surpass his old man. "I felt that I had to accomplish something personally," he told a reporter from *TV and Movie Screen* magazine. "What would I have done if I'd gone back to Hong Kong? Nothing. I could have said, 'Bring tea,' and the servant would have brought tea. Just like that. I could have spent every day in leisure. I wanted to do something for myself—to bring honor to my own name. In Hong Kong, if I rode in a big car, people only said, 'There's Bruce Lee in his old man's car.' Whatever I did, it was a reflection of what my family had already accomplished."

Bruce was so thrilled he immediately agreed to fly down to L.A. for a screen test, despite the fact his wife was nine months pregnant.

On February 1, 1965, the first day of the Chinese New Year, Linda gave birth at East Oakland Hospital. It was a baby boy, just as Bruce had predicted. His parents gave him the English name Brandon Bruce Lee and the Chinese name *Gok Ho*, which means "National Hero." "Bruce was intensely proud to have a son," says Linda, "the first grandchild of his family." Brandon arrived in this world at a healthy eight pounds and eleven ounces with jet black hair, which quickly fell out and grew in platinum blond. "Our first child is a blond, grey-eyed Chinaman," Bruce proudly told everyone, "maybe the only one around." Like his father, Brandon quickly became a handful for his inexperienced mother. "Brandon did not sleep through the night for eighteen months. He never took to a pacifier or a special blanket, he just hollered all the time," Linda recalls, "which ironically, seems to have marked the beginning of his life's pattern."

It is an indication of how much Bruce wanted to seize his Hollywood opportunity that he did not reschedule his screen test. Three days after the delivery, Bruce left his newlywed wife and newborn son and hopped on a plane. "Bruce was a super dad, but he was not the kind who changed diapers or got up in the middle of the night," Linda explains. "He had weightier things on his mind, like building a career and paying the bills."

Jay Sebring picked up the exhausted new father from the L.A. airport. It was the first time the two men had met. They immediately bonded over Jay's muscle car, a Shelby Cobra. Along with fast cars and Asian martial arts, Jay and Bruce shared a love for fashionable clothes, stylish haircuts, and beautiful women. Sebring—a jet-setting playboy who was dating the actress Sharon Tate—was a gatekeeper for Hollywood's Cult of Cool. (Steve McQueen was the King.) The screen test at 20th Century Fox was Bruce's first step in his initiation.

Bruce met with William Dozier at his office for a pre-interview to cover the topics that would be discussed and the demonstrations to be performed. Afterward Dozier and the film crew took Bruce to a studio stage set dressed like an affluent suburban living room and sat him down in a folding chair in front of an elegant camelback sofa. Wearing a tight black suit, white shirt, and black tie with a small knot, Bruce looked like an earnest Bible salesman or a young congressional aide at a funeral. His hair was neatly parted on the left and brushed back to reveal his entire forehead and dramatic black eyebrows. Bruce crossed his legs and clasped his hands in his lap. He was visibly nervous.

As the film began to roll, Dozier, standing off-camera, gave his first instruction: "Now Bruce, look into the camera lens and tell us your name, age, and where you were born."

"My last name is Lee—Bruce Lee. I was born in San Francisco. I am twenty-four right now."

"And you worked in motion pictures in Hong Kong?"

"Yes, since I was around six years old," Bruce answered, shifting his eyes, his anxiety palpable.

Trying to lighten the mood, Dozier said, "I understand you just had a baby boy. And you've lost a little sleep over it, have you?"

Bruce chuckled ruefully, "Yeah, three nights."

"And tell the crew," Dozier continued in a light tone, "what time they shoot the pictures in Hong Kong."

"Well, mostly in the morning, because it's kind of noisy in Hong Kong you know, around three million people there. So every time when you have a picture it's mostly say 12 a.m. to 5 a.m. in the morning."

"They'd love that here," Dozier joked. "And you went to college in the United States?

"Yes."

"What did you study?"

"Ah," Bruce paused, his eyes looking up and to the right, "Ph-philosophy."

"And you told me earlier today that karate or jujitsu are not the most powerful or best forms of Oriental fighting. What is the most powerful or best form?"

"Well, it's bad to say the best, but, ah," Bruce smiled to himself, "in my opinion, I think gung fu is pretty good."

"Tell us a little bit about gung fu."

"Well, gung fu is originated in China. It is the ancestor of karate and jujitsu. It is a more complete system. And it is more fluid—by that I mean, it is more flowing. There is continuity in movement instead of one movement, two movement, and then stop."

"Would you explain the principles of a glass of water as it applies to gung fu?" Dozier asked, bringing up a topic from the pre-interview.

"Well, gung fu, the best example would be a glass of water," Bruce smiled, finally feeling comfortable. "Why? Because water is the softest substance in the world but yet it can penetrate the hardest rock or anything, granite, you name it. Um, water also is insubstantial—by that I mean you cannot grasp hold of it; you cannot punch it and hurt it. So every gung fu man is trying to do that: to be soft like water and flexible and adapt itself to the opponent."

"I see, what's the difference between a gung fu punch and a karate punch?"

"Well, the karate punch is like an iron bar—*wham*. A gung fu punch is like an iron chain with an iron ball attached to the end," Bruce chuckled, licking his lips. "And it go—*WHANG!*—and it hurts inside."

"Okay, now we are going to cut," Dozier instructed, "and in just a second we will have you stand up and show us some gung fu and some movements."

"Okay," Bruce nodded.

After a fresh reel of film was loaded, Dozier asked Bruce to act out some classic character types from Chinese Opera. Drawing from his experience watching his father onstage, Bruce successfully imitated how a warrior and scholar walk. "The scholar is a weakling, a ninety pound in Charles Atlas," Bruce chuckled, mincing in front of the camera. "He would be walking just like a girl, shoulders up and everything."

"So by the way they walk, you can immediately tell who they are," Dozier said.

"Right, the character they represent."

"Now, show some gung fu movements."

"Well, it's hard to show it alone," Bruce shrugged, dramatically, "but I will try to do my best."

"Well, maybe one of the fellas will walk in," Dozier said, playing his part in the setup. "You guys want to—"

The crew started laughing and calling out, "Go ahead, come on, get in there," as they pushed the assistant director, a balding man in his late fifties with silver hair and black horn-rim glasses, in front of the camera. He clearly was not expecting to be the butt of the joke.

"Accidents do happen!" Bruce teased.

"There are various kinds of fighting," Bruce explained to the camera. "It depends on where you hit and what weapon you will be using. To the eyes, you would use fingers." Bruce lashed out a finger strike millimeters from the man's eyes and pulled it back before the assistant director could react. "Don't worry, I won't—" Bruce assured him, and then lashed another strike at his eyes. "Or straight at the face," added Bruce as he punched at his nose. The assistant director flinched.

"Hold it just a minute," Dozier said as he stepped in front of the camera and grabbed the assistant director's arm. "Let's move the gentleman around this way so you are doing it more into the camera. Okay, swell."

As they adjusted positions, Bruce said, "And then there is bent arm strike using the waist again into a backfist." Immediately he flicked out three punches so fast they made the assistant director's neck jerk back and forth like a bobblehead doll.

"Let's have thc assistant director back up just a little bit," Dozier teased. Subdued chuckles from the crew turned into belly laughs and Bruce tried to cover his smile with his hand. Finally comfortable and feeling in control of the room, Bruce joked, "You know, kung fu is very sneaky. You know the Chinese, they always hit low." Bruce feinted to the old man's face, dropped low, and lashed a punch at his groin. The assistant director's entire body was swaying back and forth in reaction to blows too fast for his brain to register. "Don't worry," Bruce said, patting him on the arm.

"These are just natural reactions," the assistant director pleaded.

"Right, right," smiled Bruce.

"Cheat into the camera and show us again," Dozier instructed.

"There is the finger jab, there's the punch, there is the backfist—then low," he exclaimed as he linked all four strikes into a flurry that caused the assistant director to spasm with fear. "Then there are the kicks—straight to the groin, then up!" And just as fast as the punches, Bruce flicked a snap kick to the groin, and brought up a roundhouse kick to his head. "Or if I can back up," Bruce said before stepping back and snapping out a sidekick within inches of the assistant director's face.

The crew behind the camera laughed openly in appreciation and awe of Bruce Lee's speed, accuracy, and control. He had shown them something they had never seen before.

Patting the assistant director on the arm, Bruce smiled. "He's kind of worried."

"He has nothing to worry about," Dozier declared.

And with that Bruce's nerves were gone. Five years of working the stage in front of live audiences up and down the West Coast had finally paid off.

The next day, Bruce flew back to his wife and newborn son.

Three days later, seven after the birth of Brandon, Bruce Lee received a call informing him that his father was dead. The timing was not viewed as a coincidence by the family. Hoi Chuen had been sick for a long time, suffering from a terrible cough. Doctors told him the years of smoking opium had weakened his heart and lungs. When he learned there was a grandson to continue the family lineage, the patriarch of the clan was finally able to let go.

Linda was having difficulty recovering from the delivery. It had left her in a weakened state. Bruce was torn between his concern for his wife's health and his Confucian duty to attend his father's funeral. It was eventually decided that Brandon and Linda would move in with her mother in Seattle, while Bruce was in Hong Kong for three weeks from February 15 to March 6.

According to Chinese custom if a son is not present when his father dies, he must come crawling back to ask forgiveness. At the doorway of the mortuary, Bruce dropped to his knees and crawled on all fours to his father's casket, while wailing uncontrollably as tradition demanded. Bruce described the service as a "cross between Chinese custom and Catholic regulation; the whole deal was one mess of conflict." Because of Chinese tradition, Bruce couldn't cut his hair or shave: "All in all, I look like a pirate with long hair and whiskers."

Bruce's first letter to Linda was filled with worry about her well being: "One thing I'm anxious [about] is your health. I hope you will go have a check up. Never mind about the expense, your health is more important. . . . Do not forget to go to the doctor and above all do not forget to let me know of the result (like your blood count, etc.). If there is anything that has to be done, do it! Do not worry about expenses. I'll be able to pay for it."

As the eldest son, Peter helped Grace deal with the will and Hoi Chuen's estate. Bruce quickly set about spending his inheritance on gifts for himself (three tailored suits plus a top coat), Linda's mother (a purse and jade jewelry), and Linda (a wig and, most importantly, a diamond wedding ring to replace the one he had borrowed from James's wife, Katherine). "Let's hope I'll bring everything through without the customs official finding out. I can't afford to pay tax on them all," Bruce wrote to Linda. "In fact, I'm broke starting tomorrow. You'll know why when you see me: wig, ring, etc., etc., etc."

Bruce returned to America in mid-March. Peter chose to stay in Hong Kong, teach school, and look after the family.

Soon after coming home, Bruce received a call from William Dozier. Everyone had loved the screen test. Plans for *Number One Son* were under way, but it might take another two or three months until there was noticeable progress. In the meantime Dozier wanted to sign Bruce to an exclusive contract for $1,800 (the equivalent of $14,000 in 2017). How did that sound? Bruce, who was making a hundred or so per month teaching kung fu, didn't need to be asked twice. It was the biggest payday of his life.

With all this money burning a hole in his pocket, Bruce decided to take his wife and child for an extended vacation in Hong Kong to meet his family. Bruce pitched it to Linda as the honeymoon they hadn't previously been able to afford: "Baby, this trip you'll remember the rest of your life. I can promise you that. We'll buy the whole of Hong Kong." They planned to leave in early May when Brandon was old enough to travel.

Bruce and James agreed to shut down their Oakland school. After six months in business, there still were not enough students to cover the rent. At least for the moment, Bruce abandoned his plans for a national chain of kung fu schools and decided to return to the family business of acting. "Just about the time I discovered I didn't want to teach self defense for the rest of my life," Bruce explained, "I went to the Long Beach International Karate Tournament and got myself discovered by Hollywood."

Prior to the Lee family's departure, Bruce underwent a ritual familiar to new actors in Hollywood—finding an agent. On April 22, William Dozier wrote to Bruce with a recommendation: "I am taking the liberty of suggesting a reputable and honest agent for you, one William Belasco, President of Progressive Management Agency here in Hollywood." Along with the letter, Dozier included the presentation material for *Number One Son*. A few days later Bruce met with William Belasco and signed with him—his first (and last) Hollywood agent. During their conversation, Belasco informed Bruce that *Number One Son* was on hold until July. Bruce agreed to return from Hong Kong when the project restarted.

"After reading the 'presentation' I'm very enthused on the whole project and have added several ideas of my own to add more 'coolness' and 'subtleness' to the character of Charlie Chan's son," Bruce wrote back to Dozier on April 28. "This project does have tremendous potential and its uniqueness lies in the *interfusion* of the best of both the Oriental and American qualities plus the never before seen Gung Fu fighting techniques. . . . I have a feeling that this Charlie Chan can be another James Bond success if handled properly."

Concerned his family might not fully embrace his white wife, who spoke no Chinese, and towheaded baby boy, Bruce called his mother and told her she could expect to see "the only blond-haired, gray-eyed Chinaman in the world." He also touted Linda's many wonderful qualities, specifically her abilities as a cook.

They arrived on May 7 to a family still grieving. Bruce's mother was deeply depressed. The family was polite to Linda but distant, accepting her in a standoffish way. "It wasn't palsy-walsy," Linda recalls. "They would have preferred that Bruce had married a Chinese girl." All of his family's love and attention focused on little Brandon as if Linda was simply the wet nurse.

To add to Linda's discomfort, the Nathan Road apartment, while spacious by Hong Kong standards, felt tiny and overcrowded to her. There was little privacy and no way to escape the oppressive Hong Kong summer heat (80–85°F) and humidity (85–90 percent). The change in weather caused Brandon to fall ill. But even when he recovered, he was difficult. "Brandon was an awful baby," Linda says. "He cried all the time. Not sick, just ornery."

As the first grandchild in the family, Brandon was treated like a little emperor. Any sign of the slightest disturbance would cause all of the Chinese women to intervene. No matter what time of night, Bruce's mother, sister, or aunt would jump out of bed at the first whimper to soothe him. "Since we lived in such close quarters," says Linda, "Brandon couldn't be allowed to cry, or even utter a peep, without being rescued by a well-meaning grandma or auntie." Their overprotectiveness felt like an implicit rebuke of Linda's abilities as a mother. To maintain her position, Linda would preemptively walk the floors with babe in arms into the wee hours of the morning. The insufferable heat, the cramped living conditions, the awkward family dynamics, the language barrier, the sleep deprivation—it was all wearing Linda down. Worse, Brandon was becoming "the number-one spoiled child you have ever come across."

To prove to his relatives that his American wife wasn't useless, Bruce bragged about her cooking. "She can cook anything. Just you ask. You ought to try her spaghetti sauce. Just ask. It is the greatest spaghetti on the face of the earth." He went on and on until everybody was after Linda to make her world-famous spaghetti dinner. She tried to play them off but finally succumbed to the pressure.

The problem was she didn't actually know how to make spaghetti sauce. Her secret ingredient was Lawry's Original Style Spaghetti Sauce Spice & Seasonings mix, unheard of in Hong Kong. The colony didn't have any Western-style supermarkets. She had also never cooked for more than five people. Bruce invited twenty of his closest relatives and friends for this alleged feast. As the evening approached a feeling of dread came over Linda. While she did find enough tomatoes and a semblance of spices, she had never cooked with a gas stove before and quickly discovered how easily tomatoes burn. "It was awful," she recalls, "just an unmitigated disaster. The spaghetti was permeated with the taste of burned tomatoes. His family ate and smiled and made little murmuring sounds, but I could tell that they were sorry that Bruce was 'stuck' with me."

It was not the honeymoon Bruce had promised, but he was right about one thing: it was a trip that Linda would remember for the rest of her life.

While Linda looked after Brandon, Bruce sought to improve his martial arts and further his credibility as a kung fu instructor. He asked his master,

Ip Man, to help him with his next book project: a Wing Chun instructional manual. Bruce hired the Mount Tai Photography House to take two hundred photos of Ip Man demonstrating Wing Chun techniques over the course of a week. "Ip Man didn't like to be photographed, but Bruce's request was the exception," says Robert Chan. "Bruce was one of Ip Man's favorite students because of his dedication to the martial arts."

While in Hong Kong, Bruce continued to obsess over his ugly match against Wong Jack Man. "The more I think of him to have fought me without getting blasted bad, the more I'm pissed off!" Bruce wrote to James Lee. "If I just took my time, but anger screwed me up—that bum is nothing!" The more he stewed the more certain he became that Wing Chun had failed him. "My mind is made up to start a system of my own," he wrote to Taky Kimura, "I mean a system of totality, embracing all but yet guided with simplicity." Over the course of the summer, he mailed to James detailed descriptions complete with stick-figure drawings of his new style, which he summarized as "a combination of chiefly Wing Chun, fencing, and boxing."

When he wasn't developing his new style with its focus on simplicity, he was seeking out traditional kung fu instructors to teach him complex techniques for his Hollywood career. "On this trip I'll pick up some flowery [kung fu] forms and what not for the TV show," Bruce wrote to Taky. "The viewers like fancy stuff anyway." In his practice of the martial arts, he was developing a distinction between what was effective for him as a fighter (the martial) and what looked good as an entertainer (the arts). Low kicks, for example, were for fighting, while high kicks were for film.

As July approached, Bruce expected to be called back to California to begin shooting *Number One Son*, but he was beginning to learn that Hollywood is a town where many promises are made but few are kept. His agent, Belasco, notified him that *Number One Son* was on hold until Dozier completed a different TV project. "Well, I guess I wouldn't be in *Life* magazine yet," Bruce joked with Taky Kimura, "because they want to concentrate first on 'Batman.' "

In the meantime, Belasco sought to keep his new client happy by finding other roles for him. A golden opportunity had arisen with *The Sand Pebbles*—a movie about American sailors, along with a crew of Chinese coolies, patrolling the Yangtze River in 1920s China. There was a prominent part for a Chinese crewmember named Po-Han, who is drawn into a boxing match against a bullying American sailor. Belasco told Bruce the director, Robert Wise, was very interested, but Wise decided to give the part to the veteran Japanese American actor Mako Iwamatsu. It was a terrible blow since the role was perfect for Bruce and the movie starred his future student and friend Steve McQueen. If Bruce had landed the part, he would have enjoyed a much different career path. *The Sand Pebbles* went on to earn eight Oscar nominations, including Best Supporting Actor for Mako.

Disappointed with the delay in his starring TV project and the loss of a great movie role, Bruce decided to reach out to his childhood friends who were still in the Hong Kong film business. Not only did he want to brag about *Charlie Chan's Number One Son*, he also hoped to land a movie deal by leveraging Hollywood against Hong Kong—a technique he would use to great effect several years later. His pitch to producers was simple: I'm about to become the most famous Chinese actor in America; sign me now while you can still afford me. It seems his approach achieved some success. Several executives expressed genuine interest. Nothing was definite, but, as Bruce and his family boarded a plane at Kai Tak Airport for America, he believed that a movie career in Hong Kong was a viable backup option.

Bruce, Linda, and Brandon landed in Seattle in early September 1965 and moved in with Linda's mother, stepfather, and grandmother. It was unclear how long they planned to stay. Bruce was anxiously waiting for the green light on *Number One Son*. The word from Dozier was always good—"soon, real soon"—but there were continually further delays as Dozier developed *Batman* instead.

As the weeks dragged into months, the living arrangements grew increasingly uncomfortable. "Brandon was screaming all the time," Linda says. "He was spoiled rotten by this time. He would cry and it would bother my grandmother and I would get up at all hours once again to walk him so he wouldn't disturb her."

With all this free time, Bruce taught the occasional class in Seattle and made a couple of trips to Oakland, but mostly he focused on his training and developing his new style. "There was much self-analysis," Linda says. "He became self-critical again because he felt that that would help him move forward again." He read through his library of books, mostly boxing and fencing but also philosophy, looking for inspiration. He watched 16mm films of boxers like Jack Dempsey and Cassius Clay, who had recently changed his name to Muhammad Ali. Bruce loved Ali's swagger and was obsessed with his "phantom punch" knockout of Sonny Liston on May 25, 1965. "If it wasn't a fix," Bruce wrote to Taky Kimura, "Liston must have timed his rushing in with the on-coming force of Clay's punch so well that Liston was knocked out cold."

During their stay, Linda claims that her mother "really got to know and love Bruce." While Mrs. Emery may have found him charming, she worried about his lack of steady employment. Every day she came home from her job at Sears to find her son-in-law reading, watching films, or working out.

"When is your husband going to get a *real* job?" she would pointedly wonder aloud.

"I have this movie job coming up," Bruce would insist, referencing both the Charlie Chan TV show and all the Hong Kong film producers who were supposedly eager to sign him.

"Oh, yeah, yeah, yeah," Mrs. Emery would dismissively respond.

After living for four months with his mother-in-law, it was plainly time to move. Bruce decided to temporarily relocate to James Lee's home in Oakland. His financial situation had grown precarious. Between the gifts and the vacation, he had burned through the Hollywood signing money, and the prospects for *Number One Son* looked dubious. "It may be this *Charlie Chan* project which will develop fully for you, or another project," Dozier attempted to comfort Bruce, "but rest assured we shall try to come up with the best possible opportunity for you." Dozier was waiting to see the public's reaction to *Batman*, which was scheduled to premiere on ABC as a midseason replacement on January 12, 1966. If it was a success, the network would almost certainly green-light his next project.

Bruce wrote to one of his Bay Area students on December 18, 1965: "Linda and I will be coming down to Oakland to stay for a month before either going to Hollywood or Hong Kong. The 20th Century Fox deal is 85%. If that doesn't come out I have two contracts waiting in Hong Kong."

Bruce Lee's future was at a crossroads, and it all depended on Gotham City's Caped Crusader.

Bruce Lee in Kato costume visiting Thordis Brandt on the movie set of *In Like Flint*. She was playing "Amazon #6," circa August 1966. *(David Tadman)*

ten

citizen kato

To everyone's surprise (including Dozier's and ABC's), *Batman* became a phenomenon. With its campy sensibility, pun-saturated dialogue, Andy Warhol pop-art primary-colored costumes, hammy bad guys, and colorful fight captions ("Biff!" "Zlonk!" "Kapow!") that blasted across the screen, *Batman* appealed to comic-book fanboys, urban aesthetes, and stoned college kids. Dozier described it as the only situational comedy on-air without a laugh track. In early March 1966, *Batman* landed on the cover of *Life* magazine with the headline: "The Whole Country Goes Supermad."

In a town where unlikely success breeds immediate imitation, ABC's executives hounded Dozier for a follow-up series. By the end of February 1966, Dozier submitted a first draft script for *Charlie Chan's Number One Son*. A few weeks later, ABC rejected the project. It is unknown exactly why, although not hard to guess. No TV executive in 1966 was willing to risk his job by green-lighting a show starring a completely unknown Chinese actor.

While network TV's all-white facade was beginning to crack (the previous year *I Spy* became the first show to costar a black actor, Bill Cosby), the plight for Asian actors in Hollywood had been dire for a long time. The first and last Asian male matinee idol was Sessue Hayakawa in the silent era of the 1910–20s. Before sound and in black-and-white, American and European audiences, particularly white women, found his Japanese features to be exotic and titillating. He became an overnight superstar on par with Charlie Chaplin and Douglas Fairbanks Sr. with *The Cheat* (1915). It was a *Fifty Shades of Grey*–type movie about a venal stockbroker's wife (Fannie Ward) who falls into debt and borrows money from a Japanese antique dealer (Hayakawa) in return for her virtue. When she tries to pay him back the cash, he refuses and brands her on the shoulder as his property. "The effect of Hayakawa on American women was even more electric than Valentino's," reported film critic DeWitt Bodeen. "It involved fiercer tones of masochism." An American journalist quoted Hayakawa as saying, "My crientele [*sic*] is women. They rike [*sic*] me to be strong and violent."

They also liked him to be silent. The advent of talking pictures in 1927 exposed Hayakawa's thick Japanese accent, which suburban housewives found significantly less stimulating than his cheekbones, and sent his career as a romantic idol into decline until Pearl Harbor finished it off. After World War II, the only roles Hayakawa could secure were honorable villains like Colonel Saito in *The Bridge on the River Kwai* (1957).

What happened to Hayakawa reflected a broader trend in postwar American culture: Asian male characters were desexualized. As a result, Asian actors were disqualified from playing romantic leads. *Number One Son* represented a unique chance for an Asian actor to play a heroic leading man on network TV. Its rejection by ABC was a lost opportunity to undermine the emasculated stereotype and a blow to Bruce Lee's hopes of overnight stardom.

Like any good producer, William Dozier hedged his bets. He had multiple projects at various stages of development to present to TV executives. His strategy was to buy up the TV rights to various comic book, radio, and literary properties, including Charlie Chan, Batman, Wonder Woman, and Dick Tracy. For the past year, he had worked to secure *The Green Hornet*, a popular 1930s radio serial.

Created by George W. Trendle, the show's premise was simple: Britt Reid was a millionaire muckraking newspaper publisher by day and a masked crime-fighter, the Green Hornet, by night. Reid's sidekick was his faithful Japanese valet, Kato. (The radio producers changed Kato's nationality to Filipino after Japan invaded China in 1937.) Trendle conceived of the show as a modern-day sequel to his most popular invention, *The Lone Ranger*. Britt Reid was the great-nephew of the Lone Ranger, Kato was the minority stand-in for Tonto, and Reid's tricked-out car, the Black Beauty, was an update to "the great horse Silver."

In the summer of 1965, Dozier and Trendle entered into discussions about TV rights to *The Green Hornet*. "I have a superb Oriental in the bullpen for Kato," Dozier bragged to Trendle in a letter dated November 16, 1965. "He is actually an American-born Chinese but can play any sort of Oriental or Filipino. I don't think we should ever say what sort of nationality Kato is: just let him be what he looks like—an Oriental. The actor I have in mind for the role is a Black Belt Karate, incidentally, and can perform every trick in the Karate book."

In March 1966, the same month *Number One Son* was rejected, 20th Century Fox announced *The Green Hornet* was coming to television in the fall. This turn of events left Dozier to make an awkward call to Oakland. Instead of starring in his own TV series as a Chinese James Bond–type hero, how would Bruce like to play the Oriental manservant to a rich white crime-fighter? The answer was he wouldn't. "It sounded at first like typical houseboy stuff," Bruce explained to *The Washington Post*. "I tell Dozier, 'Look if you sign me up with all that pigtail and hopping around jazz, forget it.' "

The truth was Bruce didn't really have a choice. He was under contract to Dozier. Even if he could legally pass on the role, he had a young wife, an infant child, and an empty bank account. But despite having no leverage, Bruce insisted he would only take the part if it was upgraded and modernized from the radio version where Kato's biggest moments came when Britt Reid, the publisher, barked, "My car, Kato," and Kato answered, "Yessuh, Mistah Blitt." Like any good producer, Dozier reassured his actor. Kato wouldn't be a servant but a partner. In fact, Kato would be the Green Hornet's most important weapon and handle almost all of the fight scenes. It would also be the first chance for American audiences to see Chinese kung fu on national TV.

Dozier had Bruce at "kung fu." While Kato was a disappointment compared to Charlie Chan's son, it was still a unique opportunity for an unknown actor to showcase his talents and beloved native art form. And unlike most producers, Dozier meant what he promised. However, he left out one important detail—he wasn't completely in charge of the show. In order to secure the TV rights, he had been forced to give George Trendle final script approval.

For the past year, Bruce, Linda, and Brandon had stayed with either family or friends in Hong Kong, Seattle, and Oakland. In mid-March, they moved into a tiny old-fashioned apartment on the corner of Wilshire Boulevard and Gayley Avenue in the Westwood neighborhood of Los Angeles. It was the first time the young couple had lived alone since their marriage.

As soon as Bruce arrived in L.A., Dozier enrolled him in acting classes with Jeff Corey, a character actor who had been blacklisted in the 1950s. Bruce described him to friends as "the best drama coach here in Hollywood." Corey's celebrity client list included James Dean, Kirk Douglas, Jane Fonda, Jack Nicholson, Leonard Nimoy, Barbra Streisand, and Robin Williams. These lessons were the only formal acting training Bruce ever had. Corey taught Bruce about camera shots, lighting, placement, matching, and other factors involved in television production, but his primary objective was to improve Bruce's diction and reduce his Hong Kong accent. "People just couldn't understand him," says Van Williams, who was cast as Britt Reid/The Green Hornet. "He had that thick accent and he'd try to slow it down or speed it up and it was still bad." Several months of intensive instruction paid off. Bruce later joked with journalists: "You know how I got that job playing Kato? The hero's name was Britt Reid, and I was the only Chinese guy in all of California who could pronounce Britt Reid, that's why!"

Production for *The Green Hornet* began in June. Bruce was paid $400 a week ($313 take-home pay), and the first check arrived just in the nick of time. "We didn't have enough to pay the rent and other outstanding bills," says Linda. For a married couple that was used to living on $100 to $200 a month, it felt like they had won the lottery. "We thought it was all the money in the world," Linda recalls.

And they acted like it. Bruce immediately went out and purchased a brand-new blue 1966 Chevy Nova for $2,500. He then moved his family into a spectacular two-bedroom apartment on the twenty-third floor of Barrington Plaza. It was more than Bruce could afford, but he had received a tip from Burt Ward, who played Robin on *Batman* and also lived in the building—the manager was willing to cut under-the-table deals for Hollywood actors and other special tenants. In return for martial arts lessons, the manager halved Bruce's rent. This arrangement lasted for three months—Bruce taught kung fu to the manager and Burt Ward—until the owners discovered the deception and everyone was evicted. Bruce, Linda, and Brandon briefly moved to a rental house in Inglewood before switching to another rental in Culver City on August 30, 1967. In nine years of marriage this nomadic family moved eleven times.

Bruce may have felt rich, but he was actually getting screwed. He had made a classic rookie actor mistake—he signed with the agent recommended by his boss. It turned out his agent, Belasco, was good friends with Dozier, and thus struck a deal more to Dozier's benefit than Bruce's. The weekly salaries for the five permanent players were: Bruce Lee (Kato) $400; Walter Brooke (District Attorney Scanlon) $750; Wende Wagner (Miss Case) $850; Lloyd Gough (Mike Axford) $1,000; Van Williams (Britt Reid/The Green Hornet) $2,000. Despite being the second lead of the show, the Chinese guy was paid far less than the white actors. Fortunately for Belasco's physical safety, Bruce never discovered that he was making five times less than Van Williams. Dozier, perhaps feeling guilty, bumped up Bruce's salary to $550 per week on November 30, 1966.

At the end of May, Bruce and Van Williams met for the first time at a press party to promote the *Green Hornet* program. The introduction took place at a ceremonial luncheon attended by scores of television and motion picture executives and some sixty members of the press. The scene was the ballroom of the posh Beverly Hills Hotel, whose proprietors had tinted all the drinks a sickly green in honor of their guests.

Dozier opened with a lame Batman joke: "What happens if Batman and Robin are run over by a steam roller? They come out Flatman and

Ribbon." The crowd politely guffawed. Dozier told the press he intended to cash in on the Batman fad by making a motion picture about the Caped Crusader, and hoped to do one about the Green Hornet too. "What we are after with *The Green Hornet*," Dozier explained, "is *The Ipcress File* [a 1965 British espionage film starring Michael Caine] sort of technique—pace, flair, lots of gadgets and gimmickry. The Green Hornet's car, Black Beauty, will be so filled with wild gimmicks it will make James Bond's car look like a baby buggy."

Dozier then called up Adam West, the star of *Batman*, to the microphone. After joking about the media coverage of *Batman*, West introduced Van Williams and Bruce Lee. Van Williams—a tall, handsome, thirty-two-year-old Texan, who had costarred in the TV series *Surfside 6* (1962)—expressed surprise to be there. He had only signed on to the show two days prior. Bruce was so happy he looked like a kid on Christmas morning. He thanked the gathering in Cantonese.

During the question-and-answer session, one of the reporters asked Van Williams, "Do you really believe playing the Green Hornet will advance your acting aspirations?"

"The success of *Batman* made a lot of people sit up and take notice," Van Williams replied. "You know, there are a lot of fine Shakespearean actors who are starving."

Another reporter asked Bruce, "In the early days of radio, Kato was identified as a Japanese but during the war he suddenly shifted nationalities and emerged as Filipino. How do you see Kato?"

"Speaking for myself, I am Chinese," Bruce replied emphatically.

"But won't some knowing Orientals protest, since Kato is after all, a Japanese name?" the reporter followed up.

"I am a karate expert, black belt class," Bruce explained gravely. "Anyone object, I put them on their back."

Dozier jumped to his feet to intervene: "It is not really important whether Kato is Japanese or Chinese since the show is not exactly striving for reality."

Once the formalities were over Adam West and Van Williams sat down for a lighthearted TV interview with an ABC correspondent. Bruce's threat to flatten anyone who objected to a Chinese actor playing a Japanese character had clearly made an impression. The interviewer asked Van Williams, "Kato uses a form of karate, yes?"

"Yes, it's a Chinese form called gung fu," Van Williams replied. "I made the mistake of sneezing when I was too close to him and I ended up flat on the floor. He's fast, very fast."

Adam West, switching to his Batman voice, interjected, "Faster than Robin?"

"Faster than Robin." Van Williams smiled. "Faster than a speeding bullet."

"I doubt that very much," Adam West objected with mock indignation.

"Do you see any competition?" the interviewer asked.

"We'll work this out behind closed doors," West declared.

As filming began in June, *The Green Hornet* faced two major challenges. First, there was a conflict between Dozier and George Trendle, the eighty-two-year-old creator of *The Green Hornet*, over the style of the show. Hoping to ride Batman's campy success, Dozier wanted *The Green Hornet* to be a similarly silly knockoff. Dozier hired *Batman*'s head writer, Lorenzo Semple Jr., to pen *The Green Hornet*'s pilot script and wrote to Trendle to explain their vision: "I am sure you will agree that we can't do straight *Green Hornet* stories today as they were done on radio."

But George Trendle was horrified by *Batman* and refused to allow his beloved characters to be turned into clowns. "I thought when we discussed this *Green Hornet* situation that we had agreed that we would play it straight," Trendle replied. "I'm afraid you're planning on making the Green Hornet a fantastic, unreal person which in my opinion would kill the show in six months."

Unable to change Trendle's mind, Dozier had to switch *The Green Hornet* from a comedy to a drama. This decision compounded the show's second disadvantage. *Batman* had an hour of prime time every week (two half hours on back-to-back nights) to tell its stories, but ABC decided to only give *The Green Hornet* one thirty-minute slot per week. Dozier was forced to squeeze a crime drama, which is typically an hour long, into a thirty-minute sitcom's time frame. "When we started and I heard it was a half hour," recalls Van Williams, "I said, 'Uh oh, trouble.' " Dozier commissioned a pilot film for both *Dick Tracy* and *Wonder Woman* as possible midseason replacements in case *The Green Hornet* was canceled early.

The troubled production was an anxious environment for the actors who were compelled to compete for limited screen time. Bruce was still resentful about his demotion to sidekick and determined not to be treated like a houseboy. While the rest of the cast waited for their moment in front of the camera, Bruce performed stunts. He would put a dime on top a six-foot-high gimbal, jump into the air, and sidekick the dime across the stage. He would do two-finger push-ups and challenge stuntmen to arm wrestling contests. Van Williams affectionately viewed Bruce "Never Sits Still" Lee as a rambunctious, hyperactive younger brother. "He was a good kid. I knew what he was doing," Williams recalls. "He really wanted to show off what he could do. He didn't have the time to do that on-screen, because when he'd go in, he'd do one shot and it was all over. He started running around and kicking and doing this, that, and the other and showing off."

One of the ways Bruce liked to show off was to jump-kick unsuspecting people's earlobes. "I'd feel a 'twish,' " says Williams. "He had jumped into the air, reached out with his toe, and ticked me on the ear." This continued until Bruce accidentally injured one of the set designers. "He turned his head to talk to another guy just at the same time Bruce kicked him on the earlobe," Williams remembers. "He dislocated his jaw. That ended the Bruce Lee kicking on the set."

Besides status anxiety, part of what drove Bruce's nervous energy on-set was impostor syndrome. He was an amazing martial arts performer, but all his experience was onstage before a live audience. He had never done elaborate fight choreography on film—his childhood Hong Kong movies were melodramas, not action flicks. Onstage, Bruce dealt with three-dimensional space and an audience viewing from every angle. To sell a punch or kick, he had to land within millimeters of the target, what he called "non-contact gung fu." But *The Green Hornet* stuntmen were all veterans of Westerns. "It was a two-dimensional thing where you had the camera over your shoulder," says Van Williams. "You could stand three feet away from your opponent and swing, and if the guy reacted correctly and the sound effects were right, it looked perfect. Bruce could never get used to working that far apart."

Bruce insisted on close quarters combat. The stuntmen hated it. They weren't fast enough to react to him, and as a result, occasionally got banged up. "They got to the point where they didn't want to work on that show," Williams recalls. "They were tired of getting hurt." "Judo" Gene LeBell, a legendary pro wrestler, world-class *judoka*, and the stunt coordinator on-set, was assigned the task of calming Bruce down. "Bruce would hit you in ten different spots and as a stuntman you wouldn't know whether to grab your jaw and say that hurt or your stomach," says LeBell. "We did our best to slow Bruce Lee down because the Western way was the old John Wayne way where you reach from left field, tell a story, and then you hit the man. Bruce liked to throw thirty-seven kicks and twelve punches."

When reasoning didn't work, LeBell took to joshing Bruce. "In pro wrestling, they call it 'the swerve.' It's how far you can tease and get away with it," LeBell explains. "I'd tell him he put too much starch in my shirt."

One day as part of the general joking and roughhousing atmosphere on set, the stuntmen egged LeBell into picking "the little guy up." LeBell yanked Bruce onto his shoulder in a Crouching Nelson hold—upside down with one hand around the back. Then he slowly walked him around the set.

"Put me down!" Bruce yelled. "I'm going to kill you!"

"I'm not going to let you down."

"Why?"

"Because you are going to kill me."

Despite the difference in temperament, the two men became friends. "I reckon I teased him so much I eventually got him to loosen up a little," LeBell says. To Bruce's credit, he was so obsessed with perfecting his martial arts he put up with the hazing to learn from LeBell. Bruce offered to exchange lessons: kung fu for judo and wrestling. "I showed him some legitimate finishing holds, leg locks, arm locks," LeBell recalls. "He told me he used one of my holds on Chuck Norris in *Way of the Dragon*."

What finally convinced Bruce to modify his no-contact fight choreography was seeing the result on film. The pilot episode, "The Silent Gun," concluded with a big fight between the Green Hornet, Kato, and the bad guys in a darkly lit underground parking lot. Instead of correcting Bruce, Van Williams and the stuntmen decided to just let him do his thing. The next day they said to him, "Bruce, why don't you come with us and watch the dailies?"

"Oh yeah, I really want to see how that turned out," Bruce excitedly responded. "That was some of the best stuff I've done."

A big group gathered to watch the unedited footage from the previous day. When Bruce's big scene came up, it was a complete blur. The only way anyone could tell a fight was happening was from the kung fu noises. The stuntmen burst out laughing. Bruce stormed to his dressing room, slammed the door, and refused to come out.

After a couple of hours, Van Williams walked over and knocked on the door. "Bruce, what are you doing in there?"

"I'm very mad," Bruce said. "I'm so upset I don't know what to do. I'm just ruined. I can't do anything right."

"Bruce, this is what we've been trying to tell you. You have to slow it down. You can't do this stuff that you do so fast that the camera can't catch it."

Williams and Lee had a long talk and sorted out what Bruce needed to change. "By God he did slow it down and he really improved what he could do," Williams recalls. "Once he calmed down on film and stopped jumping around on-set, he got along really well with everyone. He was a very loyal friend. He never talked bad about anybody behind their back or anything else."

After the fight choreography, Bruce's next struggle was with the depth of his role. In the first several episodes he was only given a few lines of dialogue. "It's true that Kato is a houseboy of Britt, but as a crime fighter, Kato is an 'active partner' of the Green Hornet and not a 'mute follower,' " Bruce wrote to Dozier. "Jeff Corey agrees and I myself feel that at least an occasional dialogue would certainly make me 'feel' more at home with the fellow players."

He didn't need to convince Dozier, who replied it was Trendle who insisted Kato remain in the background as an ally, not a companion, like Tonto—a silent minority. But Dozier promised he would deal with Trendle and ask the writers to incorporate more material involving Kato, hoping it would offer Lee some satisfaction.

In the episode "The Preying Mantis," the writers created a Kato-centric installment. A Chinese restaurant is the target of a tong (Chinese mafia) protection racket. The show culminates with a contest between the tong leader and Kato, the first time an American TV audience ever had the opportunity to see a kung fu challenge match. The quick fight, lasting only thirty seconds, featured some spectacular flying kicks by Bruce and concluded with a deadly series of body blows that dispatched his enemy. This must have proven particularly satisfying to Bruce, since the tong leader was played by Mako, the Japanese American actor who had snagged the role Bruce coveted in the Oscar-nominated movie *The Sand Pebbles*. For the sequence, Bruce hired his disciple, Dan Inosanto, to double for Mako—the first of many times he would employ one of his students in a TV or movie project.

While "The Preying Mantis" added some depth to Kato's character, it still left something to be desired. Early in the episode, the tong leader ambushes Kato and knocks him head first into a trash can—an indignity Bruce objected to but was overruled by Dozier. Despite this show's focus on Chinatown, the Green Hornet does most of the talking. And in the final scene, everyone gathers for dinner at the restored Chinese restaurant to celebrate—except for Kato. His absence has led some fans to joke that Bruce must have been in back working as a busboy.

The Green Hornet experience taught Bruce that he couldn't rely on Hollywood to give him what he wanted even if he politely asked for it. He started pitching his own episode ideas to Dozier. In one of his plots, *The Cobra from the East*, the Green Hornet is sidelined early by a deadly poison, leaving Kato alone to rampage across town, kicking down doors and beating up bodyguards in search of the cure. His thirteen-page proposal was never used, but he would incorporate elements of it into later projects.

Batman's success turned its two leads, Adam West and Burt Ward, into unlikely sex symbols. Something about its double entendre dialogue, Spandex costumes, and codpieces gave the series an erotic cosplay vibe. The Dynamic Duo were nearly as besieged by groupies as the Beatles. Burt Ward's memoir reads like a collection of *Penthouse Letters*. Adam West's, while more discreet, alludes to how much fun he and the Boy Wonder had on and off set. Between scenes Batman and Robin competed to see who could bed Catwoman or whichever new femme fatale was introduced that week.

While the set of the Green Hornet was by all accounts far less licentious, every week still brought in a new beautiful starlet. On the fifth episode, it was Thordis Brandt, a striking statuesque blonde. Born in West Germany and trained as a nurse in Canada, she moved to Santa Monica and became one of the glamour girls of the Swinging Sixties—playing minor parts as saloon girls, spy vixens, and cocktail waitresses in TV shows like *The Girl from U.N.C.L.E.*, *I Spy*, and *Dragnet*. In the first year of her brief career, she was cast as the mob moll in the *Green Hornet* episode "The Frog Is a Deadly Weapon."

Before appearing on the show, Brandt's agent warned her that she was Van Williams's type. "I walked onto the set and Van, who was so handsome, came over to say hello," Brandt recalls. "I saw Bruce Lee standing off very shyly in the shadows. I walked over and introduced myself because I was really attracted to him. He told me I looked like a goddess. I was dumbstruck because Bruce was absolutely gorgeous!"

According to Brandt, they hit it off immediately and began seeing each other. "He had a magnetism that was indescribable," says Brandt. "Bruce was very quiet and shy but could be very aggressive if he wanted to be. He was a show-off and always wanted to flaunt his body."

One day when Bruce was between scenes on *The Green Hornet*, he called Thordis, who was working at a different soundstage on the 20th Century Fox studio lot. She was playing Amazon #6 on the movie *In Like Flint*, which starred James Coburn.

"Do you want to get lunch at the commissary?" Bruce asked.

"Sure."

Bruce walked over to her soundstage in his black Kato costume. He waved to Thordis and headed over to where she was filming. One of the producers, seeing a Chinese guy in a valet's uniform, intercepted him: "Hey, you are not allowed back here. You're supposed to park around front!"

Thordis ran over and yelled at the producer, "Do you know who he is? He is Kato on *The Green Hornet*. You don't talk to him like that. He could kick your butt!"

Instantly, the producer was all apologies. "I'm so sorry, Mr. Lee. What a terrible mistake! Please accept my apologies." Bruce shrugged and waved off the producer.

Afterward at lunch, Thordis asked Bruce, "Does that crap ever get to you?"

"No, because I know where I am going," Bruce said, tapping a finger to his head. "I'm going this way. They are going back that way."

Thordis and Bruce's liaison lasted for a few months until their pasts caught up with them. Brandt was involved in a tumultuous on-again-off-again relationship with James Arness, the forty-three-year-old, six-foot-seven-inch star of *Gunsmoke*. When he found out she was dating the Chinese actor, he hired private detectives to investigate Bruce Lee. They quickly uncovered he was married with a young child. Arness informed Brandt. She was shocked. Bruce, who didn't wear a wedding ring, had failed to tell her. "Why ruin a good thing?" Thordis ruefully notes. She ended it with Bruce and went back to Arness, whom she eventually married. Bruce didn't tell Linda about the affair, and she never found out.

Part of *The Green Hornet*'s marketing campaign strategy was to introduce Bruce Lee to America as an exotic novelty. The press's initial reaction was to play off the popularity of *Batman* and position Kato as a rival to Robin. "The newest challenge to Robin, the Boy Wonder, is Bruce Lee, a young actor and karate expert who will portray Kato, faithful sidekick of 'The Green Hornet,' " wrote *The Washington Post*. Bruce insisted he would not be portraying Kato as a subservient manservant but as an equal with superior abilities. "The Green Hornet and Kato are a partnership," Bruce said. "Actually, with my background in gung fu, they are making me the weapon. I'll be doing all the fighting. Once in a while the Green Hornet will throw some punches, but when he goes into it, it's the old American swing. I'll do all the chopping and kicking."

The press finally settled on the human-interest angle of Bruce's interracial marriage to Linda and their biracial child. It was less than a year before the Supreme Court's decision in *Loving v. Virginia* (1967) made mixed-race marriage legal across the country. A Chinese husband and a white wife was a nonthreatening novelty the mainstream media could get behind. Some of the headlines for these profiles were: "Bruce Lee: 'Love Knows No

Geography,' " "Bruce Lee: 'Our Mixed Marriage Brought Us a Miracle of Love,' " and "Bruce Lee: 'I Want My Son to Be a Mixed-Up Kid!' "

One of these articles opened with this unintentionally ironic bit of hyperbole: "There is only one thing wrong with Bruce Lee—he's perfect! He's a perfect husband, perfect father, and perfectly cast in the role of Kato." Another puff piece began with a profound question: "How does it happen that two people from the opposite ends of the earth meet, fall in love, establish a true and contented union, and bring up their children as a triumph of human grace?" Yet another focused on the Christ-like child: "Bruce Lee and his wife, Linda, are the parents of one of destiny's children. His name is Brandon; he is Oriental and Occidental; he has eyes like ripe black cherries; his hair is blond; his personality is a fascinating blend of the thoughtfulness of the East and vigor of the West."

The reviews of *The Green Hornet*'s premiere episode, "The Silent Gun," on September 9, 1966, were far less fawning than the pre-publicity. Comparing it harshly to *Batman*, the critics were severe about the decision to treat *The Green Hornet* as a somber drama rather than as a camp comedy. *The New York Times* delivered this cutting assessment: "The adventures of the latest comic strip hero are purposely being played straight rather than for laughs and the show, accordingly, is just sluggish old hat rather than divertingly awful. Van Williams portrays the Hornet as a crime buster serving out a sentence." *Variety* wrote: "*The Green Hornet* is unrelieved straight melodrama with none of the pop gags which, for better or worse, are sprinkled in the *Batman* script and which account for at least a measure of its initial success."

For a brief moment, the show looked like it might succeed, despite the negative reviews. *The Green Hornet*'s ratings on ABC beat its rivals in the same time slot—*The Wild Wild West* (CBS) and *Tarzan* (NBC)—for the first three weeks, but then it quickly slipped behind the competition. "I think there was a great deal of curiosity about it at first, particularly because of the great success of *Batman*," Dozier explained, "and apparently now that the audience has sampled *Green Hornet*, they are more inclined to prefer what they see on *Wild Wild West* and *Tarzan*."

Despite the overall gloom, there was a silver lining for Bruce Lee. Kato proved to be a more popular character than the Green Hornet. His character received way more fan mail from kids, like Ricky McNeece of Clinton, Iowa, who asked for a Kato mask for a school project in the hopes his teacher would give him an "A." Even negative reviews had some positive things to say about Kato's fighting ability: "Those who watched him would bet on Lee to render Cassius Clay senseless if they were put in a room and told that anything goes." More importantly to his future, Bruce and Kato were embraced by the small but growing American martial arts community, who had never before seen their art performed on-screen by one of their own. Overnight, Bruce Lee became the most famous martial artist in the country with profiles in *Black Belt* magazine and invitations to headline karate tournaments—a far cry from the 1964 Long Beach International Karate Championships two years earlier where he was a virtual unknown.

Despite the tepid ratings, ABC did not cancel and replace *The Green Hornet* midseason, but instead let it limp along in the hopes its audience share might improve. For his part, Dozier did everything he could to save the show. He begged ABC to give them an hour block of time. When that failed, he began filming two-part episodes. He also wrote to Trendle asking permission for the Green Hornet and Kato to cross over as "visiting heroes" on *Batman* as a last-ditch gimmick. The two-part telecast was scheduled for March 1 and 2, 1967, because the network's decision about renewing *The Green Hornet* would be made by the end of March.

In the story, Britt Reid visits Gotham City for a publisher's convention where he meets up with Bruce Wayne. As two rich WASP scions, they happen to be old boarding school buddies, but neither knows the other's secret identity. When the Green Hornet and Kato stumble upon a crime involving forged stamps, they swing into action, but Gotham authorities assume the duo is part of the conspiracy. After Batman and Robin confront the Green Hornet and Kato, a big fight ensues until everyone realizes they are on the same side and they join forces to stop the real criminals.

In the original script the Green Hornet and Kato lose the brawl to Batman and Robin. After all, it was their show. But when Bruce read that, he threw the script to the ground and walked off the set. "I'm not going to do that," he declared. "There's no way that I'm going to get into a fight with Robin and lose. That makes me look like an idiot!" His complaint made its way up to Dozier, who came down from his office to hear it out. Bruce was adamant: "There's no way anybody would believe that I would get in a fight with Robin and lose. I refuse to do it. It will make me look like the laughing stock of the world."

Dozier asked Van Williams his opinion. Personally, Williams didn't care if the Green Hornet lost a fight to Batman or not, but he backed up his loyal sidekick: "I agree with Bruce."

"Fine it will be a draw," Dozier decided. "Nobody wins or loses, a Mexican stand-off. Can you live with that, Bruce?"

"Okay," Bruce replied.

Bruce and Burt Ward (Robin) were friends. When they lived in the same apartment complex, Bruce shared some basic kung fu techniques with him. But Bruce heard that Ward was telling people he was a black belt like Bruce, and it offended him. "Bruce was very popular with the kids, and they were asking Robin, 'Can you do that thing that Kato does?' " Van Williams recalls. "And Robin would say, 'Oh, yeah, I'm a black belt. Watch this: EEW-WHA-HA!' and he'd do this little stance, which was a joke."

Before shooting began, Bruce told everyone, "I'm going to light into Robin and show him how it is really done and then we'll see how great a black belt you are, boy!" By the time filming started, Burt Ward was shaking in his Spandex. As an insurance policy, he begged *Batman*'s stuntmen to intervene if Bruce tore into him.

Bruce swaggered onto the set with a stern expression. He silently paced back and forth, refusing to kid around with the crew, which was very unusual. "Bruce was always joking and playing around," Williams says. After some warm-ups, he shifted into a fighting stance, clenched his teeth, squinted his eyes, and stared down Robin from behind his Kato mask. Ward as Robin stood a good distance away and tried to make small talk. Bruce ignored him. Finally, the director shouted, "Action!"

With his killer expression and dead eyes, Bruce inched his way toward his prey. Ward slowly backed away, crying out, "Bruce, remember this is not for real. It's just a show!"

As Kato crowded Robin into a corner, Ward began flapping his elbows and jumping around in a circle. One of the stuntmen in back whispered, "It's the black panther and the yellow chicken."

Hearing that, Bruce burst out laughing. "I couldn't keep a straight face anymore," Bruce recalled. Van Williams, Adam West, and the entire crew howled at the practical joke. Rumors that Burt Ward wet himself are unconfirmed. "Lucky for Robin that it was not for real," Bruce said. "Otherwise, he would have been one dead bird."

When the show aired, the announcer declared it, "A Mexican standoff, a dead heat, a photo finish," but Bruce made sure to adjust the fight choreography so he came off better. After a few exchanges of punches and kicks, the fracas finished with Kato delivering a spinning hook kick to Robin's face that sent him flying over a desk.

The crossover broadcast never generated the volume of fan letters or the bump in ratings that Dozier and Trendle had hoped for. "It was dumb," Van Williams says. "*Batman* was playing the thing for laughs and we were playing it straight and it just didn't work at all." In April 1967, ABC announced it would not renew *The Green Hornet* for a second season.

"Confucius say, '*Green Hornet* to buzz no more,' " Dozier wrote to Bruce at his home in Inglewood. "I'm sorry, as I know you must be. You worked very hard, and very well, and I believe you made a lot of friends for yourself, as well as respectful admirers. It has been a great joy to me, both personally and professionally, to work with you."

Lee graciously replied to Dozier: "I'd like to take this opportunity to thank you personally for all that you've done to start my career in show business. Without you, I would never have thought about being in Hollywood. I've gained tremendous experience from *The Green Hornet* and believe I've improved steadily since the first show—that of minimizing and hacking away the unessential. My attitude in this business is to take things as they are, and to look up to the sky 'with feet firmly on solid ground.' "

And just like that Bruce Lee became that most common of fauna in Southern California: the unemployed actor. "When the series ended I asked myself, 'What the hell do I do now?' "

In the center: Dan Inosanto, Kareem Abdul-Jabbar, and shirtless Bruce Lee. Los Angeles Chinatown class photo, circa 1968. *(David Tadman)*

Mike Stone, Joe Lewis, Bruce Lee, and Ed Parker on the set of *The Wrecking Crew*, summer 1968. *(David Tadman)*

eleven

jeet kune do

With his acting career in doubt, Bruce Lee returned to teaching kung fu. As filming for *The Green Hornet* was winding down, he opened the Los Angeles branch of the Jun Fan Gung Fu Institute in Chinatown at 628 College Street. The open house seminar was held from 8 to 9 p.m. on February 9, 1967. Dan Inosanto—an assistant instructor for Ed Parker who had been training secretly with Bruce for a year—quietly invited a large group of Parker's senior students to the event. For an hour, Bruce explained his philosophy and what he would be teaching. He occasionally would call somebody up to demonstrate one of his points. "You could see his superiority, and it was obvious he was ahead of a whole lot of people," says Bob Bremer, a student of Parker's. "I jumped ship right then."

After the seminar, everyone else jumped ship as well. It caused some hard feelings. "They nicknamed us 'the turncoats,' " says Bremer. The close-knit group of defectors included Dan Lee, Jerry Poteet, Bob Bremer, Larry Hartsell, Richard Bustillo, Pete Jacobs, and Steve Golden. "Parker wasn't thrilled with the situation," says Golden. "But for the last year before I left,

Ed was spending more and more time dealing with Hollywood, serving as Elvis Presley's bodyguard. He was not teaching me. So who left whom?" Bruce named Inosanto his assistant instructor. Dan tried to maintain ties by teaching six days a week for both Parker and Bruce, but after several months it became too much and he joined Bruce full-time.

Like his very first *kwoon* in Seattle, Bruce conceived of his L.A. branch more as an exclusive private club than a commercial school. New students had to be sponsored by an existing member, and the first six months were a tryout. The Chinatown *kwoon* didn't have any signage out front, the windows were covered with the pink window cleaner Glass Wax, the front door was kept locked, and there was a secret knock: three raps, a pause, and then two raps. "I don't want too many in my organization," Bruce explained. "The fewer students I have and the harder it is for anyone to join will give my club more prestige and importance. Like anything else, if it's too popular and too easy to join, people won't think too highly of it."

For the first few months, Bruce ran the school like a boot camp. He focused on physical conditioning: fitness, flexibility, and basic punching and kicking drills. Members trained four times a week. The two-hour sessions were always grueling. Quite a few people quit after a few weeks. "Bruce was testing our sincerity and willingness to train hard," says Dan Lee (no relation). "The fitness program finally eased off at the fourth month, and he began training those who remained."

Bruce's club was the opposite of a strip mall Karate McDojo. There were no uniforms, no ranks, no colored belts, no bowing, and no titles. Everyone was on a first-name basis: Bruce was Bruce; Danny was Danny. Partly as a joke, but mainly to dramatize his philosophy in physical form, Bruce erected on a table near the front door a miniature tombstone inscribed with the words: "In memory of the once fluid man, crammed and distorted by the classical mess."

Classes, which averaged twelve students, started with stretching and calisthenics before proceeding to basic techniques: footwork, punching, kicking, trapping, and a lot of questions and answers. "He emphasized footwork, footwork, footwork, and more footwork," says Jerry Poteet. "He was trying to get us to be more mobile." The second half of the two-hour classes was spent on hard sparring. "It was always intense and combative," says Bustillo.

During breaks, he would show his students 16mm films of classic boxing matches, slowing it down during key moments. "Okay, now, watch where the punch is coming from," Bruce would narrate. "It's not the hand or the arm, it's the waist, and it's BOOM!" Classes often incorporated music. Joe Torrenueva, who worked as a hairstylist for Jay Sebring, would play his Latin conga drums to demonstrate rhythm and timing. Bruce was very hands-on. He made sure everyone was doing everything correctly—it had to be precise. He examined every student carefully, tested and recorded their progress in a notebook. After a few months, he handed out typewritten notes with his observations and a supplemental training program for each of them. "To my surprise, they were all different," says Dan Lee.

Bruce's goal was to improve his students' skill level to the point where they were good enough to spar with him. Once this was accomplished, he turned over most of the day-to-day teaching at the school to Inosanto, who was better with larger groups, and shifted to private lessons with a select group of senior students—Ted Wong, Dan Lee, Jerry Poteet, Herb Jackson, Mito Uyehara, Bob Bremer, and Peter Chin. Ted Wong, who spoke Cantonese, became Bruce's protégé. Herb Jackson fixed the equipment and served Bruce his tea. Bruce would wait until Jackson left the room and then joke, "I always wanted a Caucasian houseboy."

Every Wednesday evening, the crew converged in Bruce's kitchen at his Culver City rental home. They were greeted by his friendly Great Dane, Bobo—a slobbering, clumsy 150-pound dog who knocked down anything in his way, including chairs, lamps, and even four-year-old Brandon. Neither Bruce nor Linda could control him. "We even had him at a training school," Linda smiled. "He's the only dog I know that ever flunked out."

The ranch-style house had a great room with a high ceiling that was so big Bruce converted half of it into a gym with a speed bag, heavy bag, and other specialized equipment. After warming up on the bags inside the house and covering fundamentals like broken rhythm and bridging the gap, the crew headed outside to the fenced-in backyard to spar. Bruce was one of the first martial arts instructors to introduce protective gear—boxing gloves, headgear, chest protectors, and shin guards. In traditional karate dojos, students would spar bare-fisted and stop their punches an inch before making contact. Bruce believed "touch sparring" was unrealistic, calling it "swimming on dry land," and insisted on full contact. "Bruce's way of training was overpowering," recalls Mito Uyehara. "When he tired me out, he would then pick on Ted Wong. Bruce would never quit until we did. He enjoyed seeing both Wong and myself giving up."

Bruce didn't charge any money for these backyard sessions, because they weren't really lessons. He was experimenting with new methods, tactics, and techniques to create his own system of martial arts, and his students were, in their own estimation, his "kicking dummies."

On July 9, 1967, Bruce gave his new approach to the martial arts a Cantonese name, *Jeet Kune Do*. He came up with the Chinese term first and then asked a UCLA linguistics professor to translate it for him into English—"stop fist way" or, more broadly, "the way of the intercepting fist."

"What does that mean?" Dan Inosanto asked Bruce as they drove down the highway.

"There are three opportunities to strike an opponent: before he attacks, during his attack, or after he attacks," Bruce explained. "Jeet Kune Do means to intercept before he attacks—to intercept his movement, his thoughts, or his motive."

Appropriately for a Eurasian born in America and raised in British colonial Hong Kong, Jeet Kune Do was a hybrid system, mixing East and West. "You have to go outside your environment to achieve something better," he told Dan. "Some people will say, 'Hey, that's a Korean kick. We can't use that kick.' But I don't care. It all belongs to mankind."

From boxing Bruce took its superior footwork and from kung fu its kicks. But what made his fusion unique, rather than just another kickboxing amalgamation, were the major elements he adapted from fencing. His brother Peter, whom Bruce revered and envied, was an elite fencer in high school and taught Bruce some of the basics. But it wasn't until Bruce moved to America that he took the sport seriously. "I can remember at the beginning showing him the art of fencing and he could get nowhere near me with a sword," recalls Peter. "When he came back in 1965 for my father's funeral, we went at it again and I could not touch him. That's the way Bruce was: always secretly practicing." Bruce also became fascinated with fencing theory. His library contained sixty-eight books on fencing—his favorites were by Aldo Nadi, Julio Martinez Castello, and Roger Crosnier. The term *Jeet Kune Do* or "stop fist way" came from the fencing technique "stop hit." In his notes, Bruce described Jeet Kune Do as "fencing without a sword."

Unlike boxers, who place their weak side forward, Bruce used a fencer's on-guard position: strong side crouching forward, right hand extended as if holding a sword, and left heel raised and cocked to explode off the blocks when bridging the gap. His favorite attack was the finger jab to the eyes—the technique he used against Wong Jack Man. "Faced with the choice of socking your opponent in the head and poking him in the eyes, you go for the eyes every time," Bruce wrote in his notes. "Like a fencer's sword that is always in line, the leading finger jab is a constant threat to your opponent." In Wing Chun, Bruce had been taught to fight in close and use trapping techniques (*chi sao*—sticky hands) to control his opponent. With Jeet Kune Do, he stepped back to a fencer's distance and lunged forward to attack before leaping backward to safety.

Jeet Kune Do was Bruce Lee's personal expression of the martial arts. Like a custom-made suit, he tailored it to take advantage of his innate aggressiveness, preternatural reflexes, and uncanny ability to read an opponent. "Sparring with Bruce was so frustrating because he would be on you before you could even react," says Jhoon Rhee, the Father of American Tae Kwon Do. One evening when Bob Bremer complained that Bruce was simply too fast for him, Bruce explained it wasn't an issue of speed: "There's a split second when you are not with me and somehow I seem to know when that is." Jesse Glover, his first student in America, says, "The thing that made him so effective was the fact that he could pick up a potential movement before it happened. Many of his advanced concepts were based on this type of detection. The question is how much of his thinking at this stage of his development is transferable to the average person." Bruce's problem as a teacher was that he could pass on his ideas, but not his talent, and you needed both for Jeet Kune Do to work.

Bruce knew by heart the "Ave Maria" and other Catholic prayers. He could recite long biblical passages from memory. Despite his resistance, the Catholic Brothers at La Salle had pounded Christianity into his head. But unlike his mother, he was not a believer. He was an atheist—perhaps because he could not tolerate the idea of an authority higher than his own. When asked by *Esquire* magazine if he believed in God, Bruce replied, "Ah, to be perfectly frank, I really do not." If his friends brought up the subject, he would joke, "I don't believe in anything. I believe in sleeping." He was practical by nature, a bit of a materialist—all traits in the Hong Kong tradition.

Yet Bruce had a spiritual, even a mystical, side to him. He was a seeker and a bibliophile. He haunted the philosophy section of bookstores looking for answers. One of his early career dreams, before he realized he could make a living as a kung fu instructor, was to own a used bookstore. His personal library would grow to more than 2,500 books. "Bruce carried a book with him wherever he went," says Linda. "I frequently saw him sitting quietly reading while there was household uproar all around him—children crying, doors slamming, conversations taking place everywhere. Bruce was able to read a book while performing a series of strenuous exercises." In his notepads, Bruce copied down passages from his favorite authors: Plato, Hume, Descartes, and Aquinas from the Western tradition; Lao-tzu, Chuang-tzu, Miyamoto Musashi, and Alan Watts from the Eastern.

One of his most important influences was the renegade Indian mystic Jiddu Krishnamurti. Selected at age fourteen by the occultist Theosophical Society as the predestined "World Teacher," Krishnamurti was groomed to become its leader and "direct the evolution of mankind towards perfection." In 1929 at the age of thirty-four, he shocked his adoptive cult by renouncing his role as the World Teacher, arguing that religious doctrines and organizations stood in the way of real truth. "I maintain that truth is a pathless land, and you cannot approach it by any religion. A belief is purely an individual matter, and you cannot and must not organize it. If you do, it becomes dead, crystallized; it becomes a creed, a sect, a religion, to be imposed on others."

Krishnamurti's teachings reinforced Lee's instinctive rejection of universal truths and traditions in favor of individual ones. In a 1971 TV interview with Pierre Berton, Bruce adapted Krishnamurti's words to the martial arts: "I do not believe in styles anymore. Styles separate men, because they have their own doctrine and then the doctrine becomes the gospel truth. But if you do not have styles, if you just say, 'Here I am as a human being. How can I express myself totally and completely?' Now this way you will not create a style—because a style is a crystallization—this way is a process of continuing growth."

The irony was Bruce had created a distinct style of martial arts. His response was to insist that Jeet Kune Do was his personal system, and his students needed to follow their own path. He was a guide, not a teacher. "Jeet Kune Do is merely a name used, a boat to get one across the river," Bruce said, "and once across, is to be discarded, and not to be carried on one's back." Employing the paradoxical structure of Zen koans, he called Jeet Kune Do "the style of no style" and made his school slogan: "Using No Way As Way; Having No Limitation As Limitation."

"It was the sixties," Dan Inosanto jokes. "Everybody talked that way."

Bruce was not interested in politics but he sensed the countercultural mood of the country and applied it to the martial arts. "Everyone was questioning our government. We didn't believe they were leading us down the right path," Inosanto explains. "Bruce was antiestablishment—the voice of the sixties. He questioned everything. He said, 'If you don't question it, you can't grow.' "

Over time, Jeet Kune Do became less about specific stances or fighting techniques and more about a philosophical approach to the martial arts and life. Question tradition but be practical: "Adapt what is useful, reject what is useless." Find your personal truth: "Add what is specifically your own." And continue to evolve. "He once told me that Jeet Kune Do in 1968 will be different in 1969," recalls Inosanto. "And 1969 Jeet Kune Do will be different than 1970." In contrast to Chinese Confucian reverence for the past and deference to the collective, Bruce drew deeply from the American ideal of individualism, philosophy of pragmatism, and focus on the future—in order to form a more perfect person.

Fists and feet were weapons to use physically against an opponent and spiritually against one's own ego, greed, and anger—a means of self-defense and self-enlightenment. "In this respect, Jeet Kune Do is directed toward oneself," Bruce said. Krishnamurti stated as his goal, "I am concerning myself with only one essential thing: to set man free." Similarly, Bruce declared, "The final aim of Jeet Kune Do is toward personal liberation. It points the way to individual freedom and maturity."

When it came to training, Bruce Lee was on the cutting edge of the fitness revolution. He was the first martial artist to train like a modern athlete. At that time, traditional stylists thought it was sufficient to repeat basic techniques as their primary form of exercise. It was a widespread view. Professional football players in the 1960s considered weightlifting to be dangerous and detrimental—many NFL teams banned it. Bruce recognized that strength and conditioning were crucial to becoming the ultimate fighter.

After his exhausting fight with Wong Jack Man, Bruce redoubled his efforts to improve his endurance. "An out-of-condition athlete, when tired, cannot perform well," Bruce explained. "You can't throw your punches or kicks properly and you can't even get away from your opponent." From boxing, he borrowed skipping rope and roadwork. Every morning he would run four or five miles through his neighborhood with his Great Dane, Bobo. "Jogging is not only a form of exercise to me," Bruce said. "It is also a form of relaxation. It is my own hour every morning when I can be alone with my thoughts."

Since he was a teenager, Bruce had lifted weights, but he didn't become serious about it until his Oakland years. His students James Yimm Lee and Allen Joe were pioneers in the early era of bodybuilding and showed him basic lifts and general exercises with weights. Bruce was interested in strength not size; he wanted to be ripped not bulky, recognizing that speed is more important to power than mass. "James and I were into heavy weight training," Allen Joe says, "but Bruce went with lighter weights with higher repetitions." In his garage, Bruce installed an isometric machine, squat rack, bench press, dumbbells, and grip machine for his forearms.

Bruce was a fanatic about training and he had the free time to do it. As one of his L.A. students enviously noted, "To Bruce every day seemed like a weekend because he never had a steady job like most of us." From Monday to Sunday he routinely did the same thing: He jogged in the morning and then sharpened his martial tools with five hundred punches, five hundred finger jabs, and five hundred kicks. In the afternoon, he spent time in his library—reading philosophy books, calling up his agent or his pals. In the early evening he lifted weights three nights per week.

Even when he wasn't officially training he was training. While watching TV, he curled dumbbells. While driving his car, he would repeatedly punch a small *makiwara* board—much to the distress and anxiety of his passengers. He turned every activity into martial arts play. "When I'm putting on my pants," Bruce said, "I'm doing a balancing act."

All of this exercise put a tremendous strain on his fragile frame. He spent hours every week practicing a rapid sidekick even when his knees were hurting. As a result, his knees always made a clicking sound when he whipped his foot out. He sweated profusely as if constantly on the verge of overheating. "Bruce Lee always seemed to be wet. Even in an air-conditioned room, as soon as he gesticulated, he would quickly perspire," says Mito Uyehara. "One night he rode his exercycle for 45 minutes without stopping. When he got through he was completely drenched. Even the floor beneath him was so wet that it had to be mopped right away."

To help his body recover, he began using an electrical muscle stimulator machine. Karate champion Mike Stone, who learned about the device while teaching karate to Los Angeles Rams football players, introduced Bruce to it. "It's minor electric shock treatment that you put on your muscles to increase their pulse and repetition," Mike Stone says. "The NFL used electro-stim machines to rebuild injured areas. Bruce believed it would enhance his skill and ability. But he went over the top. One to ten, he would crank the dial up to seven or eight, enough to curl his hair." Bruce continued to use the electro-stim machine for the rest of his life—freaking out friends and colleagues, particularly the Chinese in Hong Kong. "When I got to the door of his office, I didn't dare go in, because he was wearing a headband with a bunch of electrical cables attached to it," recalls Bolo Yeung, the beefy bad guy in *Enter the Dragon*. "My immediate reaction was 'Are you crazy?' "

Bruce was equally adventurous in his diet. He believed in the curative powers of ginseng and queen bee honey. He subscribed to all the fitness magazines of the day—*Strength & Health*, *Ironman*, *Muscle Builder*, *Mr. America*, *Muscular Development*, and *Muscle Training Illustrated*—and purchased many of the faddish fitness supplements they advertised. Several times a day he took a high-protein drink made up of Rheo Blair Protein Powder, ice water, powdered milk, eggs, eggshells, bananas, vegetable oil, peanut flour, and chocolate ice cream. He haunted health food stores and bought tons of vitamins, in particular anything promoted by Jack LaLanne. Along with protein smoothies, he also blended raw hamburger beef and drank it. "The thing that really scared me was when he was drinking beef blood," recalls movie star James Coburn.

His obsession with training and nutrition was not only about performance but also aesthetics. His passion may have been the martial arts but his profession was acting. At that time if you had a barrel chest like William Holden or Robert Mitchum, you qualified as a hunk. (Once when asked how he maintained his then envied physique, Mitchum replied, "I breathe in and out all of the time. And once in awhile I grudgingly lift something—like a chair.") Bruce wanted to play heroic leading roles, and he knew, as an Asian man with a shorter frame and slighter build, he needed to outwork his white counterparts to create a musculature that immediately conveyed power in the visual medium of movies.

"He was a little pudgy and had a little baby fat on him when I first met him," recalls Van Williams, the star of *The Green Hornet*. "He didn't have muscle definition. He wanted that badly. That's what he really started to work on once he got the role of Kato." From little definition in *The Green Hornet* (1966), he created a hypertrophied body that looked like it was sculpted out of marble in *Way of the Dragon* (1972). "From the Oakland period to the days in Hollywood when I went to see him, his body changed," says George Lee, one of his Oakland students. "He was much more developed and it was amazing he could develop a body as quick as he did."

The change in his physique was so dramatic it has led some to speculate about steroid use. While it is possible he tried them, there is no evidence to suggest regular use. Bruce loved to show off all his new experiments, even cow's blood, but no one recalls him ever mentioning steroids. If he used them, he kept it secret, and there was no reason back then to be ashamed of steroids. They had been approved by the FDA for human use in 1958 and were considered safe until the 1980s. Anabolic steroids dramatically increase muscle mass and as a result cause large gains in weight. But Bruce's weight remained steady—never rising above 145 pounds. He was shredded, not pumped like Arnold Schwarzenegger. His incredible muscular definition was the result of constant training and cutting his subcutaneous body fat down to almost zero.

American audiences may have shrugged at *The Green Hornet*, but it was adored by the martial arts community, who claimed Bruce Lee as its first breakout star. Mito Uyehara, the publisher of *Black Belt* magazine, quickly realized the benefit of associating his magazine with Bruce's celebrity. In October 1967, Mito published a glowing profile: "A vibrant personality with piercing black eyes and a rather handsome face full of animation, unlike the inscrutable poker-face expressions Westerners usually associate with the Oriental." For Bruce's part, he viewed *Black Belt*, the leading martial arts magazine in the country, as an excellent platform to promote himself and his message: "Classical methods, which I consider a form of paralysis, only solidify and condition what was once fluid." As their mutually beneficial friendship deepened, Mito touted his talents as an instructor.

One day in 1968 the offices of *Black Belt* came to a screeching halt as the best college basketball player in the country walked into the display room to browse over some books. Standing at seven-foot-two-inches, his name was Lew Alcindor, although he would later change it to Kareem Abdul-Jabbar. Alcindor had just returned to Los Angeles from New York to finish his senior year at UCLA. In New York he had studied Aikido and wanted to continue his training.

"Do you have any books on Tai Chi?" he asked.

"Sorry, we don't," Mito answered. "But if you would like to know about any Chinese martial art, I know someone who can help you."

"Who's that?"

"Have you ever heard of Bruce Lee?" Mito asked. "He was Kato on TV's *Green Hornet* series."

"No, I never watch those shows."

That night Mito drove over to Bruce's house to tell him the big news: "Guess who is going to be your next student?"

"Who?"

"Lew Alcindor!" Mito exclaimed as if unwrapping an expensive gift.

"Who's that?"

"What? Everyone knows Lew Alcindor," he said, incredulous. "He's the most sought-after college athlete in the country today."

"How would I know him?" Bruce shrugged. "Shit, I don't know anything about basketball, baseball, or football. They only time I ever got close to an American athlete was when I had to walk across the football field in college." Bruce paused for a moment and stared at Mito. "What's so special about this Alcindor guy?"

"He'll be the highest paid athlete coming out of college," Mito replied. "For someone that tall, he's supposed to be real smooth and quick."

"How tall is he?"

"He claims to be seven-foot-two but many think he's closer to seven-foot-four."

Suddenly five-foot-seven Bruce pulled out a chair and jumped on it. "Linda, get a measuring tape," Bruce called out. She held it to the floor as Bruce stretched the tape until he came to seven-foot-two. He dropped the tape but left his hand extended in midair, eyeing the distance from the floor to his hand.

"Hell, he's not that tall," he scoffed. "I'd like to meet him. I wonder how it feels to spar a guy that tall. Can you arrange for me to see him?"

About a week later, Lew and Bruce got together. Bruce was stunned to see what seven-foot-two looked like in the flesh. He was so awed by Alcindor's height that he kept muttering, "Boy, I never realized anyone could be so tall."

Alcindor told him he was interested in Tai Chi. "Forget Tai Chi. It's for old men in parks," Bruce declared. "You should learn Jeet Kune Do."

Alcindor lost all interest in Tai Chi and became Bruce's private student during his final year at UCLA. "I saw Bruce as a renegade Taoist priest," says a chuckling Abdul-Jabbar. "He was into spirituality and it was heavily influenced by Taoism. But you couldn't put him in that box—he was beyond that. We worked on specific things, footwork for example, how to use the dummy or hitting the bag."

They also sparred. "Lew was too slow. He could never touch me," Bruce told Mito. "But he has such long arms and legs, it was impossible for me to hit his face or body. The only target open was his lead knee and shin. In a real fight, I would have to bust his legs." Bruce was amazed by Alcindor's physical abilities: "The sonovagun has powerful legs. He kicks like a mule. And he sure can leap. He jumped toward a basketball rim and hit it with a front kick."

When the Milwaukee Bucks drafted Alcindor in 1969 for $1.5 million, he went to Bruce for help. He wanted to add thirty more pounds of muscle to compete against bulkier centers like Wilt Chamberlain. Bruce put him on a special diet and gave him a weightlifting program. "Being in the best shape you can be will absolutely enhance all aspects of your game on the basketball court," Bruce told Lew.

After Alcindor moved away, Bruce stayed in touch. In the back of his mind, Bruce kept imagining how to choreograph a fight scene with Big Lew on film. "With me fighting a guy over seven feet tall, the Chinese fans would eat it up," Bruce told Mito. "It would be something they've never seen before. I can picture their reactions when I do a sidekick straight to his face."

Although Bruce's role as Kato gave him Hollywood cachet in the martial arts community, the most esteemed martial artists of that era were the karate point fighting champions. In these contests held across the country, blows were only allowed above the waist, not to the legs or groin. Attacks to the torso could be full force, but anything to the head was halted before making contact. Contestants could be penalized for striking too hard to the face. Once a competitor landed a punch or kick to the torso or face, the judge jumped in, separated the fighters, declared a point, and then restarted the contest.

Bruce had no interest in competing under point fighting's restrictive rules, what he called a "one touch and run game." He grew up fighting in kung fu challenge matches where contestants pounded on each other until somebody was unconscious or verbally submitted. But to gain the respect of the martial arts community he needed to associate himself in some way with the karate champions.

Bruce Lee was introduced to Mike Stone at the 1964 Long Beach International Karate Championships after Stone beat Chuck Norris and won the tournament. When Bruce opened his Chinatown school in 1967, he invited Stone to visit. After demonstrating the basic concepts and techniques of Jeet Kune Do, Bruce said to Mike, "You know this school is pretty far away from where you live. Maybe you could just come over to my house. I have a little gym set up. We can work out together in the backyard. Say once a week or something like that."

Mike was interested but hesitant. He had been losing recently and was keen to pick up some new tricks to help him start winning again. Like every good-looking guy in L.A., he was also eager to get into the movie business and viewed Bruce as a good connection. But Stone was one of the country's three best karate fighters—along with Joe Lewis and Chuck Norris—and he didn't want anyone to think Kato was better than him. Knowing Stone couldn't publicly accept a formal teacher-student relationship, Bruce carefully phrased it as "working out together" rather than "private lessons." With that face-saving understanding, Mike finally agreed.

In their first session on September 30, 1967, Bruce sought to establish his superiority. He challenged Mike to an arm wrestling contest. Then he asked Mike to hold the heavy bag. "Stand with your back to it, and I'll kick it," Bruce said. "I want to show you how much power I have." It continued in this vein for the rest of the night.

Mike kept coming back. There were seven lessons over a six-month period. Bruce admired Stone's skill at karate forms (*katas*) and taught him a Wing Chun form. They also studied old boxing films and books about the martial arts. Stone's favorite part of each four-to-five-hour session were the conversations the two men held over a bowl of noodles.

Interestingly, they never sparred. Bruce frequently sparred with his other students but not Mike. Instead these two competitive and proud men worked out together, while simultaneously studying each other—looking for weaknesses, strategizing how to best the other. "When you stand with another man or watch him, me as a fighter, I'm already picking him apart," Stone says. "In my mind, I am looking for the opportunities, for the openings, for the habitual things that he does."

Both of them were certain they could beat the other guy. From Stone's perspective, Bruce was a talented martial artist with some interesting ideas, but not a real fighter because he didn't compete in karate point fighting tournaments. In the opposite corner, Bruce didn't think much of karate point fighters, because karate was a derivative and inferior style of kung fu and point fighting was not much more than an aggressive game of tag. But neither of them put their certainty to the test, because there was no upside. If Mike won, Bruce would stop training him and Mike would lose a useful Hollywood connection. If Bruce won, Mike would stop training with him and Bruce would lose a high-profile, reputation-enhancing "student."

Despite their egos, the sessions were a lot of fun and filled with laughter. "Bruce was like a kid as far as his enthusiasm and bubbly personality were concerned," recalls Stone. "He was always clowning around and cracking jokes and just keeping everybody in good spirits. He was great that way."

While training with Bruce, Stone became increasingly interested in translating his popularity as a champion karate fighter into a career in entertainment. To that end, he formed a nightclub act with Joe Lewis, the top heavyweight point fighter, and Bob Wall, who would later play the bad guy O'Hara in *Enter the Dragon* (1973). At the end of the act, Lewis and Stone would give a karate demonstration. One evening, Lewis noticed that Stone's style of fighting had changed.

"I'm working out with this Chinese guy named Bruce Lee," Stone explained. "He wants to work with you. You should go down and start taking lessons with him."

Joe Lewis first ran into Bruce Lee at *Black Belt*'s offices. Lewis, who also had a big but fragile ego, was there to complain about how *Black Belt* had misspelled his name in the previous issue. As he was leaving, Bruce chased him into the parking lot: "Ah, Joe, Joe, Joe, let me talk to you for a second." For the next thirty minutes, Bruce launched into a discourse about why Jeet Kune Do was superior to Lewis's style and how it could help him improve his results in karate tournaments. Lewis, who was already a champion, stood there politely and ignored everything Bruce said. "I was an American fighter and didn't think much of kung fu fighters, because most of them didn't fight. Instead, they indulged in constant practice of their many long forms, painting the air with their fingers," Lewis explains. "Also I didn't respect little guys."

Despite this bad first impression, Stone was able to convince Lewis that it was worth his while to train with Bruce. Like Stone, Lewis also wanted to get into the movie business. He called up Bruce and arranged for a lesson on January 25, 1968. "Once a week I would go and take a private lesson with Bruce and spend the whole rest of the week working on what he was showing me. And it actually in a great way improved my fighting style," says Lewis. "I was already a two time national champion before I started working with Bruce. He helped accelerate my career. In 1968, when we were working out extensively, I won eleven consecutive Grand Championships without a loss. What Bruce showed me enabled me to do that. He was a true master and master teacher. But I'd say his main quality was his charm. He could charm anybody."

The success of the 1964 Long Beach International Karate Championships led to an explosion of karate tournaments across the country. After *The Green Hornet*, all of the promoters wanted Kato as their headline performer. For the 1967 Long Beach Championships, Ed Parker featured Kato extensively in his advertisements. Over ten thousand spectators came—a record crowd at a karate tournament—many of them young kids who had dragged their fathers along. After Bruce's demonstration (one-inch punch, closing the gap, sparring with full protective gear), the crowd gave him a huge standing ovation and then about half the audience left. They weren't interested in karate, just in Kato.

At a tournament in Fresno he was mobbed by riotous fans, who scratched, kicked, and gouged to get near him. The experience terrified him. There were so many people he felt powerless to protect himself. "A surprising number were young women," Linda notes.

At the 1967 All American Karate Championships, Bruce had a ringside seat in Madison Square Garden for one of the seminal point fighting contests: middleweight Chuck Norris versus heavyweight Joe Lewis for the grand championship. Like Lewis and most American karate stars of the era, Chuck Norris began studying the martial arts when he joined the military and was stationed in East Asia. Norris, who grew up with an alcoholic father, was nonathletic, scholastically mediocre, and debilitatingly shy as a child. The martial arts gave him a sense of structure, discipline, and self-confidence, and he threw himself into competitions with a singularity of focus.

The introverted Norris wore an all-white karate gi with a black belt. The brash Joe Lewis was in a white top and black karate pants with a red belt. They faced each other in a horse stance, left legs forward and fists at their waists. For the first few seconds the only movement was Norris shifting his shoulders from left to right. As soon as Lewis raised his left foot to feint a kick, Norris leapt forward with a sidekick that Lewis blocked. Over the next ten seconds, Lewis slowly inched toward Norris, backing him to the edge of the mat. Lewis suddenly jumped at Norris with a sidekick that Norris blocked. Norris immediately countered with a sidekick of his own followed by a punch and another sidekick that landed on Lewis's torso. The judge scored a point to Norris, who held off Lewis for the rest of the match to eke out a one-point victory.

When the tournament ended at 11 p.m., Chuck Norris and Bruce Lee were introduced to each other. As they headed to the main lobby, they ran into a horde of fans waiting to pounce and were forced to make a hasty exit through a side door. After discovering they were staying at the same hotel, they walked back together, talking the entire time about the martial arts and their philosophies. Norris was exhausted—he had fought thirteen matches in the past eleven hours—but the conversation was so engaging he followed Bruce up to his room where they began working out and exchanging techniques. "The next time I looked at my watch, it was 7:00 a.m.! We had worked out together for seven hours!" recalls Norris. "Bruce was so dynamic that it had seemed like only twenty minutes to me."

As Norris left the room for some much-needed sleep, Bruce said, "When we get back to Los Angeles, let's start working out together."

On October 20, 1967, Norris began training with Bruce in the secluded backyard of his modest home in Culver City. Because Norris was, like Mike Stone, sensitive about status, he would later insist that these were "workouts" rather than "private lessons"—two equals exchanging techniques rather than a teacher-student or coach-fighter relationship. "Bruce didn't believe in high kicks. He kicked only below the waist. I finally convinced him that it was important to be versatile enough to kick anywhere. Within six months he could kick with precision, power, and speed to any area of the body," Norris claimed. "In return, he taught me some kung-fu techniques, including linear or straight punches that I was able to use in my repertoire." (In fact, Bruce learned how to high kick as a teenager in Hong Kong; Norris may have helped refine his technique.)

One of Norris's most vivid memories was of a kicking bag shaped like a man in Bruce's garage. "Kick the guy," Bruce urged. "Kick him in the head."

"Well, I don't know," Chuck demurred. "My pants are pretty tight."

Bruce kept at Chuck until he finally gave in. He threw a high kick and ripped his pants all the way up the back. They fell down to his ankles. He reached down to pull them up as Linda walked in. "I had to go home hanging onto my pants," Norris recalled. "I haven't worn anything but double knit since then!"

Bruce continued to give demonstrations and appear as the headliner at karate tournaments across the country. He became close friends with Jhoon Rhee and attended his Washington, D.C., championships every year. "In 1967, we had 8,000 audience members, an unheard of number," recalled

Rhee. "Bruce really helped me gather the crowds." Rhee was so thankful for Bruce's help over the years, he invited Bruce to join him for an all-paid martial arts demonstration tour of the Dominican Republic in February 1970.

All of these free trips expanded Bruce's horizons. And his high-profile private students enhanced his reputation. But neither the tournament promoters nor the karate champions were paying Bruce. His Chinatown school was, at best, a break-even operation, and he was finding it difficult to land another lucrative acting gig. He and his family had grown used to a certain lifestyle during the flush *Green Hornet* period, and now he was struggling to maintain it. Bruce Lee desperately needed another source of income.

Bruce Lee sipping a Presidente beer in the Dominican Republic, 1970. *(David Tadman)*

Meeting James Coburn at Hong Kong's Kai Tak Airport, April 1973. *(David Tadman)*

twelve

sifu to the stars

The popularity of Kato as a character allowed Bruce to supplement his income with paid appearances across the country. He was invited to perform at fairs, malls, and public parks. He appeared at store openings and rode on floats, often in Kato's dark suit, chauffeur's cap, and black mask. His asking price quickly rose to $4,000 for an afternoon's visit. But after *The Green Hornet* was canceled, big-money invites for Kato slowly dried up.

As opportunities to monetize Kato appeared to be ending, several businessmen approached Bruce with an offer to open a nationwide franchise of "Kato Karate Schools." They would fund it, and he would add his name, prestige, and expertise to the chain. It was his college career dream served on a silver platter. Instead of spending years adding new schools one city at a time, he would instantly have an empire.

The hitch was it went against everything he had come to believe about the martial arts. Jeet Kune Do was supposed to be the physical expression of one's individuality in combat, not hamburgers to be homogenized for mass consumption. From the uniforms to the uniform curriculum, Bruce hated everything about Karate McDojos. He only liked to teach small groups of highly talented and motivated students—mostly so they could help him get better. He also knew from trying to balance three schools in Los Angeles, Oakland, and Seattle how much time and effort a nationwide chain would consume. It would effectively end his acting career and turn him into a corporate executive.

And yet it was a lot of money—enough, perhaps, to secure him and his family financially for life. He tortured over the decision before finally turning it down. "I could have made a fortune," he explained to friends. "But I didn't want to prostitute my art for the sake of money." It was a huge gamble on Hollywood, made at a moment when his prospects didn't look good. But Bruce had an alternative strategy that fit with his personal philosophy and would also advance his acting career. Instead of turning his art into a mass-market commodity for Kato-loving suburban teens, he would craft it into a boutique luxury item for celebrities.

Jay Sebring, hairstylist to the stars, was the key to his plans. Seeing how Sebring had fancied up a two-dollar haircut and sold it to the famous for fifty bucks, Bruce realized he could do the same with private kung fu lessons. He asked Sebring to speak to his celebrity clients. An obscure Chinese actor didn't have the juice to connect with Hollywood's elite. He needed Sebring, who whispered in their ears as he clipped their bangs, to vouch for him.

As soon as Bruce and his family moved to Los Angeles in mid-March 1966, two months before filming started on *The Green Hornet*, he began giving Sebring private kung fu lessons. In return Sebring helped him put together a marketing list. "I'll be giving private lessons before the series starts," Bruce wrote to one of his Oakland students. "The prospective students are so far Steve McQueen, Paul Newman, James Garner, and Vic Damone. The fee will be around $25 an hour [$190 in 2017 dollars]."

Despite Sebring's best efforts, there were no takers. Nobody in the movie industry had ever heard of Bruce Lee or kung fu. As filming began on *The Green Hornet*, Bruce focused on the all-consuming task at hand and let the idea of becoming *sifu* to the stars slip to the backburner. Maybe Kato would be his ticket to fame, fortune, and a fabulous film career. Once Dozier informed him that "*Green Hornet* to buzz no more," Bruce's spirits collapsed. He realized he needed to make some serious decisions, but he was uncertain what to do.

One day he dropped by Dozier's offices to seek advice about his stalled acting career. He ran into Charles Fitzsimons, the co-producer of *The Green Hornet*.

"You finding any acting work?" Fitzsimons asked.

"Nothing," Bruce said, sitting down. "I'm worried."

"Why don't you use your talent to teach celebrities kung fu?"

"I tried to get some clients before *The Green Hornet*," Bruce said. "But no one was interested."

"How much were you asking?"

"$25 an hour. Was that too much?"

"It was too little," Charles said. "You are Kato now. You've got a screen credit. You should be charging $50."

"Man, you are crazy!" Bruce exclaimed.

"If you sell a hot dog for $2, nobody will think it is special, but if you charge $8.50, people are going to think it must be the best hot dog in the world, and they will buy it if they can afford it."

"Who will spend that kind of money on kung fu?"

"Your potential clients are all the writers, actors, directors, and producers in this town suffering from middle-aged, macho syndrome. Rich guys who want to appear tough and virile. They've got money to burn, and if you don't take it, they'll spend it learning karate from someone else."

"I don't know," Bruce said. "You really think they'd pay $50 an hour?"

"You have to charge an outrageous figure, because that is the only thing that will impress them."

On February 29, 1968, Bruce went out and printed up new business cards: Bruce Lee, Jeet Kune Do, Professional Consultation and Instruction: $150 per Hour, Non-Professional Tuition: $500 for Ten Sessions. He handed Jay Sebring the cards and asked him to repitch his clients. Within weeks, Kato from *The Green Hornet* landed his first celebrity student, Vic Damone.

Vic Damone was a handsome Italian crooner in the mold of Frank Sinatra and Dean Martin. A big band singer, actor, and television presenter, Damone was best known for songs such as "On the Street Where You Live" from *My Fair Lady* and "You're Breaking My Heart." Like most other Italian boys from Brooklyn, Damone had boxed a little in high school. Now everyone was talking about karate. Elvis Presley was high kicking onstage between songs. Sebring, who cut Damone's hair, touted Bruce's talents as a self-defense instructor, and Damone decided to give him a try.

Sebring and Bruce drove to Las Vegas to see Damone sing at the Sands. Damone booked them a suite and comped their stay. In the afternoons all three of them worked out together on the Sands's empty stage. As Bruce covered basic techniques, he explained his three-part strategy for combat. "If someone confronts you, first you stun him with a shot. Boom! Now, if he comes at you again, then you cripple him by breaking his kneecaps. If he still continues, then you go for the throat and kill him. So you stun, you cripple, and then you kill."

Damone was intrigued with the simplicity and directness of Bruce's approach. His boxing coaches had taught him to set up an opponent—jab, jab, feint, feint, jab—until he dropped his guard and then you could finally whack him one. "But with kung fu you don't go through all of that," Damone says. "You just go right to the kill."

Of all the things Bruce taught Damone, the most useful were about relaxation. "You've got to relax," Bruce would insist. "Once your body is relaxed, almost like a limp rag, you can throw anything and you'll be surprised how deadly it is. If you tighten up before you throw a punch, it will be weak. Keep your body loose and it'll be like a whip." Damone never had to stun, cripple, or kill anybody, but Bruce's relaxation techniques improved his singing. "Whenever I had a hard piece like 'MacArthur Park,' I would relax like Bruce taught me," Damone says. "The vocal cords would work and the voice would just flow out, just so beautiful. Bruce helped me in a lot of ways. He really was a hell of a wonderful, sweet guy."

The lessons continued on and off for about a year. Damone would come over to Bruce's house whenever he was in Los Angeles, and Bruce made a handful of trips to Las Vegas. It was during one of those Vegas forays that Bruce Lee became a legend in his own lifetime.

After finishing class, Bruce, Jay, and Vic decided to hit the Sands' Chinese restaurant for dinner. As they were walking across the casino, they ran into Sammy Davis Jr.'s humongous bodyguard, Big John Hopkins. Damone and Big John began chatting about different things. Big John, who was smoking a cigarette, reached up to scratch his forehead with the cigarette still in his hand. All of a sudden, Big John shot out his hand to wave hello to someone walking directly behind Bruce. Quicker than Damone could blink, Bruce, who misinterpreted the wave as an attack, knocked the cigarette flying from Big John's hand, kicked out one of his legs to knock him off balance, locked up both his arms at his sides, bent him backward until he was helpless, and went right at his throat with the points of his fingers.

"Oh my God!" Damone shouted, stepping between them. "Whoa! Hey! Whoa! What are you doing?"

"What do you mean?" Bruce looked at Damone quizzically. "He was trying to hit me."

Now Big John, as big and tough as they come, became very gentle: "No, no, no, I wasn't gonna hit you. I was waving at somebody behind you."

"Oh, okay," said Bruce, letting Big John free. "I'm sorry."

As Big John was regaining his composure, he said, "Jesus Christ, who the fuck are you?"

"This is Bruce Lee," Damone said. "This is Jay Sebring."

"I'm so sorry," Big John said, before pausing to reflect. "What the hell did you do to me? Because all the sudden I'm standing here and I'm helpless."

To smooth things over, Damone patted Big John on the shoulder and invited him to join them for dinner. During the meal, Big John peppered Bruce with so many fawning questions about Jeet Kune Do that Damone finally leaned over to Sebring and whispered, "I've never seen John kiss ass like this."

It was a great story and Damone loved telling it to all his friends, who loved telling it to all their friends. Like a game of telephone the story grew with each retelling until it became mythological.

In the later versions of the tale, it was Frank Sinatra who invited Bruce Lee to Las Vegas to learn more about kung fu. When Bruce arrived in town, he was brought up to Sinatra's suite by Vic Damone. Sinatra had become very interested in the martial arts because of *The Manchurian Candidate* (1962), but he thought a lot of the mystique was exaggerated. A good tough American street fighter, he insisted, could always beat an Oriental karate man, because Asians were smaller and thinner. Bruce politely disagreed. "Well, how can we test this?" Frank asked. "I mean without anybody getting hurt." Bruce looked at Sinatra's two massive bodyguards and said, "Why don't we put one bodyguard by the door, and the other across the room smoking a cigarette. Let's see if they can stop me from kicking it out of his mouth. Would this be an acceptable test of what the martial arts can do?" Sinatra nodded, excited. After Bruce left the room, Sinatra told his bodyguards, "Look, I don't want you to hurt him, cause he's small and Chinese, but I wouldn't mind if either one of you knock him on his ass. Give him a good shot. Let's settle this once and for all." Everyone was waiting, and then BLAM! The door not only flew open, the damn thing came off the hinges, blasting the first bodyguard out of the way. Hurtling across the room, Bruce high kicked the cigarette out of the second bodyguard's mouth and sent it whistling past Sinatra's face. "What do you think now?" Bruce asked. "Holy shit!" Sinatra exclaimed.

The fact that this story bore little resemblance to the truth, or even plausibility, didn't seem to matter. Nobody fact-checked it with Sinatra or Damone. When the legend becomes fact, print the legend. This tall tale made Bruce Lee the most sought after martial arts instructor in Hollywood.

"Whether that story was true or not, I didn't know," recalls Oscar-winning screenwriter Stirling Silliphant. "But that was the story I heard at a Hollywood party. It was circulating all over Hollywood at the time. And it was good enough for me. I decided Bruce was going to be my man."

Stirling Silliphant was the Aaron Sorkin of his day, as successful in TV as in movies. He had just been nominated for an Academy Award for *In the Heat of the Night* (1967). A fencer in college, he was, at the age of fifty, suffering from middle-age, macho syndrome. For weeks he tried to track down Bruce Lee without success, until he stopped by Sebring's for his monthly haircut.

On March 18, 1968, Silliphant called Bruce and said, "I am Stirling Silliphant. I have been looking for you for weeks. I would like to study with you."

"I don't really teach. I have one or two students only," Bruce said, playing hard to get.

"Can we meet to discuss it?" Silliphant anxiously asked. "I really want to study with you. So does my friend, Joe Hyams. Do you know him? He's the most important columnist in town. Writes for *The Saturday Evening Post*. Married to Elke Sommer. Just published a best-selling biography of Humphrey Bogart. We want to buy the ten-lesson package."

"Where do you want to meet?" Bruce asked, still noncommittal.

"Columbia Pictures," Silliphant said, hoping this would convince the young actor to accept him as a student.

"I'm free for lunch on March 20."

When they met, Bruce took one look at Silliphant, fifty, and Hyams, forty-four, and said, "Forget it. You've never studied the martial arts before. You're too old to start."

Silliphant was taken aback. As an A-list writer-producer, who hired lots of actors, he assumed Bruce would jump at the chance to have him as a pupil. But if anything, the initial rebuff just made Silliphant more eager. "You don't know anything about me," he huffed. "At USC I had the fastest reflexes of anyone ever tested. I have incredible eyesight. Tests show I have a highly competitive attitude. I'm a winner. I was three years varsity fencing at USC and we won the Pacific Coast championship. All you have to do is teach me to apply my attitude. Instead of sword hitting, it'll be my body hitting."

"You were a fencer?" Bruce smiled, raising an eyebrow. "Show me."

Silliphant lunged back and forth with a steak knife as his sword. After a minute, he asked, "What do you think?"

Bruce leaned back, appearing to consider: "You are too old, but your stance with just a slight alteration is almost like Jeet Kune Do. After watching your movements, I think I can teach you."

Bruce turned to look at Joe Hyams: "Why do you want to study with me?"

"Because I saw your demonstration at Ed Parker's Championships and was impressed with your demonstration, and because I heard you are the best."

"You've studied other martial arts?"

"For a long time," Hyams answered. "I served in the South Pacific during World War II. I started studying martial arts to stop guys from beating me up for being Jewish. But I stopped some time ago and now I want to begin again."

"Would you demonstrate some of your techniques?"

Hyams jumped up for his audition and ran through several *katas*, or forms, from other disciplines.

"Do you realize you will have to unlearn all you have learned and start over again?" Bruce asked.

"No," Hyams said, crestfallen.

Bruce smiled, placed his hand on Hyams's shoulder, and said: "Let me tell you a story my *sifu* taught me. A professor once went to a Zen master to inquire about Zen. As the Zen master explained, the professor would frequently interrupt his remarks, 'Oh yes, we have that too . . .' and so on. Finally the Zen master stopped talking and began to serve tea to the professor. He poured the cup full and then kept pouring until the cup overflowed. 'Enough,' the professor once more interrupted. 'No more can go into the cup!' 'Indeed,' answered the Zen master. 'If you do not first empty your cup, how can you taste my tea?' "

Bruce studied Hyams's face. "You understand the point?"

"Yes," he said. "You want me to empty my mind of past knowledge and old habits so that I will be open to new learning."

"Yes," Bruce said, and then addressed Hyams and Silliphant. "I think I can teach you both."

Hyams and Silliphant started their twice-a-week lessons on March 25 at Hyams's house. Bruce focused on the basics but quickly had them sparring each other. "It was probably a ridiculous sight: two middle-aged men wearing headgear and boxing gloves pummeling each other in the driveway of a suburban home," Hyams recalls. Bruce, acting as umpire-coach, would observe and critique: "Focus! Relax!"

Hyams's favorite times were the conversations after class in his backyard over a glass of fruit juice. "These few moments were precious to me," Hyams says, "because, invariably, I gained insight into one or both of my friends."

Hyams took seventeen lessons over two months before quitting. Silliphant continued to train privately with Bruce for the next three years. "It was a very rewarding and beautiful time," Silliphant recalls. "It really began to open me up in terms of martial arts and physical contact." Silliphant was enthralled with Bruce—a man crush. "I owe my spirituality to Bruce Lee," Silliphant says. "In my lifetime, I never met another man who was even remotely at his level of consciousness. Because of Bruce, I opened all my windows."

Early in their training, Bruce criticized Silliphant for being too timid: "Your defenses are good, but your offense is weak. Your attacks lack emotional content."

"When I fenced in college, I scored 90 percent of my touches via counterattacks," Stirling said. "I prefer to react."

"Bullshit," Bruce replied. "That's a technical rationalization. There's something in you, something deep in your mind that stops you from attacking. You have to rationalize that the other guy is attacking you, so then it's okay to knock him off. But you don't have the killer instinct; you're not pursuing him. Why?"

Silliphant thought about this for weeks and weeks. Finally, he said to Bruce, "My father, a pure Anglo, never once in his life held me in his arms or kissed me. In fact, I've never in my life touched a man or had any body contact with another male. I'm not homophobic or anything, but, ah, I just, um, haven't ever done it."

The two men had been working out all afternoon. They were sweating and had their shirts off, wearing black Chinese pajama pants only.

Bruce stepped toward Silliphant and said, "Put your arms around me."

"Hey, Bruce," Silliphant protested, "you're all sweaty, man."

"Do it!" he demanded.

So Silliphant put his arms around his *sifu*.

"Pull me closer," Bruce said.

"Jesus, Bruce!"

"Closer!"

Silliphant could feel Bruce's vibrant life force. He felt good and alive, and it was as if a steel wall between them had been blown away. When Silliphant opened his arms, Bruce stepped back, studying him.

"You have to love everyone," Bruce said, "not only women, but men as well. You don't have to have sex with a man, but you have to be able to relate to his separate physicality. If you don't, you will never be able to fight him, to drive your fist through his chest, to snap his neck, to gouge out his eyes."

When Bruce was a teenager at La Salle, he recruited a gang from his fellow classmates. In Seattle, he had a formed a crew out of his kung fu students. In Hollywood, he repeated the same pattern. Stirling Silliphant became Bruce's most important patron and cheerleader—the man who would do the most to advance his career.

James Coburn—along with Steve McQueen and Charles Bronson—was one of the tough-guy action stars of the era. He appeared in supporting roles in movies like *The Magnificent Seven* (1960) and *The Great Escape* (1963) until the James Bond parody film *Our Man Flint* (1966) made Coburn a star. To prepare for the role of Flint, he began studying karate.

Aware of Coburn's growing fascination with the Asian arts, Stirling Silliphant called him to tout his new master: "Look, I've met a young Chinese boy who's really sensational—he's got the magic kick; he's got the magic!" After several weeks, Silliphant finally had the chance to introduce Bruce to Coburn at a Hollywood party. It was a small but impressive gathering with just about every guest a major player in the movie industry. With Bruce present, the topic of conversation quickly turned to the martial arts.

"I had a few lessons while making the *Flint* series," Coburn said to Bruce. "What do you think of that instructor the producer used?"

"I know who you're referring to," Bruce hesitated, before answering. "Let me put it this way. If I were to classify all the instructors in the country, I'd have to place him pretty far down the bottom."

"You should show James your famous one-inch punch," Silliphant said, mischievously.

"Sure," grinned Bruce. "Stand up."

Bruce positioned Coburn several feet in front of a chair and asked him to hold a seat cushion against his chest for protection. Coburn was so tall Bruce decided to add an extra inch to the punch. As soon as Bruce blasted him, Coburn went flying back, sprawled into the chair, toppled it over, and rolled into the corner of the room. The shock on Coburn's face as he wobbled to his feet was so complete the room burst into laughter.

It took a few seconds for Coburn to regain his composure and realize what had happened. Suddenly, his face lit up and he blurted out: "Let's go! Let's go to work."

"Anytime," Bruce replied. "But I want to let you know that it's not cheap."

"I don't care. I want to start right away. How about tomorrow?"

"Sure," Bruce nodded. "I can start you off even if it's a Sunday."

On November 1, 1968, Bruce went to Coburn's mansion for their first lesson. It looked like a museum. Coburn collected Asian antiques—vases, statues, and paintings from India, Japan, and China. They worked on the basics: a few punches and kicks to assess Coburn's level. The next week Coburn came to Bruce's house and they started in earnest: twice a week for the next six months.

"Bruce always had this energy," Coburn recalls. "It was always exploding on him. We'd work out together for an hour and a half and at the end of that time, he'd be filled with force. You really felt high when you finished working out with Bruce." Coburn enjoyed the physical aspect but he was more interested in the esoteric side of the martial arts. After working out, they would hang out and talk about philosophy, psychology, and mysticism.

"We'd do a thing Bruce called 'bridging the gap,' " Coburn says. "It's the distance from your opponent you have to stand in order to score—it's how close you can get in and move away fast enough not to get hit in return. It amounts to constant observation of your opponent and constant observation of yourself, so that you and your opponent are one—not divided. And while you were picking up this physical bridging of the gap, you were learning to overcome certain psychological barriers at the same time."

Coburn was so enthusiastic he converted one of the rooms in his mansion into a gym to match Bruce's. As the months went by, the two seemed inseparable. Coburn became Bruce's most dedicated Hollywood student, taking 106 private lessons with him over a three-year period.

Steve McQueen and Jay Sebring were best friends—two straightforward, street-smart, self-made men. For 1960s Hollywood, they embodied the ideal of masculinity: cool, tough, and dangerous with just a hint of vulnerability.

When Sebring bragged that Bruce Lee was the best fight instructor he had ever met, McQueen was, at the age of thirty-seven, eager to meet him. Their first training session took place at McQueen's mansion, nicknamed the Castle, on August 25, 1967.

Bruce was impressed with McQueen's determination and resilience. "That guy doesn't know the meaning of quitting," Bruce told a friend. "He just keeps pushing himself for hours—punching and kicking for hours without a break—until he is completely exhausted." During one class, they were training in McQueen's big courtyard paved with rough sandstone rock, and Steve tripped and cut open his big toe. It was a bloody mess with a big piece of flesh dangling.

"We'd better stop," Bruce suggested

"No," McQueen responded. "Let's keep on training."

Over the first year, the private lessons were sporadic. McQueen was the biggest box office star in Hollywood and frequently out of town. "Steve would be damned good if he could work out more, but the sonovagun never stays home," Bruce said. "If he's shooting, he'll be stuck at a location for as long as five months, returning for a couple of days in between. If he's not working, he'll be somewhere in the desert, driving his dune buggy or motorcycle."

Even more than Steve's busy schedule, the biggest difficulty Bruce faced as McQueen's teacher was gaining his trust. "When I first saw him, I couldn't understand that guy," Bruce told a friend. "He was so suspicious of me." McQueen came from a broken home. His father abandoned the family before Steve was six months old. His alcoholic mother cycled through abusive boyfriends. She sent Steve away first to family members and then later, when he became a rebellious teenager, to reform schools.

Over time Bruce and Steve slowly became friends. "They really connected," says Linda, "because they were the same kind of guy, rough and tumble coming from similar backgrounds." Both had a parent who was an addict; both were smart but had done poorly in school; both were teenage troublemakers who roamed the streets in gangs. "If I hadn't found acting," McQueen later admitted to a reporter, "I would have wound up a hood." They were angry, aggressive, hypercompetitive alpha males—Lee of the charming, showboating variety, and McQueen the hard, isolate, stoic type. "It took quite a while before I got to know him," Bruce said of McQueen. "But once he accepted me as a friend, we became real close."

"Sometimes I'd feel rotten and the phone would ring, and it would be Bruce," McQueen recalled. "I don't know why he called. He would just say, 'I just thought I should call you.' "

Steve McQueen became like an older brother to Bruce in Hollywood. Their relationship was a mixture of mutual admiration and mutual envy. McQueen longed to possess Bruce's fighting prowess, while Lee wanted to be as big a star as McQueen. More than anyone else in Tinseltown, McQueen served as Bruce Lee's role model. From Steve he learned that the star, not the director as in China, is dominant. McQueen replaced directors he didn't respect and chewed through producers. He bent everyone on-set to his will. And he cut a wide swath through the female population of actresses, groupies, production assistants, makeup artists, housewives, hitchhikers, waitresses, and hatcheck girls.

As Bruce's career counselor, McQueen told him not to worry about acting lessons or joining one of the drama playhouses: "You will develop your own acting style over time. The most important thing is to meet the right people in the industry and impress them."

Bruce had difficulty networking because he disliked Hollywood parties. As a relatively obscure TV actor and the only Asian guest, he frequently felt like a lowly outsider. "Bruce and I went along to one or two during his lean period, partly because one never knew what opportunities might suddenly present themselves," Linda Lee says. "The trouble with film parties is that the stars want to be at the center of things and Bruce was too much his own man, too conscious of his own worth, to join in the fawning, adulatory chorus that tends to surround the Big Name. And Bruce, on first meeting, was always so polite and courteous that I think most of them got the impression that he was simply there to take away the dishes."

When he became fed up with being ignored or treated like a Chinese busboy, Bruce would grab the spotlight by giving a performance. "Inevitably, at some time during the evening, when I turned round and looked for

Bruce, he would be in the center of a group, doing push-ups or performing his coin trick or holding the floor on philosophy or the martial arts," Linda recalls. "I used to marvel at the look of amazement on everyone's faces. They simply weren't ready for Bruce."

Another reason why Hollywood partygoers often mistook Bruce for the help was he didn't smoke cigarettes and rarely touched alcohol. "I'm not that type of cat," Bruce told *Fighting Stars* magazine. As drunken revelers puffed away and downed cocktails, he remained dead sober with a cup of tea in his hands. It led many to believe he was a teetotaler—a myth that continues to this day. In fact, he did occasionally partake, he just didn't imbibe very often or very much. Alcohol didn't sit well with him.

"I tried twenty times to get him to drink," says Bob Wall, who costarred in *Enter the Dragon*. "One time I got him to sip wine. He spit it out. It wasn't his thing." Andre Morgan, who worked with Bruce in Hong Kong, confirms this: "Bruce was not a drinker. He drank a little *Shaoxing* wine at dinner, but he wasn't hitting the bottle like people in Hollywood hit the bottle." Joe Lewis adds this story: "There was this time in about 1969 that Bruce was at the house and my wife fixed him a drink—some kind of sweet, syrupy thing. And Bruce drank it and then he got unbelievably sick. He turned red, he was sweating, sweat was running all down his face. And we helped him to the bathroom. He threw up and threw up and threw up still more."

Based on these anecdotes, it seems likely that Bruce Lee suffered from alcohol flush reaction. It is more colloquially known as the Asian Glow, because over 35 percent of East Asians suffer from it. Affected persons lack an enzyme needed to metabolize alcohol. After one or two drinks, they turn red in the face, start sweating, and feel nauseated.

Finding himself in the foreign land of late-1960s hard-partying Hollywood, Bruce needed to adapt. Because boozing with the boys was a nonstarter, he had to find a different way to fit in. Fortunately, there was another social drug becoming popular at that time that Bruce's body could metabolize and his brain could enjoy.

When rising screen idol Robert Mitchum was arrested in 1948 at what Federal Bureau of Narcotics agents alleged was a marijuana smoking party, he gave his occupation as *former actor*. He believed his movie career was finished. Facing the press, he said, "I guess it's all over now. I'm ruined. This is the bitter end." He was right to be pessimistic. For decades, the American government had been vilifying cannabis as a gateway drug and racially stigmatizing its association to Mexican laborers and black jazz musicians. Even Hollywood, a long-standing bastion for stoners, had supported the propaganda with *Reefer Madness* (1936) and *The Devil's Weed* (1949).

But Mitchum's conviction proved a boon to his career, casting him as a rebel both on-screen and in real life. On the other coast, the Beats, a group of mostly white intellectuals and writers who frequented the jazz clubs of New York City, began to evangelize marijuana as a device to enhance literary visions, most famously in Allen Ginsberg's *Howl and Other Poems* (1956) and Jack Kerouac's *On the Road* (1957). Ginsberg wrote in the November 1966 issue of *Atlantic Monthly*, "Marijuana is a useful catalyst for specific optical and aural aesthetic perceptions." The Beat prophets led to the Beatnik proselytizers, which led to the counterculture hippies. By the mid- to late 1960s, marijuana had become pervasive, especially in Hollywood.

It was Steve McQueen who turned Bruce Lee on to marijuana. It quickly became his drug of choice—Puff the Magic Dragon. After a training session with one of his celebrity clients, Bruce would light a blunt and talk philosophy. "He'd want to get high and have a ball, listen to music," James Coburn recalls. "Blowing Gold was one of his favorite things." Herb Jackson, one of Bruce's senior students, says that Bruce kept a box of marijuana cigarettes in his garage.

"It was different and scary," Bruce said of his first experience getting stoned. "I was feeling pretty high when Steve gave me a cup of hot tea. As I placed the cup to my lips, it felt like a river gushing into my mouth. It was weird. Everything was so exaggerated. Even the damn noise from my slurping was so loud it sounded like splashing waves. When I got into my car and started to go, the street seemed like it was moving real fast toward me. The white centerline just flew at me and so did the telephone poles. You just notice everything more sharply. You become aware of everything. To me, it was artificial awareness. But, you know, this is what we're trying to reach in martial arts, the 'awareness,' but in a more natural way. Better get it through martial arts, it's more permanent. It doesn't make sense to be on pot all the time."

Joe Lewis recalls an anecdote that shows how marijuana helped Bruce socialize in this new environment: "Hell, back in Hollywood, I saw Bruce doing dope right in front of me. One time, he walked into my place and started passing out these huge joints the size of big cigars. I said, 'Bruce, that's not the way you do it. You just roll one little one and pass it around.' He tells me, 'No need to share. I want everyone to have their own.' And he thumps his chest like he did in the movies, real big and proud. Everybody thought that was funny. That was Bruce, all right. Bruce to a T. But it's not like anybody thought that anything was wrong with all that. It was the sixties and seventies. We thought it was innocent. Everybody was doing drugs."

Everybody in the movie industry might have been doing drugs, but most martial artists—largely ex-servicemen—were not. To them, real men got drunk, not high. "Judo" Gene LeBell remembers going over to Bruce's house for a lesson and becoming upset at all the pot smoke. "I never went back to his house," he says, still angry fifty years later. When the topic of marijuana use was raised with Dan Inosanto, he looked down at his hands, shook his head, and sighed, "Bruce said, 'It raises the consciousness level.'" But ever the loyal disciple he felt the need to add, "I don't think Bruce was as much a user as people make it out to be."

Beyond its consciousness-raising appeal, Bruce's fondness for cannabis—at first he used marijuana and then later switched to hash—may have involved an element of self-medication. "Never Sits Still" had been hyperactive and impulsive since his childhood. Marijuana and hash seem to have served as a kind of chill pill. Bob Wall remembers working out with Bruce Lee at his Kowloon Tong home in Hong Kong in 1972. "He was funnier than hell because the minute we were done he would have a hash brownie," he says. "We'd be philosophizing and talking away. He'd finish it. Immediately, I could almost see him chewing his fingers off, right? Then he'd go for another one. Because he couldn't sit, he'd be out the door. He was just fucking hyper like a motherfucker. But after two brownies, he was mellow. He became a normal human."

By the end of 1968, Bruce was the hottest self-defense instructor in Hollywood. He was so overwhelmed with requests he printed up new business cards: Bruce Lee's Jeet Kune Do, Professional Consultation and Instruction: $275 per hour, Ten Session Course: $1,000, Instruction Overseas: $1,000 per week plus expenses. "I used to charge $500 for a ten hour course, and people flocked," Bruce later told a reporter. "I even doubled the prices and people still kept coming. I had no idea so many people were interested in Chinese boxing. It was a very profitable thing to do."

To his core of Stirling Silliphant, James Coburn, and Steve McQueen, Bruce added two top directors, Blake Edwards (*Breakfast at Tiffany's*, *The Pink Panther*) and Roman Polanski (*Rosemary's Baby*, *Chinatown*), a successful TV producer, Sy Weintraub (*Tarzan*), and a casino magnate, Beldon Katleman. As these A-listers padded his bank account, they also offered him a glimpse into the lifestyles of the rich and famous. "The first time I went to Katleman's place, I was greeted by his butler who had a heavy British accent and dressed exactly like British butlers in the movies," Bruce recalled. "He took me through the huge mansion to the backyard with a full-sized tennis court and an Olympic-sized pool. It was the biggest damn backyard I've ever seen. I never knew anyone could be that rich."

When Steve McQueen was just starting out he had a chance to hang out with Frank Sinatra and saw the private jets, limousines, red carpet events, screaming fans, opened doors, and fawning admiration. "I want some of that," McQueen whispered to his wife. Now it was Bruce's turn to feel the same way.

What Lee wanted more than anything was a new sports car. He neglected his old Chevy Nova, hardly ever cleaning it. The only thing he liked about the junker was the sticker on the back window with the inscription: "This Car Is Protected By The Green Hornet." "Only a few hundred were printed," he proudly said. "I tried to get more but even I couldn't get any."

Jay Sebring would let Bruce race his Shelby Cobra along Mulholland Drive—the twisty two-lane road along the ridgeline of the Santa Monica Mountains. "I don't know how fast," Linda laughs, "but I didn't want to know." Bruce admired the Cobra, but what he really desired was a Porsche 911S Targa, because McQueen had one. On August 26, 1968, he visited

Bob Smith's Volkswagen-Porsche dealership in Hollywood for a test drive. As soon as he got home, he called up McQueen in Palm Springs.

"Steve, I'm going to get a Porsche like yours," Bruce declared.

"Look, Bruce, let me take you for a ride in mine when I get back," Steve said with a note of caution in his voice. "It's a really hot car, but if you don't know what you are doing you can get into a lot of trouble with this thing."

"Okay," Bruce excitedly said.

McQueen was a world-class driver—he could have made his living as a Grand Prix driver—while Bruce was by all accounts a menace behind the wheel. ("He was just way too fast for me," says Dan Inosanto. "It would scare me.") Bruce was expecting a joy ride, but McQueen hoped to frighten Bruce out of buying a Porsche. Steve picked up Bruce and drove up the San Fernando Valley to Mulholland Drive.

"Okay, Bruce, you ready?" Steve said, focused intently on the road.

"Yes, I'm all set. Let's go!"

Steve peeled away, grinding through the gears as he twisted and turned along the winding, dangerous path high in the mountains.

"What do you think of this power, Bruce?" Steve shouted over the roar of the engine.

Bruce said nothing.

"Now watch this!" Steve yelled as he slalomed from the side of the mountain to the edge of the precipice. "Isn't that great, Bruce? See how it handles. Now watch how I slide it!" Steve put the Porsche into a tail slide as he went right to the edge. "Isn't that great, Bruce?"

No reply.

"Now watch this, Bruce. Sucker will do a mean 180," Steve announced as he geared it up, spun it around, and finally stopped the car. He looked over and said, "Well, what do you think, Bruce?" But Bruce wasn't in the passenger seat. Steve looked down and saw Bruce huddled in the deep footwell with his hands over his head. "Bruce?"

"McQueen you sonovabitch!" Bruce shouted as he pulled himself back into the seat. "McQueen, I bloody kill you! I kill you, McQueen! I gunna kill you!"

Steve saw the look of rage on Bruce's face and it terrified him. He knew how deadly Bruce could be when he was angry. So Steve put the pedal to the metal and raced back up Mulholland Drive as fast as he could.

"Bruce, calm down!" Steve shouted.

"Steve, slow down," Bruce cried out. "Slow down!"

"You won't hit me will you, Bruce?" Steve pleaded.

"No, no."

"You won't touch me, will you?"

"No, no."

"You won't hurt me will you?"

"No, no! Just stop the car. Stop the car!"

Steve finally pulled over to the side, and Bruce said, "I will never drive with you again, McQueen. Never!"

Afterward Bruce told a friend: "If you think I'm a fast driver, you should ride with Steve. One afternoon while coming down Mulholland, he must have thought we were on a racetrack because he was going at least 60 around the curves. You know I don't usually get scared that easy, but Steve sure made me shit that time. I kept praying that he doesn't hit a stone or there'll be no tomorrow."

It wasn't the terror ride that scared off Bruce from immediately buying a Porsche, but rather Linda telling him she was pregnant again. A second child meant more practical concerns. Linda and Bruce decided they needed to upgrade their family's living situation. On August 27, 1968, Bruce went over to McQueen's Castle to ask for advice. He had never bought a home before. McQueen offered to have his business manager help Bruce and Linda with the search.

With his income from private lessons and residuals from *The Green Hornet*, Bruce and Linda approached a realtor about finding a nice house in the mid-$20,000 range. "We didn't know much about the housing market in Southern California," Linda says. "I was not prepared for the kind of location or property for that sum of money. Eventually, we realized we would have to upgrade our housing budget."

Their realtor highly recommended a house at 2551 Roscomare Road in the upscale neighborhood of Bel Air. Initially, Bruce and Linda were uncertain. The 1,902-square-foot, three-bedroom, two-bath ranch home, built in 1951, needed a lot of work. It also cost $47,000, which was way over their budget. But Bruce adored the exclusivity of Bel Air, and McQueen's business manager told them it was a steal: "With the tax refund it is better to own in Bel Air than rent in Culver City." When Bruce called Steve for his opinion, McQueen offered to cover the $10,000 down payment. "Boy, that was a lot of money, and he was just gonna give it to me with no strings attached," Bruce later said. "I had to turn him down because I'd feel obligated. But it was nice of him and I sure appreciated it. That Steve is too much."

They applied for a home loan on September 9, and it was approved on September 13, 1968. "With the mortgage payments, property taxes, and insurance, we were in way over our heads," Linda says. "It doesn't matter if you can deduct money from your taxes in April, if you can't make your mortgage payments in October."

Bruce's students from his Chinatown school helped him move on September 28 and 29. He had trouble sleeping the first few nights. "It was so quiet that I could hear a pin drop," Bruce said. "I heard strange noises in my backyard and on my roof. The next morning I saw animal tracks. I didn't know they came from wild animals until my neighbor told me. It's kinda funny, all these years I lived in L.A. and never dreamt that wild animals roamed so close." Bruce quickly fell in love with his new home's location: "This place is terrific. I'm away from the heavy city traffic and still can get to any place in Los Angeles quickly. Sometimes, I just sit in my backyard and gaze at the ocean watching the sun slowly set. Civilization seems so far away."

Just as in Culver City, Bruce converted his Bel Air home into a martial arts training center. On the patio, under the eaves of the house, he hung huge red kicking backs, a top and bottom bag, a square hitting pad strung by elastic cords, a squat machine, a leg-stretching device, a variety of weights and assorted kicking and striking pads. He filled the garage with so much training equipment that he had to park his Chevy Nova on the street. Once everything was set up, he held private lessons at his Bel Air home with his senior Chinatown students and his Hollywood clients. All the activity raised some eyebrows in the fancy neighborhood. Brandon, who was four years old, made friends with a boy on the next block named Luke. He frequently invited Brandon over to his home but refused to visit Brandon's. When Linda asked Luke's mother why, she confessed that Luke was afraid of all the strange equipment and the people yelling and hitting each other.

One of the attractions of the house for Bruce was its close proximity to Mulholland Drive. ("Good for the guys," Linda says, "but bad for children.") If anything, the ride with McQueen had increased Bruce's desire for a Porsche. The more Bruce stared at his dilapidated Chevy Nova with its faded paint job in front of his brand-new home in his fancy Bel Air neighborhood the more embarrassed he became of the eyesore. But he was already overextended with the house. Then out of the blue, Bruce received a windfall. His mother sold one of the apartments in Hong Kong that his father had bought after the war. Bruce's share of the profits was $7,000. It just so happened that a 1968 Porsche 911S Targa cost $6,990. It was like fate, a sign from Heaven. On December 7, 1968, barely two months after moving into a house he couldn't afford, Bruce bought a red 911 Porsche from Bob Smith.

He immediately raced over to Chuck Norris's karate school in Sherman Oaks. He screeched into the parking lot, locked the brakes, and slid into the curb. Inside the school, Norris, his business partner, Bob Wall, and his chief instructor, Pat Johnson, heard this awful crashing noise and ran outside expecting to find an accident. Instead, they saw a brand-new Porsche sitting at a cockeyed angle on the curb and Bruce Lee standing next to it with his arms folded across his chest just looking it over as proud as he could be.

"Guys, check out my new car," Bruce said.

"Bruce, it's beautiful," Norris said, "but we thought something had happened."

"Nah, nah, it's fine. Chuck, come along, I'm going to take you for a ride in my Porsche."

Norris froze in terror: "Ah, Bruce, I've got to run back to my other school. I've got lessons to teach. See you later, but remember you owe me a ride."

"Pat, jump into the car."

"Well, my classes are about to start," Pat Johnson hedged. "Another time, okay?"

"Bob, come on."

"Bruce, I have an appointment," Bob Wall lied. "I'm gonna sell somebody a lesson."

"Okay, next time," Bruce said, so delighted with his new car he didn't realize they didn't want to ride with him. "I'll see if Lewis is home."

"Great, Bruce, great," they said, as Bruce jumped into his Porsche and peeled away.

The purchase of the Porsche stretched the family's financial situation to its limits, but Bruce felt compelled to show McQueen he was his equal. "It was extravagant," Linda admits, "when we were hardly making mortgage payments. It was an extravagance, but it made Bruce happy."

The arrival on Saturday, April 19, 1969, of a healthy baby girl made Bruce even happier. Shannon Emery Lee was born at Santa Monica Hospital. "The second time I had decided it was going to be a girl," Bruce told everyone, "so we only chose a girl's name." Bruce wrote down in his daytime planner Shannon's weight and length—six pounds, six ounces, and nineteen inches. Shannon quickly had her doting father wrapped around her little finger. His friends noted a change in attitude. He became more attentive.

One day when he visited the *Black Belt* offices looking depressed, Mito Uyehara asked, "What's wrong, Bruce?"

"I feel real bad today," Bruce confided. "I was clipping my daughter's nails and accidentally cut her finger. When she started to scream and I saw the blood dripping, I went crazy. I didn't know what to do. Lucky that Linda was around. Man, I felt really bad. She's so tiny and I had to hurt her."

On May 30, 1969, Grace Ho arrived at Los Angeles International Airport to see her newest grandchild. She traveled with Robert, who was entering college in the fall. From the other side of the terminal, Bruce spotted his younger brother and charged over to greet him. After they embraced, Bruce took a step back to look Robert up and down.

"Jesus, you're *skinny*!" Bruce bellowed. "Don't tell anyone you're my brother—you'll embarrass me!"

"Don't tease him," Grace interjected.

"How much do you weigh?"

"108."

"108 pounds? No good! I need to train you."

While Bruce was away, Robert had become one of Hong Kong's biggest teen sensations with his boy band, the Thunderbirds. They made a couple of top 10 hit singles for EMI, the most popular of which was "Baby Baby, You Put Me Down." Anders Nelsson, who fronted a rival band, says, "He was like the David Cassidy of Hong Kong. Pretty boy, pretty boy." When the rumors that he was leaving for college in America proved true, his lovelorn female admirers were distraught. Robert told *The China Mail*, "I hope my fans will understand I have to think about my future."

Robert was more famous than Bruce had ever been as a child actor, but as the youngest sibling he still had to obey his elders. The day after his arrival Robert was roused out of bed by his big brother, who handed him a pair of tennis shoes. "We are going for a three-mile run," Bruce said.

Robert lasted for less than a mile before dropping away. He staggered back to Bruce's Bel Air home and threw up, his face completely white. For the next two weeks, Bruce put Robert through his boot camp. He made him eat his special egg, peanut butter, and banana protein shakes three times a day. He had him lifting dumbbells every day. Robert's weight jumped from 108 to 124 pounds, but Bruce realized there was little hope of turning his little brother, the sweet-singing lover, into a street fighter.

"Since you have no talent for the martial arts and no strength to beat anybody up," Bruce finally said, "there's only one skill I want to teach you: how to run away."

Robert was annoyed but couldn't help but burst out laughing.

Grace and Robert stayed until the end of the summer. In their eyes, Bruce must have seemed a great success. To all outward appearances, Bruce Lee was the model immigrant—a homeowner in Bel Air with a Porsche, two cute kids, and a lovely Caucasian wife. That it was all built on a mountain of debt and teetering on the brink of collapse made Bruce's story a prototypically American one. "It was a very difficult time for us," Linda says. The arrival of Shannon made Bruce unbelievably happy and extremely anxious. "I have to be more concerned for my family now," Bruce admitted to a friend. "First time in my life I am worried about where the money will come from if anything happens to me."

Sharon Tate and Bruce on the set of *The Wrecking Crew*, summer 1968. *(David Tadman)*

Steve McQueen and Sharon Farrell in *The Reivers*, October 1968. *(Bernd Lubowski/ullstein bild/Getty Images)*

thirteen

bit player

The cancellation of *The Green Hornet* dropped Bruce from a salaried player on a regular series down to a fringe actor, a freelancer—sustaining himself on bit parts, dreaming of the big one just around the corner. Unlike his white colleagues, who could show up any day of the week to play Ambulance Driver or Ranch Hand or Criminal Suspect #3, Bruce often had to wait months to compete for the handful of roles in any given year written specifically for an Asian actor.

After six months without any serious prospects, Bruce landed his first post-Kato part in *Ironside*, a lukewarm police procedural starring Raymond Burr as a wheelchair-bound detective. In the episode "Tagged for Murder" (October 26, 1967), Bruce played a karate instructor, the son of a GI whose dog tags are a clue in a murder mystery. With only a few minutes on-screen and less than a dozen lines of dialogue, it was not a big enough part to even qualify for a "guest star" mention in the opening credits but rather as a "co-star" in the end credits.

In his one scene, a detective shows up at Bruce's school and observes a basic martial arts demonstration between Bruce and "Judo" Gene LeBell—a bit of exoticism shoehorned into the plot. Its highlight: LeBell attempts to hip toss Bruce but instead Lee jumps over his shoulder and flip throws Gene. This pro wrestling sequence was choreographed by LeBell, who was impressed by Bruce's athletic abilities. "I could pick him up, spin him around, and Bruce would come down in position to counterattack," LeBell recalls. "I'd tell him, 'You're so great you could be a world-class stuntman. We'd have you double all the kids.' Then he'd get mad."

The next year, 1968, was a long dry spell for Bruce's television career. He only had one big audition. "My agent called to let me know of a CBS proposal for a one hr. series—kind of like 'I Spy' called 'Hawaii 5-O,' " Bruce wrote to a friend. "Looks good. Will let you know what develops." Bruce went up for the role of Detective Chin Ho Kelly. Much to his disappointment, he lost the part to Kam Fong Chun, an eighteen-year veteran of the Honolulu Police Department and community theater actor. *Hawaii Five-O* was the lone drama on American TV to feature multiple Asian characters in major roles. (Sadly, the same can be said of its reboot, launched four decades later in 2010.) If Bruce had landed it, he would have experienced a much different career trajectory. Kam Fong Chun played Detective Chin Ho Kelly for the next ten years from 1968 to 1978.

It took over fourteen months before Bruce was on television screens again with a guest-starring role on *Blondie*, a short-lived sitcom based on the comic strip. In the episode "Pick on Someone Your Own Size" (January 9, 1969), Bruce once again played a karate instructor who teaches the show's protagonist Dagwood Bumstead how to defend himself against a bully. The kicker: when Dagwood finally faces off against the bully in his karate stance and screams "Yosh!" the bully takes the same pose and yells back "Yosh!" Dagwood looks into the camera and whimpers, "Uh-oh."

The entire training sequence was filmed at Bruce's school in Chinatown. The director, Peter Baldwin, questioned Bruce about a particularly dangerous-looking kick he planned to deliver to the show's star.

"Is it safe?" Baldwin asked. "Can you control it?"

"Do you trust me?" Bruce asked.

"Yes," Baldwin naively replied.

"Stand perfectly still and don't move," Bruce said, before suddenly twirling and lashing out a spinning back kick. His foot stopped millimeters from Baldwin's nose.

"He won me over with that move," the director recalls. "We went on to shoot a wonderful scene."

During this period, Bruce lost out on a number of roles in Westerns, because he refused to wear a Chinese pigtail, or queue. "Most of those shows want me to wear a queue and I won't do that. I don't give a damn how much they pay me. Wearing those queues is real degrading," he explained. "When the Manchus ruled China, they forced the Chinese natives to wear those damn pigtails to mark them as women."

The only Western to let him keep his Jay Sebring hairstyle was *Here Come the Brides*. Based on *Seven Brides for Seven Brothers* (1954), it was a comedy, set in the 1870s, about the lumberjacks in the frontier town of Seattle and the one hundred women imported from the East Coast to keep the men from leaving. In the episode "Marriage, Chinese Style" (April 9, 1969), a Chinese secret society arranges for a bride from China, Toy Quan, to marry one of its members, Lin Sung, played by Bruce Lee. But Lin Sung, who is intent on breaking away from traditional customs, refuses to marry a woman he has never met. His decision sets the convoluted plot into motion.

The role was unique, because it was the only time in Bruce's adult career where he didn't play a martial arts master. In fact, his character was a bit of a coward, constantly being threatened or bullied. As a result, Bruce had the chance, as an actor, to work with a different palette of emotions—alarm, humiliation, and fear.

Behind the scenes, he was helped into character by his first experience on horseback. Before filming, the director pulled Bruce to the side and asked him, "Have you ever ridden a horse before?"

"No, never," Bruce said with some trepidation. "I've never even seen one up close."

"Don't worry about it," the director attempted to reassure his nervous actor, "the animal we've got is real tame."

As one of the handlers brought over his steed, Bruce blurted out, "Holy shit! I'm not gonna ride that damn thing. It's too big!"

"There is nothing to fear," the director said, soothingly. "He is very gentle, totally harmless, a complete professional."

It took several minutes of pleading and reassuring words from the director and the rest of the crew to cajole Bruce into the saddle. The horse remained perfectly motionless as the handler explained how to use the reins to control the horse. "But you probably won't even need them," said the handler, "because he is so friendly."

The moment the handler completed his instructions and stepped away, the horse bolted. Bruce's cowboy hat flew off his head as he held on to the reins for dear life. "I started to yell, 'Whoa!' but the damn horse never listened," Bruce recalled. "When it finally stopped, I was far down the field. I got off as fast as I could and was ready to throw stones at it. I walked back to the shooting site and the damn horse was already there, waiting for me. When the guys saw me—how pissed I was—they started to laugh. I was so mad I couldn't laugh. I swore I would never ride a horse again, but that director got me to ride it for several more takes. He said that he couldn't find a stand-in for me. That bastard."

Bruce never appeared in a Western or rode a horse again.

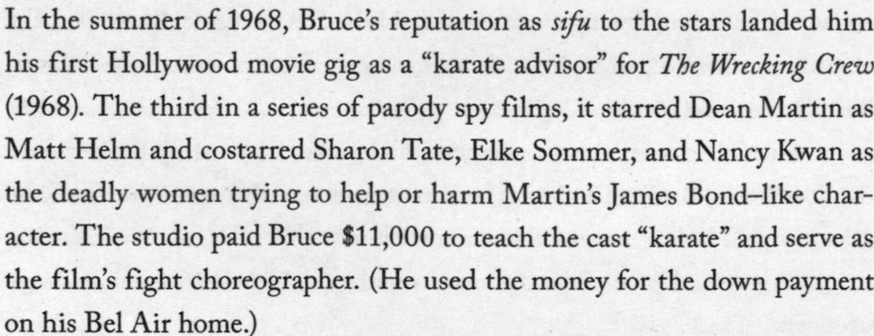

In the summer of 1968, Bruce's reputation as *sifu* to the stars landed him his first Hollywood movie gig as a "karate advisor" for *The Wrecking Crew* (1968). The third in a series of parody spy films, it starred Dean Martin as Matt Helm and costarred Sharon Tate, Elke Sommer, and Nancy Kwan as the deadly women trying to help or harm Martin's James Bond–like character. The studio paid Bruce $11,000 to teach the cast "karate" and serve as the film's fight choreographer. (He used the money for the down payment on his Bel Air home.)

All of the female costars had already heard about their new teacher. Sharon Tate used to date Jay Sebring. Elke Sommer was married to Bruce's former student, Joe Hyams. And Nancy Kwan, who starred in *The World of Suzie Wong* (1960), was the most famous Hong Kong actress working in Hollywood. Bruce quickly charmed all of them. Nancy Kwan and Bruce developed an older sister–younger brother relationship. He would ask her for advice about his acting career. Sharon Tate, who was now married to Roman Polanski, invited Bruce over for dinner, telling her husband, "The two of you will get along like a house on fire." They did—Polanski became one of Bruce's regular clients. "Sharon and Nancy were pretty good students," Bruce said. "They were doing side kicks with just a minimum of teaching."

Bruce had less success with Dean Martin. "I tried to teach him how to kick," Bruce said, "but he was too lazy and too clumsy." He was also too drunk. Martin's personal assistant carried a shoulder-strapped portable bar to keep him well lubricated during filming. Bruce realized Martin required someone to double him for his fight scenes. As the karate advisor, Bruce was given the authority to design the fight scenes and hire the extras necessary for them. This was his chance to bring his two worlds together and pay off his high-profile karate friends.

He hired Mike Stone to double for Dean Martin, Ed Parker to play a guard, Joe Lewis to play a thug who attacks Martin's character, and Chuck Norris to deliver one line of dialogue and a high kick. When Bruce called Norris, he said, "There's a small role that you'd be good for. You'll play Elke Sommer's bodyguard, fight Dean Martin, and have one line. Are you interested?" Bruce didn't need to ask Norris or any of the other karate champions twice.

The day before Chuck Norris's screen debut was Ed Parker's 1968 Long Beach International Karate Championships on August 4, 1968. The martial arts world was buzzing about a potential fifth contest between Chuck Norris and Joe Lewis. In their four previous encounters, Norris had won the first three but Lewis had upset him in their fourth. Would Norris revenge his loss and recapture his title as the best karate fighter in America or had the torch passed to Lewis?

But the much-hyped matchup was not to be. Lewis was disqualified in the early rounds for intentionally injuring one of his opponents. In the finals, Norris was scheduled to compete against Skipper Mullins, the number three nationally ranked fighter. The two of them were good friends. In the locker room before the match, Norris told Skipper, "I have my first part in a movie tomorrow, so beat on my body but try not to hit me in the face. I don't want to go on the set looking like I've been in a brawl."

"OK," Skipper smiled, "but you'll owe me one."

To further merge his movie and martial arts worlds, Bruce Lee arrived at the finals with a special guest in tow—Steve McQueen. As the crowd applauded their arrival, Lee and McQueen took their seats of honor in the front row. When Norris made his way to center stage, Bruce called him over to meet McQueen.

"Good luck with the fight," McQueen said, "and with your scene tomorrow."

"Thank you," Norris said, slightly in awe.

Skipper and Norris went into the ring and bowed. Skipper immediately threw a round kick, one of his favorite moves. Norris anticipated this and blocked it, but this time Skipper followed up with a back fist, a technique he had never used before. The unexpected move caught Norris completely by surprise and flush in his left eye. After an intense struggle, Norris managed to win by one point, leaving the tournament with the trophy and a big black eye.

It took the makeup man two hours to hide Norris's shiner. For his film debut, Norris was only required to say, "May I, Mr. Helm?" Dean Martin was to enter the nightclub, hand Norris his gun, and walk to a booth. Norris had spent two weeks practicing the line, but when the cameras rolled and Dean Martin walked toward him, he felt his throat tighten and the words whisper out of his mouth. He assumed his movie career was over, but fortunately the director thought it was fine.

Chuck Norris, Joe Lewis, and Ed Parker had walk-on roles and filmed for a day or two, but Mike Stone, as Dean Martin's double, was on-set for nine weeks and paid $4,500. Despite Martin's drinking, Stone found him to be "easy to work with, really likeable, always approachable." Bruce was also a blast on-set. "This guy was an absolute clown," Stone says, "so wonderful, such a tremendous sense of humor, a practical joker, really like a kid.

Between shooting, he would show you these push-ups, play jokes with coins, magic tricks and stuff."

Stone enjoyed Bruce on-set, but he had heard a rumor about Bruce that really bothered him. Prior to filming, Mito Uyehara, the publisher of *Black Belt*, had alerted Stone that Bruce was telling people he was one of the reasons why Stone, Lewis, and Norris were winning tournaments. Stone couldn't believe it. "I was a champion before I met Bruce."

Bruce and Mike roomed together while they were filming on location in Idyllwild, California. One night as they were about to go to sleep, Stone brought up what Uyehara had told him.

"Bruce, listen, I heard something and it's kind of bothering me," Stone began, "so I just want to say it and I don't believe it's true, but I still have to say it."

"Well, what is it?" Bruce asked.

"Well, Mito pulled me to the side one day at lunch and said you are telling people that Chuck, Joe, and I are winning karate tournaments because we are working with you. Now I don't think that's very accurate because we were already successful champions when we met you."

Caught by surprise, Bruce became defensive: "Is that what you really believe, Mike? Is that what you believe?"

"No, but I heard it and I wanted to ask you directly."

"Mike, is that what you really believe?" Bruce angrily asked again.

"No, Bruce, I don't believe you said it," Mike said, trying to mollify the situation. "It was probably just a misunderstanding."

"But is that what you really believe?" Bruce repeated, unwilling to let it go.

Mike and Bruce continued working together on the movie, but that argument cooled off their friendship. Bruce stopped training with Stone and never hired him for another movie project. In Bruce's view, he had given Stone numerous private lessons for free and yet Mike refused to be grateful. Bruce wasn't telling people he had made Stone, Norris, and Lewis champions; he was saying he had helped them become better champions. He was livid that Stone "really didn't believe" that Bruce deserved any credit for his success.

When he got back to Los Angeles, Bruce let Mito Uyehara know how he felt: "These guys, just because they're designated as 'champions,' don't want to be classified as my students. They want to learn from me but want others to feel that they are equal or almost equal to me. And they want me to say that they are 'working out' with me. To me, working out is for them to contribute also but they don't; it's all one-sided. I have to teach them and that's not working out."

Unlike Mike Stone, Joe Lewis never had any problem giving Bruce credit for his instruction or calling Bruce his "teacher." Lewis and Lee's friendship ended for a different reason.

Joe's wife was a beautician. On December 1, 1969, she went over to Bruce's house to put highlights in his hair. When she came home, she told Joe that Bruce had aggressively made a pass at her. Lewis became enraged. He immediately jumped into his car and drove over to Bruce's home to confront him. He went up to the back door and banged on it. When Bruce opened it, Joe accused him: "My wife says you made a pass at her."

Bruce took one look at Joe, turned to his wife, and said, "Linda, come here. I want you to hear this."

The instant he called Linda over, Joe realized his wife had lied to him and he had been set up. "She was extremely jealous of all my relationships with my male friends. She systematically, covertly set about ending all of my friendships," Lewis recalls. "I felt like a fool. My wife had set me up before this incident, and I immediately knew she had nailed me again. I felt used, tricked, betrayed. I felt there was no way I could ever make this up to Bruce." Lewis dropped his head in shame, turned around, and left. When he got home, his wife said Bruce was lying, but he didn't believe her. Their brief marriage ended soon afterward.

In his daytime planner, Bruce wrote: "Joe Lewis over regarding his wife. End friendship!" When Bruce later decided to hire an American karate champion for *Way of the Dragon* (1972), he cast Chuck Norris, since he was the only one Bruce still liked. That film launched Norris's career, turning him into a household name. Stone and Lewis tried but never made it in the movie business.

Prior to *The Sopranos* and the advent of the Golden Age of Television, the boob tube was considered a vast wasteland. While modern stars bounce between TV and cinema like they are interchangeable content platforms, movie actors used to prefer unemployment to television work. And TV actors had almost zero chance of breaking into the movies. Over the six-year run of *Rawhide* (1959–65), Clint Eastwood was arguably the most famous actor on TV and yet he had to go to Italy to make several spaghetti westerns (*The Good, The Bad, and The Ugly*) to prove to Hollywood he was a bankable movie star.

Even if he had been white and spoke flawless English, Bruce Lee's dream of becoming the world's biggest box office star would have been the longest of long shots. He had been a sidekick on a ratings-challenged TV series that had barely lasted one season. In the two years since then, his career had stalled. His only hope against hope was his celebrity clientele. Every class he taught was a paid audition with some of the most powerful men in the industry. He needed one of them to believe in him so much they would force the studios to give him a movie role.

It was Stirling Silliphant who finally came to Bruce's rescue. Fresh off an Oscar win for *In the Heat of the Night* (1967), he was hired to adapt Raymond Chandler's hardboiled novel *The Little Sister.* The title was changed to *Marlowe*, and James Garner was cast as the eponymous detective Humphrey Bogart had made famous in *The Big Sleep* (1946). To shoehorn Bruce into the movie, Silliphant simply invented the character of Winslow Wong, a mob henchman. "By the time of *Marlowe*, I had seen so many parodies of a thin guy with a weasel face and a fat guy with a black suit come into offices to threaten people that merely seeing such types enter a room would send me into gales of laughter," Silliphant recalls. " 'So,' I thought, 'let's send in one of the world's greatest martial artists and have him demolish Marlowe's office.' "

This was Lee's first ever cameo in a Hollywood movie, the big break he had spent the past two years struggling toward.

On August 21, 1968, Bruce began filming his two brief appearances. In the first three-minute-long scene, Lee, as Winslow Wong, struts into Marlowe's office wearing a brown suit and a turtleneck. Winslow has been sent by his mob boss to stop Marlowe's investigation into a blackmail case. To get the detective's attention, he immediately sidekicks a hole in his wall and karate chops a coatrack into kindling. Marlowe pulls a gun. Winslow Wong scoffs, "You won't need that," saunters over to his desk, and lays down $500.

"For that you can kick the ceiling in," Marlowe wisecracks.

Winslow tells Marlowe to back off: "You are not looking for anybody, you cannot find anybody, you don't have time to work for anybody, you have not heard a thing, nor seen a thing."

"And what do I do for an encore?" Marlowe asks.

"Nothing, keep on doing nothing for a reasonable length of time, and I will come back and place five more like these on your desk side by side."

"And for whom am I doing all this nothing?"

"Winslow Wong, that is I."

"I like a man who uses good grammar," Marlowe replies.

Silliphant wanted to give his *sifu* some snappy dialogue to showcase his acting chops. It nearly backfired. In the back-and-forth patter, Bruce comes off as stiff and nervous, over-enunciating certain lines and mispronouncing others. Sharon Farrell, who played Orfamay Quest, remembers how much Bruce struggled with the scene. "Bruce was fine in life, but when he got in front of the camera, he had problems," Farrell says. "He tried too hard."

Whatever his difficulty with the dialogue, Bruce came alive for the demolition of Marlowe's office—the primary reason he was hired. When Marlowe turns down Winslow's bribe, he flies into action: splintering a bookcase, shattering a door, and, most spectacularly of all, jump kicking an overhead light hanging from an eight-foot ceiling. "Since Bruce had the physical capability of doing the whole enchilada in one continuous ballet of directed violence, I didn't want to cut into it," says Silliphant. "Director Paul Bogart agreed, and of course, I rank the scene as one of the foremost martial arts scenes ever to appear in an American film."

Bruce told a friend: "Smashing the lamp was no easy trick. That was the hardest stunt in the whole movie. I had to jump real high and didn't have any help either—just a small running space to get my body up there. But it was spectacular, huh? Oh, the glass wasn't real. That's a typical Hollywood gimmick. Yep, it's made of sugar."

In Bruce's second and final scene, Winslow Wong confronts Marlowe in a high-rise building and invites him out to the windswept terrace. This time wearing a white suit and Cuban boots with elevated heels, Winslow attacks with a series of jumping kicks as Marlowe retreats and insults him for being a paper tiger. Marlowe ends up on the railing overlooking the city far below and taunts, "You're light on your feet, Winslow. Are you just a little gay, huh?" The camera cuts to a close-up of Bruce's face as he becomes enraged. He charges Marlowe with a flying sidekick. Marlowe, who has been setting Winslow up, dodges at the last second. The force of Winslow's attack carries him over the side of the building and down to this death. "The scene was a real gimmick," Bruce told friends. "I only jumped over a three foot wall."

Marlowe was Bruce's first chance to play a villain on-screen. He hoped the flashy moves he demonstrated would convince the studios to cast him as the hero.

If Bruce's challenge was to invent a Hollywood role for himself that didn't yet exist (the Asian kung fu hero), Sharon Farrell faced the more common problem of too much supply for too little demand. Every year thousands of beauty queens from every Podunk town in flyover country arrive by the busload hoping to make it big in Hollywood. A perfect example of the archetype, Farrell was from Cedar Rapids, Iowa, and she had spent the decade of the 1960s slowly climbing her way up from starlet roles in TV shows—like "The Actress" in *Naked City* (1961) and "Kitty Devine" in *The Beverly Hillbillies* (1965)—to more serious acting parts in films. *Marlowe* was only her second significant movie role. Although she wasn't the female lead, her character, Orfamay Quest, is the "Little Sister" of Raymond Chandler's title and she is the one who sets the creaky plot into motion when she hires Marlowe to find her brother. It was a much bigger part than Bruce's.

When she first laid eyes on Bruce Lee she had no idea who he was. Sharon was heading toward her car in the MGM parking lot after a wardrobe fitting when she noticed him bopping along about twenty feet away. "He stopped and it was kind of scary at first and then he started grinning like a little kid, and then he started to laugh, and then he started coming towards me. His smile was just like he had swallowed the sun," Sharon recalls. "It was like he recognized me. I couldn't move. I just started grinning, and he was grinning. It was just joyous and funny. It was like 'Oh, my God.' "

Bruce walked over and charmed Farrell, who was in a bad marriage and looking for a little fun. "I was just miserable," Sharon says. She had recently married her manager, Ron DeBlasio, believing it would advance her career—only to discover after their vows that he wanted her to be a traditional wife.

Bruce offered to drive Sharon to her car. She agreed. Bruce circled around the block several times, mischievously refusing to stop at her car.

"Well, what were you going to do?" he asked.

"I've got some shopping I want to do."

"Okay, we'll do it together," he said.

Bruce was wearing black jazz stretch pants—tight through the thighs and flared at the ankles. Sharon told Bruce she liked them. "Well, let's get some for you," Bruce said. They drove to Capezio and she bought a few pairs. Then they returned to her little one-bedroom apartment on Harper Avenue, just below Sunset Strip, that she had lived in before her marriage.

Bruce flipped through her collection of records, looking for cha-cha music. "I was cha-cha champion of Hong Kong," he said. "Let me show you."

"I know how to cha-cha," she said, smiling.

They danced around the room—until Sharon tripped over a chair and injured her leg.

"Oh, let me fix you," Bruce said. "I give a great massage."

He proceeded to pick her up and carry her to the bed. As he was rubbing her leg, one thing led to another.

"He was the first man I had ever been with who had such a beautiful body. Those abs—his muscles were so defined, it was as if they were chiseled," Sharon recalls. "Bruce was the most incredible lover I've ever been with. He was just so knowledgeable about a woman's body."

The next day she woke up to find Bruce making a breakfast drink: raw eggs beaten up with some salt and Worcestershire sauce. Sharon wondered what she had gotten herself into. She wanted a cup of coffee and some time to wake up, but Bruce was happily whistling away.

"Where are your vitamins?" Bruce asked. When she admitted she didn't use them, Bruce told her about all the vitamins and supplements she should be taking. After convincing her to drink down the egg mixture, they drove to a popular health food store on Sunset Strip. Bruce loaded her shopping cart with vitamins, explaining every one and why exactly Sharon needed to take them.

Sharon and Bruce continued their affair throughout the filming of *Marlowe*. "We just were hot and heavy when we could get away," Sharon remembers. "He would say, 'I'm coming over,' and he'd just show up and then he'd drag me into the bedroom."

When they weren't in bed together, Sharon tried to sketch him. "But he wouldn't sit still at all. He was always exercising," she recalls. "He was like a wiggle worm. It made me so mad. Then I would jump down and start trying to beat him up. He was just so much fun." The only thing that bored her about Bruce was his philosophizing. "When he got kind of preachy about flowing like water, I didn't get that," Sharon says. "He would sit and talk about stuff and sometimes I would just tune out."

The honeymoon period didn't last long. Bruce was happily married; Sharon was not. Bruce had no intention of leaving his spouse; Sharon did. One night when he was talking fondly about his family, Sharon started crying.

"What's the matter?" Bruce asked, swooping her up into his arms.

"I know you have a sweet family and a sweet wife and we are so wrong to be doing this but I want to enjoy what we have for just a little while longer," Sharon said, ashamed at how trapped she felt. "I don't expect any commitments or promises and I don't want to do 'confessions' today. I know this is where our conversation is headed."

After *Marlowe* wrapped in September, they agreed to stop seeing each other, but it was a difficult promise to keep. They attempted to focus on their work. Sharon had multiple auditions for a major role in an upcoming movie, and Bruce was busy teaching his celebrity clients. "I missed him horribly but I was trying to do the right thing," Sharon recalls. "I didn't call him or ask to see him."

On September 19, 1968, Steve McQueen invited Bruce to an early screening of *Bullitt*, the movie that would cement his status as the King of Cool. A week later McQueen flew to a location shoot in Carrollton, Mississippi, a tiny town of 250 people, to star as Boon Hogganbeck in *The Reivers*, a comedy based on William Faulkner's Pulitzer Prize–winning novel.

After several telephone calls to arrange the trip, Bruce followed McQueen to Mississippi to serve as his personal kung fu trainer on October 12. McQueen needed to get into tip-top shape for the October 18 premiere of *Bullitt*. Bruce had his own hidden reason for wanting to visit the set—Sharon Farrell. She had been auditioning to play the female lead in *The Reivers* and had landed the part of McQueen's love interest, Corrie—a hooker with a heart of gold.

When Bruce spotted Sharon next to her trailer, he snuck up behind her and put his hand over her mouth. "Why didn't you return my calls?" Bruce asked. "Did you really think I wouldn't be able to find you?" Bruce dragged her into her dressing room and they made love as quietly as possible, hoping no one would hear them.

Afterward, Sharon had a confession to make. She had already hooked up with Steve McQueen. "I'm just using him to get over you," she said. "But we can't do this again, Bruce. I'm so sorry."

"I understand," Bruce sighed and smiled sadly. "He's such a star. I understand, but I will be one too. Can't you wait for me?"

"It doesn't have anything to do with waiting for you, or you being a star," she protested. "It's not because he's a star and you're training him and you're doing small parts. I'm doing small parts too."

"Come on, Sharon. This is a big movie, *The Reivers*," Bruce snarled. "You are a big star now."

Sharon winced. "Even though I'm Steve's love interest in this movie, the Winton Flyer has a bigger role than me—the little boy, Mitch, and even Rupert Crosse, all have bigger parts than me."

Bruce just stared angrily at her.

"What about your relationship with Steve? What if he finds out about today? He could have you blacklisted all over town," Sharon pleaded. "Oh Bruce, I'm in such a mess. Go home to your wife, but kiss and hold me first, then just go."

Bruce left Farrell's trailer. He avoided her for the rest of the week. Sharon didn't see him again. Her decision tormented her. "I almost went with Bruce. If he had just pushed a little harder, I fear I probably would have walked out of that dressing room with him and never looked back," Sharon recalls. "Bruce took me to the moon and back. He just turned me inside out. But he was married and didn't have a pot to pee in. Steve was so successful—he was my protector. He helped me get away from Bruce. I was in lust with Steve, but Bruce was the love of my life."

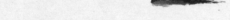

Every marriage is unique and deals with the topic of extramarital affairs in its own way. Bruce's approach was to broach the subject hypothetically.

"If I ever had an affair with a woman," Bruce once said to Linda, "it would be something that happened spontaneously. I would never plan or decide to have a mistress or anything of that nature."

"Uh huh," Linda replied, taken aback.

"If that ever happens," Bruce quickly added, "and if you ever find out about it, I want you to know that it has absolutely no importance at all. All that matters to me is you and the children. Infidelity has no real bearing on a marriage. Fleeting attraction for another female has no significance regarding a matter so fundamental as a marriage."

"Oh yeah?" she asked, growing upset.

"Men are like that," he said.

"Hmmm." Linda paused, before firmly and emphatically stating her red line. "If you ever leave me for another woman, I won't hang around forlornly waiting for you to come back. I'll be gone—like a flash."

"Would you?" Bruce asked, a little nonplussed.

"You're darned right, I would," she said. And Bruce knew she meant it.

None of Bruce's Hollywood pals was faithful. The Mad Men double-standard era of the 1950s had come to a boil with the Swinging Sixties free love ethos. Stirling Silliphant was married four times. Steve McQueen's wife, Neile Adams, was aware of his many affairs: "I told him as long as you don't flaunt it, I can handle it." Roman Polanski's second wife, the actress Sharon Tate, confided to one of her girlfriends that she and Polanski "have a good arrangement. Roman lies to me, and I pretend to believe him." Even Chuck Norris, the right-wing evangelical Christian of the bunch, had an illegitimate child, which he confessed to in a chapter in his memoir entitled "A Sin That Became a Blessing." Bruce clearly had his friends in mind when he responded to a journalist's question about the bad behavior in show business by joking: "Well, let me put it this way, to be honest and all that, I'm not as bad as some of them. But I'm definitely not saying I am a saint."

Much to Silliphant's and Bruce's disappointment, *Marlowe* did not launch his movie career. Released on October 31, 1969, it was a dud at the box office and drubbed by the critics. *Variety* wrote, "*Marlowe* is a plodding, unsure piece of so-called sleuthing in which James Garner can never make up his mind whether to play it for comedy or hardboil." Roger Ebert reserved his only praise for Bruce Lee's two scenes, although he didn't deem him important enough to use his name or get his ethnicity right: "Somewhere about the time when the Japanese karate expert wrecks his office (in a very funny scene), we realize Marlowe has lost track of the plot, too. *Marlowe* becomes enjoyable only on a basic level; it's fun to watch the action sequences. Especially when the karate expert goes over the edge."

Despite being a flop in America, MGM decided to release *Marlowe* in Asia three years later after Bruce became famous in Hong Kong. "They are going to give me top billing," Lee bragged to a journalist. "I really don't know how I'm going to explain that to Garner when I get back to Hollywood."

He never had the chance to tease James Garner. But he did try to rekindle his relationship with Sharon Farrell. They ran into each other by accident at a Beverly Hills doctor's office in 1973. Lee Marvin was also in the waiting room. "He gave me his phone number," Sharon says. "Lee Marvin looked away when Bruce grabbed me and kissed me." Bruce was finally the big star he promised Sharon he one day would be. But Sharon lost the piece of paper. "I thought I put it in my purse, but I couldn't find it afterwards," she says. "I must have dropped it on the floor."

Stirling Silliphant and Bruce working on the screenplay for *The Silent Flute* at Silliphant's Pingree Production offices, circa May 1970. *(David Tadman)*

Stirling Silliphant, Bruce Lee, and James Coburn greeted with flower leis in India, February 1971. *(David Tadman)*

fourteen

the silent flute

Steve McQueen may have stolen Bruce's girl, but Bruce still needed him. For months he had been lobbying Steve about making a martial arts movie together. Bruce knew no Hollywood studio would back a kung fu flick with him in it unless there was also an A-list star attached. In response to Bruce's entreaties, McQueen had been cautious and noncommittal about the idea.

Bruce's plan was to get a firm commitment from McQueen on the Mississippi set of *The Reivers*. After his tryst and breakup with Sharon Farrell in her trailer, Bruce approached McQueen and told him that Stirling Silliphant was eager to write the script. "Will you star in it?" he asked.

"You should talk to my business partner, Robert Relyea, first," McQueen dodged.

Bruce sat down with Relyea, who was also the executive producer on *The Reivers*, and made his pitch: Steve McQueen to star, Stirling Silliphant to write, and Bruce Lee to costar in the first ever martial arts movie made in America. To illustrate the concept, Bruce showed Relyea his boyhood stack of Hong Kong kung fu comic books. "This will be the next big trend in films," Bruce said. "All we need is the financing."

Robert Relyea didn't think it was a good career move for McQueen. He tried to gently turn Bruce down, but when Bruce didn't take the hint and kept pushing, Relyea finally exploded: "Stop bothering me, Kato, and forget this crap about starring in movies. Just concentrate on keeping our star in shape. And do yourself a favor. Throw away those stupid comic books—they're a waste of time!"

A less determined man might have given up, but, after returning from Mississippi, Bruce met with Silliphant and argued that they should pitch McQueen together. He was certain the two of them could convince Steve to say yes.

Once McQueen agreed to a meeting, they went to the Castle to explain the story concept: Cord the Seeker embarks on a journey to discover the true nature of the martial arts. Along the way, Cord must defeat several enemies—Blind Man, Rhythm Man, Monkey Man, and Panther Man—who represent greed, fear, anger, and death. There would be tons of great fight scenes. McQueen would, of course, be the hero, Cord, while Bruce would play all four of the enemies.

"Hmm," Steve paused. "Do you have a script yet?"

"No," Bruce said, "but Stirling is the best screenwriter in Hollywood."

"If you sign on," Silliphant said to McQueen, "I'll write it."

"I don't know. My schedule is pretty booked at the moment," McQueen said, trying to be polite. "I couldn't get involved right now. But once you have a script, I'll read it."

As McQueen hedged, Bruce tried to keep his cool. This project was his ticket to a Hollywood movie career. He was desperate to get it made. He had a Bel Air home, a Porsche, and a young family—none of which he could afford at his current income level. Without McQueen on board, Silliphant would drop out and then Bruce would be back to square one.

Bruce pressed Steve to accept the deal. This was a tactical mistake. McQueen was a loyal friend but he was not a generous actor. He fired directors who didn't make him look good, writers who didn't give him the best lines, and actors who were taller than him. He stole scenes from his male costars and slept with his female leads. Bruce may have believed he was Steve's kung fu master, but McQueen saw him as a high-priced personal trainer who had forgotten his place.

"Let's face it, Bruce, this is a vehicle to make a big star out of you, and I gotta be honest with you, I'm not in this business to make stars out of other people," McQueen finally replied. "I love you, buddy, but you're just going to be hanging on my coattails and I'm just not going to do that. I'm not going to carry you on my back."

Having been slapped down, Bruce left the mansion in a rage. As he stood in the courtyard with Silliphant, he looked up at the windows, raised his fist, and shouted, "I'm going to be bigger than he is. Who the hell is he to tell me he won't do this film with me? I'll be a bigger star than Steve McQueen!"

After McQueen's refusal, Bruce fell into a funk. He started avidly reading self-help books: Napoleon Hill's *Think and Grow Rich!*, Norman Vincent Peale's *The Power of Positive Thinking*, and Dale Carnegie's *How to Win Friends & Influence People*. His favorite author was Hill, who advised his readers to write down a goal and recite it over and over, morning and night.

On January 7, 1969, Bruce wrote down his life goal. Entitled "My Definite Chief Aim," his ambitious and uncanny prophecy reads: "I, Bruce Lee, will be the first highest paid Oriental super star in the United States. In return I will give the most exciting performances and render the best of quality in the capacity of an actor. Starting 1970 I will achieve world fame and from then onward till the end of 1980 I will have in my possession $10,000,000. I will live the way I please and achieve inner harmony and happiness."

The first part of his prediction was a reaction to McQueen's rejection, while the last line was pure wishful thinking. Despite their many side benefits, fame and fortune rarely lead to inner harmony or happiness—as Bruce would soon discover. McQueen had made Lee lose face in front of Silliphant. The American part of Bruce read self-help books, set down goals, and looked to the future. The Chinese half required revenge.

Paul Newman was to Steve McQueen what McQueen was to Bruce

Lee—the older brother he loved, envied, and ached to defeat. "It was a weird 'professional sibling rivalry,'" writes Marshall Terrill, McQueen's best biographer. "Throughout his career, McQueen used Newman as a measuring stick for his success and vowed that one day he would catch up with Newman. Steve's fierce competitiveness would drive him ever onward."

If McQueen didn't want to be in his movie, Bruce would offer the part to Paul Newman. He asked Jay Sebring, who cut Newman's hair, to recruit Paul as a kung fu student. Once they started training together, Bruce planned to pitch his project. But it didn't happen. For unknown reasons, Newman never became one of Bruce's students. Without McQueen or Newman, Bruce's movie project appeared dead in the water.

Seeing that Bruce was in a terrible emotional and financial state, Silliphant agreed to stick with the project. "Bruce was bereft," Silliphant recalls. "This crazy film was not just a passing fancy. It became an obsession; this was his road to stardom." They still needed a star, so on January 13, 1969, Bruce and Silliphant met for lunch and called James Coburn. They offered him the part of Cord and, to sweeten the deal, the chance to direct his first movie. Coburn, who loved Bruce and always wanted to direct, jumped at the chance. The three men quickly signed off on the organizational chart: Silliphant and Coburn would co-produce, Coburn would direct and play the lead, and Bruce would play all four of the costarring roles and choreograph the fight scenes.

"Will you write it?" Bruce eagerly asked Silliphant.

"No, I'm up to my ears in work and I don't have time to do it," said Stirling, who had recently signed to write a Japanese samurai movie. "I could talk to my nephew, Mark. He's a hip, young screenwriter—very talented. He'll get it."

Bruce was hesitant. Coburn was a successful actor, but he was not on Steve McQueen's level. To get a studio to finance the project, they needed a first-rate screenplay.

"Let's meet with Mark next week to discuss the project," Coburn suggested. "Do you have a working title, Bruce?"

"Not yet. Let's call it 'Project *Leng*' for now," Bruce said. "*Leng* means 'beautiful' in Cantonese."

Seven days later Bruce, Jim, and Stirling met with Mark Silliphant to discuss Project *Leng*. Bruce left the meeting deeply concerned about Mark's ability to deliver. After considering the issue, Bruce decided to write the outline himself. Over the next month, Bruce followed the same schedule: in the mornings, he listened to motivational tapes, read out loud "My Definite Chief Aim," and visualized becoming the highest-paid Oriental superstar in the United States. In the afternoons, he wrote the treatment for Project *Leng*.

On February 28, 1969, Bruce met with Stirling and Coburn at Silliphant's office to present his new story ideas and argue that Mark should be replaced with a veteran screenwriter. Stirling and James liked the presentation but were less enthusiastic about removing Mark. He was working on spec (i.e., for free), while a veteran screenwriter would demand to be paid up front. Since Bruce didn't have any money, the fee would fall on Silliphant and Coburn. After some back-and-forth, they finally agreed with Bruce, who later wrote to a friend: "We will speed up the process as soon as the professional comes up with the treatment. Everything is going big gun."

The prospect of being fired by his famous uncle lit a fire under Mark, who pleaded with Stirling not to replace him. Stirling relented. Mark could keep working on the project in secret. If what he wrote was good, Stirling would show it to Coburn and Lee. Stirling warned his nephew to write fast. There was only a small window of opportunity when Bruce would be distracted from his obsession with Project *Leng*. Stirling had found another way to help Bruce Lee make his mortgage payments.

After *Marlowe*, Silliphant's next screenplay was *A Walk in the Spring Rain*, a love story starring Ingrid Bergman and Anthony Quinn. He snuck a fight scene into the script and convinced Columbia Pictures to hire Bruce as the fight coordinator. "Since the story was located in the Tennessee Mountains, I couldn't write any Orientals into the fight because they simply don't have

Asians down there in Gatlinburg," Silliphant explains. "But I did bring Bruce to Tennessee to choreograph the fight."

On April 17, 1969, Bruce arrived in Gatlinburg to stage the scene with two local stuntmen—big redneck types, who resented that Silliphant had brought in an outsider. They took one look at this 135-pound, bespectacled Chinese guy and scoffed, "A stiff breeze would blow him over."

"This little guy, pound for pound, can rip a lion's ass," Silliphant told them, "so you better not mess with him."

"Bullshit," they replied.

"We better clear this up," Silliphant said, "because he's your boss and you are working for him."

Silliphant explained the situation to Bruce and suggested a demonstration. Without hesitation, Bruce grabbed a kicking shield from one of his bags.

"Okay, one of you guys hold this shield," Bruce said to the two stuntmen. "I'm going to give it a little kick. But I suggest you brace yourself first, because, you know, I kick pretty hard."

"Sure, buddy, sure," they chuckled.

"Hey, let's make this interesting," Silliphant interjected, "and stand them next to the swimming pool."

"Cool, man, cool," the stuntmen said.

The first guy held the air shield loosely next to his chest and grinned at his friend. With no movement, no run, nothing, just standing in front of the guy, Bruce flicked out a sidekick that catapulted the stuntman into the middle of the pool.

The second stuntman didn't believe it. "No way. That's a trick. Some kind of Chinese magic," he said, picking up the shield and bracing himself like a linebacker. "Try that shit on me."

Bruce's next kick sent the second one nearly to the end of the pool, almost missing the water. As the stuntmen climbed out of the pool, rubbing their chests, their attitudes were completely adjusted. "These guys came up Christians! Instant baptism!" recalls Silliphant. "They became slaves of Bruce, and Bruce loved it."

While they were in Tennessee, Stirling informed Bruce that he had given his nephew a second chance to work on the project. After they returned to Los Angeles, Stirling, James, and Bruce met with Mark over lunch on May 12, 1969, and told him what they wanted. Six weeks later, Mark sent them his treatment for the project. No one liked it. On July 25, Mark was fired a second time, and the three principals agreed to find a professional screenwriter. Their search, however, was delayed by what happened the night of August 8, 1969.

On August 7, 1969, Jay Sebring visited Steve McQueen to give his friend a trim in the living room of the Castle. Sebring planned to check in on his former girlfriend, Sharon Tate, the next night, and he invited McQueen to join him. Steve, who had also dated Sharon, agreed. Tate was eight and a half months pregnant, and her husband, Roman Polanski, was stuck in London finishing a screenplay. Sharon had been semiseriously complaining to all her friends about how her husband had left her alone with two annoying houseguests: Voytek Frykowski, an old friend of Polanksi's from Poland, and his girlfriend, Abigail Folger, heiress to the Folger coffee fortune.

The next night Sebring planned to pick up McQueen, but Steve canceled at the last moment when he unexpectedly ran into a former lover and decided to spend the evening with her instead. Sebring drove to Tate's home alone.

At the Spahn Movie Ranch on the outskirts of Los Angeles County, Charles Manson told his hippie cult followers: "Now is the time for Helter Skelter." Borrowed from the Beatles song, it was Manson's term for what he prophesied was the coming apocalyptic race war between blacks and whites. He hoped to incite the revolution by killing some wealthy white people and pointing the blame at black militants. Manson told his young followers Tex Watson, Susan Atkins, Patricia Krenwinkel, and Linda Kasabian: "Go to the former home of Terry Melcher and kill everyone on the premises." (Melcher, a well-known record producer, had snubbed Manson, an aspiring musician.) Manson didn't know exactly who lived there, but said they were "entertainment types." Late at night on August 8, 1969, the four Manson cult members drove to Melcher's former home—currently being rented by Sharon Tate and Roman Polanski.

Shortly after midnight, Tex Watson, Susan Atkins, and Patricia Krenwinkel entered the house while Linda Kasabian waited outside. Through a frenzied and horrific combination of shooting, stabbing, beating, and hanging, they murdered Sharon Tate and her unborn baby boy, Jay Sebring, Abigail Folger, Voytek Frykowski, and Steven Parent, an eighteen-year-old visitor. Before leaving, Susan Atkins dipped a towel in Sharon Tate's blood and used it to scrawl "Pig" across the front door in a vain attempt to make the crimes look like the work of black militants.

The grisly massacre rattled the nation, terrorized Hollywood, and signaled the end of the 1960s peace and love era. The Tate murders became the single biggest crime story since the kidnapping and murder of the Lindbergh baby in 1932. Within hours, the carnage in the Hollywood Hills was front-page news across the world, elbowing aside the triumphant return of the Apollo 11 astronauts from the moon and the investigation of Senator Edward Kennedy's mysterious accident at Chappaquiddick. "This hit the movie community very deeply," recalls Warren Beatty. "The collective response to these killings was what you might expect if a small nuclear device had gone off." Writer Dominick Dunne says, "People were convinced that the rich and famous of the community were in peril. Children were sent out of town. Guards were hired."

The personal and physical proximity of the murders shook Bruce to his core. Jay Sebring was one of his closest friends in Hollywood and largely responsible for launching his acting and private kung fu teaching careers. Bruce had taught Sharon Tate how to kick for *The Wrecking Crew*, and Roman Polanski was a client. Bruce and Linda had been guests at their home. "That was a very scary and horrible time, because our friends had been murdered," Linda recalls. "It also happened just a couple of canyons across from where we lived. The sense was there were crazy people out there randomly killing."

On August 13, 1969, Bruce attended Sharon Tate's funeral with Joe Hyams at 11 a.m. After lunch, they went to Jay Sebring's funeral at 2:30. It was a sad and frightening day for the attendees, which included Paul

Newman, Henry Fonda, and James Coburn. Afterward, Bruce told a friend, "The house was only a couple miles away. Boy, when things like that happen in your own backyard, it scares the hell out of you, especially when you have a family. From what I picked up at the funeral, what they did to the victims was awful. Even the papers couldn't describe it. It was just too brutal."

For three months, the police investigated the murders without any suspects. Bruce remained hypervigilant, taking extra precautions around the house. Polanski, who was crazed with grief, tried to catch the killers. He was convinced somebody in his own circle—possibly a jealous husband—was responsible. The police had found a pair of horn-rimmed glasses that no one could identify on the floor not far from Sharon's and Jay's bodies. Had the killer or killers dropped them? Polanski went to an optician's outlet on Beverly Drive and bought a Vigor lens-measuring gauge—a gadget the size and shape of a pocket watch—to aid his private investigation.

To protect himself, Polanski continued his self-defense lessons with Bruce. Several days a week they worked out at the Paramount gym. One morning, Bruce quite casually mentioned, "I've lost my glasses."

"I never liked your old pair anyway," Polanski said. "After class, why don't I drive you to my optician's and buy you a new frame as a gift."

On the drive over, Polanski's heart raced. Bruce was part of the circle of friends, but he was also, as the only Asian, an outsider looking in. He knew how to use a gun and was an expert in bladed weapons. He had the strength and skill to overpower multiple victims. Perhaps Sebring had invited him over and something had gone terribly wrong. Perhaps he was secretly in love with Tate and had snapped.

When they arrived at the eyeglasses store, Bruce selected new frames and told the clerk his prescription. Polanski breathed a sigh of relief. "As I had hoped," Polanski recalls, "his prescription bore no resemblance to the lenses found at the scene of the crime." Polanski never revealed to Bruce his brief suspicions. In their mutual grief, the two men became extremely close. Polanski later invited Bruce to his chalet in Gstaad, Switzerland, for a weeklong ski vacation and Jeet Kune Do training seminar.

A month after the crime, Silliphant and Coburn put up $12,000 ($80,000 in 2017 dollars) to hire a screenwriter named Logan. He took three months to complete a screenplay for Project *Leng*. Once again, no one liked it. "He brought in a script," recalls Silliphant, "that was mostly science fiction and screwing. None of our plot. So we fired him."

Having already failed twice, Bruce and Coburn pleaded with Silliphant to write the script. He relented but under one condition. "Okay, I'll write the goddamned thing," Silliphant said. "But I'm not going to do it alone while you guys are off fishing. We are going to meet three nights a week in my office from 5–7 p.m. We will dictate the scenes and ideas to my secretary and get it down."

Now over a year into this project, they met religiously through March, April, and May of 1970—twenty script meetings in total. "Bruce and Jimmy contributed enormously and richly to the texture of the script, so that you could smell it," recalls Silliphant. "It was there, and we all got excited." The three men brought radically different flavors to the stew. Bruce filled it with Taoism, Zen Buddhism, and his Jeet Kune Do philosophy, Coburn sprinkled in some mystical Islamic Sufi parables, and Silliphant added some meditations on the timeless state of mind from T. S. Eliot's *Four Quartets*.

The result, which they entitled *The Silent Flute*, was the most ambitious and avant-garde kung fu screenplay ever written. Instead of the typical revenge-driven story line, it was a metaphysical meditation on the meaning of the martial arts. Coburn explained: "The martial arts are used as a tool to portray the self-evolution of man."

In the final draft, the hero, Cord, seeks the Bible of Martial Arts, which contains the secrets of unarmed combat. He must fight his way through three trials, representing Ego, Love, and Death. His guide is Ah Sahm, a blind man who symbolizes his unconscious and plays a flute only Cord can hear. At the end of his bloody journey, Cord rejects the Bible, which represents organized religion, unifies with Ah Sahm, and disappears into nirvana.

The screenplay's structure is pure Joseph Campbell's *The Hero with a Thousand Faces*, the dialogue groovy, trippy, and stained with pot smoke, and the level of sex and violence extreme even by modern standards. The gruesome murders of Sharon Tate and Jay Sebring haunt every page. One scene includes a crucified, decapitated woman with a rose sticking out of her neck; others feature intestines being ripped from a giant black man and a beautiful young boy's brains leaking from a crushed skull. Cord's second trial (love) involves an elaborate lesson in tantric sex with a beautiful concubine. The scene's description reads in part: "Lying together fully relaxed, she parts with her fingers the lips of her vulva and partially inserts his penis." The concubine then says, "These two labia are the fire in the middle. We will lie thus for awhile until we are prepared for the inexpressible experience of unity we call *samsara* when time and eternity become one."

But wait, there's more. The authors intended for the movie to be filmed in three locations (Thailand, Japan, and Morocco) and six languages (Thai, Cantonese, Arabic, Japanese, Urdu, and English). With their script complete, all they needed was a Hollywood studio crazy enough to finance an X-rated, multimillion-dollar, multilingual, mystical, martial arts movie.

Before they had a chance to pitch any studios, Bruce Lee was sidelined with a potentially career-ending injury. On August 13, 1970, exactly one year after Tate's and Sebring's funerals, he placed a 125-pound barbell on his shoulders and bent over from the waist while keeping his back straight—a "Good Morning" exercise. On this particular day, for whatever reason, Bruce failed to warm up properly, and something snapped in his back. At first he only felt a mild twinge of discomfort, but over the next few days, the pain became more severe, forcing him to seek out a doctor. After extensive examinations, the final diagnosis was that he had injured his fourth sacral nerve, permanently.

The doctors prescribed three months of bed rest followed by three more months of rehab. He asked if he would be back to normal after six months. They told him to forget about kung fu: "You will never kick high again." For Bruce Lee, this was like a death sentence. The martial arts were his whole life and livelihood. How was he going to realize his Definite Chief Aim? What would he do for work? How would his family survive?

For three months, Bruce was confined to a bed—an exquisite form of torture for someone as hyperactive as "Never Sits Still." He only left the house for his weekly treatment of cortisone injections. It was a hell of mental anguish, physical agony, and financial stress. "I really got scared because I just got Shannon and I spent a lot of money on doctors for my treatment," Bruce told a friend. "I'm not afraid for myself because I can always exist, but when you have others to feed, it scared me a lot."

As he lay flat on his back unable to act or teach, the bills piled up. Even before the injury, Bruce had overextended himself and failed to save a penny for a rainy day. He had gambled everything on *The Silent Flute*—a project entirely dependent on his physical health. As the family's prospects for solvency went from dim to dismal, Linda made a decision.

"I'm going to work," she told Bruce.

"Absolutely not," her proud patriarchal Chinese husband replied. "You already have a job: wife and mother. It would be a disgrace and loss of face for my wife to work."

"I'm getting a job," she insisted. It was one of the few times she ever stood up to him. Linda almost always let Bruce have his way, unless his bullheadedness was harmful to the children. Protecting them was her first priority.

Without a college degree, past work history, or qualifications of any kind, she applied for a job at an answering service. Under past experience on the application, she put down: secretarial chores for my husband's business. "It was true enough," Linda reflects. She got the minimum-wage job and worked evenings from four to eleven with an hour commute each way. She fed five-year-old Brandon and sixteen-month-old Shannon dinner at three before leaving Bruce to look after the kids. It was his first time changing a diaper. To save face, Bruce insisted they never tell anyone that his wife was working. He developed an elaborate scheme of excuses for why Linda was not at home if anyone called or came over: she is shopping or visiting friends. Linda would come home after midnight to find Shannon, Brandon, and Bruce asleep. "But Bruce would often leave me beautiful notes of love and appreciation, which made it all worthwhile," she says.

Seeing him so despondent and worried, Linda said to her husband,

"Perhaps it would have been easier for you to achieve your goals if you had not had the responsibility of me and the children."

"No matter what, no matter how bad times are and how bad they become," Bruce replied, "I want you to know that the most important thing in my life is to have you and the children around me."

Trapped in bed, Bruce's brain roamed free. For inspiration, he read all the works of Krishnamurti. Then he began to write. He filled eight notebooks with script ideas, quotes from his favorite authors, and commentary on the martial way. He wrote constantly, putting into words his training methods and philosophy of Jeet Kune Do. He later considered turning his notes into a book but ran out of time. After his death, Linda published some of his notes as *The Tao of Jeet Kune Do*, the best-selling martial arts book of all time.

Once he could walk again, Bruce began slowly rehabilitating by trying a little bit of resistance training to strengthen his muscles. He also utilized some Eastern medicine, like acupuncture. Bruce decided the doctors were wrong. He would practice martial arts again, and he would accomplish this through hard work and positive thinking. On the back of one of his business cards, he wrote "Walk On!" and placed it on the stand next to his desk for motivation.

After five months, Bruce began working out moderately and resuming light training. To the shock of his physicians, Bruce was soon able to do everything he could before. He could kick high. He was his old self with one exception: his back remained a chronic source of discomfort for the rest of his life. He simply decided it would not stand in his way, pushed through the pain, and once again was able to lead what appeared to outsiders to be his normal lifestyle.

After much discussion, Silliphant and Coburn agreed that the only studio executive audacious enough to back an X-rated mystical martial arts movie was Ted Ashley, the new chairman of Warner Bros. He had been hired to turn around the failing studio by focusing on the counterculture youth market and had recently enjoyed great commercial success with the *Woodstock* documentary (1970). Silliphant intended to pitch *The Silent Flute* as the *Easy Rider* (1969) of fight films.

As one of the most famous screenwriters in town, Silliphant was able to convince Ashley to invite him and Bruce Lee to an exclusive dinner party at Ashley's Beverly Hills mansion. "It was strictly for the most important people in the movie industry," Bruce bragged to friends. "These men have enormous power to make a movie or kill it. Some actors would give their right arm to be invited." As proof of the movie's concept, Silliphant asked Bruce to give a short kung fu demonstration for the VIP crowd. He immediately took control of the room. "I vividly recall Bruce astonishing us with his demonstrations of various kicks and breaks," recalls Ted Ashley. "It took my breath away! It was one thing to know that there is something called 'martial arts,' but it was another thing entirely to be two or three feet away from it."

Having wowed the boss, Silliphant submitted the screenplay to Warner Bros. "They instantly loved it," Silliphant claims. Perhaps, but in Hollywood talk is cheap; true love is measured in money. Warners would make the film but not with a single American dollar. The entire movie had to be filmed in India where Warner Bros. had huge sums of frozen funds. The Indian government did not allow American film studios to remit the money they made at Indian box offices back to the United States; it could only be used to make movies in India. The problem was no American producer or director wanted to film in a country as impoverished as India, so the money was trapped. Ted Ashley told Silliphant, "The rupees are sitting in India. You guys go over and figure it out."

On January 29, 1971, they flew first class from Los Angeles to Bombay (Mumbai) to scout locations for the next two weeks. Coburn and Silliphant arrived with grave reservations—both had been to India before and didn't think the subcontinent was right for their film. Bruce was eager and filled with hope. On the plane flight from Bombay to New Delhi, Bruce worked out his nervous energy by repeatedly punching a thick notebook in his lap.

"Hey, man, you've been doing that for an hour now," Coburn finally complained. "Can't you stop it for awhile?"

"I've got to keep in shape," Bruce apologized.

From New Delhi, they were driven north to the desert on the border with Pakistan. As the star, Coburn was seated up front with Silliphant and Lee was sitting in back. "The road is terrible!" Bruce wrote to Linda. "And driving is a nightmare." Hour after hour on patchy dirt roads was extremely rough on Bruce's back. To distract himself, Bruce started singing pop songs under his breath, mile after mile. Coburn finally turned around and said, "For Christ's sake will you stop that. You're driving me crazy." When Coburn turned back, Bruce shook his fist at the back of Coburn's head.

They stopped at a dumpy dive for lunch but the food was inedible. Bruce ordered a couple of lamb chops, which he couldn't chew. He threw his food to a starving dog that had been watching them. Instantly, from the kitchen, three Indian waiters came out with sticks and brooms and started beating the dog and took the meat away. Bruce stood up indignantly, intent on pounding the waiters into the dirt. Coburn grabbed Bruce's arm and shook his head. The cook came over and said, "Pardon me, Sahib, but you don't understand. Our children have no food, and to give it to a dog is wrong." Tears welled up in Bruce's eyes. "I thought I saw poverty in Hong Kong when I was growing up, but it was nothing compared to India," Bruce later told a friend. "I never realized how good we live until I went there. Flies all over the place. Starvation, very common. People and kids, begging for food, some lying along dusty roads, dying from lack of food."

From northern India, they flew south to Madras (Chennai). Bruce would point out of the window: "Hey, it's beautiful down there. We can shoot down there."

"You can't put a crew down there," Coburn said. "What are we going to do, parachute them into the jungles? Where are we going to put the generator? Where are we going to live?"

Besides adequate locations, they also hoped to find talented local martial artists for the fight scenes to avoid the cost of flying in foreign stuntmen. In Madras, they held tryouts for local fighters. Nine Indian martial artists showed up. Bruce stood in front of the group and said, "Now, let's see where you are at—what you can do." All of a sudden, it was utter chaos. The nine guys just started beating the hell out of each other. Within seconds, one guy was streaming blood from his mouth. Bruce held up his hand and shouted, "No, no! Hold it a minute! Look, this is what I mean." Without any warm-up and with a bad back, Bruce gave a little demonstration that left them awestruck. They had never seen anything like it. When he finished, they all went down on their knees.

"What do you think?" Coburn asked him afterward. "Can we use any of them?"

"No way," Bruce said. "It would take me at least three years to train any of those fellows to the right level."

At the airport as they waited for the flight to Goa, Bruce noticed a group of Indian boys staring at him. They had never seen a Chinese man in person. He called them over and began performing magic tricks, snatching coins from their hands or making a fork disappear. More boys gathered. Bruce demonstrated kicks, punches, and kung fu forms for the kids. The boys laughed and applauded. Coburn, who preferred to travel quietly, sighed in annoyance.

They arrived at the beaches of Goa to find them overrun by Western hippies from America, Germany, France, and Britain, beautiful long-haired young people lying around naked. "God knows how but all the hippie kids knew who Bruce Lee was," recalls Silliphant. "They must have seen him in *The Green Hornet*. They knew him more than they knew Coburn." The hippies invited them to hang out. For two days, Silliphant, Coburn, and Lee smoked Nepalese hash and talked about how to adapt their screenplay for India. Coburn didn't think it was possible, Silliphant was ambivalent, and Bruce anxiously tried to convince them that they could shoot around bad locations. "Warner Bros. wants to do it. Why wouldn't we do it?" Bruce argued. "To hell with the locations, we can make this work. We will make this work."

Warner Bros. had paid for the entire trip out of blocked rupees and made all the arrangements. At every hotel, James Coburn, as the director and star, was given the biggest suite, while Silliphant, the lowly writer, and Lee, the no-name Chinese actor, were put in adjoining closet-sized rooms. The lumpy bed in the Goa Hotel irritated Bruce's back. By the time they flew to Bombay for their last night before returning home, the pain was excruciating. A chauffeur drove them from the airport to the Taj Mahal palace. Coburn was checked in to a suite the size of a house. "It was embarrassing, you could put an entire production company in this thing," Silliphant recalls. "Of course, he wasn't apologizing; he was a big star. This is his due, right?" Lee and Silliphant once again had tiny rooms. Bruce was indignant. This was the final blow and he became enraged.

"One day I will be a bigger star than McQueen and Coburn," Bruce declared to Silliphant.

"You are Chinese in a white man's world," Silliphant told Bruce. "There's no way."

On February 11, 1971, they departed from Bombay divided. Coburn was convinced India was completely wrong for the project artistically. Silliphant didn't think India was ideal, but was certain kung fu movies were the next big trend and believed it was worthwhile to get a jump on the market. Bruce couldn't afford to let the project die. Coburn and Silliphant offered to help him with his money problems, but Bruce was too proud and refused.

When Coburn told Warner Bros. the movie couldn't be made in India, the studio jettisoned the project—it was blocked rupees or nothing. Bruce was furious, bitter, and brokenhearted. He felt betrayed by his closest Hollywood friends. "Coburn screwed it up," Bruce declared with anger in his voice. "He didn't want to go back to India so he told Warner Brothers that India had no good locations. He killed the whole damn project. I was counting so heavily on that movie. It was my one chance of a lifetime. Shit, if I knew he was gonna do that, I wouldn't have had him as a partner."

Even after Coburn and Warner Bros. dropped out, Bruce refused to give up on *The Silent Flute*. He couldn't admit defeat or let the fantasy go. "*Silent Flute* is moving along fine," he assured his Oakland student Leo Fong. "We ran into some problems in location, but we should know real soon on the official date." Bruce met with other producers. He pitched Roman Polanski: "If you ever want to direct a meaningful martial arts movie. . . ." For months he kept at it without results. "Nothing new developed with *Silent Flute*," he wrote to his L.A. student Larry Hartsell on June 6, 1971. "It's a matter of time."

Slowly, piece by piece, the dream died.

James Franciscus (Mike Longstreet) and Bruce Lee (Li Tsung) between takes on *Longstreet*, June 1971. *(ABC Photo Archives/ABC/Getty Images)*

Practicing *chi sao* (sticky hands) on *Longstreet*, June 1971. *(ABC Photo Archives/ABC/Getty Images)*

fifteen

the way of longstreet

While Bruce Lee was desperately trying to get Hollywood to make its first ever kung fu movie, he received some unexpected East Coast competition from the most unlikely of sources: a young, struggling Jewish comedy writer from Brooklyn named Ed Spielman. Ed wrote and sold jokes to Phyllis Diller and Johnny Carson. But ever since watching Akira Kurosawa's 1956 classic *Seven Samurai* as a teenager, Spielman's real passion was Asian culture. While Bruce was studying philosophy at the University of Washington, Ed was one of five students in Brooklyn College's Chinese language department. As an extracurricular he studied Japanese karate and, after he graduated, Chinese kung fu.

Still obsessed with Kurosawa, Spielman decided to write his first treatment for a movie about Miyamoto Musashi, Japan's most famous samurai. In the first draft, Musashi travels to the Shaolin Temple in China and befriends a Shaolin monk, who teaches him kung fu. Sometime in 1967, Spielman gave the story to his comedy-writing partner, Howard Friedlander, a graduate of New York University film school.

"The story of that monk just resonated with me. I loved that character," Friedlander says. "I suddenly got this idea—it burst in my brain—and I turned to him and said, 'Ed, it's a Western.' And he said, 'What?' And I said, 'It's a Western. The Shaolin monk—bring him to the West.' And his mouth dropped open. He realized that was it." They went to Friedlander's apartment and started writing the outline. Spielman came up with the idea of making Kwai Chang Caine a half-American, half-Chinese Shaolin monk. "That guy is me," Spielman says. "That Caine character is me in a way, just like Siegel and Shuster did Superman. He was always Eurasian; he always didn't fit in." When it was finally done, they entitled their treatment: *The Way of the Tiger, The Sign of the Dragon*.

In 1969, Spielman and Friedlander submitted a portfolio of their jokes to Peter Lampack, a young agent at William Morris. Into the middle of the packet, Spielman slipped their movie treatment about a Eurasian Shaolin monk, who roamed the American West of the 1880s, righting wrongs with pacifist, Eastern philosophy and if that failed, kicking serious cowboy butt. "I didn't think much of the comedy material quite frankly," Lampack recalls, "but I was quite taken with their story of a half-Chinese, half-Caucasian boy, because it was a completely fresh idea."

Fired up with youthful enthusiasm, Lampack tried and failed to generate interest inside William Morris. Undaunted, he took it out to market himself, pitching it to every studio and producer in Hollywood as a James Michener–type tale about an exotic locale that an American audience could understand. "I took fifty rejections," Lampack says. "I was young enough and idealistic enough not to realize that a mixed-race protagonist was not high on the list of priorities for most studios, because there was a substantial prejudice, then, in the United States, following World War II, and the immediate decades following—an anti-, if not an overt but subtle, anti-Oriental sentiment."

The only person to take an interest in the treatment was Fred Weintraub, a forty-one-year-old executive at Warner Bros. Formerly the owner of the Greenwich Village nightclub the Bitter End, Weintraub was close friends with Ted Ashley. When Ashley was hired to revive Warner Bros., he put Weintraub in charge of a development fund earmarked for countercultural, youth-appealing projects like Columbia Pictures' *Easy Rider* (1969). Weintraub's first act was a million-dollar bet on a documentary about a music concert in upstate New York. Released March 26, 1970, *Woodstock: 3 Days of Peace and Music* made so much money at the box office it saved Warner Bros. from bankruptcy.

One of his next projects was Spielman and Friedlander's treatment for *The Way of the Tiger, The Sign of the Dragon*. "I liked the idea and gave the boys something like $3,800 to write a screenplay," recalls Weintraub. The boys turned in the screenplay on April 30, 1970. As soon as Weintraub read it, he was sold. "Now I just had to sell the Warner Bros. honchos on the idea of a kung fu western," Weintraub says.

During a trip to L.A., he decided to study the source material for the script, whose lengthy title had been changed to a Chinese word hardly any American had ever heard before: *Kung Fu*. He camped out in the Warner's vaults to watch "some of these Chinese 'chop-socky' films that were becoming popular in Asia, but which had so far gone little seen in America." While underwhelmed by their execution, Weintraub was inspired by their potential. "For the most part, the films were a mess: unbearably long with incomprehensible stories, bargain-basement production values, and insipid, badly dubbed dialogue. But in the last ten minutes of each film, there would be some kind of battle where a single heroic martial arts master dressed in white would take on a swarm of black clad attackers and defeat them all with lightning fast kicks, flips, and punches—knocking my socks off in the process."

Fred shared his enthusiasm for the potential of kung fu movies with his old friend Sy Weintraub (no relation). Sy, who had made a fortune producing the Tarzan movies and TV series, was one of Bruce Lee's private students. He told Fred he had to meet his young Chinese instructor. "That's how I first came face to face with Bruce Lee. Although chest to face would be more accurate, since at 6'2" I towered over the 5'7" martial artist and sometime actor," Weintraub says. "At the time I met Bruce I had never seen any of his TV work. To me he was just a sweet, bright, well-spoken young man, who was extremely knowledgeable about his craft—martial arts, not acting—and anxious to apply his skills to a movie career."

After chatting with Bruce, Weintraub realized he had found the perfect actor for the difficult-to-cast part of Kwai Chang Caine, the Eurasian kung fu master. Several names had been floated in association with the project. Spielman's choice was James Coburn. "He walked beautifully," Spielman says. "He was king for a theatrical. I thought he would have been a slam dunk." But it was Weintraub's project and he wanted Bruce. "We talked about it a lot," Weintraub says.

For a brief moment, it was a go project on the verge of production—"They were going to take us to Durango, Mexico, for the Western scenes," says Friedlander, "and Taiwan for the Chinese sequences"—until March 1, 1970, when Richard Zanuck and his partner, David Brown, were hired as senior executives at Warners. As with almost all Hollywood studio change-overs, the first thing these stepfathers did was to dash against the rocks all the babies of any rival executives lest they grow up into hits and their biological fathers take credit for their success. "It was Zanuck-Brown who came in, and they just canceled the project," Friedlander says. "I'll never forget that." Despite his success with *Woodstock*, Weintraub couldn't save *Kung Fu*. He appealed the decision all the way to the top, but "even Ted Ashley, my best friend and head of the studio, passed on the film. The general consensus was that the public would not be willing to accept a Chinese hero." With one racist swipe, *Kung Fu* was cast down into Development Hell, where previously promising projects are sent to torment the hopes and dreams of their creators.

With *Kung Fu* canceled, Fred Weintraub began looking for another project for Bruce, whom he viewed as a special talent. The treatment for a film called *Kelsey* caught his eye. "It's a story I loved. There's a tribe called the Mandan in North Dakota and they had blue eyes. But some of them also looked Chinese," Weintraub says. "I was trying to figure out something that might work for Bruce. I was crazy."

Set in 1792, the story is about a tall, rugged trapper (Kelsey) who is searching for a hidden path through the Dakota territories that, legend has it, runs through the lands of the Mandan people. In Act I, Kelsey is betrayed by a French-Canadian rival (Rousseau) and left for dead. He stumbles back to the trading post and recruits an old military buddy (Woody) and a Chinese mercenary (Lee) to track down Rousseau. In Act II, they discover the Mandans, fight several ritualized challenge matches with their braves, and bed down for the winter with several of their blue-eyed squaws. In Act III, Kelsey, Woody, and Lee battle it out against Rousseau and his outlaws. In the final, countercultural twist (circa 1971), the three heroes refuse to return to the trading post and choose to live with the Mandans instead.

Kelsey is the primary source material for *Enter the Dragon* (1973). In *Kelsey*, Lee is Chinese, Kelsey is white, and his old buddy, Woody, is black. "I had the actor Woody Strode in mind," Fred says. The three heroes in *Enter the Dragon* are also white (Roper), black (Williams), and Chinese (Lee; conveniently the same name). And their interrelationships are also the same. In *Enter the Dragon*, Roper and Williams are old war buddies, while Lee is a warrior they have just met.

The difference is the hierarchy of the heroes. In *Kelsey*, Lee has 13 lines, Woody 31, and Kelsey 115. Not only is Lee not the lead, he's not even the second most important character. Introduced as "an expert in the martial arts," Lee's first act is to bring Kelsey some tea. In other words, Lee is Kato—the nearly silent kung fu expert and Asian manservant to the white hero. Weintraub believed in Bruce's talent, but he still didn't think a Chinese actor could carry a Hollywood movie.

In the end, it didn't matter. Weintraub submitted the *Kelsey* screenplay to Warner's honchos on March 26, 1971. It was returned with extensive notes. A second draft was submitted on April 28. Despite the changes, *Kelsey* was quickly rejected. It was too weird even for Warner Bros. "God, I never got anywhere with it," Weintraub says.

After the failure of *Kelsey*, *Kung Fu*, and, most heartbreakingly, *The Silent Flute*, Bruce became so disillusioned with Hollywood he started to lose faith. He felt helpless, unable to shape his own destiny. "He began to believe what we kept telling him, which is that you will never be a superstar," says Stirling Silliphant. "You will always be: 'Bruce Lee, stick around and we'll keep working you into things.' " One day Bruce grabbed his six-year-old son, Brandon, and warned him to never become an actor: "When you grow up, you are going to be the biggest producer in Hollywood and you are going to call the shots and you will tell everybody who can be a star and who cannot be a star. No one is going to tell you that because you are Chinese you cannot be a leading man."

Seeing his *sifu*'s frustration and worried he might abandon Hollywood, Silliphant devised a new strategy to make Bruce Lee a movie star. "I thought if we got him a TV series of his own," Silliphant says, "he could get very very hot and that would make the bridge into films." An opportunity to put this plan into action arrived when Tom Tannenbaum, the head of Paramount TV, hired Silliphant to adapt Baynard Kendrick's mystery novels about Duncan Maclain, a blind private investigator who worked with his German shepherd and his household of assistants to solve murders. The plan was for the show, renamed *Longstreet*, to air the first two-hour episode as an ABC Movie of the Week and if audiences responded, turn it into an ongoing series.

Bruce later claimed creative credit for the original idea, telling Mito Uyehara, "The idea of *Longstreet* indirectly came from me. I always had in mind that someday I'd like to act in a movie in which I would be a blind fighter. I mentioned that to Silliphant several times and that's how he got the idea of using a blind detective as the leading character. My idea came from the Japanese movie, *Zatoichi: The Blind Swordsman*."

Silliphant set up a lunch meeting between Lee and Tannenbaum on September 30, 1970. Bruce clearly charmed Tannenbaum, because four days later he wrote in his daily planner, "Will Make TV series."

Silliphant didn't try to make Bruce the star of *Longstreet*. Although he took great liberties with the source material—about the only thing the TV show has in common with the novels is that the lead character, renamed Mike Longstreet, is a blind detective—Silliphant didn't turn Longstreet into a sightless Chinese fighter. He didn't even work Bruce into the pilot TV movie. As with *The Silent Flute*, Silliphant didn't believe Bruce was ready to carry a project yet. In person, Bruce had the charisma and raw energy of a potential star, but that magnetism hadn't translated to the screen. His Kato was bland, his acting in *Marlowe* stiff. Bruce needed the right vehicle, but he also needed to dig deeper as an actor. He needed a breakout performance.

After the *Longstreet* pilot movie aired on February 23, 1971, Tannenbaum ordered four episodes to be filmed before the show's premiere on September 16, 1971. Silliphant, who was the executive producer, decided to dedicate the third episode to Bruce and his personal style of martial arts. He even went so far as to name the episode "The Way of the Intercepting Fist"—the English translation of *Jeet Kune Do.* His goal was to showcase Bruce's talents in the best possible light as a calling card to help Bruce land his own TV show.

Silliphant's strategy was brilliant in its simplicity: he would have Bruce Lee play Bruce Lee. Silliphant, with Bruce's help, wrote the role of Li Tsung as an Asian antique dealer and kung fu master. Li Tsung ends up teaching kung fu to Mike Longstreet, played by James Franciscus.

In the opening of "The Way of the Intercepting Fist," the blind Longstreet is attacked by three longshoremen who want to stop his inquiries into their thefts at the New Orleans port. Out of nowhere, Li Tsung (Bruce Lee) intercedes, dispatching the thugs with kung fu strikes and spinning back kicks.

"What did you do to them?" Longstreet asks.

"They did it to themselves," Li Tsung responds.

"Who are you?"

"Li, Li Tsung," he says in James Bond fashion and pats Longstreet on the shoulder. "May it be well with you."

When Longstreet asks Li Tsung to teach him this ancient art of ass-kicking, Li Tsung refuses.

"I'm willing to empty my cup in order to taste your tea," Longstreet pleads.

"Your open-mindedness is cool, but it doesn't change anything. I don't believe in systems, Mr. Longstreet, nor in method. Without system, without method, what's to teach?"

Silliphant clearly had a blast writing this episode with Longstreet as his stand-in. As he later said, "What I did was simply to take many of the things Bruce had taught me and put them into the script." After all those very expensive private lessons, Stirling must have been delighted that he could write them off as a business expense.

During Longstreet's first session, Li Tsung pulls out a kicking shield and asks him to kick it. Then he hands the shield to Longstreet. "I want you to feel the difference when I put my body behind it." Li Tsung blasts Longstreet back five feet into a chair behind him, which he flips over landing head over heels.

Longstreet's friend Duke Paige (played by Peter Mark Richman), who has been observing skeptically, asks, "What is this thing you do?"

Li Tsung launches into what amounts to a thinly veiled Jeet Kune Do infomercial. "In Cantonese, *Jeet Kune Do*, the Way of the Intercepting Fist. Come on touch me anywhere you can," Li Tsung says and then sidekicks at Duke's knee. "To reach me you must move to me. Your attack offers me an opportunity to intercept you. In this case, I am using my longest weapon, my sidekick, against the nearest target, your kneecap. This can be compared to your left jab in boxing, except it is much more damaging."

Bruce is energized and dynamic throughout these training sequences, fully embodying the character he had spent the last several years creating. In short, he's a star. Bruce was not a method actor who becomes the roles he plays, but a classic Hollywood leading man who turns every character into a version of himself. "I am a personality and each role I play shares a bit of that personality," Bruce later told the Hong Kong press. "I think the successful ingredient in it [*Longstreet*] was because I was being Bruce Lee. I was free to express myself." He expanded on this point with another interviewer: "When I first arrived [in Hollywood] I did *The Green Hornet*. As I looked around I saw a lot of human beings, as I looked at myself I was the only robot there, because I was not being myself."

For the rest of the episode, Silliphant would often let Longstreet deliver some of Bruce's favorite quotes. When, after much struggle, Longstreet finally does a decent kick, Li Tsung cries out in approval, "Yes! Now how did it feel to you?"

"Like I didn't kick. IT kicked," Longstreet replies, uttering a line that

Bruce would later repeat in *Enter the Dragon*—"When there is an opportunity, I do not hit. IT hits all by itself."

As Longstreet's confidence grows, he decides to challenge the longshoreman who beat him up to a rematch. He walks into their waterfront pub and lays down his challenge: "I'm coming down to Pier 6 one week from today, twelve noon sharp, and I'm personally going to kick you in the river."

Li Tsung objects to Longstreet using his art for violent purposes and refuses to continue his lessons. "You have a quarrelsome mind, Mr. Longstreet. Unless you learn to calm it you will never hear the world outside."

Longstreet appeals, "Li, I want you to believe it is more than just learning to defend myself. There were a couple of times there when you were teaching me that I felt my body and my head really were together. It's funny that out of a martial art, out of combat I'd feel something peaceful, something without hostility, almost as though if I knew Jeet Kune Do, it would be enough simply to know it and by knowing it never have to use it."

"Do you always know the right thing to say?" Li Tsung jokes, agreeing to prepare him for his challenge match with the longshoreman.

As the day approaches, Longstreet desperately tries to cram years of self-defense training into a few hours. When he complains that there is too much for him to remember, Li Tsung delivers Bruce Lee's most famous line: "If you try to remember you will lose. Empty your mind. Be formless, shapeless, like water. Now you put water into a cup, it becomes the cup; put it into a teapot, it becomes the teapot. Now, water can flow or creep or drip or CRASH! Be water, my friend."

Over the years, this "Be water, my friend" passage has become every Bruce Lee fan's favorite saying—his iconic tagline. After *Longstreet* aired, Bruce did a television interview with Pierre Berton, Canada's top TV journalist. Since it is the only TV interview with Lee still extant, every Bruce Lee documentary uses clips from it. During their chat, Berton asked Bruce, "Can you remember the key lines by Stirling Silliphant? You wrote there are some lines that express your philosophy. I don't know if you remember them or not." Bruce replies, "Oh, I remember them. I said, 'Empty your mind. Be formless, shapeless like water. Now if you put water into a cup, it becomes the cup; you put water into a bottle, it becomes the bottle; you put it in a teapot, it becomes the teapot. Now, water can flow or it can crash. Be water, my friend.' Like that, you see?" Since then, every Bruce Lee documentary edits out Berton's prompting and presents just the portion where Bruce is saying "Empty your mind . . . ," as if he were a Zen mystic and not an actor quoting a line written by an Oscar-winning screenwriter.

In the final training sequence, the night before the big fight, Li Tsung tells Longstreet he will never be ready unless he changes his attitude: "Like everyone else you want to learn the way to win but never to accept the way to lose. To accept defeat, to learn to die is to be liberated from it. So when tomorrow comes you must free your ambitious mind and learn the art of dying."

Silliphant based this scene on one of his private lessons with Bruce. "He had me running up to three miles a day," Silliphant recalls. "So this morning he said to me we're going to go five. I said, 'Bruce, I can't go five. I'm a helluva lot older than you are, and I can't do five.' He said, 'When we get to three, we'll shift gears and it's only two more, and you'll do it.' I said, 'Okay, hell I'll go for it.' So we get to three, we go into the fourth mile, and I'm okay for three or four minutes, and then I really begin to give out. I'm tired, my heart's pounding, I can't go anymore and so I say to him, 'Bruce if I run anymore,' and we're still running, 'if I run anymore I'm liable to have a heart attack and die.' He said, 'Then die.' It made me so mad that I went the full five miles."

As with *Marlowe*, Bruce also served as the fight coordinator on the *Longstreet* episode. "Bruce was the advisor and would suggest whatever had to be done," says Peter Mark Richman. "He was not just a guy who hung around doing nothing but was always working out."

While shooting the episode from June 21 to July 1, 1971, Bruce also established a daily class to instruct the entire crew in Jeet Kune Do. "Bruce Lee was next door teaching Karate during the Longstreet episodes. All the actors went to study with him. He was in incredible shape and very popular. He would do splits above the ground by putting his legs on one desk and another with nothing underneath, all kinds of incredible things," says Louis Gossett Jr., who played Sergeant Cory. (It was so unusual to have both an Asian American and an African American actor cast in prominent roles on a TV show that *The New York Times* review made a point of mentioning it: "The Chinaman lends a deft touch of exotica. . . . The police detective, played by Lou Gossett, is black.") James Franciscus was particularly grateful for Lee's instruction: "Bruce taught me enough basics so I looked like I knew what I was doing. I really didn't, but . . ."

In keeping with the show's theme, Bruce not only gave physical lessons to the actors but also offered philosophical teaching. Marlyn Mason, who played Mike Longstreet's assistant, Nikki Bell, remembers Bruce's wisdom fondly: "He was just the dearest man. He changed my life in three words. He said to me, 'Don't say a word, just listen and think about it.' And I listened, and he said, 'What is, "is." ' I thought, 'That's pretty simple,' but I didn't say anything. I began to think about it, and I don't think there's a day that passes that I don't think about him because it literally changed my life."

Peter Mark Richman was less impressed. When asked what he thought Bruce was trying to put across on the show, he answered, "It was kind of horseshit philosophy. The writer Stirling Silliphant had the idea he would be someone who was knowledgeable in Eastern philosophy." Marlyn's and Peter's differing reactions reflect the split people had to Bruce's philosophizing. Some found him profound; others thought it was a marketing gimmick. It is entirely possible that it was a little bit of both. Bruce was very serious about philosophy but for someone as self-aware as he was, he had to realize the benefit it added to his persona in an era where the Beatles were learning Transcendental Meditation at Indian ashrams.

The quality actors appreciate most in their colleagues is the ability to listen and react. These are skills Bruce still lacks in *Longstreet*. Whenever he is in a scene where the other actors are talking and he is not the center of attention, he looks visibly uncomfortable. But in the Jeet Kune Do lessons where he is in charge and the scene is all about him, he absolutely dominates. You can't take your eyes off him. It is the difference between a character actor and a star. *Longstreet* was Bruce Lee's breakout performance, the moment he began to realize his potential as a screen performer. He still had work to do, but the moments when Bruce Lee was being "Bruce Lee" are electric.

With a loving eye, Silliphant had finally managed to capture on-screen what had so captivated him about Bruce in real life. And his plan to use this episode as a calling card to get Bruce his own show looked well on its way to success. The excitement inside Paramount over the episode was palpable. On July 10, 1971, Bruce wrote to a friend to share the good news: "Finished shooting 'Longstreet'—be sure to watch it in Sept. I did a good job on it. In fact, Tom Tannenbaum, head of Paramount's TV department, has just contacted me for a development of a TV series for me. Also, he wants me to be a recurring character in Paramount's 'Longstreet.' This happens so fast I don't know what to think—must have done a good job!? Well, what more can I say but that things are swinging my way."

act iii

the returned

> "In this world there are only two tragedies. One is not getting what one wants, and the other is getting it."
>
> —*Oscar Wilde*

Run Run Shaw with his female stars on the backlot of Shaw Bros., 1976. In the middle with the pixie haircut is Betty Ting Pei. *(Dirck Halstead/Getty Images)*

Andre Morgan, John Saxon, Raymond Chow, and Bruce Lee, February 1973. *(Stanley Bielecki Movie Collection/Getty Images)*

sixteen

the last mogul

A year before *Longstreet* while he was still writing *The Silent Flute* screenplay with Coburn and Silliphant, Bruce received a surprise early morning phone call from a Hong Kong radio station wanting to do a live on-air interview. On this morning in mid-March 1970, his initial impulse was to curse them for waking him up so early, but being a professional charmer he quickly agreed, not realizing its significance. Afterward he told his friend Mito Uyehara, "Do you know we spent a full hour on the phone from Hong Kong to my house? Boy, that call must have cost them a mint. But it serves them right for waking me up so early. Can you imagine me talking to thousands of people way over there. I think it's the first time any radio station has done that."

Mito asked, "What did you talk about?"

"Nothing important," Bruce answered. "I really don't know why he wanted to talk to me. First, he asked me if I'm gonna go back to Hong Kong and I said, 'Soon.' Then he asked me if I'm doing any movie right now, and if I ever planned to do one in Hong Kong. I told him that I would if the price is right. You know, my Chinese is pretty lousy now, but hell, if it's good enough for a disc jockey, it's good enough for the listeners."

A week later Bruce was scheduled to make a short trip to Hong Kong. He hadn't visited the colony in over five years. The purpose of his visit was to arrange a visa for his mother to live in America. She was getting older and wanted to be closer to the majority of her children—Robert, Agnes, and Phoebe lived in San Francisco and Bruce was in Los Angeles, while only Peter remained in Hong Kong.

On March 27, 1970, Bruce landed in Kai Tak Airport with five-year-old Brandon. As surprised as he was by the live radio interview, the reception he received upon exiting the plane came as a complete shock. A throng of reporters was waiting. Bruce assumed there must be some big shot on the plane with him, until he heard a chorus calling his name, "Mr. Lee! Mr. Lee!" The press cornered him and asked him the same questions he'd been asked by the disc jockey. Bewildered, Bruce politely answered and agreed to pose with two actresses flanking him on either side while photographers snapped away.

"Shit, I didn't know what was going on," he told Mito afterward. "But I ain't griping. I never had so much attention since the *Green Hornet* days. It's good for my ego. I couldn't believe that one hour over the radio had made me some kind of celebrity in Hong Kong."

It took him several hours to discover the real reason for all the attention. *The Green Hornet* had recently aired on Hong Kong TV and had become so popular with locals they nicknamed it *The Kato Show*. "After I found out, it finally dawned on me as to why the interview over the radio and why the crowd was there. My mom had told the papers about my coming and they printed it. *Green Hornet* was a big hit with the people there," Bruce happily recounted, "and they kept replaying it for months. When I first saw it, I couldn't stop laughing especially watching Van [Williams] speaking Chinese. It was funny! I guess I'm the only guy who ventured away from there and became an actor. To most people, including the actors and actresses, Hollywood is like a magic kingdom. It's beyond everyone's reach and when I made it, they thought I'd accomplished an incredible feat."

The prodigal son had returned as the hometown hero made good.

Everybody wanted a piece of him. "I had a good time even if it was very hectic. My mom's place was bombarded constantly by the guys from TV and the newspapers," Bruce said. "They came not just for me. My mom for the first time in her life got her share of publicity, too. She really dug it."

The biggest request came from the late night talk show, *Enjoy Yourself Tonight*—Hong Kong's version of *The Tonight Show Starring Johnny Carson*. For the first fifteen minutes, the host and Bruce joked around. After years practicing with the American media, Bruce was at his best—relaxed, charming, irreverent. "Talk shows like that are easy to do," Bruce said afterward. "You don't have to memorize anything and can joke all night. There's no serious discussions—everything is light."

After the interview portion, Bruce gave one of his well-honed kung fu demonstrations. He was eager to show off all he had learned since leaving home. He did some two-finger push-ups. With a leaping kick, he snapped in half four one-inch boards suspended from the ceiling by a rope—a particularly difficult stunt. While the crowd was still howling with applause, Bruce led five-year-old Brandon out, and he broke some boards too. Now the Chinese crowd, who adore children, went wild. Just as Bruce's father had him acting in a movie by the age of two months, Bruce was introducing his young son to the family business.

For the grand finale, two assistants were brought out. "The station was so thrilled to get me, they asked me if I needed anything," Bruce recalled. "All I asked for, and got, were two karate black belts." Bruce asked one karate guy to hold on to a kicking shield and directed the other black belt to stand behind him, explaining that if the kick knocked his partner backward, he should grab him. "The stage was small but I felt it was enough to generate some power in my kick," Bruce recounted with relish. "I had to stand less than five feet away, but I kicked that mother perfectly, lifting that guy off his feet, driving him back hard. The second guy didn't expect the guy to fly at him and didn't brace himself. But even if he were ready, no way he could have stopped him. That guy was going too fast. You should have seen the expression of all the people. It was funny when the guys crashed into the props, knocked everything down. The stagehands were all shook up and ran all over the place trying to get the props back. But the two guys on the floor made me laugh the most. They were so shocked; they had the dumbest look on their faces. Man, the whole place was a comical mess."

Hong Kong audiences had watched countless kung fu demonstrations, but they had never seen anything quite like this before. And they had never seen anyone quite like Bruce on their TV screens—his charisma, his energy, or his swagger, which he had honed from close study of Steve McQueen, the King of Cool. "He was so lifelike, even on the screen," recalls Michael Hui, one of Bruce's classmates from La Salle. "He looked like he could step out from the television into your living room." What Chinese audiences were used to seeing were stiff contract actors dressed up and sent out to mouth the studio line under threat of punishment if they strayed. What they saw in Bruce was a free man, unshackled of any institution or even, seemingly, the constraints of two thousand years of Confucianism. "He was a very straight-forward, very Westernized, very gung-ho, can-do spirit," says Ang Lee, director of *Crouching Tiger, Hidden Dragon*. "Unlike the repressed Chinese zigzagging attitude."

Bruce Lee was something new. And no one recognizes the new faster than children. The most important kid watching the show that night turned out to be David Lo, the son of director Lo Wei. As Bruce was joking in the interview, David ran into the other room to grab his father. Lo Wei, who worked for Golden Harvest Studios, was impressed with what he saw. Afterward he called his boss, Raymond Chow, and suggested he watch it. Bruce might be someone worth pursuing. It took Chow a week or two to get a copy of the episode. "Not only was I very impressed by his technique and great form, I was most taken by his eyes," recalls Chow. "Those eyes could express so much intensity."

Raymond viewed Bruce as an interesting prospect, an actor with enough potential to be worth giving a tryout. He tried to track Bruce down, but it was too late. Bruce had already returned to America on April 16, 1970. For the moment, Raymond Chow would have to continue his bitter fight against Run Run Shaw, Hong Kong's last movie mogul, without the assistance of Bruce Lee.

In the decade since Bruce moved to America, Hong Kong's movie landscape had completely transformed. In the 1950s, it was a tiny cottage industry with a handful of bigger studios and dozens of independent production companies. By 1970, it was dominated by one man, Run Run Shaw.

Born on November 23, 1907, near Shanghai, Run Run was the sixth of seven children of a wealthy textile merchant who owned an old vaudeville hall. Run Run and his two older brothers, Run Me and Run Je, were more excited by the possibilities of the entertainment industry than textiles and decided to turn the theater around by staging their own plays. Run Je wrote a Robin Hood–style melodrama, *Man from Shanxi*, and staged it in the dilapidated hall. On opening night the lead actor plunged through the rotten planks of the stage, and the audience laughed, thinking it was intentional. The boys took notice and rewrote the script to include the pratfall as a stunt. They had a hit, and in 1924 they turned *Man from Shanxi* into their first film.

As mainland China became increasingly unstable in the 1930s, the brothers decided to move their operation to Singapore. "We were more interested in distribution than in filmmaking," Run Run remembers. "We bought one movie theater and then expanded our interests in that direction until we owned 120 theaters in Singapore and Malaysia alone." Their string of cinemas became known as the Mandarin Circuit, snaking from Hong Kong through Taiwan, Vietnam, Laos, Thailand, Burma, Korea, Malaysia, Singapore, the Philippines, Indonesia, and Western cities with large Chinese communities like San Francisco.

When the Japanese overran Singapore on February 15, 1942, the Shaw brothers were more prepared for the ensuing disaster than the British Army. They had already liquidated most of their assets and buried more than $4 million in gold, jewelry, and currency in their backyard. After Singapore was liberated, they dug up their hidden treasure and used it to reestablish their empire. "The pearls were a little brown, the watches rusty, the banknotes mildewed, but the gold was nice and yellow," Run Run Shaw recalled. "We were still rich."

Having secured a virtual monopoly on theatrical distribution, the brothers turned their sights to content. With the fall of mainland China to the Communists, Hong Kong was now the movie capital of the Chinese-speaking world. Run Run moved there in 1957 to expand the family's empire. In 1961, two years after Bruce Lee was sent to America, he completed his studio on a windy hill overlooking Hong Kong's Clearwater Bay. He named it Movietown, and it was the largest privately owned studio in the world. The forty-six-acre lot was a completely self-contained operation. All Shaw Bros. films were planned, written, acted, directed, cut, dubbed, and dispatched from one of the ten studios, sixteen outdoor sets, and three sound rooms. Film was processed in the Movietown laboratory; sets were built in the Movietown factory. Nothing was purchased that could be manufactured; nothing manufactured was used only once.

The same was true of its actors. Like MGM and other golden-era Hollywood studios, Movietown had its own acting academy, the Southern Dramatic School, which taught aspiring thespians how to dance, kiss, and fight. Thousands applied, a few hundred were accepted; and of those, only one out of fifty graduates was offered an ironclad Shaw Bros. contract. Once signed, Run Run's power over the house actors would have made Darryl Zanuck choke on his cigar in envy. The contract lasted up to six years with a base pay of $200 per month without any fringe or medical benefits. Actors and actresses had no say over scripts, directors, or costars. Almost all had to live in Movietown's high-rise concrete dormitories. Fraternization between the sexes, drunkenness, and drugs were strictly forbidden on pain of unemployment. About the only way to break the contract was to quit the profession or the country.

With his monopoly on distribution and lock on cut-rate talent, Run Run began pumping out movies, more than forty per year—overwhelming independent producers. "The Chinese film industry was at its lowest level then," Run Run explained. "Films were made in seven or ten days and were of very poor quality and the turnover was small. I held to the idea that in this part of the world where the Chinese population is so large, there had to be a market for quality films." While Run Run's films were of higher quality, the real key to his success was what he had learned as a boy when the audience laughed at the actor who fell through the rotten stage planks: The customer is always right. Unlike the didactic social message movies of Bruce's childhood in the 1950s, Shaw's films pushed no political agenda. "If they want violence, we give them violence. If they want sex, we give them sex," Run Run declared as his corporate mission statement. "Whatever the audience wants, we will give them. I particularly like movies that make money."

Having studied moviegoers from the perspective of a theater owner, Run Run concluded, "Every type of film has its period of popularity. After some time, people get tired of the same sort of film." When Run Run arrived in 1957, musicals were hot and starred effete romantic male leads. Then in late 1964, the fickle public's affection shifted to the bloody Japanese samurai movies (*chambara*). Run Run quickly began churning out his own savage sword-fighting copies (*wuxia*), filled with vengeful superheroes able to leap, somersault, and levitate in defiance of gravity. "Sometimes we do overdo [the violence] a little, especially in the sword movies," Run Run admitted. "But actually, the Chinese audience, and in fact most other audiences, love violence."

The popularity of *wuxia* sword-fighting films declined in 1968 after Communist China's premier, Chou En-lai, declared that Japan was the new imperialist force in the East. Suddenly it became unfashionable to imitate samurai films. As he had done before, Run Run Shaw turned on a dime. With Chinese nationalism as the new trend, Shaw Bros. simply switched to the uniquely Chinese art of kung fu. Hong Kong cinema had a deep tradition of kung fu movies; the most popular of which was the long-running Wong Fei-hung film series. Shaw Bros. revived this tradition with a distinctly anti-Japanese twist to suit the mood of the times with *The Chinese Boxer* (1970)—the first major movie to devote itself entirely to the art of kung fu.

The idea for *The Chinese Boxer* originated with Hong Kong's biggest male action star and Shaw academy graduate, Jimmy Wang Yu, who wrote, directed, and starred in it. "That picture was my idea, and I made the script. I am the leading actor, because I had a good idea," Jimmy says. "Everybody said karate was so powerful and Chinese kung fu is so powerful, why don't you put them into one film?" In the movie, Wang Yu plays a kung fu student whose teacher is killed by Japanese karate fighters. Wang Yu's character dons a mask and challenges the Japanese to combat, defeating them in a series of bloody duels to the death with his "Iron Palm" technique. The resulting felicitous combination of ethnic chauvinism and traditional kung fu was a smash hit at the box office, becoming the second most popular Chinese movie in Hong Kong history. Its success marked the switch from supernatural *wuxia* sword-fighting films to the body-centric unarmed combat of kung fu movies—setting the stage for Bruce Lee's rise to fame.

Bruce was well aware of *The Chinese Boxer*. He attended a special screening in L.A.'s Chinatown with Steve McQueen and Kareem Abdul-Jabbar. Victor Lam, a Chinese producer who attended the screening with them, claims, "From watching Wang Yu, Bruce learned how to show off his technique on film." While it is debatable if Wang Yu, whose athletic background was swimming, had anything to teach Lee about kung fu choreography, Jimmy's success seems to have triggered Bruce's hypercompetitive nature. Just as Bruce dreamed of replacing Steve McQueen as Hollywood's biggest box office star, he would soon try to eclipse Jimmy Wang Yu in Hong Kong. Anything Jimmy had done first, Bruce set out to do bigger and better.

But before that could come to pass, Shaw's grip on the Hong Kong film industry had to be broken. By the end of the 1960s, Run Run had achieved a near monopoly on Chinese film production by defeating his main rival, Cathay Films. Facing no external enemies, all seemed secure. It was a trusted lieutenant that ended Shaw's empire.

Raymond Chow graduated with a journalism degree from Shanghai's St. John's University in 1949, the same year Mao Zedong and his Communist revolutionaries took over the country. Wisely predicting that the new government wouldn't be particularly hospitable to an independent press, Raymond, along with most of Shanghai's creative talent, fled to Hong Kong, where he worked as a cub reporter for the newly launched *Hong Kong*

Tiger Standard. The pay was so low he had to take up part-time work to survive. "At one time I was holding down seven jobs," Chow says.

In 1951, Chow took a better-paying job at Hong Kong's Voice of America office, which was the propaganda arm in America's war against Communism in Asia. The United States had backed the strongman Generalissimo Chiang Kai-shek against Mao Zedong in China's civil war. When the Generalissimo lost and fled to Taiwan, America established its rearguard operations in Hong Kong. Raymond was hired to set up the Mandarin-language broadcasting program for Voice of America.

In 1958, he decided to transfer the skills he had acquired as an American spin doctor to the job of head of publicity for Shaw Brothers Studio. Movie marketing proved to be even more dishonest work than government propaganda. Two months in, Raymond told Run Run he was resigning because he couldn't sell the dreck Shaw Bros. was making. Impressed by his nerve, Run Run said to the young publicist, "You think you can do a better job? I'll make you head of production."

Along with his partner, Leonard Ho, Raymond Chow had a strong run. He was the one who signed off on Jimmy Wang Yu's *The Chinese Boxer*. "I showed the script to Mr. Raymond Chow," Jimmy says. "He let me try it. Actually, Mr. Run Run Shaw didn't bother his mind about it."

By the late 1960s, Shaw Bros. was facing the same existential threat that nearly bankrupted several American movie studios—color television. Cinema attendance began declining at the same time costs were increasing. Run Run—being the kind of tough businessman who would pull the gold out of your teeth and charge you for doing it—decided to shift toward television, downsize movies, and reduce production budgets. "Shaw was thinking of cutting down the operations and using half of the manpower and capital to go into television," says Raymond. "I didn't quite agree with that."

Raymond offered Run Run a deal. He would set up a production company, Golden Harvest, under the umbrella of Shaw Brothers Studio. Golden Harvest would make half its movies, Shaw Bros. would be the distributor, and they would split the profits. Since Golden Harvest's movies would be pushed through Shaw's chain of movie theaters, Run Run could downsize production, and Raymond didn't need to go into sales and distribution.

Even though Golden Harvest was part of Shaw Bros., the new production company still had to compete internally with Shaw's old movie division for talent. As the former head of production, Raymond knew when everybody's ironclad contracts with Shaw Bros. were about to expire. He went around quietly whispering in the best directors' and actors' ears that they should not renew with Shaw, they should move to Golden Harvest instead. Since he didn't have any money of his own, Raymond promised them a percentage of the profits.

Several of the directors Raymond secretly approached went back to Run Run and said, "My contract is about to expire, and you better give me a better deal than I'm getting from Golden Harvest." Run Run confronted Raymond about stealing his best talent. Raymond denied it. "No, don't be ridiculous." Although still suspicious, Run Run believed Raymond, whose nickname was the Smiling Tiger. There the matter might have rested if not for one man—Jimmy Wang Yu.

The success of *The Chinese Boxer* had made Jimmy Wang Yu the colony's biggest box office star and number one heartthrob. Jimmy wanted to join Golden Harvest and get a share of his box office success, but he still had several years on his contract with Shaw Bros. To solve this dilemma, Jimmy decided he would publicly break with Run Run. Raymond tried to dissuade him, but Jimmy went ahead with his plan. Shaw was furious. Feeling betrayed by his most trusted protégé, Run Run canceled the deal with Golden Harvest, fired two of Raymond's top lieutenants, forced Raymond to come to the office for another week before firing him too, and finally for good measure sacked a few other innocent executives just to emphasize his point: rebellion would not be tolerated.

Meanwhile, Jimmy Wang Yu fled to Taiwan. To cut off any income and force him to return, Run Run sought an injunction from a Taiwanese court and took out advertisements in the local press warning producers that Jimmy could not legally work.

Raymond, on the street and broke, turned to everyone and anyone who had an axe to grind with Run Run Shaw—not a short list. Most significant was Shaw's old nemesis Cathay Films. They gave Raymond their

Bruce Lee's Dutch-Jewish great-grandfather, Mozes Hartog Bosman, circa 1880. *(Courtesy of Andrew E. Tse)*

His Chinese great-grandmother, Sze Tai, circa 1890. *(Courtesy of Andrew E. Tse)*

His great-uncle Sir Robert Hotung with Queen Mary at Wembley, 1924. *(Courtesy of Andrew E. Tse)*

His grandfather Ho Kom Tong with decorations, 1925. *(Courtesy of Andrew E. Tse)*

In re:

LEE JUN FON, alias BRUCE LEE, native born citizen of the United States, for citizen's Return Certificate, Form 430. (Male)

....

State of California)
City and County of) ss
San Francisco)

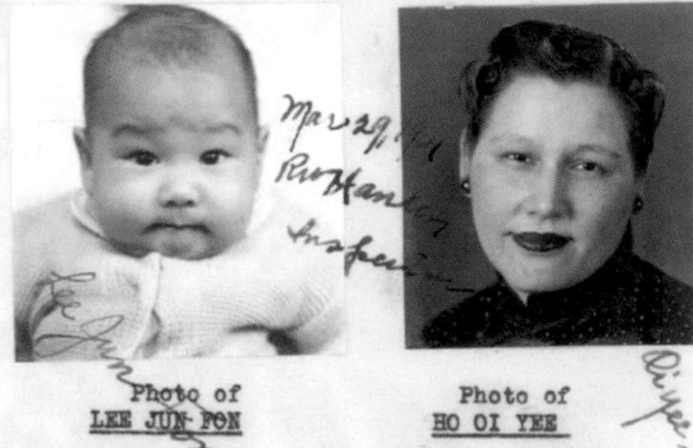

Photo of LEE JUN FON

Photo of HO OI YEE

HO OI YEE, being first duly sworn, deposes and states as follows:

That she is a temporary resident of the United States; that she was duly admitted to the United States by the United States Immigration Authorities at the Port of San Francisco, California, incident to her arrival from China, ex SS "President Coolidge", on the 8th day of December, 1939, No. 39707/8-25;

That she is the mother of LEE JUN FON, alias BRUCE LEE, who is applying for a citizen's Return Certificate, Form 430, at the Port of San Francisco, California; that the said LEE JUN FON, alias BRUCE LEE, was born in the United States;

That affiant has attached her photograph and that of her said son, LEE JUN FON, alias BRUCE LEE, hereto for the purpose of identification;

That your affiant makes this affidavit for the purpose of aiding her said son, LEE JUN FON, alias BRUCE LEE, in obtaining a citizen's Return Certificate, Form 430.

Ho Oi Yee

Subscribed and sworn to before me this 5th day of March, 1941.

Albert K. Chow
Notary Public in and for the City and County of San Francisco, State of California.

Application for citizen's Return Certificate for three-month-old Bruce Lee, photographed beside his mother, Grace Ho, March 1941.

(Courtesy of National Archives at San Francisco)

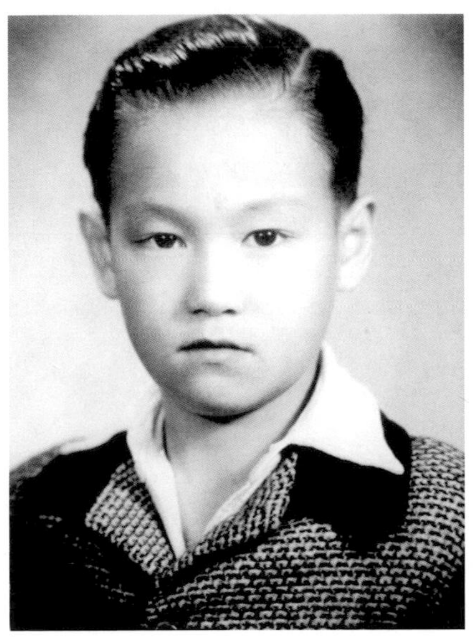

Bruce Lee, circa 1946.

(Courtesy of Hong Kong Heritage Museum)

Peter, Agnes, Grace, Phoebe, Robert, and Bruce, circa 1956.

(Michael Ochs Archive/Getty)

Bruce, bottom row, to the right of his teacher.
La Salle class photo, circa 1950.
(Ng Chak Tong)

Bruce, bottom row, fourth from the left, wearing glasses.
St Francis Xavier class photo, circa 1958.
(Courtesy of Johnny Hung)

With Robert Lee at the cha-cha championships, 1958. *(David Tadman)*

CHA CHA FANCY STEPS

1) Number one	23) Kick step
2) " two	24) eight step
3) " three	25) ∠ 2 step go
4) " four	26) ∠ 4 step go
5) " five	27) 2 step style
6) " six	28) 3 " "
7) " seven	29) Number 4 (3)
8) " eight	30) Rubbing & double
9) slide step	31) Change alone
10) New step (1)	32) B step
11) New step (2)	33) "B" side step
12) change	34) New ∠
13) changing	35) waltz step
14) square step	36) mambo style
15) Tango step (1)	37) side step
16) " (2)	38) straight side step
17) 3 step backward	39) New side step
18) Banana boat	40) wave step
19) shake step	41) circle step
20) starting step (1)	42) "A" step
21) " " (2)	43) "B" "
22) "Poof" step	44) "C" "

Bruce's cha-cha notebook, 1958. *(Courtesy of Hong Kong Heritage Museum)*

Playing a troubled teenager in *The Orphan*, 1960. *(Michael Ochs Archive/Getty Images)*

Bruce and Peter Lee with Ruby Chow's
dog in Seattle, circa 1960.
(David Tadman)

Practicing *chi sao* ("sticky hands") with his father, Li Hoi Chuen,
in Hong Kong, summer 1963. *(David Tadman)*

Tombstone displayed at his
Los Angeles Chinatown school, 1967.
(Courtesy of Hong Kong Heritage Museum)

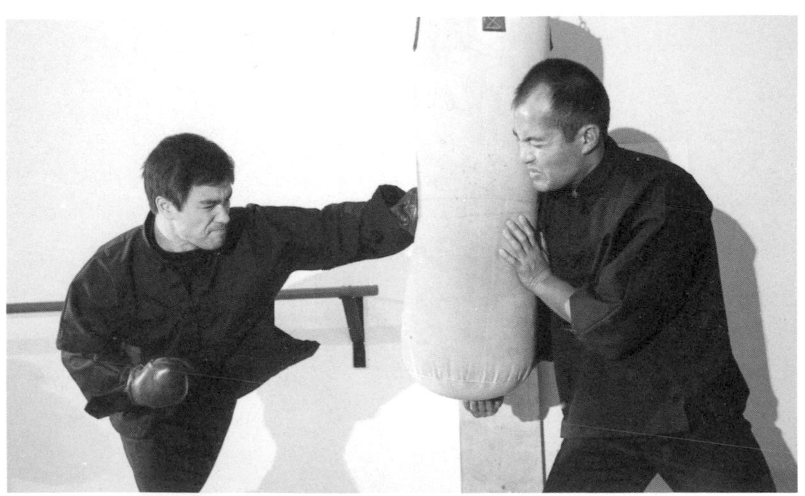

With Dan Inosanto holding the heavy bag, circa 1968.
(David Tadman)

Jay Sebring at Joshua Tree, circa 1966.
(Courtesy of Anthony DiMaria)

Bruce's first and last time on a horse. With Linda Dangcil and Robert Brown in *Here Come the Brides*, April 9, 1969. *(ABC Photo Archives/ABC/Getty Images)*

With Brandon, Linda, and Shannon, circa 1970.

(Courtesy of Hong Kong Heritage Museum)

SECRET

My Definite Chief Aim

I, Bruce Lee, will be the first highest paid Oriental super Star in the United States. In return I will give the most exciting performances and render the best of quality in the capacity of an actor. Starting 1970 I will achieve world fame and from then onward till the end of 1980 I will have in my possession $10,000,000. I will live the way I please and achieve inner harmony and happiness

SECRET

Bruce Lee
Jan. 1969

Bruce's life goal, January 1969.

(Courtesy of Hong Kong Heritage Museum)

The only sex scene of Bruce's career, in *The Big Boss*, 1971.

(Michael Ochs Archives/Getty Images)

With Bob Wall in *Fist of Fury*, 1972.

(Entertainment Pictures/Alamy Stock Photo)

With Chuck Norris in *Way of the Dragon*, 1972.
(Concord Productions Inc./Golden Harvest Company/Sunset Boulevard/Corbis/Getty Images)

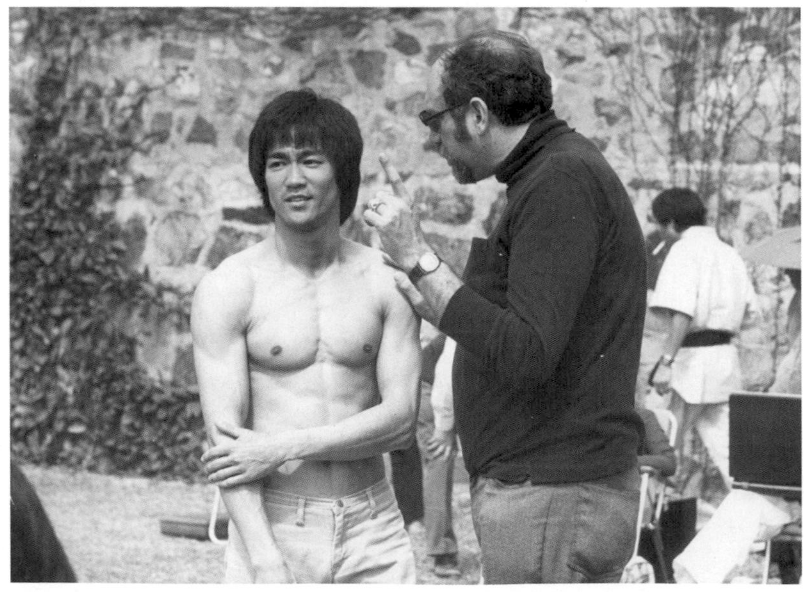

With producer Fred Weintraub on the set of
Enter the Dragon, February 1973.
(Stanly Bielecki Movie Collection/Getty Images)

Brandon Lee in *The Crow*, March 1993.
(Entertainment Pictures/Alamy Stock Photo)

Shannon and Linda Lee attend Hollywood Walk of Fame Star to Honor Bruce Lee at 6933 Hollywood Boulevard, April 28, 1993.
(Ron Galella, Ltd./WireImage/Getty)

Bruceploitation flick starring Bruce K.L. Lea, 1976.
(Everett Collection/Alamy Stock Photo)

The world's first Bruce Lee statue was erected in Zrinjevac City Park, Mostar, in Bosnia-Herzegovina, November 27, 2005. *(kpzfoto/Alamy Stock Photo)*

abandoned, barnlike production studio with soundstages, built initially to house a modest textile mill, perched precariously on a hilltop on Hammer Hill Road. In three short months, Raymond raised enough money to open Golden Harvest for business.

It wasn't great business. Shaw Bros. still controlled the best movie theaters on the Mandarin Circuit; Golden Harvest had to make do with second-run dives. Run Run was able to keep most of his A-list directors. The best Raymond could poach was Lo Wei, a competent, if not particularly brilliant, craftsman, who would later direct Bruce's first two movies. Golden Harvest's top star, Jimmy Wang Yu, was still under contract with Shaw Bros. and could not legally work for anybody else in Hong Kong. So Raymond sent Jimmy to Japan to make a movie with Japan's top action hero, star of the *Zatoichi* Blind Swordsman films, and Bruce Lee's favorite actor, Shintaro Katsu. The movie they co-produced was *Zatoichi Meets the One-Armed Swordsman* (1971).

The problem was the One-Armed Swordsman was a valuable Shaw Brothers property. Jimmy Wang Yu had already played the role for Shaw Bros. in the hit films *The One-Armed Swordsman* (1967) and *Return of the One-Armed Swordsman* (1969). "That was salt in the wound," says Andre Morgan, who worked for Golden Harvest, "because it confirmed to Run Run that Raymond was the Benedict Arnold of Chinese showbiz." Run Run sued Golden Harvest for copyright infringement, fully intending to bleed Raymond's start-up studio dry with legal fees.

To sum up, money was tight, distribution was tough, his talent pool was shallow, his biggest star was a wanted man, and he was facing the legal wrath of the monopoly studio in town. Raymond Chow was a man in desperate need of a savior.

After Bruce's departure from Hong Kong in late April 1970, Raymond Chow was able to track down his phone number in L.A. Bruce was surprised to get the call. He didn't know Chow, but he had heard of him. They started chatting and seemed to hit it off. Raymond asked him if he would consider making a movie in Hong Kong. As with the radio interview, Bruce joked, "If the money is right." They continued talking, but Bruce mostly focused on all the current Hollywood projects he was working on. It was apparent he wasn't particularly interested in Chow's offer. Bruce was fully committed to *The Silent Flute.*

A year later on April 10, 1971, Bruce called Raymond back. *The Silent Flute*, *Kung Fu*, and *Kelsey* had collapsed. He couldn't make his mortgage payments. His back injury was still bothering him. He needed the money.

"What is your best film, do you think?" Bruce asked Raymond.

"I like most of my own films. I won't say they are the best. Looking back I can always find something to improve," Raymond replied, "but I'm happy."

"What about Jimmy Wang Yu's *The Chinese Boxer*?" Bruce asked.

"That is one of the most successful action pictures we have ever made."

"I can do better," Bruce asserted.

"Oh really?" Raymond said, charmed.

"Yes, if you really want to make good kung fu films you should . . . ," Bruce said and proceeded to explicate all the things he would do differently.

"Yes, yes," Raymond placated. "But if you help me, together, I am sure, we can build something." Feeling positive about the conversation, Raymond concluded by saying, "Well, I'll send somebody over to sign a contract with you."

"You are not coming?" Bruce asked, slightly taken aback.

"Well, I'm busy with other things. You know, since we agree on most things on the phone, I'll send a producer over to see you."

They may have agreed on many things, but Bruce wasn't certain he really wanted to sign a contract with Golden Harvest, a struggling studio with finances as shaky as his own. With an offer from Raymond Chow on the table, Bruce decided to approach Chow's mortal enemy, Run Run Shaw. He reached out to his childhood acting friend, Unicorn Chan, who worked for Shaw Bros., for an introduction. "Unicorn and Bruce wrote letters in the 60s and brought up the idea of him coming back," says Bruce's brother Robert.

Bruce sent Unicorn a letter, in a mixture of English and Chinese, to give to Run Run Shaw stating his interest and his stipulations. "Bruce made three demands," recalls Unicorn Chan: "(1) The salary be US$10,000 per movie, (2) He must have the right to make changes in any script given to him, and (3) He must have total control over fight choreography." For an unproven and relatively unknown movie actor, it was an aggressive opening bid. "Bruce Lee wanted too much money to do a film with us," explains Lawrence Wong, a producer with Shaw Bros. "Because if we paid him, we would then have to upgrade all of our other contract stars accordingly."

After some internal debate, Run Run's counteroffer was $5,000 per movie without any mention of script approval or fight choreography control. Linda says that Bruce laughed when he saw the reply, but he didn't reject the offer outright. He wired Shaw to ask about his two ignored stipulations. For Bruce, having control over the quality of the final product was more important than the money. Run Run's paternalistic reply was, "Just tell him to come back here and everything will be alright." This made Bruce furious. He might be broke, but he was a free man and wouldn't be owned by Run Run Shaw.

If Raymond Chow wasn't Bruce Lee's first choice, Bruce wasn't Raymond's first draft pick either. At the time, Bruce wasn't anything more to Raymond than an interesting prospect, a charming guy with some impressive kung fu skills who had appeared as the chauffeur in a mediocre American TV show four years ago. The person he really wanted to sign was Hong Kong's most famous female action star, the actress Cheng Pei Pei—the "Queen of the Swords." She had achieved stardom as a swordswoman in King Hu's *Come Drink with Me* (1966). According to Hong Kong movie lore, Run Run Shaw grew extremely fond of his leading lady, but she resisted his advances. This only stoked his ardor and he pursued her even more intently. To escape his clutches, Cheng Pei Pei first fled to Taiwan and then later to Los Angeles where she got married. To Raymond Chow, not only was Cheng Pei Pei a bankable star, unlike Bruce Lee, but adding her, along with Jimmy Wang Yu, to his stable would be a coup in his war with Run Run Shaw.

The producer sent to bring her back was Liu Liang Hwa (Gladys to her friends). A former actress herself, Gladys was the wife of director Lo Wei. While Gladys was in L.A., she stayed at Cheng Pei Pei's house. Bruce, the prospect, was invited over to visit. "Bruce would come to our house to pick up Gladys. He had quite long hair and always smelled of incense," Cheng Pei Pei recalls, using the polite euphemism for pot smoke. "My husband thought Bruce was a bit of a hippy!"

Gladys was unable to sign Cheng Pei Pei. She wasn't ready to return to movies yet, although she would eventually have a long and varied career, including the role of Jade Fox in *Crouching Tiger, Hidden Dragon* (2000). And it was not entirely certain when Gladys returned to Hong Kong if Bruce would sign either. Raymond was offering more money than Shaw—$15,000 for a two-picture deal. But it was risky going with a shaky start-up. Golden Harvest could go bankrupt before the films were even made or Raymond might refuse to pay up or the movies could turn out to be so terrible that Bruce would regret appearing in them.

Bruce consulted with Stirling Silliphant to solicit his advice.

"Don't take this," Silliphant said. "Don't go."

"I need the money," Bruce replied.

"Look, if you are going to do it, ask for the money up front and insist on a first-class round-trip ticket," Silliphant argued. "I don't have to tell you about Chinese producers. You're going to get over there, and you're not going to get your money and no return ticket and you're not going to be able to get home. You'll be stuck and your family is here."

"No, I trust Raymond Chow," Bruce said, "and I will be back."

On June 28, 1971, Bruce signed with Golden Harvest to make two films: *The Big Boss* and *King of the Chinese Boxers* (later changed to *Fist of Fury*). Once they were finished he intended to return. Contrary to popular myth, Bruce had not given up on Hollywood. Despite his many recent disappointments, the positive experience of *Longstreet* had reignited his optimism about his future career prospects in America. He even believed he could resuscitate the *Silent Flute* project. Two days before his departure, he wrote to a friend, "Am leaving for H.K. this Sunday morning to do two features. Will be there for 4 months. When I come back I'll be busy with the possible shooting of *Silent Flute*, a movie (with Fred Weintraub), and the TV series we will be working with Paramount during my 4 months stay in Hong Kong."

Bruce did not hold out great hopes for the two Golden Harvest movies he was about to make. Before he signed the contract, Bruce prepared by watching a whole bunch of Hong Kong kung fu movies. "They were awful," Bruce said. "It is possible to act and fight at the same time, but most Chinese films have been very superficial and one dimensional." While he was certain he could do better, Bruce did not expect that these two flicks would have any effect on his Hollywood career. His deal with Raymond Chow was not part of his career path but a momentary side trip to resupply his depleted bank account. He signed the deal for the money. It was as simple as that.

Throwing down the Big Boss, played by Han Ying-Chieh, in *The Big Boss*, August 1971. *(Michael Ochs Archives/Getty Images)*

Director Lo Wei and Bruce on location in Thailand, August 1971. *(David Tadman)*

seventeen

the big boss

Bruce Lee was not supposed to be the star of the movie that would turn him into a star. By the time he signed Golden Harvest's two-page contract on June 28, 1971, preproduction had already begun on *The Big Boss*, and James Tien, who was being groomed as the Next Big Thing, was already cast in the lead. Raymond Chow offered to produce a different film specifically for Bruce, but he couldn't afford to wait. Chow reluctantly agreed to shoehorn him into the movie.

As soon as Bruce finished filming the "Way of the Intercepting Fist" episode of *Longstreet* he gave Linda $50—all the cash he had left after paying off old debts—and hopped on a Pan Am flight headed for Hong Kong on July 12. Raymond Chow had wanted Bruce to fly directly to Thailand, where *The Big Boss* was being filmed, to avoid a layover in Hong Kong, because Chow was afraid Run Run Shaw might try to poach Bruce from Golden Harvest. "Bruce refused; he was determined to stamp his authority on his productions from the outset insofar as was reasonable. It wasn't a question of ego; it was a question of making it clear from the outset that he was his own man," Linda says. "He stayed at the airport only long enough to greet a friend and to show he was not going to be moved around like a pawn."

After this display of independence, Bruce flew on to Bangkok where he stayed for a few days before being driven on July 18 to Pak Chong, a tiny, impoverished village on the edge of a national park. For a city boy like Bruce, it was a steep descent from Bel Air to Pak Chong. He wrote to his wife in the first of fourteen homesick letters: "The mosquitos are terrible and cockroaches are all over the place. . . . The food is terrible, this village has no beef and very little chicken and pork. Am I glad I came with my vitamins. . . . I miss you a lot but Pak Chong is no place for you and the children. It's an absolute underdeveloped village and a big nothing." His weight dropped from 145 pounds to 128. To try to maintain his energy, he popped so many vitamin pills a rumor went around—and made its way into the tabloid press—that Bruce was on drugs throughout the shoot.

The gravest danger he faced was not, however, from nature but from man. The cast and crew were equal parts envious and resentful. Most were friends with James Tien, and it appeared that Bruce had been brought in from Hollywood to steal his spotlight. If anyone remembered the Little Dragon, it was from the black-and-white weepies he made as a child where he played a spunky orphan. *The Big Boss* was to be a violent action flick. It would be as if Macaulay Culkin disappeared after *Home Alone* and then showed up as an adult to play Jason Bourne. Then there was the issue of Bruce's salary. The budget for the entire film was less than US$100,000. The rest of the actors were making at most $400. Bruce was being paid $7,500. The only bigger line item in the budget was for fake blood. "We heard that they'd spent all this money on Bruce Lee and we were going, 'Who *is* this guy?' " remembers Zebra Pan, a stuntman for Golden Harvest.

Before he had a chance to win over his colleagues, Bruce had to deal with the director, Wu Chia-Hsiang, who had already been filming James Tien's scenes for a week. Wanting to see what all the fuss and money was about, Wu Chia-Hsiang threw him into a fight scene against the Big Boss's underlings. Director Wu wanted Bruce to engage in extended routines of punches, blocks, kicks, sweeps, locks, throws, and acrobatic flips. Hong

Kong kung fu movies drew their fight choreography from Cantonese Opera, which often had combat scenes of fifty separate movements or more.

But unlike the stuntmen on set, Bruce had never studied Cantonese Opera. He was primarily a street fighter. He viewed traditional kung fu fight choreography as staid and unrealistic. It was the old way, the way of his father; Bruce was the new. When facing three opponents, Bruce wanted to crescent kick one to the head, spinning hook kick another, and roundhouse kick the third with each kick a knockout blow—a whirling dervish of destruction. "In Mandarin movies, everybody fights all the time, and what really bothered me was that they all fought exactly the same way," Bruce complained. "Wow, nobody's really like that!"

Director Wu was aghast. Chinese audiences expected long, elaborate fight scenes; they didn't want realism. He believed Bruce was a con man—he only knew three kicks! Director Wu, who came up in the Chinese movie system where the director was the Big Boss and the actors were the factory workers who were expected to obey, told Bruce to give him more action: "I want you to fight more. I want action. This is not enough." Bruce, who came up in the Hollywood star system of Steve McQueen, told Director Wu he would direct his own fight scenes.

At an impasse, they both called Raymond Chow in Hong Kong.

"This director is rubbish," Bruce said. "When I fight these underlings, I should get rid of them with three kicks. If it takes a long time to dispatch these peons, then what should I do when I meet the head villain? I'll have to fight him for a whole hour."

"You've been swindled," Director Wu complained to Chow. "You told me this guy was very good, but he can't fight. All he knows are three kicks. I call him 'Three Leg Lee.' "

Both sides had a point. Having lived in the East and West, Bruce wanted to bridge the gap. On *The Green Hornet*, he saw the excessive use of the John Wayne punch as boring and knew he could excite an audience by spicing it up with kicks. Bruce made Western fight choreography more complicated. But when he watched the Chinese films, he realized they needed to be simpler. They were so intricate that they lacked any realism and therefore any sense of danger or visceral engagement for the audience. Director Wu was also correct that Bruce was not a classically trained Cantonese Opera graduate. Bruce knew way more than three kicks, but he had not spent his youth, unlike the stuntmen and other action stars of his era, drilling dozens and dozens of traditional kung fu forms from dawn to dusk.

Chow had a tough decision to make. The movie needed a director, but he had already invested $7,500 in Bruce Lee. Before deciding whom to fire, Chow watched the daily rushes. He saw in Bruce's moves the expertise that Director Wu had missed. "Actually, his three legs were astonishing, very good," Chow says. He was so impressed he decided to turn the insult into a compliment. Golden Harvest marketing material for *The Big Boss* hyped the "Amazing Three Leg Lee." (When Bruce later acquired a reputation as a ladies' man, the tabloid press had a field day with this nickname.)

Raymond called the on-set producer, Liu Liang Hwa (Gladys)—the same woman who had recruited Bruce in L.A. and was the wife of director Lo Wei—to ask her advice. Gladys told Raymond that Director Wu was an ill-tempered man who had alienated most of the crew. She had a self-interested suggestion for how to solve the crisis. Her husband had recently finished filming a movie for Golden Harvest in Taiwan. Why not bring Lo Wei to Thailand to replace Director Wu? Chow agreed. Bruce was relieved to no longer have to deal with Director Wu, but the fifty-two-year-old Lo Wei would prove an even more difficult challenge.

When he was a younger man, Lo Wei was a matinee idol in Shanghai. After the Communist takeover in 1949, he fled with the rest of the Shanghai movie community to Hong Kong where he remade himself into a director and was eventually hired by Shaw Bros. While he may have lacked the visual genius of Hong Kong's best director, King Hu, he was still a highly valued craftsman, who cranked out seventeen profitable movies for Shaw in less than six years. It was a coup for Raymond Chow to poach him from Shaw Bros. If there was anyone who could rescue a troubled movie shoot it was Lo Wei.

As a director, Lo Wei retained the arrogance and narcissism of a former screen star. His nickname around the studio was "Orson Welles" for his booming baritone voice, his weight, his ego, his temper, and his tendency to cast himself in his own movies. (He gave himself the role of Chief Inspector in Bruce's next movie, *Fist of Fury*.) Having spent his life on movie sets, Bruce picked up on this right away, writing to his wife, "Another director (a fame lover) just arrived supposedly to take over the present director's job. It really doesn't matter, as long as he is capable as well as cooperative."

Lo Wei didn't believe in cooperating with his actors. He demanded deference and obedience. He also must have expected a bit of gratitude from Bruce. After all, it was his son who had noticed Bruce on TV, it was Lo Wei who told Raymond Chow to hire Bruce, and it was his wife who had gone to L.A. to recruit him.

Kowtowing to authority figures was not Bruce's forte. Just as he had with Ruby Chow, Bruce refused to use Lo Wei's title when addressing him, a shocking breach of etiquette on a Hong Kong movie set. Instead he just called him "Lo Wei." This failure to give him face irritated Lo Wei immensely. Lo Wei's wife, Gladys, tried to intercede. "Our conflicts began with little things," Lo Wei recalled in a 1988 interview. "He liked to call me by my full name when we were on set. He'd shout 'Lo Wei! Lo Wei!' So my wife said to him, 'How can you call him by his full name? He is much older than you. If you want to sound more intimate or familiar then call him "Uncle Lo." If you want to sound more polite then simply call him "Director Lo." ' "

Lo Wei was even more taken aback when Bruce tried to get involved with the direction and production sides. Bruce felt, rightly, that Hong Kong movies were far behind those made in Japan and America and wanted to improve them. Lo Wei preferred to do things as they had always been done. By most accounts, Lo Wei was a hands-off director, not overly invested in the details of his movies. While the actors were filming scenes, he often turned up his radio to listen to horse and dog races. If someone disturbed him during a race or his horse lost, he would bellow in rage. For a perfectionist like Bruce, this negligent approach to directing was offensive. In a letter to his wife, Bruce wrote, "The film I'm doing is quite amateur-like. A new director has replaced the uncertain old one; this new director is another so-so one with an almost unbearable air of superiority."

Bruce "Three Leg" Lee also clashed with the veteran stunt director on set, Han Ying-Chieh, who was also playing the role of the villainous Big Boss in the movie. As Bruce and Han Ying-Chieh were fighting each other in front of the cameras, they were also battling behind the scenes for control over the style of the fight choreography. Han Ying-Chieh wanted the theatrical, mimetic Cantonese Opera movements; Bruce insisted it be as realistic as possible, even going so far as to actually hit his costars. Han remembers being kicked by the Little Dragon: "His grasp of timing and space was excellent, but he threw his punches and kicks too hard. The time my face got grazed by a kick of his, though it was painful, I still consider myself lucky."

The final result was a series of compromises between the two men's styles. Bruce was able to introduce certain elements that would become part of his iconic image—spinning high kicks, quick knockouts, and even tasting his own blood. (One of his students, Larry Hartsell, had told Bruce about a bar brawl where he had tasted his own blood and terrified his opponents. Bruce loved the story and adopted it into his repertoire.) Han Ying-Chieh included certain stereotypical features from Hong Kong action movies, like trampoline jumps and a handful of extended classical kung fu back-and-forth sequences.

Faced with a defiant actor, director Lo Wei wasn't sure what to do. He couldn't fire him. His only recourse was to leverage the competition between Bruce and James Tien over who would end up the star of the movie. When Bruce had insisted on being part of a movie that already had a lead, Raymond Chow realized he had a backup plan if Bruce lacked the charisma to carry the movie. "This was the subtlety of it," says Andre Morgan. "If you look at the movie carefully, you will see the movie starts out with two stars, because they wanted to screen-test Bruce, see if he was real or not. Then halfway through, they made a decision. 'Who to kill, and who to keep alive?' "

Before the decision was made, Lo Wei was able to play them off each other. Early on Lo Wei fought with Bruce over the exaggerated Cantonese

Opera pantomime techniques that Bruce loathed. "Lee would fight for three or four scenes. I told him to do this and that. Told him how he needed to fight. He wasn't willing to fight anymore," Lo Wei recalls. "The next day we really needed to film him fighting. Lee's few moves weren't going to cut it! But then I had an idea. When I arrived on set in the morning, I told Lee to take a seat next to me, and rest. Then, I called James Tien in. I decided to film him fighting instead of Lee. I had Tien jumping on the trampoline, doing falls, and doing flips for the camera. Lee sat next to me all morning. He thought it wasn't right. Tien was fighting too much. Lee probably thought that Tien would replace him as the star of the film. So after that day, Lee was a bit more cooperative, a bit more willing to fight for the camera."

Around this time, Bruce seems to have gained a slightly greater appreciation for Lo Wei. In a letter to his wife, he grudgingly wrote, "The shooting is picking up steam and moving along much better than it was. The new director is no Roman Polanski but as a whole he is a better choice than our ex-director." And Lo Wei must have come to appreciate Bruce Lee's star potential, because he decided to kill off James Tien at the end of Act I, and give the rest of the movie to Bruce.

Lo Wei claims that when he arrived in Thailand the screenplay for *The Big Boss* was only three sheets of paper, likely an exaggeration but not by much. Hong Kong movies were often started with just a basic idea of the plot—the director and producers improvised the rest during filming. With details seemingly pulled from his own biography, Bruce plays Cheng Chao-an, a reformed troublemaker who has been sent away to a foreign country (Thailand) to work in an ice factory. His promise to his mother not to fight again is embodied by a jade pendant he wears around his neck. He is greeted by James Tien's character, the leader of the workers, who immediately beats up some bullies while Bruce watches and pulls on his pendant in frustration. The ice factory is actually a front for a drug smuggling operation. When two workers discover some heroin packed in blocks of ice, they are secretly executed and their bodies hidden in the ice. James Tien confronts the Big Boss about his missing workers and threatens to go to the police. The Big Boss's minions kill him in a gruesome battle.

From this point on, Bruce shifts from sidekick to hero of the movie. Unlike in real life, his character is a country bumpkin, easily fooled. The boss makes him the foreman and at a banquet plies him with alcohol and Thai prostitutes, leading to Bruce's first ever sex scene on film. Upon entering the bedroom, he rather innocently passes out while the Thai prostitute undresses and snuggles next to his sleeping body. It is only after he discovers the body parts of the workers frozen in blocks of ice that he realizes he's been duped. Bruce later told reporters, "The character I played was a very simple, straightforward guy. Like, if you told this guy something, he'd believe you. Then, when he finally figures out he's been had, he goes animal."

Making the decision to confront the Big Boss and his almost certain death, Bruce's character, Cheng Chao-an, throws all his worldly goods into the river. In the original, director's cut version of the movie, Cheng Chao-an then heads back to the brothel for one last bit of fun. He picks out a prostitute, pushes her onto the bed, and strips naked (the headboard of the bed conceals his private parts). It was the only nude sex scene of Bruce's film career. After the prostitute falls asleep, Cheng Chao-an steals a package of rice crackers from her bed stand and heads off to the Big Boss's estate.

This scene, along with about five minutes of other X-rated material, was cut from the Cantonese-language and international versions released in Hong Kong and the West primarily to appease the censors. But it also made commercial sense: test audiences were upset that the hero of the film postponed his revenge for sex and crackers. In the edited version, Bruce's character suddenly appears in front of the Big Boss's estate inexplicably eating rice crackers.

The final climactic battle was filmed during the crew's last three days in Pak Chong. It proved difficult for Bruce. First, he had to face down the Big Boss's German shepherd. Bruce loved dogs but had a phobia about attack dogs. Lo Wei seemed to enjoy his star's discomfort. "We borrowed the dog from a military barracks. Everyone was afraid of it. He was a mean dog," Lo Wei remembers. "Lee tried to fight, but he wasn't doing well. He refused to be filmed. 'I'm not kidding! You can't film me!' In the end there was nothing we could do. The dog was staring him down. Lee had a frightened look on his face. We all laughed at him. He's such a great hero. How can he be afraid of one dog? So we brought in a second dog, which we put under anesthesia while we were filming. It was pretty cruel of us. The dog would pass out, and we'd need seven or eight people to throw him around in front of the camera."

Bruce had suffered some minor wounds throughout the shoot—a cut finger on a cheap piece of glass—but the most time-consuming injury turned out to be a sprained ankle. He wrote to Linda, "I've gone through two days of hell. I sprained my ankle rather badly from a high jump—which required a drive of two hours to Bangkok to see a doctor—consequently I caught the flu (Bangkok is hot and stuffy and the traffic is a 24 hr. jam). Anyways, with fever, cold, aches and pain, we used close-ups while I dragged my leg to finish the last fight." For the film, they added a moment where the Big Boss, played by the fight director Han Ying-Chieh, cuts Bruce's leg to explain his limp.

While Bruce was filming in the remote village of Pak Chong, Paramount TV sent repeated telegrams to Golden Harvest's Hong Kong offices trying to track him down. Before he had left Los Angeles, four episodes of *Longstreet* had been filmed. The original plan was for Bruce's episode, "The Way of the Intercepting Fist," to air third in the lineup. But Tom Tannenbaum, the head of Paramount TV, liked it so much he decided to make it the season opener during Fall Premiere Week on September 16, 1971. This decision created a dilemma for Tannenbaum. With Bruce's character Li Tsung playing such a prominent part in the pilot, viewers would naturally expect him to be a recurring character in the series. But Bruce had not signed the multi-episode deal Tannenbaum had offered him prior to his departure. Paramount was desperate to get him under contract and back to America to film more episodes.

After several failed attempts to speak by phone, Tannenbaum finally was able to reach Bruce in Bangkok. To entice him to return, he offered Bruce $1,000 per episode for three more episodes of *Longstreet* and promised to develop a TV show specifically for Bruce to star in called *Tiger Force*.

" 'Longstreet' is such a success that reaction is instantaneous whenever my character comes up," Bruce excitedly wrote to Linda. "So Paramount is asking me to reappear and stay as a re-occurrence character. In the meantime Tannenbaum is working on 'Tiger Force.' "

Bruce agreed to fly back to Hollywood after *The Big Boss* wrapped to film the additional episodes of *Longstreet*, but he didn't think $1,000 was enough. He sent a telegram to Tannenbaum asking for $2,000 per episode. "Who knows what the future might hold?" Bruce explained in a letter to Linda. "There comes a time when you have to advance or retreat—this time I can always retreat to my Hong Kong deal."

As he waited several weeks for a reply, his letters to Linda grew increasingly anxious. "Disregard the consequences, I am firm in my ground of 'it's about time to raise my worth,' " Bruce wrote. "Tell Brandon when I go to Bangkok, I'll pick him up some toys and send them to him—unless the Paramount deal doesn't come through. Who knows what will happen? At any rate, one way or other I don't mind too much. The future looks extremely bright indeed. Like the song says, 'We've only just begun.' "

When he finally heard from Paramount, his relief was palpable. Tannenbaum agreed to $2,000 per episode for three episodes and Bruce would only be required on-set for a maximum of nine days. Now Bruce could afford to buy presents for his children and his wife. "You will see my 7th anniversary gift—a his and her present," he wrote to Linda. "Should have one and a half grand when I return—I hope anyway." The his-and-her anniversary present was a pair of matching rings. "Bruce sometimes forgot my birthday," Linda says, "though he was generally very good about our wedding anniversary."

All of Paramount's telegrams and transpacific telephone calls to the Golden Harvest offices had a side benefit. They transformed Bruce in Raymond Chow's eyes into a hot Hollywood property. "It's funny," Bruce later told reporters, "but when Paramount sent telegrams and telephoned Hong Kong for me, boy, the producers there thought I was an important star. My prestige must have increased threefold."

And it wasn't just Hollywood increasing his stature. Spies on the set of *The Big Boss* were reporting back to Run Run Shaw that Bruce Lee was the real deal. Realizing he had made a mistake letting Bruce slip away, Run

Run tried to steal him from Raymond. "Golden Harvest is terribly shaken now for Shaw Brothers has been calling me and writing for me to work with them instead," Bruce wrote to Linda. "They are using all means to get me. One thing is for sure, I'm the super star in H.K."

In the last few days of filming in Pak Chong, Raymond Chow visited the set to meet his "superstar" for the first time in person. He was eager to reaffirm their relationship. Bruce was his usual confident self, telling Raymond, "You just wait, I'm going to be the biggest Chinese star in the world."

Bruce's confidence was infectious. Golden Harvest made *The Big Boss* the flagship of its turnaround efforts. Raymond threw much of his remaining capital into marketing the movie: buying extensive ads and throwing a lavish welcoming party for Bruce and the crew when they returned to Hong Kong's Kai Tak Airport on September 3, 1971. Reporters gathered to get a first look at Raymond Chow's new talent. Having spent years mastering how to charm Western reporters, Bruce effortlessly won over the Hong Kong press. When they asked him how he would compare himself to Hong Kong's biggest action star, Jimmy Wang Yu, hoping to stir up a rivalry, he carefully ducked the question: "I know everyone has seen Wang Yu's performances in other films. *The Big Boss* will be in theaters soon, so I invite everyone to watch it and make their own comparisons—isn't that better than for me to try to brag?"

He then deftly gained their sympathy with an amusing story of the prejudice he faced as a Chinese man in America: "One day, I was mowing my lawn when an American walked by and asked me how much I charged for the service. I said to him, 'I am doing this for free, but when I'm done cutting the grass, I'm going to sleep with the woman inside the house.' " And then he appealed to the reporter's sense of Chinese patriotism: "In America, I am always playing sidekicks and villains, using Eastern martial arts as a kind of sideshow. But here in Hong Kong and Taiwan, I think our martial arts films have been too heavily influenced by the Japanese, such that I feel suffocated. I want to show them what we can do!"

Even questions about his conflict with Lo Wei didn't throw Bruce off his charm offensive. "It's true that Lo Wei and I often argued on the set, but it was all for the purpose of making *The Big Boss* the best movie we could," Bruce told the reporters. "Since we are both strong-willed, it was inevitable that there would be some 'butting of heads,' but these were always about the work, and were not personal; I do not think it will be a problem for us to work together again in the future."

Lo Wei was less diplomatic. He told the press that Bruce was spoiled and arrogant, saying he acted as if everyone were beneath him. And he began whispering in reporters' ears that it was really he who had taught Three Leg Lee how to fight on film.

Fortunately, Bruce didn't read what Lo Wei said about him in the papers. With Paramount and Shaw Bros. vying for his services, he was focused on using this leverage to his advantage. Bruce demanded that Raymond delay his next film so he could return to Hollywood to film three episodes of *Longstreet*. Chow also agreed to fly Bruce's family back to Hong Kong and set them up in an apartment with no strings attached—originally Chow had insisted that Bruce perform in a short film about Jeet Kune Do in exchange for Linda's airfare. For the rest of his career, Lee employed this simple strategy of playing his various suitors off each other: Chow versus Shaw and Hong Kong versus Hollywood. By the time he got on a plane to return to Los Angeles on September 6, 1971, Bruce had every reason to believe he had finally become the master of his destiny.

The day after his arrival in L.A., Bruce was back on set shooting his role in three different *Longstreet* episodes: "Spell Legacy Like Death" (episode 6), "Wednesday's Child" (episode 9), and " 'I See,' Said the Blind Man" (episode 10). They were not written by Silliphant, who was busy working on the screenplay for *The Poseidon Adventure* (1972). Instead they had been assigned to other less-talented writers and finished prior to Bruce's return. The writers did last-minute revisions to give Bruce the equivalent of a "walk through" part—sticking him in the background, tossing him a few trivial lines of dialogue.

The opening of the sixth episode, "Spell Legacy Like Death," jumps right into a training session between Bruce's character, Li Tsung, and James Franciscus's Mike Longstreet without any reference to where Li Tsung has been for the last five shows. They are even wearing the same workout clothes from the pilot. The inside joke for the writers was about whether Bruce was going to rejoin the cast on a permanent basis. After Longstreet receives a blackmail call from a bomber threatening to blow up a major bridge, Li Tsung offers to help. "You joining the team, Li?" asks Longstreet. Li Tsung replies, "It is always more rewarding to be a participant instead of an observer." When the bomber demands that Longstreet come alone with the blackmail money, he leaves his kung fu master behind. As he departs, Longstreet repeats the inside joke: "You going to hang in here a while, Li?"

His next *Longstreet* episode, "Wednesday's Child," is a flashback to *The Green Hornet*. Li Tsung becomes the blind detective's chauffeur. At the end of the show, Li Tsung blasts through the bad guys with a series of spinning and flying kicks. Compared to four years prior, Bruce's skills as a martial arts performer have improved dramatically and his ability to clearly deliver English dialogue has vastly improved. But he is still playing the manservant to a rich white master.

In "Spell Legacy Like Death," Bruce has nineteen lines; in "Wednesday's Child," it's twelve; by the third and final of his Longstreet episodes, " 'I See,' Said the Blind Man," he's got five. He holds a punching bag while Longstreet lets off some steam. He has no role at all in the plot. After such a promising start, Li Tsung as a character has become a step back from Kato. He's less important than Longstreet's guide dog. In the majority of scenes, Bruce is seen in reaction shots while the other characters are talking, and he is usually looking down with his arms defensively crossed. Linda says that Bruce found his role in these three episodes to be "anticlimactic." (He probably used a more colorful adjective.)

Bruce fought for every line of dialogue. As a practical joke, he would hide behind the office door of Joel Rogosin, the head writer on the series. When Rogosin walked in, Bruce would grab him from behind, wrap his arms around him, and say, "I need more lines in the script!" Rogosin remembers, "He was smaller than I was but extremely strong. If he grabbed you, you stayed in his hold until he decided to let go. I would say, 'Whatever you want.' He was a delight."

Despite his disappointment in the number of lines he was given, Bruce remained a lively and entertaining member of the cast, clowning around between takes. "He would take all the air out of his body and then he would begin to inflate himself. He would begin to take in air; he would kind of balloon up," says Marlyn Mason, who played Nikki Bell. "And we had such fun watching him. We would say, 'Blow yourself up, blow yourself up.' "

The *Longstreet* pilot episode aired on September 16, 1971. *The New York Times* delivered its verdict three days later. It was mixed for the show itself but a rave for Bruce's performance.

> In the first episode, "The Way of the Intercepting Fist," Longstreet wastes no time in getting mugged by some waterfront hijackers. He is rescued by a Chinese youth, Li Tsung, who demolishes the thugs with a spectacular demonstration of something resembling super-karate. It turns out to be an ancient Chinese art of self-defense and, naturally, Longstreet wants to cram in a few lessons.
>
> Li, well played by Bruce Lee, turns out to be a sort of disciplined superboy, providing a Robin for Longstreet's Batman and given to heavy salutations like "May it be well with you." Inner peace is Li's secret weapon: "You've got a quarrelsome mind, Mr. Longstreet. Unless you learn how to calm it, you will never hear the world outside."
>
> There is, in other words, a little something for everybody. The blind hero elicits instant sympathy. . . . The Chinaman (who emerges impressively enough to justify a series of his own) lends a deft touch of exotica with advice on how to "learn the art of dying."

Bruce was ecstatic. He told a friend, "Boy, am I glad it was so favorable." In an interview a year later, Bruce proudly repeated the quote, almost word-for-word, from memory, "*The New York Times* said, like, 'The Chinaman incidentally came off quite convincingly enough to earn himself a television series,' and so on and so forth."

Audiences also loved Bruce's performance. "We had more fan mail on that episode than on any of the other shows we did in the series," says Silliphant. "And the fan mail that came pouring in was all for Bruce."

After filming the three extra episodes of *Longstreet*, Bruce was done with the show. It had served its purpose. The pilot had grabbed the attention of the public and earned him an endorsement from *The New York Times* for his own TV show. And Bruce already had two solid TV prospects in development: Paramount's *Tiger Force*, and, much to the surprise of everyone including Bruce, Warner's *Kung Fu*.

While Bruce was in Thailand filming *The Big Boss*, Fred Weintraub had an idea for how to revive *Kung Fu*—instead of a feature film, turn it into an ABC Movie of the Week. If Warner's movie division couldn't appreciate *Kung Fu*'s brilliance, he'd just give it away like secondhand clothes to its TV people. Weintraub marched the *Kung Fu* screenplay over to Tom Kuhn, head of the Warner Bros. TV division.

As Kuhn was sitting in his office, he heard his secretary saying to someone, "You can't just walk in there."

As he looked up, he saw this huge guy walking toward his desk. "Who are you?" Kuhn asked.

"I'm Fred Weintraub," Weintraub said, as he plunked down the *Kung Fu* screenplay on his desk.

Reading the title, Kuhn joked, "I've never heard of 'kung fu,' but it sounds like something I had for lunch. I think I got some on my tie."

"Just read it," Weintraub replied. "You'll like it."

Tom Kuhn loved it, but it was a movie script—too long and expensive to produce for television. Kuhn called Weintraub. "Fred, this is fabulous," Kuhn said. "I'd love to do it, but I can't afford it for television."

"Tear out every other page," Fred suggested.

Kuhn started laughing. "Fred, we're going to be friends for life."

ABC loved the script too. Warner Bros. and ABC announced their TV deal for *Kung Fu* on July 22, 1971.

Back in New York City, Howard Friedlander, who had written the original movie screenplay with Ed Spielman, heard about the TV deal after running into a friend on the street. "I remember this very clearly like it happened ten minutes ago. I was walking east on 54th Street in Manhattan. I had about two dollars in my pocket. I was broke, and I was alone. I bumped into a friend, and he says, 'Hey, I see they're making your movie.' I looked at him like he was nuts. I said, 'What movie?' He says, 'Oh, that *Kung Fu* thing, it's in the trades.' Well, I couldn't get to a newsstand fast enough, and I sprang for a copy of *Variety*. I started flipping through it until I found that Warner Bros. was making *Kung Fu*. And I got to a phone—a pay phone, there were no cells in those days. And I called Ed and I called [our agent Peter] Lampack, and we had a meeting, and Lampack called the West Coast and found out they were making this, as a TV movie."

Bruce heard about the TV deal for *Kung Fu* after he returned to America in September. ABC had scheduled the air date for February 22, 1972. Kuhn planned to start production on December 15, 1971. The casting process was already under way, but they had yet to find the right actor to play Kwai Chang Caine, the Eurasian kung fu master.

The buzz about Bruce's performance in *Longstreet* had already reached the ears of Ted Ashley, the president of Warner Bros. Once he learned that Tom Tannenbaum at Paramount was developing a TV series specifically for Bruce, Ashley decided to steal Bruce away. "It was because of *Longstreet* that Ted Ashley and Warner Bros. became interested in him," says Silliphant.

Two days after the *New York Times* review of *Longstreet* hit the newsstands, Bruce was called in for a meeting with one of Ashley's underlings, Jerry Leider. After the meeting, Ashley phoned Kuhn personally to lobby for Bruce. "Ashley called me and congratulated me on the sale of *Kung Fu* and asked me to see Bruce as a possible lead," Kuhn recalls. "Ted was looking to further Bruce's career." Kuhn's office scheduled an appointment with Bruce for 3:30 p.m. on September 24, 1971. It wasn't a formal audition but a casual meet-and-greet. For all intents and purposes, the part was Bruce's to lose. All he had to do was convince Kuhn.

A more cautious soul might have opted for a low-key approach, but the fiery Bruce made a bold choice for his entrance. He walked into Kuhn's office, kicked the door shut with his foot, dropped his gym bag on the floor, pulled out a nunchaku, and started swinging it at Kuhn.

"What are you doing?" Kuhn asked in terror as the sticks whipped around his face.

"Don't move," Bruce said.

"Don't worry, I'm not going anywhere," Kuhn said. "Put that goddamn thing down."

Bruce stopped whirling the nunchaku and stuck out his forearm. "Feel my arm," he demanded.

Tom did. It was like a rock. "Okay, please sit down," Kuhn said. "Take it easy."

Once Kuhn got Bruce to put the nunchacku away, they had a thirty-minute meeting that was half business, half personal. Despite the frightening introduction, Kuhn found himself won over by Bruce's charm, charisma, and wit. "I just wanted to get a feel for the guy and a sense of how he came across. We talked about his Hong Kong movie, *The Big Boss*," Kuhn remembers. "His presence was just mesmerizing. I really enjoyed my time with him. His energy was just fantastic. He was entertaining and he was a character."

On first blush, Bruce seemed perfect for the part. After all, he was the only actor in Hollywood who was also a Eurasian kung fu master. But the role of Kwai Chang Caine, the half-American, half-Chinese Buddhist monk, as written had a very different flavor from Bruce's personality. "The concept of the series was a man who was not involved, a man who avoided action at almost any cost, a very quiet, seemingly passive man," says John Furia, a producer on the show. Caine was not the type of man who would, for example, burst into an audition and start swinging a nunchaku. "It did occur to me that this part was rather cerebral," says Kuhn, "a guy who only fights when he's absolutely cornered." Even Fred Weintraub, who lobbied for Bruce to get the job, noted that Warners needed an actor "to portray the sense of quiet serenity that Caine possessed, a quality that driven and intense Bruce was not known for."

But for Kuhn, the biggest problem with Bruce as Kwai Chang Caine boiled down to one thing—his accent. "By the end of the half hour I really liked the guy, but frankly I had trouble understanding him," Kuhn says. "It was fun, but my conclusion was that we'd have to loop the hell out of this guy for an American television audience to understand him. And you can do that with a movie, but you can't do it on an every-week basis with a television show. You have to take yourself back to 1971. Television was pretty primitive back then. You only had the three networks. Things that weren't easy for that mass audience to absorb, either audio-wise or visually, their tendency was just to change the channel."

After the meeting, Kuhn called Fred Weintraub. "What the fuck was that?" Kuhn laughed. "He nearly caved my skull in with a pair of clubs."

"That was Bruce Lee," Weintraub replied. "What do you think about him for *Kung Fu*?"

"He's amazing," Tom gushed. "I've never seen anything like that. But getting him the lead is still going to be a long shot. He might be too authentic."

After considering it some more, Kuhn decided Bruce wasn't right for the role. He called up Ted Ashley to inform him.

"I understand," Ashley said. "It's your gig, your choice."

With Bruce scratched off the top of the list and no other viable Eurasian actors in Hollywood in 1971, the producers had to decide between powdering an Asian actor's face or applying eye makeup to a white actor—as Hollywood had done so many times in its yellow-face tradition. But in that increasingly racially charged era, the white producers and executives knew that would be problematic. Kuhn says, "We sought out every Asian in Hollywood, because you didn't have to be super bright to know what was coming." Among the Asian actors considered were Mako, who guest-starred on *The Green Hornet* with Bruce, and George Takei, who played Sulu on *Star*

Trek. "We read everyone, but none of them really measured up. There wasn't one guy who showed up who we thought, 'This guy can carry a series,' " Kuhn says. "Mako had a thick accent, and Takei was not the physical type."

Having discarded the Asian half of Caine's ancestry, they turned to the American side and began auditioning white actors. "David Carradine came in to read and he was just bouncing off the wall. I don't know what he was on that day, but he was on lots. I called his manager afterwards and said, 'You know, even if he were fabulous'—and he did actually give a pretty good reading—'you can't do a television series with a guy who's stoned all the time,' " Kuhn remembers. "But we still couldn't find anybody, and we were maybe two weeks away from production, and I didn't have a lead. All the other parts were cast, and the next time his manager called I said, 'You know what, send him in. What have we got to lose?' So David came in, completely straight, gave an incredible reading, and bottom line, we finally hired him. And that was the last time I ever saw David Carradine straight."

Carradine signed for the role sometime in late November 1971. When word got out, George Takei and the Association of Asian Pacific American Artists (AAPAA) filed a formal complaint for unfair hiring practices. Kuhn says, "He kind of tried to organize the Asian actors against what was going on with *Kung Fu*." They wanted David Carradine replaced with an Asian actor and a Chinese historical advisor hired. Kuhn agreed to their second demand but not the first. "We had an Asian advisor, kung-fu guy on the show, David Chow, and as much Asian involvement as we could get, but David Carradine was to be the star of the show." The Asian acting community was not pleased with the compromise, but pragmatism outbid ideology. There were so few opportunities for Asian actors in Hollywood they decided it was better to have a show on the air with lots of secondary roles for Asian actors, but a white lead, than no show at all. James Hong, who was the president of the AAPAA, says, "As the show went on, we realized it was a great source of employment for the Asian acting community."

Kuhn turned out to be correct in his assessment of Carradine: he was perfect for the part and a huge risk. With its countercultural story line of pacifist Orientals threatened by aggressive Caucasians, *Kung Fu* was a surprise cultural hit, especially among college kids protesting the Vietnam

War. Carradine was nominated for a Best Actor Emmy in 1973 and a Golden Globe in 1974. But despite its critical and popular success, the show was canceled soon after Carradine was arrested for attempted burglary and malicious mischief in 1974. While high on peyote and completely naked, Carradine broke into a neighbor's home and accosted two young women—allegedly assaulting one while asking if she was a witch. The young woman sued him for $1.1 million and was awarded $20,000. It was not the kind of press a network wants for an actor playing a wise, gentle Buddhist monk.

Despite Tom Kuhn's concern about Bruce's accent, Ted Ashley saw star potential in him and, perhaps more important, didn't want to lose him to Paramount. He was worried Bruce would make *Tiger Force* once he discovered he wasn't getting the part of Kwai Chang Caine. In early October 1971, a month before David Carradine was officially cast in *Kung Fu*, Ashley offered Bruce an exclusive development deal to create his own TV show. The advance was an eye-popping $25,000 (or $152,000 in 2017 dollars)—enough money to pay off most of his mortgage.

Bruce had a pitch ready. Since *The Green Hornet*, he had been writing movie and TV ideas in his notebooks. On one page he brainstormed a Chinese hero by time period and type of job: "Western: (1) San Francisco sheriff (partner of a blind man?). Modern: (1) bounty hunter, (2) agent, (3) detective, (4) embassy intrigue?" On the next page, he expanded a little on the Western idea: "San Francisco: (1) Sheriff X, presiding, (2) Ah Sahm, a ronin (unofficial deputy of Sheriff X—take care of office for room and board)."

He later developed this into a seven-page, typed TV proposal. The title of the show was *Ah Sahm*, which was also the name of the lead character. The story was set in the Old American West. Ah Sahm was a Chinese kung fu master who traveled to America to liberate Chinese workers being exploited by the tongs. In each episode Ah Sahm helped the weak and oppressed as he journeyed across the Old West.

The striking similarities between *Ah Sahm* and *Kung Fu* (both are Eastern Westerns) has led some Bruce Lee biographers to mistakenly assume they were the same project or that Bruce was the author of *Kung Fu*. In fact, they are distinct. Ah Sahm is full Chinese, not half-American, half-Chinese, like Kwai Chang Caine, and Ah Sahm is not a Shaolin monk—he is a warrior. Unfortunately, the proposal for *Ah Sahm* does not have a date, so it is unknown if Bruce typed it before or after he read the *Kung Fu* screenplay written by Ed Spielman and Howard Friedlander.

Once Ashley offered Bruce the development deal, Bruce submitted his proposal to Warner Bros. with one alteration. He changed the title from *Ah Sahm* to *The Warrior*. According to Linda, Bruce did not sign the contract for Warner's development deal before he returned to Hong Kong. He wanted to wait and see how *The Big Boss* did at the box office. If it did well, it would strengthen his negotiating position. As it turned out, *The Big Boss* succeeded beyond his wildest expectations.

Smashing Japanese bad guys in *Fist of Fury*, March 1972. *(National General Pictures/Getty Images)*

Final leap into gunfire in *Fist of Fury*, March 1972. *(Bettmann/Getty Images)*

eighteen

fist of fury

Bruce, Linda, six-year-old Brandon, and two-year-old Shannon flew to Hong Kong on October 11, 1971. They changed their clothes before they landed, because Bruce expected a handful of reporters would greet them. They didn't imagine that Raymond Chow would arrange for the actors of *The Big Boss* to create a celebratory cavalcade of lanterns for them as soon as they stepped off the plane. This hero's welcome gave Bruce the sense of a triumphant return.

Even more than Bruce, Raymond Chow needed a hit. His first five films had done poorly at the box office. With his studio under immense pressure from Shaw Bros., Chow's future largely depended on the success of *The Big Boss*. From staged events to advertising to media exposure, Chow pulled out every stop to publicize the movie. Leading up to the October 29 premiere, Bruce's life was a whirlwind of print, radio, and TV interviews. Chow wanted to reintroduce the Little Dragon to an older audience who might remember him as the spunky child actor from 1950s black-and-white weepies. Having done everything they could to promote the movie, both Raymond's and Bruce's fates rested on the outcome of its opening night.

Raymond, Bruce, and Linda entered the theater with some trepidation. Hong Kong audiences were a notoriously tough crowd to please. They would very vocally curse a bad movie. Some would even bring knives to the theaters and, if they were disappointed, express it by slicing up their seats. "As the movie progressed we kept looking at the reaction of the fans," Bruce recalled. "They hardly made any noise at the beginning, but at the end they were in a frenzy and began clapping and clamoring. Those fans are emotional: if they don't like a movie they'll cuss and walk out." As Bruce heard the audience cheering his character throughout the movie, he grew increasingly relaxed and confident. By the time his first ever sex scene arrived, he leaned over to Linda and joked, "Part of the fringe benefits."

In the audience for the premiere was the famous Hong Kong movie critic and film historian Mel Tobias. "I didn't know who Bruce Lee was. It was just by accident that I saw the first show. I had a guest from Manila and he wanted to see a midnight show, and the midnight show was *The Big Boss*," Tobias recalls. "When the film ended there was about ten seconds of silence. They didn't know what hit them, and then they started roaring. When they saw Bruce Lee, they were just completely stunned. And then the applause afterwards, which was thunderous. And the feeling I had: This guy is going to be *IT.* The way he projected the Oriental and the Asians gave us a sense of identity."

Bruce began the evening with modest hopes. "I didn't expect *The Big Boss* to break any kind of record," he confessed. "But I did expect it to be a money maker." The crowd's reaction overwhelmed him. "That night every dream that Bruce had ever had came true as the audience rose to its feet with thunderous, cheering applause," Linda says. "In less than two hours of action on the screen, Bruce became a glittering star, and as we left the theater we were absolutely mobbed."

The box office numbers were stunning and completely turned around Golden Harvest's fortunes. Shown in only sixteen Hong Kong theaters, *The Big Boss* took in $372,000 Hong Kong dollars in its first day and passed the magical HK$1 million mark in just three days. Over its three-week run in local theaters, *The Big Boss* grossed HK$3.2 million. *The China Mail* estimated that 1.2 million Hong Kongers out of a population of four million paid to see the movie. To add a patriotic, hometown flair to the success, *The Big Boss* also smashed the previous box office record held by *The Sound of Music.* A local Chinese newspaper crowed: "The Julie Andrews film had been local film distributors' wildest dream at the box office since it hit the screen in 1966." Julie Andrews's husband, Blake Edwards, was one of Bruce's celebrity students. Bruce had gone from teaching stars to being one.

Since he was three months old, Bruce had acted in twenty-three movies. None of them enjoyed anything like the fantastic success of *The Big Boss.* Most had been failures. What made this movie different? Certainly it wasn't the quality of the production. In a 1988 interview, director Lo Wei reflected, "Now that I think about it, *The Big Boss* really was a crappy film. I didn't have much time. I just wanted to get it done, no matter how sloppily or whatever."

One key to its popularity was Bruce's fight sequences. Unlike most action stars who train for a few months for a movie, Bruce was an expert martial artist—a master of the art. Everyone else in *The Big Boss* looks like they are playing patty-cake, while Bruce is a demonic whirlwind. Hong Kong audiences, who had been raised on kung fu fare, knew the real deal when they saw it. To prove that his fights were not bolstered by trick photography, Lee and Lo Wei used extra-long takes—some lasting for twenty seconds and more. "What Lee would do was choreograph a fight and let the camera run so you knew it wasn't phony," says Michael Kaye, another Golden Harvest director. "Remember, Lee was dealing with a local audience who knew kung fu and they would have been able to tell if it was phony."

But being the real deal is not enough. Plenty of great martial artists have bombed on-screen. What is effective in the ring is rarely exciting on film. Bruce made his bones in Hollywood as a fight choreographer and he knew how to make his particular skill set look spectacular on celluloid. Call it enhanced realism. On film, he knocks out three baddies with three spinning head kicks—something not even Bruce Lee could do in real life, but on film audiences believed he could. As a critic for *The Washington Post* put it, "Bruce Lee in motion is an exhilarating sight to behold—explosive, graceful and amusing. Lee gets an audience response I haven't heard since Steve McQueen's motorcycle ride in *The Great Escape*. His performance [has] Cagney-esque cockiness and early Steve McQueen nonchalance."

After twenty-five years as a working actor, Bruce had finally learned how to invest actions with emotions. The transformation from the pleasant manservant Kato in *The Green Hornet* to a berserker in *The Big Boss* was dramatic. For the first time since he was eighteen years old in *The Orphan*, Bruce had been given the starring role. Over this period of struggle and rejection and hard work, he had managed to acquire the X-factor, the indefinable quality that sets Marilyn Monroe—a "star"—above Sir Laurence Olivier—merely a "great actor." Paul Heller, co-producer of *Enter the Dragon*, says, "Bruce had an intensity which the camera caught. Some actors can be brilliant actors but the camera doesn't love them—the camera loved Bruce. Bruce's energy, his raw talent and his excitement all came through the camera and onto the screen." Bruce found a way to access the tremendous life force he possessed—"I can feel it sort of bubbling and roaring up inside of me," he told friends—and translate it onto the screen. "I had more confidence as I had just done *Longstreet*," he explained.

Bruce's electrifying performance tapped into the unconscious yearnings of the public. Hong Kong's population in 1842 was seven thousand. In 1971 it was four million. The vast majority were mainland Chinese who had fled successive waves of disasters. Hong Kong was essentially a high-functioning refugee camp run by British businessmen. If anyone needed a shot of ethnic boosting it was the Hong Kong Chinese, who suffered from not only an inferiority complex but also an identity crisis: Were they Chinese migrants or British colonial subjects or both or what? Robert Clouse, who directed *Enter the Dragon*, argues, "Bruce did more for the Chinese psyche than any dozen politicians and martyrs. This acted as gut-level therapy for millions of overworked and underprivileged people. Bruce rekindled a feeling of pride and literally brought his countrymen to their feet screaming and cheering in hundreds of theaters. They suddenly felt better about themselves and could take another day with a little less pain and prejudice."

The phenomenal success of *The Big Boss* was also due to a shocking external event that set off a firestorm of Chinese nationalism right before its premiere. It involved, of all things, a territorial dispute over some tiny abandoned islands in the South China Sea. The Diaoyu Islands were seized along with Taiwan by the Japanese during the First Sino-Japanese War (1895) and renamed the Senkaku Islands. After World War II, these empty islands were placed under the administrative control of the United States. A 1969 United Nations survey identified possible oil reserves in the area. China, Taiwan, and Japan immediately claimed the forgotten islands, stirring up bitter memories. On June 7, 1971, Richard Nixon announced his decision to give the islands to Japan. *The Big Boss* was released on October 30. On November 29, the U.S. Senate approved an amendment stating that America would defend Japan in the case of an attack on the Senkaku Islands.

The Chinese felt deeply betrayed. There were protests and outraged editorials. "I remember it as if it was yesterday," says Marciano Baptista, a Eurasian classmate of Bruce's brother Peter at La Salle. "The Americans did a very stupid thing giving the Senkaku Islands to Japan. You could've been Chinese from anywhere, any denomination, any persuasion, any political background—they all supported China on the Senkaku. One of the problems with Hong Kong is we never had an identity until after 1971 when we were forced to choose. We began to have a Chinese identity because they gave the islands to somebody else."

In an environment of rising ethnic nationalism, Bruce had heroically defended his fellow Chinese workers in *The Big Boss* and Chinese audiences loved him for it. In his next movie, *Fist of Fury*, he would make this nationalism explicit and the public would love him even more. But first, he would have to endure his own very personal and very public humiliation at the hands of the Americans.

Bruce wasted no time in leveraging the success of *The Big Boss* to pivot back to Hollywood. The day after the premiere, he wrote a letter to Ted Ashley, increasing his demands for the *Warrior* development deal. "In addition to our [previous] agreement, I should have a minimum of 4 months off a year to make features in Hong Kong," he wrote, "and I should have participation in the TV series itself and merchandising."

For an interview with the English-language *Sunday Post-Herald*, dated November 21, 1971, Bruce discussed the *Warrior* project. "I should find out within a week whether this thing is on. If so, I will hustle back to Hollywood," Bruce said. "It's a really freaky adventure series about a Chinese guy who winds up in the American West in 1860. Can you dig that? All these cowboys on horses with guns and me with a long, green hunk of bamboo, right? Far out. What's holding things up now is that a lot of people are sitting around in Hollywood trying to decide if the American television audience is ready for an Oriental hero. We could get some really peculiar reactions from places like the Deep South."

Bruce received an international call from Warner Bros. on November 25, 1971. It was a double body blow of bad news. Since Warners could only justify producing one Eastern Western, they had decided to make *Kung Fu* and reject *The Warrior*, and they were going to cast David Carradine as the lead, not Bruce Lee. The loss of a starring role and his development deal in one call was a bitter pill to swallow. "He was supremely disappointed," Linda says. "We were not in very good financial shape at that time. So this would have been a major breakthrough."

The Hong Kong press was calling Bruce "the ultimate Mid-Pacific Man"—a term at that time for a Westernized Chinese. It was an apt phrase. Bruce wanted to straddle the globe—to bring Western professionalism to Hong Kong movies and Chinese culture to American TV. The danger for him was being caught in the middle of the ocean with nowhere to call home. He was rejected for *Kung Fu* because of his thick Chinese accent. He worried about being too Western for Hong Kong audiences. "There were some scenes in *The Big Boss* where I really didn't think I was Chinese enough," Bruce said. "You really had to do a lot of adjusting."

Being caught between two cultures was the theme that attracted Canadian TV's most popular journalist, Pierre Berton, when he came to Hong Kong looking for the appropriate subject to interview on December 9, 1971.

Berton discovered that everyone was talking about this previously unknown actor who had just broken Hong Kong's box office record and was bragging that he was about to become the first Oriental to ever star in an American TV series.

For his introduction, Berton framed Bruce as a man torn between East and West: "Bruce Lee faces a real dilemma. He's on the verge of stardom in the United States with a projected TV series on the horizon, but he's just achieved superstardom as a film actor here in Hong Kong. So how does he choose, the East or the West—the kind of problem that most budding movie actors would welcome."

At this moment, Bruce must have realized he faced another dilemma. Unaware that *The Warrior* had already been rejected, Berton intended to make it central to the twenty-five-minute-long interview. Bruce had to decide if he was going to admit he didn't have an American TV series on the horizon or try to dodge the subject.

For the first half of the interview, Berton delved into other topics before returning to his central framing device: "There's a pretty good chance that you'll get a TV series in the States called *The Warrior*. Isn't that where you use the martial arts in a Western setting?"

Bruce initially tried to avoid this question by bringing up a different TV project: "Well, that was the original idea. Paramount—you know, I did *Longstreet* for Paramount, and Paramount wants me to do a television series. On the other hand, Warner Brothers wants me to be in another one. But both of them, I think, they want me to be a modernized type of a thing, and they think that the Western idea is out. But I want—"

"You wanted the Western," Berton interjected, before pressing again. "Are you going to stay in Hong Kong and be famous, or are you going to go to the United States to be famous, or are you going to try to eat your cake and have it too?"

"I am going to try to do both, because, you see, I have already made up my mind that in the United States I think something about the Orientals, I mean, the true Orientals should be shown."

"Hollywood sure as heck hasn't," Berton agreed. "Let me ask you, however, about the problems that you face as a Chinese hero in an American series. Have people come up in the industry and said, well, we know how the audience is going to take a non-American?"

"Well, such questions have been raised. In fact, it is being discussed, and that is why *The Warrior* is probably not going to be on, I think, because unfortunately, such things does exist in this world, you see?" Bruce said, finally admitting the truth. "They think that business-wise it's a risk, and I don't blame them. I mean, in the same way, it's like in Hong Kong, if a foreigner comes and becomes a star, if I were the man with the money, I probably would have my own worry of whether or not the acceptance would be there."

For his final question, Berton asked Lee, "Do you still think of yourself as Chinese, or do you ever think of yourself as North American?"

"Do you know how I want to think of myself?" Bruce responded. "As a human being, because I mean, I don't want to sound like, you know, as Confucius say, but under the sky, under the heaven, man, there is but one family. It just so happened, man, that people are different."

A week after the Berton interview Bruce penned a gracious concession letter to Ted Ashley. "I am sorry to hear about the outcome of 'The Warrior.' Well, you cannot win them all, but damn it, I am going to win one of these days," Bruce wrote, before suggesting some ways the two men could still work together. "I feel Warner can definitely create a martial arts script, preferably for feature, tailored for me. And maybe Warner can help in releasing my [Hong Kong] movies in the States. I am daily improving in my acting and as a human being, and my dedication will definitely lead me to my goal. Any fair and rightful assistance from you will be deeply appreciated."

Since Bruce had bragged so extensively about the *Warrior* deal with Warner Bros. to the Hong Kong media, he needed a face-saving way to avoid directly admitting he had been rejected. In this endeavor he was greatly aided by the Chinese-language press with whom he was still enjoying a honeymoon period. On December 18, 1971, *The Hong Kong Standard*, which had been launched in 1949 "to give a Chinese voice to the world," ran the headline: "Bruce Lee Can Stay On in HK." Under a smiling photo of the actor ran this caption: "Bruce Lee . . . an Oriental first." The article stated: "Bruce Lee has been given permission by Warner Brothers of America to remain in Hong Kong for another six months. Warner Brothers are planning a new television series, The Warrior, with Bruce Lee taking the leading role—the first time an Oriental actor has been given such an honor. It is understood that Warners have now decided to delay the start of The Warrior." Once the six-month "delay" came and went, the Hong Kong press never brought up the topic of *The Warrior* again.

Prior to the premiere of *The Big Boss*, Bruce planned to make one more film with Golden Harvest and then return to America for good to star in *The Warrior* or *Kung Fu*. "His contract with Raymond Chow called for a second film, *Fist of Fury*," says Linda. "His intentions were, vaguely, to finish this film for Chow, then return to Hollywood and consider several of his television offers." But the rejection by Warner Bros. and the incredible success of *The Big Boss* had changed his calculations. He decided to extend his stay in Hong Kong. In December 1971, Bruce sold his Bel Air home and his Porsche and relocated his family to the Waterloo Hill neighborhood in Kowloon.

Bruce's next movie, *Fist of Fury*, nearly foundered over clashes with director Lo Wei. It began with the first draft of Lo Wei's "script," which the director had scribbled in the typical slapdash fashion of Hong Kong cinema. Having spent months carefully crafting the screenplay for *The Silent Flute* with Coburn and Silliphant, Bruce was disgusted by what he considered a lack of professionalism. He refused to begin filming until a detailed screenplay was written, bringing production to a screeching halt. Bruce was still only a contract player, but he was already acting like he was Steve McQueen. "Raymond spent the weekend rewriting the script," Andre Morgan says. "When Bruce saw the new script and saw it was going to work and he was going to have more input on the fight scenes, he agreed to make the movie."

The story Raymond Chow, Lo Wei, and Bruce agreed upon was based on the life and legend of Master Huo Yuanjia. He was the founder of the famed kung fu school *Jing Wu* ("Excellence in Martial Arts"). Huo Yuanjia became a national hero in 1902 when he challenged a Russian wrestler who had called China "The Sick Man of Asia." The Russian immediately apologized for his remarks. In a country ravenous for heroes, Huo Yuanjia became an overnight legend. His life was first fictionalized in the seminal novel *Modern Chivalry Heroes*, by the founding father of the martial arts genre, Ping Jiang. In the novel, Huo beats martial arts champions from Russia, Japan, and England—restoring pride to his people. At the end, he is killed by the trickery of the Japanese.

Fist of Fury cleverly avoided retelling this tale—what the Chinese call "warming over yesterday's rice"—to focus on the fallout after his death. Instead of playing Huo Yuanjia, as one might expect, Bruce Lee was cast as his top student, Chen Zhen. Bruce explained to reporters, "That is more interesting because Huo Yuanjia is sort of limited as a character for a film because you've got to follow how his history goes."

In the movie, Bruce, as Chen Zhen, arrives late for his master's funeral. After the burial a delegation of Japanese judo students shows up with a mocking gift: a sign that reads "Sick Man of Asia." Out of fear of the consequences (the school is located in the Japanese-controlled concession of Shanghai), the Chinese kung fu disciples restrain themselves. But Bruce, appropriately playing the hothead of the bunch, goes alone to the Japanese school to return their gift with an extra helping of his furious fists. After beating the stuffing out of everyone in the room, he rips the sign into pieces and says in the Chinese version, "Now you listen to me, I'll only say this once, the Chinese are not the sick men of Asia!"

While a Hollywood movie would likely have ended on this triumphant moment, Chinese fatalism turns the flick into a cautionary tale about the cycle of violence. After Bruce humbles and humiliates the Japanese, they attack his school, severely injuring his friends. While Bruce is killing the Japanese sensei, who poisoned his master, the sensei's students are slaughtering his friends. Upon returning to his school to discover the horror his righteous revenge has wrought, Bruce is surrounded by police. Instead of running or being taken into custody, he charges the police with a flying kick. Guns fire. The frame freezes. The End.

Bruce was extremely proud of the final scene. "At the end I died under the gunfire," he said. "But it's a very worthwhile death. I walk out and I say 'Screw you, man! Here I come!' Boom! And I leap out and leap up in the air, and then they stop the frame and then ba-ba-ba-ba-ba-bang!—like *Butch Cassidy and the Sundance Kid*."

Bruce may have refused to start filming until the screenplay was finished, but he'd never been one to sit still. While the production was delayed, he boldly took it upon himself to make a solo trip to Japan to entreat his matinee idol to join his movie. Arriving in the Roppongi district of Tokyo, the Little Dragon went to the offices of Shintaro Katsu, the forty-year-old star of the *Zatoichi* film series.

"Mr. Katsu, I hold you in high esteem, cinematically and otherwise," Bruce flattered. "I want to act with you, and I want to learn from you." He proceeded to pepper Katsu with dozens of questions about how he made his movies.

Beyond the opportunity to be near his idol, Bruce wanted to work with Katsu because he had starred with Jimmy Wang Yu in *Zatoichi Meets the One-Armed Swordsman*. Bruce considered Jimmy an unworthy rival—an actor pretending to be a tough guy, not a serious martial artist—and had developed a real contempt for him. If Bruce could get Shintaro Katsu to appear in *his* movie and it did better than Jimmy Wang Yu's, it would establish him as the bigger of the two men.

This was particularly important because *Fist of Fury*'s themes were lifted wholesale from another Jimmy Wang Yu movie, *The Chinese Boxer* (1970), which had been produced by Shaw Bros. In that film just as in *Fist of Fury*, noble Chinese kung fu students must defend themselves against dastardly Japanese karate and judo masters. If *Fist of Fury* was a hit, Bruce could stick it to both Jimmy Wang Yu and Run Run Shaw with one punch.

Unfortunately, Katsu refused. "I am so terribly sorry, but I cannot act with you," Shintaro Katsu told Bruce. "I am contractually bound." As a consolation, Katsu offered Bruce two actors from his troupe: Riki Hashimoto, a former professional baseball player, who ended up playing the villainous sensei, and Jun Katsumura, a former professional wrestler, who was cast as the sensei's bodyguard.

Even in the best of circumstances, the relationship between the Japanese and the Chinese can be tricky. *Fist of Fury* was the first time a Hong Kong studio had hired Japanese actors to play the villains in an overtly anti-Japanese movie. To avoid having their two Japanese guests balk at what was being asked of them, the Chinese hit upon a simple solution: they never gave them a copy of the screenplay. "We were acting but we didn't have a script at hand," remembers Jun Katsumura. "There was no plan but I'd heard something about what the story was about. I understood what to do."

Director Lo Wei gave Hashimoto and Katsumura their marching orders. "He told us to be odious. That is what he ordered us to do," Riki Hashimoto says. "I mainly played villains in Japanese films, so I used that experience. I tried to make my character as evil as I could." They decided to approach the project aloofly and simply do their duty, consoling themselves with the thought that no one in Japan would ever want to see a movie that cast their people in such a negative light.

Just as Bruce had been stunned by the impoverished conditions in rural Thailand, the Japanese felt filming for Golden Harvest was like slumming in the Third World. "The location was run-down. And I thought, 'Can you really shoot here?' " Katsumura recalls. "It was that bad."

The Japanese actors were also shocked by how rough-and-tumble the action choreography was. "When you have a fight in Japan, it's like dancing at a certain tempo. It has a flow and is easy to understand," Hashimoto says. "Over there they just do it directly. They don't care if it hurt or somebody got injured. I admired that. It makes it very hot-blooded." Jun Katsumura learned this lesson the hard way when he was choreographing his scene with Bruce. "He told us about his martial arts and took his shirt off. He played with his muscles and showed me his tricks," Katsumura says. "Then I did my karame—karame is when you restrain an assailant. Then he jumped to his feet, and he was kicking and punching for real! They really hit each other in Hong Kong movies. I thought you had to be careful."

What didn't surprise them was the conflict between Bruce and Lo Wei. "It is common, also in Japan, for the director and the lead actor to argue. That wasn't strange," Katsumura reflects.

After the phenomenal response for *The Big Boss*, both Bruce and Lo Wei jockeyed in the press to claim sole ownership of its success. Lo Wei gave himself the nickname "The Million Dollar Director." He also told reporters that he taught Bruce how to fight in front of the camera. After reading Lo Wei's quotes in the newspapers, Bruce stormed onto the set to confront his director in front of the entire cast and crew, including a young stuntman by the name of Jackie Chan.

"You called yourself 'The Dragon's mentor,' " Bruce yelled, shaking his head in fury.

"The quote was out of context," Lo Wei said.

"It's in the paper, isn't it?" Bruce said with a dangerous edge in his voice.

"I never said I taught you how to fight," said Lo, waving his hands in an attempt to calm down his star. "I only said I showed you how to fight for *the cameras*. The skill, the talent, that's yours, Bruce. At most I, ah, gave you a little polish."

Jackie Chan and the rest of the stuntmen watched in discomfort, afraid the argument might come to blows. As the two men stared at each other, the director's wife, Gladys Lo, stepped in between them. She placed her petite hand gently on Bruce's shoulder.

"Please, Little Dragon," she said, "don't take what my husband says so seriously. There is no insult in his words. Everyone knows that you are the master, and we are all just students!"

Bruce's gaze softened and his shoulders relaxed. Lo Wei slowly took a sideways step that placed his bulk behind the slim body of his wife.

"All right, Madame Lo," Lee said finally. "Out of respect for you, I'll forget that this happened. But if your husband ever talks to reporters about me again, I'll give *him* a lesson on how to fight."

Bruce walked off to the side of the set, shaking his head. When he was out of earshot, Lo Wei waved his hand anxiously at the rest of the crew. "Was that a threat?" he asked, his face betraying a mix of fear and annoyance. "Did he threaten me? All of you are witnesses."

Seeing Lo Wei hiding behind his wife, the crew turned away from him in disgust and resumed their previous conversations.

After this argument, Bruce banned Lo Wei from directing any of his fight scenes in *Fist of Fury*. He decided he would handle them all himself to make certain no one could ever again take credit for his work. This posed a problem. Han Ying-Chieh, who had served as action director and also played the villain in *The Big Boss*, had been hired as the fight choreographer for *Fist of Fury*. "Technically, Han Ying-Chieh was still the chief choreographer," remembers Zebra Pan, who was a stuntman on the set. "Then we all came in to shoot that opening scene, the one where Bruce beats up all the Japanese in their dojo. Han Ying-Chieh says, 'Okay, Bruce, let's try this . . . ,' and Bruce goes: 'No, how about this . . . ?' And for the first time started to really *do* Bruce Lee, to do all the stuff with multiple kicks and the nunchaku and everything. We were just knocked out by it and after that Han Ying-Chieh just kept quiet."

As Hashimoto and Katsumura discovered quickly, Bruce wanted to make film fighting as close to real fighting as possible by eliminating any fakery. He didn't want to use camera angles and depth of field to give the illusion of a blow being struck; he actually wanted to hit his costars—*action cinéma vérité*. As a consequence, Bruce preferred to cast martial artists rather than actors in his movies. For the part of the Russian wrestler bad guy, he picked Bob Baker, one of his Oakland students. Baker had no acting experience, but he could take a punch. "We did actually hit each other in most of the fight scenes," Baker recalls. "We were really sparring."

This quest for realism extended to the smallest details. Bruce choreographed a moment in his fight with Baker where he is trapped between

Bob's legs and has to bite him to get free. This was a pedagogical moment from Bruce's Jeet Kune Do philosophy: do whatever is necessary to win. The trouble with the scene was Baker wasn't giving a realistic enough reaction to Bruce's bite. Baker says, "I wasn't an actor. I didn't know how to respond to it. He really had to bite me." Bob was so surprised he yanked his leg away with all his might. "I just about pulled Bruce's teeth out. He put his hand over his mouth."

Perhaps as payback, Bruce set up his student for a real-life test of skill. At the end of a late night of filming, Bruce was leaving the set with Bob by his side. One of the Chinese stuntmen came up to Bruce and challenged him, saying he didn't think Bruce's kung fu was as good as the movies made it look. Following Chinese kung fu custom, Bruce said, "I am the master. If you want to fight me you have to fight my student first." Unfortunately for Bob, the conversation was taking place in Cantonese and he didn't understand a word of it. Suddenly, the stuntman lunged at Bob, who despite his surprise reacted immediately and decked the stuntman, ending the fight in one blow.

Fist of Fury was the first and only time Bruce shared an on-screen kiss with a costar, the twenty-year-old actress Nora Miao. She had been hired by Golden Harvest a year earlier after responding to a newspaper ad recruiting actors. There were only two other actresses under contract at the fledgling studio, and executives wanted to groom Nora for swordswoman roles. (The two stereotypical parts for young actresses were either passive love interests or swordswomen.) Lo Wei took Nora under his wing, eventually adopting her as his goddaughter.

She first appeared alongside Bruce in *The Big Boss*. She was visiting the set during a break from filming another movie, and Lo Wei decided to give her a walk-on role as the ice-lolly hawker, whom Bruce protects from some thugs harassing her. It was her first time meeting Bruce face-to-face, but they had heard of each other. While Bruce was in America, Nora had been a close teenage friend of his brother Robert. "I knew his family well," Nora says. "Robert and I went dancing, partying and hung out together with his mum and sister. I visited his home often. They often mentioned Bruce Lee." When they finally met, Nora says, "We felt that we had known each other all our lives even at first sight. Of course, he had heard of me. It was like 'Oh my younger brother's buddy has become a star.' "

When Robert became a teen pop sensation, he was romantically linked in the press to Nora. It is not clear if they were in fact boyfriend and girlfriend or just pals, but after *Fist of Fury*'s release the tabloids became enamored of the love triangle story line—older brother returns home and poaches his younger brother's girl. Hong Kong film historian Bey Logan has joked, "Maybe there was a Kennedy thing: Marilyn Monroe, Robert, and Jack."

If there was any sexual spark between Bruce and Nora, it's not evident on celluloid. Their on-screen kiss may be the least convincing in film history.

While Bruce was in America honing his stage persona, a younger generation of future kung fu action stars was perfecting their entertainment skills the traditional Chinese way. Boys whose parents were so poor they couldn't afford to raise them were sold to the China Drama Academy where they studied Cantonese Opera under unbelievably harsh conditions. Training could go on for as long as eighteen hours a day and included weapons training, acrobatics, kung fu, singing, and acting.

The most talented of the China Drama Academy's younger students were organized into a performance troupe called the Seven Little Fortunes. As the boys grew older and less cute, they were replaced and had to look for work elsewhere. Many of them migrated into the movie business to work as stuntmen.

The Little Fortunes were resentful and jealous of the buzz surrounding Bruce Lee until they saw *The Big Boss*. "We were prepared to hate the film.

We really wanted to," Jackie Chan says. "After all, this overseas Chinese guy had come in out of nowhere, was making hundreds of times our salaries, and had Hong Kong eating out of the palm of his hand. We wanted to, but we couldn't. The film was everything the movies we were making weren't. And even though *The Big Boss* may not seem very impressive today, for us then, it was a revelation. When we gathered in the evenings to drink and talk, the conversation always ended up turning the same way: what did Lee have that we didn't? What was the secret of his success?"

When word went out that Golden Harvest was looking for stuntmen for Bruce's second movie, the Little Fortunes clamored to study the secret of his success up close. Jackie was hired as a bit player; Yuen Wah, another ex–Little Fortune, served as Bruce's stunt double, performing all the acrobatic flips that Bruce had never learned how to do; and Sammo Hung—the Big Brother of the troupe, both in terms of status and physical girth—was hired by Golden Harvest as the stunt coordinator. Prideful and pugnacious, Sammo Hung was not content to simply watch from a distance. In a story that has become legendary, Sammo apparently ran into Bruce in a hallway at Golden Harvest during filming. As they got to talking about kung fu, they started to argue about certain finer points, and then, as martial artists are wont to do, they began to show each other certain techniques. It wasn't quite a full-out challenge match, but there was some light contact involved. Sammo walked away convinced that Bruce was the genuine article, but his pride wouldn't allow him to say that Bruce was better. "Sammo says it was even, but there were no witnesses, so who can confirm or deny?" Jackie Chan diplomatically notes.

Hong Kong was light years behind Hollywood in terms of screenwriting, directing, and production values, but its one competitive advantage was this group of stuntmen who were as physically talented as they were courageous. Just as he had as a teenager in Hong Kong and again as a young man in Seattle, Bruce began to form the stuntmen into his gang, winning them over with his charisma, loyalty, and generosity.

Instead of retreating with the bosses, he ate his lunches with the stuntmen, charming them with off-color jokes and his refusal of special treatment.

"Lee was always given something more gourmet. He would ask the production management: 'Why is that person eating "marinated pork rice" while I get "marinated chicken liver"?' " remembers Henry Wong, a production assistant. "The person from the production management said, 'Oh, because you're the boss.' Lee got a bit angry with him and said, 'Don't talk about me being the boss or not, I can eat what everyone else eats. There's no need to treat me differently. Next time—this is the last time—don't treat me special.' "

Even after filming ended, he continued to socialize with the stuntmen. One day he ran into Jackie Chan on the streets of Tsim Sha Tsui. "Where are you heading?" Bruce asked.

"Oh Bruce, I'm going to play bowling," Jackie replied.

"Can I go with you?"

"What? Yes!"

Jackie had intended to take the bus, but he immediately hailed a taxi for Hong Kong's newest superstar. When they got out of the taxi, Jackie felt like a hero. The crowd started screaming, "Bruce Lee! Bruce Lee!" Jackie immediately acted as Bruce's bodyguard. "Go away, go, go go," Jackie shouted at them. "No autographs! No photos!"

In the bowling alley, Bruce sat down in his bell-bottom jeans and high-heeled Cuban boots and watched Jackie roll strike after strike.

"Do you want to play?" Jackie asked.

"Jackie, I think I'm leaving," Bruce said, unwilling to be upstaged by a stuntman. "I have to meet someone."

"Ah, okay," Jackie replied, disappointed.

Jackie Chan was not the only stuntman to serve unofficially as Bruce's bodyguard. Ip Chun, the son of Bruce's master, Ip Man, recalls: "Lee always went jogging in the mornings and before evenings. He would always go with several stuntmen and would never go alone, because he would often encounter those who wanted to challenge him, and he would ask the stuntmen to take the challenges and he would go home himself."

Like with any good gang leader, Bruce offered the stuntmen protection and support. He paid their medical bills. "If a fighter was injured and the company didn't compensate enough, Bruce would give him one or two thousand Hong Kong dollars, which was a lot at the time," recalls Ip Chun. He secured higher salaries. "When times were tough, he'd tell the boss—and we'd all get a raise," says Angela Yao Ming, one of his costars in *Enter the Dragon*. And he even promised he would bring some of them back with him to America. "He said he was going to take ten of us to Hollywood," recalls Yuen Wah, his stunt double. Like with any good gang member, the stuntmen offered Bruce their undying loyalty. "All the kung fu stuntmen in Hong Kong really worshipped him," says Robert Chan, a childhood friend.

If the stuntmen were like his schoolboy followers, then his bosses were the teachers he had defied as a teenager. "He got along really well with the low-level people on set. But he was extremely impolite to his boss," Bolo Yeung, who costarred in *Enter the Dragon*, says. "In the real world, it's always the reverse: kiss up to your boss, and act like a tyrant to the people below you. Lee was just the opposite. He was kind to those below him, and mean to those above him." Raymond Chow was like the school principal. "Bruce used to roar at his superiors. He'd shout, 'Raymond Chow, get over here!' Bruce wouldn't even look him in the eyes as they spoke." Lo Wei was the PE instructor who had switched Bruce with a blade of grass. Lo Wei whipped Bruce with words, mocking him behind his back as "The Master of Anxiety." Bruce frequently confronted Lo Wei and challenged his authority. "After Lo Wei had given everyone their basic instructions for the scene, he liked to listen to the racing on the radio," says Lam Ching Ying, a stuntman. "He'd be sitting in his director's chair, getting all excited over his horse winning or losing. Finally Bruce storms over to him: 'What are you doing? Okay, everybody go home!' In fact we didn't wrap but Bruce made his point!"

Bruce was so frustrated with Lo Wei that he began plotting how to get out from under his thumb. While he was acting and choreographing his fight scenes, he also managed to find time to study every aspect of the filmmaking process, asking countless questions. He wanted to be in complete control over every aspect of his career. "His ultimate goal was to be a film producer, like Raymond Chow," says Chaplin Chang, who worked on *Way of the Dragon* and *Enter the Dragon*.

Fist of Fury was the last movie on Bruce's contract with Golden Harvest.

His plan was to direct, produce, and star in his next Hong Kong film. To realize his outsized ambitions, he needed *Fist of Fury* to smash the box office record of *The Big Boss*.

The house was packed at the Queen's Theatre for *Fist of Fury*'s premiere on March 22, 1972. If *The Big Boss* tapped into Chinese anxiety about their place in the world, *Fist of Fury* was a pure adrenaline shot of patriotism into their hearts. When Bruce delivered the line "The Chinese are not the sick men of Asia," the entire audience as one people rose to their feet and howled their approval. "Oh my God, in one screening they tore out the seats and threw them around they were all so excited," Nancy Kwan recalls.

Fist of Fury introduced several elements that became inseparable from Bruce's iconic image. It was the first time he demonstrated the nunchaku, the weapon the press would refer to as "Bruce Lee's singing rods of death." It was the first time he introduced his catlike screeches while attacking. He adopted the exaggerated emotional acting style of Japanese samurai films (*chambara*). And he perfected his movie fighting style: a series of high chain kicks punctuated by dramatic pauses to build tension.

Interestingly, none of these was particularly Chinese: nunchakus were an Okinawan weapon, unknown previously in China; *chambara* was Japanese; high chain kicks were used in Korean Tae Kwon Do, not Chinese kung fu; and his animal screeching was something he made up himself. "When people asked him why he shouted like this," recalls one of his stuntmen, "he said, 'This is what I do during a real fight.' " But it made no difference to the Chinese crowds. He had defended their honor on-screen and therefore in their hearts. He represented something new—the way the Chinese wanted to be, not who they were—strong, powerful, cocky, and utterly fearless.

The movie dominated the Hong Kong box office. Within thirteen days, it topped *The Big Boss*'s record of HK$3.5 million and in its first month grossed a whopping HK$4.3 million. From there it swept across Asia. In the Philippines, it ran nonstop for more than six months, and the government was eventually pressured into limiting the importation of foreign films to protect the local movie industry. On its opening night in Singapore, excited fans filled the streets outside cinemas causing such extensive traffic jams that officials postponed its release for a week until arrangements could be made to corral the crowds. When it finally was shown, scalpers were selling $1 tickets for $15.

Two years later on July 20, 1974, *Fist of Fury* was even released in Japan. It did remarkably well considering the content. No one was more surprised than his Japanese costars, Riki Hashimoto and Jun Katsumura. "The story of *Fist of Fury* itself made fools of the Japanese. So I thought that it would not be shown in Japan. But *Enter the Dragon* and *Way of the Dragon* were big hits in Japan, so they distributed *Fist of Fury*," Jun Katsumura says. "There are many young Japanese who are crazy about Bruce Lee. If I'd know he'd become such a superstar, I would have been friendlier with him and fooled around more. I regret that I didn't."

Bruce and Betty Ting Pei on the Hong Kong Colosseum studio set for *Way of the Dragon*, June 1972. *(David Tadman)*

nineteen

concord

If you want to know what is in a poor man's heart, see what he buys when he gets rich. Bruce was by no means wealthy at this point. He was a contract player and had been paid a flat fee, $15,000, for his work on *The Big Boss* and *Fist of Fury*. Most of that money was used to pay off old debts. It was Raymond Chow and Golden Harvest who reaped the rewards of their gamble on Bruce. *The Big Boss* alone earned over $16 million in 2017 US dollars. When a reporter asked Run Run Shaw about his decision not to sign Lee, he shrugged gloomily. "He was just an actor. How could I know?" Bruce was not rich, but his credit was good. "I'm really enjoying the position I'm at now," Bruce rejoiced to friends. "I could go down to any bank right now and get a loan for as much as I want, up to six million dollars, with just my signature."

The first thing he wanted to buy with his unlimited line of credit was control. On December 1, 1971, Bruce and Raymond signed a contract establishing a new satellite company called Concord Productions. Bruce derived the name from the Roman goddess of harmony, Concordia, and not, as some have suggested, the supersonic jet Concorde, which debuted in 1969.

The symbol for the company was the red and gold yin/yang sign Bruce had used for his Jeet Kune Do studio in Los Angeles. Raymond Chow and Bruce were the two halves of the Taoist whole: Bruce was in charge of the creative side, Chow the business operations. Profits would be split 50/50.

The agreement was not the first of its kind in Hong Kong. Raymond Chow had set up similar "satellite" company deals with Jimmy Wang Yu and Lo Wei in order to entice them to leave Shaw Bros. for Golden Harvest. But those had been kept quiet to avoid further antagonizing Run Run Shaw. Bruce's deal was the first to be made public. When other stars heard, they clamored for similar arrangements, marking the beginning of the end for Shaw's contract system. As with kung fu movies, Bruce popularized a trend that had already begun before he returned to Hong Kong.

With a new company came a new office. For the first time in his life, Bruce was now a white-collar worker. Bruce's office at Golden Harvest's studios on Hammerhill Road was a former costume and set design closet, maybe 130 square feet. He installed a desk, chairs, and a set of Olympic barbells so he could constantly pump weights. To remind him of his lean past, he kept on his shelf a broken pair of glasses he had Scotch-taped as a young man in America because he couldn't afford to have them repaired. He also pinned to one wall a poster of two vultures with the caption: "Patience my Ass. I'm gunna kill something." On another wall, he had installed wallpaper worthy of the Playboy Mansion—drawings of hundreds of bare-breasted women of all different ethnicities.

From Steve McQueen, Bruce learned that being a celebrity wasn't just about big box office but looking like a star in real life. "Image is important," McQueen told him. "To be successful, you have to look successful." Fashion conscious since he was a teen, Bruce went on a shopping spree. "He liked clothes and enjoyed buying them," Linda says. In Hollywood, he had burnished his Oriental otherness by wearing kaftans, dashikis, and Nehru jackets. In Hong Kong, he emphasized his Westernized persona by sporting Elvis-style sunglasses, bright flowered shirts, big-lapeled leather jackets, and bell-bottom jeans, which helped partially conceal the four-inch platform shoes he wore to make himself seem taller. For special occasions, he bought a floor-length mink coat. It was the 1970s.

Status-conscious Hong Kongers, who often live in tiny apartments, flash their wealth with luxury cars. It had broken Bruce's heart to sell his Porsche. After *Fist of Fury*, he acquired a red Mercedes 305SL convertible. Since Bruce had no money of his own, Raymond Chow advanced Bruce the funds out of Concord's future earnings. "Raymond was Bruce Lee's piggy bank," says Andre Morgan. Bruce would go much deeper into debt for his next major purchase.

When Bruce, Linda, and the kids first moved to Hong Kong, Golden Harvest put them up in an apartment at 2 Man Wan Road, Sunlight Garden, Kowloon—a fifteen-minute drive from Bruce's childhood home. For a Hong Kong family in 1971, the flat was quite spacious: it had two bedrooms, a living and dining room, and a Chinese kitchen. But compared to his Bel Air home, it was tiny. "A lot of the modern conveniences I had been used to, such as a washer and dryer, were missing," Linda says. "Our clothes were washed by hand and hung out on the window on bamboo poles to dry." The apartment was situated on the thirteenth floor and the elevator rarely worked. Linda and Bruce used this as an exercise opportunity—running up and down the stairs. "Our neighbors thought we were a bit strange," she says.

Adding to Linda's feeling of being cramped was Wu Ngan, his childhood friend. Bruce moved him into the apartment as his manservant. When Wu Ngan married, his wife joined as well. As the live-in servants they cleaned, cooked, and washed the clothes by hand. While the arrangement may have made Linda uncomfortable, Bruce was quite proud of it. "All the years I've been with Linda, she was always busy," Bruce bragged to friends. "Now that we can afford to hire help, I finally got her to take it easy. We have enough servants and maids to do the housework."

A cramped apartment was fine for a contract actor, but not for Hong Kong's biggest box office star. After *Fist of Fury*'s success, Raymond secured a loan for Bruce to purchase what passes for a palace in densely packed Hong Kong, a 5,700-square-foot, two-story, eleven-room, gray concrete home on 41 Cumberland Road in the tony suburb of Kowloon Tong—one of the very few neighborhoods with freestanding houses instead of apartment high-rises. Like all the other houses in the area, it was cordoned off by eight-foot stone walls and a wrought iron gate as if the neighborhood was preparing for the Communist hordes to invade. The furnishings in Bruce and Linda's home were a mix of Western and Chinese modern, in beaming bright colors, and carefully collected pieces of Chinese art. Bruce had an extensive collection of martial arts weapons he loved to display and demonstrate. The huge front yard of Bruce's new home had a Japanese garden and an extended driveway for his Mercedes and any other car he might add to his collection. While not the biggest house on the block, it was palatial by Hong Kong standards. (In 2011, it was put on the market for US$23 million.)

Having leapt up the social ladder, Bruce and Linda worked to situate their children in their new city and place in life. Two-year-old Shannon was sent to a high-end nursery school to prepare her for private kindergarten entrance exams. By the age of three, she was wearing a uniform, carrying a box bag, and learning Chinese characters.

Bruce wanted to send six-year-old Brandon to his old school La Salle. But he was afraid they wouldn't accept his son because they had expelled him. He appealed to Raymond Chow to accompany him to La Salle to plead his case.

"Why don't you just go?" Raymond asked him. "I mean, now that you're very well known."

"Yes, I'm very famous," Bruce said, "and infamous."

"What happened?" Raymond asked.

"I was very well known for fighting," he admitted, before shaving the truth a bit. "Actually, it was not all my fault. A lot of times, people picked on me and, you know, I just had to fight."

"So nothing to do with your son's schooling?"

"No, no, no, no. La Salle is very straight. The brothers are very strict," Bruce pleaded. "So, if you come with me, my son will have a better chance."

Raymond relented and went with Bruce to La Salle. The Catholic Brothers turned out to be overjoyed to see him. They had heard of his accomplishments and were very welcoming to their prodigal son. Brandon was admitted without any mention of the sins of the father. "See? All these people take me seriously now," Bruce delightedly remarked to Raymond.

It wasn't long, however, before Brandon was following in his father's foot (and fist) steps. Within a few weeks, he was already getting into fights. "Brandon is the biggest and only white kid in his class. And we're already getting complaints that he's beating up on the other kids," Bruce proudly told his friend Mito Uyehara. Mito noticed that Linda was "rather perturbed by Bruce's attitude at that moment."

Having achieved success, Bruce invited his mother-in-law to visit them in Hong Kong. "She was so proud of me," Bruce smiled, "because wherever we went, we were given the V.I.P. treatment. I guess that's the first time in her life she had that kind of attention."

Bruce looked at his life, and it was good. With a daughter in preschool, a son at La Salle, a devoted wife, and a flourishing acting career, he had in many ways re-created his own childhood—and one-upped his father in the process. His father was a well-known Cantonese Opera actor; Bruce was the biggest movie star in Hong Kong. His father had taken care of the family in a well-apportioned apartment with servants; Bruce was living in a mansion with servants. "He used to call me at two or three in the morning," says Nancy Kwan, "and tell me how good he was feeling and how finally he was making money and he could buy anything he wanted."

It was all coming together for him. But if he wanted to be like every other successful Hong Kong man—like his father and grandfather—he needed one more thing.

On March 21, 1972, Bruce, Linda, and Raymond went out for a celebratory dinner at Hugo's restaurant in the Hyatt Regency Hotel. It was Linda's birthday and the night before the premiere of *Fist of Fury*. They were all filled with anxiety, anticipation, and high hopes. As they were leaving the hotel, they bumped into the sultry twenty-five-year-old Taiwanese actress Betty Ting Pei.

Betty had recently returned from a six-month stay in Switzerland where she had married and quickly divorced a handsome Swiss man. "I was not that happy, but not brokenhearted either," Betty says. "It's because I didn't know what love was."

Raymond, who while at Shaw Bros. had signed Betty to a five-year contract, made the introductions. "Bruce was very happy to look at, you know, look at me," Betty smiles. "The feeling was quick contact."

Despite the initial sparks, or perhaps because of them, the married movie star waited nearly two weeks before making contact again. And he couldn't even do it himself. "Raymond called me at the President Hotel and said, 'Bruce and I are downstairs in the Chin Chin Bar,' " Betty remembers. "I was very excited. For sure he likes me, right? But it's funny. I didn't really want to go out, because I had no makeup. I didn't know what to wear.

"When Bruce first approached me, he offered me a part in his next movie, *Yellow Faced Tiger*," Betty says. It must have been an enticing offer. Betty's contract with Shaw Bros. had expired, she hadn't worked in the past six months since leaving for Switzerland, and she had expenses. "We didn't make lots of money back then, but I lived like a movie star," Betty says. "I drove a Mustang. Everybody knew who I was."

Having been in show business for a long time, she says she wasn't naive. "I didn't believe he wanted to work with me. I think to myself he probably just wants to be boyfriend and girlfriend." One clue may have been the body language. "We're talking and right away he's holding my hand and telling me how pretty I am." Betty reveals that the charismatic star didn't need to work so hard. "He was so famous. He had done so much better than me. I didn't feel like I could compare with him," she says. "There was no human being like Bruce. It is difficult to explain except that I knew that he got me. He got me right away, just like he could control me right away. I was like, 'I'm with him.' "

Betty ran back to her room to call her mother. "Guess who I met? Lee Little Dragon!" But her mother was unimpressed. "She just ignored me. She didn't care. She didn't know who Bruce was."

As the flashy new kid in school, the media couldn't get enough of Bruce. The press coverage during this honeymoon period was so overwhelming that it led to press coverage about the press coverage. A special article in *The*

Daily News reported with some chagrin, "In two short weeks in December [1971], four special reports of Lee Little Dragon were published, and his face appeared on the cover of magazines no less than seven times. Though many stories and rumors about Lee Little Dragon have become common knowledge, they are still not enough to satisfy the fans, who are continually interested in more reporting on his background. As a result, almost any story with any connection to him is seen as valuable."

One of the stories the media couldn't resist was the supposed bad blood between Bruce Lee and Jimmy Wang Yu, Hong Kong's two biggest action stars working under the same roof. "Wang Yu was the established force," Andre Morgan says, "Bruce Lee was the new gunslinger coming to town." The tabloids feverishly reported how they were on the verge of setting up a challenge match to see who was the better fighter. "Each is King in his own jungle," wrote *Fanfare*, a Singapore newspaper. "It's like persuading two proud tigers to live in the same cage peacefully." Raymond Chow, as a savvy promoter, did nothing to discourage this story line. "All of this stuff about threatening to punch each other out," Morgan says, "whether they really intended to or not, it didn't matter, because it sure made for good copy, didn't it? It got the fans' adrenaline pumping."

Behind the scenes, they did in fact talk trash about each other. "Bruce used to mouth off about Jimmy. It was always, 'Well, he's not really a martial artist. I'm a real martial artist,' " Morgan recalls. "Wang Yu's dismissive was, 'I'm the number one star and I'm an all-around athlete. I was an Olympic swimmer. I can do swords. I can do martial arts. I ride horses. What's the big deal? I do everything.' "

While Raymond saw the value in hyping the rivalry, he didn't want his two most valuable stars actually coming to blows. He carefully made sure Bruce and Jimmy were never in the same room together. "Raymond didn't want Bruce to be in the position where he had to look Wang Yu in the face and confront him as to who was the biggest, baddest gunslinger," Morgan says. "There was a lot of testosterone flying around back then."

Wang Yu had another way to put down Bruce. While *The Big Boss* and *Fist of Fury* may have done better than *The Chinese Boxer* at the box office, Jimmy had written, directed, and starred in his movie. In contrast,

Bruce had merely been the actor in two movies that borrowed heavily from Jimmy's work. As far as Jimmy was concerned, Bruce was riding on his coattails. "*The Chinese Boxer* was my idea. I wrote the script. It was the first kung fu movie," Jimmy said. "Because of it, a lot of directors copied my idea and wrote very similar scripts. So therefore Bruce Lee had the opportunity to come back to Hong Kong to make a successful picture."

A man as proud and competitive as Bruce Lee couldn't let this stand unanswered. After the incredible success of Lo Wei and Bruce's first two movies, Raymond Chow naturally wanted to team them up again for a third. The project he set into motion was called *Yellow Faced Tiger*. In *Fist of Fury*, Bruce had played Chen Zhen, the student of the legendary kung fu master Huo Yuanjia. For this follow-up movie, Raymond wanted to cast Bruce as Huo Yuanjia, whose nickname was "Yellow Faced Tiger" because he suffered from jaundice. Bruce initially agreed but very quickly began having second thoughts about working with Lo Wei again. The director had been telling anybody who would listen that he was responsible for Bruce's success. Jimmy Wang Yu was telling anybody who would listen that he was a real filmmaker while Bruce was merely a copycat actor. Making another film with Lo Wei would just confirm their criticisms.

The solution was both simple and ambitious. Bruce would write, direct, and star in his own movie. For good measure, and to best Jimmy, he'd compose the music too. If that wasn't enough, he'd set the movie in Rome, so it would be the first Hong Kong movie to ever film in the West. The Little Dragon decided to call his directorial debut *Enter the Dragon* for obvious branding reasons. It was not until Bruce decided to use *Enter the Dragon* as the title for his first Warner Bros. movie that the name was changed to *Way of the Dragon*.

Bruce first had to untangle himself from *Yellow Faced Tiger* and Lo Wei. According to Lo Wei's recollection of events, he had initially been preparing to make a movie with Sam Hui, one of Bruce's close friends, when Raymond Chow ordered him off that project and onto *Yellow Faced Tiger* with Bruce. "I dropped my original plans and hurried to write Lee's script," Lo Wei claims. After the script was finished and arrangements had already been made to film in Japan, Raymond called Lo Wei to inform him that Bruce no longer wanted to make the movie. A meeting between the star and his director was set up at Her Ladyship restaurant.

"We'll be underway soon," Lo Wei said to Bruce. "The visas are all approved."

"The thing is," Bruce replied, "this script isn't so great."

"What do you think the problem is?" Lo Wei asked.

"I think the script is the problem."

"What part of the script seems to be the problem then?" Lo Wei asked.

"The whole thing."

"You need to think this through," Lo Wei said, testily. "For *The Big Boss* I had to do things roughly. In Bangkok, that terrible place, we slapped the film together, but we still made money! *Fist of Fury*, we were in the same boat, and we made even more money. For *Fist of Fury* we didn't even have a script! We only had three sheets of paper for the whole film! Now, *this script* is very well written! I think it will be an absolutely fine film, so I am not worried about it."

"I still think the script doesn't work," Bruce said.

"Then we'll do it like this: you tell me which parts you don't like and we can change them! You're the star. We can change the script so you're happy with it. I want you to be happy with it too. All we need to do is talk it over!"

"I still can't put my finger on which part I don't like."

"You still don't know?!" Lo Wei erupted. "The 3rd scene? Or the 5th scene? The 7th scene? The 8th? Where's the problem with the dialogue? Is it the plot? The ambiance? The development of the story? Come on, you have to have a reason! You can't just say there's something wrong, you need to back it up."

"I need to go home and look it over again," Bruce replied. "I'll tell you tomorrow."

"You need to write it out for me," Lo Wei jousted, trying to pin Bruce down. "We will change the script according to what you think."

"I'll have it for you by tomorrow," he said. "No, not tomorrow, three days. Give me three days."

Bruce left abruptly, and Lo Wei headed back to the office. Three days passed, then a week, then two. Bruce didn't come by the office or call Lo Wei, who realized something was wrong. He asked around and heard that Bruce wanted to direct his own movie. Furious, he decided to scrap the entire project, but Golden Harvest had already invested in it—arrangements had been made—so Raymond insisted that Lo Wei find a replacement for Bruce.

"I want Jimmy Wang Yu," Lo Wei said, no doubt aware of how much this would irritate Bruce.

"Wang is so busy!" Chow replied, trying to cut Lo Wei off.

"Just try him!" Lo Wei insisted. "If you say I am the one directing, he'll probably do it."

Chow flew to Taiwan where Jimmy was filming another movie. He signed on. When the press heard that Lo Wei was going to Japan with Wang Yu, not Lee, a reporter showed up to Lo Wei's office to probe this juicy angle.

"Bruce Lee won't be going?" the reporter asked and then laughed at Lo Wei. "How can you make a movie without Bruce Lee?"

"I was already making movies before I met Lee!" Lo Wei flared, and the media gleefully ran with the story of an acrimonious split between the Million Dollar Duo. Bruce Lee was out and Jimmy Wang Yu was in.

When Bruce read the newspapers, he was furious. He had been dragging his feet but hadn't actually turned down the project. They had replaced him behind his back and made it public, causing him to lose face. He didn't want to work with Lo Wei again, but he also didn't want Jimmy Wang Yu to either. Their movie would be competing with his. What if *Yellow Faced Tiger* did better at the box office than *Way of the Dragon*? People would say that Lo Wei was responsible for Bruce's success.

Bruce decided he wanted to make both films and completely undercut Jimmy Wang Yu. He called up Lo Wei and asked why he had been replaced.

"I couldn't get ahold of you. You were supposed to get in touch with me after three days, remember?" Lo Wei pointedly said. "This is the first time that I have heard from you in a month!"

"I never said I didn't want to do the film."

"But you didn't tell me this for close to a month now!" Lo Wei shouted.

"Why did you choose Jimmy Wang? Was that Chow's idea?" Bruce asked, already suspicious of Raymond's motives.

"No! You are a celebrity! Me? I am a famous director. I have self-respect. You told me three days. You didn't contact me for almost a month. It's tasteless. I didn't know what you were thinking, so all I could do was replace you."

"Are you trying to make me look bad?" Bruce asked.

"No, I am not trying to make you look bad. I know you're about to start filming your own movie. I know. At most, I replaced you. Can we just forget about it? If no one brings it up, then it's not a problem."

"Don't you think you and Wang don't go together well?"

"Of course not," Lo Wei said.

"I think you switching me out for Wang means you're a 'low gamble,' " Bruce said, using a Cantonese insult. "How about if we do it like this: I'll go with you to Japan. You won't replace me. I'll be in your film."

"This won't do. You think you can just ignore me for weeks. I have already promised someone else. I can't just switch again now. How does that make me look?"

According to Lo Wei, Bruce lost his infamous temper and started cursing him.

"Now, Bruce Lee, consider your status in society: you're a movie star, a cultural worker, how can you curse at me this way?" Lo Wei scolded in a patronizing tone.

Bruce cursed him one last time before slamming down the phone.

That argument ended the most successful director-star partnership in Hong Kong film history. Afterward they avoided each other whenever possible and never met face-to-face. If they ran into each other at the office or on a movie set, they would turn their back and walk away.

Lo Wei and Jimmy Wang Yu went to Japan to make their movie. Bruce Lee went to Rome to make his. It was a showdown to see who was Golden Harvest's biggest star.

Bruce and Nora Miao in Rome for *Way of the Dragon*, May 1972. *(David Tadman)*

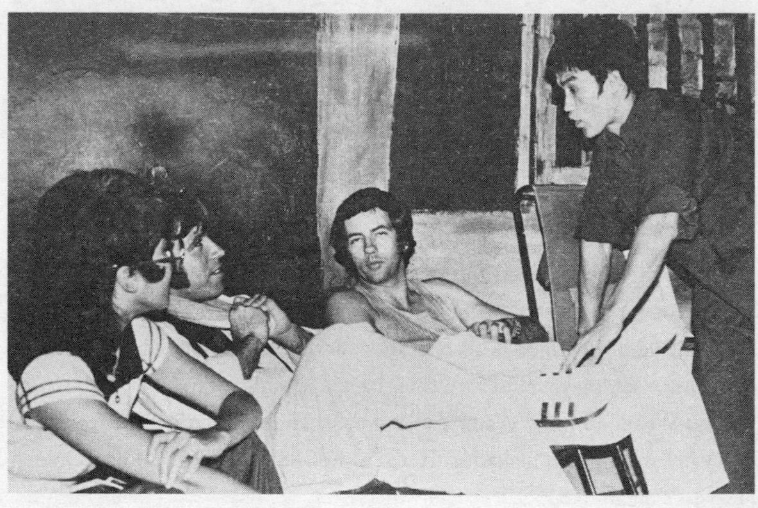

Betty Ting Pei, Chuck Norris, Bob Wall, and Bruce Lee at Golden Harvest studios during filming of *Way of the Dragon*, June 1972. *(David Tadman)*

twenty

spaghetti eastern

Way of the Dragon was the first screenplay Bruce wrote by himself. The biggest hurdle he faced was linguistic. "He found that he had left Hong Kong so long ago, he had a little trouble writing the script in Chinese," says Chi Yao Chang, the assistant director on the film. Bruce joked about being caught between two worlds, "It is quite funny really. I bought this English-Chinese dictionary originally to help me find the suitable English words when I first went to the United States when I was 18. Now I find that I have to use it to find the Chinese words which I have in mind." To help his creative process, Bruce first dictated his ideas onto a tape recorder mostly in English. Then he and Chi Yao Chang translated these oral notes into Chinese scenes as the script developed.

Bruce's initial story concept for *Way of the Dragon* was based on *The Warrior,* the TV series he had pitched to Ted Ashley—a nineteenth-century Chinese kung fu master flees from the failing Qing Dynasty to San Francisco where he protects Chinese immigrants from exploitation. Ironically, just like Warner Bros., Bruce ended up rejecting his idea. Concern over the cost of filming a period piece in America persuaded him to switch the story to the present day and look for a cheaper location.

Up until this point, no Chinese director had ever filmed in the West. Adamant that he be the first, Bruce began looking at European cities, finally settling on Rome. Kirk Douglas's Colosseum battle in *Spartacus* (1960) gave Bruce the idea for a final fight between himself and a Western bad guy. More important, Italy fit with his Eastwood strategy of conquering Hollywood.

When Clint Eastwood was unable to jump from TV to film, he made several cheap spaghetti westerns in Italy. Bruce believed Hong Kong could be for him what Italy was for Clint Eastwood—a bank shot back to Hollywood. "I'll go to Hong Kong and make it big there," Bruce confidently told an American friend. "Then I'll come back here and be a superstar like Eastwood. You just watch me." Bruce intended *Way of the Dragon* to be his spaghetti eastern, the movie that would gain him traction in the West.

It took Bruce about a month to finish a rough draft. In this modern European update of his original *The Warrior* conceit, a Chinese restaurant in Rome is being threatened by the Italian mafia. The owner appeals to his uncle back in Hong Kong to send reinforcements. He dispatches his nephew, Tang Lung, whose name means "China Dragon." (The Chinese name for the film is *Powerful Dragon Crosses the Sea*.) Drawing on his own experiences as a new immigrant to America, Bruce conceived of Tang Lung as a naive country bumpkin from the New Territories. "He is a simple man, but he likes to act big," Bruce told a reporter during filming. "He doesn't really understand a metropolis like Rome, but he pretends that he does." Tang Lung is a fish out of water, and as a result Bruce pioneered a new trend in Hong Kong cinema—the kung fu comedy—which Jackie Chan would later perfect. Tang Lung is looked down upon not only by the Westerners but also by his own more sophisticated city-slicker Chinese cousins. His secret weapon is his mastery of kung fu. "Well it is really a simple plot of a country boy going to a place where he cannot speak the language but somehow he comes out on top, because, he honestly and simply expressed himself," Bruce laughingly told *Esquire* magazine, "by beating the hell out of everybody who gets in his way."

While Bruce was working on the script, his old screenwriting mentor Stirling Silliphant arrived at Kai Tak Airport on April 10, 1972. Silliphant was researching another movie but also had hopes of reviving the *Silent Flute* project. Bruce had hopes of impressing Stirling with what a huge star he had become. Bruce greeted him at the airport with Raymond Chow, beautiful Golden Harvest actresses Nora Miao and Maria Yi, and a gaggle of reporters and TV crews in tow to record how Hollywood was visiting the island kingdom to kiss the new prince's ring. "Every time there was a newspaper report about some black or white guy coming all the way from the States to be in a film with Bruce Lee," Andre Morgan says. "Wow! That's a lot of face for the Chinese."

Bruce took Stirling on a stroll through the streets that turned into a parade. "He was followed by hundreds of people," Stirling recalls. "They were just flocking, yelling, trying to get next to him. Bruce was wearing a fantastic three-piece white Brioni suit and walking like a king, smiling at people. It was beautiful. God, it was beautiful." Bruce wanted Stirling to see *Fist of Fury* in the theaters with a Chinese crowd. "You couldn't believe the way the people watched that film," Stirling says. "They were silent and then they yelled. And when he was kicking the Japanese around they loved it."

After returning to the States, Silliphant wrote Bruce a letter dated April 20, 1972, discussing *The Silent Flute*. At this point it seems that Stirling and Bruce were both interested in reviving the project. "I can't begin to tell you how gratifying it is to see your phenomenal success. I truly hope that I'll be able to get back to Hong Kong later this year and that we can put THE SILENT FLUTE before the cameras. Believe me I'll be working on it."

While Bruce and Raymond Chow were coequal partners in Concord, it was a satellite company of Golden Harvest. In effect Chow was still Bruce's boss. As an employee, Bruce's only leverage was to threaten to quit. When Bruce tried to convince Raymond to let him direct his own movie instead of working with Lo Wei on *Yellow Faced Tiger*, he feinted toward Run Run

Shaw. They had a meeting that was leaked to the press, which reported that Shaw Bros. was offering Bruce a lucrative deal. The ensuing furor forced Run Run Shaw's press secretary to issue a vague denial: "I don't disregard the possibility that we may sign Lee, he's certainly commercial, but if Shaw Bros. does sign Lee, it would not be this year." Fearing he might lose his biggest moneymaker, Raymond caved and allowed the untested Bruce to direct his first film. From this point on, whenever Bruce had a major conflict with Chow, he would meet with Shaw.

Bruce began auditioning dozens of actresses and pop stars for the female costarring role. Interestingly, one actress who never got a chance was Betty Ting Pei. Bruce blamed the decision on his boss.

"Ah, um, everything is already fixed," Bruce tried to explain. "Raymond wasn't so keen on you playing the part."

"It doesn't matter," Betty said. "As long as we are together."

"I like your new hair cut. It looks good shorter," Bruce said, changing the subject. "Where do you get it styled? I want a new look for *Way of the Dragon*."

"Anthony Walker did it," Betty said. "I'll set up an appointment before you go to Rome."

The actress Bruce finally settled on was Nora Miao, his costar from *Fist of Fury*. His decision was driven primarily by a desire to undermine Lo Wei. Raymond had assigned Nora to costar with Jimmy Wang Yu in *Yellow Faced Tiger*, the movie Bruce had turned down. This would have made *Yellow Faced Tiger* essentially a sequel to *Fist of Fury* with the same team, except for Jimmy instead of Bruce in the lead. Bruce insisted that Raymond pull Nora from Lo Wei's project and give her to him. Raymond sided with his star actor over his star director.

When Lo Wei found out, he was fit to be tied. "Lo Wei was very angry, even with me," Nora says. "He thought I went to Rome because Bruce was famous. I said that was not true, I only did what the company told me to. I did not even understand why they sent me." As recompense for the loss of Nora, Lo Wei demanded that Chow give him one of the character actors Bruce wanted, Lee Kwan. When the Little Dragon found out that Raymond had acceded to Lo Wei's demands, it was his turn to blow hot. "Bruce was swearing in Cantonese and English. It was shocking, the worst street language," says Chaplin Chang, who served as a production manager on *Way of the Dragon*. "He vowed that one day he would run his own studio."

Still furious about Nora, Lo Wei lashed out in the press. He told the Singapore newspaper *New Nation* that Jimmy Wang Yu, not Bruce Lee, was the number one star of Hong Kong cinema. Bruce responded that his success had nothing to do with Lo Wei's direction and he would prove it with *Way of the Dragon*.

After a nineteen-hour TWA flight, Bruce, Raymond, production manager Chaplin Chang, and cinematographer Tadashi Nishimoto landed in Aeroporto Leonardo da Vinci on May 5, 1972. They checked into the Hotel Flora at Via Veneto for the remainder of their stay until May 17.

The four men had several days free before Nora Miao and the rest of the Hong Kong film crew arrived. They decided to do some sightseeing and shopping. The group went to Pisa to see the Leaning Tower. "On the way we stopped at a 'Gucci' boutique," recalls Chaplin. "Bruce and Raymond found themselves enthralled at the high-class fashion on display and bought many items of clothing. I remember Bruce buying a very high quality Italian leather jacket, and remember thinking how soft the leather was."

The group quickly grew tired of Italian food, and the shabby Chinese restaurants in Rome didn't do their native cuisine any justice. Nishimoto happened upon a Japanese restaurant, The Tokyo, which wasn't half bad. It quickly became their favorite place to eat and drink sake. "One day in the restaurant after drinking three small cups of sake, a waiter handed Bruce a towel to wipe his face," remembers Nishimoto. "Realizing he had wiped away his contact lenses by accident, out came his sunglasses and he happily talked on." Sake turned out to be the only type of liquor Bruce could consume in quantity, and it became his favorite beverage as the pressures of fame grew heavier.

When Raymond and Chaplin Chang met with the Italian film company providing support for the Chinese crew, one of Raymond's first questions was how much per diem, or daily allowance, he should pay his people in Rome. "The lady said it is normally about 70,000 or 80,000 lira per day," Chaplin says. "But she added that since we were all men and we might want to enjoy girls, 100,000 lira would be better. So Raymond agreed to 100,000."

This moment, or perhaps the ensuing research into the subject, seems to have inspired the prostitute scene in *Way of the Dragon*. Having been scolded for not trying hard enough to fit in and be friendly, Bruce's naive bumpkin character, Tang Lung, inadvertently lets himself get picked up by an Italian hooker in the Piazza Navona. It is not until she walks out of the bathroom of the hotel room naked that he realizes his mistake and flees in terror—a scene that caused knowing Hong Kong audiences aware of Bruce's reputation to chuckle.

For the part of the prostitute, Bruce selected Malisa Longo after seeing her photo in a magazine. "Honestly, I had doubts about working on that film, because the role which was offered to me was too small," Malisa Longo says. "In Italy Bruce was a nobody and totally unknown." She initially thought Bruce was conceited until "he gave me a smile, which kinda broke the ice." When they were shooting the nude hotel scene, "Bruce was very nervous and electric, as you can see in every frame of the scene," Longo says. "With me Bruce was very gentle and sweet. Even when he was with many other people he was always seeking my eyes. I know I liked him very much."

One person who may not have appreciated their mutual fondness was Nora Miao. "She was very reserved," says Longo. "After she finished work on the set she always disappeared." Nora had arrived with the second crew several days earlier. As the only girl she had developed a playful dynamic with the boys. "We had nothing to do after dinner. We thought, 'Let's have some fun,' " Nora remembers. "They asked me to stand in the street to see if someone would pick me up, because we knew that young men in Rome liked to make passes. They said, 'Just stand there.' I was up for some fun. Before long a sports car drove past, and then reversed back. As the car pulled over and the window turned down, I fled to where they waited for me. We played jokes like this, and we really had a lot of fun making the film with Bruce."

According to Nora, these games of pretend extended to her relationship with Bruce. An Italian producer kept winking at her during filming. "Why does he do that all the time?" she asked Bruce. "It is really disgusting."

"No problem," Bruce said. From then on, Bruce sat next to Nora during meal times. He would hold her hand, get her food, and be really nice to her. When they walked, he would put his arm around her shoulder. The producer stopped winking and making clucking sounds. "He thought I was Bruce's girlfriend," Nora says. "He dared not wink anymore."

Her story does explain the dozens of photos of Bruce and Nora canoodling in Rome. But when two beautiful young costars making a movie in an exotic foreign city playact at being lovers, the line the between pretense and reality can vanish quickly. Certainly everyone else involved in the production believed they crossed it. "One morning we all came down for breakfast," Chaplin Chang recalls. "We were there, then Bruce, and then Nora came down. The waiter stared at Bruce. They looked like they had done something very intimate." Andre Morgan says, "It was a fling. What happens on a film location is no big deal."

Paying homage to the visual style of Sergio Leone's spaghetti westerns, Bruce planned a dramatic introduction for the bad guy, Colt, as he steps off the plane at Rome's airport. He had asked Chuck Norris to play the role. "I was aware that an appearance in a movie—even one made in Hong Kong—could get me heightened visibility, which might draw more students to our [karate] schools," Norris says. "I had no thought that it might be the start of a new career for me."

Chuck brought with him not only his résumé as America's top karate champion, but also a surprise stowaway—his assistant instructor and business partner, Bob Wall. "Chuck gets off the phone with Bruce and says he's going to Rome to be in a movie," Wall remembers. "You're not fucking going alone. We're partners. So I paid my own way." Wall claims that Bruce was "thrilled" to see him, because "he loved me." According to Chaplin Chang, Bruce was less than pleased and had a few choice words about his uninvited guest. "Bob's arrival caused a bit of unhappiness. When we were back at the hotel, Bruce said, 'Why did Norris bring this guy?' " Chaplin recalls. "Given the way he talked about Bob, it was clear Bruce didn't like him." In the end, Chuck convinced Bruce to give Bob a role.

Because it was illegal to film in the Colosseum, the Chinese crew had to bribe the right officials and pretend to be tourists, carting in their cameras in bags. The guards only allowed the guerrilla filmmakers a few hours to film a few exteriors and establishing shots: Chuck looking down at Bruce, Bruce running around, Chuck and Bruce meeting face-to-face. Mostly the cinematographer Nishimoto took still photos with a Hasselblad camera that gave the Chinese production team back in Hong Kong the right perspective to create the columns and backdrops to re-create the Colosseum at Golden Harvest's studios. It was in Hong Kong that the bulk of the fight scene was choreographed and shot over an intensive three-day period.

Having captured as much of Rome as they possibly could in twelve days, Bruce, his Chinese team, Chuck Norris, and Bob Wall arrived at the Kai Tak Airport at 3 p.m. on May 18, 1972. Linda and Shannon were there to greet Bruce along with a group of reporters. At the press conference, Bruce was as glib and charming as ever. Rumors had swirled that the inexperienced filmmaker was running over budget. When asked how much money he had already spent on the film, Bruce dodged, "I have not estimated the expenditure and never worry about it. I believe if it is worthwhile to spend the money, then I spend it. Otherwise I would not waste the money, as the first priority is to think what is reasonably needed, and then the profit will follow."

"How much profit will your next movie make at the box office?" asked another reporter. Just as Muhammad Ali liked to hype his fights by predicting which round he would knock out his opponents, Bruce enjoyed boasting of how much money his movies would make. In response to the question, Bruce immediately raised five fingers, meaning HK$5 million.

Another reporter followed up: "In *The Big Boss* you used the famous 'three kicks' and it took HK$3,000,000 at the box office, then there was the nunchaku you used in *Fist of Fury* and that achieved the HK$4,000,000 mark, so I ask you, what weapon will you employ in your latest movie to reach your prediction of HK$5,000,000?"

"Mark my words, you will find out soon enough," Bruce teased. (He planned to use two nunchakus at the same time.)

Seeing the slight-of-frame star sitting next to the larger Westerners, a reporter asked, "Do you and Mr. Norris have a fight scene in the movie?"

"Will Chuck Norris and I fight in the movie?" Bruce smiled. "Did you think we would make love?"

Almost everyone burst out laughing, but a few reporters were offended. Referring to this joke, Kam Yeh Po at *Starry Night News* criticized Bruce as "arrogant" and "spoiled by his sudden stardom." His editorial marked the beginning of the end of Bruce's honeymoon period with the Hong Kong media. Fawning press coverage began to give way to more critical assessments.

Since *The Big Boss*, Bruce had been challenged by dozens of attention-seeking kung fu dilettantes in the press. Chuck Norris's arrival in Hong Kong stirred a patriotic wave of challenges to the American. Unused to being publicly called out, Norris was upset, but Bruce told him to forget about it. "It's a no-win situation," Bruce counseled. "All these guys want is publicity." But Bob Wall, a hot-tempered Irishman, was having none of it. He gave a statement to the press accepting any challenge on Chuck's behalf and proposing they hold it on the late night talk show, *Enjoy Yourself Tonight*. "My instructor, Chuck Norris, has been challenged. Now Chuck is a much better fighter than I am, so I want you, whoever you are, to fight me first to see if you qualify to face him. Our fight will be held on TV so everyone in Hong Kong can see it, because I'm going to beat you to death."

Unsurprisingly, there were no challengers waiting for them when Bruce, Chuck, and Bob showed up at the studio of *Enjoy Yourself Tonight* on May 19, 1972. So instead of a live death match, the crowd was treated to Chuck Norris demonstrating his karate on Bob Wall. Then Bruce jumped up to show off a few lightning-fast kicks while Chuck held a focus mitt for him.

Afterward, they sat down on the couch for the interview portion. The host, Josiah Lau, asked Bruce in Cantonese, "Is it true what is said in the newspapers that these Westerners are also your students in the States, and although you instruct them, they have won many karate championships? I think your kung fu must be very powerful."

With a grin, Bruce waved his hands and avoided the bait. "Now, don't play games with me, I have never told anyone they are my students. We are good friends and when we have time we get together and discuss martial arts."

Switching to English, Josiah Lau posed the question to Chuck Norris. "Many people said that you two were Bruce's students, but Bruce has denied this, he said that you were just friends. So which is true?"

Chuck Norris gave an answer so perfect he must have known about the question beforehand and crafted his response with utmost care. "The fact is we are too bad to be his students, and he is too good to be our teacher." Chuck smiled, as the crowd burst into laughter and appreciative applause at his face-giving, Chinese-like humility. "Nevertheless, we admire his kung fu and even though he doesn't treat us as students, we still take him as our teacher."

"What do you think of Bruce Lee?" Josiah Lau asked.

"He is a lovely man, a well-educated man," Norris said, "and, in addition, of all the martial artists I have met, he is the best."

It is no wonder that of all the martial artists Bruce had met he loved Chuck Norris the most.

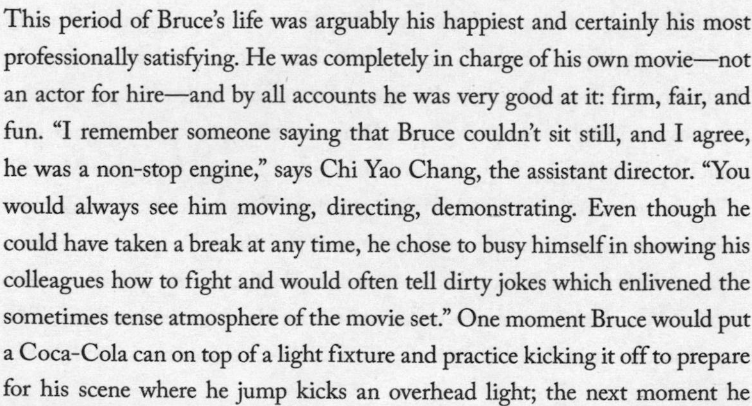

This period of Bruce's life was arguably his happiest and certainly his most professionally satisfying. He was completely in charge of his own movie—not an actor for hire—and by all accounts he was very good at it: firm, fair, and fun. "I remember someone saying that Bruce couldn't sit still, and I agree, he was a non-stop engine," says Chi Yao Chang, the assistant director. "You would always see him moving, directing, demonstrating. Even though he could have taken a break at any time, he chose to busy himself in showing his colleagues how to fight and would often tell dirty jokes which enlivened the sometimes tense atmosphere of the movie set." One moment Bruce would put a Coca-Cola can on top of a light fixture and practice kicking it off to prepare for his scene where he jump kicks an overhead light; the next moment he would ask Anders Nelsson, who was in the film, to pull out his guitar and play his favorite song, "Guantanamera," as he sang and danced along. "In one day I played that song seventeen times," says Nelsson. "I really hate that song now."

Like any good gang leader, Bruce rewarded loyalty and shared his success with his crew. He gave three of his childhood friends—Robert Chan, Unicorn Chan, and his manservant, Wu Ngan—roles as waiters in the restaurant. "He made sure I was treated with respect along with all the other men who worked side by side with him," says Wu Ngan. Because Unicorn Chan was struggling in the movie business, Bruce credited him as "assistant fight choreographer" to help boost his career. With Chuck Norris and his childhood friends surrounding him, he had merged his two worlds—America and China. Everything he had worked so hard to achieve was coming together for him. "Bruce was a very fun guy, always laughing and having a good time, and he liked to show off on set," says Jon T. Benn, who played the mafia boss. "There were some pretty girls on the set and he liked to flirt, and when we were ready to shoot he was a perfectionist."

One of the pretty girls hanging around the set was Betty Ting Pei. Whatever his relationship with Nora Miao was in Italy—pretend or an on-location fling—it ended upon their return to Hong Kong. Bruce continued his affair with Betty. "I was with him all the time at the studio," Betty says. "Everybody there knew I was his girlfriend." Their relationship was becoming serious enough that Bruce was far less discreet than usual. He would take her on dates out in public. "I ran into them a couple of times at the Chin Chin Bar," says Anders Nelsson. "Bruce was engrossed with Betty. You could see there was magic. They were like the couple that can't stand to be apart—touchy-feely, gazing into the eyes." Andre Morgan concurs, "Bruce was quite taken with Betty. She was very glamorous in her own right."

When Bruce first called up Chuck Norris to be in his film, Chuck jokingly asked, "Who gets to win?"

"I'm the star," Bruce laughed. "But I promise you the fight will be the highlight of the film."

"Okay, but only this one time," Norris joked. "How do you want me to prepare?"

"What do you weigh?" Bruce asked.

"162 or 163."

"I'm almost 140," Bruce said. "I want you to gain twenty pounds."

"There's only three weeks before filming!" Norris protested. "Why?"

"It will make you look more formidable as an opponent."

While there may have been some truth in his explanation, it couldn't have been lost on Bruce, who had spent his life working in film, that twenty pounds of extra fat would soften Chuck's muscular definition in sharp contrast to Bruce's ripped physique. "One of the reasons Chuck doesn't like to talk about *Way of the Dragon* is because he thinks he looks like a fat moose," says Bob Wall. Additional weight would also slow down Norris's movements in comparison to the already lightning-quick Lee. As the star, director, and producer, Bruce wasn't above stacking the deck in his favor.

Bruce's thirteen pages of detailed notes and stick figure drawings for the Colosseum fight were partially inspired by the second and third rounds of Muhammad Ali's boxing match against Cleveland Williams (1966). "Bruce would play the Williams fight over and over on the little eight-millimeter movie projector he had," says Joe Lewis, one of Bruce's karate champion students. "He would study the way Ali punched, the way he moved. Bruce emphasized mobility. Karate people were using stationary stances." From this foundation, he worked with Chuck to add kicks, throws, and other martial art techniques over three long days of shooting at Golden Harvest's Colosseum set. All the while, Bruce instructed Chuck on the differences between fighting in the ring versus fighting on film—sport versus entertainment martial arts. "We got a good lesson from Bruce," Bob Wall remembers. "When you fight for real, you don't let somebody know they've hurt you. But because it is a staged fight scene somebody's not going to hurt you, but you have to convince the audience that they did. So it's a reverse."

Bruce had promised Chuck their scene would be the highlight of the film, and he was correct. Whatever one thinks of *Way of the Dragon*, and opinions vary wildly, the overwhelming consensus is their battle is one of the best fight scenes ever put on film. In retrospect, much of its allure is that it pits the two most famous martial artists of their generation against each other. But the reason for its enduring appeal runs deeper. Unlike Jackie Chan and Jet Li, who grew up as entertainers, Bruce was a martial arts instructor and innovator for many years. He approached the scene like a teacher with a pedagogical purpose. At the beginning he is losing to Norris because he is stuck in the classical style. On the verge of defeat, he adapts to his circumstances and begins to freely express himself—shuffling, bobbing and weaving, and turning the tide of the fight. The entire scene is a Jeet Kune Do tutorial. He wasn't just filming a fight scene; he was making a philosophical argument about how martial arts should be taught and practiced.

Along with merging the physical and the mental into the scene, Bruce was also able to invest it with unusual emotions for a kung fu flick. There is a playful sense of humor when they wag their fingers at each other and when Bruce rips a handful of hair from Chuck's burly chest and then has trouble wiping it from his hands. Whereas most kung fu fight scenes were driven by revenge and mutual hate, the two warriors, who were old friends in real life, faced each other with mutual respect. At the end when Chuck's arm and knee are broken, Bruce's eyes plead with him to quit. When Chuck refuses, Bruce's face reflects remorse at having to kill him. Afterward Bruce covers Chuck's dead body with his uniform and kneels in a gesture of respect and grief.

When Norris left Hong Kong on June 13, one third of the film was still incomplete. Already behind schedule and over budget, Bruce was going to miss the original summer release date. He didn't complete principal photography until July 23, when postproduction could finally begin.

Most Hong Kong movies used canned music to keep costs down. Bruce insisted on hiring musicians to create an original score and personally sat in for one session and played a percussion instrument. The movie had been shot on 35mm with no sound. The voices were all dubbed later in various languages—Cantonese, Mandarin, English. Bruce asked to dub his own voice for the English version. "This had never happened where a movie star wanted to do this," says Ted Thomas, a British disc jockey and voice actor. "He couldn't do it. Not surprising, because it's not an easy technique. The other voice actors got pissed off, because they were being held up and Bruce didn't mean much to them. Bruce asked, 'Aren't you going to let me do it?' I said, 'No, no, we have guys who do it professionally.' So he got pissed off about that." To appease the star and director, Thomas let Bruce dub the voice of the African American henchman who threatens the Chinese waiters in the restaurant.

With his movie too late for the summer blockbuster season and 40 percent over budget, Raymond Chow convinced Bruce to film a Winston cigarette advertisement to recoup some of the cost overruns and promote the movie for its release in the dead zone of winter. The plan was for Bruce to film a three-minute martial arts demonstration, and have it paired with a three-minute weightlifting demonstration by Bolo Yeung. It was 1972—cigarettes were still considered healthy, even for athletes.

Bruce called up Bolo. "He said he was planning on doing a Winston cigarette commercial," Bolo says. "The next day I went to Golden Harvest to film the commercial." Bruce never smoked cigarettes—marijuana yes, tobacco no—believing, correctly, that they were bad for a fighter's lungs. After reconsidering the matter, Bruce decided against filming an original martial arts demonstration for the commercial. As a compromise he agreed to let edited clips from *Way of the Dragon* be used in the Winston ads. The tagline: "When you talk about fighting, you're talking about Bruce. When you talk about flavor, you can't beat Winston."

Bruce had bet everything—his finances, his reputation, and his new company—that his directorial debut would be a hit. He had broken with Lo Wei, racked up an immense debt with Raymond, and bragged to the press that his movie would make HK$5 million. "The money we were spending was being advanced to us on the strength of profits that were not yet realized," Linda says. "That made it doubly important *Way of the Dragon* was successful." Despite all this, he avoided many of the promotional appearances he had happily done for *The Big Boss* and *Fist of Fury*, because the press had begun printing negative articles about him. Feeling snubbed, the media criticized him even more as *Way of the Dragon*'s release date—December 30, 1972—approached.

In the end, it didn't matter that Bruce scaled back his promotional activities. It didn't matter that the movie wasn't released in the summer blockbuster season. All that mattered was Bruce Lee starred in the movie. His fans came out in droves. In its opening weekend alone, it sold over HK$1 million in tickets. By January 13, 1973, it had broken *Fist of Fury*'s record and went on to fulfill his prediction, reaching HK$5,307,000.

This was not the comparison Bruce cared about most. He wanted to see how his movie did against the project he had turned down. One month after *Way of the Dragon*, Lo Wei and Jimmy Wang Yu released their movie. It barely made HK$2 million at the box office. The victory made it clear that Lee Little Dragon had eclipsed Jimmy Wang Yu as the undisputed box office champion of East Asia.

"The reaction to *Way of the Dragon* was better than we expected. We were a little bit worried," says Louis Sit, the studio manager at Golden Harvest. "The people liked it because Bruce Lee was a Chinese hero fighting all the foreigners. At that time, Hong Kong was starting to develop into an international city, so that in all walks of life, like manufacturing and finance, they wanted to challenge foreigners. Why can't we be better than them? Bruce may have been fighting foreigners physically but at that time all of Hong Kong and Asia was fighting foreigners in all types of businesses. It was a feeling that everyone shared."

Despite the commercial success of *Way of the Dragon*, Bruce was dissatisfied with its overall quality. While he was certain it was infinitely better than Lo Wei and Jimmy Wang Yu's movie, he feared sophisticated Western moviegoers would find it amateurish. Bruce invited Peter, and his wife, Eunice Lam, to attend a special screening. After it was over, Bruce quietly asked his older brother, "How was the film?"

"Ah, um, the music was quite good," Peter said, damning it with faint praise.

Bruce pulled back like he'd been struck. Eunice put her hand on his, trying to think of something kind to say to soften the blow. Bruce's palms were clammy. She remained silent.

Bruce decided *Way of the Dragon* was not good enough to be his spaghetti eastern—his ticket back to Hollywood. He did not want it released to the West. When he discovered that Raymond Chow, without his knowledge, had sold the distribution rights to North America, he erupted. "There was a big scream out at the studio when Bruce found out," says Andre Morgan. "He felt that Raymond Chow had betrayed him."

Bruce was self-critical enough to realize he had much room for improvement as a filmmaker. He intended to make the ultimate martial arts movie in his next attempt.

The Big Boss, *Fist of Fury*, and *Way of the Dragon* were commercial, revenge-driven genre flicks. For his next film, he wanted to focus on his philosophy—a martial *way* rather than a martial *art* movie. He had tried this once with *The Silent Flute* in Hollywood. Still bitter about its failure, he rewrote the script specifically for a Chinese audience. He removed Silliphant's Freudian symbolism and focused on cultural references Asian audiences would understand. He entitled his Sinicized version *Northern Leg Southern Fist*. In China, northern styles of kung fu are famed for their kicking techniques and southern for their striking. A master of both would be the complete Chinese martial artist.

In an eighty-page Butterfly Steno Notebook, Bruce handwrote the story treatment for *Northern Leg Southern Fist*, including some dialogue, camera angles, and drawings. Following closely the plot structure of *The Silent Flute*, the treatment opens with a challenge match between the hero and his kung fu classmates versus students from a rival style. The hero and his buddies lose badly, because they have been taught the "classical mess." The distraught hero—painfully realizing, just as Bruce had with Wing Chun, that his "fighting style is artificial and restraining"—sets off to find the Bible of Martial Arts to become a true master. On his Holy Grail quest, he is accompanied by the theme song, "What Is the Truth of Martial Arts?," and a lovestruck girl, referred to as "Our Girl Friday," whom he ignores, naively believing his quest is too important for romantic distractions. He quickly takes up with a master of Southern Fist to train during the day and a Northern Leg master to train at night. In a restaurant braggarts insult the hero's teachers. He challenges them to a fight, using first his southern striking style and then his northern kicking style. He is holding his own but not winning. It is not until a mysterious Old Man sitting at a nearby table suggests "Use hands and feet" that our hero combines the two and is victorious. Afterward he chases down the Old Man and crows, "I have created a style of my own!"

If this were a patriotic Chinese kung fu movie, it might have ended here. The hero would have symbolically unified the north and south—historically the dividing line in China. But Bruce had a new truth he wanted to deliver, a sermon he wanted to preach. The Old Man serves as a mouthpiece for Bruce's Jeet Kune Do philosophy. "Styles separate people rather than unite them," the Old Man scoffs, as flute music plays in the background. When the hero begs the Old Man to instruct him, he waves him off: "I am not a teacher. I am a signpost for a traveler who is lost. It is up to you to decide the direction."

Flashing forward in time, the hero arrives on the island where the Bible of Martial Arts is kept by a famous monk. Like in *The Silent Flute*, the hero has to compete against other martial artists and pass several tests to become the new Keeper of the Bible of Martial Arts. Fortunately for him, he has mastered the Old Man's Jeet Kune Do philosophy and easily defeats his Southern Fist and Northern Leg teachers. He is offered the Bible and the job of Keeper. In *The Silent Flute*, the hero rejects the book outright and never looks inside, but in Bruce's recycled version he examines it. "Slowly the hero takes the book and he opens it page by page, which is all blank, and that's when he turns to the last page with the mirror set on it and sees himself." After learning the secret, the hero rejects the job offer: "A live person is more appealing than this book." As he heads back, he grabs "Our Girl Friday" and kisses her. The other failed applicants plead, "What is the secret of the book?" The hero refuses to answer, instead ending the movie with this wan quip, "I can tell you one thing. Pay more attention to your girlfriend."

Of Bruce's oeuvre, *Northern Leg Southern Fist* was the most personal and autobiographical—the purest distillation of everything he had experienced, learned, and believed—down to the mirror. "He always had this idea if he was ever to open another school. When you walked through the door, there would be these large red curtains and then a sign that said, 'Behind These Curtains Lies The Secret,' " says Bob Baker, who costarred in *Fist of Fury*. "And then when you opened the curtains there was just a full length mirror. And that would be the way you get into the school."

It was heady stuff for a kung fu movie and very much of its era, but it was not commercial. According to Andre Morgan, Bruce frequently discussed his *Northern Leg Southern Fist* treatment with Raymond Chow. Hollywood studio mogul Samuel Goldwyn liked to say about preachy movie ideas, "If you have a message, send a telegram." Chow was a little more diplomatic. "Raymond's reaction was that it was a little too intellectual for Chinese audiences' taste," recalls Morgan, "and needed to wait for Bruce to become a more established star."

Chow's arguments convinced Bruce that *Northern Leg Southern Fist* was a step too far for Chinese audiences at this point in his career. Bruce agreed to shelve it for a later date. "I'm dissatisfied with the expression of cinematic art in Hong Kong. I believe I have a role. The audience needs to be educated and the one to educate them has to be somebody who is responsible," Bruce told the *Hong Kong Standard*. "We are dealing with the masses and we have to create something that will get through to them. We have to educate them step by step. We can't do it overnight. That's what I'm doing right now. Whether I succeed or not remains to be seen. But I just don't *feel* committed, I *am* committed."

With *Northern Leg Southern Fist* on hold, Bruce was left scratching for a way to educate the Chinese audience about his philosophy. In the back of his mind he had a vague idea for a movie. The most successful part of *Way of the Dragon* was his fight scene with Chuck Norris where his Jeet Kune Do philosophy of adaptation was embedded within the fight scene itself. "I hope to make multi-level films in Hong Kong," Bruce told the press, "the kind of movies where you can just watch the surface story if you like, or you can look deeper into it." If the fight scene with Chuck was his crowning achievement so far, why not multiply it?

Bruce's initial notion for his next project, entitled *Game of Death*, was that a group of five elite martial artists are hired to retrieve a stolen Chinese national treasure from the top floor of a five-story wooden pagoda in South Korea. The catch: each level is guarded by an expert martial artist of a different style who they must defeat to move up a level. (If the idea seems hackneyed that is because the conceit has since been ripped off by countless action flicks and video games.) At each level, one of Bruce's compatriots would first attempt to defeat the guard and end up dead because he could not liberate himself from the classical mess. Then Bruce would step in, adapt to the guard's style, and beat him.

To underline his philosophical theme, Bruce already had the first image of the film in mind. "What I want to show is the necessity to adapt one's self to changing circumstances. The inability to adapt brings destruction," he explained to a Singaporean reporter for *New Nation*. "As the film opens, the audience sees a wide expanse of snow. Then the camera closes in on a clump of trees while the sound of a strong gale fills the screen. There is a huge tree in the center of the screen, and it is all covered with thick snow. Suddenly there is a loud snap, and a huge branch of the tree falls to the ground. It cannot yield to the force of the snow so it breaks. Then the camera moves to a willow tree, which is bending with the wind. Because it adapts itself to the environment, the willow survives. It is the sort of symbolism, which I think Chinese action films should seek to have. In this way I hope to broaden the scope of action films."

Bruce had the opening image, the theme, and the third-act action sequence. What he did not have was a story. Plenty of Hong Kong kung fu movies of that era were put into production with less. *The Big Boss*'s script was only three pages long, but it was, unlike *Game of Death*, revenge-driven—a red-blooded motivation with which mass audiences could viscerally relate. *Game of Death* was an allegorical quest movie for an unknown item—a kung fu *Pilgrim's Progress*.

His bosses had not intended to hire a missionary. They wanted to make money, not a statement. Raymond Chow's reaction to funding Bruce's didactic project was, to put it politely, "cautious optimism." Bruce must have sensed the caution more than the optimism, because he reacted the way he always did when Chow resisted his plans: he ran to Run Run Shaw. He didn't just have a meeting this time. Instead he publicly went to Shaw Bros. for a wardrobe test in full costume, makeup, and hair as an ancient Chinese warrior.

When the photos of Bruce in costume were deliberately leaked to the press, it appeared that he was not only going to leave Golden Harvest for Shaw but he was also planning to film his first period picture for them. Newspapers gleefully reported that Run Run had offered Bruce a staggering fee for the movie and when Bruce brushed it aside sent him a signed open contract with a request that Bruce fill in his own figures. When *The China Mail* asked Bruce if he would make his next movie with Shaw Brothers, he replied, sounding more like a mercenary than a missionary, "It can be produced by Shaws, Golden Harvest, or any film company. It has never been my intention to be tied to a particular company."

Raymond Chow believed Bruce was only using Shaw to improve his negotiating position with Golden Harvest, but with so much money in the pot he didn't want to call Bruce's bluff. "When an actor becomes very popular," Raymond says, "you cannot really throw the book at him the way you want." Bruce's feint to Shaw secured the green light from Chow for *Game of Death*.

Rather than fleshing out the script, Bruce immediately began filming the pagoda sequence because former student Kareem Abdul-Jabbar had a brief window of availability in late August 1972. Abdul-Jabbar, who had already won an NBA championship and MVP award in his first three years with the Milwaukee Bucks, had a few free weeks before the next season started. Bruce was delighted—he had wanted to make a movie with Kareem since they had trained together in Los Angeles. "With me fighting a guy over seven feet tall, the Chinese fans would eat it up," he had predicted.

What happens when a five-foot-seven guy fights a seven-foot-two guy, even if that shorter guy is Bruce Lee? "I was trying to get a perfect kick to Kareem's jaw and I must have kicked at least 300 times that day," Bruce said. "You know how high his chin is, huh? I had to really stretch my legs. Well, I finally pulled a groin muscle." Bruce was nearly injured again when he fell off the set during a stunt. "I had to catch him," Kareem remembers, "and we had a good laugh about that because he ended up in my arms like a baby." Kareem also witnessed Bruce dealing with a challenger: "A stuntman wanted to challenge Bruce while he was in the middle of a conversation. He put him on his back pretty quickly. People decided not to try that any more."

In Bruce's scheme for the movie, Kareem was the guardian of the fifth and final floor—the Big Boss. As for who was on the other four floors beneath, Dan Inosanto says that Bruce "kept changing it often" based on who was available. Bruce mailed a China Airlines ticket to Inosanto, who took a leave from his teaching job to play the defender of the third floor. "His movie-making is like his fighting," Inosanto says. "He just did it. He didn't know until the night before exactly what he was going to do. Then he put it together. He made up the story details as he went along, spontaneously. That's the way *Game of Death* was."

For the defender of the fourth floor, Bruce hired Korean Hapkido expert Ji Han Jae, whom Bruce had first met at a martial arts demonstration in the United States in 1969. Jae had just started as a martial arts actor for Golden Harvest and was readily available. According to several accounts, Bruce was frustrated working with the inexperienced Jae, who respectfully says, "Bruce was a good movie actor. My level and his level was different, so that's why there was a little bit of a gap."

Several names were floated for the guardians of the first two floors, including Taky Kimura (his Seattle instructor) and Wong Shun Leung (his childhood Wing Chun teacher). He even tried to talk James Coburn into participating while he was visiting Hong Kong, but Coburn politely refused.

Bruce only filmed the top three floors and a few outdoor scenes before he set the project to the side. Overall, it came to about ninety minutes of rough footage, which he edited down to about thirty minutes of finished material.

In its original form, Lee and two fellow martial artists—James Tien (his *Fist of Fury* costar) and Chieh Yuan (a Hong Kong stuntman)—arrive on the third floor and encounter Dan Inosanto playing a Filipino master of *escrima* dressed in traditional garb. Bruce is wearing what has become his most iconic outfit: a skintight canary yellow jumpsuit with a black racing stripe. It was inspired by the ski jumpsuit Roman Polanski lent Bruce during their ski vacation in Gstaad, Switzerland. Even the costumes were meant to support the movie's thesis that the martial artist had to be better than the martial tradition. "I'm dressed in a typical Muslim outfit. Everybody is in traditional garb," Inosanto says. "But Bruce looks like the modern jet set."

As the trio face off against Inosanto, Chieh Yuan attacks first with a large wooden log, but is defeated. Bruce pulls out a whiplike bamboo short staff and quickly disarms Inosanto. "The bamboo sword," he lectures Chieh, "is very much more flexible, more alive." Then Bruce engages in a riveting nunchaku duel with Inosanto, who in real life had introduced Bruce to the weapon. After Bruce wins, the trio rush to the fourth floor where they encounter Hapkido master Ji Han Jae, who soundly whips both James Tien and Chieh Yuan. While Bruce steps forward to finish the job, his two companions dash up the fifth and final floor where they are strangled to death by the towering Kareem Abdul-Jabbar and tossed back down the staircase like rag dolls. After Bruce defeats Ji Han Jae, he steps over his dead compatriots and heads upstairs, going eyeball–to–belly button with Kareem.

Unlike the two exemplars of traditional martial arts—Inosanto (Filipino *escrima*) and Ji Han Jae (Korean Hapkido)—Kareem is a master of "no style" or Jeet Kune Do, just like Bruce. Symbolically, then, Lee is battling his Jungian shadow, and he is unable to gain the upper hand until he discovers his shadow's weakness: Kareem's damaged eyes are supersensitive to sunlight. Bashing through the tower's window panels, Bruce blinds Kareem and puts him into a chokehold. After snapping his neck, he exhaustedly climbs to the highest level where he presumably uncovers the tower's mysterious item. The camera does not follow Bruce to the final floor and therefore does not reveal the MacGuffin. What the audience can see is Bruce staggering back down the staircase, seemingly stunned by his awesome discovery. Bruce toyed with several ideas for the item—the Bible of Martial Arts, a mirror—but was unable to resolve what it should be. He planned to film the treasure reveal scene after he made the decision.

From a fight choreography perspective, the battles on each level are intricate, unique, and compelling. They demonstrate Bruce's mastery of the craft. He also achieves a better tonal balance between light slapstick humor and violent action than he did in *Way of the Dragon*. His two foolish companions serve as comic relief: it's Bruce and the Two Stooges. Lee had clearly improved as a filmmaker.

As Bruce continued shooting the pagoda scenes for *Game of Death* from late August to mid-October 1972 without a script, he struggled to come up with a complete screenplay. He tried to hire several writers, including famous *wuxia* novelist and screenwriter Ni Kuang, to help him develop the story elements, but none of the writers was available. He was suffering from writer's block, which was no doubt exacerbated by the pressures, distractions, and temptations of overnight fame.

Waiting impatiently to be interviewed, circa 1972. *(David Tadman)*

twenty-one

fame and its discontents

When *The Big Boss* was released on October 3, 1971, Bruce suddenly became the most famous person in Southeast Asia. At first, he felt the thrill of victory. After a lifetime acting in movies, he had finally achieved his dream of superstardom. "In Hong Kong, I'm bigger than the fucking Beatles," Bruce would brag to his friends back in L.A. In less than a year, however, the pressures and burdens of extreme fame were beginning to wear him down. He couldn't walk down the street without being surrounded by a crowd. If he wanted to shop for clothes, the store had to close lest he be besieged. When he went to a restaurant, people would press their faces against the windows to stare at him.

"The biggest disadvantage," Bruce admitted to *Black Belt* magazine, "is losing your privacy. It's ironic but we all strive to become wealthy and famous, but once you're there, it's not all rosy. There's hardly a place in Hong Kong where I can go to without being stared at or people asking me for autographs. That's one reason I spent a lot of time at my house to do my work. Right now, my home and the office are the most peaceful places. Now

I understand why stars like Steve [McQueen] avoid public places. In the beginning I didn't mind the publicity I was getting. But soon, it got to be a headache."

When Alex Ben Block, a reporter for *Esquire* magazine, asked Bruce if fame had changed him, he replied: "Well, it's changed in the sense that it's like I'm in jail. I'm like a monkey in the zoo. I like to joke a lot, but I cannot speak as freely as I could before. But it hasn't changed me basically. It doesn't make me feel proud or that I am any better than I was. I'm basically the same [said with a laugh] damn old shit."

Worse than the loss of privacy was the increased sense of danger. It seemed like everyone wanted to challenge him to a fight. Once he jumped into a cab, and the driver turned around and asked, "Do you want to fight? Your kung fu isn't so good." He stopped going out in public alone and hired certain trusted stuntmen as his bodyguards.

One afternoon a deranged stalker jumped over the wall of his Kowloon Tong mansion into his garden where Brandon and Shannon were playing. The guy screamed that he wanted to fight Lee Little Dragon. "How good are you?" he shouted. "Show me how good you are!" Given that two of his friends, Jay Sebring and Sharon Tate, had recently been killed by the Manson gang, he was both terrified and infuriated. "This guy was invading my home, my own private home," Bruce angrily recalled. "I kicked him harder than I ever kicked anyone. I gave him my all."

Afterward Bruce made sure his children had minders at all times so they would not be kidnapped. "Bruce was very concerned about his children being unescorted," Linda says. "It's not like America where your kid just goes out the door. He was very careful."

The triads were not as involved in the Hong Kong movie business in the early 1970s as they would later become in the 1980s and 1990s, because Run Run Shaw had a monopoly over the industry. But there were still some shady characters hiding in the shadows outside the glare of the klieg lights. A few of them visited Bruce after *Fist of Fury* became a smash. "I had people stop by my door and just pass me a check for HK$200,000. When I asked them what it was for, they replied, 'Don't worry about it, it's just a gift to you.' I didn't even know these people, they were strangers to me," Bruce told *Fighting Stars*, an American martial arts magazine. "When people just pass out big money—just like that, you don't know what to think. I destroyed all those checks, but it was difficult to do because I didn't know what they were for."

As a sign of his increased wariness, Bruce began wearing a hidden belt buckle knife. More tellingly, Bruce Lee, the world's most famous evangelist of unarmed combat, began carrying a gun for protection. "He became very paranoid," says James Coburn, who visited Bruce in Hong Kong. "He had this impenetrable aura, this shield around him for ten, maybe twelve feet. Anybody who came within that area was real suspect and they had to watch out."

As Bruce increasingly closed himself off, one of the only ways to reach him was through his childhood friends. Since they had known him before he was famous, he still trusted them completely. Aside from Wu Ngan, his manservant, his oldest and dearest friend was Unicorn Chan. They had grown up in the movie business together. Bruce had sent money from America to help Unicorn when he heard his family was in financial trouble. Unicorn had introduced Bruce to Run Run Shaw when he was struggling in Hollywood. Bruce had given Unicorn a role in *Way of the Dragon* and credited him as assistant fight choreographer to boost his bumpy career. They were what the Chinese call *lao guanxi*, old friends who are forever exchanging favors.

Aware of their relationship, an independent movie company, Xinghai Corporation, approached Unicorn and offered him the leading role in his own movie if he could convince Bruce to appear in it with him. Bruce refused, having no interest in playing a bit role in a shoddy flick. But he didn't want his old friend to lose this chance, so, as a compromise, he agreed to choreograph some of the action and to personally help promote the film.

Bruce duly spent one day on-set directing a fight sequence and another at a press conference to publicize the upcoming release of *Fist of Unicorn*. What he didn't know was that the Xinghai producers had secretly filmed his participation with hidden cameras. They took this footage and ineptly inserted it into the movie to make it appear as if Bruce had a role and then used his image extensively in their marketing campaign, even going so far as to claim that *Fist of Unicorn* was "Directed by Bruce Lee." When Bruce found out he had been duped, he was enraged and sued the producers. Unicorn Chan denied any knowledge of what had been done. "Bruce was angry at himself for having fallen into the trap more than he was angry at Unicorn personally," says Andre Morgan.

Whether Unicorn knew or not, Bruce realized that unscrupulous people would use his friends to get to him. This made him almost as wary of them as he had become of strangers. On August 12, 1972, Bruce wrote to Mito Uyehara: "Well dear friend—lately 'friend' has come to be a scarce word, a sickening game of watchfulness toward offered friendship—I miss you and our once simple lunches together and our more joyful communications."

Everywhere he went in public, Bruce found himself plagued by paparazzi. Initially he tried to be patient, but the relationship grew increasingly antagonistic. Once when he was leaving a television studio he found himself surrounded by a melee of paparazzi. Even after he posed for several minutes, they demanded more. "You've got thousands of shots," he said angrily. When he tried to escape the throng, they pushed him back. In the ensuing scuffle, he knocked a camera out of a photographer's hands. The next day the headlines blared that Lee mistreated cameramen.

Used to glowing puff pieces, Bruce was surprised and wrong-footed when the press began to turn on him. "Lee was often angry at the media," remembers Robert Chan, a childhood friend and costar in *Way of the Dragon*. "He said to me many times, 'I can't work today. Did you see what they reported?' He would yell and then walk out."

Beyond the media slings and arrows universal for all celebrities, Bruce had to deal with the issue particular to crossover performers: racial purity. Bruce's movie persona was the invincible Chinese hero, defender of his people. In *The Big Boss*, he had defended Chinese migrant workers against vicious Thai bosses. In *Fist of Fury*, he had defended Chinese honor against the insults of the Japanese. And in *Way of the Dragon*, he defended a Chinese restaurant from Western criminals.

But how Chinese was Bruce Lee really? The question haunted much of the coverage of him at the time—and still lingers over his legacy. Sure he was raised in Hong Kong, but he was born in America, went to college in America, spent a dozen years living in America, and then came back with a blue-eyed wife and two Eurasian children, speaking rusty Cantonese, and spouting a bunch of foreign ideas.

When a Chinese reporter asked him, "Do you think that an inter-racial marriage will face unsolvable obstacles?" Bruce answered: "Many people may think that it will be. But to me, this kind of racial barrier does not exist. If I say I believe that 'everyone under the sun' is a member of a universal family, you may think that I am bluffing and idealistic. But if anyone still believes in racial differences, I think he is too backward and narrow. No matter if your color is black or white, red or blue, I can still make friends with you without any barrier."

This post-racial sentiment didn't sit well with many Chinese who were still struggling to find their pride as a people after centuries of colonial rule. If Bruce refused to be a "Yellow Power" Chinese nationalist, then some in the press would do it for him. Chinese newspapers insisted on spelling his last name in the Chinese way, "Li," no matter how many times he told them it should be spelled the American way, "Lee." A Taiwanese newspaper went so far as to publish an article supposedly penned by Bruce Lee himself in which "Bruce" writes, "I am Chinese and I have to fulfill my duty as a Chinese. . . . My identity as Chinese is beyond all doubts. . . . That I should become an American-born Chinese was accidental. . . . The truth is: I am a yellow-faced Chinese, I cannot possibly become an idol for Caucasians. . . . A Chinese is, and always will be, a Chinese."

This anxiety about Bruce's Chinese-ness flared into a full-fledged controversy over, of all things, facial hair. Very few Han Chinese men can grow a full beard—even a thin mustache can take weeks to cultivate. To the Chinese, body hair is associated with otherness. (A popular Chinese joke goes, "Why are foreigners so hairy? Because when we were human, they were still monkeys.") Because of his European ancestry, Bruce could grow a thick beard. He had gotten in the habit of not shaving when he was in America where no one thought anything about it. But in Hong Kong, a beard made Bruce look like Genghis Khan's cousin—a Mongol villain in a period movie. It reminded his Chinese fans that he was "mixed blood."

When a Hong Kong magazine ran a photo of Bruce seeing off his family at the airport on January 12, 1972, his bearded face shocked the public. Hong Kong's *Radio and Television Daily* criticized his appearance as a bad influence on the young and a threat to the social order:

> His flower shirts, multi-colored pants, sports shoes, and sandals, have already inspired many imitators. But who would have expected that this newly-minted, barely-thirty superstar would grow a full beard? In fact, Bruce's beard is reminiscent of nothing so much as the "hippies" who recently caused such a stir in America; this look is not nearly as handsome as his old one. The contrarian Bruce, however, not only didn't mind, he even jokingly predicted, "Now the number of beards in Hong Kong is about to double." In fact, we need only look around to see the effect. Have not many people, especially the young, already begun to imitate his hairstyle, his fashion, and even his gestures? Might it be that our relatively Westernized society might be about to shift yet further in the direction of the Stars and Stripes?

Another group threatened by Bruce's Western ways were his old Wing Chun classmates. When he created Jeet Kune Do, Bruce broke with his "mother art." For years he kept it a secret from them. It was not until he was about to move back to Hong Kong that he wrote a letter to his Wing Chun instructor, Wong Shun Leung, confessing his heresy. "Since I started to practice realistically in 1966 (protectors, gloves, etc.), I feel that I had many prejudices before, and they are wrong. So I changed the name of the gist of my study to Jeet Kune Do. Jeet Kune Do is only a name. The most important thing is to avoid having bias in the training," he wrote, before carefully crediting Wong Shun Leung and Ip Man for his new creation. "I thank you and Master for teaching me the ways of Wing Chun in Hong Kong. Actually, I have to thank you for leading me to walk on a practical road."

Upon his return, Bruce, whom Ip Man had nicknamed "Upstart," went to his master's school to demonstrate the superiority of Jeet Kune Do. Standing in the small room with Ip Man and a dozen or so Wing Chun students, some new to him, some he had known since he was a teen, Bruce asked for a volunteer to spar with him. After much hemming and hawing and staring at their feet, a junior student was cajoled into agreeing. "The guy was so baffled by my moves," Bruce triumphantly told Mito Uyehara. "I kept moving in and out, letting go kicks and punches, never gave him a chance to recover balance. I guess he got so frustrated because every blow I let go would have hit him if I didn't control it. JKD is too fast for Wing Chun." The next junior student fared even worse. "I kept throwing fakes and he kept biting. Once he got suckered and almost fell on his face. I didn't even touch him."

After watching two of their kung fu brothers get humiliated, the senior students adamantly refused to spar with Bruce. "Those mothers, they chickened out. I sure would have liked to have sparred them," Bruce complained. "These were the same guys who gave me a bad time when I first studied Wing Chun. I was a skinny kid of 15 and these guys even then were already assistant instructors to Ip Man. Well, I guess they saw enough and didn't want to make an ass of themselves."

Wong Shun Leung wasn't in attendance that day, but he heard the complaints: Lee Little Dragon made his Wing Chun brothers lose face; he claims his style is better than Wing Chun; someone should teach him a lesson.

After *The Big Boss* came out in theaters, Bruce excitedly called Wong Shun Leung, "Have you seen my movie?"

"I have not," replied his old teacher.

"I will send you tickets," Bruce responded immediately. "You have to see it. My kung fu is at a different level. My fighting is different from what I learned before. I'm so quick very few people can touch me anymore."

"I know nothing about your progress in kung fu," his teacher responded, coolly.

After receiving two tickets from Bruce, Wong finally went to see the movie with his top student, Wan Kam Leung. Bruce called the day after they went, an excited and proud student seeking his teacher's approval. "So Older Brother Leung, did you watch the movie?"

"Yes, I did."

"Now my kung fu skills are really good now, right? My legs are quick, huh?"

"Your punches hit the target *slowly* but pull back *quickly*," Wong replied. This was a pointed criticism. A good Wing Chun student's punches were supposed to hit the target *quickly* and pull back *slowly*. He was saying that Bruce's punches were weak.

Surprised and a little hurt, Bruce responded defensively, "Well, what you see in the movies is different from reality."

"Then let's try it sometime," Wong said, laying down a challenge.

Arrangements were postponed while Bruce worked on his other films. It was not until he finished *Way of the Dragon* nearly a year later that Bruce invited Wong to visit him at his new mansion in Kowloon Tong. The ostensible purpose was to discuss *Game of Death*—Bruce wanted to offer Wong a part as one of the five pagoda defenders—but the real reason was to see if the student had surpassed his teacher.

Thirty-seven-year-old Wong Shun Leung arrived with his senior student, Wan Kam Leung. After Bruce showed off his mansion, they went to his "kung fu room" filled with sandbags, punching bags, and specially designed equipment, like his electric muscle stimulator. Bruce demonstrated his prowess on all the machines. He kicked a tennis ball hanging six feet in the air three times in a row without lowering his leg. And then as a final flourish swept his kicking leg, which still hadn't touched the ground, over to a towel hanging on a chair, grabbed it with his foot, and brought it back to his face to wipe off the sweat.

Cockily, he turned to Wong Shun Leung and accepted his challenge from the previous year: "Okay, let's see what you have really got. Would you like to make some movements?"

"If it is only for research, it will be fine. If it is a competition, I will not do it," Wong replied, establishing the rules for the duel—light sparring was acceptable, but he would not participate in a no-rules brawl, like the one Bruce had with Wong Jack Man.

"Okay," Bruce accepted.

They faced off against each other. Wong Shun Leung was wearing a long-sleeved Montagut shirt. Bruce was in a T-shirt. Bruce turned into a southpaw stance and leaned on his back leg with his front right foot loose and his front right fist at his waist. They stared at each other for a long time. Neither man wanted to hurry or make a mistake. Suddenly Wong dashed forward and delivered a low kick to Bruce's knee, a classic Wing Chun opening move. Anticipating it, Bruce switched his stance and punched at Wong's face. Wong partially blocked it with his left hand and sent his right at Bruce's throat, but Bruce's deflected punch thumped Wong in the chest before Wong's fist could reach its target. Point to Bruce.

"You try to hurt my knee? You are smart," Bruce teased. "Fortunately, I am accustomed to this trick. OK, let's try again."

This time Bruce started bouncing on his toes—dancing, shuffling like his character in his movies. He flicked out several rapid right jabs, causing Wong to step backward and block. After dodging several, Wong slipped a jab and punched with his left hand at Bruce's chest. Bruce knocked his hand away. Expecting this, Wong pulled back his left hand to block and used his right hand to pierce at Bruce's throat. At the same moment, Bruce turned his outstretching right fist into an open palm and slapped Wong lightly across the face. A fraction of a second later, Wong's fingers tapped Bruce in the throat.

Bruce jumped back and said, "Leung, actually I hit you first. Do you think so?"

"Don't take it so seriously." Wong smiled. "Who hit who first is not the most important thing. It is the strength of the strike that matters. You are right. Your hand hit first, but my protecting hand had already dissolved much of your power. Truly, if you strike with all your force, I may not be able to stand it, but if the power is greatly reduced, the strike will not be effective. More importantly, my hand grasped your throat. If we had really fought, surely you would know who would have been hurt worse."

After this close exchange, Bruce stopped using just his hands and began employing his superior kicking techniques. The two men continued to lightly spar and heavily banter between exchanges for about five more minutes. When they had finished, Bruce invited Wong Shun Leung and his student, Wan Kam Leung, to a nearby coffee shop on Prince Edward Road.

"Older Brother Leung, your handwork is excellent. If I hadn't stepped back fast enough, I would have lost to you," Bruce said, before grinning. "But fortunately, you are too slow."

"Your kicking technique is remarkable," Wong shot back. "If only your foot had been able to touch me once."

As the joshing continued, they turned to Wan Kam Leung for his verdict. "You are of a similar level," he diplomatically replied.

More than forty years later, Wan Kam Leung does not need to be so tactful. "If I really had to pick a winner, I would say Bruce won," he declares now with a smile. "To be honest, if Bruce used all his strength to hit my master, there is no way he would not collapse. His legs were really powerful. I don't think there is anyone that can endure one of his kicks. Bruce and my master shook hands after the coffee and Bruce told him he should come visit him again when he was free. After we got back to the studio, my master took off his shirt and I had to massage him with some Chinese herbal ointment. His arms were black-and-blue. Good thing my master wore a long-sleeve shirt so Bruce couldn't see his bruises."

While Bruce and Wong Shun Leung remained friendly after their "exchange of techniques," not every Wing Chun student was satisfied that Bruce's impertinence had been avenged. When he was on Hong Kong TV to promote *Way of the Dragon*, Bruce was asked what he thought of traditional kung fu styles. "If a martial artist wants to seek the truth in combat, the dead traditional form cannot confine him," he responded. "The training method of Chinese martial artists today is like teaching people to swim on dry land." Many Wing Chun stylists interpreted this, quite rightly, as a public slap in the face—and a financial threat. Martial arts instruction is a tough business with narrow margins. If even a small fraction of students bailed on their traditional masters to study Jeet Kune Do, their schools might be forced to close.

The China Star, a Hong Kong tabloid, ran a multipart series supposedly written by Ip Chun, the son of Ip Man, about what Bruce was like as a teenage kung fu student. In the fourth part, Ip Chun wrote that he had seen the young Bruce Lee get knocked down by an opponent during training due to a flaw in his technique. The flaw in the story was Ip Chun never trained with Bruce when they were teenagers. He didn't arrive in Hong Kong until 1965, long after Bruce had moved to America.

Taking this article as a public insult, Bruce angrily confronted Ip Chun to ask if he had really said what had been printed. Ip Chun denied everything, blaming the reporter who had ghostwritten the article in his name. Bruce tracked down and accosted the reporter.

As Hong Kong's first genuine superstar, Bruce was the bread and butter of tabloids like *The China Star*. Its owner and editor, Graham Jenkins, a hardbitten Australian newspaperman of the Rupert Murdoch mold, published a follow-up story, filled with mock outrage, saying that Bruce had threatened the paper's informant and had forced him to change his story. Now they had managed to make Bruce look like a punk and a bully. Further enraged, Bruce sued *The China Star* for libel. "His logic was if you don't draw the line, it's just going to go on and on," says Andre Morgan. But it did go on and on. Having baited the bull, every thrash of his horns was fresh copy. *The China Star* gleefully wrote about the lawsuit.

As the controversy grew, other newspapers began reporting that Bruce had disrespected his master, Ip Man, and Ip Man was angry at Lee, quoting Wing Chun students who were avenging Bruce's slights. In traditional Confucian culture, children, students, and disciples were supposed to be deferential and devoted to their parents, teachers, and masters. The Cultural Revolution in mainland China (1966–76) was upending that power relationship with children turning on their parents, students on their teachers, and disciples on their masters. Its reverberations were being felt in Hong Kong, terrifying the authorities. By espousing individual freedom and a rejection of tradition, Bruce had aligned himself philosophically with the youth revolt. Rumors of a troubled relationship with Ip Man became a kind of shorthand for these larger societal rifts. Conservative outlets, who lionized Bruce as a Chinese hero after the patriotic *Fist of Fury*, were now painting him as too Western, too modern, not Chinese enough.

Bruce was experiencing a good old-fashioned public relations crisis: the drip drip drip of negative stories was damaging his brand. Anger and retaliation had failed to stem the erosion—if anything it had made it worse—so, as a proponent of adaptability in combat, he switched to his other great character strength, charm. The truth was Bruce respected Ip Man, and Ip Man liked Upstart. Whatever larger critique he was making in public, Bruce was extremely polite and solicitous to Ip Man in person. Whatever reservations Ip Man may have felt about Bruce's public remarks about traditional kung fu, he was clever enough to appreciate that having the most famous martial arts actor in Asia as one of his disciples was a net positive for him. To quash the rumors of a rift, Bruce invited Ip Man out for *yum cha* (afternoon tea and *dim sum*) at a restaurant near Kowloon Park.

While they ate, Bruce smiled at Ip Man and asked, "Do you still treat me as your student?"

Ip Man quickly replied, "Do you still treat me as your *Sifu*?"

Both men laughed.

After they were done, Bruce said, "*Sifu*, we haven't gone for a walk together in a long time. How about we take a walk?" They strolled along the very busy Nathan Road so the public could see that their relationship was good.

A natural disaster allowed Bruce to reestablish his image as a defender of the Chinese people. On June 18, 1972, a devastating landslide near Po Shan Road killed sixty-seven people, seriously injured twenty others, and destroyed two buildings. Borrowing from American programming, Hong Kong TV ran its first ever twenty-four-hour celebrity charity telethon, Operation Relief. With Bruce front and center, it raised over HK$7 million. Bruce brought on Brandon to break some boards. He also donated HK$10,000 to the cause. The clear message: Bruce is a proud Chinese father who helps the people in their time of need. His generosity garnered him plaudits from the press.

His charm offensive might have squelched the negative coverage if not for another unfortunate event. On December 2, 1972, Ip Man died, and Bruce Lee failed to attend the funeral. For three thousand years burial rites and ceremonies have been central to Chinese culture. Missing your master's funeral is the equivalent of spitting on his memory. The press lambasted Bruce. A widely circulated cartoon showed Lee at Ip Man's shrine saying, "Sorry, Master, I am too busy making money to go to your funeral ceremony."

The media had no difficulty finding Wing Chun disciples to criticize him as a disrespectful renegade who cared more about fame than traditional Chinese values. One senior student said: "As for why Bruce Lee didn't show up when his own *Sifu* passed away, it's pretty hard to understand. As the founder of Jeet Kune Do and a big movie star, perhaps it was just too inconvenient!" Another added, "When someone passes away, the traditional values my country holds dear demand one pay one's respect."

Even his former teacher, Wong Shun Leung, piled on: "As for the fact that he didn't show up for *Sifu*'s funeral, this was definitely a breach in terms of the decorum of the martial arts world. People shouldn't forget their 'roots.' After all, even if you break off on your own and start a great new martial art of your own, you'll never forget the foundations you built with your teachers. As for Bruce's behavior on this occasion, I don't know if perhaps he was going through a difficult time or felt awkward, but I still think he should have shown up or provided some expression of sympathies. It is certainly very difficult for a person not to let fame get to him!"

What is quite remarkable about all their criticism is they knew exactly why Bruce didn't attend the funeral—he didn't know Ip Man had died. Ip Man was a minor martial arts teacher at the time. His death was only reported in the Chinese-language newspapers, which Bruce rarely read. The only way for him to find out was for his former Wing Chun brothers and sisters to inform him, and they purposely did not. "You know those sonovabitches, they live right in the city and never called me!" Bruce fumed in private to friends. "Dammit, they carried their jealousy too far. I found out about his death three days later. Shit, I feel real bad and disappointed." Ip Man's son, Ip Chun, eventually admitted as much: "When my father passed away, I got out the phone book to try to call Bruce, but someone prevented me from doing so, and I never did."

One almost has to admire the elegance of the Wing Chun students' revenge. Bruce had made them lose face by forming his own style and publicly criticizing traditional kung fu. When Ip Man died, they deliberately did not tell him about the funeral, making him lose face with his fans. Bruce could not publicly defend himself, because to do so would be to admit how fraught his relationship was with his former Wing Chun brothers.

All Bruce could do to mitigate the crisis was to belatedly show his respects. On the seventh day after a Chinese funeral, the equivalent of a wake is held at the person's home, because it is believed that the spirit of the dead comes back on that day. It was set for 8 p.m., but Bruce showed up at seven to make sure he was the first one there. He humbly apologized to Ip Chun and the rest of Ip Man's family for missing the funeral.

All of the pressures of fame—the constant harassment, the backstabbing, the rifts with old friends, the concerns over his own and his family's safety—might have made Bruce wonder if it was all worth it, except for one bit of amazing news. The moment he had been relentlessly working toward for the last seven years had finally arrived. Warner Bros. called with an offer to make Bruce Lee the star of his very own Hollywood martial arts movie.

Jackie Chan getting his neck snapped by Bruce Lee in *Enter the Dragon*, February 1973. *(Photofest)*

twenty-two

blood & steel

Despite Warner's rejection of the *Kelsey* film project about the Mandan tribe, producer Fred Weintraub continued to believe that a movie with Bruce Lee had commercial potential. After Bruce went to Hong Kong, Weintraub established a production company, Sequoia Pictures, with his partner, Paul Heller, on the Warner Bros. lot. Weintraub asked Bruce for examples that would bolster the case for a Hollywood-backed kung fu movie. When Lee sent him a copy of *The Big Boss*, Weintraub knew he had a winner. More than Lee's electric performance, it was those box office numbers. Weintraub was convinced he could cover Warner's costs by preselling the East Asian foreign markets (Hong Kong, Singapore, Taiwan, Thailand, and Japan) while producing a film of sufficient quality to attract a Western audience.

Weintraub and Heller approached Dick Ma, Warner Bros. head of Far East distribution and the only Asian American senior executive at the studio. Up until this point, Hollywood had sold movies to the Chinese market but had never worked with Hong Kong. Dick Ma, who had been tracking the success of Shaw Bros. and Golden Harvest, lent his support to the radical idea of the first ever Hollywood–Hong Kong co-production. With Ma's encouragement, Weintraub and Heller banged out a seventeen-page story treatment about three heroes (a white guy, his black friend, and a Chinese mercenary) who enter evil Han's martial arts tournament and end his drug-dealing, slave-trading ways.

They entitled the project *Blood & Steel* and pitched it to Warner's president Ted Ashley. He was intrigued but cautious. The TV series *Kung Fu* had been a surprise critical success for the studio but it was not a ratings champ. Ashley wasn't completely convinced that American audiences were ready for a Chinese hero. Ashley called Lee in July 1972, while Bruce was working on *Way of the Dragon*, to sound out his interest in the project. After their phone conversation, Bruce wrote Ashley a follow-up letter in which he made a you-need-me-more-than-I-need-you argument:

> *Dear Ted,*
>
> *Presently, H.K. will be my base of operations as my films are enjoying "unbelievable" success, breaking all time records one after another. . . . If Warner develops something specific for me, I'm sure my special brand of action will sock it to them. . . .*
>
> *Financially, I am secure; unheard of offers have been made to me. Ted, I have gone through the interesting experience of being Number One in Mandarin films. Fame and fortune, and I mean by any standards, are mine. . . .*
>
> *The way I look at it, and honestly feel about it, is that this Chinaman will definitely invade the States in a big way, one way or another. I am sure, if you give this matter a fair and serious thought, something will be worked out to our mutual benefit.*

Ted Ashley didn't get to be president of Warner Bros. by rushing blindly into uncharted territory. He agreed to give Weintraub the paltry amount of $250,000 for the film. It was pocket change—the budget for *The Exorcist*, also filmed in 1973, was $11 million. Weintraub knew he would need at least $500,000 to film the movie, but ever the dealmaker, he agreed, hoping he could convince Raymond Chow to pony up another $250,000 in return for a split of the profits. In mid-October, he flew out to negotiate with Chow.

While Weintraub was away, Paul Heller hired novice screenwriter Michael Allin to turn the treatment into a screenplay. According to Heller, the inspiration for the script came from a favorite comic strip of his youth, *Terry and the Pirates*: "It was about China and the Orient and the mystery and dragon ladies." According to Allin, who knew nothing about kung fu or Hong Kong, the inspiration was a little more obvious: "I stole from James Bond. It's an homage." The slim, eighty-five-page script was cranked out in three weeks, in large part because they skipped all the action sequences, writing in those empty spaces, "This will be choreographed by Mr. Bruce Lee."

In Hong Kong, Fred Weintraub was having less success. As he maneuvered toward a signed deal, the wily Raymond Chow politely deflected him at every turn. To justify spending $250,000 of his own money, Chow kept demanding more and more foreign territories: Singapore, Thailand, Taiwan. After a week of conceding one country after another, an exhausted Weintraub finally concluded that Chow was bargaining in bad faith, afraid that if the movie was made, Hollywood would steal Bruce, his cash cow. On his final night in Hong Kong, Weintraub met Chow and Lee for dinner at a Japanese restaurant. Word got out that Bruce was in the establishment, and thousands of fans appeared. "I saw the opportunity to play one final card," Weintraub says. "'Bruce, I'm leaving tomorrow because we couldn't strike a deal. It's too bad Raymond doesn't want you to be an international star.' Raymond—dropping the facade of cordiality—stared at me with sudden, all-consuming hatred. In that instant he knew he had lost. Bruce said, 'Sign the contract, Raymond.'"

For his part, Raymond Chow insists his reluctance was purely tactical: "Both Bruce and I had already talked about the whole thing. All we wanted was a fair deal. It's very difficult for an independent producer to get a really fair deal with a major studio."

Having finally secured his long-cherished dream of a starring role in a Hollywood kung fu movie, Bruce shelved *Game of Death*. "It was a relief to everyone because it gave Bruce time to work on what the story was going to be," says Andre Morgan, who was promoted to associate producer at Golden Harvest. On October 29, 1972, Bruce flew to Los Angeles to work on the fine print of the contract. Warner Bros. put him up in a luxury suite at the Beverly Hills Wilshire Hotel.

Bruce immediately phoned all his old friends and invited them over to his suite. Half the fun of success is showing it off. One call in particular he had been waiting a long time to make was to Steve McQueen. He ended up leaving a message for McQueen, who was out, to phone him at the Beverly Wilshire. Steve knew Bruce wanted to brag. Instead of calling him back, McQueen messengered an 8x10 glossy photo of himself, autographed, "To Bruce Lee, my biggest fan, Steve McQueen." For days, McQueen dodged Lee's irate calls. "That chicken, he knows what I'm going to tell him so he's hiding," Bruce complained to friends. When they finally talked, Bruce half-seriously shouted, "Steve, you dirty rat, I am a star now too. I am a movie star! Don't you send me this stuff!" McQueen howled with laughter.

After settling into his posh digs, Bruce asked to meet with the American creative team. Budget constraints largely dictated the American hiring process. Bob Clouse, who had made only two feature-length movies, was selected as the director because, according to Weintraub, "we could get him for a ridiculously low price." Bruce found Clouse to be low-key and quiet—a good listener who was open to Bruce's suggestions. He signed off on Clouse. He was less enthusiastic about the screenwriter, Michael Allin.

The entire Hong Kong team had reservations about the script for a variety of reasons, ranging from the cost to film certain scenes to hoary stereotypes about the Chinese. Bruce's main concern was that the Americans would film and edit the movie in such a way that the white guy would look like the star and Bruce would be the sidekick. The screenplay had been written with three multiracial (or "international" as they used to say) heroes, because the producers didn't believe an American audience would watch a movie with a relatively unknown Chinese actor as its sole hero. Williams, the strutting Blaxploitation character, is the first and only hero killed off, per standard Hollywood storytelling, in the movie. Bruce's character, conveniently named Lee, is the same throughout the movie: he starts and ends as a highly efficient killer. Only the white character, Roper, has a narrative arc. He begins as a cynical rogue (a precursor to Han Solo), who discovers his moral compass and heroic nature after his black friend, Williams, is brutally murdered. From his own personal history, Bruce had good reason to fear that once Warners screen-tested *Blood & Steel* in Glendale and reedited it to suit suburban tastes that Roper would be turned into the Green Hornet and Lee would end up as Kato.

When he first met with Allin, Bruce said, "We've got to rap, man! I'm at your service! I'm at your service!" The scene Bruce wanted to rap about was at the cemetery where his character, Lee, talks to the tombstone of his murdered sister. Allin had included a deaf old lady who is sweeping leaves as Lee is promising his sister he will avenge her death. "Why cut away to the old woman? I want to stand there and talk to my sister. Why do I have a person stealing the scene from me?"

Allin then made a common novice-screenwriter mistake. Instead of agreeing immediately with the star ("You don't like the old lady? She's gone!"), he defended his work. "It was a wonderful little scene," he recalls. "I was really proud of it."

As Allin tried to explain that the old lady was deaf and the symbolic importance of deafness, suddenly Bruce perked up. "Ah, I see. She's sweeping the leaves like I'm going to sweep away the bad guys!"

"Yes!" Allin cried. "Okay, Bruce, that's the way it's gonna—yes, yes! That's the way to play it! You look at her and your subtext is: 'I've got to go now because I've got bad guys to sweep up.' "

"Yes, I really like that!" Bruce exclaimed.

Allin was pleased he had saved the scene from a meddling actor, but Bruce was upset Allin wouldn't just do what he was asked. Bruce didn't say anything to Allin. Instead he went to Weintraub and declared, "Either he goes, or I do." Weintraub agreed immediately because he had no intention of actually firing Allin. To keep costs down, he had promised Allin a trip to Hong Kong in lieu of payment for the screenplay. Weintraub, who had a producer's ability to compartmentalize, told Bruce that Allin was fired and he never told Allin that Bruce wanted him fired.

Negotiations over the contract proved equally contentious. Bruce made concessions on his salary but demanded script approval and directorial control of the fight choreography. Not wanting any confusion about who was the real star of the movie, the Little Dragon also demanded that the movie's title be changed from *Blood & Steel* to *Enter the Dragon*. "He was extremely obstinate and exacting," says Weintraub. "The requests he made exceeded the decision-making power of an actor, encroaching on the territory of the producers and directors. Some of the higher-ups at Warner Brothers actually suggested I find someone to replace Bruce."

The two sides were unable to come to a final agreement before Bruce was scheduled to depart from L.A. and he left without a signed contract. Buoyed by his recent success, Bruce appeared unconcerned. As his friend Peter Chin commented after driving Bruce to the airport that day, "When *The Silent Flute* was rejected, Bruce felt like it was the end of the world, but today, he said to me, 'I only have to give the word and ten production companies will make a movie with me. If Warner doesn't want to sign with me, it's their loss.' "

Bruce's confidence proved well placed. Before he had even arrived in Hong Kong, Ted Ashley sent a telegram stating that Warners would take Bruce's ideas into consideration and come back with a new offer in a week. On November 23, 1972, after a few more revisions, Bruce finally signed a contract with Warner Brothers. Filming would begin in January and last eighty days. Bruce would direct all the fight choreography. Warners refused to give him final approval over the script but fudged the issue by agreeing to send over the director and a "script supervisor" ahead of filming to give Bruce time to consult with them on how to make the film appeal to both a Western and Chinese audience. Warners was adamant that the film be called *Blood & Steel*. Bruce figured he could fight over the title at a later date and believed he wouldn't have much trouble getting the changes to the script he wanted—after all, the producers had agreed to his demand to fire the original screenwriter, Michael Allin.

All of the actors were also hired on the cheap. Newcomer Jim Kelly was a last-second replacement for the Shaft-inspired character, Williams, after another African American actor, Rockne Tarkington, pulled out over money. He accused the producers of underpaying the black man. "We were colorblind," Weintraub jokes. "We paid everyone poorly."

Bruce initially offered the role of Han's evil bodyguard, Oharra, to Chuck Norris, but he refused. One movie getting beat up by Bruce Lee was more than enough for the proud Norris, who had vowed he would never appear in another film unless he was the hero.

Hoping to appeal to Chuck's competitive nature, Bruce said, "If you don't take this part, I'm going to give it to Bob Wall."

"Bob will do a great job," Norris replied.

The only person to receive an almost competitive salary ($40,000) was John Saxon (Roper). With the other roles filled by Wall (Oharra), Kelly (Williams), and Lee (Lee), Weintraub needed at least one name actor that Western audiences would recognize and Saxon had a background in karate. Saxon's agent predicted that the movie would be "a little crappy thing with a Chinese actor that nobody will ever see." Saxon was persuaded to get on the plane only after Weintraub promised him he would be the real star of the movie.

Casting on the Chinese side was significantly less fraught. What seemed a paltry amount in Hollywood was untold riches in Hong Kong. It was also a chance to work on the first Hollywood co-production with the Little Dragon, the biggest star in Hong Kong. Angela Mao Ying, star of the hit *Lady Kung Fu*, happily agreed to play Su Lin, the sister of Bruce's character (Lee), who chooses to commit suicide rather than be violated by Oharra and his men. Bolo Yeung (Bolo) was a budding actor. Shih Kien, who was famous for playing the villain in a series of movies about Hong Kong's most popular hero, Wong Fei-hung, was Lee's choice to play the one-handed, cat-stroking Mr. Han. The choice was deliberate: Bruce wanted to signal to his Chinese audience that he was the inheritor of Wong Fei-hung's mantle.

The role that proved most contentious to cast was Mei Ling, the undercover agent who is Lee's contact on Han's Island. Bruce had promised the role to Betty Ting Pei. Their relationship had grown more serious. She had sublet an apartment in his neighborhood of Kowloon Tong, only fifteen minutes by foot from his home. When asked if she had moved there on purpose, she said with a smile, "It was a coincidence."

When producer Paul Heller and director Robert Clouse arrived in Hong Kong in December 1972 and went with the whole crew to scout locations in Repulse Bay, Bruce invited Betty to accompany them. At lunch she sat next to Paul Heller. "He called me Dragon Lady," Betty says. "Everybody knew I was the girlfriend of Bruce Lee." Chaplin Chang, the assistant director, remembers, "Betty was telling Paul how talented Bruce was. Ra Ra Ra. A lot of things in praise of Bruce Lee."

The next week Bruce changed his mind and gave the role to another Betty—Betty Chung, a popular singer. Given that it was a simple part with only a few lines, it's not clear why Bruce didn't want his girlfriend to play the part. Maybe he thought it was too indiscreet. Betty Ting Pei refuses to explain: "It is too difficult to say. It would take too much energy."

Having lost a promised part in *Way of the Dragon* to Nora Miao and a role in *Enter the Dragon* to Betty Chung, Betty Ting Pei got into a heated argument with Bruce. Afterward, he broke off their relationship and banned her from the Golden Harvest lot. Betty was brokenhearted and despondent. One evening she swallowed a handful of sleeping pills and called her mother. An ambulance rushed Betty to Queen Elizabeth Hospital. Betty's mother angrily marched down to Golden Harvest to confront Bruce Lee. Executives intercepted her as she loudly announced that her daughter had tried to commit suicide. They shooed her away, dismissing it as a publicity stunt from an actress who had lost a part in a major movie. As if to prove them right, Betty's mother then invited reporters into her daughter's hospital room. Betty didn't answer their questions but let them take photos. On December 23, 1972, *New Lantern Newspaper* ran the headline, "Betty Ting Denies Suicide Attempt Yesterday," and continued, "Ting had her stomach pumped after making a mistake in taking her medication. Refusing to answer any questions, Ting, wearing a pair of sunglasses, only let the reporters get a glimpse of her bitter smile."

The newspaper never mentioned Bruce by name, but he got the message. Everyone was gossiping about it. His friend Mito Uyehara, back in America, heard the rumors and asked Bruce what happened. "That dumb girl took several pills and said that she's in love with me and gonna kill herself if she can't have me," Bruce replied in a classic nondenial denial. "Shit, I can't do much in that kind of situation. There are too many crazy people."

On John Saxon's first day in Hong Kong, in January 1973, Lee invited him to his home and asked to see his sidekick. Standing in the middle of the room and feeling a little foolish, Saxon flicked out a few kicks.

"Not bad," Bruce said. "Now let me show you mine."

As he had done so many times before, Bruce handed Saxon a padded shield to hold against his chest and placed a chair several feet behind him. Then Bruce did a hop, skip, and a jump and blasted into the shield. Saxon went flying back on his heels and landed in the chair, which shattered. He was in shock for a few moments. Bruce ran over with a concerned look on his face.

"Don't worry," Saxon said. "I'm not hurt."

"I'm not worried about you," Bruce said. "You broke my favorite chair."

And that's when John Saxon realized he was not going to be the star of the movie.

Bruce was equally aggressive about the screenplay. He didn't view *Blood & Steel* as a potential masterpiece but as a B-movie knockoff being made at sweatshop labor prices. The movie's purpose was to get his foot into Hollywood's door and showcase what he could do—a demo reel, a proof of concept. "It was supposed to be his first international film and a sampler of greater things to come with bigger budgets, better sets, and more action," says Andre Morgan. Bruce was afraid the end product wouldn't be good enough even for that limited purpose. He began making demands of

Fred Weintraub for major script changes. What Lee didn't know was that Weintraub had secretly brought the screenwriter, Michael Allin, over and installed him at the Hyatt Hotel with a directive to keep his head low and avoid the actors. Through Weintraub as an intermediary, Bruce was unwittingly arguing with Allin over his script yet again.

Unable to get the changes he wanted to the screenplay Bruce boycotted the first day of production. He then didn't show up on the second or the third or the fourth. For a film on location with a tiny budget, this was a disaster. Weintraub sent Bob Clouse out to shoot random, B-roll footage of Hong Kong. He also tried to reassure his Warner bosses that everything was fine. When they discovered what was happening, they sent Bruce a screenplay for a completely different movie. Bruce met with Clouse, whom he'd come to trust, to discuss ditching *Blood & Steel.* Weintraub threatened Warners he would walk if they didn't stop interfering.

"Bruce was under enormous emotional pressure: Was the film going to be good enough or not? He wanted it to be more Chinese than American," Linda says. "He was certainly distraught at times. At one moment, he would be feeling real high and ready to go. Ten minutes later, he would be in the depths of depression about it all. I had to psych him up at times."

It took twelve days for the two sides to come to terms. Weintraub agreed to an extended flashback that showed Lee's sister being murdered by Han's bodyguard, Oharra. Bruce was also promised the chance to direct an opening sequence that would establish his character as a Shaolin Temple monk. Beyond his concern that the Americans would reedit the movie to make John Saxon the star, Lee was deeply worried about how the movie would be received by his Chinese fan base. The Americans had conceived of Bruce's role as the Chinese James Bond, which seemed unproblematic to them. But to the Hong Kong Chinese, James Bond was an agent of the British imperial government. When Bruce was growing up, the only people the average Chinese hated more than the British were the Chinese police officers who enforced, often corruptly, their unequal laws. In the script as originally conceived, a British agent (Braithwaite) recruits Lee to arrest Han, who is evil but also Chinese. Bruce had reason to fear his fans would view him as selling out to the West by playing a sellout. By shifting the emphasis from a British operative to a Shaolin monk, who was avenging his sister's murder, Bruce was once again playing a heroic defender of the Chinese people.

The length of his boycott and the anxiety it caused was evident on Bruce's face when he arrived on-set for his first scene—a simple exchange of dialogue with actress Betty Chung (Mei Ling). He was suffering from a nervous facial tic. It took twenty-seven takes before it disappeared. Finally filming could begin in earnest.

Michael Allin had arrived in Hong Kong on January 3, 1973. He began working on changes to the script from his room in the Hyatt, having been told there wasn't space in the studio for him. One day he was at the bar when Robert Clouse came in and said, "You've got to get out of here."

"Why?" Michael asked.

"I'm going to have a meeting with Bruce and he can't see you."

"Why? This is my bar. This is my hotel. What's happening here?"

"Nothing's happening. You've just got to get out of here," Clouse said, refusing to explain. Michael hid around a corner and watched as Bruce and Linda joined Clouse for a lunch meeting.

Two weeks later, Allin noticed a picture of himself, Clouse, and Lee in a Chinese newspaper. He took the article to the hotel's publicist, whom he had befriended during his stay, and asked her to translate what it said.

She quietly read it and said, "I don't want to tell you."

"No, we are friends," Allin pleaded. "Please tell me."

"It says here that Bruce Lee has sent the American writer home in disgrace."

In Bruce's efforts to reassure his Chinese fans that he hadn't sold out, that he was in charge of this Hollywood production not the Americans, he had told the Chinese press the story about how he made the producers fire the screenwriter.

Allin realized why he had been kept hidden in his hotel room away from

Bruce. Upset and angry, he decided to take a one-day vacation to Macau. On Saturday morning, he headed to the Star Ferry Terminal.

Sometimes fate has a wicked sense of humor. That same morning Bruce decided to check out Golden Harvest's marketing for *Way of the Dragon*. Wearing a velvet suit and platform boots, he also went to the Star Ferry Terminal to look at his movie posters plastered on the walls.

Allin first saw the crowd that surrounded him, and then he made out Bruce with his back turned to him. He was on a collision course. He walked up, and Bruce turned around.

"Michael!" Bruce exclaimed, shocked to see Allin.

"Bruce," Michael replied.

Bruce walked up to him and pointed his finger at his face. "Son of a gun," he said, his steam rising. The crowd avidly followed the encounter.

"Yep, nice to see you, Bruce," Michael said to defuse the situation and then hurried away to catch the hydrofoil to Macau.

Bruce was apoplectic. He had told the press he'd fired the screenwriter. What if they discovered it wasn't true? What a loss of face! Worse, he had been deceived. He thundered through the Golden Harvest offices accusing everybody of lying to him. "We were all saying to him, 'No. Really? He's in town? Are you sure?' " Andre Morgan remembers. When he cornered Weintraub, Bruce jumped on top of an apple box to stare him in the eyes, stuck his finger in his face, and let the dragon roar, summoning every English and Chinese curse word in his vast repertoire. Bruce in full rage was a terrifying sight, but he had enough control that he didn't hit Weintraub. He made it clear he was done with this film, stormed off the set, went home, locked himself in his den, and called Warner Bros. to inform them he was pulling out of the movie.

Allin came back that night to find Weintraub at the bar. "It was the only time I ever saw him drunk in all the years I've known him," Allin recalls.

"What did you do to Bruce?" Weintraub asked Allin.

"I didn't do anything to Bruce!" Allin said. "What happened?"

"It's my fault. I told him you were gone and he saw you. He's walked off the picture."

"What are you going to do, Fred?"

"Well, the first thing is you've got to leave."

It took several days to cajole Bruce back onto the set. If Hollywood executives are good at anything, it's getting talent to do what they want with a well-practiced mixture of sweet talk laced with veiled threats about breach of contract. Bruce knew if he blew this chance he might not get another one. And while it had taken longer than he originally thought, he had managed to run off the screenwriter in disgrace. He agreed to work with Clouse but refused to speak to Weintraub for a long time.

Allin flew to Maui to cool his heels. "I was so furious," he recalls.

A week later, Weintraub called Allin. "You've really got to save us. You remember that scene where you write about the black swan? The one where Roper and Han are touring the grounds and have this wonderful dialogue about the black swan?"

"Yeah," Allin said, trying to stifle his anger.

"We've looked all over Asia. We've gone all the way to Australia and we can't find a black swan. Michael, we need you to rewrite the scene. Please, I've got a secretary on the line. I know you can do it. Just—"

"Fred, let me think," Allin said. He put down the phone, went outside to the beach, and took a dip in the ocean. Twenty minutes later, he picked up the phone. "Fred, you still there?"

"Yes, yes, you got it?" Fred asked.

"Yes, I do."

"Yes, the secretary is waiting to take it down."

"Okay, it's very simple. Are you listening?"

"Yes, yes, yes. Everybody's listening."

"Get a duck that can act," Allin said and then hung up the phone.

While Lee fought with the producers, the American and Chinese crews were battling with each other. The problem was the Americans didn't realize how much English the Chinese crew actually understood. "One day we were shooting the scene where Bruce Lee, John Saxon, and Jim Kelly transfer from the little sampans to the big boat," says Morgan. "We didn't have walkie-talkies. We were using megaphones to cue. Someone yelled, 'Cut.' Out on the sampan, they didn't hear and kept going. Bob Clouse goes, 'Fucking Chinese.' The continuity guy, who's this little old man, says in Cantonese, 'That's the last insult I'm going to take from these fucking foreigners.' With that, he takes his clipboard and he's coming over to hit Clouse from behind. We had to grab him and pull him off the roof."

The Americans' frustrations focused on the archaic equipment and the Chinese tendency to say yes even when they meant no. The Chinese disliked the Americans' arrogant attitude and tendency to yell at underlings. But despite their differences, a mutual respect between the two groups eventually grew. "We admired how systematic the Americans were," says assistant director Chaplin Chang. "In Hong Kong, everything was either make it or get by with it."

The Americans grew to appreciate the Chinese resourcefulness, hard work, and courage. One sequence called for henchmen to chase Angela Mao Ying, playing Lee's sister, along the edge of a canal until she kicks one of them into the water. Weintraub and Clouse decided to shoot the stunt from the top of a two-story building about twenty feet away from the canal. They took five of the stuntmen to the top of the building to map out the shot. After they explained what they wanted through an interpreter, each of the stuntmen backed away from the building's edge, shaking their heads. "We were surprised by their trepidation," says Weintraub. "It was a short, four-foot drop, a pretty standard stunt." Finally, one of the men stepped forward and said, "Okay, I'll do it, but it's going to be hard to reach the water from here on this roof." Weintraub says, "I was dumbfounded. Not only because they all thought we were crazy enough to ask them to take such a hazardous fall but also because one of them was actually crazy enough to do it."

Realizing how valuable the stunt crew was to the success of the movie, Lee was exceedingly loyal and solicitous, continuing his tradition of eating a box lunch with them every day instead of dining in the hotel restaurant with the Americans. It was a kindness remembered by one of the dozens of stunt boys who worked on the movie. "He was very good to us, the little people,"

Jackie Chan says. "He didn't care about impressing the big bosses, but he took care of us." Watch closely during the battle scene in Mr. Han's underground compound and you can spot Lee whipping a young Jackie Chan around by his mop of black hair and snapping his neck. During the first take, he accidentally cracked Chan in the face with his nunchakus. "You can't believe how much it hurt," Chan remembers. "As soon as the cameras were off, Bruce threw away his weapon, ran over to me and said, 'I'm sorry, I'm sorry!' and picked me up. Of all the things Bruce did, I admire him most for his kindness that day."

Accidents are inevitable on a kung fu movie set. A particularly painful injury was sustained during Bruce and Bob Wall's climactic fight. The scene called for Wall to break two glass bottles and jab one at Lee, who would kick the bottle out of Wall's hand and follow up with a punch to the face. After several rehearsals Bruce's kick missed, Bob failed to drop the shattered bottle, and Bruce's fist slammed into its jagged edge. "Bruce was very angry with Bob Wall," says Chaplin Chang, who drove Lee to the hospital. "He said, 'I want to kill him.' But I don't think he meant it." Morgan says, "Was Bruce pissed off? Yes. But he knew it was an accident. He was mostly angry because we were going to lose two days of shooting."

The rumor that Wall purposely injured Lee and Lee intended to murder Wall was fed to the Hong Kong press to hype the movie. By the time Bruce came back to the set, his ever-loyal Chinese stunt crew expected their champion to exact revenge. Although he came up with a face-saving excuse—"I can't kill Bob, because the director needs him for the rest of the movie"—Chinese honor required some form of payback. The scene called for Lee to sidekick Wall hard enough in the chest to send him flying into a crowd of Han's men. Bruce didn't hold back. "They put a pad on Bob," recalls stuntman Zebra Pan, "but he took off like he'd been shot when Bruce kicked him! And Bruce insisted on 12 takes!" The force of Lee's kick was so great that Wall flew into the crowd, breaking a stuntman's arm. "We're talking complex break—bone through skin," says Wall. "That's when everybody went, 'Holy shit!' I don't think they realized how hard Bruce was hitting me until then."

Navigating the tricky terrain of Chinese face required the producers to turn some tricks when it came to hiring Han's harem for the banquet scene. No Chinese actresses were willing to play prostitutes in an American film, so producers were forced to hire the real thing. Responsibility for soliciting the prostitutes fell to Morgan, who knew his way around Hong Kong's nightspots. The difficulty wasn't finding them—along with Bangkok, Hong Kong was an R&R pit stop for American soldiers serving in Vietnam—it was convincing them to take part in the movie. "Never mind what they did for a living. That stayed between them and their customers. But if you commit it to film, how do you know your mother's and father's friends are not going to see it?" Morgan says. "They wanted to be paid more than I would've paid them if I wanted to sleep with them. To them, the indignity was far greater." When the stuntmen discovered how much the prostitutes were being paid, they nearly went on strike.

In the scene in which the three heroes are offered their choice of harem girls, the white guy (Saxon) selects the white madam (played by Ahna Capri), the black guy (Kelly) selects four prostitutes, while the Asian guy (Lee) picks his fellow undercover agent (Chung) for a chaste discussion of strategy. The Chinese James Bond was celibate. "He was a Shaolin monk," says Michael Allin. "He was always meant to be: 'You have offended my family and you have offended the Shaolin Temple.' "

Sexual adventures continued off-screen too. "Jim Kelly screwed everything that moved in Hong Kong," says Paul Heller. "He ended up in the hospital with bloated testicles. We had a harness for him to hang over the acid pit for his death scene, but he couldn't wear it, because he was so sore. We had to specially make a cargo net for him."

It was 1973 and everyone on-set seems to have enjoyed the era's sexual freedom, including the Shaolin monk. "Once in a while Bruce would say, because we had a bunch of Chinese girls there, 'Why don't we go out with some of them?' " says Saxon.

The final scene Clouse and the American crew filmed with Bruce in Hong Kong was the climactic battle between Lee and Han in the funhouse hall of mirrors. In the original script Han committed suicide before Lee could capture him. Both director and star felt this was a disappointing ending and spent much of the shoot trying to come up with a better idea. One day after having lunch at the Repulse Bay Hotel, Clouse and his wife, Ann, walked into a clothing boutique. "The hall had all these thin mirrors, which I watched shatter her image as she walked by them, and I said, 'Oh, ho—that's it!' " Robert Clouse remembers. For Clouse, it was a way to put Lee's much younger character at a disadvantage to the older Han (the actor Shih Kien was sixty) and make the final confrontation competitive and suspenseful for the audience. For Bruce, it was a chance to demonstrate the importance of "adaptability" in fighting—Lee breaks the mirrors to differentiate between the real Han and his reflections.

Two truckloads of mirrors were purchased for $8,000 and set up so every camera angle displayed multiple reflections. As they filmed in the oppressively hot, mirrored maze for two days, Bruce went all out, forcing Shih Kien at one point to call out, "Take it easy, son—this is only a movie." Clouse says, "Toward the end of filming, Bruce was approaching complete exhaustion."

The American team wrapped and flew out on March 1, 1973. Bruce kept the mirrored room set and continued filming with a small Chinese crew in the blistering heat for another four days, seeking to perfect the ending. "Bruce by that time was so wound up he didn't want to quit," says Paul Heller.

Bruce then went back to the beginning of the film to add the opening scenes at the Shaolin Temple, which he wrote and directed himself. To increase the wow factor, he began with a challenge match between himself and heavyweight stuntman Sammo Hung. It looked more like ultimate fighting than a kung fu battle—the two men face off wearing nothing but Spandex shorts and padded gloves. "During rehearsal we didn't do anything, we just talked. 'You punch, I punch, yada, yada. Okay, ready? Action,' " Sammo says. "One take. One take. It was very fast, only a day and a half."

After the fight sequence, Bruce inserted a dialogue exchange with the abbot of the Shaolin Temple. Always seeking to educate his audience, Bruce's on-screen character preaches Lee's off-screen philosophies: "When my opponent expands, I contract, and when he contracts, I expand, and when there is an opportunity, I do not hit." He holds up a fist. "It hits all by itself."

In a few brief minutes of film, Bruce had deftly managed to shift the emphasis of his character from a British agent to a traditional Chinese hero and to take ownership of the movie. "After you saw the opening sequences, you knew who the real star was," says Andre Morgan.

There was only one battle left.

When executives at Warners watched a rough cut of the movie, they immediately sensed they had a blockbuster on their hands. "When we saw it, we knew we had something," says Leo Greenfield, head of Warner's distribution. "God did we know." Their confidence was greatly boosted in March when Warner Bros. purchased and distributed its first Hong Kong–produced kung fu movie—Shaw Brothers' *Five Fingers of Death.* Run Run Shaw's chop-socky flick became a surprise hit with young and urban audiences, setting the stage for Bruce to exploit. If *Five Fingers of Death*, a subtitled movie with an entirely Chinese cast, could generate decent box office returns in America, how much greater was the potential for a multiracial kung fu flick filmed entirely in English?

Ted Ashley gave Weintraub another $300,000 for *Blood & Steel*'s post-production costs. He also set into motion plans for a sequel. Realizing this was his moment of greatest leverage, Bruce insisted Warner Bros. change the title to *Enter the Dragon* to make it clear that he, Little Dragon, was the star of the movie. Weintraub hated the title: "It sounded like a family film." Ashley wasn't happy either: "While *Enter the Dragon* seems logical in that it permits the next picture to be called *Return of the Dragon*, the title gives the impression of a monster movie." A series of polite but firm telegrams criss-crossed the Pacific Ocean over the next several months. As a compromise, Ashley proposed to Lee: "After spending a full two hours with our advertising department, it has been resolved that the title which will give the picture the broadest dimensions is *Han's Island*." On June 8, 1973, Bruce shot back: "Do think it over carefully because *Enter the Dragon* suggests the emergence (the entrance) of someone (a personality) that is of quality. Time is pressing, Ted. Do please send me the two scripts so I can work them over."

Bruce's reference to the two scripts was a subtle jab. Warners had already commissioned two follow-up screenplays for a potential franchise. But Bruce had made it clear through back channels that if the first one wasn't called *Enter the Dragon* he would never make another picture with Warner Bros. again. On June 13, Ashley capitulated. "As requested we have given the title still further thought and have taken greatly into account your preference as well. The title will therefore be *Enter the Dragon*. Love to you and Linda." Even Fred Weintraub eventually came around. "In retrospect I can't imagine it being called anything else. As a former adman I should have recognized the value of branding in the first place."

The grind of filming *Enter the Dragon* caused Bruce to lose twenty pounds, February 1973.
(David Tadman)

twenty-three

knockin' on heaven's door

A man of lesser ambition might have pulled back on the throttle or, at the very least, taken a vacation, but Bruce Lee had worked too hard for this moment to slow down now. He wasn't content to be the first Chinese man to star in a Hollywood movie; he wanted to be the biggest box office draw on the planet, bigger than Steve McQueen. "He was involved in such a whirlwind of activity that the goals he originally set out to achieve were rapidly being replaced by even higher goals," says Linda. "I tried to talk him into easing up, but he would cut me short by saying, 'The biggest detriment to relaxation is to say: I must relax.' By this stage, he had convinced himself that he was relaxing when he was working."

The constant exertion was taking its toll. All of his friends remember Bruce as looking gaunt and exhausted. In the previous two months, he had lost twenty pounds, dropping from 140 to 120. "The pupils of his eyes were enlarged, making his eyes seem very dark," says Sammo Hung, who costarred in *Enter the Dragon*. "His complexion was gray and pallid," remembers Charles Lowe, the assistant director on *Enter the Dragon*. "He was tired and dizzy much of the time."

When the stress became too much, Bruce would go out for long dinners with one of a handful of trusted friends. He and Charles Lowe often went to the Japanese restaurant Kane Tanaka because it had private rooms. "He liked the calm atmosphere of the restaurant," Lowe recalls. Despite his aversion to most types of alcohol, Bruce had developed a taste and tolerance for sake. "He could really drink sake," says Lowe. "He could drink ten or twenty of those incredibly tiny sake cups."

Bruce kept burning the candle at both ends, because this was his moment of greatest opportunity. If he didn't seize it, he was terrified it might pass him by. He had achieved a modicum of fame earlier in his career with *The Green Hornet* and watched it slowly evaporate to the point where he couldn't pay the mortgage on his house. That wasn't going to happen to him again. This time everything had to be perfect.

The early buzz from *Enter the Dragon* turned Bruce into a hot commodity. MGM wanted Lee to costar opposite his childhood idol—Elvis Presley, who was a black belt in karate. The Italian producer Carlo Ponti asked Bruce to costar in a movie with his wife, Sophia Loren. Run Run Shaw offered him $500,000 for his next picture, but Bruce didn't think it was enough. "If Marlon Brando can get $2 million, so can I," he told a stunned John Saxon. Warner's president Ted Ashley desperately wanted to lock Bruce into a multi-film contract to turn *Enter the Dragon* into a franchise. On April 22, 1973, Bruce wrote Ashley a letter warning him he wouldn't come cheap: "Nowadays, my offers for doing a film have reached the point which I guarantee will both surprise and shock you. . . . Because of our friendship, I am holding up my money-making time—like ten offers from hungry producers—to look forward to our meeting. You see, Ted, my obsession is to make, pardon the expression, the fuckingest action motion picture ever made."

Yet another offer was a blast from the past. Stirling Silliphant had signed a multi-picture deal with 20th Century Fox, and as part of it had secured a green light for *The Silent Flute*. On April 18, James Coburn flew to Hong Kong to lobby Bruce into rejoining the project. Bruce had grave reservations.

Having starred in *Enter the Dragon*, he had little interest in going backward and playing the sidekick to Coburn's hero. And he still had plans to make *Northern Leg Southern Fist*, his Chinese knockoff of *The Silent Flute*. But he kept his misgivings to himself and gave Coburn the royal treatment, promising he would seriously consider the project. "Bruce was pretty politically savvy," Andre Morgan says. "Coburn was a big deal in Hollywood."

The more other producers offered him the less satisfied Bruce became with Raymond Chow. Bruce erupted over a story printed in Golden Harvest's house-written fan magazine that said Chow not only had discovered Bruce Lee but was "like a babysitter" to him. Mostly they fought over money. After the incredible success of *Way of the Dragon*, Bruce was expecting wagonloads of cash to roll up to the doorstep of his mansion. Instead it arrived in trickles. Raymond argued that it was taking time for the theater owners to remit the money to Golden Harvest and besides much of it was earmarked to pay back the loans Bruce had taken out for his mansion, Mercedes, and mink coat. Bruce believed that Chow was cheating him and delaying his rightful share of the profits.

Bruce needed the money soon because he had recently ordered a customized convertible Rolls-Royce Corniche from England. He also wanted to protect his family financially in case something happened to him. On February 1, 1973, while filming *Enter the Dragon*, he took out a five-year limited life insurance policy from American International Assurance Company in the amount of US$200,000. On April 30, 1973, after the movie finished and all the huge offers began flooding in, he took out a second, much larger policy from Lloyd's of London in the amount of US$1,350,000. It was a huge sum ($7.5 million in 2017 dollars) based largely on his future earning potential rather than his current net worth. One of the ironies of Bruce's short life is that it was needed so soon.

May 10, 1973, was a typical Hong Kong summer day, muggy and oppressive. The temperature was 78°F and the humidity was 93 percent. After lunch, Bruce drove over to Golden Harvest studios on Hammer Hill Road, to "loop lines" for *Enter the Dragon*. The dubbing room had an air conditioner, but it had been turned off to avoid having its noise ruin the soundtrack. Bruce spent about thirty minutes inside this ovenlike room, before excusing himself to go to the bathroom. He felt faint and his head hurt. In the stalls, he pulled out a bag of Nepalese hash and ate some of it.

While in the bathroom, Bruce became disoriented and collapsed face-down on the floor. The sound of approaching footsteps roused him. Unwilling to appear weak, even in this moment, he pretended that he had lost his glasses and was groping around for them. A studio worker helped him up, and the pale, sweating star wobbled back to the dubbing room on rubbery legs. The moment he stepped inside the scorching room he fainted again, losing consciousness. Then he vomited his lunch of spaghetti and his body began convulsing.

A frightened stagehand ran across the parking lot to Raymond Chow's office and told him that something was wrong with his star. Chow told his secretary to call Dr. Donald Langford, an American at Baptist Hospital, and ran to the dubbing room, where he found Bruce having difficulty breathing. He was gurgling and shaking in spasms. "Rush him to the hospital immediately," Dr. Langford urged.

Four workers carried Bruce to Raymond Chow's car, and they drove him to the hospital. Bruce was in a bad state. He was sweating, shaking, and convulsing. One of the employees put a metal spoon between his teeth to prevent him from biting his tongue.

Dr. Langford was waiting outside for Raymond Chow when he pulled up with the unconscious and unresponsive movie star in his back seat. Three other doctors were summoned, including a neurosurgeon, Dr. Peter Wu. Bruce appeared to be suffering from an extremely high fever, his breathing was sporadic, and his shuddering body was bathed in sweat.

Raymond's secretary phoned Linda Lee. "Bruce is sick and they are taking him to the hospital."

"What's the matter?" Linda worriedly asked.

"Oh, I think it's a stomach upset," she replied in stilted English.

Believing it was something minor, Linda set off for Baptist Hospital, about a five-minute drive from their home. When she arrived, Bruce was gasping and every breath seemed to be his last. "Will he be okay?" she asked, terrified.

"He is very sick," Dr. Langford replied.

Dr. Langford was prepared to do a tracheotomy if Bruce stopped breathing again. His body continued to convulse violently. It took several doctors and nurses to hold him down, because he was extremely strong and difficult to control.

Failing to get any response from Bruce, Dr. Peter Wu, the neurosurgeon, examined him and deduced cerebral edema (swelling of the brain). Dr. Wu administered Mannitol to reduce the swelling. Preparations for surgery were made in case the drug didn't work, but after two and a half hours, Bruce began to regain consciousness. First he was able to move a bit, then he opened his eyes, then he made a sign, but could not speak. He recognized his wife and made signs of recognition but could not talk. Later he was able to speak but it was slurred, different from the usual way he talked. By the next day, he was able to remember aloud and joke.

"Bruce was in a very critical condition," says Dr. Peter Wu. "If he had not been brought to the hospital in time, he would have died from severe brain edema. It was sheer luck that experienced medical people were available to help him."

When Bruce was finally able to speak coherently, he told Linda, "I felt very close to death. I exerted my will and told myself, 'I'm going to fight it—I'm going to make it—I'm not going to give up.' I knew if I surrendered, I would die."

On May 13, Dr. Peter Wu met with Bruce for a personal history to determine what had caused the cerebral edema. During the conversation, Bruce admitted he had eaten hash immediately before his collapse. "I advise you not to eat it again," said Dr. Wu. "You've already had a very bad time with the drug. The effects are likely to be worse the next time."

"It's harmless," Bruce scoffed. "Steve McQueen introduced me to it. Steve McQueen would not take it if there was anything dangerous about it."

"Is Steve McQueen a medical authority?" asked Dr. Wu.

Bruce was upset that the Hong Kong doctors blamed the hash for his collapse. When Dr. Wu scheduled an angiogram for the next day to examine his brain more extensively, Bruce refused and demanded to leave.

"Please take the brain tests," urged Dr. Wu.

"No, I want to be discharged," Bruce insisted. "I will take the tests in the United States."

After his release, Bruce made arrangements to travel to L.A. for a second opinion. He didn't trust that the Hong Kong doctors knew what they were talking about, especially when it came to cannabis. In 1973, Hong Kong had very little experience with marijuana. It was considered an evil Western hippie drug. Research since then has proven that cannabis does not cause cerebral edema or lead to death. "There are no receptors for THC in the brainstem, the part of the brain that maintains breathing and heart rate," says Dr. Daniel Friedman, a neurologist at NYU Langone Medical Center, "which is why it is very near impossible to die directly from a THC overdose unlike heroin or barbiturates."

When Bruce arrived in Los Angeles, he went to see Dr. David Reisbord, a neurologist at UCLA. On May 29 and 30, Bruce was given the full battery of tests available to patients of that era: a complete physical, a brain flow study, and an electroencephalogram (EEG). As he awaited the results, Bruce called John Saxon, his costar in *Enter the Dragon*, to tell him he had come to town for medical tests.

"What's the matter?" Saxon asked.

"I've been fainting."

"Why? Are you okay?"

"Maybe if the tests don't work out, there isn't going to be a Bruce Lee."

After nervously waiting three days for the verdict, the news was good. Dr. Reisbord gave Bruce a clean bill of health. He had found no abnormalities in his brain functions and nothing wrong with his entire body. In fact, Reisbord told Bruce that he had "the body of an 18-year-old." Reisbord concluded that Bruce had suffered from a grand mal idiopathic, which means a seizure with no apparent cause. Dr. Reisbord prescribed the drug Dilantin, which is commonly used to treat epilepsy. "None of Bruce's family ever suffered from epilepsy, even in a mild form, and Bruce had never suffered from it either," Linda asserts. "Dr. Reisbord told me that at no time had Bruce suffered from epilepsy." A diagnosis of epilepsy requires at least two separate incidents. This was the first time Bruce Lee had suffered a seizure.

The Hong Kong neurosurgeon blamed the hash. The L.A. neurosurgeon didn't know what caused the collapse. Neither of them considered a far more common cause for collapse, seizure, and death in young, healthy men—heat stroke. The fatality rate for young athletes and soldiers who suffer heat stroke is 3–5 percent. It is the third most common killer of athletes and rises to first during the hottest months of summer. A common finding in the autopsies of patients who have died from heat stroke is cerebral edema.

The two criteria for diagnosing heat stroke in a patient are: 1) a core body temperature above 104°F, and 2) central nervous system (CNS) dysfunction, which includes headache, nausea, vomiting, diarrhea, dizziness, loss of balance, staggering, irrational or unusual behavior, combativeness, delirium, collapse, loss of consciousness, and coma. Seizures also frequently occur, especially when the body is cooling.

On May 10, Bruce experienced almost every symptom of CNS dysfunction associated with heat stroke. While exerting himself in a sauna-like room, Bruce began to feel dizzy and nauseous. This was followed by staggering, collapse, loss of consciousness, vomiting, and seizures. Since the medical records are no longer available, it is unknown if the doctors measured his core temperature, but their reports that Bruce was "suffering from an extremely high fever and his body was bathed in sweat" strongly indicate that he was dangerously overheated.

While Bruce's friends had long noted his vulnerability to heat ("Whenever he got overheated," said his first American student, Jesse Glover, "his control would fade."), there may have been specific reasons why he was particularly susceptible during this period. Heat stroke researchers have identified several risk factors: sleep deprivation, physical and mental exhaustion, extreme weight loss, alcohol use in the previous twenty-four hours, illness in the previous two weeks, and dehydration.

According to his wife, Bruce was sleep deprived. By all accounts, the stress of filming *Enter the Dragon* had drained him physically and mentally. He had lost 15 percent of his total body weight in the previous two months and he had minimal body fat to start. His friends say he was drinking alcohol more frequently, although there is no evidence he imbibed the night before his collapse. And a month prior to his collapse, Bruce underwent surgery to have the sweat glands removed from his armpits, because he felt his dripping pits looked bad on-screen. Without these sweat glands his body would have been less able to dissipate heat.

If Bruce Lee's collapse was the result of heat stroke, then his doctors misdiagnosed him. They caught the post-cooling complication of cerebral edema but didn't grasp or treat its cause. "There was less awareness of heat stroke in 1973 than there is now. Even now heat stroke treatment and care is not known by every physician," says William Adams, MS, director of Sport Safety Policies at the University of Connecticut's Korey Stringer Institute, which specializes in the prevention of sudden death from heat stroke and is named after the twenty-seven-year-old Minnesota Vikings football player who died from heat stroke in 2001. "His doctors might have taken his temperature and mistook it for a high fever and not realized it was heat stroke instead."

After his near-death experience, the positive test results were like a shot of adrenaline. Bruce immediately returned to his old optimistic, energetic, confident self. He rushed over to the apartment where his mother and his younger brother, Robert, were staying in Los Angeles. "He looked skinny, he looked a little tired," Robert remembers. "He said, 'You know what? The doctors tell me I have the body of an eighteen-year-old.' He then showed off his latest invention—a three-in-one kick, which was extremely fast and powerful."

He called up Chuck Norris for lunch at his favorite restaurant in Chinatown. "I passed with flying colors," Bruce announced proudly. "The doctor said I had the insides of an eighteen-year-old boy."

"What did he think caused you to pass out?" Chuck asked.

"He didn't know. Probably overwork and stress."

Bruce went on to tell Chuck about all of his accomplishments and the offers he was receiving for movie deals. "They're offering me blank checks for my next movie. Imagine it, I can fill in any amount I want if I'll just sign with them." He laughed delightedly and tossed a piece of Peking duck into the air with his chopsticks and neatly caught it. "You watch. I'm going to be the first Chinese film actor to become internationally famous. Before long I'll be bigger than Steve McQueen."

Mito Uyehara, the publisher of *Black Belt* magazine, visited Bruce and Linda at their bungalow in the Beverly Hills Hotel. "He was very jovial because he had just been informed, after four days of rigorous medical examinations, that he was in top physical condition," Uyehara says. "But to me, he seemed awfully run down. In all the years I knew him, I never saw him in such an emaciated condition before."

"Yeah, I've lost a lot of weight from working day and night," Bruce explained. "During the day, I'm at the studio and at night I'm writing scripts for my next movie as well as reading books on the whole damn business of movie production. Yeah, it's real fun and many times I'm so absorbed that I even forget to eat or sleep."

While Bruce may have been acting like nothing was wrong, Linda was still upset and worried. Bruce proudly showed Mito a clipping that was written by eight-year-old Brandon in a Hong Kong newspaper. Linda snapped at her husband, "I hope we can return to Los Angeles as soon as possible. The kids can't have a normal life there." The public rebuke, uncharacteristic for Linda, suggests a long-simmering argument. She had never liked living in Hong Kong. She wasn't happy with how the limelight had changed her husband and was terrified of what it might do to her children. Bruce nearly dying was the last straw for her.

Director Robert Clouse took Bruce to a special screening of a rough cut of *Enter the Dragon*. The work print had no music, no fades or dissolves, nor any sound effects. It didn't matter. Everyone knew a winner when they saw one. After the film ended, Bruce looked over at Clouse for a few seconds before bursting into a grin. "We've got it." Lee knew the world was his for the taking.

Bruce stopped by producer Paul Heller's house afterward. While he was there, Michael Allin, the screenwriter Bruce had banished from Hong Kong, rang the doorbell. Heller called out, "Bruce, a friend of yours is here." The two former opponents shook hands and chatted as if nothing had happened. "The picture was going to be such a fucking success that there was no hatchet to bury," Michael says. "It was over."

Confident that *Enter the Dragon* would be a blockbuster, Bruce made some major life decisions. He acquiesced to his wife's wishes to move the family back to America. Bruce decided he would split his time between America and Hong Kong, making one Hollywood and one Chinese movie per year. This way he could keep his Asian fan base happy and expand his fame internationally. Having his family on another continent would also allow him a great deal more freedom when he was in Hong Kong.

Bruce also decided to make a movie with Shaw Bros. He wrote a personal letter to Run Run Shaw: "As of now, consider September, Oct. & November, a period of three months reserved for Shaw. Specific terms we will discuss upon my arrival."

Then he called up Stirling Silliphant to tell him that he was turning down *The Silent Flute*. Bruce was still resentful that Silliphant and Coburn had abandoned the project when he needed it the most. "We were kind of starving then," Linda says. "After he is wildly successful they say, 'We are ready to do it.' "

"You can't afford me," Bruce told Silliphant. "I'm being offered a million dollars a picture."

Silliphant was surprised and upset that Bruce was turning him down. "I thought I was close to Bruce and all I'd have to do was call and he'd agree," Stirling recalls. "I was amazed by his reaction."

"I won't carry Jim [Coburn] on my shoulders," Bruce said, echoing a line Steve McQueen had used on him. As they continued to argue, Bruce asked, "Will you make the movie without me?"

"We will," Silliphant angrily said.

"Where will you find anyone to replace me, to play five parts?" Bruce asked.

"We will get five different actors to replace you," Silliphant said. "If you were to rejoin the project, I was going to suggest that you only play one role. Playing five roles would be old Hollywood Lon Chaney stuff."

"You can't afford me anyways," Bruce repeated.

At the end of the testy conversation, they agreed to have dinner together, but Bruce called back the next day to cancel it. He wrote a note to James Coburn: "Spoke to Stirling and I told him that between you and him I'll thrust our silent flute in your hands."

After flying back to Hong Kong in early June, Bruce reignited his relationship with Betty Ting Pei. Betty had not heard about Bruce's collapse, and he didn't tell her he had nearly died. "I didn't know," Betty says. "He didn't want me to worry. He told me he was the strongest man in the world." Instead he gave her a gift. "He brought me a keychain," she coyly says now. According to tabloid reports at the time, attached to the keychain were the car keys to a brand-new Mercedes-Benz.

While Bruce's letter to Run Run Shaw indicates that he intended to make at least one movie with Shaw Bros., his business interests were still intertwined with Raymond Chow and Golden Harvest, which owned the rights to *Game of Death*. If Bruce wanted to finish his philosophical pet project, he couldn't leave just yet. Excitement for the movie, which still didn't have a complete script, increased after George Lazenby, the Australian actor who had recently played James Bond in *On Her Majesty's Secret Service* (1969), called up the studio. He claimed to have seen *Fist of Fury* in America and said he wanted to work with Bruce. In truth, Lazenby had blown all his Bond money and only came to Hong Kong because he had heard its movie industry was happening. For Bruce and Raymond, this was a chance to cast "James Bond" in *Game of Death*. Bruce began working on how to fit Lazenby into the story line and decided to spend the rest of the summer trying to complete the picture. He left open the option of making a flick in the fall with Shaw Bros.

As Bruce was fielding million-dollar offers from European producers, Ted Ashley, who knew about Bruce's collapse, made an emotionally clever proposal: $100,000 a year for as long as he or Linda should live if he made five more movies with Warner Bros. "Frankly speaking, I am interested in this scheme," Bruce told *The China Mail* in an article on June 28 headlined, "Bruce Lee Scoops a Superstar Salary." "It gives me security in the years ahead and makes taxation much easier. Besides, it doesn't bar me from working with any other studio." And then, with a laugh, he added, "I have great confidence in the studio. I think it will outlive me."

For Bruce, the underlying appeal was obvious: it was another insurance policy for his family. For Warners, it was a chance to lock in his talent. They were already grooming him as their next big star. To promote *Enter the Dragon*, Warners had booked him on *The Tonight Show Starring Johnny Carson* in August.

All of this good fortune didn't make Bruce any less combative. One of his greatest irritants was director Lo Wei, who continued to slight him in the press. The afternoon of July 10, 1973, Bruce was in his office at Golden Harvest getting high on hash when he heard that Lo Wei and his wife were in the screening room. Bruce rushed into the darkened room, confronted Lo Wei about the insults, and dished out a few of his own, calling the director "a beast in human clothes." "Bruce was slightly stoned and Lo Wei cursed him back in Cantonese," Andre Morgan says. "Bruce threatened to punch him and then we had to pull them apart, literally. He was close to decking him." As Bruce was hurried out of the room, everyone tried to calm him down. It might have worked, if Lo Wei's wife, Gladys, hadn't confronted Bruce and reprimanded him.

Enraged again, Bruce pushed past Raymond Chow and Andre Morgan, rushed into the screening room again, and unsheathed a knife hidden in his belt buckle. He pointed the blade at Lo Wei—just like as a teenager he had pulled a knife on his PE teacher. "Do you believe I could kill you with this knife?" Bruce asked. Seeing the level of escalation, Raymond Chow and Andre Morgan once again dragged Bruce out of the room. Lo Wei ran to the phone and dialed 999 (Hong Kong's equivalent of 911). Once the police arrived there was a general panic. Bruce gave Andre Morgan the knife and belt buckle. Morgan scurried out a back door and down a secret passage to hide it.

The police interviewed Lo Wei first. "What is the situation?"

"Lee Little Dragon was threatening me with a knife."

"Alright, you'll have to come with me to the station," the deputy said.

Lo Wei laughed derisively. "Don't you get it? I am the one that has been threatened here. I am the plaintiff. You're telling me to go to the station? Why doesn't Lee go to the station?"

"He has a lawyer."

"And you are implying that I don't?"

A different officer came over and played good cop. "Hey, Mr. Lo, now don't jump to conclusions! That knife you were talking about, Lee got rid of it. We can't find it. Come on, you're all colleagues! Don't make such a mountain out of a molehill!"

"I didn't provoke him!" Lo Wei protested. "He's not getting away with this so easily!"

"What do you want us to do about it then?" the good cop asked.

"I just want to know that my life won't be in danger again!"

The officers went over to Bruce and told him if he wanted to settle the matter now he needed to write a letter admitting his mistake and vowing not to ever threaten or harm Lo Wei. By this point a group of reporters, tipped off by the police, had gathered outside the studio. Wanting to avoid further embarrassment and loss of face, Bruce agreed to sign the note. When the police took the letter to Lo Wei to see if it was satisfactory, Lo Wei, ever the director, couldn't help but insist on a new line. "Little Dragon must add: 'If anything happens to me and I am injured, he will be held responsible.' " It was too late for Bruce to back out now. Reluctantly he signed the updated version of the letter.

To calm the situation, Raymond Chow invited Lo Wei and his wife out to dinner. They left through a back door. Bruce went out front to give his version of events to the press. He denied having pulled a knife on Lo Wei, ridiculing the accusation. "If I wanted to kill Lo Wei," he said, "I would not use a knife. Two fingers would be enough." A year prior when Bruce was the fresh new thing, this might have worked, but he had developed a reputation and the press had soured on him. The newspapers and cartoonists criticized him. He was cast as the unruly son acting disrespectfully toward an aging father.

The next night Bruce had a scheduled TV interview with Ivan Ho, a popular talk show host. Upset at the newspaper coverage, Bruce told Ivan during their pre-interview meeting that he intended to deny he had pulled a knife on Lo Wei and demonstrate on Ivan why he didn't need a knife to hurt someone. "I will punch your arm only," Bruce explained to Ivan. "When I hit you, you will feel some strength. Don't panic, it won't hurt your shoulder. But don't try to resist. Just relax and go with the blow and you'll be alright. The audience will love it when you fall on the sofa."

During the live interview, Bruce denied using a knife, said it was ridiculous to suppose he would need one against an old man like Lo Wei, and asked Ivan Ho to stand up so he could show why. As they had practiced, Bruce snapped a blindingly fast punch at Ivan Ho's shoulder and Ivan went flying onto the sofa. Their skit worked as planned but the effect on the audience was not what Bruce anticipated. The punch was so fast it looked like Bruce had hit the popular host in the face. "The result was shocking," Ivan Ho says. "Onlookers thought it was real. They were unaware of our pre-arranged set up. It seemed serious."

Bruce took another round of criticism in the morning newspapers for "bullying" a popular TV personality. For someone who was so good at charming people, Bruce was off his game. It is impossible to know if it was the sudden fame, the mental stress, the physical strain, or lingering neurological damage from his collapse, but something was wrong with Lee.

A week later, on July 19, Raymond Chow and Bruce Lee had a lunch meeting with Nancy Kwan, the star of *The World of Suzie Wong* and his student and friend from *The Wrecking Crew*. They wanted her to play the female lead in *Game of Death*. But Bruce was unable to focus on the task at hand. Irritable and frustrated, he loudly criticized Chow for refusing to pay him the money Bruce believed he had earned. "He was saying that Raymond wasn't being fair to him," Nancy recalls. "I didn't even want to listen to it but he was going on and on and on about Raymond. He said, 'I'm not getting what I deserve.' "

"Bruce, what are you doing?" Nancy interrupted when she couldn't take it anymore. "You need to behave yourself. You are criticizing Raymond, but everyone is talking about you and Betty. You shouldn't act like this."

"Oh Nancy, it doesn't mean anything," Bruce tried to play it down. "It's just a fling."

"Everyone is talking."

"It's just a fling. I'll get rid of her. She doesn't mean anything to me. I have plenty of girls."

"Think about your wife," she said, scolding him like an older sister. "She is an American over here alone with two kids."

"I love my wife," Bruce said, stung by her words.

"But it can't be very nice for her, an American over here, and everyone is talking," Nancy continued.

Chow chimed in, "She's right, Bruce."

"Shut up, Raymond," Bruce snapped. "What do you know? It's just a fling."

Bruce Lee's altar at Kowloon Funeral Parlour, July 25, 1973. *(David Tadman)*

twenty-four

the last day of bruce lee

The morning of July 20, 1973, Bruce typed a letter to his American attorney, Adrian Marshall, about several big deals on the table including the multi-picture offer from Warner Bros. and a proposal from Hanna-Barbera to create an animated series based on his life. There were also offers for books, clothing, and endorsements. Bruce Lee was building an empire.

After finishing his letter and posting it, Bruce left his mansion in Kowloon Tong and drove to Golden Harvest's studios. He met with George Lazenby, the Australian James Bond, to further discuss his participation in *Game of Death*. As the only native English speaker at the studio, Andre Morgan joined them. Since Bruce had already shot much of the ending of the film, the goal was to come up with ways to work Lazenby into the story. "We sat around shooting the shit," Morgan recalls.

After the meeting, Bruce swung by Raymond Chow's office to say that he wanted Lazenby in *Game of Death*. Chow suggested they all go out to dinner to formalize the deal. Bruce returned to Morgan's office. He pulled out his bag of hash and offered some to Andre. They both had a nibble.

Bruce and Andre were supposed to take George out to lunch, but Bruce had other plans and canceled. He wanted to visit Betty Ting Pei's apartment for a "nooner." The studio's driver took Lazenby back to his hotel. Bruce promised to be back at the studio in the afternoon to settle how much money they were going to offer Lazenby.

Bruce jumped into his Mercedes and drove away. He arrived at Betty Ting Pei's second-floor apartment at 67 Beacon Hill Road around 1 p.m. It was a one-bedroom with parquet flooring, wooden walls, and thick blue curtains. They spent the next several hours alone together. "I was his girlfriend," Betty says. There was some sex and some hash, but no alcohol or harder drugs. Mostly Bruce was hyped about his meeting with George Lazenby and what it meant for his movie. He offered Betty the role of the love interest. Betty claims she resisted the idea, because she didn't feel comfortable playing his girlfriend on-screen while being his mistress in real life. "I never wanted to make the movie," she says. "I would feel kind of embarrassed to face someone I love."

Raymond Chow arrived at Betty's apartment around 6 p.m. It is not entirely clear why. Chow and Morgan had been waiting all afternoon for Bruce to return to Golden Harvest to work out the deal offer for Lazenby. Perhaps Raymond called Bruce to inquire when he would come back and Bruce told Raymond to meet him at Betty's place. If Betty was reticent about accepting a role in the film, perhaps Bruce wanted Raymond to help him convince her. Or maybe he just needed a chaperone to drive them to dinner to avoid public suspicion.

It was a scorching day—the temperature at 90°F and the humidity at 84 percent—the hottest day of the month. "Bruce wasn't feeling very well," Chow recalls. "I wasn't feeling very well either. I think we had some water, and then he was acting." In Bruce's bubbling enthusiasm over *Game of Death*, he jumped up and performed scene after scene. "He was always very active," Raymond says. "In telling the story, he acted out the whole thing. So, that probably made him a little tired and thirsty. After a few sips he seemed to be a little dizzy."

Immediately after feeling faint, Bruce complained of a headache. It was nearing 7:30. They were supposed to pick up Lazenby for dinner. Betty had already changed her clothes and was ready to go, but the pain in Bruce's head had grown worse. When Bruce said he wanted to rest, Chow jumped up awkwardly and tried to leave. "Raymond thought it was an excuse," Betty recalls with a smile. Betty gave Bruce one of her Equagesic pills—a common prescription pain medication. She says this wasn't the first time: "Bruce had taken them before."

Raymond suggested he go first and they could come later. Bruce went into Betty's bedroom, undressed, and sank into her mattress lying on the floor like a futon. Betty shut the door to the bedroom, went into the living room, and sat down on the couch to watch TV. Raymond departed around 7:45 to pick up Lazenby at the Hyatt and drive him to a Japanese restaurant at the Miramar Hotel.

After thirty minutes waiting at the bar with Lazenby, Chow called Betty's apartment. She told him Bruce was still asleep and Raymond and George should have dinner without them. When Raymond finished his dinner with Lazenby at 9:30, he telephoned Betty again. She said Bruce was still asleep, but she would try to wake him. Afraid of disturbing him, Betty opened the door slowly, crept into the bedroom, kneeled down beside him, and whispered, "Bruce, Bruce." He didn't stir. She pushed his shoulder and said a little louder, "Bruce, Bruce," but he still didn't wake up. Panic rising, she shook him and shouted, "Bruce! Bruce!"

Betty called Raymond back at the restaurant in hysterics—she couldn't wake him. Raymond told her to calm down. He would drive over to the flat immediately. Raymond flashed back to May 10, when Bruce had nearly died of a cerebral edema. He called Dr. Langford, the doctor who had saved Bruce's life, at home, but his line was busy. Raymond raced across town to Betty's apartment. This was before cell phones, so at stoplights Raymond repeatedly jumped out of his car to use a pay phone to redial Langford, whose line remained busy. (He later learned that Langford's daughter was on the phone with her boyfriend.)

When Chow arrived at the apartment, he found Bruce undressed, lying flat on her mattress, and Betty crumpled next to him in a state of shock.

"Bruce, Bruce, Bruce," Betty kept calling out, her voice hoarse.

Bruce Lee did not respond. Raymond Chow realized he was too late. His star was already dead.

As he stood there looking down on Bruce's lifeless body and Betty's sobbing frame, the enormous danger of the situation must have dawned on

Raymond. The most famous man in Hong Kong was dead in his mistress's bed, and the two of them were the only witnesses. The scandal would consume them. The press would blame them. It could end their careers, maybe even put them in legal jeopardy. If Raymond's original imperative was to save Bruce's life, now his immediate goal was clear: Bruce Lee had to die somewhere else besides his mistress's apartment.

Raymond re-dressed Bruce's body. He buttoned up his shirt, put on his European-style trousers, and laced up his high-heeled platform boots. Chow may have considered moving the body—Bruce's home was only a five-minute drive away. He may also have considered driving the body to the hospital himself—Baptist Hospital, where Bruce had gone on May 10, was only a three-minute drive in the opposite direction. The death of a superstar at home or at a hospital would shock but not scandalize the public.

Ultimately, Chow decided to bring in a doctor. He told Betty Ting Pei to call her personal concierge physician, Dr. Eugene Chu Poh-hwye, who worked at Baptist Hospital. Betty implored Dr. Chu to come over to her apartment to treat a friend in need of help. She did not tell the good doctor the name of the patient or his condition.

When Dr. Chu arrived, he found Bruce Lee lying in bed deeply comatose and not rousable. His pulse was not perceptible and the heartbeat was not audible. There was no respiration and no sign of life. He tried to revive Bruce for ten minutes without success.

At this point, it must have been abundantly clear to Dr. Chu that Bruce Lee had died before he arrived. It seems likely that Raymond explained to Dr. Chu the gravity of the situation and pleaded with him to drive Bruce's body to Baptist Hospital, which was only half a mile away, in order to limit the number of witnesses. Instead Dr. Chu decided to call an ambulance to treat a person who had "collapsed." The ambulance officials were not told it was Bruce Lee or that he was already deceased. Dr. Chu insisted that the "patient" be taken to Queen Elizabeth Hospital, which was twenty-five minutes away, rather than the much closer Baptist, presumably because he didn't want to bring this radioactive scandal to his place of employment. He would go along with the ruse but only so far.

Before the ambulance had even arrived, Raymond, the veteran producer, took control of the production. He told Betty not to say anything to the press. Then he called Bruce's wife at her home: "Would you go to the Queen Elizabeth Hospital right away, Linda. Bruce is on the way there—in an ambulance."

"What's the matter?" Linda demanded.

"I don't know—something like the last time."

It took seven minutes for the two paramedics and the ambulance driver to arrive at the scene around 10:30 p.m. The senior paramedic, Pang Tak Sun, found the patient, who he didn't immediately recognize, lying on his back on the mattress on the floor. Pang couldn't find a pulse and the patient wasn't breathing. He performed CPR and gave artificial oxygen. There was no change in the patient. The paramedics carried him to the ambulance. Raymond Chow and Dr. Chu jumped in back with them. The paramedics continued to treat Bruce's lifeless body during the lengthy ride to Queen Elizabeth. Pang later explained why he continued treatment long after there was any hope of success: "As a first aid man even if a person was apparently dead, I have invariably to treat him or her as a still living person and apply my first aid."

Linda arrived at Queen Elizabeth fifteen minutes before the ambulance. When she asked about her husband, the man at the front desk said, "Somebody must be joking—we don't know anything about it." She was about to call home when she saw Bruce being wheeled past her into the emergency room. He appeared unconscious to her. A team of doctors began massaging his heart. "It never occurred to me that he might die, let alone that he might already be dead," she recalls. After a minute or so, they suddenly rushed Bruce upstairs and she had to run after the gurney to an intensive care unit. The team injected drugs directly into Bruce's heart and applied electric shock. Someone tried to pull Linda away, saying, "You don't want to see this," but she struggled free and insisted, "Leave me alone—I want to know what's happening." Then she noticed that the EKG machine recording Bruce's heart was flatlined. The doctors finally gave up the macabre charade of trying to revive a man who had died long before he arrived at the hospital. On some level Linda knew the truth but she still couldn't admit it to herself. She asked one of the doctors, "Is he alive?" He shook his head.

Linda wandered along the corridor by herself. The head of the medical team asked her if she wanted an autopsy. "Yes, I want to know how he died," she said.

A little after 11:30 p.m. telephones across Hong Kong started ringing with the news: Bruce Lee was dead at the age of thirty-two. The cause of death was unknown.

A call was made to Charles Sutcliffe, Hong Kong's new police commissioner. He was hosting a party at his home on Victoria Peak for prominent members of the media. As soon as word spread, all of his guests headed for the door. "Come back after it's over," Sutcliffe told the reporters as they bolted for Queen Elizabeth Hospital.

One of Sutcliffe's guests was Ted Thomas, the British disc jockey who interviewed Lee in 1971. By the time Thomas and his colleagues arrived, the police had already cordoned off the hospital. A scrum of TV cameramen and newspaper reporters were staking out the entrance. "Nobody got in," Thomas says.

Without any official announcement, rumors swirled among the journalists outside the hospital about how Bruce Lee had died. At nearby pay phones reporters frantically called their sources. One of them reached Charles Lowe, the assistant director on *Enter the Dragon* and Bruce's sake drinking buddy.

"Someone told me Bruce Lee died in a fight," the reporter said. "Can you confirm?"

"Rumors!" Lowe replied with a sinking feeling. "It's just a rumor."

"He was beaten up by ten or twenty people in Tsim Sha Tsui," the reporter continued, "or maybe you already know?"

"You're crazy!" Lowe shouted and hung up.

Worried, he called over to Bruce's residence. Eight-year-old Brandon picked up the phone. "Is your dad home?" Lowe asked.

"No home," Brandon said in Cantonese.

"Where is he?"

"Movie! Movie! Movie!"

As Raymond and Linda approached the doors of the hospital to leave, the entrance lit up with the flashes of photographers' bulbs. Seeing they were trapped, they retreated. Raymond telephoned his wife and asked her to pick them up. Realizing the media would swarm Bruce's home, Chow then called Dr. Langford, who lived nearby, and asked if he and Linda could stop by his house.

Linda suddenly insisted on going back to see her husband one more time to make certain that he was really gone. Standing next to his body, she says, "I felt an incredible strength surge through my body and spirit. The determination and courage of Bruce himself passed to me. In a flash I knew what lay ahead and how I should deal with everything in the best possible way for Bruce, Brandon, and Shannon."

At 12:30 a.m., the police arrived at Betty Ting Pei's apartment. They did not tell her that Bruce was dead. Deeply upset, she could not bring herself to ask about his condition. After the ambulance had left her apartment building, she had called her mother and her younger brother, who were there comforting her as the police searched the premises. They found no sign of struggle or a physical altercation. The mattress on the floor was neatly made up. They put into evidence three glasses on the living room table, two half-empty bottles of 7-Up and Schweppes Ginger Beer, and an opened tinfoil package of Equagesic pills. Betty gave a full statement to the police. Given the consistency of Raymond's and Betty's later testimony, it seems likely he had already coached her in what to say. She was a professional actress and skilled at memorizing her lines.

Raymond had successfully raised Bruce Lee from the dead just long enough that he could officially die somewhere besides Betty's apartment. To complete the cover-up, he needed to stage-manage one other player in this morbid drama.

He arrived with Linda at Dr. Langford's house around 1 a.m. Linda was distraught. She didn't know what to do, what to tell the reporters. She loved her husband and was enormously proud of him.

"What do you know about Bruce and other women?" Linda asked Dr. Langford. "Was he a philanderer?"

"To the best of my knowledge," Dr. Langford answered carefully, "he had no other relationships."

"The Hong Kong press will devour him," Linda said. "How do I keep them from saying tawdry things?"

Linda deliberated with Raymond in Dr. Langford's living room. Together they decided what statement they'd give to reporters.

Andre Morgan received a call from Raymond Chow in the middle of the night. He rushed over to Golden Harvest where Chow was already in full damage control. Morgan was assigned to write the English-language press releases, while Raymond authorized the releases to the Chinese media. After some internal debate, Golden Harvest settled on the wording of its written statement: Bruce Lee collapsed at his home while walking in his garden with his wife, Linda. Golden Harvest mourns the loss of a great star.

Around the same time Queen Elizabeth Hospital released its formal explanation: the actor Bruce Lee died of an acute cerebral edema. The cause of the edema is yet unknown.

Based on these two accounts, the Hong Kong press reported to the public that their hero had died from a brain edema of unknown origins while strolling in his home garden with his beloved wife. "We wanted to protect Bruce's image and reputation and to protect Linda's and the children's feelings," explains Morgan. "We were not stupid enough to believe that we were not going to get tagged out. It was a matter of how long we could delay."

This fabricated version of Bruce Lee's death held up for three days.

H. S. Chow, an intrepid reporter who had profiled Bruce Lee multiple times for *The China Mail*, was suspicious of Golden Harvest's picturesque account and began calling his sources. Every Hong Kong hospital kept a written ambulance log listing pickup addresses. It took only two days for Chow to find the right ambulance log, track down the driver, and convince him to talk.

Ambulance #40 had picked up Bruce Lee from a second-floor apartment at 67 Beacon Hill Road, but Bruce's home was at 41 Cumberland Road. After a few more phone calls, H. S. Chow discovered that the occupant of the Beacon Hill Road apartment was Betty Ting Pei. "Bless H. S. Chow's heart," says Morgan. "We later hired him to be one of Golden Harvest's PR flacks."

In 1973 Hong Kong had four English-language dailies and 101 Chinese papers, all fighting for a circulation totaling one and a quarter million readers. Out of this cutthroat environment was born the notorious "Mosquito Press"—sensationalist scandal sheets that "print with a sting." The discovery of the cover-up—Hong Kong's most famous star actually died in the flat of an attractive actress—caused the Mosquitoes to swarm. Under the headline "Who's Lying on Li's Death," *The China Mail* wrote, "Film star Bruce Li spent his last hours at the flat of beautiful actress Ting Pei—not at his own home as was previously reported." Reacting to the revelation, *The China Star* splashed across its front page: "Bruce Lee Shock."

Having been tagged out so quickly, Raymond Chow stopped taking press calls and tried to regroup. Betty was left alone in her apartment to face the media. She made the foolish error of doubling down on the initial fabrication. "On Friday night when he died I was not at home—I had gone out with my mother," she claimed to reporters. "I last met him several months ago when we came across each other in the street." Bruce's older brother, Peter, supported her story and dismissed *The China Mail*'s allegations as "fantasy."

To contradict her assertion, the tabloids interviewed Betty's neighbors, who confirmed that Lee had been a regular weekly visitor to her apartment for months prior to his death. *The China Star* ran a double-entendre headline: "Betty Ting Pei's Fragrant Chamber Killed the Dragon."

After days of mauling in the press, Raymond, in coordination with Linda and Betty, came up with a new cover story. In a classic example of rolling disclosure, they admitted what could not be denied and denied what the press could not prove. To protect Bruce's reputation as a family man for Linda's and the children's sake, not to mention the large investment Golden Harvest had made in the soon-to-be-released *Enter the Dragon*, they refuted any romantic relationship between Bruce and Betty. To avoid legal jeopardy for Betty and Raymond, they maintained that Bruce had died at Queen

Elizabeth Hospital. All of this required concocting a new timeline. It could not be admitted that Bruce was alone with Betty. He needed a chaperone.

According to Linda's new account, "it was around noon on July 20, 1973, and I was prepared to leave our Kowloon house to lunch with a girlfriend. Bruce was in his study. He told me that Raymond Chow was due to come over that afternoon to talk about script ideas for *Game of Death*, and that they would probably dine later with George Lazenby. Bruce was his usual industrious self when I left him. That was the last conversation I ever had with my husband."

Raymond, who was Bruce's business, not his writing, partner, claimed that he arrived at Bruce's house at 3 p.m. Together they worked on the script for *Game of Death* until 5 p.m. before they drove to Betty Ting Pei's apartment to offer her a leading role in the movie. It was a business meeting and nothing else. Betty and Bruce were just friends.

At 7 p.m. Bruce complained of a headache. At 7:30 it grew worse and Betty offered him one of her Equagesic pills, which consists of 325 mg of aspirin and 200 mg of meprobamate—a mild muscle relaxant. Bruce went into Betty's bedroom to lie down. Raymond left to pick up Lazenby.

After Raymond called several times to inquire about Bruce, Betty discovered she couldn't wake him. Raymond drove over to the flat immediately. When Raymond arrived at the apartment, Bruce appeared to be very sound asleep. His attempts to rouse Bruce failed. Betty called her personal physician, Dr. Eugene Chu Poh-hwye to come over to her apartment and treat a friend. After Dr. Chu examined Bruce, he called an ambulance and instructed the paramedics to take Bruce to Queen Elizabeth Hospital. Bruce was officially declared dead at the hospital at 11:30 p.m.

This updated version of Bruce Lee's death would hold up for thirty years.

Bruce's older brother, Peter, identified the body at the mortuary of Queen Elizabeth Hospital at 2:30 p.m. on July 23. In accordance with Linda's wishes and the police investigation, a full autopsy was performed after the identification by Dr. R. R. Lycette. "The body is that of a well-built Chinese male of about 30 years of age and is 172 cm in length," states Dr. Lycette's autopsy report. His examination found no evidence of foul play. "The scalp is free of bruising and the skull shows no evidence of fracture or injury, either recent, or old. There are no recent or old needle marks." His heart was normal as were the blood vessels in his brain. Bruce didn't die of a heart attack or a brain aneurysm. The only abnormalities Dr. Lycette could find were congestion in the lungs, intestines, and kidneys, and swelling in the brain. "The brain is very tense beneath the covering dura. The brain weighs 1,575 grams. A normal brain weighs up to 1,400 grams."

His conclusion: "Congestions and edema of the brain (i.e. excessive fluid accumulation), were the immediate cause of death. The congestion of the lungs and other organs is strongly suggestive of the brain edema first stopping respiratory function, while the heart continued to pump blood into the body's arteries, which were dilating because of lack of oxygen. The edema finally caused failure of cardiac centers in the brain and stopped the heart."

While Dr. Lycette was certain that an acute cerebral edema (brain swelling) killed Bruce, the reason for the edema was a mystery. "The findings provide no definite evidence as to the cause of the cerebral edema." The last line of the autopsy did suggest a line of investigation: "It is possible that the edema is the result of some drug intoxication."

What led Dr. Lycette to this conclusion were the two items he found in Bruce's stomach: remnants of the Equagesic pill and small traces of cannabis (hash). Suspecting cannabis, Dr. Lycette met with Dr. Donald Langford and Dr. Peter Wu, the two doctors who had saved Bruce's life on May 10. Langford and Wu were already convinced cannabis was responsible for his first collapse. They persuaded Dr. Lycette it was the leading candidate for his death on July 20. "I believe the most likely cause of death is cannabis intoxication," Dr. Lycette wrote in a letter, "either due to drug idiosyncrasy or massive overdose."

Almost as soon as Dr. Lycette discovered hash in Bruce's stomach, someone in his office leaked it to the press. Surprisingly, in a colony which in 1973 recorded the seizure of 1,748 kilos of opium, 399 kilos of morphine, and 50 kilos of heroin, cannabis was still regarded by the Hong Kong police, press, and public as a major evil—a deadly Western hippie drug that turned kids against their parents. The tabloids broadcast that Bruce Lee had been using marijuana before he died. The story had all the elements for a perfect scandal: sex, drugs, deception, and death. "The Hong Kong press simply went wild," Linda recalls.

Bruce's afternoon rendezvous with Betty was turned into a drug-fueled orgy. Starting with the leaked marijuana story, the press piled on substance after illegal substance, turning him from a fitness freak into a junkie. The tabloids reported as fact to their credulous readers that Bruce had died from an overdose of "707," Hong Kong's equivalent of Spanish Fly—a supposedly potent sexual stimulant in the days before Viagra. Then they linked Bruce to a cornucopia of other drugs ranging from LSD to heroin to cocaine. On July 25, *The Oriental Daily* wrote, "It has come to our attention that a straw and several paper baggies full of powder were found by Lee's deathbed."

Starting with "scarlet woman" Betty, the press piled on starlet after starlet, turning Bruce from a superhero into a superstud. "The press decided they could add some spice to the story by not only including Betty Ting, but all his 'other mistresses,' " says Andre Morgan. "What they did was to go back through all the files and got every photograph of him with a well known actress posing together. They had five pages of him with different chicks, you know, the arm around, smiling, the whole bit. The stories were rampant, stories about him dying from an overdose, dying from screwing too much, dying with an erection, dying from being hacked to death by young thugs, poisoned by his servant. There was one story that he wasn't really dead."

Many admirers simply could not accept that someone as young and vital as Bruce Lee had departed. *The China Mail* reported that Malaysians in Penang believed news reports of his demise were a ghoulish publicity stunt for *Game of Death*: "The fans have been entering into heated argument over the issue and are even placing bets."

Because Bruce blurred the line between his life and his big-screen persona, many of his fans wanted to transform his death into one of his movies. "There are some who think Japanese martial artists might have taken a hand in Lee's death. Besides the traditional Japanese-Chinese rivalry, Lee always saved his special venom for Japanese karate and judo," wrote Alex Ben Block in the first biography of Bruce Lee (1974). "In Japan there is a tradition of assassins known as Ninja. Every Ninja was an accomplished pharmacist, skilled in preparing different poisons."

If it wasn't ninjas, it might have been a jealous kung fu master armed with the magical superpower of the delayed death touch—*dim mak* in Cantonese. "A Malaysian named Kay Wah Lee has dedicated most of his adult life to studying the ancient delayed-death-strike system," wrote Block. "He claims it's possible to walk down the street, lay his hand on a victim, and two years later to the day (or whatever elapse of time is desired), the victim will die."

While the press entertained these kung fu movie fantasies, most of the scandal sheets reveled in carnal conspiracies. "During a recent taxi ride in Taiwan, the conversation steered around to Lee's death," wrote Don Atyeo in the second Bruce Lee biography (1975). "'Ah yes,' nodded the cab driver knowingly, 'too much sex.' Which in a nutshell sums up much current popular Eastern sentiment."

Rumors that Lee died with an erection were so prevalent that tabloid reporters bribed their way into the mortuary to snap photos of his cadaver. "I paid the morgue beautician HK$1,500 to let me take pictures of Lee's corpse," says Patrick Wang, founder of the *Kam Yeh Pao* tabloid. "After snapping his face, I tried to photograph further down his body. The woman shoved me aside and dragged me out of the morgue, saying that I would get her fired."

While Patrick Wang wasn't able to prove priapism, his photographs of Bruce's face did show bloating. When film from Bruce's Hong Kong funeral also captured a swollen and distorted face underneath the glass of his coffin, it set off a new round of conspiracy theories: a bloated face proved Bruce was poisoned! According to Andre Morgan, the explanation was more prosaic—Bruce's face was swollen because of a botched embalming job. "Most bodies in Hong Kong are cremated because burial spots are so expensive," Morgan says. "The truth is they were really awful embalmers."

After Bruce's Hong Kong funeral, Linda Lee issued a public statement from Kai Tak Airport before leaving to bury her husband in Seattle. She implored the press and populace to stop speculating about Bruce's death. "Although we do not have the final autopsy report, I have no suspicion of anything other than natural death," she said. "I myself do not hold any person or people responsible for his death. Fate has ways we cannot change. The only thing of importance is that Bruce is gone and will not return." A Golden

Harvest representative pleaded, "Now that a great star is dead, it's the wish of most film people to let him die a hero. The reports, if true, will undoubtedly ruin his image. And they will break the heart of numerous Lee fans."

Brokenhearted Hong Kong fans were furious that Linda was taking Bruce's body to Seattle. "There was a lot of hostility, anger, and suspicion," says Morgan. "Suspicion there had been foul play, that it was all a setup, that he had been kidnapped." In an attempt to allay these suspicions, Golden Harvest sent a cameraman to film Bruce's funeral in Seattle and send back the footage for news reports in Hong Kong, but it only made matters worse.

To legally transport his body from Hong Kong to America, Bruce's coffin, which had a white silk interior and a protective glass enclosure around his body, was sealed inside a lead-lined shipping container and then laid inside a wooden shipping crate. When the crate was opened in Seattle it was discovered that the coffin had rubbed against the lead lining during transport, severely marring the exterior. When the casket was opened, Andre Morgan saw that the white silk interior had been stained blue from Bruce's suit. "The freight area of a 747 is not pressurized," Morgan explains. "Before we left, the glass had sealed the 89 degree and 98 percent humidity Hong Kong air inside the coffin. When the 747 leveled off at 38,000 feet, the air condensed on the glass and started to drip. It was like a small rainstorm inside his coffin." Morgan decided a new coffin was needed and purchased the closest model available: "It was slightly darker brown with a pleated velvet interior."

Sharp-eyed viewers back in Hong Kong noticed the casket was different and accused Golden Harvest of switching the bodies. "It all spun out of control," says Morgan, "from what were very easy things to explain." Attempts to clarify only led to more speculation. The scratched and stained casket was taken as a sign that Bruce's soul was not resting peacefully. Suddenly, everyone became a soothsayer looking for omens. Some blamed bad *feng shui*: On July 18 a typhoon struck Hong Kong and carried away the *feng shui* reflector—a small octagon wooden frame—Bruce had installed on his roof, but, before he could replace it, he was dead. Others believed he was cursed: when Lee Little Dragon took up residence in the neighborhood of Kowloon Tong, which is Cantonese for "Nine Dragon Pond," it caused anger and rivalry among those magical beasts, who struck him down.

All of this fevered speculation had real-world consequences. The press hounded Betty Ting Pei. "It seems that people want me to die," she lamented to *The China Star*, "and if this continues, I just don't want to live on. Bruce is dead. Why don't you leave it at that?" When her appeals for mercy failed to stop the onslaught of negative stories, she threatened to sue the press if the libel continued. In response, one of the tabloids ran a front-page headline: "Betty Ting, Sue Us!" over a fresh list of disclosures, causing the twenty-six-year-old to lock herself in her apartment. One of her close friends revealed, "She doesn't do much of anything except watch television."

The virulence of the coverage and the festering stew of suspicion quickly took a turn for the truly frightening. Students in Kuala Lumpur demonstrated carrying placards that read: "Betty Killed Bruce." Rumors began spreading in Hong Kong that a hit had been taken out on her life. In early August, a bomb threat was called in to the police. They discovered in a public square a suspicious brown paper package covered in Chinese writing: "Betty Ting knows the cause of Bruce Lee's death." The bomb turned out to be a hoax, filled only with rubbish, but over the next few weeks three more fake bombs were planted across the city with such messages as "Revenge for Bruce Lee."

The British colonial government could safely ignore a celebrity scandal, but bomb threats were another matter. Memories of the 1967 leftist riots, which endangered British control of Hong Kong, were still raw. A minor labor dispute had sparked a violent revolt. Pro-Communist Chinese radicals, who wanted to push the British out and rejoin mainland China, planted real bombs, mixed with even more decoys, throughout the city—over eight thousand in total by the end. Pro-British politicians, journalists, and police officers were killed, as were many innocent victims.

As concern grew that the current situation might spiral into widespread strife, the government felt compelled to act. Officials ordered a full-scale investigation into Bruce Lee's death.

Widow says she was aware Li sometimes took cannabis

Bruce Li took very good care of his health and would not have been so foolish as to take cannabis more than "just occasionally."

This was stated by Mrs Linda Li at the resumed hearing of the inquest into the death of actor Bruce Li in Tsun Wan Court yesterday.

Earlier, she admitted before the Coroner Mr Elbert C. K. Tung, that she was aware of the fact that her husband took cannabis occasionally.

She said she learned about this when her husband collapsed in a film studio in May this year.

Mrs Li said during a conversation between a Dr Peter Wu and her husband, cannabis was mentioned and Li admitted he took a leaf of cannabis before he collapsed.

Dr Wu told Li it was harmful for him to take drugs.

Li subsequently went to the United States for a thorough examination and discussed the effects of cannabis with a neurologist who stated it was not harmful if it was taken in moderation.

The neurologist, Dr David Reisbord, felt that cannabis had nothing to do with Li's collapse.

Mrs Li noted that after the examination, her husband continued to take cannabis occasionally and there were no after effects.

Medical reports on Li by Dr Reisbord were submitted to Mr Tung by Crown Counsel Mr J. Duffy.

Mr Duffy said Dr Reisbord would not be coming to Hongkong to give evidence.

It was stated in Dr Reisbord's report that Li was given a prescription for a convulsive disorder which had to be taken three times a day.

He took it regularly up to the day he died, said Mrs Li.

She denied that Li had ever had epilepsy.

"The word was never used and the subject was never raised by myself, Bruce Li nor Dr Reisbord," she said.

When asked by Mr Duffy whether Li had ever taken any form of drugs, Mrs Li said several years ago Li hurt his back in the United States and occasionally took a pain-killing drug.

She added that the pain-killing drug was prescribed in the United States and is known in Hongkong as "Doloxene." The drug caused no side effects.

She said her husband was in a good health up till May this year, although he did show signs of being tired.

When asked whether Li worried about his health, she replied that a doctor had once told Li that he was as fit as an 18-year-old boy.

When asked by Mr D. Yapp of Deacons, who is holding a watching brief for the American International Assurance Company, if she was aware Li took cannabis before he came to Hongkong in 1972, Linda's counsel, Mr Brian Tisdall of Johnston Stokes and Masters, immediately objected to the question on the grounds that it was irrelevant.

After a minute of heated argument between the two counsel, Mr Tung over-ruled Mr Tisdall's objection.

Mrs Li replied that she was not aware.

She agreed that she only learned about this after she came to Hongkong, but not soon after she arrived.

Mr Tung then reminded Mrs Li that she did not have to answer any questions that might tend to incriminate her.

She said it was between March or April that she became aware of the fact that Li was taking cannabis.

At the start of the hearing, Mrs Li told the court that on the day of Li's death she left the house alone at about 12.30 pm.

When she left Li appeared to be "fine and fit", Mrs Li said.

She said Li told her that he would be having a meeting with Mr Chow and would probably not be home for dinner.

Mr Raymond Chow, the head of the Golden Harvest film studio, caused a minor commotion in court when he denied in his testimony that he had ever spoken to the press about the place in which Li had died.

This immediately drew response from about 40 reporters covering the inquest.

"Within an hour or so after Li was certified dead, I gave a statement to the police stating all the facts. I can say that the statement I gave is what I said in court." Mr Chow said.

At an earlier hearing, Mr Chow had told the court that Li was found unconscious in actress Betty Ting-pei's house in Beacon Hill Road.

However, it was reported in all the newspapers and on television that Mr Chow had said Li died at his home in Cumberland Road.

Mr Tisdall explained that at the time there was a great deal of stress and the remarks were made with the permission of Mrs Li.

Earlier, Mr Chow admitted that he had told an ambulanceman escorting Li to Queen Elizabeth Hospital that Li had an attack that was something like epilepsy.

He said, however, that he could not remember whether he had mentioned it to a doctor at the casualty ward because of the confusion.

Mr Chow recalled that on May 10 while he was working in his office at the Golden Harvest studio, one of his employees rushed into his office and said Li had collapsed in the dubbing studio.

"Li had been working there the whole day, so I asked someone to call a doctor and I rushed into the studio.

"I saw Li was having difficulty in breathing, he was making a loud noise and was shaking," Mr Chow said.

"I called Dr Langford at the Baptist Hospital and he told me to rush Li to the hospital immediately," Mr Chow said.

Mr Chow agreed with Mr Tisdall that in all the films Li made as an adult, they involved a great deal of fighting.

He noted that Li had received accidental blows during the shooting of the films.

During the last completed picture, "Enter the Dragon" Li had received accidental blows during the shooting session

MRS LI AND HER LAWYER, MR BRIAN TISDALL.

South China Morning Post article after Linda's testimony at the coroner's inquest, September 18, 1973. (*Courtesy of Steven Hon/*South China Morning Post*)*

twenty-five

the inquest

The legal mechanism for the investigation of Lee's demise was a coroner's inquest—a court inquiry presided over by a judge and three jurors. Rarely used, except in high-profile cases like Jimi Hendrix's death in London, its stated purpose was to categorize the type of death—suicide, homicide, natural causes, or accidental—for any future legal proceedings. For example, a determination of homicide would be a prerequisite for a criminal trial, while a ruling of suicide might allow the life insurance company to avoid paying out a settlement.

In calling for an inquest, the government's goal was not to find *the* explanation for Bruce Lee's death but to provide *an* explanation—something palatable, preferably not scandalous, that would placate the masses. Hong Kong was a colony, not a democracy. British officials didn't care why some Chinese kung fu actor had died; they cared about quelling the unrest and maintaining control. To achieve their objective, the government needed to give the appearance of openness and thoroughness while quietly manipulating the outcome behind the scenes. An interdepartmental memo was circulated warning civil servants against talking to the press.

On September 3, 1973, all the actors in this rigged courtroom drama arrived with their own lawyers and their own secrets. The magistrate of the inquest, Judge Elbert Tung, and the public prosecutor, Joseph Duffy, represented the government's interest in creating the facade of a fair and transparent proceeding. Raymond Chow, Betty Ting Pei, and their individual lawyers wanted to maintain the fiction that Bruce and Betty's relationship was purely professional, while at the same time deflecting blame for his death. Linda and her lawyer needed to deny that Bruce was a longtime cannabis user, because there was yet another party invested in the outcome of the inquest: the insurance companies.

Just before his death, Bruce had taken out two major life insurance policies: one from American International Assurance Company (AIA) in the amount of US$200,000 on February 1, 1973, and the second from Lloyd's of London for US$1,350,000 on April 30, 1973. Insurance companies hate paying out policies that have run for thirty years, let alone only three months. AIA sent its own lawyer, David Yapp, to the inquest to try to nullify the policy by proving that Bruce had lied on the application. One of the questions was: "Have you ever used illegal drugs?" On February 1 Bruce had answered, "No." To void the policy, the AIA insurance lawyer needed to prove Bruce began using cannabis prior to February 1, 1973. To secure the insurance money, Linda had to deny it.

When Betty Ting Pei, Raymond Chow, and Linda Lee arrived at 9 a.m. at Tsun Wan Court, the scene was as chaotic as the O. J. Simpson trial. They were greeted by over a hundred reporters and several thousand noisy fans held back by police barricades. The parking lot and four surrounding roads were all blocked off to traffic, and the entrance to the courthouse was tightly controlled by the police, who escorted the witnesses through the crowds.

The courtroom gallery, with room for two hundred people, was packed to the gills with members of the press and public. At 10:20 a.m. the inquest began with the swearing in of the three-man jury who would decide the case—Fun Kee Wai, Robert Frederick Jones, and Kan Yuet Wan Ramon. The magistrate, Judge Tung, explained the case to the jurors: "The goal will be to determine the manner of death of American citizen, Bruce Lee, through consideration of the testimony of related parties. This determination will further act as the basis for any subsequent legal action." Because it seemed likely that Bruce's May 10 collapse was linked to his July 20 death, the judge said that the court would be calling upon the doctors who treated Bruce in May. He then narrowed down the possible manner of Bruce's death to seven categories and informed the jurors to choose from them: murder, manslaughter, justifiable homicide, suicide, natural causes, accidental death, and unknown.

The first witness to take the stand was Bruce's older brother, Peter Lee. "The last occasion I saw him was in April 1973 when he came to my house," Peter said, and then added as if to rule out the possibility that Bruce was drug-addled or suicidal, "He was behaving perfectly normal on that occasion."

The only lawyer to question Peter was the insurance company's representative, Mr. David Yapp. "Did you know that your brother was in the habit of taking cannabis?"

"No, not that I know of," Peter claimed.

The second witness was Raymond Chow. He stuck to his revised version of events. He went to Bruce's home at 3 p.m. for a two-hour script meeting. Then they went together to Betty Ting Pei's apartment at 5 p.m. for a two-and-a-half-hour business meeting to offer her a role in *Game of Death*. At 7:30 p.m., Bruce complained of a headache and Betty gave him one of her Equagesic pills. Feeling unwell, Bruce said he wanted to lie down. Raymond left alone to have dinner with George Lazenby. After several calls between Raymond and Betty, Raymond went over to the apartment and found Bruce looking like he was peacefully asleep. "I and Miss Ting shook him but still could not wake him up," he told the court. They called her personal physician, Dr. Eugene Chu Poh-hwye. When he couldn't revive Bruce, an ambulance was summoned and Bruce was delivered to Queen Elizabeth Hospital where he was declared dead at 11:30 p.m. Raymond concluded by saying, "I saw him almost every day. There was nothing unusual about his behavior. He was not depressed. I don't think that he had any domestic problems."

After the lunch break, the most famous mistress in Hong Kong took the stand. The already intense atmosphere in the courtroom rose to an even higher pitch as the crowd pointed and whispered. Betty Ting Pei's testimony, delivered in a halting and uncertain voice, supported Raymond's. She maintained the fiction that it was purely a business meeting and she and Bruce were merely industry acquaintances. "The last occasion I saw Bruce Lee prior to the 20th July 1973 was about a month before that date," she insisted, despite quotes in the press from her neighbors saying Bruce was a frequent visitor to her apartment.

The doctor who examined Bruce at Betty's apartment, Dr. Eugene Chu, was the next to testify. He was questioned by the insurance lawyer. "Did anybody explain to you what was supposed to be wrong with the deceased when you saw Bruce Lee?" asked David Yapp.

"I was told that Bruce Lee developed a headache, had been given some tablet for the headache and he took that. He also had a nap. Subsequently, they tried to wake him up but they could not rouse him."

"Did you ascertain what sort of tablet was give to Bruce Lee?"

"On the tin foil pack was the word Equagesic. It is a mild tranquilizer with analgesic effect. It is stronger than an aspirin. Taking one such tablet usually is quite harmless unless the patient is hypersensitive to it."

Despite weeks of wild and varied speculation over Bruce's demise, this was the first time anyone had ever suggested hypersensitivity to Equagesic as a possible cause of death. This theory would gain traction later in the inquest.

The crowd of reporters and onlookers around the courthouse was even bigger on the second day. The inquest was front-page news in every newspaper, tabloid, and TV show in the colony. The press clearly intended to squeeze as much coverage as they could before they lost their favorite subject forever.

The first witness was senior paramedic Pang Tak Sun. His ambulance had received the call at 10:30 p.m. and been informed it was a "person collapse case." Along with a junior paramedic and the ambulance driver, they went up to the second-floor apartment. Inside he claimed, "There were three males, one female and one patient in that flat. One of the males was rather young."

His testimony caused a murmur from the press. Up to this point, the only people who were reported in the apartment that night were the patient (Bruce Lee), the woman (Betty Ting Pei), and two older men (Raymond Chow and Dr. Eugene Chu). Who was this third man? The paramedic's very specific memory of a younger male became a dramatic subplot throughout the rest of the inquest. Both Raymond Chow and Dr. Eugene Chu later denied under oath that there was another man in the room. Was the paramedic mistaken or were Chow and Chu lying? It was catnip for conspiracy theorists—the young man in Betty Ting Pei's apartment the equivalent of the second gunman on the grassy knoll.

After this bombshell, the paramedic raised eyebrows again with his description of Bruce Lee: "When I first saw the patient he had his shirt on him but I cannot remember the color. He was also wearing European style trousers. His shirt was buttoned but I don't remember whether it was buttoned up to his neck. He was tidily dressed."

It was Linda Lee's lawyer, T.S. Lo, who seized upon this detail: "When you arrived at the scene you said the patient was tidily dressed?"

"Yes."

"Did he appear to be lying peacefully and no sign of struggle?" asked Lo.

"That is right."

"Did he have his shoes on?"

"They were boots with lifts."

Newspaper reports that Bruce's body was found fully dressed sparked yet another wave of conspiratorial chatter across the colony. It was taken as proof that the scene was staged—Bruce had died somewhere else and been moved to Betty's bed. Maybe the unidentified young man had helped transport the body.

The second witness of the day was Dr. Chan Kwong Chau, the casualty ward doctor who first treated Bruce at Queen Elizabeth Hospital. "There was no heartbeat, no respiration, both pupils were dilated and not reactive to light," he testified. "On clinical grounds I would say the patient was dead." Despite this fact, Dr. Chau tried to resuscitate Bruce for five to ten minutes before sending him off to the emergency ward upstairs.

Dr. Chau was followed by Dr. Cheng Po Chi, the emergency ward doctor, who testified: "Following my examination my observations were that he had no pulse, no respiration. At that juncture I thought he was dead. It was the ward procedure that even if we thought that the patient was dead we still would make the last efforts to revive the patient." Dr. Cheng gave Bruce an adrenaline shot to the heart. There was no response. Bruce Lee was certified dead at 11:30 p.m.

It was like a ghoulish game of hot potato. Bruce's body had been passed from Dr. Chu at Betty's apartment, to the ambulance paramedics, to the casualty ward, to the emergency ward, before finally everyone had to officially admit that the most famous man in Hong Kong was actually dead.

After lunch the forensic pathologist and the police detective who went to Betty's apartment that evening testified that there was no evidence of foul play. "I could not see any signs of a fight or struggle having taken place," said the forensic pathologist. "I was unable to see any obvious poisoning substances in the flat. There was no evidence that the deceased was killed by physical violence."

The judge announced that the next court date would be pushed back two weeks to September 17. He didn't reveal why, but the reason would end up having a significant impact on the proceedings.

Despite the delay, interest in the case remained high. On the morning of September 17, a line of reporters and curiosity seekers stretched out of Tsun Wan Court starting at 6 a.m. and continued to swell in numbers until the court opened at ten. The crowds had come to hear the mistress, Betty Ting Pei, and the wife, Linda Lee, testify on the same day.

It was a fraught moment for the young widow filled with potential pitfalls. To get the life insurance money, Linda needed to deny under oath that she had any knowledge of Bruce's cannabis use prior to his application for the AIA policy on February 1, 1973. She further wanted to argue that cannabis was not the cause of death. The insurance lawyer's goal was to prove that Bruce had lied on his application. Failing that, the insurance company wanted to establish cannabis as the cause of death. If Bruce died of illegal drug use, they could tie up any payout in further litigation.

During the two-week intermission, Linda had dismissed her previous attorney, T.S. Lo, and replaced him with Brian Tisdall, an aggressive young lawyer who also happened to represent Golden Harvest. Bruce had hired him previously to sue *The China Star* for libel.

When the public prosecutor, Joseph Duffy, asked Linda about Bruce's collapse on May 10 and use of cannabis, she responded: "He was treated by Dr. Langford and Dr. Peter Wu. I was present when my husband told Dr. Wu he had taken cannabis on that day. But when he received a check-up from neurologist Dr. David Reisbord in the United States, Dr. Reisbord said that taking a small dose of cannabis was not harmful and had nothing to do with his collapse."

Linda went on to testify that Bruce only took two prescription medications: Dilantin, the antiseizure drug prescribed by Dr. Reisbord, and Doloxene, a pain relief drug that combines an opioid and aspirin. "He only used Doloxene when his back was bothering him. He did not suffer any ill effects when he took it," she said. "His health between the time he collapsed in May and his death appeared to be good except he was more tired. He attributed his collapse in May to overwork and exhaustion."

At the end of her testimony, Linda submitted into evidence a letter from Dr. Reisbord, who had reviewed the autopsy report at Linda's request. Reisbord concluded: "No definite cause of death can be established. It would appear to be highly unlikely that the traces of cannibinoids found in the patient's stomach contributed to his demise. There have not been any reliable reports of human fatalities attributable to marijuana."

The insurance lawyer, David Yapp, tried to get Linda to admit that Bruce used cannabis prior to his life insurance application on February 1, 1973. "You came to live in Hong Kong in February of 1972?"

"Yes."

"Before you came to Hong Kong in February 1972 were you aware that your husband took cannabis occasionally?"

Linda's attorney, Brian Tisdall, jumped to his feet. "Objection! Leading question."

The insurance lawyer whirled on Tisdall: "Please don't interrupt my questions for the witness."

The two attorneys continued to bicker until Judge Tung intervened: "I will allow this line of questioning, but the witness is free to refuse to answer any potentially misleading questions. Do you wish to answer, Mrs. Lee?"

She nodded and then asserted, "I was not aware."

"The knowledge that he took cannabis occasionally was known to you only after you came to Hong Kong?" the insurance lawyer asked.

"Yes."

"At what point did you learn that he used cannabis?"

Once again, Tisdall objected to this line of questioning, and, after another heated argument between the two lawyers, the judge delivered his decision: "Though the witness has a right not to answer questions which may tend to incriminate herself, because these questions are not of that nature, she must answer truthfully."

"On March or April 1973," Linda claimed, selecting a month right after the life insurance application was submitted, "I was first aware that he took cannabis occasionally. In fact it was on that occasion that he told me he started taking cannabis."

As soon as Linda finished her testimony, reporters rushed out of the courthouse to file their articles for the afternoon newspapers. *The China Mail*'s front-page headline trumpeted: "Bruce Took Cannabis—Linda."

Raymond Chow was re-called to the stand. The first lawyer to question him was Brian Tisdall, who was officially serving as Linda's attorney but in reality was Golden Harvest's mouthpiece. Suggesting to Linda that she hire Tisdall as her lawyer was a brilliant maneuver on Raymond's part, as it allowed the two men, without appearing to be colluding, to present to the court and public an alternate theory of the case.

"You agree that all Bruce's films involved a great deal of physical activity and a lot of fighting?" Tisdall asked, laying the groundwork.

"Yes."

"During the making of the films were you aware that Mr. Lee might receive blows which he didn't mean to receive, and that these blows could be quite severe?"

"From time to time."

"During the making of the last completed film, *Enter the Dragon*, did he receive such blows?" Tisdall asked, plugging Golden Harvest's upcoming Bruce Lee movie.

"Several times," Raymond answered without hesitating.

"When would that be?"

"February or March 1973 at least three or four times," Raymond replied. "Once was in the face accidentally by another actor with his fist. He was hurt very much on that occasion. He had to go back to my office to rest for about one hour before he could continue his work."

"During your career as a producer have you heard much about karate and other forms of martial arts?"

"Yes."

"Have you ever heard that people might receive a blow and that the effect was not discovered until quite some time later?"

"Yes, I have heard of that."

All in all, it was an ingenious pre-rehearsed set piece. Since Bruce's death, the press had been busy disfiguring his public image as a martial arts superhero by castigating him as a drug-addicted sex maniac—a Chinese Charlie Sheen. The inquest's inquiry into cannabis as the cause of death was only further solidifying this negative perception in the public mind. By floating brain damage from a concussion sustained while filming a dangerous fight scene, Chow was inventing a heroic death. Linda had a life insurance policy she needed to secure; Raymond had a movie he needed to sell.

The insurance lawyer, David Yapp, was not duped by Chow's attempt to divert attention from drugs. After Tisdall sat down, Yapp immediately turned the questioning back to cannabis.

"You agree that Bruce Lee formed a very important part of your company's activities?"

"Yes."

"Did you take a great interest in his activities and welfare?"

"Yes."

"Presumably when he collapsed in May 1973 you were very interested to find out why he collapsed?"

"Yes."

"Were you ever informed that before he had collapsed he had taken some cannabis?"

"No."

"When did you first hear that Bruce took cannabis?"

"In this court on 3rd September 1973," Raymond said with a straight face.

Annoyed that Chow was refusing to cooperate (everyone who knew Bruce Lee knew he enjoyed marijuana and hash), the insurance lawyer attacked Raymond's credibility. "Did you make a statement in public about the place where the deceased was found collapsed which was quite different from what you told us in this inquest?" David Yapp asked, referring to Golden Harvest's initial press release that falsely claimed Bruce had collapsed at home while walking in his garden with his wife.

"I did not make any statement about that aspect to the press."

At this bald-faced lie, loud boos rained down from the reporters packed into the courthouse. Chow had fooled them once; they were not going to sit silently while he attempted it again. There was such an uproar the judge had to call for silence before turning to Chow to ask the same question again: "Did you release any public statement?"

Raymond carefully dodged the magistrate's query: "Within one hour or so after the deceased was pronounced dead, I made a statement to the police of all the facts. The statement to the police was the same as the evidence I have given in this court."

Dr. Eugene Chu was the witness who had to follow Raymond's tough act. He tried to explain why he sent Bruce to Queen Elizabeth Hospital instead of the nearer hospital, Baptist, where he also happened to work. "I sent him to Q.E.H. not because I thought he was dead but because I believed the facilities were better at Q.E.H. When I saw Bruce Lee in the bed, he had no pulse, no heartbeat and no respiration."

This bizarre assertion was quickly vivisected by Linda's attorney, Brian Tisdall. "If he had no pulse, no heartbeat and no respiration, would the superior facilities at Q.E.H. be of any importance?"

"I thought it would be better to send him to Q.E.H. to try to revive him even though he appeared to be hopeless," Dr. Chu claimed.

"Did you think there was a hope to revive him?"

"Not much."

That was the end of Dr. Eugene Chu's humiliating ordeal. When he died forty-two years later, his obituary in the *South China Morning Post* noted, "Dr. Chu never spoke another word about the night of July 20, 1973, when Lee breathed his last."

Once Dr. Chu stepped down, the crowd in the courtroom gallery began buzzing. The next witness scheduled to take the stand was Betty Ting Pei, who had been waiting in court all day. Much to everyone's surprise the public prosecutor, Joseph Duffy, rose to his feet and said, "The crown counsel does not require the presence of Miss Betty Ting Pei to give any more evidence." The magistrate agreed and Betty was dismissed.

Audible gasps erupted from the onlookers and grumbles from the reporters. Betty was the star witness and headline news. For those who were suspicious that the inquest was a sham, this was further evidence. If the government really wanted to know why Bruce Lee died, why wouldn't they re-call the last person to see him alive? There were plenty of questions that needed answers and contradictory testimony that needed untangling. Did Bruce and Raymond really arrive at her apartment together? Did Bruce consume cannabis while at her apartment? Why wasn't an ambulance called earlier? Why was Bruce fully dressed when the paramedics arrived? Was there a mysterious young man in the apartment? Did anyone attempt to move the body prior to the arrival of the paramedics? Why did Dr. Chu insist on sending him to Queen Elizabeth instead of Baptist Hospital?

Instead of asking any of these questions, the public prosecutor and the judge just let Betty Ting Pei walk away.

The next day was devoted to the testimony and questioning of one witness: the government's chemist, Dr. Lam King Leung. For six hours, he went into extended and excruciating detail over every single test that was completed for the autopsy. According to Dr. Leung's report, blood tests proved that Bruce had taken one pill of Equagesic and a small amount of cannabis. Neither was in an amount sufficient for an overdose. Further tests for every type of poison and drug known to mankind—including mercury, arsenic, bismuth, antimony, lead, alcohol, morphine, and Spanish Fly—were negative. Bruce didn't overdose, and he wasn't poisoned.

If one strategic goal of the coroner's inquest was to bore the public into submission, the plan worked. By the end of the day, the atmosphere in Tsun Wan Court had calmed significantly and the pack of reporters waiting outside the courthouse had thinned out dramatically.

To quell the unrest over Bruce's death, the government needed a socially acceptable explanation. The problem was the medical experts didn't agree. The Hong Kong–based doctors—Dr. Donald Langford (the American doctor who had treated Bruce on May 10), Dr. Peter Wu (the Chinese neurologist who saved Bruce's life on May 10), and Dr. R. R. Lycette (the coroner from New Zealand)—all believed cannabis was the cause of Bruce Lee's death. On the American side, however, Dr. David Reisbord, the UCLA neurologist who had examined Lee after his May 10 collapse, correctly pointed out that there had never been a substantiated case of death from cannabis. Based on the available evidence, Dr. Reisbord believed the cause of death was unknown and unknowable.

The government's solution was to bring in a world-famous pathologist from London, Professor Robert Donald Teare. His busy schedule was the reason the inquest had been delayed for two weeks. Teare was a professor of forensic medicine at the University of London and a guest lecturer at the Metropolitan Police (Scotland Yard) training college. Bruce Lee's case was perfect for the limelight-seeking professor, who gravitated toward high-profile celebrity deaths. He had also supervised the autopsies and testified at the coroner inquests of Jimi Hendrix (1970) and Brian Epstein (1967), the manager of the Beatles. He was billed to the Hong Kong press and public as a real-life Sherlock Holmes.

After reviewing the coroner's findings and studying the evidence, Teare privately called in the other expert witnesses for a come-to-Jesus meeting. "Professor Teare, Dr. Wu, Dr. Lycette, and myself, we met on one of the upper floors of Queen Elizabeth," recalls Dr. Langford. "It was not exactly a dress rehearsal for the trial, but it was a chance for him to caution us about how Hong Kong was really on the spot and how we were not considered to be a world forensic pathology center, that there had been no studies authenticating the possibility of a death from cannabis—and that we must not do anything to put the local medical community on the spot. If one was going to decide that the chemicals in marijuana were dangerous and could be lethal, then that conclusion shouldn't be decided in some little bitty, insignificant backwater like Hong Kong. We were not asked to perjure ourselves, but we were cautioned that the whole world would be watching. At the time I viewed this as tampering with the witnesses."

Having read the testimony and looked at the evidence, Professor Teare had developed an alternative hypothesis as to the cause of death—one that had been mentioned in passing once during the inquest by Dr. Chu but never brought up again—hypersensitivity to Equagesic. Professor Teare sought to sway the three doctors to his theory. He failed with the American and the Chinese doctors but succeeded with the New Zealand coroner.

After the tedious chemistry testimony of the previous day, the crowds had mostly departed. By the morning of the fifth day, the courtroom was relatively cold and empty. The first witness was Linda Lee. She returned to the stand to submit into evidence a report from Dr. Ira Frank from UCLA entitled "Clinical Studies in Cannabis." Dr. Frank's conclusion was the same as Dr. Reisbord's—there were no substantiated cases of cannabis as a cause of death. The trace amounts of cannabis found in Bruce's Lee's stomach were irrelevant to his demise.

The only question for Linda came from one of the jurors: "Was the reason you sought out this report from the doctors in Los Angeles because of the insurance?"

"No," she averred, "it was because I want to clarify the real reason for my husband's death."

Next up was Dr. Langford, who hesitantly proposed cannabis as the cause of Bruce Lee's first collapse on May 10. "At the time in my mind, I felt that there was a possibility his condition was due to drug ingestion," he said, before immediately qualifying his theory. "It may or may not have been drug intoxication."

Dr. Langford's decision to hedge on cannabis was partly due to the warning delivered by Professor Teare. But he was also influenced by his friendship with Bruce and Linda. The two families were neighbors, and Linda and Dr. Langford were in the same Cantonese class. He knew the life insurance company was trying to nullify Bruce's policy because of cannabis. "I had considerable sympathy for Linda wanting to get the money she felt was rightfully hers to raise those kids," Dr. Langford later explained.

In contrast, Dr. Peter Wu, the Chinese neurologist, didn't know the Lee family personally, and he certainly wasn't going to back down because some British professor had tried to big-foot him. Dr. Chu's clinical diagnosis was "cerebral edema and poisoning by cannabis suspected."

Brian Tisdall, Linda and Golden Harvest's attorney, aggressively attacked Dr. Wu's assertion that cannabis was the cause of death. "Do you have any personal experience with cannabis?" Tisdall asked.

"No, not at all."

"Had any cases involving cannabis?"

"No."

"From your theoretical knowledge would you say that cannabis is a potential killer by itself?"

"It could be by itself."

"In what circumstances?"

"If it was used excessively or if a person has a hypersensitivity towards it."

"In saying that what information or reading material are you relying upon?"

"In the pharmacological text books. My knowledge was mainly derived from text books from my student days." Dr. Wu hesitated before conceding, "I am not in the position as an expert to talk about cannabis."

Tisdall had no further questions for Dr. Peter Wu. None of the other attorneys chose to cross-examine him, not even the insurance lawyer. The destruction of his credibility was too complete. He was dismissed.

After a lunch break, Dr. R. R. Lycette, the coroner from New Zealand, took the stand. He summarized his autopsy report. There were no signs of external injury or needle marks. The only thing abnormal was the swelling of Bruce's brain. His conclusion was "edema of the brain (i.e. excess fluid accumulation) was the immediate cause of death." Because he could not find any natural causes for the edema, he briefly flirted with the cannabis theory. "But when I learned that there were no authenticated cases of deaths from cannabis," he said, "I came to the conclusion that [Lee's] death was not due to cannabis intoxication."

Having excluded cannabis and any other type of poison, Dr. R. R. Lycette was left to deduce: "Bruce Lee died from some form of hypersensitivity. I feel the most likely substance was one of the components of Equagesic." Dr. Lycette did not mention Professor Teare or the fact that he was parroting Teare's theory. "Fatal aspirin hypersensitivity has been ascribed to having swallowed just one tablet, but it is very rare."

He finished by saying that he considered Bruce's two collapses on May 10 and July 20 to be linked. "I think the May episode was consistent with a non-fatal attack of the same illness which killed Mr. Lee in July." Dr. Lycette hypothesized that Bruce may have taken the pain medication Doloxene, which also contains aspirin, prior to his collapse on May 10.

The previous day's testimony by the coroner, Dr. Lycette, had firmly set up the hypersensitivity to Equagesic theory. On day six, it was left to the final witness to drive it home—Professor Teare. As with all the other experts, Professor Teare began with his credentials: "I have specialized in forensic medicine for the last 35 years. During that time I have performed about

90,000 post-mortems and given evidence in 18,000 inquests." Those were incredible numbers, which the Hong Kong newspapers reported as fact without doing the math. To achieve what he claimed, Professor Teare would have had to perform 7 autopsies and testify in 1.5 inquests every day, seven days a week, 365 days a year for 35 years.

Hong Kong officials wanted a palatable explanation to hand to the public, and Professor Teare, who was not prone to caution, humility, or self-doubt, did not disappoint. Teare agreed with the coroner's assessment that Bruce's death from cerebral edema on July 20 was linked to his collapse on May 10. He also concurred that, "There was no ordinary natural disease in this case." He then proceeded to eliminate cannabis as the suspect with a flourish: "I have never come across any case of allergic or hypersensitivities to cannabis. In my opinion the fact that cannabis was taken shortly before the onset of his illness in May and cannabis was also found in his stomach on 20th July 73 was a pure coincidence. So far as acute cerebral edema is concerned taking cannabis or taking a cup of tea or coffee would be identical."

Having discarded cannabis, he turned to the two drugs in Equagesic, aspirin and meprobamate. Professor Teare argued: "In my opinion the cause of death was acute cerebral edema due to hypersensitivity to either meprobamate or aspirin or possibly the combination of the two." He concluded, "This sort of hypersensitivity is very rare indeed."

With that, the final witness of the inquest was dismissed. Judge Elbert Tung made a special point of thanking Professor Teare for traveling from so far away to testify. The court was adjourned until the following Monday morning when the jury would begin deliberations.

On the seventh day of the inquest, Judge Tung laid out his instructions to the three-man jury: "The key witnesses in this case are the medical and forensic experts, such as Doctors Lycette [coroner] and Lam [chemist], as well as Professor R. D. Teare," the judge said, before emphasizing, "who traveled a long way to be here." He did not mention Dr. Langford or Dr. Peter Wu, the two medical experts who supported the cannabis theory.

The judge then explained the seven possible choices for cause of death, as one would expect, but then he added, in what reads like an example of leading the jury, his own opinions as to which choices were credible and which were not:

1. **Murder:** Intentionally and maliciously causing the death of another. Since there is no evidence to support this in this case, we may rule it out.
2. **Manslaughter:** Causing the death of a person without intent to harm. Since the death clearly was not a direct result of anyone else's actions, we may rule it out.
3. **Justifiable Homicide:** Unrelated to the current case, and therefore not under consideration.
4. **Suicide:** All the evidence points to the idea that Bruce Lee had no motivation or tendency to harm or kill himself, and there is nothing else, such as a will, to indicate that he intended to die. Therefore, the probability of this is extremely low.
5. **Death by Natural Causes:** Though Doctors Lycette and Lam performed exhaustive testing on the body of Bruce Lee, they could find no evidence of a natural disease or disorder that might lead to the death of Bruce Lee. My opinion is that "natural causes" should be excluded from consideration, in accordance with the opinion of the three medical experts who testified.
6. **Accidental Death:** According to legal definitions, there is not a clear line drawn between "accidental death," "death by misadventure," and "death by disaster." In my view, "death by misadventure" involves a greater degree of "bad luck" than does "accidental death."

Perhaps worried that the jury wouldn't get the message he was delivering, the judge went on:

> Given that the body of Bruce Lee showed no outward signs of injury, and that the police found no signs of a struggle or traces of poison at the apartment, and in view of the testimony of three medical experts stating that Bruce's death was caused by cerebral edema, a verdict of "accidental death" is worth considering.

In fact, the opinion of medical expert, Professor Teare, is that cannabis could not have led to the death of Bruce Lee, either by chronic or acute poisoning. Dr. Lycette further notes that certain drugs or combinations of drugs can sometimes lead to fatal allergic reactions, and that there are cases of allergic reaction to aspirin. Though aspirin only makes up one-half of the content of "Equagesic," it is quite possible that the combined action of the aspirin and meprobamate in Equagesic caused the allergic reaction.

Of course, cases of this sort of reaction are also extremely rare; therefore, if the jury accepts the judgment of Professor Teare, the causes of death would be classified as either "accidental death" or "death by misadventure." If the members of the jury still have doubts about the testimony and analysis presented, then they should choose the seventh option: "cause of death unknown."

After being more or less told how to decide the case, the three-man jury didn't have any doubts. It took them less than five minutes of deliberation to reach a verdict: "Death by Misadventure." The longest coroner's inquest in the colony's history was concluded with its shortest jury deliberation. The swiftness of the verdict was so surprising many of the reporters were caught off-guard. They had gone outside for a smoke break. At 11:15 a.m. on September 24, 1973, Judge Tung accepted the verdict and announced that the inquest into the death of Bruce Lee was officially closed.

For the public, it remained open. Many fans were reminded of the opening scene of *Fist of Fury* where Lee falls grief-stricken on the coffin of his dead kung fu master. "Would you tell me what teacher died of?" Bruce's character asks bitterly in that scene.

"It was pneumonia," a fellow student replies.

"And you believe that?"

The grief-stricken Chinese public could not accept that their invincible hero, a thirty-two-year-old man at the height of his physical powers, had died from an aspirin. While the inquest had achieved the government's goal of quelling the more extreme outbursts (there were no more protests or bomb threats), Bruce's death remained a hot topic of debate. The jury had ruled on the manner of death—Misadventure—but not the cause. On that subject, Bruce's fans, who read the inquest transcripts published every day in the papers, could see that the experts were bitterly divided. The judge, coroner, and famous pathologist had argued for hypersensitivity to aspirin. Two of Bruce's Hong Kong doctors believed it was cannabis. And his American neurologist was convinced the cause was still unknown. Given the conflicting expert opinions, new theories and speculation were published in magazines and newspapers. When Linda Lee and Betty Ting Pei showed up together at a test screening of *Enter the Dragon*, it only added grist to the rumor mill, even causing some to suspect a murder plot.

To this day, there is no consensus on the cause of Bruce Lee's death. "Without a doubt, the most widely asked question which has been addressed to me over the years has been 'How did Bruce Lee die?' " says Linda Lee.

On July 20, 1973, Bruce Lee died from heat stroke. It is the most plausible scientific theory for his death. Consider the timeline.

Ten weeks earlier on May 10, 1973, Bruce Lee collapsed after working in a boiling hot room. He displayed multiple symptoms of central nervous system dysfunction (nausea, vomiting, staggering, collapse), and his temperature was dangerously elevated—the two diagnostic criteria for hyperthermia. Bruce had a long history of being vulnerable to heat. His risk factor was increased by sleep deprivation, extreme weight loss, and the recent surgical removal of his armpit sweat glands.

July 20, 1973, was the hottest day of the month in tropical Hong Kong. In Betty Ting Pei's small apartment, Bruce demonstrated scene after kung fu scene from *Game of Death*. "In telling the story, he acted out the whole thing," Raymond Chow says. "So, that probably made him a little tired and thirsty. After a few sips he seemed to be a little dizzy." Just like on May 10, Bruce exerted himself in a hot enclosed space and ended up feeling faint and suffering from a headache—two early signs of heat stroke. He wandered into Betty's bedroom, fell onto her bed, and never got up again. "A person who has suffered one heat stroke is at increased risk for another," says Dr. Lisa Leon, an expert in hyperthermia at the U.S. Army Research Institute of Environmental Medicine. "Patients experience multi-organ dysfunction during the hours, days, and weeks of recovery, which increases risk for long-term disability and death."

Of the minor drugs in Bruce's stomach on July 20, neither cannabis nor meprobamate is known to cause cerebral edema. The only possible suspect is aspirin. The Mayo Clinic lists the potential reactions to aspirin as "hives, itchy skin, runny nose, red eyes, swelling of lips, tongue or face, coughing, wheezing, shortness of breath, and anaphylaxis—a rare, life-threatening allergic reaction." More commonly caused by bee stings and peanut allergies, anaphylaxis can result in fatal cerebral edema. When Professor Teare and Dr. Lycette were theorizing about hypersensitivity to aspirin, they were talking about anaphylactic shock.

But anaphylaxis, a severe allergic reaction, is almost always accompanied by other symptoms—an enflamed trachea, neck, tongue, and lips, as well as hives and red itchy skin in and around the mouth. In fatal cases, the swelling of the throat blocks the airway resulting in asphyxia and cerebral edema. The paramedics and doctors who treated Bruce the night of July 20 did not find any inflammation of Bruce's tongue or throat. Nor did the coroner, Dr. Lycette, during the autopsy. Bruce Lee was a hard-core martial artist who took aspirin for pain most of his adult life. While it is possible he suddenly developed a life-threatening allergy to aspirin at the age of thirty-two, the odds that he died from anaphylactic shock without any of the associated symptoms are vanishingly small.

Compared to aspirin allergies, heat stroke is a far more common killer of young athletic men. It is the third most common cause of sudden death in sports activities and rises to first during the hottest months of summer. In the United States alone, an average of three high school and college football players die every year of heat stroke. Korey Stringer, a twenty-seven-year-old professional football player, collapsed on a Minnesota Vikings practice field on a sweltering July afternoon in 2001. His death prompted immediate changes regarding heat stroke prevention throughout the NFL. There was even less awareness of hyperthermia's dangers in 1973 than 2001. Even now proper treatment is not known by every physician.

While it is impossible to know for certain what caused Lee's death, hyperthermia is the most likely explanation. If it was heat stroke, then Bruce Lee died doing what he loved most—performing kung fu in front of an appreciative audience.

From the moment he was cast in his first movie as a two-month-old, Bruce Lee spent his time on this earth entertaining and educating others. With an intensity rarely seen before or since, Never Sits Still squeezed an entire lifetime's worth of accomplishments into thirty-two short years. His death was not a tragedy, because his life was a triumph. "Even though I, Bruce Lee, may die someday without fulfilling all of my ambitions, I feel no sorrow," he told a Hong Kong reporter in 1972 as if anticipating his own eulogy. "I did what I wanted to do. What I've done, I've done with sincerity and to the best of my ability. You can't expect much more from life."

A contestant in the Bruce Lee Talent Search at Burbank Studios, California, circa 1978. *(Frank Edwards/Getty Images)*

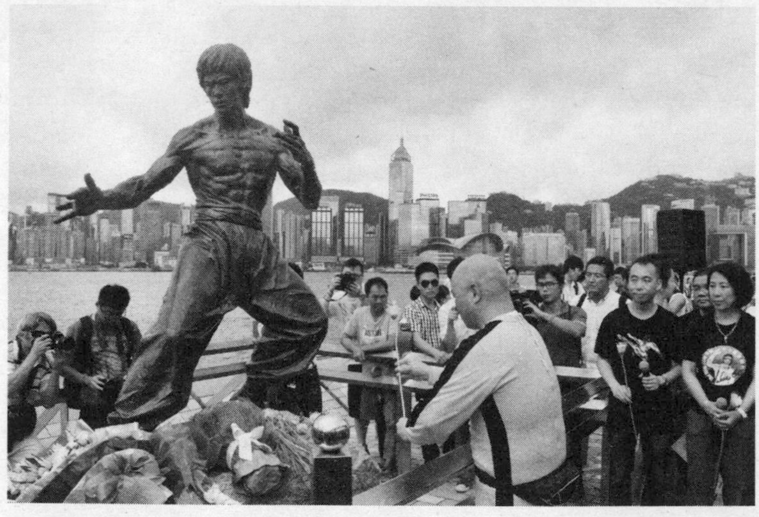

Fans place flowers at Lee's bronze statue in Hong Kong on the fortieth anniversary of his death, July 20, 2013. *(Kyodo News/Getty Images)*

epilogue

the legend

In August 1973, two teams of Chinese lion dancers paraded down Hollywood Boulevard toward Grauman's Chinese Theatre for the Los Angeles premiere of *Enter the Dragon*. A raucous crowd, which had begun to form the night before, wrapped around the block. "Riding in the back of the limousine, I saw lines and lines of people, and the lines didn't end," remembers John Saxon, who played Roper. "I asked my driver, 'What's going on?' and he said, 'That's your movie.' "

Saxon wasn't the only one sucker-punched by *Enter the Dragon*'s success. Even New York critics, who wrung their hands at the film's violence, sensed its power. *The New York Times* declared, "The picture is expertly made and well meshed; it moves like lightning and brims with color. It is also the most savagely murderous and numbing hand-hacker (not a gun in it) you will ever see anywhere." In *The Village Voice*, William Paul confessed, "In my most civilized right-thinking frame of mind, I'd like to dismiss the film as abhorrently grotesque masculine fantasy, but I have to admit that deep down in the most shadowy recesses of my subconscious the fantasy struck a responsive chord."

Enter the Dragon struck a responsive chord across the globe. Made for a minuscule $850,000, it would gross $90 million worldwide in 1973 and go on to earn an estimated $350 million over the next forty-five years. Fred Weintraub joked that the movie was so profitable the studio even had to pay him. Michael Allin recalls, "Warner's lawyer sent me a letter saying, 'The picture will be well into profit'—and here's the phrase I love—'by anybody's formula.' The picture made so much money they could not sweep it under the rug. The rug had too big a bulge."

Released less than a month after Lee's two funerals, *Enter the Dragon* made him in death what he stated as his "Definite Chief Aim" in life—the first and highest-paid Oriental superstar in the United States. It also made him bigger than Steve McQueen. While filming *Enter the Dragon,* Lee told Weintraub his goal was for their film to be more successful than McQueen's *The Getaway,* then also in production. "If I could send Bruce a telegram in heaven," said Weintraub, "it would read *Dragon* outgrossed *Getaway* everywhere."

While the TV series *Kung Fu* and Shaw Brothers' *Five Fingers of Death,* released on March 21, 1973, cracked open the door, it was Lee's performance in *Enter the Dragon* that blew it off its hinges—launching an entirely new genre of film in the West. Cheaply made Hong Kong kung fu flicks, what *Variety* would call "chopsocky," became a cultural phenomenon, breaking out of the urban grindhouses into suburban multiplexes. "Everybody was kung fu fighting," sang one-hit wonderboy Carl Douglas, "Those cats were fast as lightning." His 1974 song "Kung Fu Fighting" sold eleven million copies. In New York City, there were as many as thirty different Hong Kong flicks playing at one time.

All of Bruce's previous Golden Harvest movies—*The Big Boss, Fist of Fury,* and *Way of the Dragon*—received wide releases and grossed nearly $50 million. Three episodes of *The Green Hornet* were stitched together, prefaced with footage from Lee's screen test, and released as a theatrical movie in November 1974. "Mr. Lee, who played Kato, the kung fu artist and faithful houseboy to the Green Hornet (Van Williams), gets star billing now as the result of the huge popularity of the kung fu films he made in Hong Kong before his death last year," wrote Vincent Canby in *The New York Times.*

Since Bruce died before he became internationally famous, fans were ravenous for details about his life. "I knew so little about him and wanted to know so much," wrote a young woman from New Jersey to *Black Belt* magazine. "Suddenly, he is dead, and I just can't accept it. It's as if I knew him, and now I never will." Hundreds of fan magazines were published with fictionalized accounts of his heroic deeds. More than a half dozen memorial albums and quickie biographies were cranked out. There was even a tacky biopic, *The Dragon Dies Hard* (1975), which asserted that Lee got his martial arts start when some hoods tried to muscle in on his *Washington Post* newspaper delivery route.

An entire posthumous industry was born in 1973, complete with merchandising—pendants, action figures, T-shirts, sweatshirts, and posters of Bruce Lee to place on dorm room walls next to Che Guevara. Martial arts magazines, like *Black Belt* and *Fighting Stars*, once small-scale newssheets, became glossy publications, complete with mail-order advertisements for anything from a $132 stainless steel tri-fork to a $5.95 Bruce Lee Punching Puppet. Even Robert Lee attempted to cash in with a folk album dedicated to his brother, *The Ballad of Bruce Lee*. "Not since James Dean died in the crash of his silver-grey Porsche," wrote Kenneth Turan, the movie critic for the *Los Angeles Times*, "has any Hollywood star received this kind of send-off to Valhalla."

Bruce Lee became the Patron Saint of Kung Fu, worshipped like a demigod. Japanese teenagers cut their hair like his. The Taiwanese called him "The Man with the Golden Singing Legs," the British "The King of Kung Fu," and the Australians "The Fastest Fists in the East." Elvis Presley watched *Enter the Dragon* dozens of times and began production on his own self-financed martial arts film, which he never completed. The title of a top disco song in India was "Here's to That Swell Guy, Bruce Lee." For the rest of the decade, *Enter the Dragon* was repeatedly rereleased and each time it landed among the five top-grossing pictures of the week. A theater in Iran played the film daily until the government was overthrown in 1979. VHS tapes of *Enter the Dragon* were smuggled into Eastern Europe in the 1980s, turning Bruce Lee into a symbol of resistance to Communism.

With missionary zeal, Bruce had set out to use the medium of movies to promote the martial arts. He succeeded beyond his wildest expectations. Before Lee's death, there were fewer than five hundred martial arts schools in the world; by the late 1990s, because of his influence, there were more than twenty million martial arts students in the United States alone. In Britain, there was so much demand that crowds four-abreast would line up in the street outside the handful of commercial schools and literally throw money at the teacher to ensure a place in the next session. "Bruce Lee was, and always will be, the main reason why I must strive to reach perfection in the martial arts in my years to come," wrote a boy from South Carolina to *Black Belt* magazine.

While the rest of the world was falling in love with the late Bruce Lee, Hong Kong was experiencing a hangover. Lee had risen to superstardom in the colony as the defender of the Chinese people, their hero. His sudden death, mired in scandal, left them bereft and disturbed. "A lot of people still loved him," says W. Wong, the president of the Bruce Lee Fan Club, "but because his death was less than glorious, many felt deceived and betrayed. They felt empty because of the loss of an icon."

This disillusionment was reflected in disappointing box office numbers for *Enter the Dragon* in Hong Kong. It earned HK$3 million—the same as *The Big Boss* but two million less than *Way of the Dragon*. Even in death Bruce was still the biggest box office draw in the colony, but his fame had crested and was falling. "He's already dead," said one Chinese fan. "What's the point?"

For Hong Kong filmmakers, the point was Bruce Lee's golden punch had smashed the barrier to international markets. Prior to Bruce, Hong Kong's movie industry was the equivalent of Nigeria's today, a profitable but parochial backyard business. "After Bruce Lee, we had a great opportunity to draw attention, especially from Hollywood," says John Woo, director of *Face/Off* (1997) and *Mission: Impossible 2* (2000). "He opened the door. People around the world really started to pay attention to Chinese action movies, and the talent."

Bruce saved Golden Harvest and shattered Shaw's monopoly. "Run Run had deep pockets and owned the theaters. His strategy was to strangle Golden Harvest and bleed us to death with lawsuits," says Andre Morgan. "Bruce broke us into international markets with kung fu. It was unheard of. We could finally sell to Europe, South America, North America, and the Middle East. Raymond Chow had a pipeline of money coming in. Because we had done *Enter the Dragon*, other people were interested in doing co-productions."

Immediately, the search began for the next Bruce Lee. Anyone associated with him was signed to a movie contract and thrust in front of the cameras. Chuck Norris was the white Bruce Lee, Sammo Hung the chubby Bruce Lee, and Jackie Chan the funny Bruce Lee. None of them could topple Lee as a box office champion and international icon. Jackie Chan tried and failed to make it in America with *The Big Brawl* (1980), directed by Robert Clouse and co-produced by Raymond Chow and Fred Weintraub. It wasn't until twenty-five years after *Enter the Dragon* that Jackie finally became Hong Kong's second crossover star with *Rush Hour* (1998).

Shady independent Hong Kong producers who couldn't afford Norris, Chan, or Hung sought to cash in on the Lee phenomenon by hiring Bruce Lee look-alike actors (Lee-alikes) and changing their names to trick audiences: Bruce Li, Bruce Le, Bruce Lai, Bruce Liang, Bruce Thai, and Bronson Lee. These Bruceploitation films initially ripped off the titles and plots from his original films—*Return of Fists of Fury*, *Re-Enter the Dragon*, *Enter Another Dragon*. By the late 1970s, they gradually became their own genre, turning Bruce into a comic book superhero in flicks like *The Dragon Lives Again* (where Lee descends into Hell to fight James Bond and Dracula) and *Clones of Bruce Lee* (where Bruce Le, Bruce Lai, Dragon Lee, and Bruce Thai play four Bruce Lee clones saving the world from an army of invincible bronze men).

The best of the Bruceploitation genre turned out to be *Game of Death* (1978). Raymond Chow claims he never wanted to use the pagoda scenes Bruce had filmed in 1972 as part of a full-length movie, but distributors across the world begged him. Robert Clouse was hired to direct. Two Lee-alikes were cast—the Acting Bruce Lee and the Action Bruce Lee. Since Bruce never finished the script, a story was cobbled together like a jigsaw puzzle working backward from the finished scenes. The resulting creaky plot revolved around Billy Lo, a stuntman who refuses to sign a talent contract with the shadowy "syndicate." After they shoot him in the face and leave him for dead, he gets reconstructive surgery, fakes his demise, and takes revenge from beyond the grave. Raymond included footage from Lee's actual Hong Kong funeral in 1973. It's an uncomfortable mess until the final act switches to Lee's original footage with Dan Inosanto and Kareem Abdul-Jabbar. Suddenly, the movie is magic and a reminder why no one can ever replace Bruce Lee.

Fans across the globe ate it up. "The Rio opening was huge, one of the biggest they've ever had," Andre Morgan told reporters. "It's breaking records in Sao Paolo. Business is very, very good in Germany, and it was the number-five grosser in Japan last year, earning $8 million." Linda Lee had originally objected to using the word "Death" in the title but eventually embraced the movie. At the Los Angeles premiere held at the Paramount Theatre on June 7, 1979, she attended with fourteen-year-old Brandon and ten-year-old Shannon. Over a thousand loyal fans, dressed in traditional martial arts uniforms, held up their martial arts school banners. Mayor Tom Brady declared it Bruce Lee Day. Brandon unveiled a thirty-foot long display containing original costumes and weapons from his father's previous film roles. Bruce Lee's final project, however bastardized, was complete.

After Bruce's funeral in Seattle in 1973, Linda placed her children in the care of her sister, Joan, in Calgary while she returned to Hong Kong for the coroner's inquest. She soon discovered that Bruce had died without having drawn a will. This oversight added a complicated legal morass—an American citizen dying in a British colony—on top of an emotional and financial one. When Bruce passed, he did not have much money, but he was owed a lot. It took seven years to probate his estate. During that time, Linda and her lawyers had to negotiate with Raymond Chow and the life insurance companies. "My mom was going back and forth to Hong Kong quite a bit in the first year to take care of a lot of business," says Shannon Lee.

After things settled down a bit, Linda and the kids briefly stayed with her mother in Seattle. A few months at home reminded Linda of how much she missed Southern California. With proceeds from the estate, they moved into the affluent Los Angeles suburb of Rancho Palos Verdes. For a brief period, Chuck Norris lived two streets down. Brandon often played with Norris's two sons. Shannon and Brandon were enrolled in a private school, Rolling Hills Country Day. Linda took night classes in political science at California State University in Long Beach to complete her college degree. She eventually graduated and became a kindergarten teacher.

Her most pleasant surprise in the year following Bruce's death was the reaction of fans to *Enter the Dragon*. "When he first passed away," Linda told the *Los Angeles Times*, "we had no idea that he would become as legendary as he has." As the posthumous Bruce Lee industry sprang to life in 1973, Linda entered into the lucrative dead celebrity business, seeking to protect his legacy and profit from it on behalf of her children. She inked a book and movie deal with Warner Bros. Her paperback biography, *Bruce Lee: The Man Only I Knew* (1975), did well, but the biopic fell apart before it began production. She signed with the Ziv International agency to license Bruce's image and likeness to manufacturers of posters, T-shirts, beach towels, stationery, trophies, lamps, men's cosmetics, karate garments, dishware, glassware, jewelry, games, and toys. Zebra Books became the exclusive paperback publisher of Bruce Lee books, including *Bruce Lee's Basic Kung-Fu Training Manual* and *Bruce Lee's My Martial Arts Training Guide to Jeet Kune Do*. In death, Bruce had secured the financial future of his family.

The children lived a quiet upper-middle-class life, largely sheltered from their father's fame. They didn't study martial arts. Linda would say to them, "Don't go around telling people you're Bruce Lee's kid. Let people get to know you for who you are first."

Shannon was more like her mother: studious, sensitive, and shy. She came into her own in high school when she discovered musical theater. She attended Tulane University in New Orleans, where she majored in music and graduated in four years.

Brandon was very much his father's son. When he was eight, he told his mother he was going to grow up to be an actor. "He was a prankster, a practical joker, a daredevil, a showman," says Shannon. "He was extremely physically coordinated. One day he decided he wanted to be able to do a backflip. He had it by the third time." Brandon was also a charismatic rebel, who got expelled from his elite private high school, Chadwick, after leading protests against the administration. "He started convincing students not to go to class," Shannon recalls. He got his GED and attended Emerson College in Boston but spent all his time going to New York City in search of acting gigs. After a year, Brandon quit and moved back to Los Angeles.

All of Linda's efforts to dissuade Brandon from an acting career failed. He rented a tiny bungalow in Silver Lake, bought a Harley and a 1959 Cadillac hearse, and performed in little plays around town.

One of his girlfriends teased him, "You're not doing the whole James Dean thing are you?"

"Baby, I'm a lot more original than James Dean," he replied.

Twenty-year-old Brandon didn't want to follow in his father's footsteps and make action movies. He wanted to be a dramatic actor, but no one would hire the handsome son of Bruce Lee for serious roles. To jump-start his career, he agreed to make a few low-budget martial arts flicks. He went to his father's former assistant instructor, Dan Inosanto, for Jeet Kune Do lessons.

His first big break was, ironically enough, in *Kung Fu: The Movie* (1986). Brandon was cast opposite David Carradine as the son of Kwai Chang Caine. Over the next five years, he made several chop-socky flicks, culminating with 20th Century Fox's actioner, *Rapid Fire* (1992). During filming, Brandon hired Shannon to be his personal assistant. She had been banging around New Orleans for a couple years after graduation, singing in bands. Shannon asked her big brother about getting into acting. "It's a tough business," Brandon told her. "People treat you like a commodity, especially if you are a woman, but if you really want to do this, I'll help you in any way I can."

That same year, Universal Studios began developing *Dragon: The Bruce Lee Story*, which was based on an updated version of Linda's biography of Bruce that she rereleased in 1989. Universal optioned the book and signed a multimillion-dollar deal for the movie, video game, and merchandising rights to Bruce Lee. Rob Cohen was hired to direct, and Jason Scott Lee (no relation) to play Bruce. Cohen hewed fairly closely to Linda's version of her late husband's life. The film is a laudatory love story about an optimistic young immigrant and his adoring wife as he struggles to overcome a racially stratified system to achieve greatness. Wong Jack Man is portrayed as an evil enforcer sent to shut down Bruce's school for the high crime of teaching kung fu to white people. Bruce comes up with the idea for the TV series *Kung Fu*, but it is stolen from him and given to a white actor, David Carradine.

Since the controversy surrounding Bruce's death was off-limits, Cohen's one literary invention was an inner demon—a phantom in black samurai armor that haunts Bruce's dreams throughout the film. In the third-act finale, the demon goes after a young Brandon forcing Bruce to defeat it with a red nunchaku. Cohen justified the conceit as a metaphor about Bruce's struggle for inner peace, but it played into one of the superstitions surrounding Lee's death: The Curse of the Dragon.

Before filming of the movie began, Universal approached Brandon about playing his father, but he quickly rejected the idea. His father's legend was already a heavy enough burden without that weight. For years, he had felt like little more than a comma: Bruce's son, Brandon. Instead he landed the part he desperately wanted as the star of *The Crow*, a comic book–based story of a rock musician who returns from the grave to avenge his own murder. It was the film Brandon hoped would propel him out of the chop-socky ghetto into a mainstream movie career.

Production of *The Crow* was plagued by misfortunes. Unseasonably bad storms in Wilmington, North Carolina, destroyed some of the sets. A carpenter was electrocuted and severely burned when a crane collided with overhead power lines. A construction worker accidentally drove a screwdriver through his hand. A disgruntled employee crashed his truck into the studio's plaster shop. The situation was bad enough that *Entertainment Weekly* ran a story asking if the movie was jinxed. "I don't think this is exceptional," responded Jennifer Roth, the production coordinator. "We have a lot of stunts and effects, and I've been on productions before where people have died."

A month later while filming the last scenes of the movie, Brandon Lee was shot and killed.

By all accounts, including a police investigation, it was a freak accident, a terrible mistake—the result of inexperience, negligence, and corner cutting. "They wanted to make a $30 million movie," one disenchanted crewmember said after quitting the film, "but they only wanted to spend $12 million to do it."

For an early scene in the movie, the second unit asked the props department to provide a .44 Magnum revolver and six dummy rounds for a close-up shot. The inexperienced property master realized there weren't any dummy rounds on-set. To save valuable time, the decision was made to manufacture dummy rounds from live ones. The slugs were pulled off the casings of six live .44 bullets and the propellant disposed of. The casings were then loaded into the cylinder and the weapon repeatedly fired to discharge the primers and clear any powder residue. The slugs were reattached to the empty casings to create dummy bullets.

But, unbeknownst to the props department, one of the primers failed to detonate. When the gun was fired during the scene, the dummy bullet with a live primer triggered the powder residue with just enough force to propel the slug into the barrel of the Magnum, but no further. Afterward, the gun was returned to the props department, unchecked, for storage.

Two weeks later on March 30, 1993, the same gun with a slug lodged in its barrel was retrieved for a flashback scene where Brandon's character, Eric Draven, is murdered. The .44 Magnum was loaded with full-strength blanks—the casing of a bullet with propellant and primer but no slug. Once again, no one examined the gun. With a slug stuck in the barrel and blanks in the cylinder, it was for all practical purposes a loaded weapon. The revolver was handed to the actor Michael Massee, who played Draven's killer, Funboy. The director called, "Action." Massee pointed the gun at Lee's torso and pulled the trigger.

For a couple of minutes, no one realized something had gone horribly wrong.

An ambulance rushed Brandon to New Hanover Regional Medical Center. Despite operating for hours and transfusing more than sixty pints of blood, the surgeons were unable to save him. The damage was too extensive; the .44 slug had lodged next to his spine. Brandon Lee died of internal bleeding at 1:04 p.m. on March 31, 1993, at the age of twenty-eight.

He had planned, after filming wrapped on *The Crow*, to marry his fiancée, Eliza Hutton. The wedding was to take place April 17 in Mexico. Instead Brandon was buried on April 3 next to his father in Seattle in the plot Andre Morgan had purchased twenty years prior for Linda. "It is beyond my realm of cosmic thinking to think that it was meant to be," Linda said. "It just happened. I'm not beginning to make sense of it. I just think we were fortunate that he had as many years as he did. They say time cures anything. It doesn't. You just learn to live with it and go on."

As part of the publicity campaign for *Dragon: The Bruce Lee Story*, Bruce was given a star on the Hollywood Walk of Fame before a celebrity premiere of the movie on April 28, 1993. Speaking at the unveiling, Linda, who has an unbreakable spirit, urged the film community to take safety measures to make certain what happened to Brandon never occurred again. "Brandon very much wanted to be here," she went on to say. "He wanted to come back especially for this ceremony because, he said, his father deserved it, as well he did. We are here today to celebrate the life of Bruce Lee. And even though our happiness is tinged with sorrow for Brandon's absence, we are doubly delighted that the movie *Dragon* will be premiering tonight."

And so Brandon's death was wrapped up in Bruce's legacy. Brandon gave a breakout performance in *The Crow*—sensitive, wry, and fierce. "Lee is sensational on all counts in a performance that brims over with athleticism and ardor," wrote Peter Travers in *Rolling Stone*. The movie became a cult classic, grossing $50 million. But it was not enough to escape his father's shadow. "If Brandon had lived and made 50 great films," said Alex Ben Block, who wrote the first Bruce Lee biography, "then no one would much remember the Bruce Lee connection except as some minor footnote. But I'm afraid he is inextricably linked with his father forever." It was the son's story that became a footnote to the father's legend.

After Brandon's death, Shannon followed in her brother's footsteps, taking acting classes and studying Jeet Kune Do with Ted Wong, Bruce's protégé. "It was very difficult," she recalls, "because the timing of it all was so awful." Most starlets cut their teeth in horror films; as the daughter of Bruce Lee, Shannon started, like her brother, in chop-socky. "It's amazingly fortunate to be who I am," Shannon says, "and at the same time it can be somewhat limiting."

Her first movie, *Cage II: The Arena of Death* (1994), went straight to video. Then she costarred in *High Voltage* (1997), a slight step up in the genre. "I had a hard time putting my heart into those projects," Shannon says. "And because of that, I'm not very good in those movies. I was still in so much grief from my brother's death."

Her next part was in a Golden Harvest action flick, *Enter the Eagles* (1998), a riff on *Enter the Dragon*. They filmed in Prague. There was no script. It was chaos. "Just do it like your dad would do it," the director would say to her. "I felt so much pressure to carry on the legacy," Shannon recalls. "I would go back to my hotel room and cry a lot." After that film, Shannon's acting career stalled.

Almost as soon as he invented Jeet Kune Do in 1968, Bruce came to regret giving it a name. He could not escape the paradox that his constantly evolving "Style of No Style" was actually a coherent system with specific techniques and principles. Bruce gradually grew so concerned that Jeet Kune Do would be codified and formalized, resulting in the enslavement rather than the liberation of students, that he closed down his Chinatown school on January 29, 1970. He made his assistant instructors—Dan Inosanto in Los Angeles, James Lee in Oakland, and Taky Kimura in Seattle—promise they would never teach Jeet Kune Do in a commercial school. They could only instruct a handful of senior students informally in backyard settings.

As a result, after Bruce died and became an international icon, the hundreds of thousands of fans who wanted to become just like him had nowhere to go to learn Jeet Kune Do. Instead they flooded into whatever dojo was available to study karate, judo, Tae Kwon Do, and kung fu. During the greatest boom in martial arts history, Inosanto and Kimura kept their word and only taught privately. (James Lee died from lung cancer in December 1972.)

But a number of Bruce's other students, like Jesse Glover and Joe Lewis, leveraged their connection to Bruce to give seminars across the country. Eventually Dan Inosanto opened his own commercial school and taught his personalized version of the martial arts—a mixture of Bruce's Jeet Kune Do, Filipino Kali, and Thai kickboxing. Having appeared with Bruce in *Game of Death*, Inosanto quickly became the most recognized Jeet Kune Do instructor in the country with his mix-and-match approach referred to as Jeet Kune Do Concepts.

Linda, who had inscribed on Bruce's tombstone "Founder of Jeet Kune Do," was less ambivalent about his creation and anxious to protect it. Over the years a number of enterprising grifters, who had no connection to Lee, opened studios claiming to be authentic instructors of Jeet Kune Do. Linda felt they were damaging Bruce's legacy. On January 10, 1996, she invited Bruce's original students to a meeting in Seattle to form an organization to preserve Lee's art. The charter members, including Linda Lee, Shannon Lee, Taky Kimura, Allen Joe, and Ted Wong, became known as the Nucleus. Dan Inosanto attended the first meeting but decided he didn't want to be involved. This created a schism between Original Jeet Kune Do advocates (the conservatives who favored the Nucleus and strict adherence to what Bruce Lee taught in his lifetime) and the Concepts group (the progressives who preferred Inosanto's organization and a continual development of the art).

Martial arts instructors are a notoriously fractious, backbiting lot. It is a tribute to the universal respect in which Linda is held, and her experience as a kindergarten teacher, that she was able to unify a large portion of Bruce's students. Along with the publication of the *Bruce Lee Magazine*, the Nucleus's main activity was an annual Jeet Kune Do seminar where fans could train with his original students. The seminars were a hit with the public, but the squabbling between Nucleus members was exhausting.

After four years of refereeing the infighting, Linda decided to retire and turn the Bruce Lee Estate over to Shannon. "She approached me very gingerly," says Shannon, "because she didn't want to thrust this on me and say, 'This is your responsibility.' " Shannon was enthusiastic. Her acting career was winding down. She felt more could be done to promote Bruce's legacy and turn it into a thriving business. The Elvis Presley Estate was making over $50 million per year; Bruce Lee's less than a million.

Shannon hired the Presley Estate's lawyers and took a more aggressive approach to the dead celebrity business. She effectively disbanded the Nucleus, which was losing money. She engaged in a decadelong battle to wrestle the merchandising, licensing, and video game rights back from Universal Studios. She also established a production company, LeeWay Media, to develop Bruce Lee–specific projects: documentaries, biopics, TV series, and Broadway musicals. Along with keeping Bruce in the public's consciousness and spreading his message, one of her major goals was to make the Forbes list of Top-Earning Dead Celebrities.

The Forbes ranking is the dollar-and-cents metric of an icon's continuing star power. For years, the top five names and their earnings have been remarkably stable: Michael Jackson ($150 million), Elvis Presley ($55 million), Charles Schulz ($40 million), Elizabeth Taylor ($20 million), and Bob Marley ($18 million). In 2013, Bruce Lee became the first Asian celebrity to ever crack the list, landing in tenth place with $7 million. He was one spot behind Steve McQueen ($9 million)—continuing their rivalry into the afterlife. The next year, an endorsement deal with Mazda helped Bruce tie McQueen for ninth place with $9 million. One imagines them in heaven teasing each other over who is the bigger star.

For decades, the Hong Kong government ignored its most famous son. The kung fu star was not considered highbrow enough for a colony anxious about its self-image. Lobbying efforts by fans to turn his former home in Kowloon Tong, which was operating as a rent-by-the-hour love motel, into a museum came to naught. In frustration, the Bruce Lee Fan Club raised US$100,000 to construct a statue of Lee in a pose from *Fist of Fury*. Under pressure, officials finally agreed to place it on the Avenue of Stars, a tourist attraction on the city's harbor front. Robert Lee helped unveil the eight-foot bronze statue of his big brother on November 27, 2005, celebrating what would have been Bruce's sixty-fifth birthday. It was a belated recognition of Lee's remarkable achievements during his short life and lasting cultural impact since his death.

In an America where Chinese actors were mostly relegated to meek houseboy roles like Hop Sing in *Bonanza*, Bruce Lee overcame every obstacle in his ambition to break Hollywood's yellow glass ceiling. He became the first Chinese American male actor to star in a Hollywood movie and the first Asian since the advent of sound. It took a quarter of a century before another Chinese actor, Jackie Chan, was able to repeat this extraordinary feat.

His films launched an entirely new Chinese archetype into Western popular culture: the kung fu master. Prior to Bruce, it was only Fu Manchu, the Yellow Peril villain, and Charlie Chan, the model minority. These two tired representations reinforced the stereotype of the Chinese male as submissive, non-aggressive, and physically and sexually inferior—weak and sniveling; wily but never openly confrontational; effeminate, sexless, or gay. Smashing this emasculated image, Lee constructed a masculinity that was physically superior, excessively violent, and sexually enticing. He was the first Asian American actor to embody the classic Hollywood definition of a star—men wanted to be him and women wanted to be *with* him. With his cocky smile, come-fight-me hand gestures, and graceful but deadly moves, the chiseled Lee gave Chinese guys balls.

His pugnacious performance in *Enter the Dragon* immediately transformed Western perceptions of Asians. "We lived in Alameda, near Oakland, where the Black Panthers came from," recalls Leon Jay, a prominent martial arts instructor. "Before *Enter the Dragon*, it was 'Hey, Chink,' and after Bruce's movies came out it was like, 'Hey, brother.' " Even people who didn't like Bruce personally concede the influence his films had. "He was a self-centered asshole," says Mark Chow, Ruby Chow's son. "One thing the guy's done, though, is that nobody takes lunch money away from Chinese kids anymore because they assume they won't fight back."

As a result, Bruce's films helped change Asians' self-perception. If Bruce could defeat Chuck Norris on film, maybe they could do something similar in real life. Lee's popularity helped inspire the Asian American movement in the 1970s, which called for racial equality, social justice, and political empowerment. In Asia, his films presaged the rise of a more muscular and confident Hong Kong, Taiwan, and eventually China. The Chinese were no longer the Sick Men of Asia; they were a superpower.

Lee transformed Western filmmaking. He introduced an entirely new genre, the kung fu film, which continues to thrive, as evidenced by *The Matrix*, *Kill Bill*, and *John Wick*. His impact was even greater on fight choreography. *Enter the Dragon* not only changed who could star in action movies but how our heroes fought. Gone was the John Wayne punch. After *Enter the Dragon*, we required every action star—from Batman to Sherlock Holmes, from Mel Gibson in *Lethal Weapon* to Matt Damon in *The Bourne Identity*—to be a martial arts master, as skilled with his feet as he is with his fists.

They also needed to be ripped. Bruce popularized the physical fitness movement. Prior to his films, barrel chests were the masculine ideal. Afterward Hollywood action heroes first flirted with the pumped, steroidal look of Arnold Schwarzenegger and Sylvester Stallone before returning to the shredded, six-pack physicality Lee embodied.

Bruce was not simply an entertainer; he was an evangelist. Through the popular medium of films, he single-handedly introduced more people to Asian culture than any other person in history. Because of Bruce, millions of Westerners took up the martial arts. "Every town in America had a church and a beauty parlor," said Fred Weintraub. "After *Enter the Dragon*, there was a church, a beauty parlor, and a karate studio with a picture of Bruce Lee." Many devoted martial arts students went on to explore the Chinese philosophical underpinnings of their styles. Taoist terms like "yin" and "yang" entered the lexicon.

Ultimate Fighting Championship promoter Dana White has called Bruce Lee "the godfather of Mixed Martial Arts." Certainly the sport could never have succeeded without the incredible burst in popularity Lee inspired. Jeet Kune Do was an early hybrid experiment in martial arts cross-training. His pragmatic philosophical approach undergirds the sport: "Adapt what is useful, reject what is useless, add what is specifically your own." Bruce put the "mixed" into mixed martial arts.

But perhaps most important in this age of polarization and ethnic strife is the example he set and espoused. As a Eurasian, he faced discrimination from both sides of the East/West divide. He never let it stop him. Instead he preached a message of post-racial unity. "I think of myself as a human being, because under the sky, there is but one family," Bruce said. "It just so happens that people are different." And he practiced it. He accepted anyone who wanted to learn from him. His first student in America was Jesse Glover. "If he felt you were sincere, Bruce taught you," Taky Kimura recalls. "He didn't care what race you were."

The Hong Kong statue of Bruce Lee was the second erected in the world. The first was unveiled a day earlier in, of all places, the city of Mostar in Bosnia-Herzegovina. During the Yugoslav Civil War in the 1990s, Mostar became bitterly divided between Catholic Croats on the west side of town and the Muslim Bosniaks on the east side. After hostilities officially ended, the city decided to erect a new peace memorial. Bruce Lee was chosen over rival nominees, including the Pope and Gandhi, after a poll of residents revealed that he was the only person respected by both sides as a symbol of solidarity, justice, and racial harmony. "We will always be Muslims, Serbs, or Croats," said Veselin Gatalo of the youth group Urban Movement Mostar. "But one thing we all have in common is Bruce Lee."

afterword

I was twelve years old when my friend's family bought the first VCR in our hometown of Topeka, Kansas. I vividly remember sitting on his basement couch as my friend's older brother walked down the stairs with a tape in his hand.

The movie was *Enter the Dragon*, and it blew our minds.

We had never seen a kung fu movie before. We had no idea who Bruce Lee was. But after the movie was over, he was our hero, jumping off the screen into our imaginations. This five-foot-seven, 135-pound Chinese dude with a chiseled physique and feline swagger replaced Luke Skywalker as our ideal of total badass-ness. We put down our light sabers and picked up nunchaku, cracking ourselves in the skulls repeatedly as we tried and failed to learn how to use them.

As the spotlight of my friends' hero worship moved on to other movie, pop, and sports stars, I stuck with Bruce—someone who beneath his muscles looked as fragile and vulnerable as I felt as a skinny bullied kid; someone who was not born a deadly fighter, but who had through sheer willpower turned himself into one. I found scratched tapes of Bruce's three previous Hong Kong movies—*The Big Boss*, *Fist of Fury*, and *Way of the Dragon*—and rewound the fight scenes over and over again until they were barely watchable. I haunted the drugstores and bought copies of *Black Belt* or *Inside Kung-Fu* magazine whenever he was on the cover. I memorized every detail, many of them fanciful, about his tragically short thirty-two years of life.

In college I took up Chinese and studied the philosophers who influenced Bruce—Lao-tzu and Chuang-tzu, as well as the Western interpreters of Taoism and Zen Buddhism, like Alan Watts. I also found a kung fu instructor to begin my training. After my junior year at Princeton, I dropped out and went to the Shaolin Temple, the birthplace of kung fu and Zen Buddhism, to live and train with the monks for two years. I later turned this experience into my first book, *American Shaolin*. I spent the next two years studying the sport of mixed martial arts (MMA) of which many practitioners, including top promoter Dana White, consider Bruce Lee to be the "godfather." When I had finished my second book, *Tapped Out*, my friend Brendan Cahill suggested a biography of Bruce Lee.

It didn't seem like a particularly good idea at first. I assumed there already were several solid accounts. I was shocked to discover that the only Bruce Lee biography still in print was written over twenty years ago by Elvis Costello's former bassist.

Bruce Lee is arguably the most famous face on the planet. He is even more popular in Asia, Russia, the Middle East, and Africa than in the Western world. Hollywood has made two biopics about his life, including most recently *Birth of the Dragon* (2016). He consistently ranks in the top fifteen of *Forbes* magazine's list of "top-earning dead celebrities," along with such idols as Elvis Presley, Marilyn Monroe, and Steve McQueen. All of these iconic figures have proper biographies, except for Lee. Hardly a year goes by that a book isn't published about Marilyn Monroe. There are half a dozen biographies of Steve McQueen.

It offended me. Bruce Lee was the first Chinese American male actor to ever star in a Hollywood movie. He inspired millions of people to take up the martial arts. He deserved an authoritative biography. I set out to write it.

My methodology was fairly simple. I watched everything Bruce had ever done and took copious notes. I read everything that had ever been written about Bruce and took copious notes. And then I interviewed everyone who had ever known Bruce and was willing to talk and took copious notes.

Then I compiled these notes into a single Word document in chronological order. The final file was over 2,500 pages and a million words long.

"In building a statue," Bruce liked to say, "a sculptor doesn't keep adding clay to his subject. Actually, he keeps chiseling away at the unessentials until the truth of his creation is revealed without obstructions." Once I had my mound of clay, I chiseled away until the truth was revealed.

The process took over six years. I spent six months in Hong Kong and another two in Los Angeles and Seattle. Along the way, I interviewed over a hundred people and met with many others who were helpful in countless ways.

I am grateful I had a chance to meet and interview Bruce Lee's daughter, Shannon, and his widow, Linda Lee Cadwell. They were extremely generous with their time. I should clearly state, however, that this is not an authorized biography. Beyond granting two interviews, the Bruce Lee Estate had no involvement in this project. The content, analysis, and conclusions expressed in this book are mine alone.

In the world of Bruce Lee studies, there are five exceptional scholars: Paul Li (*From Limited to Limitless*) and Bey Logan (*Hong Kong Action Cinema*) in Hong Kong; Davis Miller (*The Tao of Bruce Lee*), David Tadman (*Regards from the Dragon: Oakland*), and John Little (the Bruce Lee Library series) in America. This book would not have been possible without their kindness, generosity, and expertise. They pointed the way. David Tadman was especially helpful with the photos. John Little, to my eternal gratitude, fact-checked the manuscript.

Andre Morgan provided crucial insight into Golden Harvest's history and Lee's last days. He was a profanely funny correspondent who kept answering my questions no matter how trivial or annoying. John Corcoran gave me an excellent tutorial on karate point fighting. I was thrilled to receive a private lesson in Wing Chun at Dan Inosanto's academy in Marina del Rey. Ed Spielman, Howard Friedlander, and Tom Kuhn walked me through the creation of the TV series *Kung Fu*. Dr. John Stern at UCLA and Duncan McKenzie (*The Death of Bruce Lee: A Clinical Investigation*) offered much needed medical expertise into the potential causes of Bruce Lee's demise. Paul Heller handed over the original *Enter the Dragon* screenplay for me to copy without batting an eye. Joe Torrenueva gave me the best haircut of my life and he didn't charge me nearly as much as he did John Edwards.

I am deeply indebted to John Little's Bruce Lee Library series for publishing so much of Lee's archives, including his letters and interviews. It is invaluable primary source material for fans and scholars of Lee. Fiaz Rafiq's *Bruce Lee Conversations*, Paul Bax's *Disciples of the Dragon*, and Jose Fraguas's *Jeet Kune Do Conversations* are fantastic collections of interviews with Bruce's family, friends, and students. It seems like everyone who knew Bruce has self-published a book about their relationship. The most useful for this project were Jesse Glover's *Bruce Lee: Between Wing Chun and Jeet Kune Do* and Mito Uyehara's *Bruce Lee: The Incomparable Fighter.* Charles Russo's *Striking Distance* is a wonderfully written exploration of Lee's time in the Bay Area.

When I began this project as a rookie biographer, Alex Ben Block, the author of *The Legend of Bruce Lee* (1974), kindly gave me a few pointers. Marshall Terrill, who wrote the excellent biography *Steve McQueen: The Life and Legend of a Hollywood Icon* (2010), was my guru and guide. He ferreted out several interview subjects I never would have discovered on my own.

I was fortunate to be hosted in Hong Kong by my dear friend, David Erro. Paul Li gave me a walking tour of the rooftops where Bruce Lee used to fight as a teenager. Bey Logan is a hilarious raconteur who does a wicked impression of Bruce. My Cantonese translator, Shirley Zhao, who is now a reporter at the *South China Morning Post*, was invaluable. Chaplin Chang is a Taoist sage. Ted Thomas nearly got me banned from the Hong Kong Club—I owe him several drinks. W. Wong, the president of the Hong Kong Bruce Lee Club, was a great guide to the Lee sites. Vivienne Chow at the *South China Morning Post* provided insight into Hong Kong's movie industry. Big Mike Leeder shared his Rolodex. Robert Chua, formerly the producer of *Enjoy Yourself Tonight*, brokered several crucial interviews. Phoebe Lee is the family historian and as fiery as her brother. Betty Ting Pei kept taking me out to expensive lunches and refusing to let me pay. It was awesome to meet Raymond Chow—now I know why they called him the "Smiling Tiger." Johnny Hung introduced me to several old boys from St. Francis Xavier.

Mark Huang, La Salle's historian, went above and beyond. Not only did he set up interviews for me with Lee's La Salle classmates, but he also continued those interviews after I had to leave.

During the process of completing this book, several of the people I interviewed have since passed away. Andre Morgan liked to joke, "As slow as you are as a writer, we'll all be dead by the time you're done." It was a delight to talk to Van Williams (1934–2016), who was extremely helpful for the "Citizen Kato" chapter. I deeply miss Fred Weintraub (1928–2017). Anytime I had a problem getting anyone in Hollywood to agree to an interview, Freddie would call that person up and growl, "Talk to the kid." In the last year of his life, Freddie visited Manhattan and took me out to lunch. "Kid," he said, "have you ever thought about directing?"

I especially want to thank my friend Brendan Cahill, who gave me the idea for the project and helped rescue it when it was in trouble. Credit also goes to my first publisher, "Wild Bill" Shinker, for signing off on it, and my current editor, Sean Manning, for throwing it a lifeline when it was lost at sea. Sean's enthusiasm is infectious. My agent, Joe Veltre, was, throughout the process, a reliable source of stability and strategy.

Finally, I can't say enough about my angelic and patient wife, Em. She encouraged me when I was down, cautioned me when I was up, and read every single page of the manuscript multiple times with a thick red pen. I couldn't have done it without her. I promise, darling, I'll handle child care for the next year.

lee family tree

Grandfather
Li Jun Biao
(Age Unkown)

Uncle
Li Zhen'en
(Age Unkown)
Died Young

Uncle
Li Zhizu
(Age Unkown)
Died Young

Husband of Fourth Aunt
Cen Liefu
(Age Unkown)
Died Young

Fourth Aunt
Li Heyi
(Age Unkown)
d. c. 1945

Fifth Uncle
Li Mantian
(Age Unkown)
d. 1940

Elder Maternal Female Cousin
Li Qiuquin
(born 1927)

Elder Maternal Male Cousin Li Fa (New Hai-quan)
(Age Unkown)

Elder Maternal Female Cousin
Li Qiuzuan
(Age Unkown)
Married Yu Ming in 1945 and moved out of Li household

Elder Maternal Male Cousin
Li Fazhi
(Age Unkown)

Elder Maternal Female Cousin
Li Qiuhuan
(born 1944–5)

SERVANTS

Disciples of Li Hoi Chuen
(male and female)
(between 25 and 35 years old)
Entered Li home in the 1950s

Driver
A Liang
(Age Unknown)
Entered Li home in 1956

Servant
Sister Mei
(about 10 in 1940)

Servant
Zhong Huan
(20 years old in 1940)
Repairman, not-in-house

Servant's Son
Wu Ngan (Enzi)
(born 1939)

Changes in household membership during '40s and '50s:

- During the '50s, the following people moved out or passed away: Li Qiuzuan, Seventh Aunt, Fourth Aunt, Grandma
- During the '50s, the following new members arrived: Disciples of Li Hoi Chuen (4), Driver A Liang

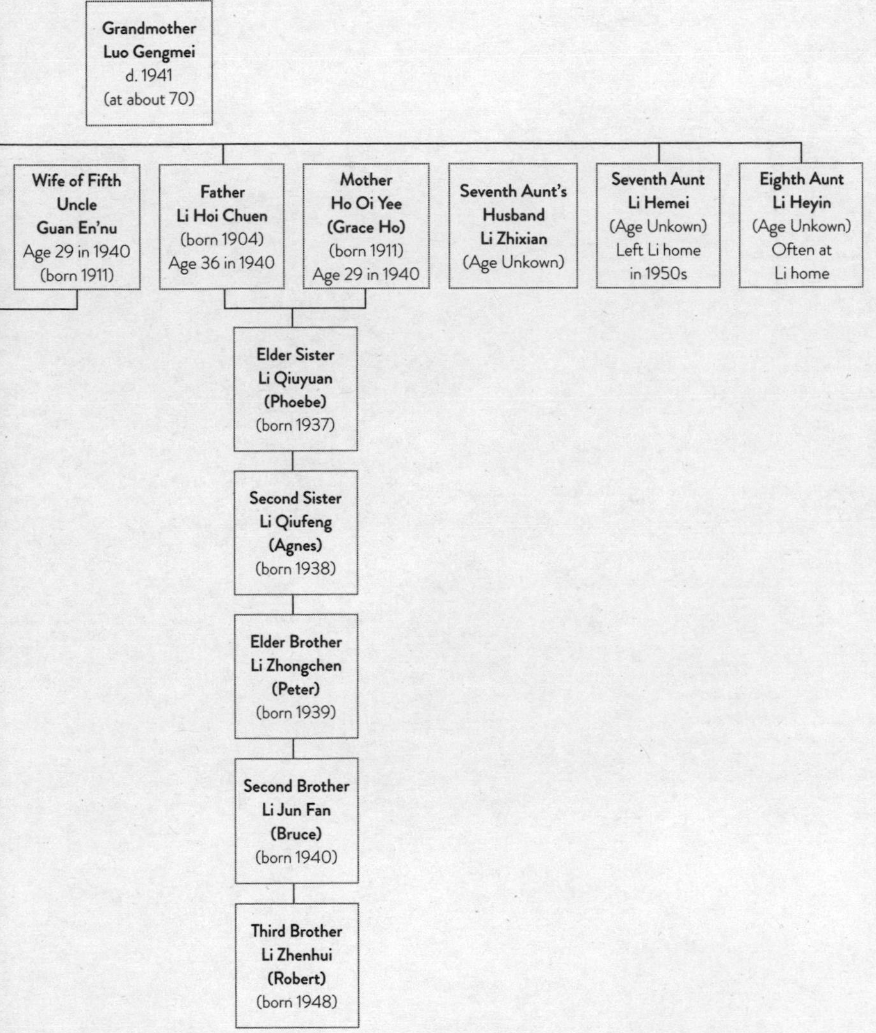

Bruce Lee's paternal family tree. Translated from Robert Lee's *Bruce Lee, My Brother*.

bruce lee filmography

Cantonese Films as a Child Actor

DATE	FILM/SERIES	NOTES
1941	Golden Gate Girl	Bruce was two months old.
1946	The Birth of Mankind	Unicorn Chan costars.
1948	Wealth is Like a Dream	His father costars.
1949	Xi Shi in a Dream	Stage name: Little Li Hoi Chuen.
1949	Lady Fan	Stage name: New Li Hoi Chuen.
1950	My Son A-Chang (The Kid)	Stage name: Dragon Li. His father costars.
1951	The Beginning of Mankind	Stage name: Little Dragon Li.
1953	The Guiding Light	Chung-luen studios' second film.
1953	A Mother's Tears	Bruce played Wang Guoliang.
1953	Sins of the Fathers	Bruce played "Big Mouth Doggy."
1953	Ten-Million People	Shot at Huada Studios.
1953	In the Face of Demolition	
1955	Love, Part One & Two	Filmed to celebrate Chung-luen's 2nd year.
1955	An Orphan's Tragedy	Based on *Great Expectations*.
1955	The Faithful Wife	

DATE	FILM/SERIES	NOTES
1955	Orphan's Song	
1955	Debt Between Mother and Son	
1956	Sweet Time Together	Bruce's first comedy.
1956	Too Late for Divorce	
1957	Thunderstorm	Bruce's first role as a refined gentleman.
1957	Darling Girl	Bruce danced the cha-cha with Margaret Leung.
1960	The Orphan	Last Hong Kong film before leaving for America.

TV Shows

1966–1967	The Green Hornet	Played Kato in 26 episodes.
Oct. 26, 1967	Ironside	"Tagged for Murder."
Jan. 9, 1969	Blondie	"Pick on Someone Your Own Size."
April 9, 1969	Here Come the Brides	"Marriage, Chinese Style."

Films as an Adult Actor

1969	Marlowe	Bruce's first Hollywood movie.
1971	The Big Boss	Filmed in Thailand. His first kung fu flick.
1972	Fist of Fury	Second film for Golden Harvest.
1972	Way of the Dragon	Bruce's directorial debut.
1973	Enter the Dragon	His first starring role in a Hollywood movie.

notes

Prologue: Tale of Two Funerals

PAGE

1 *"a carnival":* Don Atyeo and Felix Dennis, *King of Kung-Fu*, p. 76.

2 *She sent a wreath:* Ibid. Another person who did not attend was famous film and TV star Pak Yan (Amy Chan). She and Bruce had dated when they were teenagers. "People would have asked, 'Why is Pak Yan mourning Bruce Lee?' " she explained years later. "As soon as I'd seen him there, I wouldn't have been able to control myself. I would definitely have cried. People would wonder why. People would go digging stuff up, and I wouldn't want it to affect me. I have a child. It's just best to not create any problems. But I will always remember July 20, 1973." (Chaplin Chang, *The Bruce They Knew*, p. 195.)

2 *"For the scores of fans":* Don Atyeo, *King of Kung-Fu*, p. 77.

2 *"Outside the crush":* Linda Lee, *The Man Only I Knew*, p. 203. The 1926 funeral of Rudolph Valentino, who died at the age of thirty-one, sent his fans into a hysterical state of mass mourning.

3 *Linda had dressed:* Linda Lee, *The Bruce Lee Story*, p. 160.

3 *"It was a frightful time":* Don Atyeo, *King of Kung-Fu*, p. 77.

3 *Three hundred policemen . . . return to their homes:* Ibid., p. 77.

3 *"Linda has stuck to her guns":* "Lee's Body Flies to America Tomorrow," *Oriental Daily*, July 25, 1973.

4 *"I decided to bury":* Linda Lee, *The Bruce Lee Story*, p. 162.

4 *The* Los Angeles Times *wrote:* "Bruce Lee, Hong Kong Film Star, Dies at 32," *Los Angeles Times*, July 21, 1973.

4 *"a quiet and private service":* Dave Friedman, *Enter the Dragon*, p. 239.

4 *plane tickets . . . family to Seattle:* Robert Clouse, *Bruce Lee: The Biography*, p. 183.

4 *Joining them . . . for a documentary:* Interview with Andre Morgan, 2015. Originally the footage was intended only for news clips to be played for fans back in Hong Kong, but Raymond Chow used it for a full-length documentary, *Bruce Lee: The Man and the Legend* (1973).

4 *Rebu Hui:* Rebu Hui was Japanese-American and married to Hong Kong pop star Samuel Hui. Sam and Bruce were friends from grade school. Rebu and Linda bonded over being Americans married to celebrities in Hong Kong.

4 *"She kept me sane":* Linda Lee, *The Bruce Lee Story*, p. 162.

5 *Andre Morgan met:* Richard Ma, the head of Asian Distribution at Warner Bros., sent out this interoffice memo on July 24, 1973: "Bruce's funeral is arranged by Linda's mother residing in Seattle. Will be handled by Michael Schleitweiler of Butterworth Mortuary at 300 East Pine Street Seattle. Linda arriving Seattle with children and Bruce's body Thursday 26th 6:55 A.M. U.S. Time Northwest Flight Four. I understand she wants private and quiet service. No publicity." (Dave Friedman, *Enter the Dragon*, p. 239.)

5 *"as big as Arlington":* Interview with Andre Morgan, 2015.

5 *The funeral in Seattle was held:* Newspaper articles about the funeral were printed the day after on July 31, 1973.

5 *"I was unable to conceal":* Jesse Glover, *Bruce Lee*, p. 90.

5 *A contingent of Bruce's Hollywood:* Stirling Silliphant, who was devastated but also still angry with Bruce after their last argument about *The Silent Flute*, skipped the funeral. He went on a trip in his sailboat instead. (Interview with Tiana Silliphant, 2014.)

5 *generally shunned funerals:* McQueen skipped Sharon Tate's funeral after the Manson murders. Her husband, Roman Polanski, said he would never forgive McQueen for not attending.

5 *"I cared about Bruce":* Mito Uyehara, *The Incomparable Fighter*, p. 127.

5 *"In 35 years in the movie-making":* Alex Ben Block, *The Legend of Bruce Lee*, p. 125; "Pop Tune's Philosophy Marks Bruce Lee Rites," *Los Angeles Herald-Examiner*, July 31, 1973.

6 *"Bruce believed the individual":* "Pop Tune's Philosophy Marks Bruce Lee Rites," *Los Angeles Herald-Examiner*, July 31, 1973; Don Atyeo, *King of Kung-Fu*, p. 79.

6 *"When I looked into the coffin":* Jesse Glover, *Bruce Lee*, p. 90.

7 *"Farewell, brother":* Linda Lee, *The Bruce Lee Story*, p. 162.

7 *Bruce's mother, Grace Ho: Bruce Lee: The Man and the Legend* documentary.

7 *"It didn't seem right":* Jesse Glover, *Bruce Lee*, p. 90.

One: Sick Man of Asia

PAGE

11 *Ten-year-old Li Hoi Chuen:* "My father, Li Hoi Chuen, along with my uncle, Li Man Tian, went with Grandfather to Foshan to work and were apprenticed to a restaurant at the age of only ten." (Robert Lee, *Bruce Lee, My Brother*, p. 54.)

11 *a famous Cantonese Opera singer:* Interview with David Tadman, 2013.

11 *Bruce Lee's father ran:* His family lived in Jiangwei village, Shunde County, Canton Province. It was one of many villages outside the city of Foshan. (Robert Lee, *Bruce Lee, My Brother*, p. 54.)

11 *The year was 1914:* Lee Family Immigration Files, National Archives at San Francisco. Robert Lee has stated that his father was born in 1902. But on Bruce Lee's birth certificate in 1940, Li Hoi Chuen's age is given as thirty-six.

12 *neighbors believed he was cursed:* Robert Lee, *Bruce Lee, My Brother*, pp. 148–50.

12 *also a fisherman:* "When my father was little, he would go out to sea with my paternal grandfather to catch fish," says Phoebe Lee, Bruce's older sister. (Interview with Phoebe Lee, 2013.) Li Jun Bao's part-time job as a security guard has led to a family legend that he was a kung fu master. This is apparently untrue. (Robert Lee, *Bruce Lee, My Brother*, pp. 148–50.)

12 *Unlike its more staid:* Bey Logan, *Hong Kong Action Cinema*, p. 9.

12 *In 1928*: Li Hoi Chuen's Application for Non-Immigrant Visa, Hong Kong Heritage Museum.

13 *Although many have thought:* For decades, Bruce Lee biographers have asserted that Bruce's mother, Grace Ho, was half German. Robert Clouse wrote, "Grace had come to Hong Kong with her Chinese mother and German father at age 19." (*Bruce Lee: The Biography*, p. 9.) Bruce Thomas concurred, "Grace was the daughter of a Chinese mother and German father." (*Bruce Lee: Fighting Spirit*, p. 3.) Linda Lee wrote, "Grace Lee was half German and a Catholic." (*The Bruce Lee Story*, p. 20.) Even Bruce's younger brother, Robert, stated in his book, "My mother was half-German, one-quarter Chinese, and one-quarter English by blood." (*Bruce Lee, My Brother*, pp. 40–41.) Based on these incorrect statements, it was assumed that Bruce's great-grandfather Charles Henri Maurice Bosman must have been German Catholic. In fact, Bruce's mother, Grace, was one-half English, one-quarter Dutch-Jewish, and one-quarter Han Chinese. Her father, Ho Kom Tong, was half Chinese and half Dutch-Jewish. Her mother was English. Grace converted to Catholicism as a teenager. Her parents' religious affiliation is unknown, but it is unlikely either one was Catholic.

13 *He was born Mozes:* Eric Peter Ho, *Tracing My Children's Lineage*, p. 26. Mozes Hartog Bosman's father was an eighteen-year-old butcher named Hartog Mozes Bosman. His mother was seventeen-year-old Anna de Vries. The Dutch Jewish Genealogical Data Base traces the Bosman family to Levie Jacob Bosman, who was born in Germany around 1700.

13 *He shipped Chinese peasant*: Ibid., p. 33.

13 *signed "M Bosman":* Ibid., p. 26.

13 *evidenced by her bound feet:* Ibid., p. 42.

13 *Chinese surname "Ho":* Ibid., p. 45.

13 *Kwok Chung:* Ibid., p. 46.

14 *By the age of thirty-five:* Robert Hotung helped finance the Revolution of 1911, led by Dr. Sun Yat-sen to establish the Republic of China. He was knighted in 1915 for his financial contributions to the British war effort. Robert had two coequal wives. When he traveled with them to America in 1908, they were kicked out of the country for polygamy. The story ran in *The New York Times* under the headline: "Two Wives, to Be Deported: Polygamy No Harm, Says Son of Dutch Father and Chinese Mother."

14 *his younger brother, Ho Kom Tong:* There is family gossip that Ho Kom Tong was not the son of Mozes Bosman. According to these rumors, Sze Tai had an affair with a Chinese businessman while Bosman was out of the country. The reason for the suspicion is Ho Kom Tong's features were more typically "Chinese" than his brothers. In photographs, Robert Hotung looks like a member of the House of Lords, while Ho Kom Tong looks like a chubby Buddha. The problem with this argument is it is very common for Eurasian siblings to look different. Bruce Lee appears far more Chinese than his two brothers, Peter and Robert, who have distinctive Eurasian features. Moreover, it seems highly unlikely that a Chinese concubine to a European coolie trader would cheat on him—or that if she did and got pregnant, he wouldn't sell her to a brothel in San Francisco.

14 *Cantonese Opera acting:* It was extremely unusual for a man of Ho Kom Tong's stature to act on the stage, even for a charity event. At that time, acting was considered a profession for the lower orders—a step or two above prostitution.

14 *married at the age of nineteen:* Eric Peter Ho, *Tracing My Children's Lineage*, p. 139.

14 *in 1911:* Lee Family Immigration Files, National Archives at San Francisco. Robert Lee has stated that his mother was born in 1907. But on Bruce's Lee's birth certificate in 1940, Grace Ho's age is given as twenty-nine.

14 *Grace Ho's English mother:* Grace Ho's biological mother was not revealed to other members of the family. In Eric Peter Ho's very thorough family biography, he assumes that Grace Ho was Ms. Cheung's daughter. (Eric Peter Ho,

Tracing My Children's Lineage, p. 140.) But during an interview with U.S. Immigration officials in 1941, Grace Ho stated under oath that her mother was 100 percent English without any Chinese blood. (Lee Family Immigration Files, National Archives at San Francisco; Charles Russo, "Was Bruce Lee of English Descent?," *Fightland Blog*, May 18, 2016.)

14 *"She wasn't happy"*: Interview with Phoebe Lee, 2013.

14 *Grace became a socialite:* Interview with Takkie Yeung, 2013.

15 *8 Seymour Road:* Eric Peter Ho, *Tracing My Children's Lineage*, p. 111.

15 *"Just in those ten minutes"*: Robert Lee, *Bruce Lee, My Brother*, p. 41.

15 *"But Mom was very independent"*: Ibid.

15 *financially cut off:* No one seems to know the exact date of their marriage, but Hoi Chuen and Grace did have an official ceremony. "They had a matchmaker," says Phoebe Lee. "They had a paper from a witness of the marriage. And they had a wedding proclamation." (Interview with Phoebe Lee, 2013.)

16 *She dressed plainly:* Robert Lee, *Bruce Lee, My Brother*, p. 42.

16 *"My mother was very patient"*: Interview with Phoebe Lee, 2013.

16 *"My father gave all his salary"*: Ibid.

16 *Tragically, he died:* Lee Family Immigration Files, National Archives at San Francisco.

16 *adopted an infant girl:* When Li Hoi Chuen was testifying to U.S. Immigration officials in 1941, he revealed that Phoebe was adopted: "I have four children, two sons and two daughters. One of my daughters is adopted." (Lee Family Immigration Files, National Archives at San Francisco.) In my interview with Linda Lee, she confirmed that Phoebe was adopted. (Interview with Linda Lee, 2013.)

16 *bad omen insurance policy:* Robert Clouse, *Bruce Lee: The Biography*, pp. 3–4.

16 *Hoi Chuen fathered her:* Interview with David Tadman, 2013.

17 *"our genes are the same"*: Interview with Phoebe Lee, 2013.

17 *"Phoebe is my adopted"*: Lee Family Immigration Files, National Archives at San Francisco.

17 *October 23, 1939:* Ibid.

17 *Peter would live a long life:* Peter Lee died on August 15, 2008, at the age of sixty-eight.

18 *(over 600,000):* Steve Tsang, *A Modern History of Hong Kong*, p. 114.

18 *"delaying action was the best"*: Ibid., p. 115.

18 *The objective was to raise funds:* Robert Lee, *Bruce Lee, My Brother*, p. 25.

19 *"My paternal grandmother said"*: Interview with Phoebe Lee, 2013.

19 *SS* President Coolidge*:* Lee Family Immigration Files, National Archives at San Francisco.

20 *local labor leader as a Communist:* Tim O'Rourke, "Chronicle Covers: Labor

Leader Harry Bridges' Big Victory," *San Francisco Chronicle*, December 30, 2016.

20 *Built in 1924:* For photos of the Mandarin Theatre then and now: http://reelsf.com/reelsf/the-lady-from-shanghai-mandarin-theatre-1.

20 *as part of this rivalry:* Charles Russo, *Striking Distance*, p. 127.

20 *18 Trenton Street:* Lee Family Immigration Files, National Archives at San Francisco.

20 *the only medical facility:* Charles Russo, *Striking Distance*, p. 33.

20 *he left his very pregnant wife:* Lee Family Immigration Files, National Archives at San Francisco. In Robert Lee's biography of his brother, he states that his father was actually in San Francisco, not New York City, performing onstage, and he ran several blocks to his wife's bedside as soon as he heard. However, in Hoi Chuen's own testimony to U.S. Immigration officials, he stated, "I had an engagement in New York at the time of his birth, so I don't know if he had his fingerprints taken at the hospital where he was born."

21 *November 27, 1940:* Lee Family Immigration Files, National Archives at San Francisco.

21 *Le Qian Qiu Theatre:* From the 1920s to the 1940s, there were three Chinese Opera theaters in New York City's Chinatown: Le Qian Qiu, Jock Man On, and Yong Ni Shang. (Mary Ingraham, *Opera in a Multicultural World*, p. 52.)

21 *turned to a Chinese American friend:* Robert Lee, *Bruce Lee, My Brother*, p. 26.

21 *Mary E. Glover:* In some biographies of Bruce Lee, Mary Glover is identified as a doctor, but on the birth certificate only her name "Mary E. Glover" is listed without the title of "Dr." In 1940, the vast majority of physicians were male. It seems unlikely that the Chinese Hospital employed one of the few female OB-GYNs in the country.

21 *She suggested Bruce:* Paul Li, *From Limited to Limitless*, p. 1. It is unknown why Mary Glover suggested "Bruce." Maybe she just liked the name.

22 *bright Cantonese Opera paint:* Robert Lee, *Bruce Lee, My Brother*, pp. 25–26.

22 *unlucky to use the same "Jun":* Ibid., p. 26.

22 *"I can't pronounce":* Lee Family Immigration Files, National Archives at San Francisco.

22 *"Dad was very concerned":* Robert Lee, *Bruce Lee, My Brother*, p. 69.

22 *Grace, was flustered:* Tan Hoo Chwoon, *The Orphan*, p. vii.

23 *Bruce cries inconsolably: Golden Gate Girls* documentary.

23 *"a temporary visit":* Lee Family Immigration Files, National Archives at San Francisco.

23 *SS* President Pierce*:* Ibid.

23 *"Upon hearing my father sing":* Robert Lee, *Bruce Lee, My Brother*, p. 25.

24 *"Though Dad didn't much like":* Ibid., p. 27.

24 *A cholera outbreak:* Ibid., p. 28.
24 *so weak and thin:* Linda Lee, *The Bruce Lee Story*, p. 144.
24 *"I think I spoiled him":* Mito Uyehara, *The Incomparable Fighter*, p. 7.
24 *walk without stumbling:* Paul Li, *From Limited to Limitless*, p. 1.
24 *outnumbered four to one:* Steve Tsang, *A Modern History of Hong Kong*, p. 121.
25 *neighborhood opium den:* Linda Lee, *The Man Only I Knew*, p. 34.
25 *gang-raped: The Economist*, June 9, 2012, p. 88.
25 *the population dropped:* Robert Lee, *Bruce Lee, My Brother*, p. 59.
25 *Random civilians were:* Steve Tsang, *A Modern History of Hong Kong*, pp. 127–28.
25 *"Dad never talked":* Robert Lee, *Bruce Lee, My Brother*, p. 57.
26 *"The Japanese forced":* Interview with Phoebe Lee, 2013.
26 *Greater East Asia Co-Prosperity Sphere:* The Greater East Asia Co-Prosperity Sphere was a propaganda concept invented by the Empire of Japan for occupied Asian populations during 1930–45. It promised the intention to create a self-sufficient "block of Asian nations led by the Japanese and free of Western powers."
26 *moved his thirteen-member family:* Robert Lee, *Bruce Lee, My Brother*, p. 137; Phoebe Lee et al., *Lee Siu Loong: Memories of the Dragon*, p. 17.
26 *It was directly across:* Robert Clouse, *Bruce Lee: The Biography*, p. 7.
26 *loudly playing mahjong:* Robert Lee, *Bruce Lee, My Brother*, p. 58.
27 *"shake his fist":* Linda Lee, *The Bruce Lee Story*, p. 22.
27 *By the time:* Interview with Paul Li, 2013.
27 *"I was in Macau":* Interview with Fr. Marciano Baptista, 2013.

Two: Boomtown

PAGE

29 *The first to arrive:* Richard Mason, *The World of Suzie Wong*.
29 *"My parents were not":* Mito Uyehara, *The Incomparable Fighter*, p. 8.
29 *"We didn't have a sense":* Interview with Phoebe Lee, 2013.
30 *five wolfhounds:* Robert Lee, *Bruce Lee, My Brother*, pp. 60–61. One of the wolfhounds, named Bobby, was Bruce's pet. "He was always following Bruce around; he followed him to the park to practice kung fu, and he followed him to bed at night," says Robert. "That dog followed his little master around like a shadow."
30 *"They didn't talk much":* Interview with Phoebe Lee, 2013.
30 *Peter remembers that:* Alex Ben Block, *The Legend of Bruce Lee*, p. 17.
30 *"He almost had a disorder":* Robert Lee, *Bruce Lee, My Brother*, p. 32.
30 *"Why Baby":* Paul Li, *From Limited to Limitless*, p. 2.
30 *His parents discovered:* Linda Lee, *The Bruce Lee Story*, p. 26.

30 The Children's Paradise: Wendy Siuyi Wong, *Hong Kong Comics*, p. 35.
30 *"He used to spend hours"*: Agnes Lee, *Bruce Lee: The Untold Story*, p. 29.
30 *"You are really no use"*: Robert Lee, *Bruce Lee, My Brother*, p. 44. Bruce loved comic books so much that he studied drawing in college, perhaps hoping to become a graphic novelist himself. Instead, given his extroverted personality, he used his artistic talent to sketch out the elaborate fight sequences for his films, mining his childhood reading material for story ideas to incorporate into his own screenplays. In Hollywood, he carried around a stack of old Hong Kong comic books to explain to American producers his vision and pitch his ideas.
31 *Lianhua:* Stephen Teo, *Hong Kong Cinema*, pp. 4–5.
31 *"The money he had made"*: Interview with Takkie Yeung, 2013.
32 *"Bruce climbed the wooden"*: *The Brilliant Life of Bruce Li* documentary. China has a number of different hand games that are similar to rock-paper-scissors. Children play them for fun. Adults incorporate them into drinking games.
32 *"Bruce was wide eyed"*: Agnes Lee, *Bruce Lee: The Untold Story*, p. 2.
32 *Artful Dodger:* Don Atyeo, *King of Kung-Fu*, p. 11.
32 *"Cameo by Wonder"*: Robert Lee, *Bruce Lee, My Brother*, p. 71.
32 *Po-Wan Yuen:* Paul Li, *From Limited to Limitless*, p. 4.
33 *"Finally, Dad agreed"*: Robert Lee, *Bruce Lee, My Brother*, p. 72.
33 *the early 1950s:* Stephen Teo, *Hong Kong Cinema*, p. 13.
34 *"Little Dragon Li"*: Paul Li, *From Limited to Limitless*, p. 4. Bruce's screen name, Li Xiao Long (Little Dragon Li), would eventually become so famous in China that both the director of the movie, Feng Feng, and the comic book artist of the original source material, Yuan Buyun, claimed credit for it. Feng Feng's daughter has kept an old letter in which the director makes this assertion. Yuan Buyun told reporters that he heard a street performer sing, "A big dragon begets a slender dragon, and then the two become one," which planted the idea in his head. But since the opening credits of the movie and the original movie posters listed his screen name as "Dragon Li" not "Little Dragon Li," their competing claims appear to be exaggerations. One or both of them came up with "Dragon Li" and then the diminutive "Little" was added afterward. For Bruce's next movie and the rest to follow, his screen name was listed as "Little Dragon Li."
34 *King's Park:* Robert Lee, *Bruce Lee, My Brother*, pp. 28–29.
34 *"Dad also wanted"*: Ibid., pp. 108–9. In China, tens of thousands of aggressive, volatile boys are sent by their frustrated parents to the Shaolin Temple each year to learn martial arts and discipline. Kung fu is China's version of Ritalin.
35 *"I got tired of it"*: Mito Uyehara, *The Incomparable Fighter*, p. 8.
35 *"To send her children"*: Robert Lee, *Bruce Lee, My Brother*, p. 32.
35 *Grace sent her daughters:* Immediately after the occupation ended in 1945, the

first and only Catholic school in Kowloon to reopen was St. Mary's. For one year, it taught both boys and girls, so Grace sent Phoebe, Agnes, Peter, and Bruce to St. Mary's. A year later Tak Sun (at the corner of Shun Ning Road and Cheung Fat Street) reopened and all the boys at St. Mary's, including Peter and Bruce, were transferred. So technically, the first school Bruce Lee attended was St. Mary's for a year before the boys and girls were split up and he switched to Tak Sun.

35 *"Bruce was already . . . his classmates":* Robert Lee, *Bruce Lee, My Brother*, pp. 28–29.

35 *Parents began warning:* Interview with Dennis Ho, 2013.

35 *"We were playing marbles":* Interview with Anthony Yuk Cheung, 2013.

36 *"He was a real pain":* Quote provided by Mark Huang, historian of La Salle College.

36 *"Dad was very fond of Peter":* Robert Lee, *Bruce Lee, My Brother*, pp. 44–45.

36 *"Bruce was generally off with friends": Black Belt* magazine, August 1974, p. 19.

37 *leisure activity was pranks:* Phoebe remembers, "Once he handed me a book and told me I should read it because it was very special. Upon opening the book I received an electric shock! Bruce laughed and ran off." (Agnes Lee, *Bruce Lee: The Untold Story*, p. 11.)

37 *"when our maid went out":* Ibid.

37 *he and Wu Ngan . . . theater for six months:* Robert Lee, *Bruce Lee, My Brother*, p. 35.

38 *"father hated violence":* Agnes Lee, *Bruce Lee: The Untold Story*, p. 7.

38 *"Bruce did something wrong":* Interview with Phoebe Lee, 2013. Looking back on his strict upbringing, Bruce told an American reporter: "Chinese children don't argue with their parents. A Chinese boy growing up in Hong Kong knows if he disgraces himself, he brings disgrace upon all his kin—upon a great circle of people. And I think this is good." (John Little, *The Celebrated Life of the Golden Dragon*, pp. 8–11.)

38 *"Bruce was a natural": The Brilliant Life of Bruce Lee* documentary.

39 *"It helps my theater voice":* Robert Clouse, *Bruce Lee: The Biography*, p. 8.

39 *"chewing rhyme":* Robert Lee, *Bruce Lee, My Brother*, p. 152.

39 Two Opium Addicts Sweep*:* Ibid., pp. 158–59.

39 *"Dad loved to lie on the right":* Interview with Phoebe Lee, 2013.

40 *"He spent most":* Mito Uyehara, *The Incomparable Fighter*, p. 143.

40 *"an absentee parent":* Linda Lee, *The Bruce Lee Story*, p. 22.

40 *"Only rich people":* Interview with Phoebe Lee, 2013.

40 *For years Grace pleaded*: Robert Lee, *Bruce Lee, My Brother*, p. 46.

40 *classic symptoms:* http://www.phoenixhouse.org/family/how-your-substance-abuse-may-have-affected-your-child/.

40 *"You could join":* Interview with Fr. Marciano Baptista, 2013.
41 *"simple addition":* Linda Lee, *The Man Only I Knew*, p. 44.
41 *"By the time he was ten":* Linda Lee, *The Bruce Lee Story*, p. 22.
41 *50 cents:* Interview with classmates of Bruce conducted by Mark Huang, 2015.
41 *"He would often":* Ibid.
41 *"He was always talking":* Don Atyeo, *King of Kung-Fu*, p. 11.
41 *"teeth brushing":* Chaplin Chang, *The Bruce They Knew*, pp. 66–69.
41 *"hero in a chivalry movie":* Robert Lee, *Bruce Lee, My Brother*, p. 107.
42 *"mesmerizing leadership": The Brilliant Life of Bruce Lee* documentary.
42 *"From boyhood to":* John Little, *The Celebrated Life of the Golden Dragon*, p. 9.
42 *"Bruce picked on":* Interview with classmates conducted by Mark Huang, 2015.
42 *"ask Bruce twice to fight":* Linda Lee, *The Bruce Lee Story*, p. 31.
42 *"When he lost":* Chaplin Chang, *The Bruce They Knew*, pp. 66–69.
42 *rival was David Lee:* Interview with Pau Siu Hung conducted by Mark Huang, 2015.
42 *"our favorite weapon":* Mito Uyehara, *The Incomparable Fighter*, p. 7.
42 *"The communists purged":* Robert Young, "William Cheung: Hong Kong Bullies, Wing Chun Kung Fu, and Bruce Lee," Blackbelt.com, May 2, 2013.
43 *spreading corruption and violence:* "In Kowloon, it's said, everything's for sale and everyone has his price. Or hers," writes superstar Jackie Chan in his memoir. "In the hot streets of Tsim Sha Tsui, gamblers smoke thin black cigarettes and throw bundles of currency on rolls of felt; dance-hall vixens drape themselves on the shoulders of sugar daddies while scanning the clubs for fatter meal tickets to come; money changes hands everywhere, and lives are constantly shattered and remade." (Jackie Chan, *I Am Jackie Chan*, p. 21.)
43 *"The British were the ruling class":* Mito Uyehara, *The Incomparable Fighter*, p. 9.
43 *"We used to stroll":* Robert Clouse, *Bruce Lee: The Biography*, p. 14.
43 *"There were constant fights":* Interview with Steve Garcia, 2014.
43 *"'The local ginger is not hot'":* Interview with Anders Nelsson, 2013.
44 *behavior only got worse:* Paul Li, *From Limited to Limitless*, p. 7.
44 *"Cinema should entertain":* Stephen Teo, *Hong Kong Cinema*, p. 46.
44 *"Dad was very supportive":* Robert Lee, *Bruce Lee, My Brother*, pp. 75–76.
45 *He earned the equivalent:* Chaplin Chang, *The Bruce They Knew*, pp. 64–65.
45 *"a little monkey":* Agnes Lee, *Bruce Lee: The Untold Story*, p. 13.
45 *The artistic union:* Stephen Teo, *Hong Kong Cinema*, p. 47.
46 *"Bruce was very lazy":* Interview with Phoebe Lee, 2013.
46 *"simply too mischievous":* Robert Lee, *Bruce Lee, My Brother*, p. 32.
46 *"He would run":* Interview with classmates conducted by Mark Huang, 2013.
46 *"There was a P.E. teacher":* Robert Lee, *Bruce Lee, My Brother*, p. 33.
46 *"He is trying to soften":* Interview with Dennis Ho, 2013.

47 *Bruce forced one of the boys:* Out of respect for the boy, who grew up to become a successful doctor, his schoolmates refused to tell me his name.

47 *"Maybe Bruce wanted":* Interview with Dennis Ho, 2013.

47 *father grounded him:* Paul Li, *From Limited to Limitless*, p. 8.

Three: Ip Man

PAGE

49 *Triad criminality:* Just like the Italian mafia in America used to be deeply involved in boxing, the Chinese Triads in Hong Kong were enmeshed in the martial arts. To recruit teenage fighters, the Triads sponsored several kung fu clubs.

49 *Wu Gongyi was:* John Christopher Hamm, *Paper Swordsmen*, pp. 2–7. All remaining quotes in this section are from *Paper Swordsmen.*

51 *like a reform school:* Paul Li, *From Limited to Limitless*, p. 8.

51 *"Many of those boys":* Interview with Johnny Hung, 2013.

51 *"I was a punk":* Alex Ben Block, *The Legend of Bruce Lee*, p. 21.

51 *"I only took up kung fu":* Mito Uyehara, *The Incomparable Fighter*, p. 7.

51 *"Being from well-to-do . . . legs underneath":* Hawkins Cheung, "Bruce Lee's Hong Kong Years," *Inside Kung-Fu*, November 1991.

52 *due to one man, Ip Man:* An obscure figure during his lifetime, Ip Man has recently become internationally famous due to a series of blockbuster Hong Kong films: *Ip Man* (2008), *Ip Man 2* (2010), *The Legend Is Born: Ip Man* (2010), *Ip Man: The Final Fight* (2013), *The Grandmaster* (2013), and *Ip Man 3* (2015).

53 *Destitute and rumored:* The extent of Ip Man's use of opioids is still in dispute. His son, Ip Chun, told me that he only drank a mixture of water and opium very briefly as pain relief for a stomachache and then never touched it again: "He was not smoking opium at all." Some of his former students, however, have claimed that he used opium for years and switched to heroin in the mid-1950s when he became involved with a woman of questionable repute. (Benjamin Judkins and Jon Nielson, *The Creation of Wing Chun*, p. 245.)

53 *"'Relax! Relax!'":* Ibid., pp. 240–41.

53 *"an Elvis-looking youngster . . . at any price":* Wong Shun Leung, "Wong Shun Leung and His Friendship with Bruce Lee," *Real Kung Fu Magazine*, 1980.

54 *"'an impure Chinese'":* Robert Young, "William Cheung: Hong Kong Bullies, Wing Chun Kung Fu and Bruce Lee," Blackbelt.com, May 2, 2013; Fiaz Rafiq, *Bruce Lee Conversations*, p. 89.

54 *"some of them assistant instructors":* Mito Uyehara, *The Incomparable Fighter*, p. 78.

55 *He became fanatical:* Don Atyeo, *King of Kung-Fu*, p. 14.

55 *"Less than a year after Bruce":* Fiaz Rafiq, *Bruce Lee Conversations*, p. 90.
55 *"Everyone wanted to be top dog":* Hawkins Cheung, "Bruce Lee's Hong Kong Years," *Inside Kung-Fu*, November 1991.
55 *"Mom and Dad only realized Bruce":* Robert Lee, *Bruce Lee, My Brother*, p. 109.
55 *To avoid police scrutiny:* Paul Li, *From Limited to Limitless*, p. 8. In the 1950s, the Hong Kong government was very sensitive about large public gatherings in general, and especially about martial arts competitions, which could easily turn into brawls or riots. Therefore, when discussing such competitions in the news the euphemistic term "crossing hands" was used.
56 *Practitioners of Hung Gar:* In particular, Bruce's teacher, Wong Shun Leung, made a name for himself and many enemies after his notorious victory at the "Battle of MacPherson Field" against a White Crane stylist. (Paul Li, *From Limited to Limitless*, p. 8.)
56 *"The atmosphere was very tense":* Wong Shun Leung, "Wong Shun Leung and His Friendship with Bruce Lee," *Real Kung Fu Magazine*, 1980.
58 *"These are just surface-level wounds":* Robert Lee, *Bruce Lee, My Brother*, p. 113.
58 *In his diary:* Linda Lee, *The Man Only I Knew*, p. 44.
58 *"What I remember most": Brilliant Life of Bruce Lee* documentary.
58 *"If some day Bruce . . . for a long time":* Wong Shun Leung, "Wong Shun Leung and His Friendship with Bruce Lee," *Real Kung Fu Magazine*, 1980.
59 *Rolf Clausnitzer, whose:* Interview with Rolf Clausnitzer, 2013.
59 *"When he came to our school":* Don Atyeo, *King of Kung-Fu*, p. 16.
59 *"announcement of an inter-school boxing":* Hawkins Cheung, "Bruce Lee's Hong Kong Years," *Inside Kung-Fu*, November 1991.
60 *"I attacked his weak points":* Wong Shun Leung, "Wong Shun Leung and His Friendship with Bruce Lee," *Real Kung Fu Magazine*, 1980.
60 *"Bruce was unknown":* Interview with Steve Garcia, 2014.
60 *a scrappy little guy:* Over the years as Bruce's reputation has been mythologized, so has Gary Elms's. In the Hong Kong biopic *Young Bruce Lee* (2010), Gary is portrayed as a fearsome fighter.
60 *"I'd wrestle him": Inside Kung-Fu* magazine, 1994.
60 *"I spoke to the champ":* Hawkins Cheung, "Bruce Lee's Hong Kong Years," *Inside Kung-Fu*, November 1991.
61 *"When Bruce gradually":* Wong Shun Leung, "Wong Shun Leung and His Friendship with Bruce Lee," *Real Kung Fu Magazine*, 1980.
61 *"Gary was completely baffled":* Interview with Rolf Clausnitzer, 2013.
61 *"Damn it, I couldn't knock":* Ibid.

Four: Banished

PAGE

63 *"He would spend"*: Linda Lee, *The Bruce Lee Story*, p. 30.

63 *"No one had sex"*: Interview with Nancy Kwan, 2013.

63 *"It was kissing"*: Interview with Phoebe Lee, 2013.

64 *"Adolescent Bruce . . . sworn brother"*: Robert Lee, *Bruce Lee, My Brother*, pp. 93–95.

64 *"We used to go dancing"*: *Bruce Lee: Century Hero* documentary.

64 *"I was his savior"*: *The Brilliant Life of Bruce Lee* documentary.

65 *"Neither of us . . . definitive about it"*: Chaplin Chang, *The Bruce They Knew*, pp. 184–86.

66 *"She was the one real romance"*: Robert Lee, *Bruce Lee, My Brother*, p. 95.

66 *"Her dad was a friend"*: Interview with Phoebe Lee, 2013.

66 *Bruce thought of dancing:* Robert Lee, *Bruce Lee, My Brother*, pp. 99–100.

66 *"He was good at jive"*: Interview with Dennis Ho, 2013.

67 *"He didn't pick it up"*: Robert Lee, *Bruce Lee, My Brother*, pp. 99–100.

67 *"At school, I knew some Filipino"*: Hawkins Cheung, "Bruce Lee's Hong Kong Years," *Inside Kung-Fu*, November 1991.

67 *"He could barely wait . . . for the contest"*: Robert Lee, *Bruce Lee, My Brother*, pp. 101–3.

68 *"The Cha-Cha Champion"*: Being the 1958 Cha-Cha Champion of Hong Kong was analogous to being the 1983 Break Dance Champion of Minneapolis.

68 *"Since they both involve"*: Don Atyeo, *King Of Kung-Fu*, p. 24.

68 *"innate balance"*: Ibid., p. 24.

69 *Critics panned the movie:* Paul Li, *From Limited to Limitless*, p. 10.

70 *"I was getting disgusted"*: Mito Uyehara, *The Incomparable Fighter*, p. 8.

70 *"A British bigwig"*: Robert Lee, *Bruce Lee, My Brother*, p. 47.

71 *rock bottom:* The night the police came to the Li home, Hoi Chuen was away shooting a movie. When he returned the next morning from filming, Grace told him how she has been humiliated. He agreed to her demands that he stop smoking opium. (Phoebe Lee et al., *Lee Siu Loong: Memories of the Dragon*, p. 48.)

71 *Hoi Chuen detoxed:* Ibid.

71 *"It was very difficult"*: Interview with Phoebe Lee, 2013.

71 *"What are you looking at"*: "A Dragon Remembered: An Interview with Robert Lee," *Way of the Dragon* DVD extras.

72 *"Hey, either your son stops"*: Ibid. Over the years, one of Bruce's Hong Kong friends with a penchant for hyperbole has claimed that the teenage boy Bruce beat up in the street fight was the son of a prominent Triad gang boss and as a

result Bruce's parents sent him to America to avoid a reprisal on his life. This story, seemingly lifted from a Hong Kong chop-socky flick, has taken on a life of its own, appearing in otherwise sober summaries of Bruce's life (Mary Holdsworth and Christopher Munn, eds., *Dictionary of Hong Kong Biography*, p. 252). However, according to his siblings, it is untrue. The injured boy's father called the police (not something Triad gang bosses tend to do), and it was the police's threat of arrest that shocked Bruce's parents into sending him away.

72 *"No good"*: Robert Lee, *Bruce Lee, My Brother*, pp. 120–23.

72 *"Bruce didn't want to go"*: Hawkins Cheung, "Bruce Lee's Hong Kong Years," *Inside Kung-Fu*, November 1991.

72 *"Dad's intuition"*: *The Brilliant Life of Bruce Lee* documentary.

72 *"He told me once"*: Interview with Nancy Kwan, 2013.

73 *"Prior to any Hong Kong resident"*: Hawkins Cheung, "Bruce Lee's Hong Kong Years," *Inside Kung-Fu*, November 1991.

73 *"Now I try to find out"*: John Little, ed., *Letters of the Dragon*, p. 20.

73 *"I cracked up"*: Hawkins Cheung, "Bruce Lee's Hong Kong Years," *Inside Kung-Fu*, November 1991.

74 *The deal was Master Sang:* Paul Li, *From Limited to Limitless*, p. 12.

74 *"After this decision was made"*: Robert Lee, *Bruce Lee, My Brother*, p. 123.

74 *"Spent more time on Math"*: Paul Li, *From Limited to Limitless*, p. 12.

75 *"About four years of hard training"*: Linda Lee, *The Bruce Lee Story*, pp. 37–39.

77 *HK$400,000:* Tan Hoo Chwoon, *The Orphan*, p. xvii. The equivalent of US$670,000 in 2017 dollars.

77 *"No one is allowed"*: Ibid., pp. xiii–xiv.

78 *"We laughed about it"*: Agnes Lee, *Bruce Lee: The Untold Story*, p. 28.

78 *"The night before he left"*: Robert Lee, *Bruce Lee, My Brother*, p. 123.

78 *"when I've made some money"*: Linda Lee, *The Man Only I Knew*, pp. 46–47.

78 *"He asked someone"*: *Bruce Lee: Century Hero* documentary.

78 *"To dearest Bruce"*: Phoebe Lee et al., *Lee Siu Loong: Memories of the Dragon*, p. 2.

79 *"On the ship, he threw"*: *The Brilliant Life of Bruce Lee* documentary.

79 *"I saw him cry"*: Fiaz Rafiq, *Bruce Lee Conversations*, p. 97.

79 *When the ribbons broke:* Robert Lee, *Bruce Lee, My Brother*, pp. 123–24.

Five: Native Son

PAGE

83 *500 to 25,000:* Peter Kwong and Dusanka Miscevic, *Chinese America*, p. 7.

83 *Chinese became to the West:* Ibid., p. 53.

84 *"They are quiet"*: Iris Chang, *The Chinese in America*, p. 39.

84 *"Celestials":* Kwong and Miscevic, *Chinese America*, pp. 43–45.

84 *"We are inflexibly opposed":* Ibid., p. 66.

84 *"The Chinese are morally":* Iris Chang, *The Chinese in America*, p. 51.

84 *grown to 370,000:* Kwong and Miscevic, *Chinese America*, pp. 7, 67.

84 *"Why not discriminate":* Iris Chang, *The Chinese in America*, pp. 130–31.

84 *The secretary of war:* Ibid., pp. 133–34. In the Snake River Massacre of 1887, a group of white ranchers killed and mutilated thirty-one Chinese miners in Hell's Canyon, Oregon.

85 *"Be big enough to correct . . . winning wealth and respect":* Kwong and Miscevic, *Chinese America*, p. 203.

86 *"It's as pretty as any Western country":* John Little, *Letters of the Dragon*, pp. 21–23.

86 *"One bowl of shark fin soup":* After inflation, $25 in 1959 equals $212 in 2017.

87 *On May 17, 1959 . . . in San Francisco and Oakland:* Charles Russo, *Striking Distance*, pp. 14, 29–30, 47–48.

88 *"There were 30 of us":* David Tadman and Steve Kerridge, *Bruce Lee: The Little Dragon at 70*, p. 10.

88 *"I had never seen anyone as fast":* Interview with David Tadman, 2013.

89 *"We slept together":* Robert Clouse, *Bruce Lee: The Biography*, p. 25.

90 *unofficial spokeswoman:* In 1973 Ruby Chow's unofficial position became official when she was elected as the first Asian American to the King County Council.

90 *As the son of one of Ping:* "Ruby Chow, First Asian American on King County Council, Dead at 87," *Seattle Times*, June 5, 2008; Robert Clouse, *Bruce Lee: The Biography*, pp. 25–28; Bruce Thomas, *Bruce Lee: Fighting Spirit*, p. 32; Paul Bax, *Disciples of the Dragon*, pp. 34–35.

90 *It was exactly:* While there is no direct evidence that Li Hoi Chuen asked his old friend Ping Chow to treat Bruce like a fresh-off-the-boat coolie, it would not have happened without his approval.

90 *"Now I am really on my own":* John Little, *Letters of the Dragon*, pp. 25–26. Bruce would later tell his brother's girlfriend, Eunice Lam, "I used to wake up, sit on the bed and cry my heart out." (Eunice Lam, "Eunice Lam Remembers Bruce Lee," Bruce Lee Lives! Tribute Forum, April 9, 2016.)

90 *Grace, secretly sent money:* In my interview with Linda Lee, she insisted that Bruce's parents never helped him financially once he arrived in America. They completely cut him off. In contrast, Mito Uyehara, a close friend, wrote in his book about Lee, "After a few months [in America], self-reliant Bruce became disenchanted as he still had to rely on his parents for his miscellaneous expenses. He wanted to be self-sufficient because all his life he was considered the black sheep of the family. 'When I left Hong Kong, I

promised myself that I'd not depend on my parents for any kind of help, and here I was getting money from them,' Bruce told me." (*Bruce Lee: The Incomparable Fighter*, p. 12.) After interviewing Ruby Chow, Robert Clouse wrote, "Grace told Ruby she would send some money to help with his upkeep, and it was agreed that no one would tell his father about this arrangement." (*Bruce Lee: The Biography*, p. 25.)

90 *"You're not my auntie":* Robert Lee, *Bruce Lee, My Brother*, pp. 156–58. Later in life Bruce would do the same thing to director Lo Wei, calling him "Lo Wei" instead of "Director Lo." Bruce was exceedingly polite to people he liked. He was rude to authority figures he didn't respect.

91 *"Take a swing":* Jesse Glover, *Bruce Lee*, p. 17.

91 *coolie trade:* Bruce compared himself to immigrant laborers who were imported by Chinese Benevolent Associations to work undocumented in restaurants and other businesses for less than union wages.

91 *"He had no respect":* Bruce Thomas, *Bruce Lee: Fighting Spirit*, p. 33.

91 *Ruby gave structure:* Robert Clouse, *Bruce Lee: The Biography*, p. 28.

91 *vocational training:* http://seattlecentral.edu/about/history.php.

91 *With a purpose and drive:* Linda Lee, *The Bruce Lee Story*, p. 42.

91 *2.6 grade point average:* Tom Bleecker, *Unsettled Matters*, p. 33.

91 *He joined because the head instructor:* Jesse Glover, *Bruce Lee*, p. 16.

91 *His greatest desire:* Ibid., p. 52.

92 *into a super-system:* Bruce's role model was Huo Yuanjia, the founder of the Jing Wu Institute. As the first public martial arts university in China, Jing Wu hired prominent kung fu masters of various styles to provide a broad curriculum to its students. The controversial death of Huo Yuanjia became the plot line for Lee's 1972 movie, *Fist of Fury*.

92 *best kung fu artist in the world:* In 1960, Bruce still had faith in traditional kung fu. He practiced forms and felt they improved speed and power. He believed in the mystical powers of *qi* or *chi* ("internal force"). He thought the delayed death touch (*dim mak*) was possible. After less than a year living in America, he reversed his position on forms and *qi* and began to openly criticize traditional martial arts. (Jesse Glover, *Bruce Lee*, p. 40; Fiaz Rafiq, *Bruce Lee Conversations*, p. 33.)

92 *"I don't do much":* John Little, ed., *Letters of the Dragon*, pp. 25–26.

92 *"I'm saving it for dancing":* Jesse Glover, *Bruce Lee*, p. 91.

92 *Bruce Lee's first public performance:* Ibid., p. 12.

93 *fascinated by kung fu:* In Jesse's quest to find a kung fu teacher, he and his friend Howard Hall went to Oakland, California, to meet James Lee, who would later become one of Bruce Lee's assistant instructors. James asked Jesse to throw a punch at him. James countered it and blasted Jesse in the

ribs. Then he asked Jesse to punch again, countered it, and struck him in the groin. "Years later Bruce Lee told me that James Lee had said that he wanted to impress us with the fact that he could hurt us, just in case we had something up our sleeves," Jesse wrote. "Bruce also said that there was a good chance that James Lee might have been drinking." James showed Jesse and Howard a few techniques but refused to teach them more because they wouldn't be in California long enough to learn the basics of his system. When they asked James if he knew any kung fu instructors in Seattle, he said no. (Jesse Glover, *Bruce Lee*, pp. 10–11.)

93 *"Is your name Bruce Lee":* Ibid., pp. 14–15.

93 *"You are teaching black guys":* Fiaz Rafiq, *Bruce Lee Conversations*, p. 23. Bruce responded to Ruby's criticism by saying, "Well, they can beat up on Chinese anyway, at least if I teach them they're going to have some respect for us." Bruce was the first Chinese instructor in Seattle to teach kung fu to non-Chinese.

93 *"practice in secret":* Jesse Glover, *Bruce Lee*, p. 17.

94 *the southeast corner:* Paul Bax, *Disciples of the Dragon*, p. 30.

94 *"Let's get on with it":* Jesse Glover, *Bruce Lee*, p. 18.

95 *Ed was a two-hundred-pound:* Ed Hart called his favorite barroom brawl technique the Hart Attack. If things weren't going well, Ed would sink to the floor grasping his chest and apparently gasping out his last breath. Then, when his foe bent over him, Ed would corkscrew off the floor like a startled mongoose and knock the poor sucker out of his socks. (David Brewster and David M. Buerge, eds., *Washingtonians*, p. 425.)

95 *Bruce easily tied him:* Jesse Glover, *Bruce Lee*, p. 20.

95 *One of them was Skip Ellsworth:* Charles Russo, *Striking Distance*, p. 66.

95 *"During Bruce's very brief":* Paul Bax, *Disciples of the Dragon*, pp. 31–32.

95 *Lee found his recruits:* David Brewster and David M. Buerge, eds., *Washingtonians*, p. 420.

96 *"It was a beautiful performance":* James DeMile has recounted this story a number of times over the years with slight variations. See ibid., pp. 423–25; Fiaz Rafiq, *Bruce Lee Conversations*, pp. 27–28; Charles Russo, *Striking Distance*, pp. 65–66.

96 *more blue-collar young men:* Paul Bax, *Disciples of the Dragon*, p. 30.

97 *"I thought I was white":* David Brewster and David M. Buerge, eds., *Washingtonians*, p. 434.

97 *Every time they hit the dummy:* Paul Bax, *Disciples of the Dragon*, p. 35.

97 *"We were all dummies":* Ibid., p. 93; Jesse Glover, *Bruce Lee*, p. 31.

97 *Bruce was like a brilliant young professor:* This criticism is fairly universal among his Seattle crew. Ed Hart says, "I don't think Bruce liked teaching

very much. He did a lot of stuff with a few guys, but when the group got bigger, he would just tell them what to do and just stand there and watch them do it and give them some suggestions. The guy he worked out with the most was Jesse Glover. I learned more from Jesse than I did from Bruce." Howard Hall says, "James was a better teacher than Bruce. Bruce was a technician and a perfectionist, but he didn't have patience with beginners. Jimmy conveyed things better than Bruce. (Paul Bax, *Disciples of the Dragon*, pp. 22–23, 138.) To be fair, Bruce's hands-off approach was typical of traditional kung fu instruction in China. Ip Man didn't waste his time with beginners either. He worked out with his senior students, like Wong Shun Leung, and then his senior students taught the novices. Ip Man would oversee classes and make an occasional suggestion. It took Bruce several years to adjust to American expectations for more personal and involved mentoring.

98 *maximum amount of acceleration:* William Herkewitz, "The Science of the One-Inch Punch," *Popular Mechanics*, May 21, 2014.

98 *"His punch got stronger":* Jesse Glover, *Bruce Lee*, p. 55. Over the years James DeMile has claimed that he and Bruce Lee developed the one-inch punch together and no one else can do it properly. (Paul Bax, *Disciples of the Dragon*, p. 113; Robert Clouse, *Bruce Lee: The Biography*, p. 32.) It is entirely plausible that Bruce worked on his punch with DeMile, who was a boxer. Lee was constantly absorbing techniques he liked from those around him. However, DeMile's assertion that he is the only one of Bruce's students who can replicate the punch seems a bit self-serving.

98 *a 230-pound man:* Jesse Glover, *Bruce Lee*, p. 55.

98 *"I don't think Bruce ever":* David Brewster and David M. Buerge, eds., *Washingtonians*, p. 433.

98 *"I hated comedies":* Jesse Glover, *Bruce Lee*, p. 48; Fiaz Rafiq, *Bruce Lee Conversations*, p. 21.

98 *"The advantage for us":* Paul Bax, *Disciples of the Dragon*, p. 59.

98 *"I want to be rich and famous":* Jesse Glover, *Bruce Lee*, p. 38.

99 *Jesse also liked to tease:* Ibid., p. 49.

99 *put it in mothballs:* Ibid., p. 76.

99 *"Bruce would act like":* Ibid., p. 49.

99 *"without stuttering":* Ibid., p. 66.

100 *"Bruce totally loved it":* Paul Bax, *Disciples of the Dragon*, p. 41. Bruce used the gun once to rescue his brother's girlfriend, Eunice Lam, when her landlord was insulting and threatening her. Bruce came over in a rage with the Colt in his hand. As soon as the landlord saw the pistol, he bolted from the apartment. (Eunice Lam, "Eunice Lam Remembers Bruce Lee," April 9, 2016.)

100 *like a Western gunslinger:* Jesse Glover, *Bruce Lee*, p. 66.

100 *Leroy refused to play:* David Brewster and David M. Buerge, eds., *Washingtonians*, p. 437.

100 *"It was always on his mind":* Jesse Glover, *Bruce Lee*, p. 77.

100 *But the sheer size:* Ibid., p. 31.

100 *Bruce became an avid fan:* Fiaz Rafiq, *Bruce Lee Conversations*, pp. 42–43, 277.

100 *a new paradigm:* Charles Russo, *Striking Distance*, p. 67.

101 *"on top of the world":* Paul Bax, *Disciples of the Dragon*, pp. 35–36.

101 *The original ten charter members:* Jesse Glover, *Bruce Lee*, p. 47.

101 *The large room on the second floor:* Paul Bax, *Disciples of the Dragon*, pp. 35–36.

102 *"The only time I started to worry":* Jesse Glover, *Bruce Lee*, p. 71.

102 *Bruce went ballistic:* Fiaz Rafiq, *Bruce Lee Conversations*, p. 31.

102 *An incident broke out . . . "four seconds":* Paul Bax, *Disciples of the Dragon*, p. 39. There was also a fight on a ferry. When two white guys made fun of the snappy way he was dressed, Bruce mocked them back until one of the guys attacked him. Bruce easily deflected the blow and wrecked the dude with a series of punches and kicks. The guy's friend turned tail and ran. (Fiaz Rafiq, *Bruce Lee Conversations*, p. 53.)

102 *One of them was Yoichi:* Charles Russo, *Striking Distance*, p. 68.

103 *"I'm not going to let anyone prod":* Jesse Glover, *Bruce Lee*, pp. 43–45; Paul Bax, *Disciples of the Dragon*, p. 27.

105 *Yoichi swallowed his pride:* Paul Bax, *Disciples of the Dragon*, pp. 5–6.

105 *"A lot of people took exception":* Alex Ben Block, *The Legend of Bruce Lee*, p. 30.

Six: Husky

PAGE

107 *March 27, 1961:* John Little, *Letters to the Dragon*, p. 27.

107 *"We picked the right horse":* Robert Lee, *Bruce Lee, My Brother*, p. 126. It is unknown how exactly Bruce paid for his tuition, but it seems likely that Bruce's father helped to subsidize the expense. For residents, the University of Washington cost around $300 per year, or $2,500 in 2017 dollars. (https://www.uwyo.edu/oia/_files/tfrb/uwhist1617.pdf.)

107 *Only the very best:* To be fair, he probably would not have been accepted to the University of Washington if he had not been an American citizen. Admission requirements for foreign students were (and are) much more stringent. Still, given how poor and disinterested a student he was in Hong Kong, it is remarkable that he was able to graduate from high school and go on to college.

107 *"Gung Fu is a special skill":* Linda Lee, *The Bruce Lee Story*, p. 37.

108 *over 2,500 books:* Tommy Gong, *Bruce Lee*, p. 230.

108 *His GPA after:* Tan Vinh, "A Rare, Personal Glimpse of Bruce Lee's Seattle Years," *Seattle Times*, October 2, 2014.

108 *nicknamed him Beefcake:* Davis Miller, *The Zen of Muhammad Ali and Other Obsessions*, p. 92.

108 *"If you wanted him to shut":* Eunice Lam, "Eunice Lam Remembers Bruce Lee," April 9, 2016.

108 *"How would they treat":* Paul Bax, *Disciples of the Dragon*, p. 38.

109 *His focus was on the personal:* David Brewster and David M. Buerge, eds., *Washingtonians*, p. 435.

109 *Reserve Officers' Training Corps:* Until 1962, ROTC was mandatory at the University of Washington and many other land grant colleges. After successful litigation in the courts, ROTC was made voluntary during Bruce's sophomore year. (Interview with Dr. William Pola, assistant professor of military science at the University of Washington, 2014.)

109 *"Swallow that, soldier":* Linda Lee included this anecdote in her first book about her late husband, *Bruce Lee: The Man Only I Knew* (pp. 65–66). It was written in 1975 at the end of the Vietnam War and at the height of the antiwar movement. Her revised and updated version, *The Bruce Lee Story*, left out this story. It was published in 1989, after Reagan's conservative, pro-military presidency.

109 *categorized as 4-F:* Robert Lee and others have asserted that Bruce was rejected because of flat feet. (Robert Lee, *Bruce Lee, My Brother*, p. 31.) Linda Lee, however, rejected this in her first memoir about her husband: "It has been reported that Bruce was turned down because his arches were too high. In fact, his complaint was an undescended testicle." (*Bruce Lee: The Man Only I Knew*, pp. 65–66.) In my 2013 interview with Linda, she confirmed the cause was an undescended testicle.

109 *convinced he could never be a father:* Eunice Lam, "Eunice Lam Remembers Bruce Lee," April 9, 2016. Eunice wrote, "He always thought he wouldn't make women pregnant just because he had only one testis as the other one was hid in the peritoneum. He showed me it to prove it. As a student studying genetics at U.C. Berkeley, I found it to be very normal. I told him just one testis was enough to create millions of sperm and make a woman pregnant. Whether he believed me or not, I don't know."

109 *Seven years later in 1969:* Tom Bleecker, *Unsettled Matters*, p. 59. In Bleecker's scathing biography, he draws broad, unsubstantiated conclusions from Lee's cryptorchidism—claiming that one undescended testicle caused Bruce to frequently suffer from impotence, an inability to develop a mature musculature without the aid of anabolic steroids, and "psychosocial immaturity" (pp. 19–20, 38). These claims are absurd. The only two physical risks associated with cryptorchidism are infertility and testicular cancer. It does not cause impotence or stunt muscular development, and there are no proven

psychological side effects. Lee fathered two children, had an active sex life, and had the same wiry musculature in his teenage years as his two brothers.

110 *When Bruce realized his mistake:* Eunice Lam, "Eunice Lam Remembers Bruce Lee," April 9, 2016.

110 *After Pearl:* Alex Ben Block, *The Legend of Bruce Lee*, p. 30; Paul Bax, *Disciples of the Dragon*, p. 106.

110 *"If a pretty girl":* Fiaz Rafiq, *Bruce Lee Conversations*, p. 31.

110 *"R, how could we":* John Little, *Letters of the Dragon*, p. 26. Bruce also liked to charm girlfriends with philosophical aphorisms: "Dianne, To be fond of learning is to be near knowledge. To practice with vigor is to be near to magnanimity. To possess the feeling of shame is to be near energy. Love, Bruce."

110 *Japanese American sophomore named Amy Sanbo:* For Amy Sanbo's account of her relationship with Bruce Lee, see David Brewster and David M. Buerge, eds., *Washingtonians*, pp. 433–35; Tom Bleecker, *Unsettled Matters*, pp. 33–42; Robert Clouse, *Bruce Lee: The Biography*, pp. 39–40; Charlette LeFevre, "The Lady and the Dragon: An Interview with Amy Sanbo, Bruce Lee's First Love in the U.S.," *Northwest Asian Weekly*, December 1, 2007. These four sources range over a thirty-year period. The details are consistent, but the tone changes over time. As Amy Sanbo aged, her assessment became more generous and less defensive.

111 *Both of them were beautiful:* Bruce did occasionally suffer from acne. His brother's girlfriend, Eunice Lam, would tease him about it: "You think you look so good? Your face is full of tiny pimples." ("Eunice Lam Remembers Bruce Lee," April 9, 2016.)

111 *"He could get funky":* Charlette LeFevre, "The Lady and the Dragon: An Interview with Amy Sanbo, Bruce Lee's First Love in the U.S.," *Northwest Asian Weekly*, December 1, 2007. In another interview, Amy Sanbo recalled, "At the time, Bruce watched the way the blacks moved because they were such great dancers. . . . I would see him watching the way they walked down the streets. I think he would just mimic them in the beginning, and then soon he developed his own unique expression." (Tom Bleecker, *Unsettled Matters*, p. 37.) Lee's kung fu movies were extremely popular in the African American community in the 1970s. In part, it was because Bruce was a nonwhite hero sticking it to The Man, like Shaft and other blaxploitation heroes of the era. But I suspect another reason was because black audiences recognized something familiar in the way he moved and walked.

113 *"He didn't do anything":* Jesse Glover, *Bruce Lee*, p. 26.

113 *planned to open his club:* John Little, *Letters of the Dragon*, p. 27. Bruce wrote to Ed Hart in early March 1961, "I have ten students so far and the club is taking shape. Maybe in two more months, it will be opened to the public."

113 *original group dwindled:* Jesse Glover, *Bruce Lee*, p. 65. In Jesse's book he states it was Howard Hall's departure to the East Coast that ended the original club, but Bruce wrote two letters to Ed Hart in Brooklyn pleading with him to return to Seattle to save the club (John Little, ed., *Letters of the Dragon*, pp. 27–28). It is possible that both Howard Hall and Ed Hart moved to the East Coast at the same time, but it seems more likely that Jesse Glover got the name wrong.

113 *"I don't have a club":* John Little, ed., *Letters of the Dragon*, p. 28.

114 *"In every industry":* Ibid., pp. 29–31.

115 *"I found it a little difficult":* Jesse Glover, *Bruce Lee*, p. 62.

116 *"We didn't like some of the changes":* Peter Bax, *Disciple of the Dragon*, p. 114; Fiaz Rafiq, *Bruce Lee Conversations*, p. 37. Of the original crew, Taky Kimura, who was older and didn't consider himself a fighter, proved to be the most loyal. He stuck with Bruce, and in return Bruce shared with him all his best techniques.

117 *Robert, who was beginning:* Robert Lee, *Bruce Lee, My Brother*, p. 46.

117 *"No, Dad, you were right": Brilliant Life of Bruce Lee* documentary.

117 *"I had never seen a smile":* Robert Lee, *Bruce Lee, My Brother*, p. 46.

117 *"When he left":* Agnes Lee et al., *Lee Siu Loong: Memories of the Dragon*, p. 6.

118 *But instead of praising:* Jesse Glover, *Bruce Lee*, p. 19.

118 *After four years away:* Ibid., pp. 52–53.

118 *briefly considered quitting:* James DeMile (Seattle student): "He came back from Hong Kong shattered. He could hit the good Wing Chun men maybe once out of every three times they could hit him. He thought seriously about giving up martial arts." (David Brewster and David M. Buerge, eds., *Washingtonians*, p. 435.) Howard Williams (Oakland student): "Back in those early years when Bruce was going back to China to show his seniors what he had developed as far as Wing Chun, his seniors were able to get in on him as many times as he did with them. This made him very frustrated. He almost gave up the martial arts completely, but at that point he decided he was going to be even more determined, not matter what it took, to develop something no one else had. From that point on, he trained fanatically, and there was no stopping him." (Paul Bax, *Disciples of the Dragon*, pp. 138–39.)

118 *Chang Cheh:* Tan Hoo Chwoon, *The Orphan*, p xiv.

118 *Christine Pai Lu-Ming:* Eunice Lam, "Eunice Lam Remembers Bruce Lee," April 9, 2016.

119 *Amy Chan (Pak Yan):* Western kung fu film fans are most likely to remember her from *Drunken Master II* (1994).

119 *"They keep casting me":* Chaplin Chang, *The Bruce They Knew*, p. 184.

119 *"This is Hong Kong":* Agnes Lee et al., *Lee Siu Loong: Memories of the Dragon*, p. 84.

120 *"If that had been a few years ago":* Eunice Lam, "Eunice Lam Remembers Bruce Lee," April 9, 2016; Agnes Lee et al., *Lee Siu Loong: Memories of the Dragon*, pp. 76–77. Eunice Lam would later marry Bruce's brother, Peter. They divorced in the 1970s after she had an affair with her co-worker, James Wong, a famous television personality. Eunice went on to become a celebrity author.

120 *"Man, believe me":* Agnes Lee et al., *Lee Siu Loong: Memories of the Dragon*, pp. 84–85.

120 *"The ride":* Ibid., pp. 71–72.

121 *"He was a smiling man":* Ibid., p. 76.

121 *"unable to dominate":* Paul Bax, *Disciples of the Dragon*, p. 79.

121 *"What's wrong":* Agnes Lee et al., *Lee Siu Loong: Memories of the Dragon*, p. 17; Paul Bax, *Disciples of the Dragon*, p. 79. Doug Palmer asserts that Bruce was circumcised at his father's direction, but Robert says it was Bruce's initiative. It seems likely that Palmer, who did not speak Cantonese, misunderstood the situation. Circumcision was virtually unknown in the Chinese community at the time. Bruce probably decided to do it after one of his American girlfriends or buddies teased him. He was very sensitive about fitting in. Why he chose to do it in Hong Kong and not America is unknown.

Seven: Sunny Side of the Bay

PAGE

123 *"not a good person":* Interview with Linda Lee, 2013.

123 *Growing up poor:* Linda Lee, *The Bruce Lee Story*, p. 8.

124 *"he looks like George Chakiris":* Ibid., p. 7. Robert Clouse, *Bruce Lee: The Biography*, pp. 41–42. George Chakiris won the Academy Award for Best Supporting Actor for playing Bernardo, the leader of the Sharks, in *West Side Story* (1961).

125 *Initially, Linda found him:* Linda Lee, *The Man Only I Knew*, p. 21.

125 *"I don't know if I was":* Don Atyeo, *King of Kung Fu*, p. 31. She was more interested in the teacher.

125 *"I'm in the movie":* Interview with Linda Lee, 2013.

125 *"Seeing him on the screen":* Linda Lee, *The Bruce Lee Story*, p. 8.

125 *When the 1963 fall semester:* The University of Washington worked on the quarter system—autumn, winter, spring, and summer. So technically Linda enrolled for the autumn quarter, not the fall semester. Like most UW students, Bruce took classes during the autumn, winter, and spring quarters and had the summer quarter free.

125 *"He was so dashing":* Linda Lee, *The Bruce Lee Story*, p. 11.

126 *souped-up '57 Ford:* "Bruce's car was . . . especially souped up and full of gadgets—he always knew someone, either a student or a person in the car

business, who would fix up his cars this way." (Linda Lee, *The Man Only I Knew*, p. 28.)

126 *"He could always talk . . . perfect evening":* Linda Lee, *The Bruce Lee Story*, p. 12; Linda Lee, *The Man Only I Knew*, p. 29.

127 *"To the sweetest girl":* John Little, ed., *Letters of the Dragon*, p. 32.

127 *"You could sleep forever":* Linda Lee, *The Bruce Lee Story*, pp. 14–16.

128 *"techniques are smooth":* Ibid., p. 49.

128 *"Lee Hopes for Rotsa Ruck":* John Little, ed., *Words of the Dragon*, pp. 24–26.

128 *"Seven hundred million":* Linda Lee, *The Man Only I Knew*, p. 89.

129 *"I was the yin":* Linda Lee, *The Bruce Lee Story*, p. 150.

129 *James Yimm Lee was a hard:* Mito Uyehara, *The Incomparable Fighter*, p. 129; Fiaz Rafiq, *Bruce Lee Conversations*, p. 110; Charles Russo, *Striking Distance*, p. 74.

129 *With his business partner:* Al Novak was one of the pioneers of the modern martial arts scene in Northern California. Despite many traditional Chinese masters' reluctance to teach kung fu to white students in the late 1950s and early 1960s, Novak trained at a number of different schools without any backlash. Perhaps because of his size (Novak was a bodybuilder who weighed over three hundred pounds) and his personality (friends called him the "Jolly Old Man of Mayhem"), no one dared to refuse him as a student.

130 *East Wing Modern Kung Fu Club:* Fiaz Rafiq, *Bruce Lee Conversations*, p. 102.

130 *In 1962, another friend, Wally Jay:* Charles Russo, *Striking Distance*, p. 76. Leon Jay, Wally's son, says, "We got to watch Bruce do his demonstration and everything else and we were absolutely gobsmacked and stunned. We'd seen a lot of people but never anyone that dynamic. (Fiaz Rafiq, *Bruce Lee Conversations*, p. 110.)

130 *"When you get there":* Charles Russo, *Striking Distance*, p. 76. The Seattle World's Fair was held from April 21 to October 21, 1962.

131 *"James, the kid is amazing":* Ibid., pp. 78–79.

132 *The two men greeted:* Ibid., pp. 81–82.

132 *Bruce dominated James:* "I saw Bruce demonstrating with Jimmy," recalls Leon Jay, the son of Wally, "and Bruce was pretty much controlling the issue, slapping him around a bit." (Fiaz Rafiq, *Bruce Lee Conversations*, p. 110.) In the introduction to the book he produced with Bruce Lee, *Chinese Gung Fu: The Philosophical Art of Self-Defense*, James attested to Bruce's superior technique: "I was really impressed when in friendly sparring matches with Mr. Bruce Lee, I couldn't penetrate or land a telling blow or kick—even when he was blindfolded—once his hands were 'sticking' to mine." (Bruce Lee, *Chinese Gung Fu*, p. 2.)

132 *"The superiority"*: Bruce Lee, *Chinese Gung Fu*, p. 2.

133 *For the photo shoot:* The photo shoot took place sometime in the spring of 1963 prior to his return to Hong Kong in the summer and his argument with James DeMile in the fall. Jesse Glover and James DeMile had already left to form their own school but everyone was still on speaking terms.

133 *"Hurry up and fix"*: Jesse Glover, *Bruce Lee*, p. 60.

133 *"Jimmy spent years"*: Paul Bax, *Disciples of the Dragon*, pp. 165–66.

134 *"The technique of a superior system"*: Bruce Lee, *Chinese Gung Fu*, p. 88.

134 *"a dissident"*: Charles Russo, "Bruce Lee vs. Wong Jack Man: Fact, Fiction and The Birth of the Dragon," *Fightland Blog*, May 2017.

134 *"Your letter"*: John Little, *Letters of the Dragon*, p. 42.

134 *"So great was his need"*: Bruce Lee, *Chinese Gung Fu*, p. v.

134 *complete college in California:* In fact, he would tell friends that he was taking classes at the University of California. On October 30, 1964, he wrote to William Cheung, "At the present time, I'm taking courses from the University of California. By the way, I'll be getting a degree in philosophy." (John Little, *Letters of the Dragon*, p. 41.) There is no evidence that he ever took another college course after he withdrew from the University of Washington and he certainly never got a degree in philosophy. That he would concoct this story for William Cheung, who was his older martial arts brother, indicates a certain degree of embarrassment on Bruce's part that he failed to graduate from college.

135 *"How could you expect"*: Charles Russo, *Striking Distance*, pp. 1–8.

135 *"His demonstration of the ineffectiveness"*: Paul Bax, *Disciples of the Dragon*, p. ix; Fiaz Rafiq, *Bruce Lee Conversations*, p. 106.

136 *Asian martial arts etiquette:* Wally Jay recalls, "Bruce did step on many toes when he criticized the teaching of non-essential moves by various systems." (Fiaz Rafiq, *Bruce Lee Conversations*, pp. 106–7.)

137 *"Bruce knocked him over the couch"*: Charles Russo, *Striking Distance*, pp. 112–14.

137 *"The martial arts should be"*: Paul Bax, *Disciples of the Dragon*, p. 119.

137 *On July 24, 1964:* Erika Mailman, "Bruce Lee Had a Studio in Oakland," *Contra Costa Times*, April 12, 2005.

138 *"Bruce showed me some moves"*: George Lee and David Tadman, *Regards from the Dragon: Oakland*, p. xii.

138 *"Develop the tools"*: John Little, *Artist of Life*.

138 *Linda was pregnant:* In Linda's two books about her late husband, she carefully elided this crucial detail. In the dozen or so biographies about Bruce, none of the authors mentioned it. When I was trying to figure out why Bruce got married so suddenly after dropping out of college, I noticed that their

first child, Brandon, had been born (February 1, 1965) only five and half months after their wedding date (August 17, 1964). In my interview with Linda, she confirmed she was pregnant prior to the wedding. She wasn't absolutely certain whether Bruce found out before or after he left for Oakland but was inclined to believe it was before. "Did he know before he left?" she wondered. "I believe he did. Or else he came back again." Since there is no evidence of a return trip to Seattle, I assume it was before. (Interview with Linda Lee, 2013.)

138 *"was happy":* In my interview with Linda I asked, "What was Bruce's reaction when you told him?" She answered, "He was happy. He wanted a child. That was very important to him. This child would be his." I pressed, "Was he overjoyed?" "Yeah," she replied. I thought to myself, "So, he actually was a good actor." (Interview with Linda Lee, 2013.)

138 *"The idea of commitment":* Linda Lee, *The Bruce Lee Story*, p. 16.

139 *"What if I never":* Linda Lee, *The Man Only I Knew*, p. 31; Linda Lee, *The Bruce Lee Story*, p. 16; Robert Clouse, *Bruce Lee: The Biography*, p. 55.

139 *Over a series of phone calls:* Interview with Taky Kimura, 2014.

139 *"I respected Linda highly":* Ibid.; Alex Ben Block, *The Legend of Bruce Lee*, p. 33.

139 *He wrote to Linda:* Linda Lee, *The Bruce Lee Story*, p. 18.

139 *"He wanted a child":* Interview with Linda Lee, 2013.

139 *"only chose a boy's":* John Little, *The Celebrated Life of the Golden Dragon*, p. 161.

139 *"coward's way out":* Linda Lee, *The Bruce Lee Story*, p. 18.

139 *Katherine, loaned Bruce hers:* Charles Russo, *Striking Distance*, p. 126; Linda Lee, *The Bruce Lee Story*, pp. 18–19.

139 *He returned to Seattle on Wednesday . . . "It was awful":* Robert Clouse, *Bruce Lee: The Biography*, p. 55; Linda Lee, *The Bruce Lee Story*, pp. 18–19.

140 *"I'm Chinese, by the way":* Robert Clouse, *Bruce Lee: The Biography*, p. 55.

140 *illegal in seventeen other states:* Alabama, Arkansas, Delaware, Florida, Georgia, Kentucky, Louisiana, Mississippi, Missouri, North Carolina, Oklahoma, South Carolina, Tennessee, Texas, Virginia, West Virginia, and Wyoming.

140 *"If you marry":* Interview with Linda Lee, 2013; Linda Lee, *The Bruce Lee Story*, pp. 18–19; Robert Clouse, *Bruce Lee: The Biography*, pp. 55–56.

142 *Linda wore a sleeveless:* John Little, *Words of the Dragon*, p. 74.

142 *"Welcome back to the family":* Interview with Linda Lee, 2013. During our interview, Linda emphasized that not everyone in her family reacted in such a bigoted way. She said, "My father's other brother, Uncle Vern, was not present in Seattle when I got married. He lived in Boise, Idaho. He was the executive director of the YMCA, and he had a heart as big as the whole wide world. When Bruce and I got married, he said, 'Welcome to the family.' He couldn't have been more different than the other uncle, and he was also a

Christian. He just had a different view of things. I've always remained very close with his family."

142 *"You know, Mom"*: Linda Lee, *The Man Only I Knew*, p. 32.

142 *"As a bachelor"*: Alex Ben Block, *The Legend of Bruce Lee*, p. 33; Don Atyeo, *King of Kung Fu*, p. 31.

143 *"Linda is more Oriental"*: John Little, *Words of the Dragon*, p. 50.

143 *"If she is your choice"*: Chaplin Chang, *The Bruce They Knew*, p. 43; John Little, *Words of the Dragon*, p. 39.

143 *"I was certainly not"*: Linda Lee, *The Man Only I Knew*, p. 67.

143 *"We are two halves"*: John Little, *The Celebrated Life of the Golden Dragon*, p. 155.

143 *"Nobody has given"*: Paul Bax, *Disciple of the Dragon*, p. 12.

Eight: Face-off in Oakland

PAGE

145 *West Coast fair*: Don Atyeo, *King of Kung-Fu*, p. 32.

145 *Even royalty:* Taki Theodoracopulos, "Celebrity Kicks," *Esquire*, September 1980.

145 *"High Priest"*: Joe Hyams, *Zen in the Martial Arts*, p. 35; Associated Press, "Ed Parker, Karate Expert, 59," December 19, 1990.

146 *"Jimmy knew once I"*: Linda Lee, *The Bruce Lee Story*, p. 5.

146 *"Bruce was very anti-classical"*: Charles Russo, *Striking Distance*, p. 115.

146 *"Mr. Parker gave me $75"*: Interview with Dan Inosanto, 2013.

146 *"I was completely"*: Bruce Thomas, *Bruce Lee: Fighting Spirit*, p. 58.

146 *Bruce strolled in:* Charles Russo, *Striking Distance*, p. 117.

146 *"That one is the only one"*: Paul Bax, *Disciples of the Dragon*, pp. 86–87.

146 *The Long Beach Championships:* In his excellent book, Charles Russo writes, "There had been a few previous efforts to hold a national martial arts event: Arizona in 1955, and Chicago and Washington DC in 1963 and 1964 respectively. These two more-recent competitions in particular were hampered by widespread disorganization. (Chicago was a real mess)." (Charles Russo, *Striking Distance*, p. 115.)

147 *When he took the floor:* Joe Hyams, *Zen in the Martial Arts*, pp. 9–10.

147 *"He got up there . . . in Long Beach"*: Charles Russo, *Striking Distance*, pp. 119–20.

147 *"Bruce made"*: Ibid., pp. 120–21.

148 *Mike Stone, who had defeated:* Chuck Norris, *The Secret of Inner Strength*, p. 39.

148 *"My first impression"*: Interview with Mike Stone, 2013.

148 *Bruce's job was to dance:* Charles Russo, *Striking Distance*, pp. 126–28; Rick Wing, *Showdown in Oakland*, section 691–700.

148 *After several performances:* According to Charles Russo, Diana and Bruce performed several nights in Los Angeles at the Sing Lee Theatre. "I heard of tensions in L.A. as well," says Russo, referring to Bruce's criticism of traditional kung fu. (Interview with Charles Russo, 2017.)

149 *"Honored guests":* Charles Russo, *Striking Distance,* p. 131.

150 *As the two confident:* In Charles Russo's account, which is based on the memory of Adeline Fong, Kenneth blocked Bruce's strike successfully three times in a row before he raised his fists. (Charles Russo, *Striking Distance*, pp. 132–34.) In Rick Wing's version, however, Bruce failed once and then hit the volunteer with extra force the second time, causing the young man to raise his fists in anger. (Rick Wing, *Showdown in Oakland*, section 654–768.) If Kenneth had blocked Bruce three times in a row, it would make no sense for him to raise his fists. He would have been too busy basking in the crowd's cheers. Also, it would be shocking for a veteran performer like Bruce to miss once. For him to fail three times in a row stretches credulity to the breaking point.

151 *"I would like to let":* Charles Russo, *Striking Distance*, pp. 133–34. Not only what he said but also the exact phrasing he used is a hot topic of debate. Bruce spoke in Cantonese. What he said onstage was repeated and altered over countless retellings of the story. Some remember him saying, "If anyone thinks they can do better they are welcome to come onstage and try." Others recall a direct challenge: "I am better than any martial artist in San Francisco and welcome the challenge of anyone who dares to prove me wrong." (Rick Wing, *Showdown in Oakland*, section 654–768.) Charles Russo is a first-rate reporter, so his version is probably closest to the truth. Given that Bruce's goal that night was to recruit new students, it seems likely he would have said something open to interpretation as either a challenge or an invitation to join his school.

152 *His recent demonstrations:* Charles Russo, *Striking Distance*, p. 112.

152 *"Well, I'm going to open":* Interview with David Chin, 2014. Others have suggested it was David who put that idea in Wong Jack Man's head. Having learned of Wong's ambitions to open his own school, David specifically sought him out and talked him into fighting Bruce Lee. Certainly there were advantages to using someone like Wong Jack Man, who was a recent arrival and not associated with any of the local Chinatown kung fu schools, as a stalking horse. If he lost, no one in San Francisco would lose any face. For his part, Wong Jack Man would later attribute his decision to "youthful arrogance." Wong Jack Man has only ever done one interview about the fight. It was with one of his students, Michael Dorgan. ("Bruce Lee's Toughest Fight," *Official Karate*, July 1980.) He refused my request for an interview. I believe Wong Jack Man heard a version of what Bruce Lee said at the Sun Sing Theatre and, like every other martial artist in San Francisco, was

bothered by it. But it was David Chin who convinced Wong that fighting Bruce was the best way to launch a successful school. Fifty years after the event, Chin still seemed amused by how it went down.

152 *"He was real cocky":* Interview with David Chin, 2014.

153 *"the fresh, alive":* Bruce Lee, "Liberate Yourself from Classical Karate," *Black Belt*, September 1971.

153 *"The only condition":* Interview with David Chin, 2014.

153 *His new Oakland branch:* In her second memoir, Linda Lee insisted that the Oakland school was actually thriving: "Over the years I have occasionally read articles in assorted magazines which have exaggerated our poverty at this time. In fact, the Jun Fan Gung Fu Institute which Bruce and James established on Broadway initially proved quite successful. The few hundred dollars per month that the institute cleared were sufficient to cover our expenses." (Linda Lee, *The Bruce Lee Story*, p. 51.) Her account is contradicted by students of Bruce and James. Howard Williams says, "Back then Jimmy had about 10 students." (Paul Bax, *Disciples of the Dragon*, p. 137.) Leo Fong says, "Jimmy was struggling financially. There were not a lot of students. There were only about six of us in class when I attended." (Paul Bax, *Disciples of the Dragon*, pp. 123–24.) After six months, Bruce and James closed the school.

153 *His business partner:* Rick Wing, *Showdown in Oakland*, section 914–18.

153 *Bruce's pregnant wife:* Linda Lee, *The Bruce Lee Story*, p. 51.

153 *"David was saying one thing":* Paul Bax, *Disciples of the Dragon*, p. 127. Leo Fong went on to say, "After the fight, I talked to Bruce, and he agreed with me, we should go after David Chin. David Chin went into hiding after that."

154 *in early November:* No one can remember the exact date, but the first published report about Bruce Lee and Wong Jack Man's challenge fight appeared in *Ming Pao Daily* in late November 1964.

154 *"Few men had a quicker temper":* Linda Lee, *The Man Only I Knew*, p. 72.

154 *four of David's friends:* The four were Ronald "Ya Ya" Wu, Martin Wong, Raymond Fong, and Chan "Bald Head" Keung. In his mid-forties, Chan "Bald Head" was the oldest member of the group and a well-respected Tai Chi practitioner. (Charles Russo, *Striking Distance*, p. 137.) Wong Jack Man would later complain that he didn't really know any of them and that they were "only there to see the hubbub." His efforts to distance himself from the rest of the group indicate that Wong Jack Man came to believe he had been set up.

154 *"It was not a friendly . . . It's all out":* Ibid., p. 138. Over the years, Linda Lee has asserted that the San Francisco group unfurled a scroll with an ultimatum written in Chinese: "Stop teaching kung fu to non-Chinese." It is her contention that the San Francisco kung fu community was furious Bruce was giving away ancient secrets to white and black folks. In this version, Wong

Jack Man was sent as an enforcer. If Bruce Lee lost he would have to stop teaching non-Chinese and close his school. If he won, he could teach whomever he wanted. Linda's account was incorporated into the Hollywood biopic, *Dragon: The Bruce Lee Story* (1993), and has become part of Bruce's mythology. The problem with Linda's story is nobody else agrees with it. Wong Jack Man denies it. When I asked David Chin, he just laughed, "I think they just say that to make Bruce Lee look like a hero. 'Wow, yeah, he's teaching us white people.' It's totally not true." Leo Fong, who was a student and friend of Bruce Lee's in Oakland, says this tale is "bullshit." Linda has a well-earned reputation for honesty. Everyone who meets her, including myself, finds her to be thoughtful and humble. She doesn't seem like the type to invent such a defamatory story, which leads me to believe she was not the one to make it up. Bruce Lee, like many husbands, was not always completely honest with his wife. When his young, pregnant, Caucasian wife asked him why this fight was happening, he could either admit that he had insulted every single kung fu master in San Francisco or he could say something like, "They don't want me teaching kung fu to white people like you, sweetheart." By 1964 several kung fu schools in San Francisco had white students. No one tried to shut those schools down. Multiple eyewitnesses recall Bruce's performance at the Sun Sing Theatre and the effect his insulting words had on the audience. The evidence is overwhelming that this was the inciting incident for the challenge match. It seems likely that the scroll Linda remembers seeing was actually the original challenge letter written in Chinese, a language she didn't read or speak.

154 *"I suppose I should have":* Linda Lee, *The Man Only I Knew*, p. 72.

155 *in books, plays, and movies: Dragon: The Bruce Lee Story* (1993), *The Legend of Bruce Lee* (2008), *Kung Fu: The Musical* (2014), *Birth of the Dragon* (2016). The first three were authorized by the Bruce Lee Estate and portray Wong Jack Man as a villainous character. *Birth of the Dragon* is unique because it portrays Wong Jack Man as a wise Shaolin monk who tutors the rebellious Bruce Lee.

155 *a four-finger spear:* Wong Jack Man later told his students that Bruce's initial attack was a finger jab, or "spear hand." In my interview with David Chin, he remembers that it was a punch—"a sun fist." (Interview with David Chin, 2014.) Finger jabs were one of Bruce's favorite techniques and he practiced them relentlessly. They are also an excellent attack against a taller opponent since extended fingers have a longer range than a fist. For these reasons, I assume that Wong Jack Man's recollection is correct.

155 *narrowly missing his eyeball:* Charles Russo, *Striking Distance*, p. 140.

156 *"Wong Jack Man backed off":* Interview with David Chin, 2014.

156 *extremely evasive:* Rick Wing, *Showdown in Oakland*, section 1332.

156 *He turned his back and began to run:* Wong Jack Man refused my request for an interview, but he has told his students over the years that he never turned his back and ran. (Rick Wing, *Showdown in Oakland*, section 1332.) However, Linda Lee wrote in her first book that Wong Jack Man did run. (Linda Lee, *The Man Only I Knew*, pp. 71–73.) In my interview with Linda in 2013, she said, "Oh yes, he ran. He ran and he ran. There were two doors leading into a back room kind of thing and he ran in one door and out the other and in one door and out the other. They went around two or three times probably before Bruce actually got ahold of him and got him down to the ground." When I asked David Chin if Wong ran, Chin said, "Yeah, he tried to run away."

156 *sped through the narrow room:* "They went in one side and came out the other," recalls David Chin. "After Wong came back out from the [storage] room, he was front-facing Bruce Lee again." (Interview with David Chin, 2014.)

156 *windmilled a karate chop:* "Once he stopped, Wong Jack Man turned around," David Chin says, "and hit Bruce Lee with a big circle punch into the neck."

156 *The blow staggered Bruce:* Wong Jack Man later claimed that at this point in the fight he grabbed Bruce in a headlock but restrained himself before delivering the coup de grâce. Instead, Wong says, he released Bruce, believing that Bruce would give up and acknowledge that Wong had held back. "I let him go," Wong claimed. (Rick Wing, *Showdown in Oakland*, section 1421.) When I asked David Chin if he remembered Wong Jack Man putting Bruce Lee into a headlock, he said, "I don't think so." No one else at the event has ever mentioned the phantom headlock.

156 *pair of leather wrist bracelets:* They were popular among Hong Kong street toughs of that era. You can still buy them today—an advertisement on the Internet states, "These studded wrist bands can turn your forearms into devastating weapons."

156 *"Bruce was really upset":* Interview with David Chin, 2014.

157 *"Yield":* "Wong hit the showcase on a little platform. It was this old showcase window that they had for mannequins. He hit the platform and he fell," David Chin says. "Bruce jumped on top of him and he hit him and said, 'Are you going to give up?' " (Interview with David Chin, 2014.)

157 *He didn't want the story:* Rick Wing, *Showdown in Oakland*, section 1499.

157 *fight lasted about three minutes:* A man named Bill Chen has insisted to other writers that the fight lasted twenty minutes. In my interview with David Chin in 2014, he stated, "Bill Chen said the fight was twenty minutes. That's a lie. He wasn't there. Do you know how long a 20-minute fight is?"

157 *"The day before"*: Charles Russo, *Striking Distance*, p. 141.
158 *sporting a black eye:* Rick Wing, *Showdown in Oakland*, section 1580.
158 *"Diana Chang is in San Francisco"*: Ibid., section 1641–94.
158 *and* qi *in his heart: Qi* or *chi* is the Chinese word for vitality, energy, or breath. According to Chinese philosophy, everyone has a reserve of *qi* that they can cultivate through kung fu practice. Many believe that cultivated *qi* will grant special powers.
160 *"The Runner"*: George Lee and David Tadman, *Regards from the Dragon: Oakland*, p. 26.
160 *"neither crisp nor efficient"*: Linda Lee, *The Man Only I Knew*, p. 75.
161 *"It really bugged me"*: Mito Uyehara, *Incomparable Fighter*, p. 15.

Nine: Hollywood Calling

PAGE

163 *Dozier was developing:* Bey Logan, *Hong Kong Action Cinema*, p. 24.
164 *"Chinese James Bond"*: John Little, *The Celebrated Life of the Golden Dragon*, p. 18.
164 *"I need to find"*: Interview with Anthony DiMaria, the nephew of Jay Sebring, 2013.
164 *"Bruce was out"*: Linda Lee, *The Bruce Lee Story*, p. 70.
164 *Anna May Wong:* Anna May Wong, the first Chinese American film star, played a detective in a role written specifically for her. Ten half-hour episodes aired during prime time on the now defunct DuMont Television Network before it was canceled.
165 *"When I went back to the States"*: From the transcript of Alex Ben Block's interview with Bruce Lee in August of 1972.
165 *"I felt that I had to"*: John Little, *Words of the Dragon*, pp. 50–51.
165 *On February 1, 1965:* Technically, the 1965 Chinese New Year began on February 2, but Hong Kong is fifteen hours ahead of Los Angeles. When Bruce's family in Hong Kong heard the news, it was February 2. They took the timing as an auspicious sign. In my interview with Phoebe, she made a point of mentioning that Brandon was born "on the first day of Chinese New Year." (Interview with Phoebe Lee, 2013.)
165 *"National Hero"*: John Little, *Words of the Dragon*, p. 41.
165 *"Bruce was intensely"*: Linda Lee, *The Bruce Lee Story*, p. 181.
165 *"Our first child"*: John Little, *Words of the Dragon*, p. 48.
166 *"Bruce was a super dad"*: Linda Lee, *The Bruce Lee Story*, p. 181.
168 *they pushed the assistant director:* The documentary *I Am Bruce Lee* misidentifies the assistant director as George Trendle, the creator of *The Green Hornet*. While it would be fascinating if he had actually been a part of Bruce Lee's

first screen test, Trendle was eighty years old at the time. Contemporaneous photos show him to be gaunt and frail, whereas "the assistant director" looks to be in his late fifties or early sixties and reasonably healthy.

170 *a call informing him:* Robert Chan, who dated Phoebe for many years, dialed Bruce. "I called to tell him, his older brother (Peter), and his older sister (Agnes), all of whom were in America at the time," Robert recalls, "to return to Hong Kong for the funeral." (Chaplin Chang, *The Bruce They Knew*, p. 42.)

170 *opium had weakened:* Interview with Phoebe Lee, 2013. On page 48 of Phoebe Lee et al., *Lee Siu Loong: Memories of the Dragon*, Robert Lee writes, "Years of smoking opium took its toll on our father and he was not in the best of health."

170 *When he learned:* Grace Ho, who was superstitious, told author Alex Ben Block that her husband had predicted when he was thirty-four, in 1935, that he would die when he was sixty-four. (Alex Ben Block, *The Legend of Bruce Lee*, p. 37.)

170 *At the doorway:* Robert Clouse, *Bruce Lee: The Biography*, p. 62; Agnes Lee et al., *Bruce Lee: The Untold Story*, p. 26.

170 *"cross between Chinese custom . . . etc., etc., etc.":* John Little, *Letters of the Dragon*, pp. 45–46, 52.

171 *Plans for* Number One*:* Martin Grams Jr., *The Green Hornet*, p. 319.

171 *"Baby, this trip":* John Little, *Letters of the Dragon*, pp. 48–50.

171 *After six months in business:* "Bruce was a perfectionist who was determined to admit only serious students and talented pupils whom he felt were worthy spending his time on." (Linda Lee, *The Man Only I Knew*, p. 82.)

171 *"Just about the time":* Don Atyeo, *King of Kung-Fu*, p. 33.

171 *"I am taking the liberty":* Martin Grams Jr., *The Green Hornet*, p. 319.

172 *Belasco informed Bruce:* In a letter to Taky Kimura, dated May 10, 1965, Bruce bragged: "I've signed a contract with the agent, Belasco, who, by the way, is also agent for Nick Adams and many others." (John Little, *Letters of the Dragon*, p. 54.) Now long forgotten, Nick Adams was an actor who was most famous for hanging out with James Dean and Elvis Presley.

172 *"reading the 'presentation' ":* William Dozier Papers at the University of Wyoming.

172 *her abilities as a cook:* In her second memoir, Linda writes, "When we were first married I hadn't known how to cook a single thing, and then when James Lee's wife died suddenly, I became chief cook and bottle washer for a built-in family, and as a consequence, Betty Crocker and I became best friends. In the few months that had elapsed, spaghetti was about my best creation." (Linda Lee, *The Bruce Lee Story*, p. 72.)

172 *the oppressive Hong Kong summer heat:* http://www.weather.gov.hk/cis/dailyExtract_e.htm?y=1965&m=6.

172 *"Brandon was an awful baby . . . Bruce was 'stuck' with me"*: Robert Clouse, *Bruce Lee: The Biography*, pp. 64–65; Linda Lee, *The Bruce Lee Story*, pp. 71–72.

174 *"Ip Man didn't like"*: Chaplin Chang, *The Bruce They Knew*, pp. 34–35. Despite taking all the photos, Bruce never completed this Wing Chun book project.

174 *"The more I think of him"*: John Little, *Letters of the Dragon*, p. 63.

174 *"My mind is made up"*: Ibid., pp. 43–44.

174 *"Wing Chun, fencing, and boxing"*: Ibid., p. 60.

175 *"soon, real soon"*: Linda Lee, *The Bruce Lee Story*, p. 72.

175 *"Brandon was screaming"*: Robert Clouse, *Bruce Lee: The Biography*, p. 65; Linda Lee, *The Bruce Lee Story*, p. 72.

176 *"If it wasn't"*: John Little, *Letters of the Dragon*, pp. 55–57.

176 *"It may be this* Charlie Chan*"*: William Dozier Papers at the University of Wyoming.

176 *Dozier was waiting:* Alex Ben Block, *The Legend of Bruce Lee*, p. 36.

177 *"Linda and I will be coming"*: George Lee and David Tadman, *Regards from the Dragon: Oakland*, p. 44. In the standard version of Bruce's life story, he only decided to return to the Hong Kong film industry after his Hollywood career stalled out in 1970. What this letter makes clear is Bruce considered Hong Kong his backup strategy from the very beginning.

Ten: Citizen Kato

PAGE

179 *With its campy:* Matt Zoller Seitz, "Holy Influential Actor, Batman: Adam West Continues to Shape Hollywood," Vulture.com, June 10, 2017.

179 *ABC rejected:* Martin Grams Jr., *The Green Hornet*, p. 319.

180 *on par with Charlie Chaplin:* Hayakawa became the top leading man for romantic dramas. In 1918, he formed his own production company, produced twenty-three movies over three years, and netted $2 million a year in inflation-adjusted dollars.

180 *"The effect of Hayakawa"*: Daisuke Miyao, *Sessue Hayakawa*, p. 1.

180 *"My crientele [*sic*]"*: Ibid., pp. 2–3.

180 The Bridge on the River Kwai*:* Sessue Hayakawa was nominated for but did not win a Best Supporting Oscar for this performance.

180 *were desexualized:* David Eng, *Racial Castration*; Daniel Kim, *Writing Manhood in Black and Yellow*; Jachinson Chan, *Chinese American Masculinities*; Celine Parrenas Shimizu, *Straightjacket Sexualities*. The contrast between the portrayal of Asian men as emasculated in American media versus Asian women as hypersexual (geishas, massage parlor girls, etc.) has proven a rich vein for cultural studies programs.

181 *Created by George W. Trendle:* Martin Grams Jr., *The Green Hornet*, p. ix.

181 *Japanese valet, Kato:* Kato was introduced in the premiere radio episode by the announcer's opening remarks: "Britt Reid's . . . manner and appearance are those of a wealthy clubman. Mounted heads of big game, silver trophies, and various pictures in the place, show him to have been an outstanding college athlete and later something of a big game hunter. Kato himself was something of a trophy, brought back from a trip to the Orient by Britt Reid. Kato seems to serve Britt in every capacity; valet, cook, chauffeur and handyman." (Martin Grams Jr., *The Green Hornet*, p. 73.)

181 *"the great horse Silver":* Ibid., pp. 7–8.

181 *"He is actually an American-born":* Ibid., p. 318. When Dozier was later asked about Kato's nationality, he replied that the character was Korean.

181 *"It sounded at first":* Leroy F. Adams, "Batman's Boy Has a Black Belt Rival," *Washington Post*, August 30, 1966.

181 *to see Chinese kung fu on national TV:* On very rare occasions Japanese martial arts styles popped up in Hollywood movies. A Filipino houseboy used jujitsu to put the smackdown on Cary Grant in *The Awful Truth* (1937). Spencer Tracy employed some basic judo moves in *Bad Day at Black Rock* (1955), as did Frank Sinatra in *The Manchurian Candidate* (1962). I have been unable to find any examples of Chinese kung fu appearing in American movies or TV prior to *The Green Hornet* (1966). Fight choreography in Hollywood was dominated almost exclusively by Western boxing and wrestling.

182 *they moved into a tiny:* Linda Lee, *The Bruce Lee Story*, p. 73. In a letter Bruce wrote to Jay Sebring in early March, he informed Jay he planned to arrive in Los Angeles sometime around March 14–18. He needed to be in town prior to a scheduled appointment for a private acting lesson on Monday, March 21, 1966. (Letter courtesy of Anthony DiMaria.)

182 *acting classes with Jeff Corey:* Douglas Martin, "Jeff Corey, Character Actor and Acting Instructor, 88," *New York Times*, August 20, 2002. As a young actor Corey had been involved with the Communist Party. When he was summoned before the House Un-American Activities Committee, he refused to give any names and went so far as to ridicule the panel by offering critiques of the testimony of the previous witness. This behavior led him to be blacklisted for twelve years.

182 *"the best drama coach":* George Lee and David Tadman, *Regards from the Dragon: Oakland*, p. 10.

182 *"People just couldn't understand":* Interview with Van Williams, 2013. People close to Bruce, like Linda, had no difficulty understanding him and hardly noticed his accent. His screen test for 20th Century Fox is perfectly comprehensible to me. But in my interviews with his Hollywood colleagues, several of them mentioned how thick his accent was and how much trouble this

caused him while filming. Perhaps it grew worse when he was nervous, or maybe they simply had little experience with a Chinese accent.

182 *"You know how I got"*: Alex Ben Block, *The Legend of Bruce Lee*, p. 43; Don Atyeo, *King of Kung-Fu*, p. 32.

182 *"We didn't have enough"*: Linda Lee, *The Bruce Lee Story*, p. 81.

182 *"We thought it was"*: Interview with Linda Lee, 2013.

183 *1966 Chevy Nova:* Robert Clouse, *Bruce Lee: The Biography*, pp. 68–69.

183 *Barrington Plaza:* A cast sheet for *The Green Hornet* dated June 6, 1966, lists Bruce Lee's address as 11740 Wilshire Blvd. Apt. A-2308, LA #25. His phone number was 47-3-5219. (William Dozier Papers at the University of Wyoming.)

183 *Bruce, Linda, and Brandon:* Transcript of Anthony DiMaria's interview with Linda Lee for his Jay Sebring documentary. Bruce Lee's daytime planners.

183 *In nine years:* Linda Lee, *The Bruce Lee Story*, p. 50.

183 *It turned out his agent:* Interview with Joe Torrenueva, 2013.

183 *The weekly salaries:* Martin Grams Jr., *The Green Hornet*, p. 338. Technically, the actors were being paid these amounts per episode, but since it took about a week to film one show, it amounts to the same thing and is easier to understand.

183 *Despite being the second lead:* One argument that has been made for his relatively low pay is that Bruce didn't have any Hollywood credits at that time. But Wende Wagner, playing the secretary, only had a handful of bit parts on her résumé prior to *The Green Hornet*, and yet was paid more than twice as much as Bruce.

183 *Fortunately for Belasco's:* In my interview with Linda, I asked, "Did Bruce realize on *The Green Hornet* that he was getting paid so much less than everyone else?" Linda replied, "No. I didn't even know that. Was he?" "Oh yeah," I responded, very proud of my research. "Van got $2,000 an episode, Wende Wagner got $850, and Bruce got $400." "Is that right?" Linda mused with a smile. "I'm going to take that up with Van."

183 *$550 per week:* Martin Grams Jr., *The Green Hornet*, p. 319.

183 *Dozier opened with a lame:* Peter Bart, "More Chartreuse than Campy," *New York Times*, May 8, 1966.

184 *"I am a karate expert":* Bruce Lee was not a black belt in karate. He never studied the style except informally. It is possible he said this simply because it would be something a white American audience would understand. Another possibility is Bruce said, "I'm an expert in gung fu," and *The New York Times* reporter translated his quote for his readers.

184 *a lighthearted TV interview:* https://www.youtube.com/watch?v=OJKgILeaSVM.

185 *"I am sure you will . . . in six months":* Martin Grams Jr., *The Green Hornet*, p. 313.

185 *one thirty-minute slot per week:* Due to a quirk in ABC's prime-time schedule,

Batman was given two separate thirty-minute time slots every week on Wednesday and Thursday nights. The writers would split the hour-long show in half with a campy cliffhanger. These proved to be so popular the catchphrase "same bat-time, same bat-channel" entered the cultural lexicon.

185 *"When we started":* Interview with Van Williams, 2013.

186 Wonder Woman*:* Martin Grams Jr., *The Green Hornet*, p. 331. The screen presentations for *Dick Tracy* and *Wonder Woman* were both awful. Nothing came of them and the options lapsed shortly after. Here is the *Wonder Woman* pilot: https://www.youtube.com/watch?v=VWiiXs2uU1k.

186 *"He was a good kid":* Interview with Van Williams, 2013.

186 *"He dislocated his jaw":* Ibid. Williams went on to say, "He kicked some people and he got very upset about it because he didn't mean to do it."

187 *"too much starch in my shirt":* Interview with "Judo" Gene LeBell, 2013. In the 1850s, the Chinese were the first to set up laundry services for the all-male mining communities. By 1870 there were 2,899 Chinese laundries in California.

187 *a Crouching Nelson hold:* Ibid. Some people have questioned whether or not LeBell actually picked up Bruce and carried him around the set, because LeBell likes to joke around and tell tall tales. I'm not certain he did, but I know he could have. During my interview with the eighty-one-year-old LeBell, he put me in a neck crank. I couldn't move. He's a tough dude.

187 *"I reckon I teased":* Davis Miller, *The Tao of Bruce Lee*, p. 187.

187 *"I showed him":* Interview with "Judo" Gene LeBell, 2013.

188 *"I'm very mad":* Interview with Van Williams, 2013.

188 *"It's true that Kato":* John Little, *Letters of the Dragon*, p. 77.

188 *But Dozier promised he:* Martin Grams Jr., *The Green Hornet*, p. 330.

189 *spectacular flying kicks:* The two kicks were a flying spinning crescent kick and a jumping double front-snap kick. These acrobatic techniques were part of Northern Shaolin style, not Bruce's southern Wing Chun system. Bruce created a fighting style for Kato, which included jumping karate chops, based more on aesthetics than practicality.

189 *working as a busboy:* James Van Hise, *The Green Hornet Book*, pp. 61–62.

189 *"The Cobra from the East":* Martin Grams Jr., *The Green Hornet*, pp. 341–42.

189 Penthouse Letters*:* "The bathroom door opened slowly and a ravishing young woman emerged. She was wearing my Robin costume, everything except my trunks! Her piercing blue eyes filled the opening of my mask. Her large breasts stretched my crimefighting vest to the limit. She put her hands on her hips and purred, 'I'm yours, Boy Wonder. Take me!' She was a fan. I was the star. This was the moment she'd dreamed of. This was the spontaneous gratification I had come to expect." (Burt Ward, *Boy Wonder*, p. 85.)

189 *Adam West's, while more:* Adam West, *Back to the Batcave*.

190 *"I walked onto the set":* Tom Lisanti, *Glamour Girls of Sixties Hollywood*, p. 328.

190 *began seeing each other:* Despite my best efforts I was unable to track down Thordis Brandt. She only gave one public account of her affair with Bruce in Tom Lisanti's *Glamour Girls of Sixties Hollywood* (2007). I interviewed Lisanti, who remembered Brandt as believable. She also did a private interview about the relationship with one of the world's foremost Bruce Lee experts. He shared with me the details of their conversation and told me he also found her account credible. Thordis kept a contemporaneous diary detailing when Bruce called her on the phone and where they went on dates.

191 *"Why ruin a good thing":* Tom Lisanti, *Glamour Girls of Sixties Hollywood*, p. 328.

191 *Bruce didn't tell Linda:* According to Linda, it was not until after her husband died in Betty Ting Pei's bedroom that she ever considered he might have been unfaithful. "This was the first time I had ever given a thought to the idea, 'Is my husband fooling around?' " Linda wrote in her first biography of her late husband. "And all I can honestly say is that if he were, I knew nothing about it. All I know is he made me very happy; he was a good husband and a good father." (Linda Lee, *The Man Only I Knew*, p. 162.)

191 *"The newest challenge":* Leroy F. Aarons, "Batman's Boy Has Black Belt Rival," *Washington Post*, August 30, 1966.

191 *"The Green Hornet and Kato":* John Little, *Words of the Dragon*, pp. 57, 60.

192 *"he's perfect":* Ibid., p. 32.

192 *"How does it happen":* Ibid., p. 35.

192 *"one of destiny's children":* Ibid., pp. 42–43.

192 *"The adventures of the latest . . . and* Tarzan*":* Martin Grams Jr., *The Green Hornet*, pp. 331–33.

193 *Ricky McNeece:* Ibid., p. 320.

193 *"Those who watched him":* Linda Lee, *The Bruce Lee Story*, p. 74.

194 *"Fine it will be a draw":* Interview with Van Williams, 2013; Martin Grams Jr., *The Green Hornet*, p. 348; John Little, *Words of the Dragon*, pp. 72–73; Hal Lifson interview with Van Williams, 1990.

194 *" 'that thing that Kato does' ":* John Little, *Words of the Dragon*, p. 73.

195 *"Lucky for Robin":* Mito Uyehara, *The Incomparable Fighter*, pp. 70–72.

195 *"It was dumb":* Interview with Van Williams, 2013.

195 *"Confucius say":* Martin Grams Jr., *The Green Hornet*, p. 349. Dozier was far less generous with George Trendle, whom he blamed for the show's failure. "It has not been easy, George, to work around your particular brand of censorship, and I must tell you if I have my way about it again, I would never get into another deal where a basic owner of a property has any rights of final approval of scripts. I think the one thing that has been wrong with *The Green Hornet* is that we have tried too hard to make it too much like the radio series, whereas if we had been

left to our own devices we would have probably gone much more in the modern direction—and yes, even in the direction of *Batman*, which is what I think the public was expecting and also what the network was expecting. Everyone was expecting that but you, and I think we have let everyone down and apparently we have even let you down." (Martin Grams Jr., *The Green Hornet*, p. 344.)

195 *"When the series ended"*: John Little, *The Celebrated Life of the Golden Dragon*, p. 24.

Eleven: Jeet Kune Do

PAGE

197 *628 College Street:* Linda Lee, *The Bruce Lee Story*, p. 62.

197 *February 9, 1967:* Bruce Lee's daytime planners.

197 *training secretly with Bruce:* While filming *The Green Hornet*, Bruce trained Dan Inosanto, Tony Hu, and Wayne Chan in the back of Chan's pharmacy in Los Angeles's Chinatown. (Tommy Gong, *Bruce Lee*, p. 95.)

197 *"You could see"*: Paul Bax, *Disciples of the Dragon*, pp. 235–36.

197 *The close-knit group:* Fiaz Rafiq, *Bruce Lee Conversations*, p. 18. Also in attendance at the seminar were Ted Wong and Herb Jackson, but they were not affiliated with Ed Parker so cannot be categorized as defectors. (Interview with John Little, 2018.)

197 *"Parker wasn't thrilled"*: Paul Bax, *Disciples of the Dragon*, p. 187.

198 *Dan tried to maintain:* Interview with Dan Inosanto, 2013.

198 *New students:* "I was taking karate from Ed Parker in Pasadena and I had heard Dan Lee, who just made brown belt, had left and went with Bruce Lee," recalls Bob Bremer. "Soon after many top students followed. All had years of experience behind them. Bruce Lee only accepted experienced students then." (Paul Bax, *Disciples of the Dragon*, p. 247.)

198 *Glass Wax:* Interview with Joe Torrenueva, 2013.

198 *secret knock: Fighting Stars* magazine, May 1978. Full members were given a key to the gym. "I think I still have the key," Joe Torrenueva told me in our interview in 2013.

198 *"I don't want too many"*: Mito Uyehara, *The Incomparable Fighter*, p. 52.

198 *"Bruce was testing"*: Editors of *Black Belt* magazine, *The Legendary Bruce Lee*, p. 146.

198 *"In memory of"*: Linda Lee, *The Bruce Lee Story*, p. 63. Bruce came up with the tombstone idea and asked George Lee, one of his Oakland students, to work with James Lee to make it for him. "The gadget I have in mind is used to dramatize the not too alive way of the classical so called Kung Fu styles," Bruce wrote to George. (George Lee and David Tadman, *Regards from the Dragon: Oakland*, pp. 48–53.)

198 *"He emphasized footwork"*: Paul Bax, *Disciples of the Dragon*, p. 175.

199 *"Okay, now, watch"*: Interview with Joe Torrenueva, 2013.

199 *"To my surprise"*: Editors of *Black Belt* magazine, *The Legendary Bruce Lee*, p. 146.

199 *shifted to private lessons:* "The perfect sized class is two students and one instructor," Bruce explained. "That way I can work with one student while the other observes." (Fiaz Rafiq, *Bruce Lee Conversations*, p. 75.)

199 *"Caucasian houseboy"*: Paul Bax, *Disciples of the Dragon*, pp. 237–38.

199 *"We even had him"*: Mito Uyehara, *The Incomparable Fighter*, p. 52.

199 *broken rhythm:* When two fighters face each other, they typically start at a safe distance outside kicking or punching range. To land a blow, one of the fighters must "bridge the gap." By "broken rhythm," Bruce meant pausing for a fraction of a second in the middle of an attack in order to surprise or deceive the opponent.

200 *"touch sparring"*: "Without sparring, how do you know if your techniques will work?" Bruce explained to his students. "This is why I don't believe in karate sparring. Karate instructors claim that bare fist sparring is the most realistic but I don't think so. When a blow is stopped, really, you won't know if it will knock your opponent on his ass or not. I believe it's more realistic by wearing gloves and letting go with everything you've got. This way, you'll learn to throw your punches with balance, you'll know how powerful your punches are." (Mito Uyehara, *The Incomparable Fighter*, p. 42.)

200 *"When he tired me"*: Ibid., p. 53.

200 *"kicking dummies"*: Mito Uyehara, the founder of *Black Belt* magazine, wrote, "Many times I used to wonder if Bruce used his students just for his convenience, as Herb Jackson sometimes referred to himself as the 'chief kicking dummy.' I don't think Bruce intentionally tried to use his students, but outsiders might have thought so. He never charged any of us for the lessons. . . . His students had the utmost loyalty to him. They would do anything for him. None of them ever bad-mouthed him." (Ibid., pp. 52–53.) Leo Fong, one of his Oakland students, said: "Bruce would go to different people and he would try his stuff out, that's why in the process those who hung out with him learned. Basically, everybody that was close to him and worked with him were his sparring partners. He developed with his sparring partners to train himself." (Fiaz Rafiq, *Bruce Lee Conversations*, p. 69.)

200 *On July 9, 1967:* The term *Jeet Kune Do* first appears in Bruce's daily planners on July 9, 1967.

200 *linguistics professor:* Tommy Gong, *Bruce Lee*, p. 101.

200 *"What does that mean"*: Interview with Dan Inosanto, 2013; Davis Miller, *The Tao of Bruce Lee*, p. 127.

201 *"I can remember"*: John Overall, *Bruce Lee Review*, p. 169.

201 *"stop hit":* The instant after your opponent begins his attack, you launch your counterattack and "stop hit" him before his attack can land. A successful "stop hit" requires superior speed and timing.

201 *"fencing without a sword":* His protégé, Ted Wong, says, "Jeet Kune Do is more related to fencing than boxing. In fact, you read a lot of his notes that he put together, a lot of fencing terms there. So I can see that Jeet Kune Do is really fighting like a fencer. A lot of techniques come from boxing, but the way you think, the way you apply your technique, is more like a fencer." (Tommy Gong, *Bruce Lee*, p. 101.)

201 *strong side crouching forward:* Bruce was right-handed, so his dominant or strong side was his right hand and foot. For a left-hander the positions would be reversed. Boxers place their weaker hand forward (left hand for right-handers) to use the left hand jab as a pawing or probing technique and keep their stronger right hand back for power punches. With Bruce's focus on speed, he believed the stronger hand should be placed closest to the opponent, so it had less distance to travel.

201 *"Faced with the choice":* Ibid., p. 124.

201 *he stepped back to a fencer's:* Bruce's system of Jeet Kune Do included many other elements and techniques, like the straight lead punch, five ways of attack, nontelegraphy, and broken rhythm. He filled up several notebooks with his writings on these topics. Most of them are included in his posthumous book, *The Tao of Jeet Kune Do*. But the most comprehensive and comprehensible explication of Jeet Kune Do can be found in Tommy Gong's *Bruce Lee: The Evolution of a Martial Artist*.

201 *Lee's personal expression:* Bruce was extremely proud of his creation. "Bruce told me more than once that he wished that they gave Nobel prizes for the development of fighting systems," says Jesse Glover, "because he was sure that he would win one." (Jesse Glover, *Bruce Lee*, p. 83.)

201 *"Sparring with Bruce":* Mito Uyehara, *The Incomparable Fighter*, p. 41.

201 *"There's a split second":* Bremer says, "Bruce was the closest thing to a magician." (Paul Bax, *Disciples of the Dragon*, p. 239.)

201 *"The thing that made him":* Ibid., p. 20.

202 *Bruce's problem:* Alex Ben Block, *The Legend of Bruce Lee*, p. 48.

202 *He could recite:* Mito Uyehara, *The Incomparable Fighter*, p. 9.

202 *"Ah, to be perfectly":* Alex Ben Block interview of Bruce Lee for *Esquire*.

202 *"I don't believe in anything":* Linda Lee put it this way: "He believed man is a self-made product. If there is a God, he is within. You don't ask God to give you things, you depend on God for inner theme." (Alex Ben Block, *The Legend of Bruce Lee*, p. 85.)

202 *a used bookstore:* Paul Bax, *Disciples of the Dragon*, p. 37.

202 *"I frequently saw him":* Linda Lee, *The Bruce Lee Story*, p. 80.

202 *In his notepads:* Tommy Gong, *Bruce Lee*, pp. 228–29. Bruce copied down these quotes in his personal notebooks without including the sources they came from. After his death, his notes were published and, as a result, many of these passages were mistakenly ascribed to Bruce Lee himself rather than the original author. This fact-checking error gave the impression that Bruce was a genius philosopher rather than simply a well-read student of philosophy. Many of these "Bruce Lee" quotes still circle the Internet. For example, BrainyQuote.com credits Bruce Lee with this aphorism: "The key to immortality is first living a life worth remembering." The actual author was Saint Augustine. For the most complete list of misattributions, see James Bishop's *Bruce Lee: Dynamic Becoming*, pp. 191–206.

202 *renegade Indian mystic:* In addition to reading his books, Bruce went to one of Krishnamurti's public talks at the Santa Monica Civic Auditorium on March 7, 1970.

203 *"I do not believe in styles":* Bruce Lee, *The Lost Interview: The Pierre Berton Show—9 December 1971.*

203 *"Jeet Kune Do is merely":* John Little, *The Celebrated Life of the Golden Dragon*, p. 99.

203 *"It was the sixties":* Interview with Dan Inosanto, 2013.

204 *"In this respect, Jeet Kune Do":* John Little, *The Celebrated Life of the Golden Dragon*, p. 113.

204 *"The final aim of Jeet Kune Do":* Ibid., p. 95.

204 *NFL teams banned it:* "Before the 1960's weight lifting was considered dangerous and a detriment to athletes. Some NFL teams would not allow it. That all changed with the help of a man named Alvin Roy." (Thomas George, "Strength and Conditioning Coaches: The Force Is with Them," *New York Times*, June 27, 1993.)

204 *"An out-of-condition athlete":* Mito Uyehara, *The Incomparable Fighter*, p. 43.

204 *"Jogging is not":* Tommy Gong, *Bruce Lee*, p. 143.

205 *"James and I":* Ibid., p. 76. In my interview with Dan Inosanto, he told me a similar story: "We were in Santa Monica where the musclemen used to walk around, and I said, 'Doesn't that guy have a great build?' and he says, 'He might be strong but is he powerful?' I asked, 'What do you mean?' He says, 'He could be strong but if he cannot do it quickly, he is not powerful.' " (Interview with Dan Inosanto, 2013.)

205 *"To Bruce every day":* Mito Uyehara, *The Incomparable Fighter*, p. 99.

205 makiwara *board:* "Driving with Bruce was always an adventure," Chuck Norris wrote. "He kept a small *makiwara* board on his lap or on the seat next to him. Every time we were caught in traffic or came to a stoplight he would beat on the board with either his fist or his knuckles to keep his hands hard."

(Chuck Norris, *Against All Odds*, p. 50.) A *makiwara* board is a traditional Okinawan padded striking post made of rice straw bound with rope.

205 *"When I'm putting"*: Fiaz Rafiq, *Bruce Lee Conversations*, p. 72.

205 *"seemed to be wet"*: Mito Uyehara, *The Incomparable Fighter*, p. 63.

205 *"The NFL used electro-stim"*: In my interview with Mike Stone in 2013, I asked him if he believed the electro-stim machine helped. "For me, no," Mike replied. "I didn't feel really any difference. I just felt the pain that was happening at the time."

206 *"When I got to the door"*: Chaplin Chang, *The Bruce They Knew*, pp. 53–55.

206 *He subscribed:* Tommy Gong, *Bruce Lee*, p. 230. He also subscribed to *Playboy* but that, I assume, was for a different muscle.

206 *Jack LaLanne:* Linda Lee, *The Man Only I Knew*, p. 149; Fiaz Rafiq, *Bruce Lee Conversations*, p. 63. Jack LaLanne was considered the "Godfather of Fitness."

206 *"The thing that really scared"*: In her first memoir about her husband, published in 1975, Linda wrote, "He discontinued this practice before long as he was concerned about the sterility of beef blood." (Linda Lee, *The Man Only I Knew*, p. 148.) In the documentary *The Brilliant Life of Bruce Lee* (2013), Linda revised the anecdote: "We decided to try to put hamburger in the juicer to see what will happen. You get a teaspoon of red liquid out of it. He did not drink it. He was like, 'Yeah, this is not a good idea.' "

206 *"I breathe in and out"*: http://www.salon.com/2000/10/24/barrels/.

206 *"He was a little pudgy"*: Interview with Van Williams, 2013.

206 *"From the Oakland period"*: Fiaz Rafiq, *Bruce Lee Conversations*, p. 43.

207 *speculate about steroid use:* In his harsh biography, *Unsettled Matters*, Tom Bleecker claimed that Bruce Lee abused steroids for years (pp. 85–87). Since his book contains no footnotes or endnotes, I asked him during our interview if he would provide me with evidence for his assertion. He refused. Bleecker's book fanned long-held suspicions of steroid abuse. During my research for this book, I made a point of asking almost everyone who knew Bruce about it. About half strenuously denied it (Linda said, "Oh God, no. Never."), and about half started to whisper or asked me to turn off my tape recorder. The latter didn't have any evidence, but they still believed it and didn't want to be on the record tarnishing his image.

207 *approved by the FDA:* https://www.steroidal.com/history-anabolic-steroids/. German chemists in the 1930s were the first to isolate and synthesize testosterone. The Nazi government experimented with steroids on German troops, hoping to create an army of super-soldiers. The Soviet Union was the first to give steroids to its athletes. As a result, the Russians dominated strength-based Olympic sports during the 1950s. To compete, the U.S. Olympic

weight lifting team's physicians researched steroids and developed Dianabol. The FDA approved it for human use in 1958. Because steroids facilitate tissue repair, Dianabol was used to help athletes build bigger muscles and to help burn victims heal. Steroid use by weightlifters and bodybuilders skyrocketed in the 1960s. The Olympics finally banned them in 1972, but public opinion didn't turn against steroids until 1988 when Canadian sprinter Ben Johnson was discovered to have used them in his victory over American Carl Lewis. The U.S. Congress finally outlawed them in 1990.

207 *to almost zero:* One further piece of evidence against steroid abuse: In Bruce's autopsy, the coroner notes that both of his testicles were of normal size. Steroid abusers experience an atrophy of their testes. (Interview with John Little, 2013.)

207 *"A vibrant personality":* Maxwell Pollard, "Was 'The Green Hornet's' Version of Kung Fu Genuine?," *Black Belt*, October 1967.

207 *"Classical methods":* Maxwell Pollard, "In Kato's Kung Fu, Action Was Instant," *Black Belt*, November 1967.

208 *he had studied Aikido:* Fiaz Rafiq, *Bruce Lee Conversations*, p. 245.

208 *"Do you have any books":* Mito Uyehara, *The Incomparable Fighter*, pp. 105–6.

209 *"I saw Bruce as a renegade":* Davis Miller, *The Tao of Bruce Lee*, p. 134; Fiaz Rafiq, *Bruce Lee Conversations*, p. 246.

209 *"Being in the best shape":* Fiaz Rafiq, *Bruce Lee Conversations*, p. 246. Bruce also gave Alcindor financial advice: "Once you make that kind of bread you attract all kinds of people. What do you think that Muslim organization [the Nation of Islam] wants? Religion is good for you, but there's more to life than just religion. Watch your dough. Don't give it all away." (Mito Uyehara, *The Incomparable Fighter*, p. 110.)

209 *"With me fighting":* Mito Uyehara, *The Incomparable Fighter*, p. 59.

210 *"one touch and run game":* Fiaz Rafiq, *Bruce Lee Conversations*, p. 116.

210 *won the tournament:* In point fighting karate tournaments of that era, fighters would first compete in their weight class and then the winner of each weight class would face off to determine the grand champion. In the 1964 Long Beach Championships, Mike Stone beat Chuck Norris to win the middleweight division. He then went on to beat Harry Keolanui in the finals to become the grand champion.

210 *"You know this school is":* Interview with Mike Stone, 2013.

210 *Like every good-looking guy:* Since point fighting was an amateur sport, the champions still had to work as bodyguards, open karate schools, and teach private lessons to survive financially. Mike Stone became the bodyguard for record producer Phil Spector. In 1972, he met Elvis Presley and his wife,

Priscilla, backstage at one of Elvis's shows. Elvis suggested that Stone teach Priscilla karate. These private lessons led to an affair, which contributed to Elvis and Priscilla's divorce several months later.

210 *Kato was better than him:* In my interview with Mike Stone, he said, "You have to really look deep into the mentality of all of us, our thinking. We all have our personal agenda and we want to have relationships with certain people for certain reasons. . . . What would Bruce gain by having relationships with three recognizable existing champions? Wouldn't that elevate him instantaneously in the martial arts world?" (Interview with Mike Stone, 2013.)

210 *With that face-saving understanding:* In my interview with Mike Stone in 2013, he stated: "During our workouts, it was really never a teacher-student relationship. He didn't really just say hold your hand this way, do this, or do this like that." In an interview he gave in the 1970s, Stone said, "It was really an exchange of ideas more than a student-instructor relationship. There were a lot of things I wanted to pick up to improve my sparring, such as Bruce's attitude of simplicity in self-defense." (Editors of *Black Belt* magazine, *The Legendary Bruce Lee*, p. 157.)

210 *establish his superiority:* Mito Uyehara writes, "Bruce was a proud and intense martial artist and whenever he confronted another competitor, he would unintentionally 'test' him. Bruce wasn't rude or unfriendly. He was so proud of his skill that he just wanted to prove to everyone his superiority (in fighting)." (Mito Uyehara, *The Incomparable Fighter*, p. 57.)

210 *arm wrestling contest:* Mike Stone told me that he beat Bruce three times in a row in their arm wrestling contest until Bruce finally gave up. Interestingly, Van Williams told me a similar story: Bruce kept challenging him to arm wrestle, and Williams kept defeating him.

211 *There were seven lessons:* Bruce Lee's daytime planners. Stone's seventh and final lesson was April 9, 1968.

211 *aggressive game of tag:* A lot of modern criticism of point fighting is unfair. It was the only striking game in town for American martial artists. Kickboxing didn't arrive until the early 1970s. The competitors were talented karate stylists and genuine tough guys. Punches to the face were supposed to be pulled but often weren't. Injuries happened at every tournament. That said, point fighting is to mixed martial arts (or kung fu challenge matches) what touch football is to tackle. While there was a danger of getting hurt, inflicting damage was not the primary purpose of the sport. I've fought in the cage and in a kung fu challenge match, and there is no comparison to point fighting. Joe Lewis, who was considered the greatest heavyweight point fighter, eventually switched to kickboxing. "There was no defense to speak of because nobody was getting hit,"

he said of point fighting. "More than anything, it was a game of tag. How can you call that fighting?" (Davis Miller, *The Tao of Bruce Lee*, p. 120.)

211 *If Bruce won:* Bruce had learned from his fight with Wong Jack Man that no matter who wins in a private match it quickly becomes public and contested. Neither side will admit defeat. It was not in Bruce's interest for a backyard sparring match to turn into a public relations battle in the pages of *Black Belt* magazine.

211 *"Bruce was like a kid . . . named Bruce Lee":* Editors of *Black Belt* magazine, *The Legendary Bruce Lee*, p. 157.

211 *a nightclub act:* Unfortunately, their nightclub act was never filmed. I would pay big money to see these three karate point fighters croon Sinatra tunes and tell off-color jokes. The patter alone would be priceless.

212 *misspelled his name:* It is unknown how Joe Lewis's name was misspelled, but *Black Belt* probably wrote "Joe Louis," after the African American heavyweight boxing champion of the 1930–40s.

212 *"I was an American fighter":* "Interview with Joe Lewis," *Circle of Iron* DVD extras; Paul Bax, *Disciples of the Dragon*, pp. 253–54.

212 *January 25, 1968:* According to Bruce's daytime planners, Lewis took six private lessons. The final one was held on March 29, 1968.

212 *"Once a week I would":* "Interview with Joe Lewis," *Circle of Iron* DVD extras; Fiaz Rafiq, *Bruce Lee Conversations*, p. 132; Davis Miller, *The Tao of Bruce Lee*, p. 134; Paul Bax, *Disciples of the Dragon*, p. 277. Unlike Mike Stone, Lewis was much more willing to credit Bruce as one of his teachers and be publicly grateful for what Bruce taught him. But it would be a mistake to assume that Joe Lewis believed Bruce Lee was a superior fighter. Like the rest of the champion karate point fighters, Lewis believed he was the best fighter in the world. He and Bruce never sparred, but Lewis was certain he could beat him. He respected Bruce as an instructor but not as a fighter because Bruce never competed in karate tournaments. "You don't have to be a good fighter to be a good coach. Bruce Lee wasn't a fighter," argued Lewis. "People say, 'Oh, yes, he was, he was a fighter,' but we're not talking about street fighters. Street fighters have records down at the police departments. A (real) fighter has a record, he has wins, losses, knockouts and draws. If you don't have a record, you are not a fighter, that's it—it's a simple definition." (Fiaz Rafiq, *Bruce Lee Conversations*, p. 133.)

213 *sparring with full protective gear:* Mito Uyehara, *The Incomparable Fighter*, pp. 26–28. The sparring match in full protective gear was a milestone. It didn't quite work for the crowd, because it seemed too safe. But it represented the future of martial arts as a sport. Once bare-knuckle karate point fighting died out, safety gear was incorporated into most amateur and professional competitions—just as Bruce predicted.

213 *a tournament in Fresno:* Bruce was in Fresno March 4–5, 1967.

213 *"A surprising number":* Linda Lee, *The Man Only I Knew*, p. 95.

213 *stationed in East Asia:* Chuck Norris joined the Air Force in 1958 and was sent to Osan Air Base, South Korea, where he began training in Tang Soo Do. Joe Lewis joined the Marines in 1962 and was stationed in Okinawa, Japan, where he began studying Shorin-ryu Karate.

213 *introduced to each other:* In an interview given right after Bruce's death, Norris said, "After I won, I walked over to him and introduced myself." (Editors of *Black Belt* magazine, *The Legendary Bruce Lee*, pp. 148–49.) In his memoir written thirty years later, Norris flipped the status hierarchy: "As I was leaving the stadium, Bruce Lee came over to congratulate me." (Chuck Norris, *Against All Odds*, pp. 48–49.)

213 *staying at the same hotel:* After the tournament, Bruce grumbled about his accommodations. Given that he was generating rock star excitement for these karate tournaments, he began to expect rock star treatment. "Since I am the drawing power and not getting paid, at least, I expect to be treated good," he told Mito Uyehara. "But that promoter in New York was too much. He placed me in a second-rate hotel and I had to find my own transportation. Wait until he invites me again next year. From now on I ain't gonna go nowhere for nothing." When Bruce ignored the promoter's invitation the next year, the unscrupulous man went ahead and advertised that Kato would be the special guest. When Bruce didn't show up, the promoter apologized to the packed audience that his special guest couldn't make it due to another sudden commitment. "I only heard about it after the tournament was long over," Bruce complained. "I don't know how to stop these guys." (Mito Uyehara, *The Incomparable Fighter*, p. 28.)

214 *"The next time I looked":* Chuck Norris, *Against All Odds*, pp. 48–49.

214 *On October 20, 1967:* According to Bruce's daytime planners, Norris trained with him seven times. The last lesson was held on January 31, 1968.

214 *"Bruce didn't believe in high kicks":* Chuck Norris, *Against All Odds*, p. 50.

214 *In fact, Bruce learned:* Jhoon Rhee also claimed he taught Bruce how to high kick. The truth is Bruce learned how to high kick from the Northern Shaolin kung fu forms he studied as a teenager in Hong Kong. Because he didn't believe high kicks were practical in a street fight, he never incorporated them into Jeet Kune Do. However, he did think they looked cool on film. He was eager to learn how to deliver the best-looking kicks. From his 1965 screen test for *Charlie Chan's Number One Son* to his 1970s Hong Kong films, it is obvious that Bruce's high kicks evolved. In 1965, they were more compact and Chinese; by 1971, they were more extended and Korean. My guess is he adapted his sidekick from Norris's karate style and his roundhouse and

spinning hook kicks from Rhee's Tae Kwon Do. They didn't teach him how to high kick, but they helped him improve.

214 *ripped his pants:* Editors of *Black Belt* magazine, *The Legendary Bruce Lee*, p. 149.

214 *"we had 8,000":* Fiaz Rafiq, *Bruce Lee Conversations*, p. 126.

214 *Dominican Republic:* Ibid., p. 123. According to Bruce's daytime planner, he departed on February 3 and returned on February 9, 1970.

Twelve: Sifu to the Stars

PAGE

217 *His asking price:* Alex Ben Block, *The Legend of Bruce Lee*, p. 45; Maxwell Pollard, "Was 'The Green Hornet's' Version of Kung Fu Genuine?," *Black Belt*, October 1967. Adjusted for inflation, $4,000 in 1967 equals $29,000 in 2017. "You know karate guys are the only ones who don't pay me a single penny to perform," Bruce complained to Mito Uyehara. "When I was invited to a parade recently, I got paid $4,000." (Mito Uyehara, *The Incomparable Fighter*, p. 28.)

217 *"Kato Karate Schools":* Jhoon Rhee remembered the name of the chain as "Kato Karate Schools." (Editors of *Black Belt* magazine, *The Legendary Bruce Lee*, pp. 158–59.) Bruce recalled the franchise as "Kato's Self-Defense Schools." (Don Atyeo, *The King of Kung-Fu*, p. 32.) It seems likely that the businessmen approached Bruce with the more alliterative brand name, and he, as a proud Chinese, immediately objected to "Karate" in the title.

218 *"But I didn't want to prostitute":* Fiaz Rafiq, *Bruce Lee Conversations*, p. 68; John Little, *The Celebrated Life of the Golden Dragon*, p. 20. Reflecting back on her husband's decision, Linda said, "He could have become a millionaire opening a chain of Kung-Fu schools. He didn't feel it was the right thing to do because to learn his type of martial art takes very personal instruction." (Don Atyeo, *The King of Kung-Fu*, p. 32.)

218 *Seeing how Sebring:* Partial credit for the concept should also go to Ed Parker, who was already charging celebrities like Elvis Presley huge sums for private lessons. Besides poaching many of his senior students, Bruce clearly copied Parker's business model.

218 *He needed Sebring:* In a letter to Jay Sebring in early March 1966, Bruce wrote: "I need to have some private lessons going. The best would be through your introduction. I can teach the better group [more famous, wealthier] and thus not have to teach too many people. When you have the opportunity, I hope you can work on it for me. I thank you. You are a friend, Jay." (Letter courtesy of Anthony DiMaria.)

218 *As soon as Bruce:* In a letter to Sebring dated March 18, 1966, Bruce wrote: "As an instructor of gung fu let me congratulate you on your speedy progress

in Gung Fu. Your adaptation is rather fast and from past experience I'm sure with some practice you will make it in the field of martial arts. Your movements looked darn good on Thursday night. Potentially, you've got what it takes to be a Gung Fu man. Thanks again for everything."

218 *a marketing list:* Sebring also styled Bruce's hair and taught him how to cut hair. "Bruce was fanatic about his hair. He was a public person. And so he liked it just so," Linda says. "And Jay really created the look for him. But Bruce then used to cut my hair. He was learning from Jay. I had this pixie hairdo." When Linda was asked if Bruce did a good job, she started laughing: "Uh, as far as I knew back then. But when I look at the pictures, I'm not so sure." (Interview with Linda Lee conducted by Anthony DiMaria.)

218 *"The prospective students":* George Lee and David Tadman, *Regards from the Dragon: Oakland*, p. 10. The letter is dated March 31, 1966.

219 *make some serious decisions:* Linda Lee, *The Bruce Lee Story*, p. 81.

219 *"You finding any acting work":* Tommy Gong, *Bruce Lee*, p. 110; Linda Lee, *The Bruce Lee Story*, pp. 81–82; Mito Uyehara, *The Incomparable Fighter*, pp. 51–52; John Little, *The Celebrated Life of the Golden Dragon*, p. 26; John Little, "Enter the Dragon: The Making of a Classic Motion Picture," 25th Anniversary Special DVD Collection, p. 32. All of these accounts credit Charles Fitzsimons with the idea of teaching celebrities kung fu for an outrageous sum. In these versions, Bruce didn't reach out for guidance until after *The Green Hornet* was canceled. But Bruce's letters to Jay Sebring prove that Bruce and Jay came up with the plan two months before filming started on *The Green Hornet*. A year later Bruce talked to Charles, because no celebrities had signed up. Charles's contribution was to tell Bruce he wasn't charging enough. Bruce then asked Sebring to reintroduce him to his celebrity clients at the higher price point. So Bruce and Jay came up with the business plan, Fitzsimons was the consultant who fixed it, and then Sebring implemented it. Over the years Jay Sebring has received far too little credit for how much he helped Bruce's career. Since Sebring died before Bruce became famous, no Bruce Lee biographer ever had a chance to interview him. It wasn't until Sebring's nephew, Anthony DiMaria, gave me Bruce's letters to Jay that the extent of his role became clear. Almost all of Bruce's Hollywood students (Vic Damone, Steve McQueen, James Coburn, Stirling Silliphant) were Sebring's clients. Jay opened the door into the inner sanctum.

219 *On February 29, 1968:* According to Bruce's daytime planners, the cards were printed on February 29, 1968.

220 *"If someone confronts you":* Interview with Vic Damone, 2013.

220 *"But with kung fu":* Ibid.

221 *Like a game of telephone:* Telephone is a popular children's game in which players form a line and the first person whispers a message in the ear of the next person, and so on, until the last person announces the message to the entire group and compares it to the original. Outside the United States, the game is known as "Chinese whispers."

221 *In later versions of the tale:* "Audio Interview with Stirling Silliphant," *Circle of Iron* DVD extras; Jose M. Fraguas, *Jeet Kune Do Conversations*, pp. 245–46. In both interviews separated by many years, Stirling Silliphant tells the story almost exactly the same way, except in the latter version Vic Damone is the antagonist not Frank Sinatra.

221 The Manchurian Candidate*:* In preparation for the role, Sinatra studied judo. It was one of the earliest examples of Eastern martial arts in a Hollywood movie.

222 *Nobody fact-checked:* Fifty years later, I was the first person to ever tell Vic Damone how this story had grown over time. He howled with laughter: "I can't believe it. I mean, oh shit, you know? It never happened, going through a door and all that." (Interview with Vic Damone, 2013.)

222 *This tall tale:* In his book, Mito Uyehara writes that Bruce told him a slightly different version of the event: "Long before I met Bruce, I'd heard a rumor that he'd knocked down Frank Sinatra's bodyguard in Las Vegas. Loquacious Bruce normally would relate his experiences to me, but for some unknown reason, he never discussed this incident. . . . [Finally] I asked if the story was true. Bruce looked at me seriously and hesitated for a moment before he reluctantly replied, 'It wasn't Frank Sinatra's; it was Vic Damone's. No, it wasn't his bodyguard; it was the security guard at the casino. There's not much to say. I just let go a sidekick to his jaw and the big muthah just dropped. Then I walked out of the place.' Usually Bruce was eager to elaborate his experiences but that was the only time, I can recall, he really cut it brief. He never brought up the incident again. Sometimes, I just wonder if he was at fault." (Mito Uyehara, *The Incomparable Fighter*, p. 18.)

222 *"Whether that story":* "Audio Interview with Stirling Silliphant," *Circle of Iron* DVD extras; Jose M. Fraguas, *Jeet Kune Do Conversations*, pp. 245–46.

222 *He had just been nominated:* The Oscar ceremony for films made in 1967 was held in April 1968. *In the Heat of the Night* was directed by Norman Jewison and starred Sidney Poitier and Rod Steiger. The most famous quote from the movie: "They call me *Mister Tibbs*!" It won five Oscars, including Best Picture, Best Director, Best Actor, Best Writing Adapted Screenplay, and Best Sound Mixing.

223 *"I don't really teach":* "Audio Interview with Stirling Silliphant," *Circle of Iron* DVD extras.

223 *"I'm free for lunch":* Bruce Lee's daytime planner.

223 *"You're too old"*: Mito Uyehara, *The Incomparable Fighter*, p. 103.

223 *"At USC"*: Alex Ben Block, *The Legend of Bruce Lee*, p. 48.

224 *"Let me tell you a story"*: Joe Hyams, *Zen in the Martial Arts*, pp. 8–11; Bruce Lee, "Liberate Yourself from Classical Karate," *Black Belt*, September 1971. As an entertainment journalist from that era, Hyams was trained to clean up celebrity quotes to make them appear smarter than they actually were in real life. It's one of the ways he became a trusted insider. In *Zen in the Martial Arts*, Hyams has Bruce Lee speaking more like an East Asian religion major from Harvard than a street-smart Hong Konger.

224 *"It was probably"*: Joe Hyams, *Zen in the Martial Arts*, p. 78.

224 *Hyams took seventeen:* Joe Hyams trained with Bruce Lee from March 25 to May 31, 1968. In his book he does not explain why he ended his study. Shortly afterward, he took up Kenpo karate with Ed Parker.

224 *"It was a very rewarding"*: "Audio Interview with Stirling Silliphant," *Circle of Iron* DVD extras; Patrick McGilligan, *Backstory 3*, p. 351.

226 *"Look, I've met"*: Linda Lee, *The Man Only I Knew*, p. 27.

227 *"it's not cheap"*: Mito Uyehara, *The Incomparable Fighter*, p. 113; Linda Lee, *The Man Only I Knew*, p. 27.

227 *"Bruce always had this energy"*: Linda Lee, *The Man Only I Knew*, pp. 102–4.

227 *"We'd do a thing"*: Linda Lee, *The Bruce Lee Story*, pp. 83–85.

227 *seemed inseparable:* Mito Uyehara, *The Incomparable Fighter*, pp. 113–14.

227 *Steve McQueen and Jay Sebring:* Marshall Terrill, *Steve McQueen*, p. 295.

228 *"That guy doesn't"*: Paul Bax, *Disciples of the Dragon*, p. 229.

228 *"Steve would be"*: Mito Uyehara, *The Incomparable Fighter*, p. 121.

228 *"They really connected"*: Tommy Gong, *Bruce Lee*, p. 111.

228 *"If I hadn't found acting"*: Marshall Terrill, *Steve McQueen*, p. 11.

229 *"Sometimes I'd feel rotten"*: Editors of *Black Belt* magazine, *The Legendary Bruce Lee*, p. 116.

229 *mutual admiration:* Fred Weintraub, *Bruce Lee, Woodstock, and Me*, p. 233.

229 *cut a wide swath:* Marshall Terrill, *Steve McQueen*, p. 305. "Steve had floods of women," recalled one of his girlfriends. "He was always looking for the next pleasure, the next conquest. He was as self-centered as a kid on Christmas morning, yet he had such vitality. He was so much fun to be with, I found myself drawn in." (Ibid., p. 80.)

229 *"You will develop"*: *The Brilliant Life of Bruce Lee* documentary; Mito Uyehara, *The Incomparable Fighter*, p. 126.

229 *"Bruce and I went along"*: Linda Lee, *The Man Only I Knew*, pp. 107–8.

230 *"I'm not that type of cat"*: Alex Ben Block, *The Legend of Bruce Lee*, p. 83.

230 *a myth that continues:* On July 20, 2013, Johnnie Walker Whisky created a

TV advertisement that starred a CGI "Bruce Lee" philosophizing in Mandarin for the Chinese market. It immediately caused controversy, because it is widely believed that Bruce Lee never touched alcohol. The *South China Morning Post* ran an article on July 11, 2013, entitled, "Bruce Lee Whisky Advert Branded a Disgrace: Movie Legend Digitally Recreated for Johnnie Walker Commercial Despite Being a Teetotaler." The next day, the *Atlantic Wire* accused Johnnie Walker of "shamelessly using a spokesman who never drank." (Alexander Abad-Santos, "Johnnie Walker Offends by Using Bruce Lee in Chinese Ad," *Atlantic Wire*, July 12, 2013.) And Time.com referred to Lee, using a dubious choice of adjective, as "a notorious teetotaler." (Jennifer Chang, "Bruce Lee Controversially Resurrected for Johnnie Walker Ad," Time.com, July 12, 2013.)

230 *"Bruce was not a drinker":* Interview with Andre Morgan, 2013.

230 *"There was this time":* Davis Miller, *The Tao of Bruce Lee*, p. 162.

230 *Asian Glow*: Collin Lu, "What Causes 'Asian Glow?,' " *Yale Scientific*, April 3, 2011; Natasha Umer, "Here's Why You Might Turn Red When Drinking Alcohol," BuzzFeed.com, April 27, 2015; Carla Herreria, "*Fresh Off the Boat* Explains the 'Asian Flush' Phenomenon," Huffingtonpost.com, March 17, 2017.

231 *"I'm ruined":* Martin Booth, *Cannabis*, pp. 211–12.

231 *"Marijuana is a useful catalyst":* Allen Ginsberg, "The Great Marijuana Hoax: First Manifesto to End the Bringdown," *Atlantic Monthly*, November 1966.

231 *It was Steve McQueen:* In 1973 Hong Kong doctors questioned Bruce about his cannabis usage. He told them that Steve McQueen introduced him to the drug. James Coburn has claimed credit for being the first person to turn Bruce on to pot when he was interviewed for the documentary *Curse of the Dragon* (1993). Both actors smoked pot with Bruce. Since McQueen was a client before Coburn, it seems likely that Steve was first.

231 *"He'd want to get high":* Davis Miller, *The Tao of Bruce Lee*, p. 161.

231 *"It was different":* Mito Uyehara, *The Incomparable Fighter*, pp. 65–66.

232 *"Hell, back in Hollywood":* Davis Miller, *The Tao of Bruce Lee*, p. 161.

232 *"I never went back":* Interview with "Judo" Gene LeBell, 2013.

232 *" 'consciousness level' ":* Interview with Dan Inosanto, 2013.

232 *switched to hash:* Both marijuana and hash are derived from the cannabis plant and contain the same active ingredient, THC. Marijuana is the dried leaves and buds of the female plant. Hash is created through a more complex mechanical or chemical process of compressing and purifying the buds.

232 *"He was funnier than hell":* Interview with Bob Wall, 2013.

233 *"I used to charge":* Don Atyeo, *The King of Kung-Fu*, p. 33.

233 *"Katleman's place":* Mito Uyehara, *The Incomparable Fighter*, pp. 101–3.

233 *"I want some of that":* Marshall Terrill, *Steve McQueen*, p. 144.

233 *neglected his old Chevy:* "Bruce had an old Chevrolet at the time," writes Mito Uyehara. "The paint was turning dull from lack of polish. I don't think Bruce ever shined the car since he bought it." (Mito Uyehara, *The Incomparable Fighter*, p. 127.)

233 *"Only a few hundred":* Ibid., p. 107.

233 *"I don't know how fast":* Interview with Linda Lee conducted by Anthony DiMaria.

234 *"It's a really hot car":* "Memories of the Master: An Interview with Pat Johnson," *Way of the Dragon* DVD extras; Marshall Terrill, *Steve McQueen*, p. 390. After Bruce left for Hong Kong, he told McQueen that Chuck Norris should be his instructor. When Norris's film career took off, Pat Johnson became McQueen's karate teacher. The two men became extremely close friends. "Other than Ali MacGraw and his last wife, Barbara Minty, no one saw Steve more in his last decade of life than Johnson. He became his mentor, father figure, confidant, and a trusted and loyal friend." (Marshall Terrill, *Steve McQueen*, pp. 364–65.)

234 *"He was just was too fast":* According to Inosanto, Bruce was also a back seat driver: "When I'd drive, Bruce would go, 'No, no, no, you should have changed lanes before. This is way too slow. Your timing is bad.' " (Interview with Dan Inosanto, 2013.)

235 *"If you think I'm a fast":* Mito Uyehara, *The Incomparable Fighter*, p. 122.

235 *living situation:* "With Shannon on the way we decided to buy a house," Linda wrote in *The Bruce Lee Story*, p. 87.

235 *McQueen offered*: Before Bruce left the house, Steve gave him another present: a puppy from his schnauzer's litter. Bruce named it Riff. (Tommy Gong, *Bruce Lee*, p. 111.) According to Bruce's daytime planners, McQueen gave him Riff on August 27, 1968.

235 *"We didn't know much":* Linda Lee, *The Bruce Lee Story*, p. 87.

235 *cost $47,000:* The home was last resold for $648,500 in September 1991. Zillow.com estimated its value in 2017 at $1,667,748.

236 *"With the tax refund":* Mito Uyehara, *The Incomparable Fighter*, p. 127.

236 *"Boy, that was a lot":* Ibid.

236 *"With the mortgage":* Linda Lee, *The Bruce Lee Story*, p. 87; Robert Clouse, *Bruce Lee: The Biography*, p. 76.

236 *"It was so quiet":* Mito Uyehara, *The Incomparable Fighter*, pp. 123–24.

236 *block named Luke:* Linda Lee, *The Bruce Lee Story*, p. 88.

237 *"Good for the guys":* Interview with Linda Lee, 2013.

237 *received a windfall:* Robert Clouse, *Bruce Lee: The Biography*, p. 80.

237 *"Guys, check out my new car":* "Memories of the Master: An Interview with Pat Johnson," *Way of the Dragon* DVD extras. Fear of riding with Bruce seems to have been fairly universal among his friends. "He was the worst fucking driver,"

Bob Wall told me. "When I heard he died, I just assumed it was a car accident." Despite his reckless driving, Bruce was only responsible for one minor accident. According to his daytime planners, he dinged up his Porsche on January 28, 1969. Linda got into a more serious accident when she was driving the Porsche on June 3, 1969. In a letter to one of his Oakland students, Bruce wrote, "When Linda came to pick me up, the car had an accident—lucky nobody got hurt. Brandon bumped his head slightly. The car is out for a few days." (George Lee and David Tadman, *Regards from the Dragon: Oakland*, p. 36.)

238 *"It was extravagant":* Robert Clouse, *Bruce Lee: The Biography*, p. 80.

238 *"The second time":* John Little, *The Celebrated Life of the Golden Dragon*, p. 166.

238 *"I feel real bad":* Mito Uyehara, *The Incomparable Fighter*, p. 142.

239 *"David Cassidy":* Interview with Anders Nelsson, 2013.

239 *"I hope my fans . . . three-mile run":* "In the Shadow of Bruce Lee: Robert Lee: Bridging the Gap Between Individuality and a Brother's Legend," *Black Belt*, August 1974; Robert Lee, *Bruce Lee, My Brother*, p. 127.

239 *"It was a very difficult time": Brilliant Life of Bruce Lee* documentary.

239 *"I have to be more":* Mito Uyehara, *The Incomparable Fighter*, p. 142.

Thirteen: Bit Player

PAGE

242 *"Then he'd get mad":* After my interview with the eighty-one-year-old "Judo" Gene LeBell, he wrote me an email apologizing for not being sufficiently respectful of Bruce Lee's legacy: "Sorry but I should say, Bruce was the best of his time. Every man, woman, and child wanted to be the great Bruce Lee. Well not me, he was too short."

242 *"My agent called":* George Lee and David Tadman, *Regards from the Dragon: Oakland*, p. 6.

242 *"Pick on Someone":* It was the same conceit as the episode Ed Parker did for *The Lucy Show* in 1963: a bumbling white suburban type takes up an exotic Asian fighting style with lots of corny cross-cultural jokes and slapstick physical comedy.

243 *"He won me over":* John Overall, *Bruce Lee Review*, p. 83. Of all of Bruce Lee's TV performances, this *Blondie* episode is the only one that is "missing," presumed lost. There are rumors that a private collector has a copy but refuses to show it to anyone. Portions of the original script can be found in John Overall's *Bruce Lee Review*, pp. 84–86.

243 *"Most of those shows":* Mito Uyehara, *The Incomparable Fighter*, p. 73.

243 *convoluted plot into motion:* In this hackneyed episode filled with dated stereotypes about obedient Chinese women, Toy Quan is saved from being sent to a brothel when one of the white lumberjacks agrees to pay for her passage.

Because he "saves her life," she must, according to Chinese custom, marry him. He sets off to find her original Chinese betrothed, Lin Sung, to get his money back and give her away, but Toy Quan won't leave him alone. The proper white ladies of Seattle, including his girlfriend, grow increasingly suspicious of his intentions, until Bruce's character is given a chance to save Toy Quan's life, at which point she immediately switches her allegiances. "I disliked that show," says William Blinn, the story editor for *Here Come the Brides*. "It was very much like an old-fashioned *Bonanza*—you know the Oriental person saying, 'Oh, you saved my life. Therefore, blah, blah, blah, blah, blah.' And A: That's not true—it was a television myth, and B: It doesn't take you anywhere. It was such a traditional, corny western plot." (Jonathan Etter, *Gangway, Lord!*, p. 448.)

244 *"I started to yell"*: Mito Uyehara, *The Incomparable Fighter*, p. 69. The director also had difficulty finding a stand-in to loop some of Bruce's dialogue. In many of the outdoor scenes, it was necessary to rerecord his dialogue, but apparently Bruce was unavailable to loop. (One rumored explanation is he had pulled a groin muscle.) The problem was there was no actor in Hollywood who could imitate Bruce's very distinctive Hong Kong English accent. As a result, whenever Bruce opens his mouth in the episode, it is a toss-up if you will hear his actual voice or some white actor badly faking a Chinese accent. (John Overall, *Bruce Lee Review*, pp. 94–95.)

244 *paid Bruce $11,000:* Mito Uyehara, *Bruce Lee: The Incomparable Fighter*, p. 20. $11,000 is $78,000 in 2017 dollars.

244 *He used the money: The Wrecking Crew* filmed during the summer of 1968. Bruce was paid $11,000. He bought his Bel Air home on September 9, 1968. The down payment was $10,000. Money tended to burn a hole in his pocket.

245 *advice about his acting career:* In my interview with Nancy Kwan, she said, "We were both from Hong Kong so we had something in common. We could speak in Cantonese. I did take Wing Chun classes with him. He would come up to my house in Laurel Canyon and tell me about his dreams about becoming a big star. He wasn't satisfied with his life here, how it was going with the film business." (Interview with Nancy Kwan, 2013.)

245 *"like a house on fire":* Roman Polanski, *Roman by Polanski*, p. 290.

245 *"Sharon and Nancy":* Mito Uyehara, *The Incomparable Fighter*, p. 20.

245 *portable bar:* Fiaz Rafiq, *Bruce Lee Conversations*, pp. 146–47.

245 *He hired Mike Stone:* Bruce did hold an open audition for the bodyguard roles. Hundreds of martial artists showed up, but most of them were awful. Bruce became frustrated and asked Stone and Norris to give a short demonstration. "This is what I am looking for," Bruce told the crowd. "If you can't do some of these things at that level, then I'm not interested. You can leave." Half the

group immediately began filtering out. At the end of the day, Bruce hired his friends. (Interview with Mike Stone, 2013.)

245 *"There's a small role":* Chuck Norris, *The Secret of Inner Strength*, p. 57.

245 *In their four previous:* In early 1967, Chuck Norris beat Joe Lewis with a spinning back kick to Lewis's face at the Tournament of Champions. At the 1967 All American Karate Championships in Madison Square Garden (where Norris and Bruce Lee met for the first time), Norris squeaked out a win with a sidekick to Lewis's torso. At Ed Parker's 1967 Long Beach International Karate Championships, Norris won with a reverse punch against Lewis. In the 1968 U.S. Championships in Dallas, Joe Lewis finally took his revenge with a punch to Norris's solar plexus.

245 *Lewis was disqualified:* Chuck Norris, *The Secret of Inner Strength*, p. 57.

246 *Dean Martin was to enter:* For Chuck Norris's fight scene, Dean Martin was supposed to be filmed for the first stage of the fight and then doubled by Mike Stone. For the opening shot, Norris was to throw a spinning heel kick over Dean's head, but when the director called, "Action," Dean forgot to bend down. Norris hit him flush on the shoulder and sent him flying across the set. The director was horrified but Dean was good-natured about the accident. "I'm OK," he said. "Let's do it again." (Ibid., pp. 57–59.) Bruce choreographed a similar sequence for Joe Lewis, who was also supposed to kick over Dean's head. Martin would then foot sweep Lewis and nail him when he hit the floor. After what happened with Norris, Dean Martin's agent pulled Lewis to the side: "Joe, make sure you don't hit him because he's worth a lot of money." Martin had been drinking all day and showed up smashed. Lewis made sure to kick real high and real slow. He was wearing a suit and, as soon as he threw that first kick, his trousers split up the crotch. "Of course they got that on film," Lewis laughs. "That was my first ever fight scene on film." (Fiaz Rafiq, *Bruce Lee Conversations*, pp. 146–47.)

246 *paid $4,500:* Fiaz Rafiq, *Bruce Lee Conversations*, pp. 146–47.

247 *"Bruce, listen, I heard":* Interview with Mike Stone, 2013.

248 *"These guys, just":* Mito Uyehara, *The Incomparable Fighter*, p. 57. Bruce's relationship with the three karate champions and the issue of credit irritated him for the rest of his life. In an August 16, 1970, profile of Bruce Lee in the *Washington Star* (two years after his argument with Mike Stone), the author, J. D. Bethea, wrote: "At first, it was easy to dismiss Lee's filmed expertise as the same old Hollywood stuff. Ironically, he's better than he was ever portrayed on celluloid. Three of his pupils, Joe Lewis, Chuck Norris, and Mike Stone, have between them won every major karate tournament in the United States at least once. Lewis was Grand Champion three successive years. Lee

handles and instructs these guys almost as a parent would a young child. Which can be somewhat disconcerting to watch." (John Little, *Words of the Dragon*, pp. 97–98.) The article clearly gives the impression that the reporter personally watched Bruce instruct Norris, Lewis, and Stone "like a parent would a young child." But this is impossible. According to Bruce's daytime planners, he stopped training Chuck Norris on January 31, 1968. He had the falling-out with Mike Stone on the set of *The Wrecking Crew* in August of 1968. And his friendship with Joe Lewis ended on December 1, 1969. Either J. D. Bethea made up the scene or he based it on something that Bruce told him during their interview. What seems obvious is Lee wanted the public to know that Mike Stone, Chuck Norris, and Joe Lewis were his students.

248 *"My wife says you made":* Paul Bax, *Disciples of the Dragon*, pp. 270–71.

248 *never made it in the movie business:* Joe Lewis's biggest part was as the lead in *Jaguar Lives!* (1979). It was a flop. One reviewer referred to it as "a festering pile of forgotten suck." Mike Stone was cast in some bit parts during the ninja movie craze of the 1980s.

249 *vast wasteland:* Val Adams, "F.C.C. Head Bids TV Men Reform 'Vast Wasteland'; Minow Charges Failure in Public Duty—Threatens to Use License Power," *New York Times*, May 10, 1961.

249 *"By the time of* Marlowe*":* Patrick McGilligan, *Backstory 3*, p. 351.

250 *stiff and nervous:* Bruce had every reason to be anxious. Trouble with his English had limited the number of lines he was given on *The Green Hornet*. To become a Hollywood star, he knew he needed to be able to speak English clearly with a pleasing accent. While all foreign actors face this problem, it was particularly difficult for Asian actors whose accents had for years been the subject of mockery, most notably Mickey Rooney's yellow-faced burlesque in *Breakfast at Tiffany's* (1961).

250 *"Bruce was fine in life":* Interview with Sharon Farrell, 2013. To help him with his dialogue, Farrell taught Bruce an acting technique: "There's an exercise you do where you put a toothpick between your teeth and you read your lines, and you keep that toothpick there, and then you take the toothpick away. It works your tongue, and it makes it better."

250 *"the whole enchilada":* Patrick McGilligan, *Backstory 3*, p. 350.

250 *"Smashing the lamp":* Mito Uyehara, *The Incomparable Fighter*, p. 70.

251 *The force of Winslow's:* To prepare for this kicking-over-the-wall scene, Bruce went to a sporting goods store with one of his students, Ted Wong, and bought a trampoline. "He practiced the scene and asked me how it looked," says Ted. "He later took me to the movie set when that particular scene was filmed and I got to meet James Garner." (Paul Bax, *Disciples of the Dragon*, p. 225.)

251 *"The scene was":* Mito Uyehara, *The Incomparable Fighter*, p. 70.

251 *When she first laid eyes:* Interview with Sharon Farrell, 2013. Our interview was only the second time in forty years Farrell had gone on the record about her relationship with Bruce. The first was for Richard Sydenham's 2013 biography, *Steve McQueen*, p. 335.

255 *"Bruce was the love of my life":* During our interview in 2013, Farrell said, "Bruce was the most incredible lover I've ever been with." Taken aback, I asked, "Better than Steve McQueen?" She said, "Well, Steve was real macho. When he wanted you, he took you. Bruce worshipped you. He really loved you. Everything fit. It was just like magic. He was a great dancer. He took me away. He was easy, just so easy. It was just so wonderful. He was magnificent."

255 *"If I ever had an affair":* Linda Lee, *The Man Only I Knew*, pp. 162–63.

256 *"don't flaunt it":* Marshall Terrill, *Steve McQueen*, p. 102.

256 *"have a good arrangement":* Christopher Sandford, *Polanski*, p. 123.

256 *"A Sin That Became":* Chuck Norris, *Against All Odds*, pp. 171–75.

256 *"not saying I am a saint":* Ted Thomas, "Bruce Lee: The Ted Thomas Interview," December 1971.

256 Variety *wrote:* "Review: 'Marlowe,' " *Variety*, December 31, 1968.

256 *Roger Ebert:* Roger Ebert, "Marlowe," *Chicago Sun-Times*, November 25, 1969.

256 *"They are going to give":* Don Atyeo, *King of Kung-Fu*, p. 35.

257 *"his phone number":* Interview with Sharon Farrell, 2013.

Fourteen: The Silent Flute

PAGE

259 *Bruce knew no Hollywood:* Kung fu movies were not a genre back then. Hong Kong studios did not release them outside of Chinatowns until 1973.

259 *In response to Bruce's:* In April 1968, Bruce wrote to a friend, "Steve McQueen, after he completes his movie in Frisco [*Bullitt*], will get a writer and start on a Gung Fu movie with him and I in it. So this is a start toward the movie." (John Little, *Letters of the Dragon*, p. 107.) But McQueen never got around to finding a writer, forcing Bruce to approach Silliphant about the project. It seems likely that McQueen was just humoring Bruce and putting him off with talk about finding a writer.

259 *Silliphant was eager:* On September 26, 1968, Bruce excitedly wrote to a friend: "The project on Jeet Kune Do as a movie is taking another step. Stirling Silliphant (*In the Heat of the Night*) is involved to write the script. We will be getting together and roll." (John Little, *Letters of the Dragon*, p. 108.) But once again, Bruce was exaggerating to impress a friend. Silliphant would only agree to join the project on the condition that McQueen was involved.

"If Steve will do it," Silliphant told Bruce, "I will write it." (Robert Clouse, *Bruce Lee: The Biography*, p. 84.)

260 *"Stop bothering me":* Marshall Terrill, *Steve McQueen*, p. 288.

261 *"I'm going to be":* *Circle of Iron* DVD extras; Robert Clouse, *Bruce Lee: The Biography*, p. 84.

261 *He started avidly reading:* Interview conducted by phone with Mike Stone on September 12, 2013. According to Stone, he introduced Bruce to Napoleon Hill's work: "I shared Hill's book with Bruce and the idea of goal setting."

261 *On January 7, 1969:* In his daytime planners, Bruce wrote, "Make up mind to make goal."

261 *"I, Bruce Lee":* Linda Lee, *The Bruce Lee Story*, p. 96. By 1973, Bruce Lee was well on his way toward fabulous wealth and world renown, but not inner harmony or happiness.

261 *McQueen had made:* "When we left Steve's house Bruce was angry," recalls Silliphant. "He'd lost face in front of me because he had brought me to a superstar with the hope that we would come out of the meeting with a deal. He thought Steve would simply say, 'Okay, go write the script; we'll do it.' " (*Circle of Iron* DVD extras.)

262 *"It was a weird":* Marshall Terrill, *Steve McQueen*, p. 88.

262 *to recruit Paul:* In a letter from May 1969 Bruce wrote to Sebring, "Is Newman by the way ready to start?" (Letter courtesy of Anthony DiMaria.)

262 *"Bruce was bereft":* Robert Clouse, *Bruce Lee: The Biography*, p. 84.

262 *On January 13, 1969:* Bruce Lee daytime planners. On January 14, 1969, Bruce went to dinner and a movie with Coburn and his wife to firm up Coburn's commitment.

262 *The three men:* Bruce Lee daytime planners; Davis Miller, "Bruce's Lee's Silent Flute: A History," *Circle of Iron* DVD extras.

262 *"No, I'm up to my ears":* Bruce Lee daytime planners; Robert Clouse, *Bruce Lee: The Biography*, p. 84; Alex Ben Block, *The Legend of Bruce Lee*, p. 52.

263 *" 'Project* Leng' *":* John Little, *Letters of the Dragon*, p. 113.

263 *Seven days later:* They met on January 20, 1969.

263 *In the afternoons:* Bruce Lee's daytime planners. He met with Stirling Silliphant, James Coburn, and Mark Silliphant on January 20, 1969. He began listening to motivational tapes and writing the treatment on February 13, 1969.

263 *"We will speed up":* John Little, ed., *Letters of the Dragon*, p. 113. The letter was written to Jhoon Rhee on March 4, 1969.

263 *"Since the story":* Editors of *Black Belt* magazine, *The Legendary Bruce Lee*, pp. 129–30.

264 *On April 17, 1969:* He stayed in Tennessee from April 17 to April 21, 1969.

264 *"This little guy":* Robert Clouse, *Bruce Lee: The Biography*, p. 70.

265 *Sebring planned to pick up McQueen:* Marshall Terrill, *Steve McQueen*, pp. 295–96; Christopher Sandford, *Polanski*, pp. 139–40. Over the years, there have been some rumors that Sebring also invited Bruce Lee, who was friendly with Sharon, taught Polanski Jeet Kune Do, and lived only a few miles away from the Tate-Polanski home. When I asked Linda about the rumors, she said, "Not as far as I know." I did not uncover any evidence to suggest that Sebring invited Bruce.

265 *Melcher, a well-known record producer:* In March 1969, Charles Manson, who was furious over Terry Melcher's failure to deliver a record contract, went to Melcher's house on Cielo Drive, unaware that Melcher had already moved out. Manson showed up in the middle of a party given by one of the new residents, Sharon Tate. (Rob Sheffield, "Heart of Darkness: A Charles Manson Timeline," *Rolling Stone*, November 21, 2013.)

266 *Steven Parent, an eighteen-year-old visitor:* Steven Parent was visiting the property's caretaker, William Garretson, who lived in the property's guesthouse. As Parent was leaving, he stopped his car at the front gate and rolled down his window to push the button that opened the gate. Tex Watson stepped out of the bushes with a buck knife in one hand and a .22 revolver in the other. Watson slashed Parent and then shot him four times. Parent was the first person killed that night. Garretson hid in the guesthouse and survived.

266 *Before leaving, Susan Atkins*: Steve Oney, "Manson: Oral History," *Los Angeles Magazine*, July 1, 2009; Margalit Fox, "Charles Manson Dies at 83; Wild-Eyed Leader of a Murderous Crew," *New York Times*, November 20, 2017.

266 *The grisly massacre:* Marshall Terrill, *Steve McQueen*, p. 295.

266 *Chappaquiddick*: Christopher Sandford, *Polanski*, p. 155.

266 *"This hit":* Steve Oney, "Manson: Oral History," *Los Angeles Magazine*, July 1, 2009.

266 *Writer Dominick Dunne:* Marshall Terrill, *Steve McQueen*, pp. 295–97.

266 *"That was a very scary":* Interview with Linda Lee, 2013.

267 *Newman, Henry Fonda:* Christopher Sandford, *Polanski*, p. 152.

267 *"The house was only":* After the funeral, Mito Uyehara asked Bruce, "Sebring studied kung fu with you. Why didn't he fight back?" "Sebring could never get out of a situation like that," Bruce replied. "He was still too green and he wasn't that type of guy who would fight back." (Mito Uyehara, *The Incomparable Fighter*, p. 124.)

267 *For three months:* In November 1969, Susan Atkins, who was arrested on unrelated charges, boasted about the killings to fellow prisoners. They turned her in, providing the first big break in the case. On December 4, 1969, Atkins agreed to cooperate and made a deal with prosecutors. (Rob Sheffield, "Heart of Darkness: A Charles Manson Timeline," *Rolling Stone*, November 21, 2013.)

267 *hypervigilant:* Interview with Linda Lee, 2013.

267 *"I've lost my glasses":* Roman Polanski, *Roman by Polanski*, pp. 317–18; Christopher Sandford, *Polanski*, p. 158.

267 *Polanski later invited Bruce:* Bruce stayed at Polanski's chalet in Switzerland February 16–26, 1970. In his letters home to his wife, he claimed to have a miserable time: He didn't like skiing (Polanski says Bruce was a disaster on the slopes), and he didn't like Polanski's jet set guests or their hard-partying lifestyle. "The so-called jet set are kind of silly and boring. Drinking, smoking pot, and skiing is almost all they do," Bruce wrote. "In between, everyone is trying to take someone to bed. Roman, if not skiing, is always after some girls." (John Little, *Letters of the Dragon*, pp. 128–31.) Bruce Lee was not, as a general rule, averse to getting stoned or getting laid. According to Polanski, "the women were impressed by his charm and Oriental good looks." (Roman Polanski, *Roman by Polanski*, pp. 330–31.) What seemed to really bother him is that none of the guests was particularly interested in kung fu. He only began to enjoy himself after he befriended a fellow martial arts nut, Taki Theodoracopulos—a wealthy Greek-British journalist. They spent the week training together. (Taki Theodoracopulos, "Celebrity Kicks," *Esquire*, September 1980.)

268 *screenwriter named Logan*: Bruce Lee's daytime planners. Logan was hired on September 11, 1969. I could find no mention in any of the literature of Logan's last name.

268 *"He brought in a script":* Alex Ben Block, *The Legend of Bruce Lee*, p. 52.

268 *"Okay, I'll write":* Robert Clouse, *Bruce Lee: The Biography*, p. 84.

268 *Sufi parables:* Davis Miller, "Bruce's Lee's Silent Flute: A History," *Circle of Iron* DVD extras.

268 *T. S. Eliot's:* Interview with Marshall Terrill, 2013. "As for *The Silent Flute*, Stirling was trying to communicate that timeless state of mind, much as T. S. Eliot tried a similar approach with the Zen of Christianity in *Four Quartets*."

268 *"self-evolution of man":* "The Making of 'The Silent Flute,' " *Black Belt*, October 1970.

268 *In the final draft:* The date on the *Silent Flute* screenplay is October 19, 1970.

269 *crucified, decapitated woman:* Davis Miller, "Bruce's Lee's Silent Flute: A History," *Circle of Iron* DVD extras.

269 *"Lying together fully":* *The Silent Flute* screenplay, pp. 38–39.

269 *"You will never kick":* Linda Lee, *The Bruce Lee Story*, pp. 88–89; Linda Lee, *The Man Only I Knew*, pp. 14–15; Tommy Gong, *Bruce Lee*, p. 118.

270 *"I really got scared":* Mito Uyehara, *The Incomparable Fighter*, p. 93.

270 *"beautiful notes of love":* Linda Lee, *The Bruce Lee Story*, p. 95; Robert Clouse, *Bruce Lee: The Biography*, p. 73.

270 *"No matter what":* Linda Lee, *The Man Only I Knew*, pp. 163–65.

271 *For inspiration:* Ibid., pp. 118–19.

271 *He also utilized:* Tommy Gong, *Bruce Lee*, p. 118.

271 *"Walk On!":* "Walk On" had long been one of Bruce's favorite motivational phrases. It was something he wanted to pass on to Brandon. In a 1966 interview, he said, "I will teach Brandon to walk on. Walk on and he will see a new view. Walk on and he will see the birds fly. Walk on and leave behind all things that would dam up the inlet, or clog the outlet, of experience. (John Little, *Words of the Dragon*, p. 47.)

271 *After five months:* At some point after his recovery, he also drove to Las Vegas to meet a female astrologer, who had become Hollywood's favorite fortune-teller. When he returned to Los Angeles, he was jubilant. "Yeah, it cost me $40, but it was worth it. The lady said that I'm gonna be very successful very soon—anytime now and I really believe her. I can just feel it here," he chuckled, exultantly pounding his chest. "She said my success will be so great that it's almost incredible. My career will zoom so high and I'm gonna be a real big movie star." (Mito Uyehara, *The Incomparable Fighter*, p. 91.)

271 *To the shock*: Tommy Gong, *Bruce Lee*, p. 118.

271 *normal lifestyle:* Linda Lee, *The Bruce Lee Story*, p. 89. If Bruce's life is viewed as a hero's journey, then his back injury was the archetypal moment when the protagonist descends into hell, experiences the low point of his life, and is scarred with an unhealable wound—before returning to the world wiser and revitalized. In the film *Dragon: The Bruce Lee Story* (1993), his back injury serves as a central turning point in the story.

272 *dinner party at Ashley's:* Fred Weintraub, *Bruce Lee, Woodstock, and Me*, p. 29. According to Bruce's daytime planners, he had dinner with Ted Ashley on January 23, 1971.

272 *"It was strictly":* Mito Uyehara, *The Incomparable Fighter*, p. 101.

272 *"I vividly recall":* John Little, *Enter the Dragon: The Making of a Classic Motion Picture*, pp. 33–34.

272 *"They instantly loved it":* Robert Clouse, *Bruce Lee: The Biography*, p. 86.

272 *On January 29, 1971:* According to Bruce Lee's daytime planners they arrived in India on February 1 and departed from Bombay on February 11, 1971.

272 *"I've got to keep in shape":* Linda Lee, *The Man Only I Knew*, p. 24.

272 *"The road is terrible!":* John Little, *Letters of the Dragon*, pp. 142–43.

273 *"For Christ's sake":* The trip to India is drawn from these four sources: Robert Clouse, *Bruce Lee: The Biography*, pp. 87–90; Mito Uyehara, *The Incomparable Fighter*, p. 115; Linda Lee, *The Bruce Lee Story*, p. 92; Alex Ben Block, *The Legend of Bruce Lee*, pp. 52–53.

274 *smoked Nepalese hash:* In my interview with Bob Wall in 2013, he said, "Coburn told me that the whole time they were in India they were smoking dope morning, noon, and night."

275 *Coburn was convinced*: After two weeks traveling with Bruce, Coburn may have also had reservations about working with him over a longer period of time. In close quarters and under stress, the two men rubbed each other the wrong way.

275 *Coburn screwed it:* Mito Uyehara, *Bruce Lee: The Incomparable Fighter*, p. 115. According to Bruce Lee's daytime planners, he stopped teaching Coburn after the trip. They only talked on the phone.

275 *"the official date":* Bruce also wrote this delusional note to Jhoon Rhee: "*Silent Flute* is still on with Warner Bros. We are waiting to hear the next step, and should know within ten days—approval of new budget, setting up another survey trip, etc." (John Little, ed., *Letters of the Dragon*, pp. 143–44.)

275 *"meaningful martial arts movie":* Roman Polanski, *Roman by Polanski*, p. 402.

275 *"Nothing new":* John Little, *Letters of the Dragon*, pp. 145–46.

Fifteen: The Way of Longstreet

PAGE

277 *"The story of that monk": Kung Fu: The Complete Edition: From Grasshopper to Cain: Creating Kung Fu*, Warner Bros. documentary, 2003.

278 *"That guy is me":* Interview with Ed Spielman, 2013.

278 *"I took fifty rejections":* Interview with Peter Lampack, 2013.

278 *The only person to take:* To give full credit where credit is due, it was Bennett Sims who first read the treatment. A twenty-something junior executive at Warner Bros., Sims worked directly for Fred Weintraub. Sims passed the treatment to Weintraub.

278 *the Bitter End:* The roster of acts at the Bitter End was a who's who of comedy and music: Lenny Bruce, Pete Seeger, Woody Allen, Frank Zappa, Lily Tomlin, Stevie Wonder, Kris Kristofferson, Joni Mitchell, George Carlin, Bob Dylan, Phil Ochs.

279 *from bankruptcy:* During the 1960s, Warner Bros. had failed to keep up with changing tastes in movies and was bleeding money. In 1969 Steve Ross paid $400 million to buy the ailing studio primarily for its music department. He planned to sell off its movie division for parts—film library and real estate—if it didn't turn around within two years.

279 *"I liked the idea":* Fred Weintraub, *Bruce Lee, Woodstock, and Me,* pp. 3–5.

279 *"He walked beautifully":* Interview with Ed Spielman, 2013.

280 *"We talked about it":* Interview with Fred Weintraub, 2013.

280 *"It was Zanuck-Brown":* Interview with Howard Friedlander, 2013.

280 *film called* Kelsey*:* During my first interview with Fred Weintraub at his home in 2013, I asked him, "I read in this old Bruce Lee book that you had a script written for Bruce, a Western called *Kelsey*, is that correct?" Up until this question Weintraub had been trying to politely humor me but was mostly distracted

by his dog, which kept running in and out of the room. After this question, he lit up. "Oh yeah! Jesus Christ. Where did you ever get that? That's a wonderful pickup note. You're the first person to ever ask me about *Kelsey*." From that point on, I was golden. He treated me like a new talent he had discovered. Anything I needed for this biography he found for me, including digging through his archives to unearth the heretofore forgotten screenplay *Kelsey*.

280 *"I was trying":* Interview with Fred Weintraub, 2013.

281 *countercultural twist:* Kurt Wunderman, *Kelsey*, p. 111. It was basically a Kevin Costner movie, twenty years before *Dances with Wolves* (1991).

281 *"I had the actor":* Interview with Fred Weintraub, 2013.

281 *"He began to believe":* "Interview with Stirling Silliphant," *Circle of Iron* DVD extras.

281 *"When you grow up":* "Memories of the Master: An Interview with Pat Johnson," *The Way of the Dragon* DVD extras.

282 *"I thought if we":* "Interview with Stirling Silliphant," *Circle of Iron* DVD extras.

282 *Baynard Kendrick's:* The Maclain novels had already served as the basis for two films: *Eyes in the Night* (1942) and *The Hidden Eye* (1945).

282 *ABC movie:* Barry Diller at ABC TV had recently invented the Movie of the Week—made-for-TV movies that aired on the network every Sunday.

282 *"The idea of* Longstreet*":* Mito Uyehara, *The Incomparable Fighter*, p. 116.

283 *"What I did was simply":* Editors of *Black Belt* magazine, *The Legendary Bruce Lee*, p. 130.

283 *business expense:* Stirling Silliphant fled America for Thailand in the 1980s after getting crosswise with the IRS. (Interview with Marshall Terrill, 2013.)

284 *"I am a personality":* Alex Ben Block, *The Legend of Bruce Lee*, p. 90; Bruce Lee, *The Lost Interview, The Pierre Berton Show—9 December 1971*, p. 27.

284 *"When I first arrived":* Ted Thomas, "Bruce Lee: The Ted Thomas Interview," December 1971.

285 *"Can you remember":* Bruce Lee, *The Pierre Berton Show.*

286 *"He had me running":* Robert Clouse, *Bruce Lee: The Biography*, p. 72.

286 *"Bruce was the advisor":* Fiaz Rafiq, *Bruce Lee Conversations*, p. 175.

286 *While shooting the episode:* Bruce Lee's daytime planners. Rehearsals were held on June 21, 22, and 23, and filming of the episode on June 24, 25, 28, 29, 30, and July 1, 1971.

286 *"Bruce Lee was next door":* Fiaz Rafiq, *Bruce Lee Conversations*, p. 196.

286 *"The Chinaman":* John O'Connor, "In the Name of the Law Is the Name of the Game," *New York Times*, September 19, 1971.

286 *"Bruce taught me enough":* Editors of *Black Belt* magazine, *The Legendary Bruce Lee*, p. 139.

287 *"the dearest man":* Fiaz Rafiq, *Bruce Lee Conversations*, p. 176.

287 *"horseshit philosophy":* Ibid., pp. 174–75.

288 *"Finished shooting":* John Little, ed., *Letters of the Dragon,* pp. 147–48.

Sixteen: The Last Mogul

PAGE

291 *"Do you know":* Mito Uyehara, *The Incomparable Fighter,* pp. 75–77.

292 *to arrange a visa:* Bruce Lee is America's most famous anchor baby.

292 *five-year-old Brandon:* Linda Lee, *The Bruce Lee Story,* p. 96.

293 *"All I asked for":* Mito Uyehara, *The Incomparable Fighter,* pp. 76–77.

294 *"so lifelike": The Brilliant Life of Bruce Lee* documentary.

294 *"very straightforward": The Art of Action: Martial Arts in the Movies* documentary.

294 *The most important kid:* Bey Logan, *Fist of Fury,* DVD commentary.

294 *"Those eyes":* Dave Friedman, *Enter the Dragon,* p. 83.

295 *Born on November 23, 1907:* Run Run Shaw's history is drawn from three sources: Jonathan Kandelljan, "Run Run Shaw, Chinese-Movie Giant of the Kung Fu Genre, Dies at 106," *New York Times,* January 6, 2014; Don Atyeo, *King of Kung-Fu,* pp. 42–44; Stephen Teo, *Hong Kong Cinema,* p. 104.

297 *sword-fighting copies (*wuxia*): Crouching Tiger, Hidden Dragon* (2000) is the best-known modern example of the *wuxia* genre.

297 *Wong Fei-hung film series:* Between 1949 and 1960, there were 59 Wong Fei-hung movies made. At present there are 119 in total. Born in 1847, Wong Fei-hung was a Cantonese martial artist, physician, and folk hero. Nearly every major Hong Kong action star has played Wong Fei-hung: Gordon Liu, Jackie Chan, Jet Li, Sammo Hung.

297 *The idea for* The Chinese Boxer*:* Jimmy Wang Yu had become famous for his role in the *wuxia* sword-fighting flick *The One-Armed Swordsman* (1967).

297 *"That picture was my idea": Cinema of Vengeance* documentary.

298 *second most popular:* The top-grossing Chinese movie up to that point was *Dragon Gate Inn* (1967) with sales of US$470,000. *The Chinese Boxer* earned US$415,000.

298 *"From watching Wang Yu":* Bey Logan, *Hong Kong Action Cinema,* p. 27.

298 *Cathay Films:* Stephen Teo, *Hong Kong Cinema,* p. 80.

299 *"holding down seven jobs":* Vivienne Chow, "Golden Harvest's Raymond Chow Recalls Glory Days of Hong Kong Film," *South China Morning Post,* March 23, 2013.

299 *"You think you can":* Interview with Andre Morgan, 2013.

299 *"I showed the script": Cinema of Vengeance* documentary.

299 *"Shaw was thinking": The Art of Action* documentary. Another source of tension between Raymond Chow and Run Run Shaw was Mona Fong, a nightclub

singer who worked at Shaw Bros. as a dubbing singer. Run Run, who had taken Mona as one of his concubines, put her in charge of cutting movie production costs. According to Hong Kong movie lore, Chow hated having her dictate how much money he could spend. In my interview with Chow in 2013, I asked if Mona was the reason for his break with Shaw Bros. "That would be putting the matter on a very small basis," Chow told me. "There were a lot of things."

299 *Raymond offered Run Run a deal:* Interview with Andre Morgan, 2013. The idea was Golden Harvest would be kind of a United Artists operation—the talent would take a lower salary in return for a share of the profits.

300 *"No, don't be ridiculous":* Interview with Andre Morgan, 2013. Morgan added, "Being head of production requires a certain flexibility with the truth."

300 *number one heartthrob:* Jimmy Wang Yu had a scandalous affair with the wife of film director Qin Jian, who hung himself when he found out. He then married actress Jeanette Lin Tsui—the Elizabeth Taylor of Hong Kong. They became the toast of the town.

300 *Jimmy went ahead with his plan:* Andrew Morgan, who worked for years at Golden Harvest, tells a different version of the story. According to Morgan, Jimmy Wang Yu's plan was not to publicly break with Shaw but to break into Run Run's office safe and steal his contract. Raymond Chow tried to dissuade him, explaining it wouldn't make a difference because Shaw had backup copies. But Jimmy went ahead with it anyway. When the theft was discovered, the police were called. Wanted for questioning, Wang Yu fled to Taiwan. (Interview with Andre Morgan, 2018.) For his part, Raymond Chow denies the incident, stating "no such thing happened." (Interview with Raymond Chow, 2018.) Chaplin Chang, who worked for Shaw Bros. and then Golden Harvest, told Bey Logan that the contract "mysteriously disappeared." (Interview with Bey Logan, 2018.) I was unable to contact Jimmy Wang Yu, who is ill, for comment.

300 *sought an injunction:* Don Atyeo, *King of Kung Fu*, p. 40.

301 *barnlike production studio:* John Little, *A Warrior's Journey*, p. 7.

301 *"Benedict Arnold":* Interview with Andre Morgan, 2013.

302 *"What is your best film":* Interview with Raymond Chow, 2013; Bey Logan, *Hong Kong Action Cinema*, p. 31.

302 *"Unicorn and Bruce": The Brilliant Life of Bruce Lee* documentary.

303 *"Bruce made three":* Steve Kerridge, *Legends of the Dragon,* Vol. 2, p. 63.

303 *"Because if we paid":* Bey Logan, *Hong Kong Action Cinema*, p. 27.

303 *He might be broke:* Linda Lee, *The Bruce Lee Story*, p. 97.

303 *"Queen of the Swords":* In the early 1960s, the most popular *wuxia* (sword fighting) stars were women, not men. This wasn't because Hong Kong audiences were particularly progressive—quite the opposite. "At that time, acting

was considered a very low thing," Cheng Pei Pei explains. "Men preferred their wives to watch women do it." It was only after the success of *The One-Armed Swordsman* (1967), which starred Jimmy Wang Yu, that more men were cast as leads in action movies. (*The Art of Action* documentary.)

304 *"smelled of incense":* Bey Logan, *Hong Kong Action Cinema*, p. 27.

304 *"Don't take this":* Robert Clouse, *Bruce Lee: The Biography*, p. 90; "Interview with Stirling Silliphant," *Circle of Iron* DVD extras.

304 *On June 28, 1971:* "The History of the Big Boss," *The Big Boss* DVD extras; interview with John Little, 2016.

304 *Contrary to popular myth:* In the Hollywood biopic *Dragon: The Bruce Lee Story* (1993), there is a powerful scene where Bruce and Linda are sitting on the couch, grief-stricken with tears in their eyes, as they watch on TV the opening of *Kung Fu* with the credit "Starring David Carradine." Bruce leaves for Hong Kong after this rejection by a racist Hollywood establishment that cast a white actor for a part that rightfully belonged to him. In reality, Bruce left for Thailand to make *The Big Boss* on July 12, 1971. Warner Bros. and ABC did not announce the TV deal for *Kung Fu* until July 22, 1971. Casting for the show did not begin until September 1971. Bruce auditioned for the part after he had completed filming of *The Big Boss*.

304 *"Am leaving for H.K.":* John Little, *Letters of the Dragon*, pp. 147–48.

305 *"They were awful":* Linda Lee, *The Man Only I Knew*, p. 135.

Seventeen: The Big Boss

PAGE

307 *gave Linda $50:* Paul Li, *From Limited to Limitless*, p. 68.

307 *"Bruce refused":* Linda Lee, *The Man Only I Knew*, p. 135.

308 *"The mosquitos":* Linda Lee, *The Bruce Lee Story*, pp. 102–3.

308 *at most $400:* Mito Uyehara, *The Incomparable Fighter*, p. 83.

308 *"We heard that they'd":* Bey Logan, *Hong Kong Action Cinema*, p. 27.

309 *"In Mandarin movies":* John Little, *The Celebrated Life of the Golden Dragon*, p. 36.

309 *"This director is rubbish":* Interview with Raymond Chow, 2013.

310 *"Actually, his three legs": The Brilliant Life of Bruce Lee* documentary.

310 *highly valued craftsman:* Bey Logan, *Fist of Fury*, DVD commentary.

311 *"Another director (a fame lover)":* John Little, ed., *Letters of the Dragon*, p. 149.

311 *"Our conflicts began":* Chaplin Chang, *The Bruce They Knew*, pp. 23–24.

311 *"The film I'm doing":* John Little, *Letters of the Dragon*, p. 150.

312 *"His grasp of timing":* Paul Li, *Limited to Limitless*, p. 71.

312 *"This was the subtlety":* Interview with Andre Morgan, 2013.

313 *"Lee would fight":* Chaplin Chang, *The Bruce They Knew*, pp. 22–23.

313 *"The shooting is picking":* John Little, *Letters of the Dragon*, p. 151.

314 *"The character I played"*: John Little, *The Celebrated Life of the Golden Dragon*, p. 139.

314 *strips naked:* "*Big Boss* Deleted Scenes," *The Big Boss* DVD extras.

314 *X-rated material:* The original, director's cut version of the movie was released to certain Mandarin-speaking markets. Almost all the prints have been lost, although a few copies remain in the hands of private collectors. The X-rated material cut from the movie includes a clip of Bruce burying a sixteen-inch saw blade into an enemy's skull.

314 *"We borrowed the dog"*: Chaplin Chang, *The Bruce They Knew*, pp. 23–24.

315 *"I've gone through"*: John Little, *Letters of the Dragon*, p. 159.

315 *But Tom Tannenbaum:* Alex Ben Block, *The Legend of Bruce Lee*, p. 71.

316 *"Who knows what"*: John Little, *Letters of the Dragon*, pp. 153–61.

316 *" 'We've only just begun' "*: Ibid., pp. 155–57. Bruce is referring to the Carpenters' song "We've Only Just Begun."

316 *"Bruce sometimes forgot"*: Linda Lee, *The Man Only I Knew*, p. 167. This line from Linda's first biography (1975) was deleted from her second, updated version, *The Bruce Lee Story* (1989), along with anything else that might seem even remotely critical. As a result, her first book is a much more interesting read.

316 *"It's funny"*: Linda Lee, *The Bruce Lee Story*, p. 106.

317 *"Golden Harvest is terribly"*: John Little, *Letters of the Dragon*, pp. 148, 149, 157, 158.

317 *"You just wait"*: Linda Lee, *The Bruce Lee Story*, p. 101.

317 *"mowing my lawn"*: Paul Li, *From Limited to Limitless*, p. 75.

318 *short film about Jeet Kune Do:* John Little, *Letters of the Dragon*, p. 148.

319 *"anticlimactic"*: Linda Lee, *The Bruce Lee Story*, p. 106.

319 *"I need more lines"*: Joel Rogosin, "What Was It Like to Work with Bruce Lee?," *Huffingtonpost*, July 29, 2014.

320 *"He would take"*: Fiaz Rafiq, *Bruce Lee Conversations*, p. 193.

320 *In the first episode, "The Way of the Intercepting Fist:"* John O'Connor, "In the Name of the Law Is the Name of the Game," *New York Times*, September 19, 1971.

320 *"Boy, am I glad"*: Mito Uyehara, *The Incomparable Fighter*, p. 116.

321 "The New York Times *said"*: Bruce Lee, *The Lost Interview: The Pierre Berton Show—9 December 1971*, p. 27.

321 *"We had more fan mail"*: Editors of *Black Belt* magazine, *The Legendary Bruce Lee*, p. 131; Robert Clouse, *Bruce Lee: The Biography*, p. 76.

321 *As Kuhn was sitting:* Interview with Tom Kuhn, 2013.

322 *"I remember this very clearly"*: Interview with Howard Friedlander, 2013. *The Hollywood Reporter* also ran the story "Warners TV Sets Three MOWs Talking Fourth," dated July 22, 1971: "Warner Bros. Television has completed negotiations with the ABC Television network for development of three

90-minute features for the network's 'Movie of the Week' and 'Movie of the Weekend' slots and is currently in negotiations for a fourth, it is announced by Thomas G. Kuhn V-P for productions at Warners-TV. The four features are planned for the 1971-72 season. . . . The fourth property, now in negotiation, is 'Kung Fu' by Ed Spielman and Howard Friedlander."

322 *The casting process:* Interview with Tom Kuhn, 2013.

322 *"It was because of* Longstreet*":* Robert Clouse, *Bruce Lee: The Biography*, p. 76.

323 *"What are you doing":* Interview with Tom Kuhn, 2013.

323 *"The concept of the series": Kung Fu: The Complete Edition: From Grasshopper to Cain: Creating Kung Fu*, Warner Bros. documentary, 2003.

324 *Even Fred Weintraub:* Fred Weintraub, *Bruce Lee, Woodstock, and Me*, p. 28. Ed Spielman, who had seen Bruce in *The Green Hornet*, never considered him for the lead when he was writing the script for the same reason: "Bruce Lee was not right for the part, because he was not a guy with a ton of humility. He wasn't a retiring sort of guy. He should have been the Abbott at the Temple or one of the great bad guys."

324 *"loop the hell":* Interview with Tom Kuhn, 2013. Looping, or additional dialogue recording (ADR), is the process of rerecording dialogue by the original actor after the filming process to improve audio quality or reflect dialogue changes.

324 *"He's amazing":* Fred Weintraub, *Bruce Lee, Woodstock, and Me*, p. 6.

324 *"I understand":* Interview with Tom Kuhn, 2013.

325 *"As the show went on":* Herbie J. Pilato, *Kung Fu: Book of Caine,* p. 33. James Hong was a guest star on nine different episodes over *Kung Fu*'s three seasons (1972–75).

326 *an eye-popping $25,000:* Linda Lee, *The Bruce Lee Story*, pp. 106–7.

326 *seven-page, typed TV proposal:* I did not read the *Ah Sahm* proposal myself, but it was described to me in detail by a reliable source, who wishes to remain anonymous.

326 *The striking similarities:* Much of the confusion over the authorship of the TV series *Kung Fu* comes from Linda Lee's first memoir, *Bruce Lee: The Man Only I Knew* (1975). "Even before this [*Longstreet*], Warner Brothers had suddenly caught on to the fact that kung fu itself had captured the public's imagination and decided to launch a TV series," she writes. "Bruce himself had been working on the idea of a Shaolin priest, a master of kung fu, who would roam America and find himself involved in various exploits. The studio contacted him and he was soon deeply involved. He gave them numerous ideas, many of which were eventually incorporated in the resulting TV success, *Kung Fu*, starring actor David Carradine." (Linda Lee, *The Man Only I Knew*, pp. 130–31.)

327 *does not have a date:* Based on the brainstorming in his notebooks, it seems likely that Bruce came up with the original idea of a Chinese warrior righting

wrongs in the American West (an Eastern Western) on his own. It also seems probable that Bruce didn't write the full seven-page proposal for *Ah Sahm* until after Ashley offered him a development deal, which is to say, after he had already read the screenplay for *Kung Fu*.

327 The Warrior*:* As of this writing, Cinemax is currently producing *Warrior* based on Bruce Lee's original proposal. It is directed by Justin Lin (*The Fast and the Furious*) and written by Jonathan Tropper (*Banshee*).

327 *He wanted to wait:* Interview with Linda Lee, 2013.

Eighteen: Fist of Fury

PAGE

329 *This hero's welcome:* Paul Li, *From Limited to Limitless*, p. 76.

330 *"As the movie progressed":* Don Atyeo, *King of Kung-Fu*, p. 49.

330 *"Part of the fringe":* Linda Lee, *The Man Only I Knew*, p. 147.

330 *"I didn't know who Bruce":* Robert Clouse, *Bruce Lee: The Biography*, p. 108.

330 *"I didn't expect":* Don Atyeo, *King of Kung-Fu*, p. 49.

330 *"That night every dream":* Linda Lee, *The Bruce Lee Story*, p. 107.

330 *grossed HK$3.2 million:* In 1972, the Hong Kong dollar was pegged to the U.S. dollar at a rate of 5.65 H.K. dollar = 1 U.S. dollar. HK$3.2 million = US$566,372. In 2017 dollars that would be US$3.3 million. The movie cost US$100,000 to make.

331 *"The Julie Andrews film":* "The Big Boss Takes a Record Profit," *China Mail*, November 19, 1971.

331 *"a crappy film":* Chaplin Chang, *The Bruce They Knew*, p. 23.

331 *"What Lee would do":* Don Atyeo, *King of Kung-Fu*, p. 50.

331 *bombed on-screen:* See Ed Parker in *Kill the Golden Goose*, Joe Lewis in *Jaguar Lives!*, Chuck Liddell in *The Death and Life of Bobby Z*.

332 *"Bruce Lee in motion":* Gary Arnold, "Shades of Cagney, Echoes of McQueen," *Washington Post*, August 25, 1973.

332 *"Bruce had an intensity":* Fiaz Rafiq, *Bruce Lee Conversations*, p. 258.

332 *"I can feel it":* Linda Lee, *The Bruce Lee Story*, p. 130.

332 *"I had more confidence":* Don Atyeo, *King of Kung-Fu*, p. 48.

332 *"Bruce did more for":* Robert Clouse, *Bruce Lee: The Biography*, p. 102.

333 *South China Sea:* The Senkaku/Diaoyu Island dispute continues to be a source of international tension to this day.

333 *"I remember it as if":* Interview with Fr. Marciano Baptista, 2013.

333 *"In addition to our":* John Little, *Letters of the Dragon*, p. 161.

334 *"I should find out":* Jack Moore, "Bruce Lee—the $3 Million Box-Office Draw," *Hong Kong Sunday Post-Herald*, November 21, 1971; reprinted in ibid., p. 107. Four days later, Bruce gave a more defiant interview to *The China Mail*:

"To me, it doesn't really matter whether or not *The Warrior* is made. It has its advantages and disadvantages. Naturally, I am proud to be the first Chinese to star on American TV. But I find filming for TV dull and monotonous." ("Will Li Hit Hollywood or HK?," *China Mail*, November 25, 1971.)

334 *on November 25, 1971:* Bruce Lee's daytime planners.

334 *Since Warners could:* In my interview with Tom Kuhn in 2014, he said, "I don't know who at Warners would have made this call, but this was right around the time we signed David Carradine."

334 *"He was supremely disappointed":* *The Brilliant Life of Bruce Lee* documentary.

334 *"There were some scenes":* Jack Moore, "Bruce Lee—the $3 Million Box-Office Draw," *Hong Kong Sunday Post-Herald*, November 21, 1971.

336 *"I am sorry to hear":* John Little, *Letters of the Dragon*, pp. 162–63. In the same December 16, 1971, letter to Ashley, Bruce also asked for the $25,000 for his development deal: "In my commitment with Warner for 'The Warrior' dating from Dec. 71 to Dec. 72, I think I have $25,000 coming to me." It is unknown if Bruce ever signed the contract with Warners or if Warners paid him the $25,000, but it seems doubtful. The topic is never mentioned in his letters again, and Bruce never worked on another TV project with Warners to justify a $25,000 advance.

336 *On December 18, 1971:* "Bruce Lee Can Stay On in HK," *Hong Kong Standard*, December 18, 1971. Other Chinese newspapers made the case even more strongly: "Acceding to Bruce's demands, Warner Bros. agreed to push back the start of filming on 'The Warrior' for six months in order to allow Bruce to fulfill his obligations in Hong Kong." (Paul Li, *From Limited to Limitless*, pp. 85–86.)

337 *"His contract with Raymond":* Linda Lee, *The Bruce Lee Story*, p. 107.

337 *sold his Bel Air home:* He bought the Bel Air home in 1968 for $47,000 and sold it in 1971 for $57,000. (*The Big Boss* DVD extras.)

337 *"Raymond spent the weekend":* Interview with Andre Morgan, 2013.

338 Jing Wu*:* The Chinese title for *Fist of Fury* is *Jing Wu Men*. In North America it was renamed *The Chinese Connection* to play off the popularity of *The French Connection* (1971).

338 Modern Chivalry Heroes*:* Petrus Liu, *Stateless Subjects*, p. 50.

338 *"That is more interesting":* John Little, *The Celebrated Life of the Golden Dragon*, p. 142.

338 *"Now you listen to me":* "Fist of Fury Location Guide with Bey Logan," *Fist of Fury* DVD extras.

339 *"died under the gunfire":* John Little, *The Celebrated Life of the Golden Dragon*, p. 142.

339 *"Mr. Katsu, I hold":* "Master of Bushido: An Interview with Jun Katsumura," *Fist of Fury* DVD extras.

339 *a real contempt:* Bey Logan, DVD commentary, *Fist of Fury*.

340 *"He told us to be odious":* "Blade of Fury: An Interview with Riki Hashimoto," *Fist of Fury* DVD extras.

341 *After reading Lo Wei's quotes:* Jackie Chan, *I Am Jackie Chan*, pp. 167–69. Jackie Chan went on to star in several Lo Wei movies, none of which did particularly well. After Bruce's death, Lo Wei continued to insist that he taught Bruce how to fight for films. In a 1988 interview, he said, "People definitely won't believe me if I claim that Lee didn't know how to fight. But what I'll tell you is this: Lee didn't know how to fight in front of the camera. I told him to do this and that. Told him how he needed to fight." (Chaplin Chang, *The Bruce They Knew*, pp. 20–21.)

342 *"Technically, Han Ying-Chieh":* Bey Logan, *Hong Kong Action Cinema*, pp. 28–29. While Bruce choreographed all his own fight scenes, Han Ying-Chieh was allowed to design the scenes without Bruce in them. In the final film, the difference in style is obvious. Bruce's scenes are cleaner, crisper, and more explosive; the Han Ying-Chieh scenes have a pantomime feel with more circular arm movements and less contact. (Bey Logan, *Hong Kong Action Cinema*, pp. 28–29.)

342 *"We did actually hit":* Will Johnston, "Bob Baker Interview," Tracking the Dragon Convention.

343 *This was a pedagogical:* Bruce mentioned biting as an option when teaching Mike Longstreet in the premiere episode of *Longstreet*, "The Way of the Intercepting Fist."

343 *"I am the master":* Bey Logan, DVD commentary, *Fist of Fury*.

343 *"I knew his family":* "The First Lady: An Interview with Nora Miao," *Fist of Fury* DVD extras.

344 *"a Kennedy thing":* Bey Logan, DVD commentary, *Fist of Fury*.

344 *unbelievably harsh conditions:* See China's classic movie *Farewell My Concubine* (1993) for a vivid portrayal of the life of young Chinese Opera students.

344 *"We were prepared":* Jackie Chan, *I Am Jackie Chan*, pp. 166–67.

345 *"Sammo says it was even":* Ibid., p. 169.

345 *"Lee was always given":* Chaplin Chang, *The Bruce They Knew*, p. 95.

346 *"If a fighter was injured":* Interview with Ip Chun, 2013.

346 *"When times were tough": The Brilliant Life of Bruce Lee* documentary.

347 *"take ten of us to Hollywood":* Ibid.

347 *"All the kung fu stuntmen":* Chaplin Chang, *The Bruce They Knew*, p. 40.

347 *"He got along really well":* Ibid., pp. 47–48.

347 *"After Lo Wei had given":* Bey Logan, *Hong Kong Action Cinema*, p. 29.

347 *"His ultimate goal": The Brilliant Life of Bruce Lee* documentary.

348 *"Oh my God":* Interview with Nancy Kwan, 2013.

348 *high chain kicks:* Hong Kong film historian Bey Logan ascribes Bruce's chain

kicks to Louis Delgado, who trained with Bruce and was one of America's top point fighters.

348 *"he shouted like this": The Brilliant Life of Bruce Lee* documentary. There is no evidence that Bruce ever screeched like a cat in one of his street fights. During my research, I asked multiple interview subjects about the origin of his animal cries, but no one knew the answer. It seems that Bruce invented it for *Fist of Fury*.

348 *Within thirteen days:* Linda Lee, *The Man Only I Knew*, p. 150.

348 *scalpers were selling:* Don Atyeo, *King of Kung-Fu*, pp. 52–53.

349 *"The story of* Fist of Fury*":* "Master of Bushido: An Interview with Jun Katsumura," *Fist of Fury* DVD extras.

Nineteen: Concord

PAGE

351 *$16 million:* Paul Li, *From Limited to Limitless*, p. 82.

351 *"He was just an actor":* Robert Clouse, *Bruce Lee: The Biography*, p. 120.

351 *"I'm really enjoying":* Mito Uyehara, *The Incomparable Fighter*, p. 86.

351 *goddess of harmony:* Interview with Andre Morgan, 2015.

352 *wallpaper worthy: Bruce Lee, The Man and the Legend* documentary.

352 *"Image is important": The Brilliant Life of Bruce Lee* documentary; Mito Uyehara, *The Incomparable Fighter*, p. 126.

352 *"He liked clothes":* Linda Lee, *The Man Only I Knew*, p. 155.

352 *kaftans, dashikis:* Davis Miller, *The Tao of Bruce Lee*, p. 140.

353 *"piggy bank":* Interview with Andre Morgan, 2015.

353 *2 Man Wan Road:* The exact address was 2 Man Wan Road, Sunlight Garden, 13th Floor, Flat A, Kowloon, Hong Kong.

353 *"Our clothes":* Linda Lee, *The Bruce Lee Story*, p. 112.

353 *"All the years":* Mito Uyehara, *Bruce Lee: The Incomparable Fighter*, p. 141.

353 *41 Cumberland Road:* Peter Farquhar, "Bruce Lee Fans Are Worried His Hong Kong Home Is About to Be Demolished," *Business Insider Australia*, September 10, 2015.

354 *Japanese garden:* Alex Ben Block, *The Legend of Bruce Lee*, p. 85. The Japanese garden had a small stream and a stone bridge. There was no backyard as a railway ran directly behind his home. (Interview with John Little, 2018.)

354 *US$23 million:* Nash Jenkins, "Bruce Lee's Former Home in Hong Kong Faces an Uncertain Future," *Time*, September 8, 2015.

354 *By the age of three:* Linda Lee, *The Man Only I Knew*, p. 112.

354 *"Why don't you just go?":* Interview with Raymond Chow, 2013.

355 *"Brandon is the biggest . . . kind of attention":* Mito Uyehara, *The Incomparable Fighter*, p. 142.

355 *"He used to call me":* Interview with Nancy Kwan, 2013.

355 *"I was not that happy":* Interview with Betty Ting Pei, 2013. It was the first time she had revealed intimate details of her relationship with Bruce to a Western reporter. For decades she had pretended that she and Bruce were just friends.

356 *"In two short weeks":* Paul Li, *From Limited to Limitless,* p. 83.

357 *"Wang Yu was":* Interview with Andre Morgan, 2015.

357 *"Each is King":* Steve Kerridge, *Bruce Lee: Legends of the Dragon*, Vol. 1, p. 17.

358 *"I wrote the script": Cinema of Vengeance* documentary.

358 *motion was called* Yellow Faced Tiger: The name of the project was later changed to *A Man Called Tiger.* After Bruce and Lo Wei argued, Bruce decided he wanted to make *Way of the Dragon.* Lo Wei intended to replace Bruce with Jimmy Wang Yu on the *Yellow Faced Tiger* project, but Bruce would only allow it if Lo Wei changed the title to *A Man Called Tiger.* Bruce was attached to *Yellow Faced Tiger* and wanted to use it as the title for the movie he made after *Way of the Dragon.* Eventually Bruce decided to change the name of that project from *Yellow Faced Tiger* to *Game of Death.* After Bruce died, Lo Wei made *Yellow Faced Tiger* in 1974. He filmed it in San Francisco and cast Chuck Norris as the villain. The American name for the film was *Slaughter in San Francisco.* The movie is so bad it has proven a considerable source of embarrassment to Norris. "I can honestly tell you that I've never seen it," Norris says, "but I always know when it's on cable because my friends call me up and tell me about it!" (Bey Logan, *Hong Kong Action Cinema*, p. 34; Paul Li, *From Limited to Limitless*, p. 94.)

358 *changed to* Way of the Dragon: In North America, *Way of the Dragon* was retitled *Return of the Dragon*, because it wasn't released in America until after *Enter the Dragon* had become a box office sensation.

358 *movie with Sam Hui:* Bruce invited Sam Hui to a special dinner to apologize for causing delays to his movie *Iron Fist Love Song.* Sam's wife, Rebu Hui, who was Japanese American, and Linda Lee subsequently became best friends—two foreign wives of famous actors living in a Chinese city.

359 *"We'll be underway":* Chaplin Chang, *The Bruce They Knew*, pp. 5–9.

Twenty: Spaghetti Eastern

PAGE

363 *"He found that":* Steve Kerridge, *Legends of the Dragon*, Vol. 2, pp. 69–70.

363 *"It is quite funny":* John Little, *The Celebrated Life of the Golden Dragon*, 150.

363 *failing Qing Dynasty:* Paul Li, *From Limited to Limitless*, p. 95.

364 *"I'll go to Hong Kong":* Mito Uyehara, *The Incomparable Fighter,* p. 116; Don Atyeo, *King of Kung-Fu*, p. 48. "Bruce always loved to talk about how Clint Eastwood had filmed Westerns in Italy before returning to America," says James Coburn. "Just as Hollywood, which had been the best at producing such films, was nonetheless beaten to the punch by Italian shoot-em-ups,

Bruce was confident that martial arts films had the same 'import potential.' " (Paul Li, *From Limited to Limitless*, p. 95.)

364 *finish a rough draft:* Steve Kerridge, *Legends of the Dragon*, Vol. 2, p. 17.

364 *"He is a simple":* Don Atyeo, *King of Kung-Fu*, p. 30.

365 *"Every time there was":* Ibid., p. 55.

365 *"He was followed": Circle of Iron* DVD extras. For lunch the next day, Bruce brought a special present for his old Hollywood patron. "He had the two most beautiful Oriental girls I had ever seen with him. He said we were all set for the afternoon, but I had to leave early and go do a television interview I'd agreed to," Silliphant claims. "Bruce ended up with both the chicks, and next day he said to me, 'Boy, what you missed.' " (Alex Ben Block, *The Legend of Bruce Lee*, p. 115.)

365 *"I can't begin":* Steve Kerridge, *Legends of the Dragon*, Vol. 1, p. 33.

366 *"I don't disregard":* Ibid., p. 16.

366 *"Lo Wei was very angry":* "The First Lady: An Interview with Nora Miao," *Fist of Fury* DVD extras.

366 *"swearing in Cantonese":* Interview with Chaplin Chang, 2013; Fiaz Rafiq, *Bruce Lee Conversations*, p. 232.

367 *Lo Wei lashed out:* Steve Kerridge, *The Bruce Lee Chronicles: An Inside Look at Way of the Dragon*, Vol 1.

367 *production manager Chaplin:* Chaplin Chang had worked for famed director King Hu. Tadashi Nishimoto was one of several Japanese cinematographers Shaw Bros. had hired to help them catch up with the more advanced Japanese film industry in the 1960s. His credits included *The Love Eternal* (1963), *The Magnificent Concubine* (1964), and King Hu's *Come Drink with Me* (1966).

367 *"stopped at a 'Gucci' ":* Steve Kerridge, *Legends of the Dragon*, Vol. 1, pp. 88–89.

367 *"three small cups of sake":* Ibid., p. 110.

367 *only type of liquor:* Different types of alcohol seem to affect people who suffer from alcohol flush reaction differently. Based on anecdotal reporting, clear alcohols—vodka, gin, soju, sake—cause less of a negative effect than beer, wine, or whiskey. That said, the fact that three small shots of sake caused him to sweat so much that a waiter handed him a towel to wipe his face indicates Bruce continued to suffer from alcohol flush reaction—even from sake.

367 *"70,000 or 80,000 lira":* Interview with Chaplin Chang, 2013.

368 *"Honestly, I had doubts":* Fiaz Rafiq, *Bruce Lee Conversations*, p. 233.

368 *"We had nothing to do":* "The First Lady: An Interview with Nora Miao," *Fist of Fury* DVD extras.

369 *"came down for breakfast":* Interview with Chaplin Chang, 2013.

369 *"It was a fling":* Interview with Andre Morgan, 2013.

369 *steps off the plane:* To save time and cost, Bruce arranged to film Chuck Norris coming off the plane the moment he actually arrived in Rome. The Chinese

production crew paid off the right officials to allow them to set up their cameras on the tarmac.

369 *"I was aware":* Chuck Norris, *The Secret of Inner Strength*, p. 71.

369 *"Chuck gets off the phone":* Interview with Bob Wall, 2013.

369 *"didn't like him":* Interview with Chaplin Chang, 2013. *Black Belt*, September 1997, pp. 10, 11, 30.

370 *"How much profit":* Steve Kerridge, *Legends of the Dragon*, Vol. 1, pp. 195–99.

371 *Kam Yeh Po:* Paul Li, *From Limited to Limitless*, p. 96.

371 *"It's a no-win":* Chuck Norris, *The Secret of Inner Strength*, p. 73.

372 *"The fact is":* Steve Kerridge, *Legends of the Dragon*, Vol. 1, pp. 231–34.

372 *"I remember someone":* Steve Kerridge, *Legends of the Dragon*, Vol. 2, pp. 69–70.

373 *"He made sure":* John Overall, *Bruce Lee Review*, p. 175.

373 *"very fun guy":* Fiaz Rafiq, *Bruce Lee Conversations*, p. 217.

373 *"I was his girlfriend":* Interview with Betty Ting Pei, 2013.

373 *"I ran into":* Interview with Anders Nelsson, 2013.

373 *"Bruce was quite taken":* Interview with Andre Morgan, 2013.

373 *"Who gets to win":* Chuck Norris, *The Secret of Inner Strength*, pp. 71–72.

374 *"fat moose":* Interview with Bob Wall, 2013.

374 *"the Williams fight":* Davis Miller, *The Tao of Bruce Lee*, p. 125.

374 *"We got a good":* Steve Kerridge, *Legends of the Dragon*, Vol. 2, p. 27.

374 *opinions vary wildly:* Alex Ben Block, who in 1974 wrote the first biography of Lee, said of *Way of the Dragon*, "From a directorial point of view, it is a foolish, indulgent, rather routine film. In my opinion it is Lee's worst film." Don Atyeo, who wrote the second biography in 1975, said, "In this writer's opinion, it was the best thing he ever did. . . . *Way of the Dragon* is a polished piece of filmmaking by any standard." (Alex Ben Block, *The Legend of Bruce Lee*, p. 92; Don Atyeo, *King of Kung-Fu*, p. 56.)

375 *percussion instrument:* Linda Lee, *The Bruce Lee Story*, p. 127.

375 *on 35mm:* Interview with John Little, 2018.

375 *"This had never":* Interview with Ted Thomas, 2014.

376 *Winston cigarette:* Paul Li, *From Limited to Limitless*, pp. 109–10.

376 *"I went to Golden Harvest":* Chaplin Chang, *The Bruce They Knew*, p. 50.

376 *"The money we":* Linda Lee, *The Bruce Lee Story*, p. 128.

377 *Feeling snubbed:* Paul Li, *From Limited to Limitless*, p. 113. Much of the negative press focused on Bruce's relationship with Raymond Chow. The tabloids speculated that Bruce and Raymond had fallen out over money. In truth, they were arguing but mostly about control of the movie. "Raymond and Bruce were very good friends, but at the same time they also fought a lot, because Bruce liked to challenge everybody," says Louis Sit, who was the studio manager at Golden Harvest. "Raymond would never challenge Bruce about

kung fu, but Bruce would challenge Raymond about production, business, distribution, sales, PR, everything. He liked to be the boss." ("'Inside Way of the Dragon,' An Interview with Louis Sit," *Way of the Dragon* DVD extras.)

377 *barely made HK$2 million:* Paul Li, *From Limited to Limitless*, p. 113. Prior to its release, the title of Lo Wei and Jimmy Wang Yu's movie project had been changed from *Yellow Faced Tiger* to *A Man Called Tiger.*

377 *"The reaction to* Way*":* "'Inside Way of the Dragon,' An Interview with Louis Sit," *The Way of the Dragon* DVD extras.

377 *"How was the film?":* Paul Li, *From Limited to Limitless*, p. 115. After the screening, Bruce and Peter's relationship became more distant.

378 *"a big scream out":* "Interview with Andre Morgan," *The Way of the Dragon* DVD extras.

379 *"I am not a teacher":* Bruce Lee, *Northern Leg Southern Fist*, pp. 47–60.

380 *"Raymond's reaction":* Interview with Andre Morgan, 2015.

380 *"I'm dissatisfied":* Linda Lee, *The Man Only I Knew*, pp. 151–53; Alex Ben Block, *The Legend of Bruce Lee*, p. 77.

380 *"I hope to make":* Alex Ben Block, *The Legend of Bruce Lee*, p. 77.

381 *wooden pagoda*: The *Game of Death* pagoda was based on Beopjusa Palsangjeon in South Korea. (John Little, *A Warrior's Journey*, p. 73.)

381 *"As the film opens":* John Little, *Words of the Dragon*, p. 138.

382 *"cautious optimism":* Interview with Andre Morgan, 2015.

382 *"I can be produced":* John Little, *Words of the Dragon*, p. 123.

382 *"When an actor":* Interview with Raymond Chow, 2013.

382 *Bruce's feint:* Chow also agreed to cancel their previous Concord Productions contract. On August 21, 1972, Bruce and Raymond Chow signed an agreement of only six lines, the effect of which was to cancel out their Concord Productions contract signed on December 1, 1971. Bruce refused to immediately sign a new contract with Chow, leaving himself even greater room to maneuver. (Paul Li, *From Limited to Limitless*, p. 100.)

382 *"With me fighting":* Mito Uyehara, *The Incomparable Fighter*, p. 59.

382 *"I was trying":* Ibid., p. 111.

383 *"I had to catch":* Fiaz Rafiq, *Bruce Lee Conversations*, p. 248.

383 *"kept changing it":* Interview with Dan Inosanto, 2013.

383 *"His movie-making":* Editors of *Kung-Fu Monthly*, *Who Killed Bruce Lee?*

383 *"My level and his level":* Fiaz Rafiq, *Bruce Lee Conversations*, p. 251.

383 *Coburn politely*: According to John Little, Bruce finally settled on Wong In Sik, who had been one of Bruce's opponents in *Way of the Dragon*, to guard the first level, Taky Kimura to guard the second, Dan Inosanto the third, Ji Han Jae the fourth, and Kareem Abdul-Jabbar the fifth. (John Little, *A Warrior's Journey*, pp. 79–83.)

383 *rough footage:* This original footage was considered lost until it was rediscovered in the Golden Harvest archives by Hong Kong filmmaker and historian Bey Logan in 1999. Golden Harvest had taken Bruce's original thirty minutes of material, edited it down even further by eliminating Bruce's two companions, and then surrounded it with a completely different story line for their full-length version of *Game of Death* in 1978.
383 *inspired by the ski:* Interview with Davis Miller, 2013.
384 *"I'm dressed in a typical":* Interview with Dan Inosanto, 2013.
384 *As the trio face off:* Bey Logan, *Hong Kong Action Cinema*, pp. 35–37.
384 *treasure reveal scene:* Interview with Andre Morgan, 2015.
385 *Ni Kuang:* Paul Li, *From Limited to Limitless*, p. 105. Born in 1935, Ni Kuang has written over three hundred Chinese-language *wuxia* and science fiction novels, and more than four hundred film scripts.

Twenty-one: Fame and Its Discontents

PAGE
387 *"the fucking Beatles":* Interview with Joe Torrenueva, 2013.
387 *"The biggest disadvantage":* Linda Lee, *The Man Only I Knew*, pp. 153–54.
388 *"I'm in jail":* Alex Ben Block, *The Legend of Bruce Lee*, p. 99.
388 *"Do you want to fight":* Interview with Nancy Kwan, 2013.
388 *"This guy was invading":* Davis Miller, *The Tao of Bruce Lee*, p. 148.
388 *"being unescorted":* Interview with Linda Lee, 2013.
388 *"I had people":* Alex Ben Block, *The Legend of Bruce Lee*, p. 100.
389 *carrying a gun:* Don Atyeo, *King of Kung-Fu*, p. 67.
389 *"very paranoid":* Davis Miller, *The Tao of Bruce Lee*, p. 145.
389 *Bruce duly spent:* Bey Logan, *Hong Kong Action Cinema*, p. 31.
390 *"Bruce was angry":* Interview with Andre Morgan, 2015.
390 *"Well dear friend":* John Little, ed., *Letters of the Dragon*, pp. 168–69.
390 *"You've got thousands":* Alex Ben Block, *The Legend of Bruce Lee*, p. 100.
390 *mistreated cameramen:* Don Atyeo, *King of Kung-Fu*, p. 67. A Hong Kong paparazzo, Yi Bao-Yao, recalls a confrontation he had with Bruce: "As I was waiting at the television station until evening, when I finally saw Bruce hurrying into the studio. I snapped a few photos quickly so I wouldn't be left empty-handed. Who would have expected that, upon realizing he was being photographed, Bruce came charging at me, yelling and cursing? To be honest, I was a little afraid at the time, but due to my personality, I couldn't give up so easily. Instead, I said to him, 'Do you remember what you said at the airport recently about friendship among Chinese? What happened to that?' He paused for a moment and then pointed a finger at me, saying I had made him react violently like that. Just then, a good friend of mine on the set walked over

to ask Bruce if he could take a few photos, attempting to distract him from picking on me. Bruce took this opportunity to emphasize that he was very willing to pose for photos when people asked politely, but he would simply not stand for people taking photos unbidden. Just then, Bruce's brother-in-law, Yu Ming, came out of the makeup room and pointed out I was a nephew of a friend, Yi Qiushui, and that he should let me take a few portraits. At first he was surprised, then he continued grumbling about how it was my fault for baiting him. Every time I saw him after that, he very politely shook my hand, making me feel a little embarrassed about our previous encounter. (Paul Li, *From Limited to Limitless*, p. 104; Yi Bao-Yao, *Twenty Years of Movie History*.)

390 *"Lee was often angry":* Chaplin Chang, *The Bruce They Knew*, p. 156.

391 *"inter-racial marriage":* John Little, *Words of the Dragon*, p. 119.

391 *spelling his last name:* Alex Ben Block, *The Legend of Bruce Lee*, p. 100.

391 *"I am Chinese":* John Little, *Words of the Dragon*, pp. 124–30.

392 *"His flower shirts":* Paul Li, *From Limited to Limitless*, pp. 87–88.

393 *"Since I started":* Wong Shun Leung, "Wong Shun Leung and His Friendship with Bruce Lee," *Real Kung Fu Magazine*, 1980. Bruce's letter was sent on January 11, 1970.

393 *"Those mothers":* Mito Uyehara: *The Incomparable Fighter*, p. 78.

394 *"Have you seen my movie":* Interview with Wan Kam Leung, 2013.

395 *"If it is only for research . . . of a similar level":* Wong Shun Leung, "Wong Shun Leung and His Friendship with Bruce Lee," *Real Kung Fu Magazine*, 1980.

396 *"If I really had to pick":* Interview with Wan Kam Leung, 2013.

397 *"If a martial artist":* Steve Kerridge, *Legends of the Dragon*, Vol. 1, pp. 232–33.

397 *Graham Jenkins:* Don Atyeo, *King of Kung-Fu*, p. 67.

397 *"His logic":* Interview with Andre Morgan, 2015.

397 *the lawsuit:* Linda Lee quietly dropped the lawsuit after Bruce's death.

398 *The Cultural Revolution:* Across middle school, high school, and college campuses in mainland China, students were rounding up teachers and beating them, sometimes to death. (Song Yongyi, "Chronology of Mass Killings During the Chinese Cultural Revolution [1966–1976].")

398 *"Do you still treat":* Hawkins Cheung, "Bruce Lee's Classical Mess: Cleaning Up the Mess the 'Little Dragon' Left Behind," *Inside Kung-Fu*, February 1992.

399 *They strolled:* Interview with Ip Chun, 2013.

399 *"As for why Bruce":* Paul Li, *From Limited to Limitless*, pp. 111–12.

400 *"those sonovabitches":* Mito Uyehara: *The Incomparable Fighter*, p. 79.

400 *"When my father":* Paul Li, *From Limited to Limitless*, p. 112.

400 *He humbly apologized:* Interview with Ip Chun, 2013.

Twenty-two: Blood & Steel

PAGE

404 *Weintraub and Heller:* Fred Weintraub, *Bruce Lee, Woodstock, and Me*, pp. 8–9.

404 *"Dear Ted":* John Little, ed., *Letters of the Dragon*, pp. 165–66.

405 *screenwriter Michael Allin:* Michael Allin was the protégé of famed screenwriter John Milius. When Paul Heller, who co-produced *Enter the Dragon*, was developing a Western called *Pistoleros*, he couldn't afford Milius to rewrite the script. Milius recommended Allin. Heller and Allin worked on the *Pistoleros* screenplay together. It never was made, but the two became friends. When it was time to hire an inexpensive screenwriter for *Enter the Dragon*, Heller tapped Allin. After *Enter the Dragon*, Michael Allin went on to write the screenplay for *Flash Gordon* (1980)—another film with a Fu Manchu–type villain. (Interview with Michael Allin, 2013.)

405 *"China and the Orient":* Paul Heller, *Blood & Steel* DVD extras.

405 *"I stole from James Bond":* Interview with Michael Allin, 2013.

405 *"I saw the opportunity":* Fred Weintraub, *Bruce Lee, Woodstock, and Me*, pp. 10–12.

405 *"wanted was a fair deal":* Interview with Raymond Chow, 2013.

406 *"It was a relief":* Interview with Andre Morgan, 2015.

406 *"That chicken":* Mito Uyehara, *The Incomparable Fighter*, p. 126.

406 *"Steve, you dirty rat":* "Memories of the Master: An Interview with Pat Johnson," *Way of the Dragon* DVD extras. After his practical joke, McQueen followed up with a congratulatory letter, "Dear Bruce, I want to let you know two important things I've been thinking about you: Now you're a big star, but I hope you never let it change you. Second, I wish you and your family every happiness. I'm doing great right now myself—mentally and physically. Your Brother, Steve McQueen." (Paul Li, *From Limited to Limitless*, p. 108.)

406 *"ridiculously low price":* Interview with Fred Weintraub, 2013. The two feature-length movies Robert Clouse directed prior to *Enter the Dragon* were *Darker than Amber* (1970) and *Dreams of Glass* (1970).

407 *"We've got to rap":* Interview with Michael Allin, 2013.

408 *"He was extremely":* Paul Li, *From Limited to Limitless*, pp. 107–8.

408 *"When* The Silent Flute*":* Paul Li, *From Limited to Limitless*, p. 109.

409 *"We were colorblind":* Interview with Fred Weintraub, 2013.

409 *"Bob will do":* Interview with Bob Wall, 2013.

409 *background in karate:* John Saxon had studied a little bit of karate and some Tai Chi. He wasn't an advanced student, but he understood the basics.

409 *"a little crappy thing":* Fiaz Rafiq, *Bruce Lee Conversations*, p. 263.

409 *the real star:* Interview with Fred Weintraub, 2013.

409 *Bolo Yeung (Bolo):* Later in his career, Bolo Yeung would play the villain opposite Jean-Claude Van Damme in *Bloodsport* (1988) and *Double Impact* (1991).

410 *"a coincidence":* Interview with Betty Ting Pei, 2013.
410 *"called me Dragon Lady":* Ibid.
410 *"Ra Ra Ra":* Interview with Chaplin Chang, 2013.
410 *"It is too difficult"* Interview with Betty Ting Pei, 2013. Since Betty will not speak about why they broke up, there is no way to know exactly what was said during their argument. But given how Bruce reacted, many have speculated that Betty threatened to make their relationship public.
410 *Executives intercepted:* Interview with Andre Morgan, 2015.
410 *On December 23, 1972:* "Betty Ting Pei Denies Suicide Attempt Yesterday," *New Lantern Newspaper*, December 23, 1972.
411 *"That dumb girl":* Mito Uyehara, *The Incomparable Fighter*, p. 138.
411 *And that's when John:* "Did you believe you were going to be the star of the film?" I asked Saxon during our interview. He replied with a smile, "Certainly not after that first morning." (Interview with John Saxon, 2013.)
411 *"It was supposed":* Dave Friedman, *Enter the Dragon*, p. 166.
412 *"Bruce was under enormous":* Linda Lee, *The Man Only I Knew*, pp. 186–87.
413 *Michael Allin had arrived:* Interview with Michael Allin, 2013.
414 *"'No. Really? He's in town'":* Interview with Andre Morgan, 2013.
414 *When he cornered Weintraub:* Robert Clouse, *Bruce Lee: The Biography*, p. 144.
415 *"Get a duck that can act":* Interview with Michael Allin, 2013.
415 *"the little sampans":* Interview with Andre Morgan, 2013.
416 *"We were surprised":* Fred Weintraub, *Bruce Lee, Woodstock, and Me*, p. 25.
417 *"You can't believe":* Jackie Chan, *I Am Jackie Chan*, pp. 173–74.
417 *"Bruce was very angry":* Interview with Chaplin Chang, 2013.
417 *"Was Bruce pissed . . . of the movie":* Interview with Andre Morgan, 2013.
417 *"They put a pad on Bob":* Bey Logan, *Hong Kong Action Cinema*, p. 39. Bob Wall angrily denies that he ever wore a pad to protect himself from Lee's kicks. To suggest that he did is, in his view, an insult to his toughness. However, along with Zebra Pan, there are two other eyewitnesses who saw him wear a chest guard: Dave Friedman, the Warner Bros. behind-the-scenes photographer on-set, and Philip Ko Fei, a Chinese stuntman.
417 *"We're talking complex break":* Interview with Bob Wall, 2013.
418 *"Never mind":* Interview with Andre Morgan, 2013.
418 *"He was a Shaolin":* Interview with Michael Allin, 2013.
418 *"Jim Kelly screwed everything":* Interview with Paul Heller, 2013. Paul Heller told me, "Kelly ended up with a bad case of the clap." Fred Weintraub told me, "His balls got about as big as a bowling ball. I don't know what he had." Bob Wall told me, "I don't even know what Jim had. All I know is his balls swelled up."
418 *"bunch of Chinese girls":* Interview with John Saxon, 2013.
419 *"The hall had":* John Little, *Warner Brothers Enter the Dragon*, pp. 26–27.

419 *"Take it easy, son":* Bruce Thomas, *Bruce Lee: Fighting Spirit*, p. 187.
419 *"complete exhaustion:"* Robert Clouse, *Bruce Lee: The Biography*, p. 151.
419 *"During rehearsal": Blood & Steel* documentary.
419 *"When my opponent expands":* The American producers ended up cutting this exchange from the original theatrical release. "With regards to the philosophy," Weintraub says, "I feel that a little of it goes a long way with American audiences." Following an outcry from Bruce Lee fans, Warner Bros. reinserted the scene in later editions. (Bey Logan, *Hong Kong Action Cinema*, pp. 39–40.)
420 *"After you saw":* Dave Friedman, *Enter the Dragon*, p. 27.
420 *"When we saw it":* Robert Clouse, *The Making of Enter the Dragon*, p. 197.
420 *"like a family film":* Fred Weintraub, *Bruce Lee, Woodstock, and Me*, p. 18.
420 *"impression of a monster movie":* Dave Friedman, *Enter the Dragon*, p. 8.
420 *"After spending a full":* Linda Lee, *The Bruce Lee Story*, p. 132.
420 *"Do think it over":* John Little, *Letters of the Dragon*, p. 181.
421 *never make another picture:* Robert Clouse, *Bruce Lee: The Biography*, p. 161.
421 *"In retrospect I can't":* Fred Weintraub, *Bruce Lee, Woodstock, and Me*, p. 18.

Twenty-three: Knockin' on Heaven's Door

PAGE

423 *A man of lesser ambition:* John Saxon remembers: "One day I asked him, 'Bruce, what would you do if you were 6 foot 4 and 190 pounds?' He stopped and seriously thought about it before saying, 'If I was 6 foot 4 and 190 pounds, I'd rule the world.' He had great ambition." (Fiaz Rafiq, *Bruce Lee Conversations*, p. 268.)
423 *"He was involved":* Linda Lee, *The Bruce Lee Story*, p. 155.
423 *lost twenty pounds:* Mito Uyehara, *The Incomparable Fighter*, p. 79.
423 *"The pupils of his eyes":* Bey Logan, *Hong Kong Action Cinema*, p. 41.
423 *"His complexion was gray":* Robert Clouse, *Bruce Lee: The Biography*, pp. 171–72.
424 *"He could really drink sake":* Chaplin Chang, *The Bruce They Knew*, p. 111. Different types of alcohol seem to affect people who suffer from alcohol flush reaction differently. But it seems likely that drinking this much sake would still have caused Bruce's face to turn red and body to sweat profusely.
424 *"If Marlon Brando":* Fiaz Rafiq, *Bruce Lee Conversations*, p. 268. John Saxon's shocked reply: "Wow!"
424 *"Nowadays, my offers":* John Little, *Letters of the Dragon*, p. 178.
425 *"Bruce was pretty politically":* Interview with Andre Morgan, 2015.
425 *"like a babysitter":* Alex Ben Block, *The Legend of Bruce Lee*, p. 116.
425 *was cheating him:* As is often the case, they both were probably right. It does take time for theaters to pay back earnings to a studio, and Bruce had borrowed a great deal of money. On the other hand, movie producers are masters

at creative accounting, and Raymond Chow had honed his skills at Shaw Brothers. Bruce's movies were propping up Chow's struggling studio. It would have been very simple to move the costs for Golden Harvest's many failed movies onto the balance sheets of Bruce's films. When I asked Paul Heller, who co-produced *Enter the Dragon*, what his opinion of Chow was, he replied, "Raymond is a *gonif*, if you know what that word means. He is an Oriental Machiavelli." (Interview with Paul Heller, 2013.)

425 *Rolls-Royce Corniche:* Alex Ben Block, *The Legend of Bruce Lee*, p. 85.

425 *US$200,000:* Worth slightly more than US$1.1 million in 2017 inflation-adjusted dollars.

425 *Lloyds of London:* Tom Bleecker, *Unsettled Matters*, p. 99.

425 *muggy and oppressive:* Robert Clouse, *Bruce Lee: The Biography*, p. 164.

425 *The temperature:* http://www.weather.gov.hk/cis/dailyExtract_e.htm?y=1973&m=05.

426 *"Rush him to":* Alex Ben Block, *The Legend of Bruce Lee*, p. 112.

426 *put a metal spoon:* Interview with Raymond Chow, 2013.

426 *"a stomach upset":* Linda Lee, *The Bruce Lee Story*, pp. 152–53.

427 *"It's harmless":* Davis Miller, *The Tao of Bruce Lee*, pp. 157–58.

428 *"No, I want to be discharged":* Coroner's inquest of Bruce Lee, p. 68.

428 *cannabis does not cause cerebral edema:* In the recorded history of marijuana's extensive use around the globe (200 million people use cannabis at least once a year), there are only two cases where full postmortem investigations proved a link to cannabis. In both cases, the death was the result of heart failure, not cerebral edema. (Benno Hartung, "Sudden Unexpected Death Under Acute Influence of Cannabis," *Forensic Science International*, 2014.)

428 *"There are no receptors":* Interview with Dr. Daniel Friedman, 2015.

428 *full battery of tests:* Linda Lee, *The Bruce Lee Story*, p. 153.

428 *"What's the matter":* Interview with John Saxon, 2013.

428 *grand mal idiopathic:* http://www.webmd.com/epilepsy/guide/types-epilepsy.

429 *"None of Bruce's family":* Linda Lee, *The Bruce Lee Story*, pp. 153–54.

429 *healthy men—heat stroke:* In his thoughtful book, *The Death of Bruce Lee: A Clinical Investigation* (2012), Duncan Alexander McKenzie was the first person to propose heat stroke as an explanation for Bruce's May 20 collapse.

429 *The fatality rate:* Lisa R. Leon, "Heat Stroke," comprehensivephysiology.com, April 2015.

429 *It is the third:* Dr. Douglas Casa, "Cold Water Immersion: The Gold Standard for Exertional Heatstroke Treatment," *Exercise Sport Science Review*, Vol. 35, No. 3 (2007), pp. 141–49.

429 *A common finding:* Lisa R. Leon, "Heat Stroke," comprehensivephysiology.com, April 2015. As the brain overheats along with the rest of the body, the

blood brain barrier becomes increasingly permeable, allowing protein and fluid leakage into the brain.

429 *The two criteria:* James P. Knochel, M.D., "Heat Stroke," *The New England Journal of Medicine*, June 20, 2002.

429 *Heat stroke researchers:* Lisa R. Leon, "Heat Stroke," comprehensivephysiology .com, April 2015.

430 *sweat glands removed:* Don Atyeo, *King of Kung-Fu*, p. 70; Davis Miller, *The Tao of Bruce Lee*, p. 141.

430 *Without these sweat glands:* Interview with William Adams, 2015. There are few other surface areas of the body that exhibit greater sweat rates—such as the lower back, chest, and forehead—than the armpits.

430 *"There was less awareness":* Ibid.

430 *"He looked skinny":* "A Dragon Remembered: An Interview with Robert Lee," *The Way of the Dragon* DVD extras.

431 *"I passed with":* Chuck Norris, *The Secret of Inner Strength*, pp. 84–85.

431 *"He was very jovial":* Mito Uyehara, *The Incomparable Fighter*, pp. 79–81.

431 *"I hope we can":* Ibid., p. 142.

431 *never liked living in Hong Kong:* "I remember walking into a clothing store one time, and the girls were talking back there," Linda told me in our interview. "They said to each other, 'She's ugly.' I said to them in Cantonese, 'Hey, he married me, so screw you.' " (Interview with Linda Lee, 2013.)

432 *"We've got it":* Robert Clouse, *Bruce Lee: The Biography*, 166.

432 *"Bruce, a friend of yours":* Interview with Michael Allin, 2013.

432 *He acquiesced:* Linda Lee, *The Bruce Lee Story*, p. 154.

432 *"As of now, consider":* John Little, *Letters of the Dragon*, p. 182.

432 *"We were kind of starving":* Interview with Linda Lee, 2013.

432 *"You can't afford":* Alex Ben Block, *The Legend of Bruce Lee*, p. 87.

433 *"Lon Chaney":* A silent era film star, Lon Chaney was known as the "Man of a Thousand Faces" for his ability to transform himself through the use of makeup. He often played multiple roles in the same movie.

433 *to cancel it:* The reason Bruce gave to Silliphant's secretary for canceling the dinner is that he didn't want to embarrass his wife, Linda, by having her in the same room with Silliphant's new girlfriend, Tiana Alexandra (Thi Thanh Nga), a twenty-two-year-old Vietnamese American actress. (Alex Ben Block, *The Legend of Bruce Lee*, p. 115.) Tiana Alexandra had been a karate student of Jhoon Rhee, who introduced her to Bruce Lee several years earlier. How well Bruce and Tiana knew each other has been the subject of some speculation over the years. (Fred Weintraub, *Bruce Lee, Woodstock, and Me*, p. 29.)

433 *"Spoke to Stirling":* John Little, *Letters of the Dragon*, p. 180.

433 *"He brought me a keychain":* Interview with Betty Ting Pei, 2013.

433 *Mercedes-Benz:* Mito Uyehara, *The Incomparable Fighter*, p. 138. Keychains are not the customary reconciliation present given by newly minted superstars to their mistresses after a messy rift. If it wasn't a Mercedes, it was some other gift way more expensive than a keychain. When I met Betty, she was driving a gold Jaguar with a TING PEI vanity license plate.

433 *blown all his Bond money:* Bey Logan, DVD commentary, *Game of Death*.

434 *"Frankly speaking, I am":* Don Atyeo: *King of Kung-Fu*, p. 71.

434 *To promote* Enter the Dragon*:* Linda Lee, *The Bruce Lee Story*, p. 154.

434 *getting high on hash:* Interview with Andre Morgan, 2013.

434 *"a beast in human":* Robert Clouse, *Bruce Lee: The Biography*, pp. 174–76.

434 *"Bruce was slightly stoned . . . with this knife":* Interview with Andre Morgan, 2013.

435 *"What is the situation":* Chaplin Chang, *The Bruce They Knew*, pp. 11–12.

435 *"If I wanted to kill":* Robert Clouse, *Bruce Lee: The Biography*, pp. 174–76.

436 *"When I hit you": Bruce Lee: Century Hero* documentary.

437 *"He was saying that Raymond":* Interview with Nancy Kwan, 2013.

437 *"It's just a fling":* In our interview, Nancy explained, "Bruce was like that—the big cars, clothes, and girls. He had been poor for a long time, and he was just enjoying the fame and everything that went with it." (Interview with Nancy Kwan, 2013.)

Twenty-four: The Last Day of Bruce Lee

PAGE

439 *typed a letter:* John Little, *Letters of the Dragon*, pp. 182–83.

439 *They both had a nibble:* Interview with Andre Morgan, 2013. Morgan joked, "Bruce was in my office alone with me, just us two junkies."

440 *"nooner":* Ibid.

440 *Bruce jumped in his Mercedes:* It is unclear if Bruce drove directly to Betty's apartment and parked his Mercedes there or if he drove back home, dropped off his car, and walked the ten or so minutes to her apartment. There are no reports of Bruce's Mercedes being found at Betty's apartment after his death the same evening. Either he made a pit stop at home before going to Betty's or someone drove his car home after he died.

440 *one-bedroom:* "Last Day of Bruce Lee (Betty Ting Pei)," www.youtube.com /watch?v=sasL92n_OCo.

440 *"I was his girlfriend":* Interview with Betty Ting Pei, 2013.

440 *There was some sex:* "Martial arts legend Bruce Lee did have extramarital sex on the day of his death but was not killed by an aphrodisiac as has been speculated, says the woman in whose house the film star's body was found 40 years

ago." ("Dame of Death: Betty Ting Opens Up on Bruce Lee's Final Hours," *Want China Times*, October 31, 2013.)

440 *He offered Betty:* Editors of *Kung-Fu Monthly*, *Who Killed Bruce Lee?*, p. 54.

440 *"I never wanted":* Interview with Betty Ting Pei, 2013.

440 *Raymond Chow arrived:* Witnesses recalled seeing Raymond Chow's car at her apartment in the late afternoon.

440 *If Betty was reticent:* An alternative theory is that Betty wasn't resistant to the idea. After all, she was an ambitious actress with her own career to consider. Bruce had offered her parts in two of his previous movies, *The Way of the Dragon* and *Enter the Dragon*, but each time the part had gone to another actress. Perhaps when Bruce promised her a role in *Game of Death*, she didn't believe him. In this scenario, Bruce didn't need Raymond to persuade her but rather to convince her she would actually be given the part.

440 *scorching day:* http://www.weather.gov.hk/cis/dailyExtract_e.htm?y=1973&m=7.

440 *"Bruce wasn't feeling very well":* Interview with Raymond Chow, 2013.

440 *"Raymond thought it was an excuse":* Interview with Betty Ting Pei, 2013. Betty found the memory of Raymond Chow's embarrassment amusing. "He thought Bruce said he had a headache, because he wanted to have sex," she whispered to me.

441 *"Bruce had taken them before":* The coroner's inquest concluded that Bruce Lee died from an allergic reaction to the medicine in the Equagesic pill. But if Betty is telling the truth and Bruce Lee had taken one of her pills before, he couldn't have been allergic to them. If he had suffered a severe allergic reaction previously, he wouldn't have swallowed the same type of pill again that night.

441 *He later learned that Langford's*: Interview with Raymond Chow, 2013.

441 *found Bruce undressed:* It makes sense that Bruce would have taken off at least some of his clothes before climbing into his girlfriend's bed.

442 *Raymond redressed:* Testimony at the coroner's inquest strongly indicates that Bruce's body was re-dressed. Whether or not this was done because Raymond intended to move the body or simply to make Bruce more presentable is unknown.

442 *shock but not scandalize:* There have long been rumors that Chow tried to move the body. A missing shoe has been held up as evidence by conspiracy theorists. Since Chow has long maintained the fiction that Bruce was still alive at this point in time and Betty will not discuss this subject, it is impossible to know what exactly happened in these crucial moments. What we do know is that Bruce's body was not removed from the apartment until the paramedics arrived.

442 *revive Bruce for ten minutes:* Coroner's inquest of Bruce Lee, p. 12; Alex Ben Block, *The Legend of Bruce Lee*, p. 122.

442 *clear to Dr. Chu:* During the inquest into Bruce's death, Dr. Eugene Chu

Poh-hwye was asked why Bruce wasn't sent to Baptist Hospital, which was a few blocks from Betty's apartment, instead of Queen Elizabeth Hospital, which was much further away. Wouldn't time have been an important factor in saving Bruce's life? Dr. Chu replied, "I spent at least ten minutes trying to revive him. When he did not show any signs of improvement, it did not occur to me that the time was of great importance." (Alex Ben Block, *The Legend of Bruce Lee*, p. 122.)

442 *Instead Dr. Chu:* Coroner's inquest of Bruce Lee, p. 16.

443 *He told Betty not to say:* Interview with Betty Ting Pei, 2013.

443 *"What's the matter?":* Linda Lee, *The Bruce Lee Story*, p. 158.

443 *"As a first aid man":* Coroner's inquest of Bruce Lee, p. 18.

443 *"Somebody must be joking":* Linda Lee, *The Bruce Lee Story*, p. 158.

444 *"Yes, I want to know":* Linda Lee, *The Man Only I Knew*, p. 17.

444 *Victoria Peak:* Victoria Peak is a mountain on the western half of Hong Kong Island. It attracted prominent European residents because of its panoramic view and more temperate climate. For nearly a century the Chinese were not allowed to live there. The first non-European to obtain permission to build a home on "The Peak" was Robert Hotung, Bruce's great-uncle.

444 *"Nobody got in":* Interview with Ted Thomas, 2013.

444 *"Movie! Movie! Movie!":* Chaplin Chang, *The Bruce They Knew*, pp. 116–17.

445 *"I felt an incredible":* Linda Lee, *The Man Only I Knew*, p. 18.

445 *"Was he a philanderer":* Davis Miller, *The Tao of Bruce Lee*, p. 163. Here is Dr. Langford's exact quote: "Linda was distraught. She didn't know what to do, what to tell the reporters. This was a young, inexperienced woman who loved her husband and was enormously proud of him. She asked me what I knew about Bruce's relationship with women, whether or not he was a philanderer. I told her truthfully, to the best of my knowledge, that he had no other relationships. But Linda thought, quite accurately, that the Hong Kong press would devour her husband. Her major concern was how to keep tawdry things from being said. She handled herself with considerable poise and dignity. I don't think that anyone could've done better than she did. It was in my living room that she and Raymond Chow decided what statement they'd give to reporters."

446 *After some internal debate:* Interview with Andre Morgan, 2013.

446 *"We wanted to protect":* Ibid.

447 *"Bless H.S.":* Ibid.

447 *"print with a sting":* Don Atyeo, *King of Kung-Fu*, p. 78.

447 *"Film star Bruce Li spent":* H. S. Chow, "Who's Lying on Li's Death," *China Mail*, June 24, 1973.

447 *"Bruce Lee Shock":* Don Atyeo, *Bruce Lee: King of Kung-Fu*, p. 75.

447 *"On Friday night":* Ibid.

447 *double-entendre headline:* Robert Clouse, *Bruce Lee: The Biography*, p. 183.

448 *"it was around noon":* Linda Lee, *The Bruce Lee Story*, pp. 156–57. At the coroner's inquest, Linda testified under oath that the last time she'd seen her husband was at 12:30 p.m. on July 20: "He appeared fit and well at that time. He was in a happy state. He told me that he would discuss a new film with Raymond Chow that afternoon and probably would not come home for dinner." It is possible that when Bruce left Golden Harvest for his rendezvous with Betty, he made a pit stop at home to give his wife an alibi for the rest of his day, waited for her to leave for her lunch date, and then jogged over to Betty's apartment, leaving his Mercedes at his home. If this is what happened, then Linda's statement is not technically untrue. It seems more likely, however, that he simply went straight to Betty's.

448 *very sound asleep:* Coroner's inquest of Bruce Lee, p. 5.

448 *"The body is":* Autopsy Report, Forensic Division, Government Laboratory, Hong Kong, August 2, 1973.

449 *"I believe the most likely":* Coroner's inquest, evidence, letter dated August 13, 1973.

449 *Surprisingly, in a colony:* Don Atyeo, *King of Kung-Fu*, p. 87.

450 *"The Hong Kong press simply":* Linda Lee, *The Man Only I Knew*, p. 200.

450 *cornucopia of other drugs:* Don Atyeo, *King of Kung-Fu*, p. 80.

450 *"baggies full of powder":* "Bruce Dies After Meal," *Oriental Daily*, July 25, 1973.

450 *"add some spice to the story":* Don Atyeo, *King of Kung-Fu*, p. 80.

450 *"The fans have been entering":* Ibid., p. 74.

451 *"Every Ninja":* Alex Ben Block, *The Legend of Bruce Lee*, p. 134. Just to be clear: there were no ninjas, teenage mutant or otherwise, roaming around Japan, let alone Hong Kong, in 1973. Ninjas may or may not have been master poisoners in the ancient past, but the coroner found no evidence of poison in Bruce's autopsy. As for vengeful Japanese karate masters, Bruce Lee's films weren't released in Japan until after his death. When they hit the theaters, the Japanese public fell in love with him, and to this day he remains a cultlike figure in that country.

451 *"A Malaysian named Kay Wah Lee":* Ibid., p. 136. Chinese martial arts fiction (*wuxia*), like Western comic books, is filled with magical superpowers, including the delayed death touch (*dim mak*). By focusing one's internal energy (*qi*) on a vulnerable pressure point or acupuncture meridian of an opponent's body, a kung fu master supposedly could deliver a delayed death blow—the Chinese version of the Vulcan nerve pinch.

451 *"During a recent taxi ride":* Don Atyeo, *King of Kung-Fu*, p. 88. If you could die from too much sex, it would be mankind's favorite way to commit suicide. The only young, healthy people who ever perish right after sex are teenagers

in horror movies. Bruce died of a cerebral edema not a heart attack. The autopsy did not find the presence of Spanish Fly or any other aphrodisiac in his system. Oversexed is a moral condemnation parading as an explanation.

451 *"I paid the morgue beautician":* Elaine Yau, "That Bruce Lee World Exclusive, and the One That Got Away: Hong Kong News Veteran Looks Back," *South China Morning Post*, January 4, 2016.

451 *"Most bodies in Hong Kong":* Interview with Andre Morgan, 2015.

451 *"Although we do not . . . Now that a great star":* Don Atyeo, *King of Kung-Fu*, p. 81.

452 *"Suspicion there had . . . velvet interior":* Interview with Andre Morgan, 2015.

452 *The scratched and stained casket:* Alex Ben Block, *The Legend of Bruce Lee*, p. 124; Linda Lee, *The Man Only I Knew*, p. 204; Linda Lee, *The Bruce Lee Story*, p. 162.

452 *"Nine Dragon Pond":* Don Atyeo, *King of Kung-Fu*, p. 90. If Bruce had been an African American blues musician, his death would have evoked tales of a crossroads deal with the devil—his soul for fame.

453 *"It seems that . . . Revenge for Bruce Lee":* Don Atyeo, *King of Kung-Fu*, p. 81.

453 *many innocent victims:* Two of the victims were a seven-year-old girl and her two-year-old brother who opened a bomb wrapped like a gift outside their residence.

Twenty-five: The Inquest

PAGE

456 *An interdepartmental memo:* Don Atyeo, *King of Kung-Fu*, p. 84.

456 *They were greeted by over:* Paul Li, *From Limited to Limitless*, p. 160.

456 *"The goal will be":* Ibid.

457 *"I saw him almost every day":* Coroner's inquest of Bruce Lee, p. 5.

457 *The already intense:* Paul Li, *From Limited to Limitless*, p. 162.

458 *The press clearly intended:* Ibid., p. 164.

459 *the young man in Betty Ting Pei's apartment:* On May 10, 1973, Raymond Chow and several Golden Harvest employees carried Bruce's unconscious body to Chow's car, drove him to Baptist Hospital, and narrowly saved his life. When Chow received a call from a hysterical Betty on July 20 telling him Bruce wouldn't wake up, it seems likely that Chow planned to repeat the same process. While he was at a pay phone on the side of the road, he probably called one of the Golden Harvest stagehands who had helped him carry Bruce previously, and asked the young man to meet him at Betty's apartment. Once Chow and the young man arrived at the apartment, they realized Bruce was already dead. After the scandal broke in the press and Chow was caught lying about the initial story, he recognized that the presence of an unnamed young man in the apartment would appear suspicious, so Chow denied that the young man was ever there. The other possibility is the senior paramedic, Pang Tak Sun,

was incorrect and there was not an unnamed young man in the apartment with Raymond Chow, Dr. Chu, Betty, and Bruce's corpse on the night of July 20. But the paramedic's testimony was very precise, and he had no reason to lie.

459 *"When you arrived at the scene":* Coroner's inquest of Bruce Lee, pp. 18–20.

459 *helped transport the body:* A far simpler explanation is that Bruce had done what most men do at their girlfriend's apartments when they want to take a nap: he got undressed and climbed under the covers. Raymond Chow, who was trying to hide any evidence of an affair, didn't want the paramedics to find a half-naked married man in another woman's bed. So Chow re-dressed Bruce.

459 *"There was no heartbeat":* Coroner's inquest of Bruce Lee, p. 21.

460 *"Following my examination":* Ibid., p. 23.

460 *"I could not see any signs":* Ibid., pp. 27–28.

460 *On the morning of September 17:* Paul Li, *From Limited to Limitless*, p. 168.

461 *Linda went on to testify:* Coroner's inquest of Bruce Lee, pp. 31–34.

462 *"I will allow this line":* Paul Li, *From Limited to Limitless*, p. 169.

462 *"Though the witness has a right":* Paul Li, *From Limited to Limitless*, p. 170.

462 The China Mail*'s front-page:* Don Atyeo, *King of Kung-Fu*, p. 87.

463 *"Once in the face accidentally":* It is entirely possible this actually happened (accidents are frequent on kung fu movie sets), but there are no other corroborating accounts of this incident.

463 *"Yes, I have heard of that":* Coroner's inquest of Bruce Lee, p. 39.

464 *At this bald faced lie:* Don Atyeo, *King of Kung-Fu*, p. 85.

465 *"Not much":* Coroner's inquest of Bruce Lee, pp. 44–45.

465 *"Dr. Chu never spoke":* Oliver Chou, "Hong Kong Doctor, Who Tried to Revive Bruce Lee, Takes Secrets of Kung Fu Legend's 1973 Death to the Grave," *South China Morning Post*, August 14, 2015.

465 *The magistrate agreed:* Coroner's inquest of Bruce Lee, p. 47.

466 *thinned out dramatically:* Paul Li, *From Limited to Limitless*, p. 174.

467 *"upper floors of Queen Elizabeth":* Interview with Dr. Langford conducted by Davis Miller.

467 *the courtroom was relatively cold:* Paul Li, *From Limited to Limitless*, p. 176.

468 *"No" she averred:* Coroner's inquest of Bruce Lee, p. 62.

468 *"I had considerable sympathy":* Davis Miller, *The Tao of Bruce Lee*, p. 163.

469 *"In the pharmacological":* Coroner's inquest of Bruce Lee, p. 71.

469 *"there were no authenticated cases":* Ibid., p. 78. As part of Dr. Lycette's thorough research into the subject, he wrote a letter to the U.S. Armed Forces Institute of Pathology on August 13, 1973. Dr. Lycette sent the autopsy report and explained why he suspected cannabis. On August 30, 1973, the U.S. Armed Forces Institute of Pathology replied, "The postmortem findings seem to exclude a natural cause of death. [That said] it has not been possible

to confirm your opinion that death may be attributed to cannabis intoxication. Authenticated cases in which death has been attributed to cannabis intoxication are not known. There is still no fully authenticated case reported in which death from the effect of cannabis poisoning on the central nervous system has been established." (Coroner's inquest, Exhibit F.)

469 *"Fatal aspirin hypersensitivity":* Coroner's inquest of Bruce Lee, p. 80.

470 *"is very rare indeed":* Ibid., pp. 91–92.

470 *from so far away to testify:* Paul Li, *From Limited to Limitless*, p. 179.

471 *Intentionally and maliciously causing:* Ibid., p. 182.

472 *The longest coroner's inquest:* Ibid., p. 183.

472 *Many fans were reminded:* Alex Ben Block, *The Legend of Bruce Lee*, p. 123.

473 *a murder plot:* Paul Li, *From Limited to Limitless*, p. 183. The coroner's report ruled out murder by physical violence, and the blood tests ruled out murder by poison. Despite this, belief that Bruce was killed by somebody—be it ninjas, death touch kung fu masters, or Raymond Chow—remains prevalent. Any murder theory rests on the assumption that there was a massive cover-up that included the coroner, his entire office, the government chemists, etc. There has never been a shred of evidence of a cover-up. To the contrary, the coroner, Dr. Lycette, went to great lengths trying to discover the cause of death, even going so far as to write to the U.S. Armed Forces Institute of Pathology. If he had been involved in a widespread conspiracy, Dr. Lycette would not have wanted to draw attention to the case from an outside party like the U.S. Army.

473 *"Without a doubt":* Linda Lee, *The Bruce Lee Story*, p. 175.

473 *"In telling the story":* Interview with Raymond Chow, 2013.

474 *"A person who has suffered":* Lisa R. Leon, "Heat Stroke," comprehensive physiology.com, April 2015.

474 *meprobamate is not known to cause cerebral edema:* C. Charron et al., "Incidence, Causes and Prognosis of Hypotension Related to Meprobamate Poisoning," *Intensive Care Medicine*, Vol. 31 (2005), pp. 1582–86.

474 *The Mayo Clinic:* http://www.mayoclinic.org/diseases-conditions/drug-allergy/expert-answers/aspirin-allergy/faq-20058225.

474 *vanishingly small:* Other than heat stroke and aspirin allergy, the only other scientifically possible theory is epilepsy. At the 2006 meeting of the American Academy of Forensic Sciences, Dr. James Filkins argued that the cause of Bruce's death was SUDEP or Sudden Unexpected Death in Epilepsy. SUDEP, accounts for 5–30 percent of deaths in patients with epilepsy, who die unexpectedly at a time other than during a seizure. It is most common in men aged between twenty and forty. There are approximately 2,750 deaths annually in the United States. In close to 50 percent of these deaths, autopsies reveal neurological damage including cerebral edema. ("Epilepsy Could

Solve Mystery of Kung Fu Legend's Death," *The Guardian*, February 24, 2006.) The major weakness of the SUDEP theory is it is entirely based on the assumption that Bruce Lee had epilepsy. There is usually a family history of epilepsy, and it most commonly develops in children or the elderly. Bruce was a young man with no examples of epilepsy in his family. It also takes more than one seizure for a diagnosis of epilepsy, because lots of different things can cause a seizure. Prior to May 10, Bruce had no history of seizures. "Dr. Reisbord told me that at no time had Bruce suffered from epilepsy," says Linda. (Linda Lee, *The Bruce Lee Story*, p. 154.) There is also no evidence that Bruce suffered a second violent seizure prior to his death on July 20. If he did, Betty Ting Pei, sitting in the next room, didn't notice it. Finally, even if Bruce had epilepsy, the likelihood of SUDEP increases with the number of seizures. "The risk is maximal when a person has numerous seizures over years," says Dr. John Stern, a neurologist and specialist in epilepsy at UCLA, "and not much more than baseline risk for sudden death when there have only been two seizures." (Interview with Dr. John Stern of UCLA, 2015.) For all these reasons, epilepsy/SUDEP is an even less likely theory than aspirin allergy. And thus relegated to an endnote.

474 *the third most common cause of death:* Douglas Casa, "Cold Water Immersion: The Gold Standard for Exertional Heatstroke Treatment," *Exercise Sport Science Review*, Vol. 35, No. 3 (2007), pp. 141–49.

474 *three high school:* Eric Brady, "Heat-Related Illness Still Deadly Problem for Athletes," *USA Today*, August 15, 2011.

475 *Even now proper treatment:* Interview with William Adams, 2015.

475 *"Even though I":* John Little, *The Celebrated Life of the Golden Dragon*, p. 176.

Epilogue: The Legend

PAGE

477 *"Riding in the back":* Fiaz Rafiq, *Bruce Lee Conversations*, p. 267.

477 *"The picture is expertly":* Howard Thompson, "Enter the Dragon," *New York Times*, August 18, 1973.

477 *"In my most civilized":* William Paul, "Getting the Thrust of Kung Fu," *Village Voice*, April 30, 1973.

478 *"Warner's lawyer sent":* Interview with Michael Allin, 2013.

478 *"If I could send Bruce":* Alex Ben Block, *The Legend of Bruce Lee*, p. 157.

478 *His 1974 song:* Simon Braund, "Rise of the Dragon," *Empire Magazine*, August 2013.

478 *thirty different Hong Kong:* Alex Ben Block, *The Legend of Bruce Lee*, p. 158.

478 *grossed nearly $50 million:* Kenneth Turan, "The Apotheosis of Bruce Lee: An Actor Dies; A Posthumous Industry is Born," *American Film*, October 1975.

478 *Three episodes of:* Martin Grams Jr., *The Green Hornet*, p. 364.

478 *"Mr. Lee, who played":* Vincent Canby, " 'Green Hornet,' From Bruce Lee Series," *New York Times*, November 28, 1974. Canby went on to say, "He looks very young, very clean-cut and very American (in an Oriental sort of way)." Canby may have been trying to make up for the *New York Times* obituary of Bruce Lee. It was only eight lines long, one of which read, "Vincent Canby, the film critic of *The New York Times*, said that movies like *Fist of Fury* make 'the worst Italian western look like the most solemn and noble achievements of early Soviet Cinema.' " (Joel Stein, *Time 100 People of the Century*, June 14, 1999.)

479 *"I knew so little":* "1974 Black Belt Hall of Fame: Bruce Lee Martial Artist of the Year," p. 92.

479 *a tacky biopic:* Kenneth Turan, "The Apotheosis of Bruce Lee: An Actor Dies; A Posthumous Industry is Born," *American Film*, October 1975. Linda Lee, Raymond Chow, Madame Lo Wei, and Betty Ting Pei sued the producers for invasion of privacy. (" 'Dragon' Draws Suit From Bruce Lee Widow," *Variety*, June 30, 1975.) When the plaintiffs lost this suit, Linda filed a second lawsuit, seeking $13 million in damages, for appropriation of property rights. Three years later the judge ruled in Linda's favor but only awarded her $25,000. ("Bruce Lee Widow Files Another 'Dragon' Suit," *Variety*, September, 2, 1975; "Bruce Lee's Widow Wins Estate Suit," *Variety*, April 7, 1978.)

479 *small-scale newssheets:* Don Atyeo, *The King of Kung-Fu*, p. 25.

479 The Ballad of Bruce Lee*:* "Into this world came a little dragon, Bruce Lee, his hands and feet fast, powerful, and mighty," Robert Lee sang over strumming guitar. "It was easy for him to win the world's acclaim, for he was strong and his will untamed."

479 *"Not since James Dean":* Kenneth Turan, "The Apotheosis of Bruce Lee: An Actor Dies; A Posthumous Industry is Born," *American Film*, October 1975.

479 *A theater in Iran:* Davis Miller, *The Tao of Bruce Lee*, p. 154.

479 *VHS tapes:* Ilinca Calugareanu, "VHS vs. Communism," *New York Times*, February 17, 2014.

480 *five hundred martial arts:* Davis Miller, *The Tao of Bruce Lee*, p. 170.

480 *In Britain, there was:* Simon Braund, "Rise of the Dragon," *Empire Magazine*, August 2013.

480 *"Bruce Lee was, and always":* "1974 Black Belt Hall of Fame: Bruce Lee Martial Artist of the Year," p. 92. So many kids wanted to be like Bruce that sales soared for nunchakus. Most quickly realized, after cracking themselves repeatedly in the skull, how difficult the weapon is to master and wisely stored them in their closets. A few foolish hoodlums attempted to use them in the commission of crimes—causing an international nunchaku panic. "The fad

has really caught on," one Los Angeles police officer told the press in late 1973. "Every ten or fifteen blocks you see a karate school, and we've had a couple of robberies where the suspects have tried to hit their victims over the head with fighting sticks." Nunchakus were outlawed in England and several American states. (Don Atyeo, *The King of Kung-Fu*, p. 26; Alex Ben Block, *The Legend of Bruce Lee*, p. 44.)

480 *"A lot of people still"*: Interview with W. Wong, 2013.

480 *"He's already dead"*: Alex Ben Block, *The Legend of Bruce Lee*, p. 157.

480 *"to draw attention"*: Fiaz Rafiq, *Bruce Lee Conversations*, p. 331.

481 *These Bruceploitation films:* Sammo Hung satirized these Bruceploitation movies in *Enter the Fat Dragon* (1978).

482 *"The Rio opening"*: Kenneth Turan, "I Made Love To . . . And Other True Tales of the Bruce Lee Cult," *New West*, September 2, 1979.

482 *Bruce Lee's final project: The Silent Flute* was finally made into a movie in 1978. It was renamed *Circle of Iron* and starred David Carradine in the multiple roles originally intended for Bruce Lee. The movie was not nearly as ambitious or interesting as the screenplay.

482 *It took seven years:* Linda Lee, *The Bruce Lee Story*, pp. 188–89.

482 *negotiate with Raymond Chow:* The only person to report about these negotiations was Tom Bleecker, who was briefly married to Linda in the late 1980s. According to Bleecker, Bruce died with only US$23,000 in cash. His Kowloon Tong mansion was his only major asset. It was sold for $180,000, netting Linda $40,000. As for the life insurance companies, Lloyd's of London only agreed to pay out $129,000 on Bruce's $1,350,000 policy. American International Assurance Company (AIA), who sent a lawyer to the coroner's inquest, agreed to pay $100,000 on Bruce's $200,000 policy. Both companies contended that Bruce's false statement on the application forms that he had never used illegal drugs nullified the policies but settled before the case was taken to court. As for Bruce's half of Concord Productions—the profits from *Way of the Dragon*, *Enter the Dragon*, and the future value of *Game of Death*—Raymond Chow eventually paid Linda US$2,700,000. So the total value of Bruce Lee's estate, not deducting for taxation and extensive legal fees, was US$2,992,000—the equivalent of $13 million in 2017 dollars. (Tom Bleecker, *Unsettled Matters*, pp. 145–46, 155, 161–62.)

482 *"My mom was going"*: Interview with Shannon Lee, 2013.

483 *Chuck Norris lived:* Ibid.

483 *"When he first passed"*: Monica Yant, "Bruce Lee Estate Items to Go on the Block," *Los Angeles Times*, September 19, 1993.

483 *Ziv International agency:* "Ziv International Obtains License for Lee Products," *Hollywood Reporter*, September 24, 1975.

483 *Zebra Books:* "Zebra Signs with Ziv," *Publishers Weekly*, June 14, 1976. Bruce had originally intended to publish *The Tao of Jeet Kune Do* with *Black Belt* magazine's publishing arm, Ohara. He never got past the note taking stage before abandoning the project. After his death, Linda decided to publish these notes with Ohara. *The Tao of Jeet Kune Do* (1975) became the best-selling martial arts book of all time.

483 *"Don't go around":* Interview with Shannon Lee, 2013.

483 *When he was eight:* Betsy Sharkey, "Fate's Children: Bruce and Brandon," *New York Times*, May 2, 1993.

483 *"He was a prankster":* Interview with Shannon Lee, 2013.

484 *"He started convincing":* Ibid. Linda's spin on these events: "As a senior Brandon was elected student body president, but the innovations he had in mind for the school did not fit in with the administration's mindset." (Linda Lee, *The Bruce Lee Story*, pp. 182–83.)

484 *"You're not doing":* Shannon Bradley-Colleary, "20 Years After His Death on the Set of *The Crow*, I Remember Brandon Lee," *Huffington Post*, April 1, 2013.

484 *Jeet Kune Do lessons:* "Dan Inosanto told me that Brandon came in very humble," said Taky Kimura. "He started at the bottom like everybody else, took his lumps, and worked his way up. Dan said this young man had all the moves and the coordination similar to what his dad had. Dan was hopeful one day he could groom Brandon to be the leader and take over the whole thing [the Jeet Kune Do movement]." (Paul Bax, *Disciples of the Dragon*, p. 12.)

484 *"It's a tough business":* Interview with Shannon Lee, 2013.

485 *updated version of Linda's biography:* Linda's ghostwriter for her updated biography, *The Bruce Lee Story*, was Tom Bleecker. She married him in 1988 but divorced him two years later in 1990. A year later she married Bruce Cadwell, a businessman, and moved to Boise, Idaho. They are still together.

485 *The Curse of the Dragon:* Amy Longsdorf, "The Curse," *Morning Call*, May 7, 1993. Misfortune surrounding the filming of *Dragon: The Bruce Lee Story* only reinforced the death curse myth. Jason Scott Lee, who played Bruce, lost his grandmother; costar Lauren Holly, who played Linda, lost her fourteen-year-old brother in a fire; and the director Rob Cohen suffered a heart attack that nearly forced him off the project.

485 *more than a comma:* Betsy Sharkey, "Fate's Children: Bruce and Brandon," *New York Times*, May 2, 1993. In one of his earliest interviews, Brandon told *Black Belt* magazine, "I'd be talking with people and they'd invite me out for a drink. I'd be thinking, 'Does this person really like me or are they just screwing with me because I'm Bruce Lee's son?' "

485 *"where people have died":* Juliann Garey, "Disasters Plague the Set of 'The Crow,' " *Entertainment Weekly*, April 2, 1993.

486 *"$30 million movie":* Adam Smith, "The Fall of the Crow," *Empire* magazine, August 2013.

487 *Instead Brandon was buried:* The graves of Bruce and Brandon have become a tourist attraction and pilgrimage site, receiving scores of visitors every day. "As with other celebrity gravesites, Bruce and Brandon's get their share of clandestine late night visits," says Andy Koopmans, author of *The Importance of Bruce Lee*. "I've heard from many Seattle residents who grew up in town that it's always been a tradition to go 'smoke a bowl with Bruce and Brandon' at night after the cemetery is officially closed." (John Overall, *The Bruce Lee Review*, pp. 145–46.)

487 *"It is beyond my realm":* Betsy Sharkey, "Fate's Children: Bruce and Brandon," *New York Times*, May 2, 1993.

487 *"Brandon very much wanted":* Alex Ben Block, "Brandon Lee's Mom: Never Again," *Hollywood Reporter*, April 29, 1993.

487 *"Lee is sensational":* Peter Travers, "The Crow," *Rolling Stone*, May 11, 1994. Peter Rainer at *The Los Angeles Times* concurred, "Lee has phenomenal presence, and his movements are so balletically powerful that his rampages seem like waking nightmares. Lee keeps you watching *The Crow* when you'd rather look away." (Peter Rainer, "'The Crow' Flies With Grim Glee," *Los Angeles Times*, May 11, 1994.)

487 *"If Brandon had lived":* Betsy Sharkey, "Fate's Children: Bruce and Brandon," *New York Times*, May 2, 1993.

487 *the son's story:* Davis Miller, *The Tao of Bruce Lee*, pp. 166–67.

487 *"It was very difficult":* Interview with Shannon Lee, 2013.

488 *"It's amazingly fortunate":* Ibid.

488 *"I felt so much pressure":* Ibid.

488 Enter the Eagles*:* The role was created specifically for Shannon, according to a Golden Harvest representative. "It will be interesting working with Shannon. On my second film, I was with (her late brother) Brandon," said Michael Wong, her costar in the movie. "I bought two Harley Davidsons because of him. We had a day off in Los Angeles and he let me ride his Harley." (Norma Reveler, "Golden Harvest Reaping Deal with Lee's Daughter," *Hollywood Reporter*, June 24, 1997.)

488 *regret giving it:* "If people say Jeet Kune Do is different from 'this' or 'that,' then let the name of Jeet Kune Do be wiped out, for that is what it is, just a name," Bruce wrote in his notes. "Please don't fuss over it."

488 *January 29, 1970:* Tommy Gong, *Bruce Lee*, p. 167.

488 *He made his assistant instructors:* In a 1972 phone conversation with his student Dan Lee, Bruce explained, "That's why I did ban all the schools of Jeet Kune Do because it is very easy for a member to come in and take the agenda as the truth and as 'the way,' you know what I mean?"

489 *known as the Nucleus:* The Charter Members of the Nucleus were Linda Lee Cadwell, Taky Kimura, Allen Joe, George Lee, Bob Bremer, Richard Bustillo, Steve Golden, Larry Hartsell, Herb Jackson, Pete Jacobs, Daniel Lee, Jerry Poteet, Ted Wong, Greglon Lee (the son of James Yimm Lee), Chris Kent, Tim Tackett, John Little, and Shannon Lee Keasler. Shannon married Ian Keasler in 1994. Their daughter Wren Keasler was born in 2003.

489 *created a schism:* James Bishop, *Bruce Lee: Dynamic Becoming*, p. 142.

490 *She effectively disbanded:* In 2001, the Nucleus held its annual Jeet Kune Do training seminar in the Netherlands. It lost $25,000. On March 11, 2002, the Bruce Lee Estate's new lawyers sent a legal letter to Nucleus members terminating the license granted them and ordering them to cease using the names and trademarks of the Bruce Lee Educational Foundation and the Jun Fan Jeet Kune Do Nucleus. "A lot of people were really mad at me," Shannon says, "because they thought I should've stepped in and handled it differently. I'm very easygoing up to a point, and then at some point, I'm like, 'You're being a jackass, so just cut that out.' People don't take too kindly to that." (Interview with Shannon Lee, 2013; James Bishop, *Dynamic Becoming*, pp. 155–56.)

490 *tie McQueen for ninth place:* Immediately after a famous musician dies, the boost in record sales will briefly inflate their ranking. In the past two years, Prince, David Bowie, and Tom Petty have jumped into the top ten, pushing Brucc off thc list.

490 *ignored its most famous son:* "Only in his hometown is a prophet without honor" (Matthew 13:57).

490 *love motel:* Nash Jenkins, "Bruce Lee's Former Home in Hong Kong Faces an Uncertain Future," *Time*, September 8, 2015.

490 *Robert Lee helped unveil:* "Hong Kong Unveils Bruce Lee Statue," *The Age*, November 28, 2005.

491 *Chinese male as submissive:* Jackinson Chan, *Chinese American Masculinities*, p. 5.

491 *"We lived in Alameda":* Fiaz Rafiq, *Bruce Lee Conversations*, p. 114.

491 *"self-centered asshole":* David Brewster and David M. Buerge, eds., *Washingtonians*, p. 429.

491 *Asian American movement:* Jackinson Chan, *Chinese American Masculinities*, p. 7.

491 *transformed Western filmmaking:* Bruce Lee also had a huge influence on video games. The 1984 arcade video game *Kung-Fu Master* was inspired by *Game of Death*. Most of the fighting games have a shout-out to Bruce with one or more characters based on him. Kim Dragon from *World Heroes* is a martial arts actor whose special move is a Dragon kick. Jann Lee in *Dead or Alive* is named after Lee Jun Fan. Fei Long in *Street Fighter* fights like Bruce. Marshall Law, from the *Tekken* series, resembles Bruce Lee with his techniques and whoops and yells. Liu Kang in *Mortal Kombat* dresses and moves like

Bruce. *EA Sports UFC* skipped the Lee-alike Bruceploitation and simply licensed Bruce from the Estate as a character wearing yellow and black compression shorts modeled after the yellow tracksuit in *Game of Death.*

492 *greater on fight choreography:* Interestingly, Lee did not have the same impact on Hong Kong fight choreography. After the Bruceploitation period died down in the late 1970s, Hong Kong filmmakers rejected his high-impact, heightened-realism approach. They returned to elaborate Chinese Opera choreography in Jackie Chan and Jet Li movies or focused on "wire-fu" stunts in *wuxia* films like *House of Flying Daggers* (2004).

492 *"Every town in America":* Interview with Fred Weintraub, 2013.

492 *"I think of myself as":* Bruce Lee, *The Lost Interview: The Pierre Berton Show—9 December 1971.*

493 *"you were sincere":* Paul Bax, *Disciples of the Dragon*, p. 4.

493 *"Muslims, Serbs, or Croats":* Ivo Scepanovic, "Bruce Lee Beats Pope to Be Peace Symbol of Mostar," *The Telegraph*, September 12, 2004; Robert Siegel, "Bosnian City's Unique Statue Choice: Bruce Lee," NPR, September 13, 2005; "Bosnia Unveils Bruce Lee Bronze," *BBC News*, November 26, 2005.

bibliography

English Language Books

Abdul-Jabbar, Kareem. *Giant Steps: The Autobiography of Kareem Abdul-Jabbar*. New York: Bantam, 1983.

Ashrafian, Dr. Hutan. *Warrior Origins: The Historical and Legendary Links Between Bodhidharma, Shaolin Kung-fu, Karate and Ninjitsu*. London: The History Press, 2014.

Atyeo, Don, and Felix Dennis. *Bruce Lee: King of Kung-Fu*. London: Bunch Books, 1974.

Bax, Paul. *Disciples of the Dragon: Reflections from the Students of Bruce Lee*. Denver: Outskirts Press, 2008.

Bishop, James. *Bruce Lee: Dynamic Becoming*. Carrollton, TX: Promethean Press, 2004.

Bleecker, Tom. *Unsettled Matters*. Lompoc, CA: Gilderoy Publications, 1996.

Block, Alex Ben. *The Legend of Bruce Lee*. New York: Dell, 1974.

Booth, Martin. *Cannabis: A History*. New York: Picador, 2003.

———. *The Dragon Syndicates: The Global Phenomenon of the Triads*. New York: Doubleday, 1999.

———. *Golden Boy: Memories of a Hong Kong Childhood*. New York: Picador, 2004.

Borine, Norman. *King Dragon: The World of Bruce Lee*. New York: Fideli Publishing, 2002.

Brewster, David, and David M. Buerge, eds. *Washingtonians: A Biographical Portrait of a State*. Seattle: Sasquatch Books, 1988.

Burger, Richard. *Behind the Red Door.* Hong Kong: Earnshaw Books, 2012.

Campbell, Sid, and Greglon Yimm Lee. *The Dragon and the Tiger: The Birth of Bruce Lee's Jeet Kune Do: The Oakland Years*, Vol. 1. Berkeley: Frog, 2003.

———. *The Dragon and the Tiger: Bruce Lee: The Oakland Years*, Vol. 2. Berkeley: Frog, 2005.

Chan, Jachinson. *Chinese American Masculinities: From Fu Manchu to Bruce Lee.* New York: Routledge, 2001.

Chan, Jackie. *I Am Jackie Chan.* New York: Ballantine, 1998.

Chang, Iris. *The Chinese in America.* New York: Penguin, 2003.

Chwoon, Tan Hoo. *The Orphan: Bruce Lee in His Greatest Movie.* Singapore: Noel B Caros Productions, 1998.

Clouse, Robert. *Bruce Lee: The Biography.* Burbank, CA: Unique Publications, 1988.

Cohen, Rob. *Dragon: The Bruce Lee Story, The Screenplay*, October, 4, 1991.

Confucius. *The Analects.* New York: Penguin, 1979.

Damone, Vic. *Singing Was the Easy Part.* New York: St. Martin's, 2009.

Editors of *Black Belt* magazine. *The Legendary Bruce Lee.* Santa Clarita, CA: Ohara Publications, 1986.

Editors of *Kung-Fu Monthly. Who Killed Bruce Lee?* London: Bunch Books, 1978.

Eng, David L. *Racial Castration: Managing Masculinity in Asian America.* Durham, NC: Duke University Press, 2001.

Etter, Jonathan. *Gangway, Lord! Here Come the Brides Book.* Albany, GA: Bear-Manor Media, 2010.

Farrell, Sharon. *Sharon Farrell: "Hollywood Princess" from Sioux City, Iowa.* Topanga, CA, 2013.

Fraguas, Jose. *Jeet Kune Do Conversations.* Los Angeles: Empire Books, 2006.

Friedman, Dave. *Enter the Dragon: A Photographer's Journey.* Los Angeles: Warner Bros. Entertainment, 2013.

Fuhrman, Candice Jacobson. *Publicity Stunt!* Forest Knolls, CA: Wink Books, 1989.

Glover, Jesse. *Bruce Lee: Between Wing Chun and Jeet Kune Do.* Self-published: Seattle, 1976.

Goldman, Andrea. *Opera and the City: The Politics of Culture in Beijing, 1770–1900.* Stanford: Stanford University Press, 2012.

Gong, Tommy. *Bruce Lee: The Evolution of a Martial Artist.* Los Angeles: Bruce Lee Enterprises, 2014.

Grams, Martin Jr., and Terry Salomonson. *The Green Hornet: A History of Radio, Motion Pictures, Comics, and Television.* Churchville, MD: OTR Publishing, 2010.

Hamm, John Christopher. *Paper Swordsmen: Jin Yong and the Modern Chinese Martial Arts Novel.* Honolulu: University of Hawaii Press, 2006.

Handelman, Dr. Kenny. *Attention Difference Disorder: How to Turn Your ADHD Child or Teen's Differences into Strengths.* New York: Morgan James Publishing, 2011.

Ho, Eric Peter. *Tracing My Children's Lineage*. Hong Kong Institute for the Humanities and Social Studies, University of Hong Kong, 2010.

Holdsworth, May, and Christopher Munn, eds. *Dictionary of Hong Kong Biography*. Hong Kong: Hong Kong University Press, 2012.

Hopkins, Philip, and Richard Ellis. *Hyperthermic and Hypermetabolic Disorders*. Cambridge: Cambridge University Press, 1996.

Hyams, Joe. *Zen in the Martial Arts*. New York: Houghton Mifflin, 1979.

Ingham, Mike, and Xu Xi. *City Voices: Hong Kong Writing in English, 1945 to the Present*. Hong Kong: Hong Kong University Press, 2003.

Judkins, Benjamin, and Jon Nielson. *The Creation of Wing Chun: A Social History of the Southern Chinese Martial Arts*. Albany: SUNY Press, 2015.

Kael, Pauline. *5001 Nights at the Movies*. New York: Henry Holt, 1991.

Kerridge, Steve. *The Bruce Lee Chronicles: An Inside Look at Way of the Dragon*, Vol 1. Tiger Rock Publishing, 2011.

———. *Bruce Lee: Legends of the Dragon*, Vol. 1. London: Tao Publishing, 2008.

———. *Bruce Lee: Legends of the Dragon*, Vol. 2. London: Tao Publishing, 2008.

Kwong, Peter, and Dusanka Miscevic. *Chinese America: The Untold Story of America's Oldest New Community*. New York: The New Press, 2005.

Lao-tzu. *Tao Te Ching*. New York: Penguin, 1963.

Lee, Agnes, Grace Lee, and Robert Lee. *Bruce Lee, The Untold Story: Bruce Lee's Life Story as Told by His Mother, Family, and Friends*. Burbank, CA: Unique Publications, 1986.

Lee, Bruce. *Chinese Gung Fu: The Philosophical Art of Self-Defense*. Black Belt Books, 2008.

———. *The Lost Interview: The Pierre Berton Show—9 December 1971*. BN Publishing, 2009.

———. *Northern Leg Southern Fist*. Screenplay treatment.

———. *The Tao of Jeet Kune Do*. Santa Clarita, CA: Ohara, 1975.

Lee, George, and David Tadman. *Regards from the Dragon: Oakland*. Los Angeles: Empire Books, 2008.

Lee, Linda. *Bruce Lee: The Man Only I Knew*. New York: Warner, 1975.

———. *The Bruce Lee Story*. Santa Clarita, CA: Ohara Publications, 1989.

Lee, Phoebe, Robert Lee, Agnes Lee, and Peter Lee. *Lee Siu Loong: Memories of the Dragon*. Hong Kong: Bruce Lee Club, 2004.

Lee, Robert G. *Orientals: Asian Americans in Popular Culture*. Philadelphia: Temple University Press, 1999.

Lee Family Immigration Files. Scans from 12017/53752. Record Group 85, ARC 296477. National Archives and Records Administration, San Francisco.

Leong, Karen. *The China Mystique: Pearl S. Buck, Anna May Wong, Mayling Soong, and the Transformation of American Orientalism*. Berkeley: University of California Press, 2005.

Lisanti, Tom. *Glamour Girls of Sixties Hollywood: Seventy-Five Profiles*. London: McFarland, 2008.

Little, John. *Bruce Lee: Artist of Life*. Boston: Tuttle, 1999.

———. *Bruce Lee: A Warrior's Journey*. New York: Contemporary Books, 2001.

———. *Bruce Lee: The Celebrated Life of the Golden Dragon*. Boston: Tuttle, 2000.

———. *Enter the Dragon: The Making of a Classic Motion Picture*. Warner Brothers Special Edition, 1989.

Little, John, ed. *Bruce Lee: Letters of the Dragon*. Boston: Tuttle, 2016.

———. *Bruce Lee: Words of the Dragon, Interviews, 1958–1973*. Boston: Tuttle, 1997.

Liu, Petrus. *Stateless Subjects: Chinese Martial Arts Literature and Postcolonial History*. Ithaca: Cornell University East Asia Program, 2011.

Logan, Bey. *Hong Kong Action Cinema*. Woodstock, NY: Overlook Press, 1995.

Lorge, Peter. *Chinese Martial Arts: From Antiquity to the Twenty-First Century*. Cambridge University Press, 2011.

Marr, Caroline J., and Nile Thompson. *Building for Learning: Seattle's Public School Histories, 1862–2000*. Seattle School District, Seattle, 2002.

Mason, Richard. *The World of Suzie Wong*. London: Collins, 1957.

McGilligan, Patrick. *Backstory 3: Interviews with Screenwriters of the 60s*. Berkeley: University of California Press, 1997.

McKenzie, Duncan Alexander. *The Death of Bruce Lee: A Clinical Investigation*. Self-published, 2012.

———. *Mortal Dragon: The Death of Bruce Lee Explained*. Self-published, 2015.

Miller, Davis. *The Tao of Bruce Lee*. New York: Random House, 2000.

———. *The Zen of Muhammad Ali and Other Obsessions*. New York: Random House, 2002.

Miyao, Daisuke. *Sessue Hayakawa: Silent Cinema and Transnational Stardom*. Durham, NC: Duke University Press, 2007.

Morris, Meaghan, Siu Leung Li, and Stephen Chan Ching-kiu, eds. *Hong Kong Connections: Transnational Imagination in Action Cinema*. Durham, NC: Duke University Press, 2005.

Norris, Chuck. *Against All Odds: My Story*. Nashville: B&H Publishing Group, 2004.

———. *The Secret of Inner Strength: My Story*. Boston: Little, Brown, 1988.

Overall, John. *Bruce Lee Review*. Essex, England: Woowums Book, 2009.

Pendo, Stephen. *Raymond Chandler On Screen: His Novels into Film*. Metuchen, NJ: Scarecrow Press, 1976.

Pilato, Herbie J. *Kung Fu: Book of Caine*. Rutland, VT: Tuttle, 1993.

Polanski, Roman. *Roman by Polanski*. New York: William Morrow, 1984.

Rafiq, Fiaz. *Bruce Lee Conversations*. London: HNL Publishing, 2009.

Robards Coover, Darcy Anne. "From the Gilded Ghetto to Hollywood: Bruce Lee,

Kung Fu, and the Evolution of Chinese America." Diss., Clemson, SC: Clemson University, 2008.

Russo, Charles. *Striking Distance: Bruce Lee and the Dawn of Martial Arts in America.* Lincoln: University of Nebraska Press, 2016.

Sandford, Christopher. *Polanski: A Biography*. London: Century Publishing, 2007.

Scura, John. *The Best of Bruce Lee: Tracing a Career of the Most Phenomenal Martial Artist Ever—Through a Collection of Reprinted Articles from* Black Belt, Karate Illustrated, *and* Fighting Stars *Magazines*. Los Angeles: Rainbow Publications, 1974.

Segaloff, Nat. *Stirling Silliphant: The Fingers of God: The Story of Hollywood's Hottest Writer Who Rode* Route 66, *Mastered Disaster Films, and Lived His Life Like It Was a Movie*. Albany, GA: BearManor Media, 2013.

Shifren, Ester Benjamin. *Hiding in a Cave of Trunks: A Prominent Jewish Family's Century in Shanghai and Internment in a WWII POW Camp*. CreateSpace Independent Publishing Platform, 2012.

Silliphant, Stirling. *The Silent Flute*. Screenplay, October 19, 1970.

Smith, Mike. *In the Shadow of the Noonday Gun*. Windsor, January 24, 2013.

Straight, Raymond. *James Garner: A Biography*. New York: St. Martin's, 1985.

Surman, Dr. Craig, and Dr. Tim Bilkey. *Fast Minds: How to Thrive if You Have ADHD (Or Think You Might)*. New York: Penguin, 2013.

Sydenham, Richard. *Steve McQueen: The Cooler King: His Life Through His Movie Career*. Big Star Creations, 2013.

Szeto, Kin-Yan. *The Martial Arts Cinema of the Chinese Diaspora: Ang Lee, John Woo, and Jackie Chan in Hollywood*. Carbondale: Southern Illinois University Press, 2011.

Tadman, David, and Steve Kerridge, eds. *Bruce Lee: The Little Dragon at 70*. Los Angeles: Bruce Lee Enterprises, 2010.

Takaki, Ronald. *Strangers from a Different Shore: A History of Asian Americans*. New York: Penguin, 1989.

Teo, Stephen. *Chinese Martial Arts Cinema: The Wuxia Tradition*. Edinburgh: Edinburgh University Press, 2009.

———. *Hong Kong Cinema: The Extra Dimensions*. London: British Film Institute, 1997.

Terrill, Marshall. *Steve McQueen: The Life and Legend of a Hollywood Icon*. Chicago: Triumph Books, 2010.

Thomas, Bruce. *Bruce Lee: Fighting Spirit*. Berkeley: Blue Snake Books, 1994.

Tobias, Mel. *Memoirs of an Asian Moviegoer*. Hong Kong: South China Morning Post Productions, 1982.

Tsang, Steve. *A Modern History of Hong Kong*. London: I. B. Tauris, 2010.

Tse-Tung, Mao. *On Guerrilla Warfare*. BN Publishing, 2007.

———. *Quotations from Chairman Mao Tse-Tung.* 2nd Edition. Beijing: People's Liberation Army Daily, 1966.

Uyehara, Mito. *Bruce Lee: 1940–1973.* Los Angeles: Rainbow Publications, 1974.

———. *Bruce Lee: The Incomparable Fighter.* Santa Clarita, CA: Ohara Publications, 1988.

Van Hise, James. *The Green Hornet Book.* Las Vegas: Pioneer, 1989.

Ward, Burt. *Boy Wonder: My Life in Tights.* Los Angeles: Logical Figment Books, 1995.

Watts, Alan W. *The Joyous Cosmology.* New York: Vintage, 1965.

Weintraub, Fred. *Bruce Lee, Woodstock, and Me: From the Man Behind a Half-Century of Music, Movies and Martial Arts.* Los Angeles: Brooktree Canyon Press, 2011.

West, Adam. *Back to the Batcave.* New York: Berkley, 1994.

West, David. *Chasing Dragons: An Introduction to Martial Arts Film.* London: I. B. Tauris, 2006.

Wing, Rick L. *Showdown in Oakland: The Story Behind the Wong Jack Man–Bruce Lee Fight.* Self-published: San Francisco, 2013.

Wong, Wendy Siuyi. *Hong Kong Comics.* Princeton: Princeton Architectural Press, 2002.

Wunderman, Kurt. *Kelsey.* Screenplay. Fred Weintraub Family Productions, April 28, 1971.

Zhang, Yingjin. *Chinese National Cinema.* London: Routledge, 2004.

English Language Periodicals

"1974 Black Belt Hall of Fame: Bruce Lee Martial Artist of the Year." *Black Belt,* November 1974.

Aarons, Leroy F. "Batman's Boy Has Black Belt Rival." *Washington Post,* August 30, 1966.

Abad-Santos, Alexander. "Johnnie Walker Offends by Using Bruce Lee in Chinese Ad." *The Atlantic Wire,* July 12, 2013.

Adams, Val. "F.C.C. Head Bids TV Men Reform 'Vast Wasteland'; Minow Charges Failure in Public Duty—Threatens to Use License Power." *New York Times,* May 10, 1961.

Adcock, Joe. " 'Exit the Dragon' Playwright Aims to Slay Asian American Stereotypes." *Seattle Post-Intelligencer,* September 2, 1997.

Arnold, Gary. "Shades of Cagney, Echoes of McQueen." *Washington Post,* August 25, 1973.

Bart, Peter. "More Chartreuse than Campy." *New York Times,* May 8, 1966.

Berman, Eliza. "How Batman and Superman Conquered America Decades Ago." Time.com, March 24, 2016.

Block, Alex Ben. "Brandon Lee's Mom: Never Again." *Hollywood Reporter*, April 29, 1993.

———. "The Hong Kong Style: Part I." *Esquire*, August 1973.

Blum, Jeremy. "Bruce Lee Whisky Advert Branded a Disgrace." *South China Morning Post*, July 11, 2013.

"Bosnia Unveils Bruce Lee Bronze." *BBC News*, November 26, 2005.

Bradley-Colleary, Shannon. "20 Years After His Death on the Set of *The Crow*, I Remember Brandon Lee." *Huffington Post*, April 1, 2013.

Brady, Eric. "Heat-Related Illness Still Deadly Problem for Athletes." *USA Today*, August 15, 2011.

Braud, Simon. "Rise of the Dragon." *Empire*, July 2013.

"Bruce Lee Can Stay On in HK." *Hong Kong Standard*, December 18, 1971.

"Bruce Lee, Hong Kong Film Star, Dies at 32." *Los Angeles Times*, July 21, 1973.

"A Bruce Lee Museum." *New York Times*, July 8, 2008.

"Bruce Lee Remembered." *New York Times*, July 27, 2005.

"Bruce Lee's Last Moments Revealed." *The Star*, October 29, 2013.

"Bruce Lee, the Statues." *New York Times*, November 28, 2005.

Calugareanu, Ilinca. "VHS vs. Communism." *New York Times*, February 17, 2014.

Canby, Vincent. "'Green Hornet,' from Bruce Lee Series." *New York Times*, November 28, 1974.

———. "'Have You Seen Shu Lately?' 'Shu Who?'" *New York Times*, May 13, 1973.

Casa, Dr. Douglas. "Cold Water Immersion: The Gold Standard for Exertional Heatstroke Treatment." *Exercise Sport Science Review*, Vol. 35, No. 3 (2007).

Chan, Kelvin K. "Kung Fu Filmmaker Run Run Shaw Dies." Associated Press, January 8, 2014.

Charron, C., et al. "Incidence, Causes and Prognosis of Hypotension Related to Meprobamate Poisoning." *Intensive Care Medicine*, Vol. 31 (2005), pp. 1582–86.

Cheng, Jennifer. "Bruce Lee Controversially Resurrected for Johnnie Walker Ad." Time.com, July 12, 2013.

Cheung, Hawkins. "Bruce Lee's Classical Mess: Cleaning Up the Mess the 'Little Dragon' Left Behind," as told to Robert Chu. *Inside Kung-Fu*, February 1992.

———. "Bruce Lee's Hong Kong Years." *Inside Kung-Fu*, November 1991.

Chi, Paul. "The 'Asian Glow' Explained." *The Daily of the University of Washington*, March 11, 2003.

Chiao, Hsiung-Ping. "Bruce Lee: His Influence on the Evolution of the Kung Fu Genre." *The Journal of Popular Film and Television*, Vol. 9 (Spring 1981).

Ching, Gene. "Great American Great Grandmaster." *Kungfu Taichi Magazine*, January/February 2010.

———. "Keeping Secrets." *Kungfu Taichi Magazine*, January/February 2010.

Chou, Oliver. "Hong Kong Doctor, Who Tried to Revive Bruce Lee, Takes Secrets of Kung Fu Legend's 1973 Death to the Grave." *South China Morning Post*, August 14, 2015.

Chow, Vivienne. "Bruce Lee Whisky Advert Becomes a Call for Occupy Central." *South China Morning Post*, July 12, 2013.

———. "Golden Harvest's Raymond Chow Recalls Glory Days of Hong Kong Film." *South China Morning Post*, March 23, 2013.

———. "It's a Tribute, Not an Ad, Says Bruce Lee's Daughter." *South China Morning Post*, July 12, 2013.

Clopton, Willard Jr. "Kato Likes Puns, Preys on Words." *Washington Post*, May 6, 1967.

"Dame of Death: Betty Ting Opens Up on Bruce Lee's Final Hours." *Want China Times*, October 30, 2013.

Dannen, Frederic. "Hong Kong Babylon." *The New Yorker*, August 7, 1995.

Dorgan, Michael. "Bruce Lee's Toughest Fight." *Official Karate*, July 1980.

Draper, Dave. "Type Training." *Muscle Builder/Power*, May 1969.

Ebert, Roger. "Marlowe." *Chicago Sun-Times*, November 25, 1969.

Elegant, Robert S. "Oriental Films: Lots of Blood and Revenge." *Los Angeles Times*, January 14, 1973.

Endow, Ken. "Punch Lines." *Karate Illustrated*, September 1970.

Eskenazi, Stuart. "Ruby Chow, First Asian American on King County Council, Dead at 87." *Seattle Times*, June 5, 2008.

"Ex-Fighter Bob Wall Jailed for Grand Theft." *Black Belt*, September 1997.

Farber, Stephen. "Kids! Now You Can Chop Up Your Old Comic-Book Heroes with Your Bare Hands!" *Esquire*, August 1973.

Farquhuar, Peter. "Bruce Lee Fans Are Worried His Hong Kong Home Is About to Be Demolished." *Business Insider Australia*, September 10, 2015.

Fox, Margalit. "Charles Manson Dies at 83; Wild-Eyed Leader of a Murderous Crew." *New York Times*, November 20, 2017.

Garey, Juliann. "Disasters Plague the Set of 'The Crow.' " *Entertainment Weekly*, April 2, 1993.

Gee, Alison Dakota. "Dragon Days." *Los Angeles Times*, July 20, 1998.

George, Thomas. "Strength and Conditioning Coaches: The Force Is with Them." *New York Times*, June 27, 1993.

Ginsberg, Allen. "The Great Marijuana Hoax: First Manifesto to End the Bringdown." *Atlantic Monthly*, November 1966.

Gould, Jack. "Milton Berle, Yesterday's 'Mr. Television,' Returns." *New York Times*, September 10, 1966.

Graceffo, Antonio. "Master Leo Fong: From Bruce Lee to Wei Kung Do." *Kungfu Taichi Magazine*, July/August 2012.

Graham, Bob. "Enter Bruce Lee—He's Still Alive and Kicking." *San Francisco Chronicle*, July 29, 1988.

Greenspan, Roger. "Screen: In the Tradition of 'Marlowe.'" *New York Times*, October 23, 1969.

Hartung, Benno. "Sudden Unexpected Death Under Acute Influence of Cannabis." *Forensic Science International*, Vol. 237 (2014).

Hartunian, Atina. "Yip Man: Wing Chun Legend and Bruce Lee's Formal Teacher." *Black Belt*, August 12, 2013.

Herkewitz, William. "The Science of the One-Inch Punch." *Popular Mechanics*, May 21, 2014.

Hess, Amanda. "Asian-American Actors Are Fighting for Visibility." *New York Times*, May 25, 2016.

"Hong Kong Unveils Bruce Lee Statue." *The Age*, November 28, 2005.

Inosanto, Dan. "What is Jeet Kune Do?" http://elitejkd.com/what_is_jeet_kune_do.php.

"In the Shadow of Bruce Lee: Robert Lee: Bridging the Gap Between Individuality and a Brother's Legend." *Black Belt*, August 1974.

Israel, Evan. "Bruce Lee's Barber." *Fighting Stars Magazine*, May 1978.

Itzkoff, Dave. "Bruce Lee Lands on Chinese TV." *New York Times*, October 8, 2008.

Jenkins, Nash. "Bruce Lee's Former Home in Hong Kong Faces an Uncertain Future." *Time*, September 8, 2015.

Kandelljan, Jonathan. "Run Run Shaw, Chinese-Movie Giant of the Kung Fu Genre, Dies at 106." *New York Times*, January 6, 2014.

Knochel, James P., M.D. "Heat Stroke." *The New England Journal of Medicine*, June 20, 2002.

Lam, Eunice. "Eunice Lam Remembers Bruce Lee." Network54.com, April 9, 2016.

Laurent, Lawrence. "'Kung Fu,' an Eastern-Western, Finds a Place in the TV Schedule." *Washington Post*, December 31, 1972.

Lee, Bruce. "Liberate Yourself from Classical Karate." *Black Belt*, September 1971.

"Lee Group Opens Door to Asia Slate." *Hollywood Reporter*, August 8, 2006.

LeFevre, Charlette. "The Lady and the Dragon: An Interview with Amy Sanbo, Bruce Lee's First Love in the U.S." *Northwest Asian Weekly*, December 1, 2007.

Leon, Lisa R. "Heat Stroke." Comprehensivephysiology.com, April 2015.

Lian, Pang Cheng. "Inside Bruce Lee." *New Nation* (Singapore), August 14, 1972.

Logan, Bey. "Once Upon a Time in Kung Fu." *Huffington Post*, August 12, 2013.

Longsdorf, Amy. "The Curse." *The Morning Call*, May 7, 1993.

Mailman, Erika. "Bruce Lee Had a Studio in Oakland." *Contra Costa Times*, April 12, 2005.

"The Making of 'The Silent Flute.'" *Black Belt*, October 1970.

Marchetti, Gina. "Jackie Chan and the Black Connection," in *Keyframes: Popular Cinema and Cultural Studies*, ed. Matthew Tinkcom and Amy Villarejo (London: Routledge, 2001).

Martin, Douglas. "Jeff Corey, Character Actor and Acting Instructor, 88." *New York Times,* August 20, 2002.

McNary, Dave. "Bruce Lee Biopic Draws 'Adjustment Bureau' Director." *Variety,* May 30, 2014.

"Meet Bruce Lee—The Green Hornet's Buzz Bomb." *Movie Mirror,* October 1966.

Mendelsohn, Daniel. "J.F.K., Tragedy, Myth." *The New Yorker,* November 22, 2013.

Milhoces, Gary. "It Is What It Is." *USA Today,* December 27, 2004.

Miller, Davis. "Bruce Lee's Silent Flute: A History." *Circle of Iron* DVD extras, 2004.

———. "Chasing the Dragon." *Hotdog Magazine,* April 2001.

Nagourney, Adam. "Few Problems with Cannabis for California." *New York Times,* October 26, 2013.

Ni, Ching-Ching. "Time Is the One Enemy That May Vanquish Him." *Los Angeles Times,* July 31, 2003.

O'Connor, John J. "In the Name of the Law Is the Name of the Game." *New York Times,* September 19, 1971.

O'Rourke, Tim. "Chronicle Covers: Labor Leader Harry Bridges' Big Victory." *San Francisco Chronicle,* December 30, 2016.

Oliver, Myrna. "Tom Tannenbaum, 69; Longtime TV, Movie Producer." *Los Angeles Times,* December 5, 2001.

Oney, Steve. "Manson: Oral History." *Los Angeles Magazine,* July 1, 2009.

Paul, William. "Getting the Thrust of Kung Fu." *Village Voice,* August 30, 1973.

Peterson, David. "Solid Gold Wing Chun Memories." *Inside Kung-Fu,* March 1994.

Pilato, Herbie J. "Brandon Lee—His Final Days." *Inside Kung-Fu,* April 1988.

Pollard, Maxwell. "In Kato's Kung Fu, Action Was Instant." *Black Belt,* October 1967.

———. "Was 'The Green Hornet's' Version of Kung Fu Genuine?" *Black Belt,* October 1967.

Polly, Matthew. "Fake Ass White Boys: A Brief History of MMA Trash Talk in Advance of UFC 145." Deadspin.com, April 21, 2012.

Pomerantz, Dorothy. "Michael Jackson Leads Our List of the Top-Earning Dead Celebrities." *Forbes,* October 23, 2013.

"Pop Tune's Philosophy Marks Bruce Lee Rites." *Los Angeles Herald-Examiner,* July 31, 1973.

Pumphrey and Roberts. "Postmortem Findings After Fatal Anaphylactic Reactions." *The Journal of Clinical Pathology,* April 2000.

Rafferty, Terrence. "Dragon: The Bruce Lee Story." *The New Yorker,* 1993.

Rainer, Peter. " 'The Crow' Flies With Grim Glee." *The Los Angeles Times*, May 11, 1994.

Rand, Flora. "Chinese Bruce Lee Says of His American Child: 'I Want My Son to Be a Mixed-Up Kid!' " *TV/Radio Mirror*, November 1966.

Rayns, Tony. "Bruce Lee: Narcissism and Nationalism." *A Study of the Hong Kong Martial Arts Film*, the 4th Hong Kong International Film Festival catalogue, April 3, 1980.

Reveler, Norma. "Golden Harvest Reaping Deal with Lee's Daughter." *Hollywood Reporter*, June 24, 1997.

"Review: 'Marlowe.' " *Variety*, December 31, 1968.

"Robin's New Love Rival." *TV Radio Show*, October 1966.

Rogosin, Joel. "What Was It Like to Work with Bruce Lee?" *Huffington Post*, July 29, 2014.

Rubenstein, Steve. "In the Shadow of a Legend." *Black Belt*, August 1974.

"Run Run Shaw's Last Years." *The Star Online*, January 9, 2014.

Russo, Charles. "Bruce Lee vs. Wong Jack Man: Fact, Fiction and the Birth of the Dragon." *Vice, Fightland Blog*, May 2017, http://fightland.vice.com/blog/bruce-lee-vs-wong-jack-man-fact-fiction-and-the-birth-of-the-dragon.

———. "The Lost History of Bruce Lee." *San Francisco Magazine*, June 2011.

———. "Was Bruce Lee of English Descent?" *Vice, Fightland Blog*, May 2016, http://fightland.vice.com/blog/was-bruce-lee-of-english-descent.

Sansweet, Stephen J. "The Rock 'Em, Sock 'Em World of Kung Fu." *Wall Street Journal*, October 4, 1973.

Savill, Richard. "Cannabis Is Blamed as Cause of Man's Death." *The Telegraph*, January 20, 2004.

Scepanovic, Ivo. "Bruce Lee Beats Pope to Be Peace Symbol of Mostar." *The Telegraph*, September 12, 2004.

Schubiner, Dr. Howard. "Substance Abuse in Patients with Attention-Deficit Hyperactivity Disorder: Therapeutic Implications." US National Library of Medicine, National Institutes of Health, 2005.

Seitz, Matt Zoller. "Holy Influential Actor, Batman: Adam West Continues to Shape Hollywood." Vulture.com, June 10, 2017.

Sharkey, Betsy. "Fate's Children: Bruce and Brandon." *The New York Times*, May 2, 1993.

Siegel, Robert. "Bosnian City's Unique Statue Choice: Bruce Lee." NPR, September 13, 2005.

Smith, Adam. "The Fall of the Crow." *Empire*, August 2013.

Smith, Anna. "Wildest and Weirdest Star Audition Stories." *MSN Entertainment*, May 4, 2011.

Stein, Joel. "Time 100 People of the Century." *Time*, June 14, 1999.

Stewart, Kev. "Bruceploitation: The 5 Best Bruce Lee Clones in Gaming." What Culture.com, September 30, 2013.

"Swish! Thwack! Kung Fu Films Make It." *New York Times*, June 16, 1973.

Theodoracopulos, Taki. "Celebrity Kicks." *Esquire*, September 1980.

Thompson, Howard. "Enter the Dragon." *New York Times*, August 18, 1973.

Travers, Peter. "The Crow." *Rolling Stone*, May 11, 1994.

Turan, Kenneth. "The Apotheosis of Bruce Lee: An Actor Dies; A Posthumous Industry is Born." *American Film*, October 1975.

———. "I Made Love To . . . And Other True Tales of the Bruce Lee Cult." *New West*, September 2, 1979.

"Unrealized Urnings." *Playboy*, December 1995.

Varadarajan, Tunku. "The Fred Astaire of Kung Fu." *Wall Street Journal*, June 28, 2002.

Vinh, Tan. "A Rare, Personal Glimpse of Bruce Lee's Seattle Years." *Seattle Times*, October 3, 2014.

"Will Li Hit Hollywood or HK?" *China Mail*, November 25, 1971.

Wong, Shun Leung. "Bruce Lee and His Friendship with Wong Shun Leung." *Real Kung Fu Magazine*, Hong Kong, 1980.

Yant, Monica, "Bruce Lee Estate Items to Go on the Block." *The Los Angeles Times*, September 19, 1993.

Yglesias, Matthew. "Parents Really Are Harder on First Children." Slate.com, October 21, 2013.

Yongyi, Song. "Chronology of Mass Killings During the Chinese Cultural Revolution (1966–1976)." *Online Encyclopedia of Mass Violence*, August 2011.

Young, Robert. "Origins of a Dragon." *Black Belt*, July 2012.

———. "William Cheung: Hong Kong Bullies, Wing Chun Kung Fu, and Bruce Lee." Blackbelt.com, May 2, 2013.

Zimmer, Ben. "Take Note, Grasshopper, of Kung Fu." *Wall Street Journal*, January 10, 2014.

"Ziv International Obtains License for Lee Products." *Hollywood Reporter*, September 24, 1975.

Chinese Language Books

Li Zhenhui 李振 [Robert Lee]. *Li Xiaolong* 李小 [*Bruce Lee, My Brother*]. Zhuo Nan 卓男, ed. Hong Kong: Masterpiece Films, Ltd., 2010.

Li Zhiyuan 李志遠 [Paul Li]. *Shenhua Zaixian* 神話再現 [*From Limited to Limitless: The Ways of Bruce Lee*]. Hong Kong: Oriental Resources Company, 1998.

Zhang Qinpeng 張欽鵬 [Chaplin Chang] and Luo Zhengguang 羅振光 [Dr. Roger Lo]. *Tamen Renshi de Li Xiaolong* 他們認識的李小龍 [*The Bruce They Knew*]. Hong Kong: Infolink Publishing Ltd., 2013.

Chinese Language Periodicals

"丁珮昨否認自殺 Ding Pei Zuo Fouren Zisha" ["Betty Ting Denies Suicide Attempt Yesterday"]. *San Tang Yat Po*, December 23, 1972.

"丁珮鄰居縷述 Ding Pei Linju Lüshu" ["Betty Ting's Neighbors Talk"]. *Oriental Daily*, July 25, 1973.

"萬里飛屍費用萬六 Wanli Fei Shi Feiyong Wan Liu" ["Sixteen Thousand Hong Kong Dollars to Fly Corpse"]. *Oriental Daily*, July 25, 1973.

"小龍遺體明日飛美 Xiao Long Yiti Mingri Fei Mei" ["Lee's Body Flies to America Tomorrow"]. *Oriental Daily*, July 25, 1973.

"死因仍屬—謎遺孀探停屍間 Siyin Reng Shu Yi Mi Yishuang Tanting Shijian" ["Cause of Death Remains a Mystery as Lee's Widow Visits Morgue"]. *Oriental Daily*, July 25, 1973.

Documentaries

The Art of Action: Martial Arts in the Movies. Sony Pictures, 2002.

Biography—Bruce Lee: The Immortal Dragon. A&E Home Video, 2005.

Blood & Steel: The Making of Enter the Dragon. Warner Home Video, 1998. DVD extra on 25th anniversary edition of *Enter the Dragon*.

The Brilliant Life of Bruce Lee. Hong Kong Heritage Museum, 2013.

Bruce Lee: A Warrior's Journey. Warner Home Video, 2002.

Bruce Lee: Century Hero. Showbox Home Entertainment, 2004.

Bruce Lee: Curse of the Dragon. Warner Home Video, 1993.

Bruce Lee: The Legend. Golden Harvest, 1983.

Bruce Lee: The Man and the Legend. Golden Harvest, 1973.

Cinema of Vengeance. Fortune 5, 1994.

Golden Gate Girls. Blue Queen Cultural Communications, 2013.

How Bruce Lee Changed the World. A&E Home Video, 2009.

I Am Bruce Lee. Shout! Factory, 2012.

The Tao of Caine: Production and Beyond. Warner Brothers Entertainment, 2003. DVD extra on 30th anniversary *Kung Fu: The Complete Edition*.

DVD Extras

The Big Boss: 2 Disc Ultimate Edition. "The History of The Big Boss," "Deleted Scenes Examined," "DVD Commentary with Andrew Stanton and Will Johnston." Cine-Asia, 2010.

Fist of Fury: 2 Disc Ultimate Edition. "An Interview with Nora Miao," "An Interview with Riki Hashimoto," "An Interview with Jun Katsumura," "An Interview with Joe Torreneuva," "An Interview with Linda Palmer," "An Interview with Dan Inosanto," "Location Guide with Bey Logan," "DVD Commentary with Bey Logan." Cine-Asia, 2011.

Game of Death: Platinum Edition. "Bruce Lee: A Warrior's Journey—The Making of Game of Death." Hong Kong Legends, 2001.

Kung Fu: The Complete Edition. "From Grasshopper to Cain: Creating Kung Fu." Warner Brothers Entertainment, 2003.

The Way of the Dragon: 2 Disc Ultimate Edition. "Memories of the Master: An Interview with Pat Johnson." Cine-Asia, 2010.

Audio and Video

Block, Alex Ben. "*Esquire* Interview." 1972.

Corcoran, John. "Audio Interview with Co-Writer Stirling Silliphant." *Circle of Iron*. Blue Underground, 2004.

Johnston, Will. "Bob Baker Interview." Tracking the Dragon Convention, 1990. https://www.youtube.com/watch?v=aJIzyJFF-d8.

Tadman, David. "An Interview with George Lee." Vimeo.com, February 3, 2014.

Thomas, Ted. "Bruce Lee: The Ted Thomas Interview." December 1971.

index

Page numbers in *italics* refer to photographs.

about the author

MATTHEW POLLY is the national bestselling author of *American Shaolin* and *Tapped Out*. A Princeton University graduate and Rhodes Scholar, he spent two years studying kung fu at the Shaolin Temple in Henan, China. His writing has appeared in *The Washington Post*, *Esquire*, *Slate*, *Playboy*, and *The Nation*. He is a fellow at Yale University and lives in New Haven, Connecticut.